Dictionary of Literary Biography • Volume Thirty-one

American Colonial Writers, 1735-1781

Dictionary of Literary Biography

1: *The American Renaissance in New England*, edited by Joel Myerson (1978)
2: *American Novelists Since World War II*, edited by Jeffrey Helterman and Richard Layman (1978)
3: *Antebellum Writers in New York and the South*, edited by Joel Myerson (1979)
4: *American Writers in Paris, 1920-1939*, edited by Karen Lane Rood (1980)
5: *American Poets Since World War II*, 2 parts, edited by Donald J. Greiner (1980)
6: *American Novelists Since World War II*, Second Series, edited by James E. Kibler, Jr. (1980)
7: *Twentieth-Century American Dramatists*, 2 parts, edited by John MacNicholas (1981)
8: *Twentieth-Century American Science-Fiction Writers*, 2 parts, edited by David Cowart and Thomas L. Wymer (1981)
9: *American Novelists, 1910-1945*, 3 parts, edited by James J. Martine (1981)
10: *Modern British Dramatists, 1900-1945*, 2 parts, edited by Stanley Weintraub (1982)
11: *American Humorists, 1800-1950*, 2 parts, edited by Stanley Trachtenberg (1982)
12: *American Realists and Naturalists*, edited by Donald Pizer and Earl N. Harbert (1982)
13: *British Dramatists Since World War II*, 2 parts, edited by Stanley Weintraub (1982)
14: *British Novelists Since 1960*, 2 parts, edited by Jay L. Halio (1983)
15: *British Novelists, 1930-1959*, 2 parts, edited by Bernard Oldsey (1983)
16: *The Beats: Literary Bohemians in Postwar America*, 2 parts, edited by Ann Charters (1983)
17: *Twentieth-Century American Historians*, edited by Clyde N. Wilson (1983)
18: *Victorian Novelists After 1885*, edited by Ira B. Nadel and William E. Fredeman (1983)
19: *British Poets, 1880-1914*, edited by Donald E. Stanford (1983)
20: *British Poets, 1914-1945*, edited by Donald E. Stanford (1983)
21: *Victorian Novelists Before 1885*, edited by Ira B. Nadel and William E. Fredeman (1983)
22: *American Writers for Children, 1900-1960*, edited by John Cech (1983)
23: *American Newspaper Journalists, 1873-1900*, edited by Perry J. Ashley (1983)
24: *American Colonial Writers, 1606-1734*, edited by Emory Elliott (1984)
25: *American Newspaper Journalists, 1901-1925*, edited by Perry J. Ashley (1984)
26: *American Screenwriters*, edited by Robert E. Morsberger, Stephen O. Lesser, and Randall Clark (1984)
27: *Poets of Great Britain and Ireland, 1945-1960*, edited by Vincent B. Sherry, Jr. (1984)
28: *Twentieth-Century American-Jewish Fiction Writers*, edited by Daniel Walden (1984)
29: *American Newspaper Journalists, 1926-1950*, edited by Perry J. Ashley (1984)
30: *American Historians, 1607-1865*, edited by Clyde N. Wilson (1984)
31: *American Colonial Writers, 1735-1781*, edited by Emory Elliott (1984)

Documentary Series:

1: *Sherwood Anderson, Willa Cather, John Dos Passos, Theodore Dreiser, F. Scott Fitzgerald, Ernest Hemingway, Sinclair Lewis*, edited by Margaret A. Van Antwerp (1982)
2: *James Gould Cozzens, James T. Farrell, William Faulkner, John O'Hara, John Steinbeck, Thomas Wolfe, Richard Wright*, edited by Margaret A. Van Antwerp (1982)
3: *Saul Bellow, Jack Kerouac, Norman Mailer, Vladimir Nabokov, John Updike, Kurt Vonnegut*, edited by Mary Bruccoli (1983)
4: *Tennessee Williams*, edited by Margaret A. Van Antwerp and Sally Johns (1984)

Yearbooks:

1980, edited by Karen L. Rood, Jean W. Ross, and Richard Ziegfeld (1981)
1981, edited by Karen L. Rood, Jean W. Ross, and Richard Ziegfeld (1982)
1982, edited by Richard Ziegfeld; associate editors: Jean W. Ross and Lynne C. Zeigler (1983)
1983, edited by Mary Bruccoli and Jean W. Ross; associate editor: Richard Ziegfeld (1984)

Dictionary of Literary Biography • Volume Thirty-one

American Colonial Writers, 1735-1781

Edited by
Emory Elliott
Princeton University

A Bruccoli Clark Book
Gale Research Company • Book Tower • Detroit, Michigan 48226

Advisory Board for
DICTIONARY OF LITERARY BIOGRAPHY

Louis S. Auchincloss
John Baker
D. Philip Baker
A. Walton Litz, Jr.
Peter S. Prescott
Lola L. Szladits
William Targ

Matthew J. Bruccoli and Richard Layman, *Editorial Directors*
C. E. Frazer Clark, Jr., *Managing Editor*

Manufactured by Edwards Brothers, Inc.
Ann Arbor, Michigan
Printed in the United States of America

Copyright © 1984
GALE RESEARCH COMPANY

Library of Congress Cataloging in Publication Data
Main entry under title:

American colonial writers, 1735-1781.

(Dictionary of literary biography; v. 31)
"A Bruccoli Clark book."
Includes index.
1. Authors, American—18th century—Biography—Dictionaries. 2. American literature—Colonial period, ca. 1600-1775—Bio-bibliography. 3. American literature—Revolutionary period, 1775-1783—Bio-bibliography. 4. American literature—Colonial period, ca. 1600-1775—History and criticism—Addresses, essays, lectures. 5. American literature—Revolutionary period, 1775-1783—History and criticism—Addresses, essays, lectures. I. Elliott, Emory, 1942- . II. Series.
PS193.A38   1984   810'.9'001   84-13533
ISBN 0-8103-1709-5

This volume is for a few of the scholars who have increased our knowledge and understanding of eighteenth-century American literature:

Ursula Brumm
Edward Davidson
Alan Heimert
J. A. Leo Lemay
Mason I. Lowance
Kenneth Silverman

Contents

Plan of the Series ix

Foreword xi

Acknowledgments xiii

John Adams (1734-1826) 3
   Steven E. Kagle

Samuel Adams (1722-1803) 11
   Elaine K. Ginsberg

Ethan Allen (1738-1789) 14
   Martha Strom

James Allen (1739-1808) 16
   Lewis Leary

Josiah Atkins (circa 1755-1781) 18
   John C. Shields

Thomas Bacon (circa 1700-1768) 19
   Robert Micklus

John Bartram (1699-1777) 22
   William J. Scheick

Joseph Bellamy (1719-1790) 32
   Donald Weber

Robert Bolling (1738-1775) 34
   Charles Bolton

Jonathan Boucher (1738-1804) 38
   David Curtis Skaggs

John Camm (1718-1778) 47
   Homer D. Kemp

Landon Carter (1710-1778) 49
   Homer D. Kemp

Jonathan Carver (1710-1780) 53
   Daniel E. Williams

Benjamin Church (1734-1778) 60
   Jeffrey Walker

Thomas Cradock (1718-1770) 68
   David Curtis Skaggs

Charles Crawford (1752-circa 1815) 70
   Robert P. Winston

Samuel Davies (1723-1761) 72
   Paul W. Harris

William Dawson (1704-1752) 75
   Homer D. Kemp

John Dickinson (1732-1808) 77
   Elaine K. Ginsberg

Nathaniel Evans (1742-1767) 82
   William D. Andrews

Thomas Fitch (circa 1700-1774) 86
   O. Glade Hunsaker

Alexander Garden (circa 1685-1756) 88
   Amanda Porterfield

Thomas Godfrey (1736-1763) 90
   Frank Shuffelton

Jonas Green (1712-1767) 96
   Robert Micklus

Joseph Green (1706-1780) 99
   David Robinson

Alexander Hamilton (1712-1756) 101
   Robert Micklus

Jupiter Hammon (1711-died between
   1790 and 1806) 107
   Sondra A. O'Neale

Oliver Hart (1723-1795) 112
   Tony Owens

Samuel Hopkins (1721-1803) 115
   Donald Weber

Francis Hopkinson (1737-1791) 118
   William D. Andrews

Thomas Hutchinson (1711-1780) 123
   Michael P. Kramer

John Jay (1745-1829) 130
   Rick W. Sturdevant

Thomas Jefferson (1743-1826) 136
   Robert D. Richardson, Jr.

John Leacock (1729-1802) 149
   Carla Mulford

William Livingston (1723-1790) 152
   William K. Bottorff

James Maury (1718-1769) 156
   Homer D. Kemp

Contents

Jonathan Mayhew (1720-1766) 158
  Michael P. Kramer

John Mercer (1704-1768) 174
  Meta Robinson Braymer

George Micklejohn (circa 1717-1818) 176
  Robert W. Hill

Robert Munford (circa 1737-1783) 177
  Hugh J. Dawson

Jonathan Odell (1737-1818) 179
  James C. Gaston

James Otis, Jr. (1725-1783) 181
  Anne Y. Zimmer

Thomas Paine (1737-1809) 186
  Maureen Goldman

John Parke (1754-1789) 202
  Maurice J. Bennett

Benjamin Young Prime (1733-1791) 205
  Michael Robertson

Samuel Quincy of Georgia (birth date
  and death date unknown) 207
  John C. Shields

Samuel Quincy of Massachusetts
  (1734-1789) 209
  John C. Shields

James Reid (birth date and
  death date unknown) 212
  Mark R. Patterson

Samuel Seabury (1729-1796) 214
  Arthur Sheps

Michael Smith (1698-circa 1771) 218
  M. Jimmie Killingsworth

William Smith (1727-1803) 219
  William D. Andrews

Ezra Stiles (1727-1795) 226
  Alasdair Macphail

William Stith (1707-1755) 237
  Homer D. Kemp

Thomas Story (circa 1670-1742) 239
  Thomas P. Slaughter

John Trumbull (1750-1831) 241
  Arthur L. Ford

Mercy Otis Warren (1728-1814) 246
  Frank Shuffelton

George Washington (1732-1799) 253
  David Curtis Skaggs

Phillis Wheatley (circa 1754-1784) 260
  Sondra A. O'Neale

John Witherspoon (1723-1794) 267
  Christopher J. MacGowan

Charles Woodmason (circa 1720-death
  date unknown) 272
  Alan Axelrod

John Woolman (1720-1772) 274
  Thomas Werge

John Joachim Zubly (1724-1781) 291
  Louis P. Masur

Appendix I:
Eighteenth-Century Philosophical
Background 297

  John Locke (1632-1704) 299
    David Woolwine

  George Berkeley (1685-1753) 304
    John Holland

  Francis Hutcheson (1694-1746) 310
    Mark Valeri

  Thomas Reid (1710-1796) 318
    Susan Mizruchi

  Henry Home, Lord Kames
  (1696-1782) 322
    Liza Dant

  Dugald Stewart (1753-1828) 329
    Thomas F. Strychacz

Appendix II:
Eighteenth-Century Aesthetic
Theories 337

  Hugh Blair, Excerpts from *Lectures on Rhetoric and
  Belles Lettres* (1783) 339

  John Witherspoon, Excerpts from *The Works of the
  Rev. John Witherspoon* (1800-1801) 350

  William Smith, Excerpts from *A General Idea
  of the College of Mirania* (1753) 381

Supplementary Reading List 387

Contributors 391

Cumulative Index 395

Plan of the Series

... Almost the most prodigious asset of a country, and perhaps its most precious possession, is its native literary product—when that product is fine and noble and enduring.

Mark Twain*

The advisory board, the editors, and the publisher of the *Dictionary of Literary Biography* are joined in endorsing Mark Twain's declaration. The literature of a nation provides an inexhaustible resource of permanent worth. It is our expectation that this endeavor will make literature and its creators better understood and more accessible to students and the literate public, while satisfying the standards of teachers and scholars.

To meet these requirements, *literary biography* has been construed in terms of the author's achievement. The most important thing about a writer is his writing. Accordingly, the entries in *DLB* are career biographies, tracing the development of the author's canon and the evolution of his reputation.

The publication plan for *DLB* resulted from two years of preparation. The project was proposed to Bruccoli Clark by Frederick G. Ruffner, president of the Gale Research Company, in November 1975. After specimen entries were prepared and typeset, an advisory board was formed to refine the entry format and develop the series rationale. In meetings held during 1976, the publisher, series editors, and advisory board approved the scheme for a comprehensive biographical dictionary of persons who contributed to North American literature. Editorial work on the first volume began in January 1977, and it was published in 1978.

In order to make *DLB* more than a reference tool and to compile volumes that individually have claim to status as literary history, it was decided to organize volumes by topic or period or genre. Each of these freestanding volumes provides a biographical-bibliographical guide and overview for a particular area of literature. We are convinced that this organization—as opposed to a single alphabet method—constitutes a valuable innovation in the presentation of reference material. The volume plan necessarily requires many decisions for the placement and treatment of authors who might properly be included in two or three volumes. In some instances a major figure will be included in separate volumes, but with different entries emphasizing the aspect of his career appropriate to each volume. Ernest Hemingway, for example, is represented in *American Writers in Paris, 1920-1939* by an entry focusing on his expatriate apprenticeship; he is also in *American Novelists, 1910-1945* with an entry surveying his entire career. Each volume includes a cumulative index of subject authors. The final *DLB* volume will be a comprehensive index to the entire series.

With volume ten in 1982 it was decided to enlarge the scope of *DLB* beyond the literature of the United States. By the end of 1983 twelve volumes treating British literature had been published, and volumes for Commonwealth and Modern European literature were in progress. The series has been further augmented by the *DLB Yearbooks* (since 1981) which update published entries and add new entries to keep the *DLB* current with contemporary activity. There have also been occasional *DLB Documentary Series* volumes which provide biographical and critical background source materials for figures whose work is judged to have particular interest for students. One of these companion volumes is entirely devoted to Tennessee Williams.

The purpose of *DLB* is not only to provide reliable information in a convenient format but also to place the figures in the larger perspective of literary history and to offer appraisals of their accomplishments by qualified scholars.

We define literature as the *intellectual commerce of a nation*: not merely as belles lettres, but as that ample and complex process by which ideas are generated, shaped, and transmitted. *DLB* entries are not limited to "creative writers" but extend to other figures who in this time and in this way influenced the mind of a people. Thus the series encompasses historians, journalists, publishers, and screenwriters. By this means readers of *DLB* may be aided to perceive literature not as cult scripture in the keeping of cultural high priests, but as at the center of a nation's life.

DLB includes the major writers appropriate to each volume and those standing in the ranks immediately behind them. Scholarly and critical counsel has been sought in deciding which minor figures to include and how full their entries should be.

---

*From an unpublished section of Mark Twain's autobiography, copyright © by the Mark Twain Company.

Plan of the Series

Wherever possible, useful references will be made to figures who do not warrant separate entries.

Each *DLB* volume has a volume editor responsible for planning the volume, selecting the figures for inclusion, and assigning the entries. Volume editors are also responsible for preparing, where appropriate, appendices surveying the major periodicals and literary and intellectual movements for their volumes, as well as lists of further readings. Work on the series as a whole is coordinated at the Bruccoli Clark editorial center in Columbia, South Carolina, where the editorial staff is responsible for the accuracy of the published volumes.

One feature that distinguishes *DLB* is the illustration policy—its concern with the iconography of literature. Just as an author is influenced by his surroundings, so is the reader's understanding of the author enhanced by a knowledge of his environment. Therefore *DLB* volumes include not only drawings, paintings, and photographs of authors, often depicting them at various stages in their careers, but also illustrations of their families and places where they lived. Title pages are regularly reproduced in facsimile along with dust jackets for modern authors. The dust jackets are a special feature of *DLB* because they often document better than anything else the way in which an author's work was launched in its own time. Specimens of the writers' manuscripts are included when feasible.

A supplement to *DLB*—tentatively titled *A Guide, Chronology, and Glossary for American Literature*—will outline the history of literature in North America and trace the influences that shaped it. This volume will provide a framework for the study of American literature by means of chronological tables, literary affiliation charts, glossarial entries, and concise surveys of the major movements. It has been planned to stand on its own as a vade mecum, providing a ready-reference guide to the study of American literature as well as a companion to the *DLB* volumes for American literature.

Samuel Johnson rightly decreed that "The chief glory of every people arises from its authors." The purpose of the *Dictionary of Literary Biography* is to compile literary history in the surest way available to us—by accurate and comprehensive treatment of the lives and work of those who contributed to it.

The *DLB* Advisory Board

Foreword

The Glorious Revolution in England in 1688-1689 marks a significant turning point in the development of American culture. Before that event the thought and writing of those living in the New World, and in New England in particular, had begun to develop in ways that were increasingly autonomous and, from an English contemporary's viewpoint, rather peculiar. Throughout the seventeenth century the political turmoil in England and the often shrewd diplomacy of the New Englanders provided many of the northern colonists with the opportunity to develop in their writings religious ideas, political structures, and an early form of national pride, which is expressed in such a work as Cotton Mather's *Magnalia Christi Americana* (1702). Even in the southern colonies, where the ties to the Church of England and the Crown remained strong, conditions of life in the New World—the land, the natives, the distance from Europe—led to variations in taste, forms of expression, and culture that give Ebenezer Cook's *The Sot-Weed Factor* (1708) and William Byrd's *The Secret History of the Line* (written circa 1730) their particular character. By 1690 in New England the literary expression found in the Puritan jeremiad, the spiritual autobiography, and the spiritualized histories and biographies could be distinguished as having the potential for forming the foundation of a distinctive American literary tradition—a tradition that was emerging in the southern and middle colonies by the end of the century as well.

The establishment of a new, stable government in England in the 1690s, however, had a profound and lasting impact upon intellectual and cultural life in America. What Perry Miller indicated about New England in the subtitle for the second volume of his *The New England Mind* is true of all the colonies: America was transformed "from Colony to Province." Great Britain's heightened awareness of the importance of the American colonies and the increased political control that followed served to transform the colonies from a set of relatively separate entities to a subculture of Europe. Just as the increasingly watchful eyes of European governments affected the political, military, and economic activities of the colonists, so did the influential opinions of the European arbiters of literary and artistic taste set the standards and establish the forms for literature and the arts. Of course, the seventeenth-century American poets such as Anne Bradstreet and Edward Taylor had been influenced by European writers such as Donne, DuBartus, and Quarles, as well as by Shakespeare and Milton; but the Puritan writers of the seventeenth century felt neither the desire nor the obligation to imitate European models, as did the preacher-poet Mather Byles with Pope in the 1740s and American prose writers with Addison and Steele throughout the eighteenth century. As English and Scottish philosophers, critics, and men of letters elaborated the criteria for taste in literature and the arts in the eighteenth century, the American provincials strove to adhere to these standards and emulate their European betters.

As a result of these historical events, American literature really has two beginnings: one established in the austere rhetoric and sacred imagery of the sermon and the personal narrative of New England; another fostered by Enlightenment thought and neoclassical principles. While the blending of these two heritages would ultimately provide rich verbal and imaginative resources for later American writers, the situation presents the student of eighteenth-century American literature with complex questions of influences and continuities. For example, because of the powerful impact of preachers such as Jonathan Edwards and George Whitefield during the religious revivals of the Great Awakening in the 1740s, the imagery, myths, and verbal structures of the Puritan sermon remained vital elements of American writing. The sermon continued to be the most important literary form throughout the century. Thousands in the middle and southern colonies as well as in New England learned the rhetoric of sin and salvation, of personal calling and communal mission. By the 1770s and 1780s, the vision of sacred destiny depicted in the Puritan idiom became part of the political tracts and speeches of the American Revolution, present even in the works of such a rationalist as Thomas Paine.

At the same time, by the 1740s and 1750s the classics and the works of Scottish and English writers were widely available. An increasing number of American bards, among them even Congregational ministers, experimented with heroic couplets, sonnets, and odes. At the head of this new tradition in American literature stands Benjamin Franklin. With his graceful style and wit, Franklin typified the cosmopolitan ideal in both his life and his writing. Beginning in the 1760s, the colleges in America instituted major curriculum reforms, introducing the classics along with the critical and philosophical works of contemporary European thinkers, especially those of the Scottish Commonsense School of thought. So important were these figures of the European Enlightenment to American literature of the eighteenth and nineteenth centuries that this volume includes an appendix to present a review of the lives, works, and influence of the most important English and Scottish philosophers of the age.

These two heritages—New England Puritan and self-consciously American on the one hand; European Enlightenment and imitative on the other—initially stood in sharp contrast, as different as Cotton Mather from Benjamin Franklin. Throughout the century, however, there occurred a gradual and subtle blending of religious and classical elements, so that by the 1770s and 1780s young men such as Philip Freneau and Joel Barlow created nationalistic epics and satires that are neoclassical in form, but echo the Puritans in content and imagery. What precedes this aesthetic resolution, however, are four decades of literary history that continue to challenge the scholar who seeks to understand the complex intellectual and literary conditions in the mid-eighteenth century and the relationship of this period to the development of American literature and culture as a whole.

Fortunately, during the last two or three decades, significant scholarly contributions have served to increase our knowledge both of the lives and works of many early writers and of the processes whereby the elements of seventeenth-century American culture were transformed and transmitted through the thought and writing of the eighteenth century to the generation of the Revolution and beyond. Questions of continuity, influences, and American uniqueness, or lack thereof, have been foremost in much of the most important work done in this field. Though there are many distinguished scholars who have contributed to this effort, I have dedicated this volume to six scholars whose work I have found to be of greatest importance in furthering our understanding of the literature and the significance of this period of our literary heritage.

—Emory Elliott

Acknowledgments

This book was produced by BC Research. Karen L. Rood, senior editor for the *Dictionary of Literary Biography* series, was the in-house editor.

Art supervisor is Claudia Ericson. Copyediting supervisor is Joycelyn R. Smith. Typesetting supervisor is Laura Ingram. The production staff includes Mary Betts, Rowena Betts, Kimberly Casey, Patricia Coate, Mary Page Elliott, Lynn Felder, Kathleen M. Flanagan, Joyce Fowler, Angelika Kourelis, and Patricia C. Sharpe. Jean W. Ross is permissions editor. Joseph Caldwell, photography editor, did photographic copy work for the volume.

A project of this magnitude is necessarily the work of many hands, and for such a book to be also of consistent high quality requires the commitment of hearts and minds as well. Credit should go to the contributors who patiently and cheerfully endured too many impersonal form letters from me during our two years of work together. To each of you, a hearty thanks for your goodwill and fine work.

While we would not have this volume without the collective commitment of the contributors, the book certainly would never have seen print without the splendid individual performance of our editor at BC Research, Ms. Karen Rood. Ms. Rood's superb editing skills, her unwavering professionalism, and her genuine scholarly interest in the material were exemplary throughout; she is indeed a person of exceptional talents, and I have been most fortunate to be able to work with her.

Closer to home, I have been able again to count upon the assistance of the mainstay of the Princeton American Studies Program, Mrs. Helen Wright. Aiding me as she has American studies faculty since 1946, Helen helped to organize the complicated assignments for this volume of the *DLB,* and she typed and helped to mail those form letters. During the copyediting stage I received considerable assistance from my research assistant, Ms. Susan Mizruchi, who proved to be a remarkably capable editor as well as the most promising scholar I already knew her to be. Also assisting with final details and in searching for materials for reproduction in the volume has been another graduate student in the Princeton English department, Ms. Elizabeth Dant.

The skillful aid of the reference staff at the John Carter Brown Library at Brown University was essential in providing illustrations for this book. Director Norman Fiering, bibliographer Everett Wilkie, and reference librarian Susan L. Newbury have earned my gratitude.

Valuable assistance was also given by the staff at the Thomas Cooper Library of the University of South Carolina: Lynn Barron, Daniel Boice, Sue Collins, Michael Freeman, Gary Geer, Alexander M. Gilchrist, Jens Holley, David Lincove, Marcia Martin, Roger Mortimer, Jean Rhyne, Karen Rissling, Paula Swope, and Ellen Tillett.

Finally, I acknowledge the contribution of those closest to me whose understanding and support are essential to the completion of any project I assume: my children, Scott, Mark, Matthew, Constance, and Laura, and as ever, my wife, Georgia.

Dictionary of Literary Biography • Volume Thirty-one

American Colonial Writers, 1735-1781

Dictionary of Literary Biography

John Adams

Steven E. Kagle
Illinois State University

BIRTH: Braintree, Massachusetts, 30 October 1734, to John and Susanna Boylston Adams.

EDUCATION: B.A., Harvard College, 1755; studied law under James Putnam, 1756-1758.

MARRIAGE: 25 October 1764 to Abigail Smith; children: Abigail, John Quincy, Susanna, Charles, Thomas Bolyston.

DEATH: Quincy, Massachusetts, 4 July 1826.

SELECTED BOOKS: *Thoughts on Government: Applicable to the Present State of the American Colonies* (Philadelphia: Printed by John Dunlap, 1776);
Observations on the Commerce of the American States with Europe and the West Indies; Including the Several Articles of Import and Export. Also, An Essay on Canon and Feudal Law ... (Philadelphia: Printed & sold by Robert Bell, 1783);
History of a Dispute with America, from its Origins in 1754. Written in 1774 (London: Printed for J. Stockdale, 1784); enlarged edition, in *Novanglus, and Massachusettensis; or, Political Essays, Published in the Years 1774 and 1775, On the Principle Points of Controversy, Between Great Britain and Her Colonies ...*, by Adams, as Novanglus, and David Leonard, as Massachusettensis (Boston: Printed & published by Hews & Goss, 1819);
A Defence of the Constitutions of Government of the United States of America, volume 1 (London: Printed for C. Dilly, 1787; Philadelphia: Printed for Hall & Sellers, J. Crukshank, and Young & M'Colloch, 1787; New York: Printed & sold by H. Gaine, 1787); volumes 2-3 (London: Printed for C. Dilly & J. Stockdale, 1787-1788); volumes 1-3 (Philadelphia: Printed by Budd & Bartram for William Cobbett, 1797);
Discourses on Davila. A Series of Papers, on Political History: Written in the Year 1790, and then published in the Gazette of the United States (Boston: Printed by Russell & Cutler, 1805);
Diary of John Adams and *Autobiography* in volumes 2 and 3 of *The Works of John Adams*, edited by Charles Francis Adams (Boston: Little, Brown, 1850-1851);
The Earliest Diary of John Adams, edited by L. H. Butterfield, Wendell D. Garrett, and Marc Friedlander (Cambridge: Harvard University Press, 1966).

Collections: *The Works of John Adams*, 10 volumes, edited by Charles Francis Adams (Boston: Little, Brown, 1850-1856);
The Adams Papers, 26 volumes to date (Boston: Harvard University Press, 1961-);
Legal Papers of John Adams, edited by L. Kinvin Wroth and Hiller B. Zobel (Cambridge: Belknap Press, 1965).

OTHER: *A Dissertation on the Canon and Feudal Law*, by Adams, but attributed to Jeremy Gridley, in *The True Sentiments of America*, compiled by Thomas Hollis (London: Printed for I. Almon, 1768), pp. 111-143.

John Adams is still far less celebrated than many of his contemporaries, such as Washington, Jefferson, and Franklin, but after a long period of

John and Abigail Adams, August 1766; pastel portraits by Benjamin Blyth (Massachusetts Historical Society)

relative neglect he has regained a highly respected place in American history. Most of Adams's popular reputation is the result of his political activities and public offices, including his role in the first Continental Congresses and his election to the vice-presidency and presidency; however, his importance as a writer and political thinker, which was eclipsed along with his political fortunes during the early-nineteenth century, has now been securely established.

John Adams was born in Braintree, Massachusetts, where his paternal great-great-grandfather Henry Adams had settled in 1639. John's mother, Susanna Boylston, was descended from the Pilgrims who settled at Plymouth in 1621. His father, also named John, was a prosperous farmer, a town selectman, and a church deacon. This Puritan ancestry is observable in the strong emphasis on high morals, active learning, and hard work that mark most of Adam's life and writings.

John was first taught at home, next at a school run by a neighbor, Mrs. Belcher, and then at a local public school taught by Mr. Joseph Cleverly, whom Adams once called "the most indolent man I ever knew." Here the young Adams turned away from the pursuit of excellence that would be such a marked feature of his character, not only because of his "Enthusiasm for Sport" (particularly hunting), but also because his lazy and inattentive teacher failed to provide a challenging pace of study. Adams's behavior so alarmed his father, who had determined that his eldest son should go to college, that he set his son to work beside him gathering thatch in order to teach him that the professions open to an educated man were preferable to farming; however, John, who throughout his life thrived on hard work, was happier "among the Creek Thatch" than at Cleverly's school. Finally, Adams agreed to prepare for college if his father would send him to a school run by Mr. Marsh. Here Adams's zeal for hunting was replaced by zeal for learning, and in 1751 he was admitted to Harvard College.

At Harvard Adams began a series of notes and weather records that soon developed into a diary that would span more than fifty years, during a large portion of which time its author would be close to many of the most important events in American history. There were long and significant periods in which Adams neglected his diary, but for much of the time he wrote regular and extensive entries that give an effective portrait of the diarist and his time. This diary has value not only as a source of information about the life of a major historical figure, but also as a work of intrinsic merit. Indeed, it is also one of the finest diaries written in colonial America.

Adams considered improvement of his style to be one of the principal uses of the diary. In the eighteenth century the imitation of models was considered an effective way of developing one's prose style; for example, Franklin in his *Autobiography* told of imitating the *Spectator Papers,* and Adams's early diary entries show their author's attempts to learn not only from classical and contemporary European models, but also from the best American practices. Adams's diary shows his development of the balanced, rhythmic prose style so valued by writers and critics in the eighteenth century. The forceful expressions and commonplace examples that enliven the work are traceable to the "plaine style" of the Puritans. Adams had a good ear for dialogue, which helped him in characterization; and while by modern standards many of the figures he describes seem too much like stereotypes, Adams was really following forms such as the "prose character" widely used in writing of the period.

As with many diarists, Adams proved his own best character. Just as he could be forceful in his condemnation and satire of others, so he often subjected his own behavior to stern criticism. In addition Adams frequently betrayed truths about his character and its development of which he was, at best, only partially aware. The diary has a clear thematic direction determined by Adams's strong need to achieve. The pattern of its production as well as its content suggest that Adams used the work as a tool to serve his ambition, directing him toward greater and more effective actions. During periods which called for major effort, this diary keeping lapsed. Modeling himself after the hero of one of his favorite fables who chose the steep and difficult path of righteousness over that of vice, Adams would berate himself for what he called idleness and determine to begin some "uncommon unexpected Enterprize" that would surprise the world. Of course, for such sacrifices Adams expected "fame, fortune or something" in exchange. The display of such ambition in the diary invites comparison with the pursuit of excellence and virtue which Benjamin Franklin described in his *Autobiography;* however, while Franklin made himself appear modest, disarming his readers with an admission of vanity, Adams in his diary made himself seem prideful, full of high expectations for himself and scornful of the follies of others. As a result, the diary is less than successful at winning its readers' endorsement of Adams's achievements. Nevertheless, Adams's accomplishments were significant, and the creation of the diary was a major one. Adams's diary is also the earliest part of the most extensive and important multigenerational autobiographical record of any American family, as Adams's practice was passed on to his children and grandchildren.

After graduating with a bachelor's degree in 1755, Adams taught school and, from 1756 to 1758, studied law with James Putnam. In 1761, the young lawyer accompanied a friend, William Cranch, on his visits to see Mary, the eldest daughter of Reverend Smith of Weymouth. These visits led to Adams's courtship of and marriage to Mary's sister Abigail in 1764. During this courtship Adams and Abigail Smith began a correspondence that has been frequently published and cited. The early letters were highly stylized. John, adopting the pseudonym Lysander, and Abigail, the pseudonym Diana, wrote of romantic dreams, and casual banter often covered more serious concerns as when Abigail wrote requesting a "catalogue" of her faults and John proceeded to complain of such things as her walk, posture, and bashfulness. Letters written during long separations after the marriage provide insights into the events and individuals that led to the birth of the American nation. For example, in one letter Adams complained of the Continental Congress, "Every Man in it is a great Man—an orator, a Critick, a statesman, and therefore every Man upon every Question must shew his oratory, his Criticism and his Political Abilities."

Adams became active in political controversies following the imposition of the Stamp Act in 1765. His essays (later titled *A Dissertation on the Canon and Feudal Law* when Thomas Hollis included them in *The True Sentiments of America,* 1768) were published in the *Boston Gazette,* where two years earlier he had published some humorous pieces under the name Humphrey Ploughjogger. *A Dissertation on the Canon and Feudal Law,* which was also published with Adams's *Observations on the Commerce of the American States with Europe and the West Indies* in 1783, argued the existence of a largely unwritten British constitution, which superseded the tyrannical and outdated civil and ecclesiastical law of the Middle Ages. Adams, like Jonathan Mayhew, used New England's Puritan rejection of "unlimited submission to a monolithic church hierarchy" to attack the claim of the British political establishment to total authority over the colonies. The same year Adams drafted and on October 14th published in the *Boston*

First page of Adams's first diary (courtesy of Royall Tyler Collection at the Vermont Historical Society)

An 1849 painting by Frankenstein of the Adams family farm in Braintree. John Adams was born in the house on the right; after their marriage, he and Abigail Adams lived in the house on the left, where John Quincy Adams was born (Adams National Historic Site).

Gazette the "Instructions of the Town of Braintree to their Representative," which insisted that "no freeman should be subject to any tax to which he has not given his own consent." On 13 January 1866 Adams published the first of a series of letters under the name Clarendon. These letters, written in reply to others and signed with the name Pym, had been reprinted two months earlier in the *Boston Evening Post* from material that had originally appeared in the *London Evening Post*. Adams argued that the British constitution limited the king's power. While these pieces gained him some recognition, they did not lead to political office as Adams hoped.

Adams withdrew from active politics until 1770 when he agreed to join Josiah Quincy in defending the soldiers involved in the Boston Massacre. Although he opposed the stationing of these British troops in Boston, Adams could not condone mob action. He eventually won the acquittal of all but two of the soldiers, and those two were convicted only of the lesser charge of manslaughter. In June of 1774 Adams was chosen by the Massachusetts legislature as one of five representatives to the First Continental Congress.

Beginning in January of 1775, Adams again wrote a series of letters to the *Boston Gazette,* this time in response to another series written by David Leonard under the pen name Massachusettensis (Adams mistakenly believed that they had been written by Jonathan Sewall). Adopting the name Novanglus, Adams argued that America and Britain shared a common king but were "distinct states." As such, Adams concluded, they could not be controlled by Parliament except in the area of foreign trade or where they had granted "*compact* and *consent.*" In the Novanglus letters, Adams argued a principle later articulated in the Declaration of Independence: that New England derived its law and rights not from Parliamentary or English common law, but from "the law of nature and the compact made with the king in our charters." Therefore, if the king broke his part of this social contract, his action would also "annul it on the part of the people." In such a case, Adams concluded, even "open avowed resistance by arms" would not be rebellion but lawful action. When the Novanglus letters were written, Adams still disavowed any intention to seek independence, but after the first battles of the Revolution, he became one of its strongest advocates in Congress. A member of the committee appointed to draft the Declaration of Independence, Adams signed it for Massachusetts.

In Congress Adams became acutely aware of the differences among the colonies. Observing that the Southern states were suspicious of the republicanism of New England and recognizing that prospects for union would be enhanced if all the states had comparable government, Adams wrote, privately circulated, and later published his *Thoughts on Government* (1776). In this essay he supported a form of government which he knew would seem too republican for the South and insufficiently republican for New England but which he hoped would prove acceptable to both sections. Although the basic values expressed were similar to those he had long held, Adams skillfully manipulated the emphasis by stressing the advantages of a bicameral legislature in which only one house needed to be directly elected as means to provide checks and balances against the power of any group.

Adams finally left Congress in 1777 in order to return to his law practice, but he soon received word that Congress had chosen him as part of a joint commission to France. After serving there until 1779, Adams returned home and was soon involved in drafting a constitution for Massachusetts. He had only been home for a few months when he accepted commissions to treat with Great Britain on both peace and trade. In Europe Adams was instrumental in securing important loans from the Dutch and was one of the commissioners who negotiated and signed the Treaty of Paris, establishing peace with Britain. Adams stayed in Europe serving as America's first ambassador to the Court of St. James's until 1786.

During his last year in England, Adams began his *A Defence of the Constitutions of Government of the United States of America* (1787-1788). He devoted most of the work to a lengthy analysis of the history of several European states to prove that the lack of appropriate checks and balances, whether in monarchies, aristocracies, or democracies, inevitably led to a loss of liberty and frequently to disruptive violence. In his preface Adams argued that these problems might be avoided by a tripartite division of authority among separate executive, legislative, and judicial branches as well as a further division of legislative power between two houses. While in most of his earlier works Adams had been primarily concerned with the dangers of the power of government, in these proposals, he paid greater attention to the dangers of unchecked popular sentiment as well as to those from the intrusion of government on the rights of individuals. Such sentiments were later used by Adams's political opponents as evidence of aristocratic tendencies. The first volume of the *A Defence of the Constitutions of Government of the United States of America* was published in America during the deliberations of the Constitutional Convention, and, along with the constitution that Adams drafted for Massachusetts in 1779, it had a significant influence on the Constitution of the United States.

Adams returned to Boston on 17 June 1788, just as the new Constitution was about to be ratified, and the next year he was elected the first vice-president of the United States. During his first term as vice-president, news of the radicalism of the French Revolution prompted his writing of *Discourses on Davila* (1805), a warning against unlimited democracy. With a Puritan's distrust of man's inner nature, Adams suggested that benevolence was not an effective balance for the selfish affections and concluded that, as "emulation and rivalry" could not be repressed, they should be "directed to virtue and then stimulated." Because *Discourses on Davila* was a long and stiffly scholarly work (Adams, himself, called it "heavy" and "dull"), few people read it in its entirety; yet it produced great controversy. Political adversaries seized on the work as an opportunity to brand Adams as a monarchist and an opponent of the Constitution.

In 1797 a three-vote plurality in the electoral college made Adams the second president. Among the most difficult problems Adams faced during his administration was his attempt to keep America free from the war with Britain and France. The most serious threat to peace was the XYZ affair in which French agents had demanded bribes and loans from America. When these demands became known there was a movement to improve American military strength, and this action required an increase in taxes. The most serious domestic problem involved the Alien and Sedition Acts. The Alien Acts allowed the president to deport not only enemy aliens but any noncitizen who might be a threat to public order. The Sedition Act permitted the imprisonment of anyone who slandered or libeled members of the federal government.

In 1800 Adams lost the presidency to Thomas Jefferson. This loss has been attributed to several factors including taxation, the Alien and Sedition Acts and dissension within the Federalist party (especially a conspiracy led by Alexander Hamilton

Engraved broadside by Amos Doolittle, celebrating Adams's stand during disputes with France. The slogan at the top of the broadside is attributed to Charles C. Pinckney, Adams's special envoy to France (Massachusetts Historical Society).

to get Adams replaced as the party's candidate). After losing the election Adams retired to Quincy, where on 5 October 1802 he began work on his autobiography. Adams professed to be writing it for his family and not the general public; however, his obvious attempts to defend his career, which continued to be under political and personal attack, suggest that he at least considered the possibility of a wider audience. Not only does the autobiography appear more self-conscious and formal than the diary, but its style and format seem stiffer than one expects in works of this genre. During the writing of the autobiography Adams seems to have rediscovered his diary, which he had ignored for years, and relied heavily on it for the balance of the new work. However, the reworked material is far less engaging than the original in the diary.

Another important product of Adams's retirement was his correspondence with Thomas Jefferson. Jefferson and Adams had been estranged as the result of political rivalries and misunderstandings that arose as a result of them. Benjamin Rush, with whom Adams kept a long and productive correspondence, arranged a reconciliation between the two former presidents. On New Year's Day 1812, Adams wrote the first of a long series of letters in which he and Jefferson explored their personal and political principles and found themselves in surprising agreement. When, on 4 July 1826, exactly fifty years after the signing of the Declaration of

Independence, Adams lay on his deathbed, his last words were, "Thomas Jefferson survives." But Jefferson had died only hours before.

Letters:

Correspondence Between the Hon. John Adams and the Late Wm. Cunningham . . . (Boston: E. M. Cunningham, 1823);

Letters of John Adams, Addressed to His Wife, edited by Charles Francis Adams (Boston: Little & Brown, Co., 1841);

Correspondence between John Adams and Mercy Warren . . . , edited by Charles Francis Adams, in *Collections of the Massachusetts Historical Society,* fifth series, 4 (1878): 315-511;

Warren-Adams Letters, Being Chiefly a Correspondence Among John Adams, Samuel Adams, and James Warren, edited by Worthington Chauncey Ford, *Collections of the Massachusetts Historical Society,* 72-73 (1917-1925);

Statesman and Friend, the Correspondence of John Adams with Benjamin Waterhouse 1784-1822, edited by Worthington Chauncey Ford (Boston: Little, Brown, 1927);

The Adams-Jefferson Letters, edited by Lester J. Cappon, 2 volumes (Chapel Hill: University of North Carolina Press, 1959);

Adams Family Correspondence, volumes 1-2, edited by L. H. Butterfield, Wendell D. Garrett, and Marjorie E. Sprague (Cambridge: Harvard University Press, 1963); volumes 3-4, edited by Butterfield and Marc Friedlander (Cambridge: Harvard University Press, 1973);

The Spur of Fame: Dialogues of John Adams and Benjamin Rush, 1805-1813, edited by John A. Schutz and Douglas Adair (San Marino: Huntington Library, 1966).

Bibliography:

John W. Cronin and W. Harvey Wise, Jr., *A Bibliography of John Adams and John Quincy Adams* (Washington: Riverford Publishing Company, 1935).

Biographies:

Gilbert Chinard, *Honest John Adams* (Boston: Little, Brown, 1933);

Catherine Drinker Bowen, *John Adams and the American Revolution* (Boston: Little, Brown, 1950);

Page Smith, *John Adams,* 2 volumes (Garden City: Doubleday, 1962);

James Bishop Peabody, ed., *John Adams, A Biography in His Own Words* (New York: Newsweek Inc., 1973);

Peter Shaw, *The Character of John Adams* (Chapel Hill: University of North Carolina Press, 1976).

References:

Zoltán Haraszti, *John Adams and the Prophets of Progress* (Cambridge: Harvard University Press, 1952);

John R. Howe, Jr., *The Changing Political Thought of John Adams* (Princeton: Princeton University Press, 1966);

Steven G. Kurtz, *The Presidency of John Adams* (Philadelphia: University of Pennsylvania Press, 1957).

Papers:

Most of the papers of John Adams are located at the Massachusetts Historical Society in Boston, where, along with those of other members of the Adams family, they are being edited for publication by the Belknap Press of Harvard University. Microfilm copies of these papers are available at several major libraries.

Samuel Adams
(16 September 1722-2 October 1803)

Elaine K. Ginsberg
West Virginia University

BOOKS: *An Appeal to the World; Or, A Vindication of the Town of Boston* . . . (Boston: Printed & sold by Edes & Gill, 1769);
The Writings of Samuel Adams, edited by Harry A. Cushing, 4 volumes (New York: Putnam's, 1904-1908).

Samuel Adams was, according to his cousin John Adams, "born and tempered a wedge of steel to split the knot of *lignum vitae*" that tied the colonies to Great Britain. Even his Loyalist critics testified to his skill as a political organizer, writer, and molder of public opinion.

Born in Boston, Adams was one of twelve children of Samuel and Mary Fifield Adams. The elder Samuel was a brewer, a deacon in the Old South Church, and active in local politics. Adams attended the Boston Latin School and was graduated from Harvard College in 1740 with a B.A. Three years later he took his M.A. at Harvard, arguing the affirmative of the proposition "Whether it be lawful to resist the Supreme Magistrate, if the Commonwealth cannot otherwise be preserved." Adams studied law briefly, was unsuccessful in a business of his own, and then joined his father in the brewery. He married Elizabeth Checkley in 1749; she died in 1757, leaving two children. In 1764 he married Elizabeth Wells.

Following his father's example, Adams participated actively in local Boston politics. In 1748 he helped to found the *Independent Advertiser,* a short-lived weekly magazine for which he wrote on political and moral issues. By 1764 his political influence was considerable; in that year he drafted the instructions to Boston's representatives to the General Court, and in 1765 he was elected to the Massachusetts House of Representatives. He was soon the acknowledged leader of the radical party, which controlled the General Court after 1766. Although he led the opposition to the Townshend Acts and was the leader and chief organizer of the Sons of Liberty, nothing in his writings of the 1760s suggests that he was an early agitator for independence. In fact, he explicitly disavowed such an idea in a letter he drafted for the Massachusetts Assembly in January 1768, writing that the citizens of Massachusetts were "so sensible . . . of this happiness and safety, in their union with, and dependence upon, the mother country, that they would by no means be inclined to accept of an independency, if offered to them." In an article signed Alfred that was published in the *Boston Gazette* for 2 October 1769, he expressed fears that the "jealousy between the mother country and the colonies" might finally end in the ruin of "the most glorious Empire the sun ever shone upon." Nevertheless, a persistent theme in Adams's writings is the ever-present and immi-

Portrait by John Singleton Copley (Museum of Fine Arts, Boston)

Engraving by Paul Revere

nent danger of British tyranny. A letter to Christopher Gadsden of South Carolina (December 1766) is typical; after expressing satisfaction and relief at the repeal of the Stamp Act, Adams asks, "But is there no Reason to fear the Liberties of the Colonies may be infringed in a less observable manner? The Stamp Act was like a sword that Nero wished for, to have decollated the Roman People at a stroke, or like Job's Sea monster.... The Sight of such an Enemy at a distance is formidable, while the lurking Serpent lies concealed, and not noticed by the unwary Passenger, darts its fatal Venom. It is necessary then that each Colony should be awake and upon its Guard."

An issue to which Adams devoted much attention was the presence of British troops in Massachusetts. Hoping to enlist the support of every colony in demanding the withdrawal of the troops, Adams sent to sympathetic printers throughout the colonies a "Journal" recounting innumerable British "atrocities": soldiers beating small boys, harassing merchants, violating the Sabbath, and raping Boston women. By fanning Bostonians' hatred of the British troops, Adams probably contributed to the very real tragedy of 1770 known as the Boston Massacre. Yet following the trial of the soldiers involved in that incident, he continued to agitate, writing a series of articles for the *Boston Gazette*, signed Vindex, attempting to prove the guilt of the soldiers and attributing their acquittal to the shortcomings of the jury. Adams paints the scene in lurid colors, accusing the soldiers of "savage barbarity" and describing bayonets five inches deep in citizen blood. As he continued to agitate against the British troops and against the royal government, he filled the pages of the *Boston Gazette* not only with his own writing but also with items from other papers, with official documents, and with extracts from correspondence.

Educated in theology, the ancient classics, and the law, Samuel Adams was also thoroughly grounded in the total body of Whig political classics. Three basic principles undergirded his political philosophy: the natural rights of man, the particular rights and privileges granted to the British citizen under the constitution, and the rights and privileges of the colonists granted by the various charters. In the "State of the Rights of the Colonists," adopted by the Boston town meeting 20 November 1772, Adams clearly delineated the Lockian principle that all civil rights are firmly rooted in natural law: "All men have a Right to remain in a State of Nature as long as they please: and in the case of intolerable Oppression, Civil or Religious, to leave the Society they belong to, and enter into another." As late as 1794, having assumed the governorship of Massachusetts, he publicly reaffirmed his strong belief in the principles of natural law and natural rights and the compact theory of government.

Samuel Adams was a thorough Puritan who considered the most important legacy of New England's founding fathers to be their zeal and virtue. He saw in the era of political crisis surrounding the American Revolution an opportunity for "recovering the Virtue and reforming the Manners of our Country." Included in his idea of virtue was the subordination of self-interest to community interest: "It would be the glory of this Age, to find Men having no ruling Passion but the Love of their Country, and ready to render her the most arduous and important Services with the Hope of no other Reward in this Life than the Esteem of their virtuous Fellow Citizens." Subordination of self to country permeated Adams's own life and writings; he was ambitious for neither social status nor material wealth. It is said that when he left for Philadelphia to represent Massachusetts at the Continental Congress, his friends, embarrassed by the condition of his clothing, presented him with a complete new outfit and some spending money. "For my own part," he wrote in 1774, "I have been wont to converse with poverty; and however disagreeable she may be thought to be by the affluent and luxurious who never were acquainted with her, I can live happily with her the remainder of my days, if I can thereby contribute to the redemption of my Country."

Adams was a member of both the First and Second Continental Congresses and signed the Declaration of Independence. He served as a member of the Massachusetts Constitutional Convention and in 1789 was elected lieutenant governor under John Hancock. Adams became governor upon Hancock's death in 1793 and was elected to that office in 1794.

John Adams wrote in 1817 that "Without the character of Samuel Adams, the true history of the American Revolution can never be written. For fifty years, his pen, his tongue, his activity, were constantly exerted for his country without fee or reward." Samuel Adams's writings included resolutions and instructions of the town of Boston, official letters, resolutions, and appeals of the Massachusetts House of Representatives and circular letters of the Committees of Correspondence. His hundreds of articles in the Boston newspapers appeared under as many as twenty-five different pseudonyms. In addition he kept up a steady correspondence with political leaders throughout the colonies and in England. His writings, along with his other activities, were unquestionably a major propaganda force of the revolutionary era.

References:

Stewart Beach, *Samuel Adams: The Fateful Years, 1764-1776* (New York: Dodd, Mead, 1965);

Pauline Maier, *The Old Revolutionaries* (New York: Knopf, 1980);

John C. Miller, *Sam Adams, Pioneer in Propaganda* (Boston: Little, Brown, 1936);

Vernon L. Parrington, "Samuel Adams, the Mind of the American Democrat," in his *The Colonial Mind, 1620-1800*, volume 1 of *Main Currents of American Thought* (New York: Harcourt, Brace, 1927), pp. 233-247.

Papers:

There are collections of Adams's papers at the Lenox Library Association in Lenox, Massachusetts, the New York Public Library, the Massachusetts Historical Society, the Historical Society of Pennsylvania, the American Philosophical Society, the Connecticut Historical Society, and the Boston Public Library.

Ethan Allen
(21 January 1738-12 February 1789)

Martha Strom
Princeton University

BOOKS: *A Brief Narrative of the Proceedings of the Government of New-York, Relative to Their Obtaining Jurisdiction of that Large District of Land, to the Westward from Connecticut River* . . . (Hartford: Printed by Eben Watson, 1774);

An Animadversory Address to the Inhabitants of the State of Vermont . . . (Hartford: Printed by Watson & Goodwin, 1778);

A Narrative of Colonel Ethan Allen's Captivity . . . (Philadelphia: Printed & sold by Robert Bell, 1779);

A Vindication of the Opposition of the Inhabitants of Vermont to the Government of New-York, and of their Right to Form into an Independent State . . . (Dresden, N.H.: Printed by Alden Spooner, 1779);

A Concise Refutation of the Claims of New-Hampshire and Massachusetts-Bay, to the Territory of Vermont . . . , by Allen and Jonas Fay (Hartford: Printed by Hudson & Goodwin, 1780);

The Present State of the Controversy Between the States of New-York and New-Hampshire on the One Part and the State of Vermont on the Other (Hartford: Printed by Hudson & Goodwin, 1782);

Reason the Only Oracle of Man . . . (Bennington, Vt: Printed by Haswell & Russell, 1784).

A revolutionary soldier of legendary prowess and verve and the author of a number of controversial works, Ethan Allen was born to Joseph and Mary Baker Allen in Litchfield, Connecticut, the eldest of eight children. Little is known of his early life except that his preparation for college was cut short when his father died in 1755. After serving at Fort William Henry in 1757 during the French and Indian War he went to live in the New Hampshire Grants, and in 1762 he married Mary Brownson, who bore him five children (three of whom died before adulthood) before her death in 1783. The following year he married Mrs. Frances Montresor Buchanan, with whom he had three children.

Allen's talent for leadership became evident during the dispute in 1769 between New York and New Hampshire over the control of the New Hampshire Grants, which became Vermont. Remembered primarily as the "colonel commandant" of the Green Mountain Boys, a group organized during the dispute over Vermont, and as the military hero who captured Fort Ticonderoga on 10 May 1775, Ethan Allen's most respected literary achievement is *A Narrative of Colonel Ethan Allen's Captivity* (1779). Captured by the British while he was attempting to attack Montreal in September

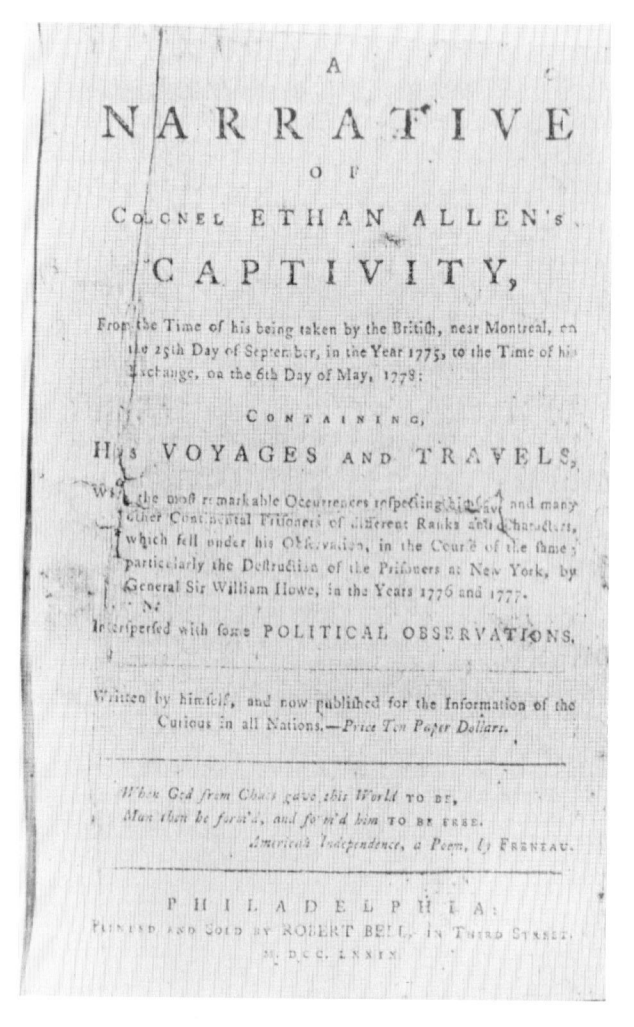

Title page for Allen's description of his life as a prisoner of war. Transported in irons to England, he was often displayed to curious members of the nobility. Allen used such occasions, he said, to deliver "harrangues on the impracticality of Great Britain's conquering the then colonies of America."

Title page for Allen's attempt to define a rational universe and his inscription in the copy he gave his second wife

1775, he was held prisoner until 6 May 1778, when he was at last exchanged for Col. Archibald Campbell. The narrative describing his captivity was a best-seller, appearing in five editions within the first two years of its publication. Promulgating the virtues of the Green Mountain Boys and condemning the British, the book's immense popularity helped to further Washington's efforts to keep the American cause alive.

Allen also wrote provocative newspaper articles, political pamphlets, and several other longer works. A substantial proportion of Allen's writings are defenses of Vermont containing arguments designed to persuade Congress to proclaim Vermont a state. The philosophical work in which he announced that he was not a Christian, *Reason the Only Oracle of Man* (1784), offended the public and was burned by its printer. The full title explains the stir caused by this first book opposing revealed religion to be published in America: *Reason the Only Oracle of Man, or a Compenduous System of Natural Religion. Alternately Adorned with Confutations of a variety of Doctrines incompatible to it; Deduced from the most exalted Ideas which we are able to form of the Divine and Human Characters, and from the Universe in General.*

Allen died in 1789 of apoplexy in Burlington, Vermont. In his last years he had settled in Sunderland, Vermont, to tend to his farms and local Vermont affairs, and his writing changed as his life became less vehemently political and more conducive to contemplation. Scholars portray Ethan Allen as a political hero, but his biographers admire his talent as a polemical writer and his consistently undaunted independence of mind.

Biographies:
Hugh Moore, *Memoir of Colonel Ethan Allen* (Plattsburg, N.Y.: O. R. Cook, 1834);

Stewart H. Holbrook, *Ethan Allen* (New York: Macmillan, 1940);

Charles Albert Jellison, *Ethan Allen: Frontier Rebel* (Syracuse: Syracuse University Press, 1969).

References:
Charles Walter Brown, *Ethan Allen of Green Mountain Fame: A Hero of the Revolution* (Chicago: Donohue, 1902);

John Pell, *Ethan Allen* (Boston: Houghton Mifflin, 1929);

Pell, Introduction to *A Narrative of Col. Ethan Allen's Captivity* (New York: Georgian Press, 1930);

John Spargo, *Ethan Allen at Ticonderoga* (Rutland, Vt.: Tuttle, 1926).

Papers:
Among the institutions that hold letters, manuscripts, and other documents are the Vermont Historical Society, the University of Vermont, the New-York Historical Society, the Connecticut Historical Society, and the office of the Secretary of State of Vermont in Montpelier, Vermont.

James Allen
(24 July 1739-1808)

Lewis Leary
University of North Carolina

BOOK: *The Poem Which the Committee of the Town of Boston Had Voted Unanimously to Be Published with the Late Oration . . .* (Boston: Printed & sold by E. Russell, 1772).

OTHER: Samuel Kettell, ed., *Specimens of American Poetry*, volume 1 includes poems by Allen (Boston: S. G. Goodrich, 1829).

James Allen, a poet of Boston, was the son of a wealthy merchant of that city. He spent three years at Harvard, but left without a degree. The rest of his life was spent in what one of his contemporaries remembered as indolent repose, writing essays and verses on local affairs that he was quick to recite at the drop of a suggestion to literary or bibulous companions but that he did not take the trouble to publish.

All of literary Boston seems to have known, talked about, and admired his poem on the Battle of Bunker Hill, which was apparently never printed and does not survive. In 1772, on the second anniversary of the Boston Massacre, he composed an ardently patriotic poem to be presented with the address delivered on that occasion by Dr. Joseph Warren. Loyalists in Boston seized upon that poem, calling it a clever ploy meant to deceive patriots and,

Portrait of James Allen by John Singleton Copley (Massachusetts Historical Society)

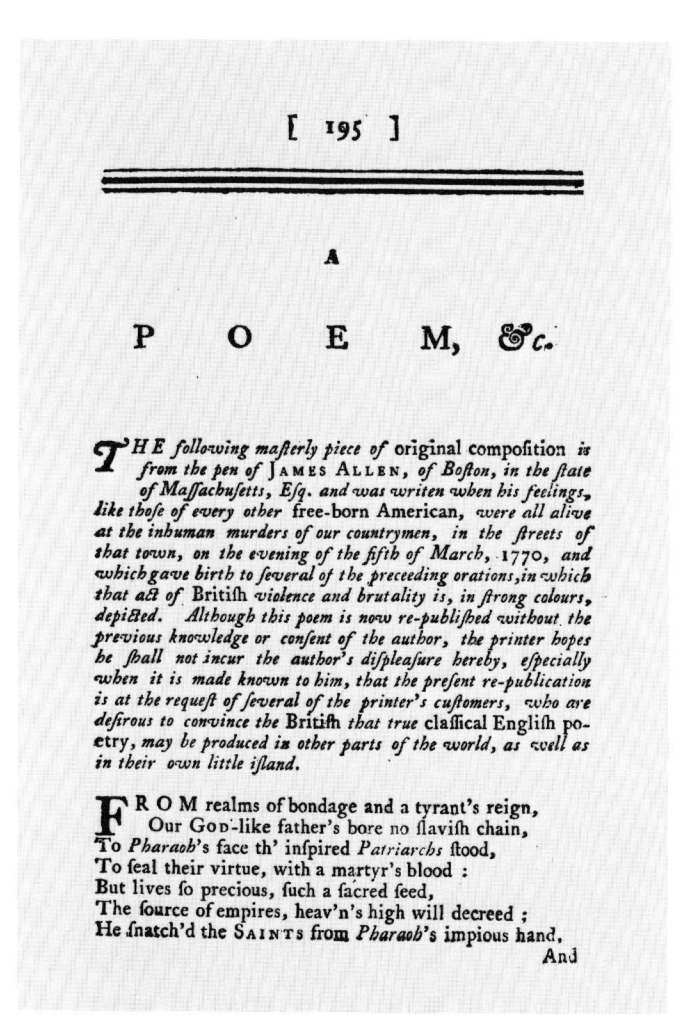

First page of Allen's poem on the Boston Massacre, as it appears in a 1785 collection of orations commemorating that event (courtesy of the John Carter Brown Library at Brown University)

to prove their assertion, printed it later in that year side by side with an earlier poem by Allen called "The Retrospect," which was as ardently pro-British as the poem on the massacre was propatriot. Allen at that time made no reply, but in 1785 allowed his poem on the massacre to be printed again in Boston, and it was also included in that year in a volume collecting orations commemorative of the massacre. Both pamphlets are extremely rare.

From December 1785 to March 1786 Allen or perhaps one of his patriot friends contributed three parts of another poem called "The Retrospect" to the *Boston Magazine,* this time affirming his allegiance to the new United States. The largest collection of Allen's verse is the five poems found in Samuel Kettell's *Specimens of American Poetry* (1829). Allen died, as he had lived, anonymously, a strange man, Boston's first literary bohemian, who was said to have written most harmoniously "when inspired by the West Indian Muses, sugar, rum, and lemon juice," and who kept his coffin in his bedchamber and sometimes slept in it.

References:

Samuel Kettell, "James Allen," in *Specimens of American Poetry,* edited by Kettell (Boston: S. G. Goodrich, 1829), I: 160-162;

Samuel L. Knapp, *Biographical Sketches of Eminent Lawyers, Statesmen, and Men of Letters* (Boston: Richardson & Lord, 1821), pp. 150-151;

Lewis Leary, "The 'Friends' of James Allen, or, How Partial Truth Is No Truth at All," *Early American Literature,* 15 (Fall 1980): 165-171;

H. E. Scudder, ed., *Recollections of Samuel Breck, with Passages from His Notebooks* (Philadelphia: Porter & Coates, 1877), pp. 190-193.

Josiah Atkins
(circa 1755-circa 15 October 1781)

John C. Shields
Illinois State University

BOOK: *The Diary of Josiah Atkins,* edited by Steven E. Kagle (New York: Arno Press, 1975).

Josiah Atkins's diary, written while the author served as an American soldier in the Revolutionary War, first in the infantry and later as a military nurse, is of importance not only to students of history, but also to students of literature; its clear, unadorned, though pleasant, style makes it one of the best journals written in America before 1800 by an author who had not had the benefit of university training.

What is known about the life of this man from Waterbury, Connecticut, is contained in the diary. Since the journal records only Atkins's experiences while serving in the military from January 1781 until shortly before his death in the middle of October of the same year, details of his earlier life must be reconstructed from descriptions he gives in the journal. He appears to have been married and the father of two children, Sally and Josiah, born while he was in service. Atkins himself was probably no older than twenty-five or twenty-six when he died. The enthusiastic devotion displayed in the diary suggests that he was a pious and active church member, probably of a conservative Congregational parish. His vocation was that of tool and instrument maker, but it is evident from the diary that in Waterbury Atkins had also practiced the letting of blood and the "drawing" of teeth.

The diary includes observations and comments on various maneuvers of Washington, General Lafayette, and Colonel St. Simon as they engaged in the campaigns which eventually resulted in the surrender of Cornwallis at Yorktown only four days after Atkins's last entry. Atkins's writings about slavery leave no doubt as to his sympathies; he is appalled to discover that some of the same citizens who have proclaimed rights and liberties for all also keep 200 to 900 slaves to labor on their Virginia plantations. At one point, Atkins records a slaves' protest march "arising from their harsh treatment." According to Atkins, blacks "flock'd in great numbers to Cornwallis, as soon as he came into these parts" of Virginia.

Atkins's strong objections to slavery seem to derive from his even stronger commitment to his God. In the same passage where he laments the hypocrisy of slaveowners, he quotes Peter 2:19: "While they promise them liberty, they themselves are the servants of corruption." He also regrets his complicity in an undertaking which not only takes him away from family and friends but also forces him into "the capacity of a soldier carrying the cruel and unwelcome instruments of war." "Oh!," he exclaims, "that I were as great as my grief, or less than my name!" Were he as great as his grief he would end the conflict; were he less than his name, Josiah, which in Hebrew means "May Yahweh heal," he could adjust to his predicament with less anxiety. Here Atkins reveals the power of his faith. He makes it a practice to observe the Sabbath by writing passages which resemble colloquies with God. These passages never become reduced to mere exercises but always appear to grow out of his spiritual needs at the time.

It is perhaps no surprise to learn that this man so concerned with his spiritual health would find great satisfaction in ministering to the medical needs of his fellows. When the opportunity arose for him to assist a physician as "doctors mate," he seized it. Serving in this capacity he could avoid the possibility of causing death and could learn more about a profession in which he had already developed a marked interest. Twice in the journal, Atkins declares, "I have such thirst for medical knowledge." On a certain occasion, disagreeing with the resident physician's decision not to bleed a patient, he writes that "the quality of blood was not lessen'd by proper bleeding." Even though this reasoning, that the quality of a patient's blood is of greater concern than its quantity, has been disproved by modern medicine, Atkins's theory reflects what was then held to be a legitimate argument for treatment. And Atkins significantly observes that he has set this incident down "for some future consideration and my own improvement."

The number of cancellations and revisions noted by Steven Kagle, the editor of the manuscript, suggests that Atkins gave careful thought to his writings, as well as to his quest for medical knowledge. Every change represents an improvement in the text. Although the diary contains not a single classical allusion (suggesting that Atkins was not university-trained), the number of biblical allusions is legion, showing definite familiarity with the King James Bible. Atkins also uses such words as *importunate, affirmative,* and *precipitation*—none of which occurs in the King James Bible, and at one point he uses the phrase *feu-de-joy* (for "feu de joie") to describe an artillery salute "on account of the anniversary of American independence." Thus, Atkins displays a more than modest reading background, one which certainly extends beyond knowledge of the Bible.

While it is unlikely that Atkins consciously intended to give his diary unity, two unifying patterns can be discerned in it. Kagle points out in his introductory remarks that Atkins's identification of himself early in the diary as a "stranger in a strange land" enables the diarist to see himself in terms of Moses and therefore to project an element of hope into his predicament. Hence when he much later seizes the opportunity to serve as a male nurse, he sees his improved condition as that of "*pilgrim* and *stranger* on earth; and may this turn my tho'ts on *seeking another and better,* even an *heavenly* one, whose builder and maker is God." Once an isolated stranger in a hostile land, this young man, because of his fulfilling service as minister to others' health, feels assured that he is on the road to heavenly reward.

The other unifying pattern is, in fact, Atkins's interest in medicine. Even prior to his assignment as male nurse Atkins occasionally mentions that he prefers to serve as amateur physic to his fellow soldiers rather than as infantryman. When the news of the opportunity for his reassignment is reported three-quarters of the way into the book, it serves as a sort of climax. The tone of the journal immediately becomes positive; there are no more pronouncements on the cruel instruments of war. Rather Atkins throws himself into his work, and even when he falls ill, this pious man of God remains positive. Thinking that an emetic agent will contribute to his cure, the young man seeks the proper chemical which will serve his purpose; "but still all availed nothing. A sad pickle I shou'd have been in had not nature given me a remedy! By the help of my finger I bro't up all the physic, and made out considerable" vomiting.

In *The Diary of Josiah Atkins,* Atkins's good humor is combined with a piety that commands respect. As documentation of the final days of the American struggle for independence, and as a commentary on the evils of slavery and the state of medicine in the eighteenth century, *The Diary of Josiah Atkins* is an important record, whose value is enhanced still more by its stylistic excellence.

Reference:

Steven E. Kagle, ed., Introduction to *The Diary of Josiah Atkins* (New York: Arno Press, 1975), pp. 1-17.

Thomas Bacon

(*circa 1700-26 May 1768*)

Robert Micklus
State University of New York at Binghamton

BOOKS: *A Compleat System of the Revenue of Ireland . . .* (Dublin: Printed by R. Reilly, 1737);

Two Sermons, Preached to a Congregation of Black Slaves, at the Parish Church of S.P., in the Province of Maryland (London: Printed by John Oliver, 1749);

Four Sermons, Upon the Great and Indispensible Duty of All Christian Masters and Mistresses to Bring Up Their Negro Slaves in the Knowledge and Fear of God . . . (London: Printed by John Oliver, 1750);

A Sermon Preached at the Parish Church of St. Peter's, in Talbot County, Maryland: On Sunday the 14th of October, 1750, for the Benefit of a Charity Working School to be Set Up in the Said Parish . . . (London: Printed by John Oliver, 1751);

A Sermon, Preached at Annapolis, in Maryland, Before a Society of Free and Accepted Masons . . . (An-

Alexander Hamilton's caricature of Thomas Bacon, from the manuscript for Hamilton's The History of the Tuesday Club
(The Milton S. Eisenhower Library, The Johns Hopkins University)

napolis: Printed & sold by Jonas Green, 1753);
An Answer to the Queries on the Proprietary Government of Maryland, by Bacon and Cecilius Calvert (London, 1764);
Writings of the Rev. Thomas Bacon (London: Religious Tract Society, n.d.; Philadelphia: Presbyterian Board Publication, 1843).

OTHER: *Laws of Maryland At Large . . . ,* compiled by Bacon (Annapolis: Printed by Jonas Green, 1765).

The Reverend Thomas Bacon, one of colonial Maryland's most prolific authors, is remembered today primarily for his sermons on charity schools and the education of slaves, and for his compilation *Laws of Maryland At Large . . .* (1765). In his own day he was also known as a poet of modest abilities, a political essayist worthy of defending Lord Baltimore's proprietary party against Franklin's attacks, and an outstanding musician.

Other than the fact that he was raised in Ireland (perhaps Dublin, where his brother, Anthony

Title page for Bacon's 1749 book, evidence of his concern for the spiritual well-being and education of black slaves (courtesy of the John Carter Brown Library at Brown University)

Bacon, M.P., attended Trinity College), little is known about Bacon's early life. Records show that he was working for the Custom House in Dublin by 1737 and that he began publishing the *Dublin Mercury,* a biweekly newspaper, by 23 January 1742. By 27 September 1742, Bacon was printing the official newspaper of Ireland, the *Dublin Gazette,* which he published only until 12 July 1743, when he began preparing for the ministry.

Following in his brother's footsteps, the Reverend Thomas Bacon sailed to America in June 1745 and shortly thereafter was appointed rector of St. Peter's, Talbot County, by the governor of Maryland, Thomas Bladen. During that time, Bacon was elected an honorary member of Dr. Alexander Hamilton's Tuesday Club of Annapolis (Bacon appears frequently as "Signior Lardini" in Hamilton's 1,900-page mock epic, *The History of the Tuesday Club*), where he was appointed club musician *con stromenti.* Bacon had a large hand in composing most of the Tuesday Club's music (much of which appears in Hamilton's *The History of the Tuesday Club*), and was so distinguished a musician that the other club members sometimes deferred performing their songs and odes until he was present. In the summer of 1755 Bacon's wife died, and soon thereafter a mulatto, Rachel Beck, accused him of rape. Bacon sued her for libel and won, but in the spring of 1756 disaster again struck when his only son, John ("John Gabble" in *The History of the Tuesday Club*), was killed and scalped during a march of the Independent Maryland Foot Company against the French at the Ohio. Toward the end of 1758, however, Bacon's life took a turn for the better when he was appointed minister of All Saints, Frederick County (at that time the most lucrative parish in Maryland), and shortly before his death in 1768 he was elected a member of the American Philosophical Society.

Bacon published numerous sermons and essays while he was living in Maryland. The more significant ones included *Two Sermons, Preached to a*

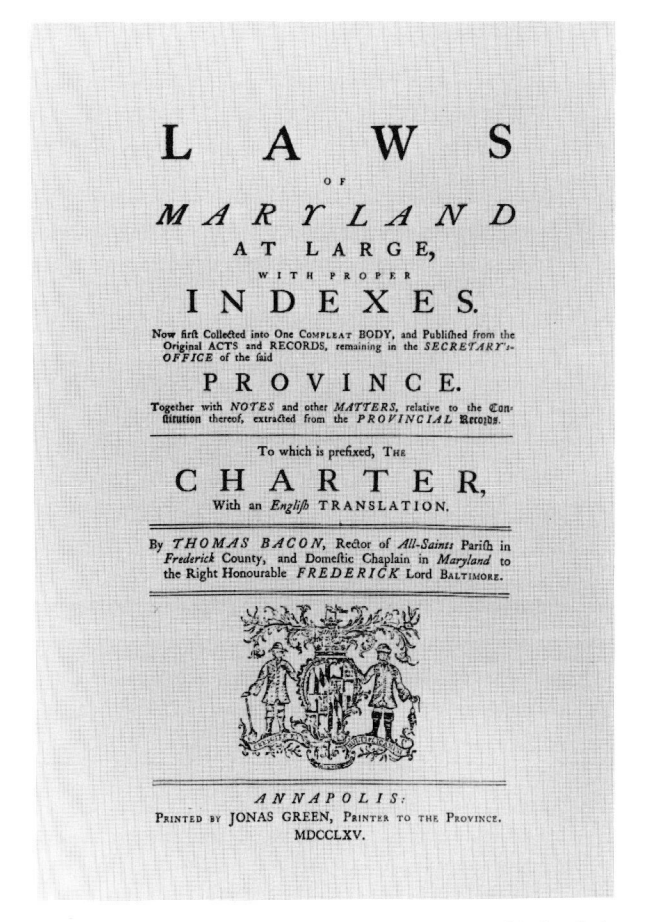

Although Bacon had a modest reputation as a poet in his day, he is best known by historians for his work compiling Maryland's laws.

Congregation of Black Slaves . . . (1749) and *Four Sermons, Upon the Great and Indispensible Duty of All Christian Masters and Mistresses to Bring Up Their Negro Slaves in the Knowledge and Fear of God . . .* (1750). These sermons, like his efforts to establish a charity school in Talbot County, evidence Bacon's sincere efforts throughout his ministerial career to help the poor. But Bacon is best remembered by historians for compiling the *Laws of Maryland . . .* and for his hand (along with Cecilius Calvert) in *An Answer to the Queries on the Proprietary Government of Maryland* (1764), which was designed to anticipate and fend off negative criticism of Lord Baltimore's administration. These works, along with his participation in the Tuesday Club, made Bacon a vital political and cultural force in colonial Maryland.

Reference:

J. A. Leo Lemay, *Men of Letters in Colonial Maryland* (Knoxville: University of Tennessee Press, 1972), pp. 313-342.

John Bartram
(23 March 1699-22 September 1777)

William J. Scheick
University of Texas at Austin

BOOK: *Observations on the Inhabitants, Climate, Soil, Rivers, Productions, Animals, and Other Matters Worthy of Notice* (London: Printed by J. Whiston & B. White, 1751).

OTHER: Journal or letter excerpts on rattlesnake teeth, salt-marsh mussels, wasps, dragon flies, and aurora borealis, in *Philosophical Transactions* (Royal Society of London), 41 (1742): 358-359; 43 (1745): 157-159, 363-366; 46 (1750): 278-279, 323-325, 400-402; 52 (1762): 474; 53 (1763): 37-38;

"An Essay for the Improvement of Estates, by Raising a Durable Timber for Fencing and Other Uses," in some copies of *Poor Richard Improved*, by Benjamin Franklin (Philadelphia: Franklin & Hall, 1749);

Thomas Short, *Medicina Britannica: or a Treatise on Such Physical Plants as Are Generally to be Found in the Fields or Garden in Great Britain,* includes an introduction, notes, and an appendix by Bartram (Philadelphia: Franklin & Hall, 1751);

"An Extract of Mr. Wm. [*sic*] Bartram's Observations in a Journey up the River Savannah in Georgia with His Son, on Discoveries," *Gentleman's Magazine,* 37 (1767): 166-168;

Journal entries for 19 December 1765-12 February 1766, in *An Account of East-Florida, with a Journal, Kept by John Bartram of Philadelphia, Botanist to His Majesty for the Floridas; upon a Journey from St. Augustine up the River St. John's,* by William Stork (London: Nicoll, 1767);

Letters, 1734-1768, in *Memorials of John Bartram and Humphry Marshall,* edited by William Henry Dillingham (Philadelphia: Lindsay & Blakiston, 1849);

"Diary of a Journey through the Carolinas, Georgia, and Florida from July 1, 1765, to April 10, 1766," edited by Francis Harper, *Transactions of the American Philosophical Society,* new series 33 (1942): 1-120.

A farmer in colonial Pennsylvania, John Bartram was one of America's pioneer botanists. As he remarked in a letter (1764), he had "in thirty years' travels, acquired a perfect knowledge of most, if not all the vegetables between New England and Georgia, and from the sea-coast to Lake Ontario and Erie." He not only identified closely with the European scientific community of the eighteenth century, developed a popular botanical garden on his estate, and played a prominent role in the propagation of New World plants abroad and Old World plants at home, but he also authored numerous reports, letters, and journals pertaining to the American wilderness. Although only a few samples of Bartram's writings survive, they apparently represent his work generally. Read only in the context of other eighteenth-century nature reportage, the extant Bartram documents may not seem particularly unique or impressive, and they hardly intimate

Portrait of John Bartram by Albert Hamson (John Bartram High School, Philadelphia, courtesy of Caroline Bartram West)

why Benjamin Franklin urged Bartram to write a natural history of the New World. Read, however, with an awareness of Bartram's dialectical manner of thought and his implicit emphasis on process—a pattern and emphasis intrinsic to his colonial culture as well—these writings evince a fascinating mode of perception.

Born on 23 March 1699, near Darby, Pennsylvania, John was the son of Elizabeth Hunt Bartram and William Bartram, whose father (John's grandfather) settled in America in 1682. When John was two, his mother died. A little later in his life, when his father and stepmother moved to Bartram lands in North Carolina, he remained in Pennsylvania in the care of one of his relatives. Succeeding as a farmer on lands inherited from an uncle, John married Mary Maris in 1723; they had two sons, one of whom died in infancy. Two years after the death of his wife in 1727, John married Ann Mendinghall; they raised nine children, one of whom died young and another of whom was William Bartram, whose *Travels* (1791) would surpass the influence and fame of any writings by his father.

Before his second marriage Bartram purchased more than one hundred acres of land along the Schuylkill River at Kingsessing, near Philadelphia. Living there in proto-Thoreauvian simplicity, he farmed, cut stone, built his own house, and, in 1729, started a botanical garden—if not the first, certainly the most popular botanical garden in colonial America and, even today, part of the Philadelphia park system. No mere farmer, Bartram experimented in his fields and his garden in the expectation of discovering ways to increase agricultural productivity. In the course of these experiments over the years, Bartram became steadily more interested in botany as a science. This development was hardly as dramatic as the account given, allegedly in Bartram's words, in Hector St. John de Crèvecoeur's *Letters from an American Farmer* (1782): "One day I was very busy holding my plow (for thee seest that I am but a simple plowman) and being weary I ran under the shade of a tree to repose myself. I cast my eyes on a daisy, I plucked it mechanically and viewed it with more curiosity than common country farmers are wont to do; and observing therein many distinct parts, some perpendicular, some horizontal. *What a shame, said my mind, that thee shouldst have employed so many years in tilling the earth and destroying so many flowers and plants, without being acquainted with their structures and uses!* This seeming inspiration suddenly awakened my curiosity for these were not thoughts to which I had been accustomed." Whatever the fictional elements in this report, the emphasis on plant "structures and uses" rings true, for Bartram's increasing interest in botany included a concern with both agricultural utilitarianism (*uses*) and botanical wonder (*structures*). This devotion to botany as an intrinsically fascinating science is unlikely to have engendered "thoughts to which [he] had been [un]accustomed" because it emanated from an abiding predisposition in Bartram; as he recalled in his sixty-fifth year (in a letter to Peter Collinson), "I had always, since ten years old, a great inclination to plants, and knew all that I once observed by sight, though not their proper names, having no person, nor books, to instruct me."

Bartram's study of botany indeed required extensive reading. Since he received a meager formal education during his youth, Bartram had to inform himself by reading. In 1738, he quipped in a letter, "I love reading [books] dearly: and I believe, if Solomon had loved women less, and books more, he would have been a wiser and happier man than he was." He became a life subscriber to the newly formed Library Company of Philadelphia and, in 1743, aided in founding a similar organization in

Drawing of Bartram's house at Kingsessing, from William Darlington's Memorials of John Bartram and Humphry Marshall *(1849)*

the township of Darby. Concerning botanic texts in particular, Bartram had to master Latin. He purchased a Latin grammar and paid for three months of instruction from a schoolmaster. Bartram, who explicitly devalued religious treatises, prized especially the numerous botanic volumes sent to him by friends and correspondents over the years. During the 1740s, for instance, he read or reread Mark Catesby's *Natural History of Carolina, Florida, and the Bahama Islands* (1748), John James Dillenius's *Historia muscorum* (1741), John Frederic Gronovius's *Flora virginica* (1739) and *Index supellectilis lapideae* (1740), Carolus Linnaeus's *Systema naturae* (1735) and *Genera plantarum* (1737), Philip Miller's *Gardener's Dictionary* (1731), and Sir Hans Sloane's *Catalogus plantarum quae in insula Jamaica sponte proveniut* (1696), among a large number of other works. During the last three decades of his life Bartram continued his habit of reading anything written about plants that he could get a copy of—finally a formidable total of books read during his lifetime.

In the course of Bartram's self-education, books provided a foundation for the more active study of botany during excursions into the American wilderness. Given his growing family and the financial uncertainties for farming, Bartram would have had little time for such journeys were not some means of patronage available. Bartram's first opportunity occurred when Peter Collinson, a London wool merchant and botanist, offered to pay Bartram to collect specimens of new plants for shipment to England. Subsequently Bartram attracted a number of subscribers over the years. Eventually he acquired friends and correspondents among leading figures of the eighteenth-century scientific community, such people as William Byrd II (American amateur physician), Mark Catesby (American naturalist and author), Peter Collinson (English merchant and botanist), John James Dillenius (German-English botanist), Jared Eliot (American minister and physician), Benjamin Franklin (American politician, scientist, and inventor), John Frederic Gronovius (Dutch physician and botanist), Peter Kalm (Finnish-Swedish professor and naturalist), Carolus Linnaeus (Swedish botanist and taxonomist), James Logan (American translator and experimenter with maize), Philip Miller (Scottish botanist and physician), and Sir

Hans Sloane (English naturalist and physician to King George II).

Membership in this international community generated the support Bartram needed, with the foundation provided by reading botanical texts, in order to indulge his personal wish to explore the American wilderness. In accord with his arrangements with Collinson, Bartram journeyed in 1735 to the source of the Schuylkill River and to the Blue Mountains of Pennsylvania. He traversed Lancaster County in Pennsylvania as well as parts of New Jersey and Maryland in 1737 and 1738. Six years later (and again in 1744 and 1753) he ranged over the Catskill Mountains along the Hudson River in New York. In 1743 he journeyed to Lake Ontario and in the following year went up the Susquehanna River in New York. Bartram traveled through Connecticut in 1755, through parts of Virginia and South Carolina in 1760, through Pennsylvania to Pittsburgh and along the Ohio River in 1761, and through sections of Virginia and South Carolina in 1762. This itinerary is only representative; for Bartram made numerous ventures into the wilderness in spite of trouble with Native Americans as a result of agitation during the French and Indian War.

And threat there was, as Bartram recollected in a letter in 1763: "Many years past, in our most peaceable times, far beyond our mountains, as I was walking in a path . . . an Indian man met me and pulled of my hat in a great passion, and chawed it all round—I suppose to show me that they would eat me if I came in that country again." The environment too, as much as its inhabitants, threatened Bartram, who tended to lose weight during strenuous journeys and who apparently suffered from a chronic malarialike illness as a result of his explorations. The extensiveness of his travels, however, convinced Bartram (as he uncharacteristically boasted in a letter to Collinson in 1763) that he knew "more of the North American plants than any others," got him appointed as King George III's botanist in 1765, and secured his election as a member of the Royal Academy of Science at Stockholm in 1769.

Bartram's self-education through reading and traveling included efforts at writing. His weak formal education left him ill-equipped for written expression, and in fact he never did learn to spell, to compose well-structured sentences, to range in vocabulary, or to devise a conscious stylistic manner. Even several of his friends and correspondents who highly regarded his knowledge—Peter Collinson and Peter Kalm, for example—explicitly criticized Bartram's apparent limitations as a writer. Sensitive to such complaints, Bartram told Collinson in 1754 that he preferred to write "not according to grammar rules, or science, but nature": "Good grammar and good spelling, may please those that are more taken with a fine superficial flourish than real truth; but my chief aim was to inform my readers of the true, real, distinguishing characters of each genus, and where, and how, each species differed from one another, of the same genus."

Bartram's evident emphasis, in this reply, falls on a language of precision. This language of "objective" natural description surfaces in Bartram's letters from the 1730s to the 1760s, in his "An Essay for the Improvement of Estates, by Raising a Durable timber for Fencing and Other Uses" (a fugitive item apparently inserted in some copies of Benjamin Franklin's *Poor Richard Improved,* 1749), and in his introduction, appendix, and notes to Thomas Short's *Medicina Britannica* (1751). This language certainly characterizes his observations printed in the *Philosophical Transactions* of the Royal Society of London. These published reports concern rattlesnake teeth (1742), salt-marsh mussels (1745), wasp nests (1745), black wasps (1750), dragon flies (1751), aurora borealis (1762), and yellow wasps (1764).

The language of these reports appears as well in *Observations on the Inhabitants, Climate, Soil, Rivers, Productions, Animals, and Other Matters Worthy of Notice* (1751), the journal Bartram kept while accompanying Conrad Weiser on a trip in 1743 through Pennsylvania and New York to Fort Oswego on Lake Ontario. Weiser was appointed to make peace between the English colonists and the Iroquois, and Bartram traveled with him to observe the "great variety of plants and other curiosities there." Although Bartram made at least three copies of the journal he kept during this trip, he had difficulty getting one to Collinson. Bartram sent Collinson a copy in 1744, but it miscarried as a result of the capture of the British transporting vessel by a French ship. This copy, however, was preserved by the captain of the pirated ship and delivered to Collinson in 1750. Collinson was disappointed by the reticence and the illiteracy of Bartram's manuscript, but he had it published, noting in his prefatory remarks that the work appears "without the author's knowledge" and that he (Collinson) "thought himself not at liberty to make any material alteration, though as it appears, many who seek only amusement in what they read, will in those places be disappointed where only are treated of the several plants with which nature has bountifully covered the hills and valleys he travers'd, with the various qualities of the soil and climate." In many places, then, in Collinson's opinion, *Observations* is a text for eighteenth-century botanic specialists, whereas in other instances it is a text of interest to the general public.

In fact, *Observations* (from which Henry David Thoreau in 1857 or thereabout copied long extracts) is Bartram's most publicly accessible work, evincing not only the manner of "objective" natural description typical of his earlier reports printed in *Philosophical Transactions* but also the voice of intrusive polemic. *Observations* exhibits an uneasy dialectic between attenuated specialized notations pertaining to nature and several *obiter dicta* concerning race, religion, and politics. Remarks about nature comprise the *background* content of Bartram's book; that is, these observations constitute the genre-implied and reader-anticipated subject matter of the work: information about climate, soil, rivers, plants, and animals. This backgrounded matter includes such memorable episodes in the narrative as an encounter with a rattlesnake, which "while provoked . . . contracted the muscles of his scales so as to appear very bright and shining, but after the mortal stroke, his splendor became much diminished," and the discovery of an unusual landscape "principally composed of rotten trees, roots, and moss, perpetually shaded, and for the most part wet[;] what falls is constantly rotting and rending the earth loose and spungy, . . . tempt[ing] abundance of yellow wasps to breed in it."

In dialectic with such background matter are Bartram's polemical comments, which comprise the *foreground* of the book; that is, these comments draw attention to themselves as apparently aberrant, disruptive of mood, destructive of generic mode, or antagonistic to reader expectations of a text devoted to observations about nature. This foreground matter principally concerns the inhabitants of the wilderness. As an English colonist, Bartram typically defames the French, whom he accuses of supplying Native Americans with weapons, of claiming territorial rights on the basis of a few forts staffed by mercenaries, and of proselytizing on behalf of Roman Catholicism, "what they call the christian religion." Sometimes he also criticizes the shortcomings of English colonists: "It were to be wished, that the *English* government in these parts had been more diligent in searching and surveying the heads of their own rivers"; similarly, "this is surely an excellent regulation for preventing traders from imposing on the *Indians*, a practice they have been formerly too much guilty of, and which has frequently involved the *English* colonies in difficulties, and constantly tended to depreciate us in the esteem of the natives."

Observations, speculations, and complaints about Native Americans contribute to the foreground matter of Bartram's book. Interest in their preparation of squash, rituals pertaining to bears, propagation, and drying of huckleberries vies with nature reportage in *Observations*. Conjectures concerning the origins of Native Americans particularly interest Bartram, who considers the theories that they descended from the Ten Lost Tribes of Israel, that they "were originally placed here by the . . . creator . . . as soon as . . . [the New World] became habitable," or that (as José de Acosta had speculated in 1590) they migrated from the Old to the New World over a land bridge or a small stretch of sea between Asia and North America. Summarizing his experience with northeastern Native Americans, Bartram writes: "they are a subtile,

OBSERVATIONS
ON THE
Inhabitants, Climate, Soil, Rivers, Productions, Animals, and other matters worthy of Notice.

MADE BY

Mr. *JOHN BARTRAM*,

In his Travels from

PENSILVANIA

TO

ONONDAGO, OSWEGO and the Lake ONTARIO,

In *CANADA*.

To which is annex'd, a curious Account of the

CATARACTS at *NIAGARA*.

By Mr. PETER KALM,

A *Swedish* GENTLEMAN who travelled there.

LONDON:
Printed for J. WHISTON and B. WHITE, in Fleet-Street, 1751.

(Price *One Shilling* and *Six-pence*.)

Title page for Bartram's travel journal for 1743. He later defended his writing style by claiming that he wrote "not according to grammar rules, or science, but nature."

prudent, and judicious people in their councils, indefatigable, crafty, and revengeful in their wars, the men lazy and indolent at home, the women continual slaves, modest, very loving, and obedient to their husbands." Bartram's attitude here is more subdued than is the general tenor of his epistolary comments on Native Americans, whose "savage cruelty" was symbolized for him in the ominous incident when his hat was chewed by a Native American expressing anger over Bartram's incursion into Native American territory. If Native Americans fare somewhat better in *Observations* than in Bartram's letters, their presentation benefits from the unadorned, understated language of the book, even of its polemical matter.

Native Americans particularly figure in the dialectical interaction between foregrounded polemic and backgrounded nature in *Observations* whenever Bartram raises the subjects of agriculture and superstition. Reflecting a belief prevalent among eighteenth-century colonial Americans of English origin, Bartram asserts that cultivation of land determines ownership. Consequently, Bartram argues, Native Americans possess no actual claim to the New World, for "whatever nature has done for them (and she is no where more bountiful) they are too lazy by any trouble of their own to improve." In his persistent notations about topography and soil Bartram implicitly celebrates this ideal of potential settlement, of the wilderness transformed, through cultivation, into productive farmland. In this vision of progressive change, Bartram the "objective" botanist and Bartram the "subjective" polemicist intersect, giving rise in *Observations* to a dialectical engagement of backgrounded nature and foregrounded social critique.

This dialectic informs as well Bartram's reflections on Native American superstitions. "They have strange notions of spirits, conjuration, and witchcraft: these are agreeable to their blindness, and want of proper education among them," Bartram writes. One or another "silly story is religiously held for truth among them," Bartram complains, recounting later in the book an illustrative episode involving his attempt to move some rocks out of his way: "I took a fancy to ascend 2 thirds of the height of a neighbouring hill, in the way I came to abundance of loose stones, and very craggy rocks, which seemed to threaten impending ruin, the soil was black and very rich, full of great wild stinging nettles, as far as I went I rolled down several loose stones to make a path for my more expeditious return. This I found the *Indians* much disturbed at, for they said it would infallibly produce rain the next day, I told them I had sufficient experience, it signified nothing, for it was my common practice to roll down stones from the top of every steep hill, and could not recollect that it ever rained the next day, and that I was almost sure tomorrow would be a very fair day. . . . Before day break it began to rain, it lasted about a hour and then ceased. The *Indians* insisted that was caused by the stones I rolled down 2 days ago, I told the *Antecoque Indians* if their observations had any truth it should have been the day before, which was remarkably fair. To this he cunningly replyed, that our *Almanacks* often prognosticated on a day, and yet the rain did not come within two days." Bartram's irritation at superstitious notions similarly surfaces in a letter to Collinson (11 June 1743), in which he repudiates the claims "of astrology, magic, and mystic divinity." This antagonism toward superstition contributes to the foreground matter of *Observations*, to the "subjective" polemical voice vying with the background matter of the text conveyed through the "objective" scientific language of measurement.

This dialectical interplay between superstition and science, agriculture and wilderness, humanity (English, French, Native American) and nature—in short, between foreground and background textual matter—might not be the product of Bartram's conscious design; but, nevertheless, even as an unconscious effect of his narrative manner it defines an intrinsic aesthetic feature of *Observations*. In fact, a dialectical mode of thought seems generally to characterize Bartram's perception of nature, a mode most evident in a letter (25 March 1762) he wrote to Alexander Garden, a South Carolinian, an amateur Linnaean botanist, and (later) a Loyalist: "What charming colours appear in the various tribes, in the regular succession of the vernal and autumnal flowers—these so nobly bold—those so delicately languid! What a glow is enkindled in some, what a gloss shines in others! With what a masterly skill is every one of the varying tints disposed! Here, they seem to be thrown on with an easy dash of security and freedom; there, they are adjusted by the nicest touches. The verdure of the empalement, or the shadings of the petals, impart new liveliness to the whole, whether they are blended or arranged. Some are intersected with elegant stripes, or studded with radiant spots; others affect to be genteelly powdered, or neatly fringed; others are plain in their aspect, and please with their naked simplicity. Some are arrayed in purple; some charm with the virgin's white; others are dashed with crimson; while others are robed in scarlet. Some glitter like silver lace;

others shine as if embroidered with gold. Some rise with curious cups, or pendulous bells; some are disposed in spreading umbels; others crowd in spiked clusters; some are dispersed on spreading branches of lofty trees, on dangling catkins; others sit contented on the humble shrub; some seated on high on the twining vine, and wafted to and fro; others garnish the prostrate, creeping plant. All these have their particular excellencies; some for the beauty of their flowers; others their sweet scent; many the elegance of foliage, or the goodness of their fruit: some the nourishment that their roots afford us; others please the fancy with their regular growth: some are admired for their odd appearance, and many that offend the taste, smell, and sight, too, are of virtue in physic." Not only is its display of sustained exuberance and prevalence of adjectives exceptional for Bartram, but this long paragraph also discloses the extensive degree to which he revels in nature's manifestation of multiple antitheses, in nature's manifestation of an essential dialectic: plants are vernal/autumnal, languid/bold, glowing/glossy, secure/free, arranged/blended, simple/elegant, white/scarlet, humble/lofty, excellent/offensive.

Dialectic, doubtless, also characterized the numerous, now-lost journals Bartram wrote over the years. It certainly informs the journal he, as King George III's botanist, kept during his journey through the Carolinas, Georgia, and Florida in 1765-1766. Two excerpts from this account were printed during Bartram's lifetime, albeit not under his supervision. Silently edited by someone—a common practice during the eighteenth century, when anonymous collaborations were legion—the entries for 5-25 September 1765 appeared (mistakenly attributed to Bartram's son) as "An Extract of Mr. Wm. Bartram's Observations in a Journey Up the River Savannah in Georgia with His Son, on Discoveries," in *Gentleman's Magazine* (1767). The entries dated 19 December 1765-12 February 1766, which Bartram seems to have separated from the main journal, were edited by someone for literacy and were appended to William Stork's *An Account of East-Florida, with a Journal, Kept by John Bartram of Philadelphia, Botanist to His Majesty for the Floridas; upon a Journey from St. Augustine up the River St. John's* (1767); four editions of this volume appeared during the eighteenth century. The complete journal from which these excerpts were drawn evinces an interesting contrast to *Observations*, written twenty-three years earlier, for the later journal modifies the dialectical manner of the antecedent work by displacing polemic with silence.

In fact, narrative silence emerges as the most striking feature of Bartram's Floridian journal. Consider these typical entries for 1765: (July 9) "observed numerous species of curious plants & found one new genus"; (July 11) "A strange new tree"; (July 17) "I found several curious species of plants in [the] savanas. . . . Saw several curious plants"; (August 7) "A great variety of curious plants"; (August 18) "found several curious plants"; (September 5) "found A very curious evergreen shrub & A very odd plant"; (October 1) "this day we found severall very curious shrubs." These observations, like so many others in the journal, are repetitively modified by the adjectives *odd, strange,* and *curious* as well as by the adverbs *nice* and *very*. Evasively nonemotional, these understated observations are punctuated by a narrative silence, a punctuation implicitly more dramatic than that required by the rules of English grammar that Bartram never learned. This narrative silence occurs precisely when the reader, whose expectations have been aroused by the evocative (if evasive) words *odd, strange,* and *curious,* anticipates subsequent details, description, or information but in the process of reading further discovers no forthcoming elucidating commentary.

Narrative silence is particularly prevalent, to an enigmatical degree, in the part of this journal treating the Floridian wilderness. Nearly three years before the trip Bartram remarked with emotion in a letter: "Oh! if I could but spend six months . . . [in] Florida"; and about a year later on at least two occasions he anxiously sought to facilitate the financing of such a journey before he, now in his sixty-sixth year, became too old to withstand the rigors of such a venture. This very emotion is precisely what is absent from the journal, a fact all the more vexing since the landscape of Florida must have been as spectacular as Bartram had anticipated; certainly it was potentially more evocative of emotion than were the topographic features and the flora he encountered during his journey to the Great Lakes in 1743. Yet, in comparison to the voices of *Observations*, the Floridian journal "resounds" with silence.

Reasons behind Bartram's silence in this later work might include the fact that while traveling he collected whole or parts of plants. Mere references in his journal to a "curious" plant could then sometimes be supplemented later by a labeled and dated collected specimen, thereby eliminating any need for a fuller verbal description. Possibly, too, his silence might in part have derived from his advanced age or from the fact that during the expedition he was ill, as he reported to Collinson in June 1766: "I hope what specimens I sent for thyself will give thee great pleasure, as many of them are entirely new; the collecting of which hath cost thy friend many score pounds, pains, and sickness, which held me constantly near or quite two months; in Florida, the fever and jaundice; and a looseness through North and South Carolina, and Georgia; yet, some how or other, I lost not an hour's time of travelling through those provinces; and when at Augustine, with the fever and jaundice, I travelled both by water and land all round the town for many miles, and to Picolata, to the Congress, although so weak as hard set to get up to bed; and during the meeting of the Governor and Indians, in the Pavilion, I was forced to sit or lie down upon the ground, close by its side, that I might observe what passed." The burden of sickness and age, and the habit of collecting might have contributed to the taciturnity of Bartram's journal of 1765-1766.

Another cause, as critics have for some time suggested in general terms, might be attributed to Bartram's Quaker heritage, eschewing emotion and advocating plain language. This heritage doubtlessly influenced Bartram's manner of expression in the Floridian journal, even though by 1758 he had been disowned by the Quakers of the Darby Meeting because he refused to believe in the divinity of Jesus Christ and even though by 1765 he was in some respects more a Deist than a Quaker. As early as 1758, in fact, he remarked to Philip Miller: "Strange it is, but very true, that many seeds of plants we take little care of, as not being of general use, will keep good in the ground for seven years or more, before they all come up, and perhaps the ground tilled every year, too; but the nutritious grains, pulse, and other esculents, that are adapted for our general support, generally come up the first year they are sown. Oh! the wisdom of Divine Providence! The more we search into it, the more wonderful we discover its powerful influence to be." This proto-Deistic observation became more pronounced in 1762, when in letters to Alexander Garden and Peter Collinson respectively, Bartram noted: "The more we search and accurately examine [God's] works in nature, the more wisdom we discover"; "My head runs all upon the works of God, in nature. It is through this telescope I see God in his glory." In short, by the time Bartram traveled to Florida in 1765-1766, his attribution of a sacramentality to nature was far more intense than at the time of his trip to the Great Lakes in 1743. Bartram's devotional wonder, in response to this sacramentality of nature, likely informs the silence of his Floridian journal, a taciturnity also reminiscent of the Quaker tradition of meetings spent in silent receptivity.

A sixth factor influencing the narrative silence of the journal of 1765-1766 might be found in Bartram's sense of his readers; for however potentially sacramental his view of creation, Bartram by his own admission (in 1741) did not "naturally delight in such solitudes" as were characteristic of his exploratory forays. Nor did he become more private by 1765; he still kept a journal for himself *and* for his friends. His friends tended to be fellow specialists, a fact leading some contemporary critics to conclude, with reason, that the reticence of Bartram's journal derives from his audience, which required no elaborative detail. But, we should note, Bartram is most silent concerning "odd," "strange" and "curious" plants, the ones unknown to him and his friends.

If the fact that Bartram's silences occur in places where even his anticipated audience cannot elaborate reduces the claim that his specialist readers account for the taciturnity of his text, it does not diminish the important role of his sense of audience. Bartram's readers were not only fellow specialists but also—and for him, more significant—they were friends. In an early letter to Collinson, Bartram revealed his conception of how friends "read" each other: "according to our friend Doctor [Christopher] Witt, we friends that love one another sincerely, may, by an extraordinary spirit of sympathy, not only know each other's desires, but may have a spiritual conversation at great distances one from another. Now, if this be truly so,—if I love thee sincerely—and thy love and friendship be so to me—thee must have a spiritual feeling and sense of what particular sorts of things will give satisfaction; and doth not thy actions make it manifest?" The element of social decorum in this remark can be discounted; for the playful politeness of manner here actually permits Bartram to make a sincere observation (in an unembarrassing fashion and with an occult undertone) about "sympathy" between friends. Bartram apparently conceived of his readers as friends whose "sympathy" enabled them—as if they were fellow Quakers engaged in a meeting of silent receptivity—to intuit and share his silent devotional wonder at nature's splendor. Perhaps by means of this "sympathetic" devotional silence, Bartram's imagined friendly readers were at once to enter and to complete the text of the Floridian journal; being drawn into the text in its places of narrative absence, or silence, the "sympathetic" reader necessarily participates in the account, even in a

Draft for a 1759 letter to botanist Philip Miller (courtesy of the Academy of Natural Sciences and the John Bartram Association) sense personally filling in the gaps of inexpressiveness and reducing the impression of narrative fragmentation given by the terse and elliptical manner of the text's language.

This silence can be described as the foreground of the Floridian journal; that is, given the expected context of nature reportage generally typical of such a document, this silence seems aberrant to the reader. Like the polemical voice of *Observations*, it functions in dialectic with the titularly declared primary concern of the work: observations about nature (the background matter) expressed in a language of precise measurement, a language emphasizing date, time, temperature, weight, size, texture, depth, distance, direction, and color. This contrast between a language of exact measurement and silence imparts to the Floridian journal—in a way reminiscent of the dialectical interaction between nature reportage and social polemic in *Observations*—a sense of improvisation, of lack of finish, of fragmentation. Indeed, in spite of their record of precise scientific information, both journals lack proportion or symmetry of external form.

What symmetry inheres in these works, in fact, lies in this very manifestation of dialect distorting their external form—a symmetry reflective of process in nature, progress in civilization and permanent revisionism in the human mind. Bartram's belief in such an ongoing revisionism (also characteristic of the philosophical, political, and religious milieu of eighteenth-century colonial America) surfaces most notably in his scientific commentary. A memorable instance occurs in a letter he wrote in 1755, in which he reported that, considering his (Bartram's) floral discoveries in the New World, "Linnaeus must make many alterations" in his famous taxonomic system. This appreciation of the need for progressive revisionism also informs Bartram's manner of writing. It underlies the dialectical modality of his journals, how their parts contest and interact as foreground and background matter. It explains, concerning external form, the tendency of these texts to appear improvised (in spite of later revisions by Bartram), incomplete, and fragmented. This appearance mirrors the processes of nature, so incompletely fathomed by the human intellect, in Bartram's opinion; it reveals (especially in *Observations*) the progressive development of European civilization in the American wilderness; it exemplifies the ongoing advancement of the human mind interacting with both civilization and nature. Nature, civilization, and the human mind are, in Bartram's works, processive; they are comprised of mere fragments of time, even as every trip into the wilderness represents a mere fragment of time. The improvisational attitude, the asymmetrical external form, and the contest between the foreground and background matter of his journals of 1743 and 1765-1766 convey an aesthetic impression of this perception of process. Principally it is embodied in the inherent dialectical structure of these narratives. If the dialectic between nature and civilization in *Observations* emerges awkwardly and produces an uneven aesthetic effect, its transformation into a dialectic between nature reportage and silence in the Floridian journal achieves a satisfying aesthetic dimension, into which the "sympathetic" reader enters in order to participate in the *process* of the text.

Bartram had a wonder to relate. This wonder of the sacramentality of nature ranged finally beyond the scientific language of precise measurement. It could be evoked only in verbal motions between scientific language and some other mode of expression. This wonder is overshadowed by the dialectical interplay of backgrounded nature reportage and foregrounded polemic in *Observations*, a somewhat didactic work. This same wonder is highlighted by the dialectical interplay of backgrounded nature reportage and foregrounded narrative silence in the Floridian journal, which includes (rather than instructs) the "sympathetic" reader in the process of its disclosures. In some remarks later appended to, but separate from, this journal Bartram notes, "many people love to tell wonders." Between *Observations* and the Floridian account Bartram instinctively discovered that the best way to tell a wonder is to make the reader participate in the text, make the reader re-create the moment of the wonderful "curious" find. Such reader-text interaction occurs in the Floridian narrative whenever the reader's "sympathy" is evoked by the author's "silence." In this journal Bartram told his friends about the curiosities of the plants and landscape of Florida less through the scientific language of exact measurement than through a silence they had to enter, a devotional silence similar to that of Quaker meetings spent in silent receptivity and to that of Bartram's experience of solitude in the wilderness. The silence full of wonders Bartram encountered in nature became, in his Floridian narrative and for his reader-friends, a silence which "told" wonders.

References:

Rose Marie Cutting, *John and William Bartram, William Byrd II and St. John de Crévecoeur: A Ref-*

erence Guide (Boston: G. K. Hall, 1976), pp. 1-35;

Ernest Earnest, *John and William Bartram: Botanists and Explorers* (Philadelphia: University of Pennsylvania Press, 1940);

Wayne Franklin, *Discoverers, Explorers, Settlers: The Diligent Writers of Early America* (Chicago: University of Chicago Press, 1979), pp. 46-57;

Josephine Herbst, *New Green World* (New York: Hastings House, 1954);

David Scofield Wilson, *In the Presence of Nature* (Amherst: University of Massachusetts Press, 1978), pp. 89-122.

Papers:
Most of the Bartram papers are held by the Historical Society of Pennsylvania.

Joseph Bellamy
(20 February 1719-6 March 1790)

Donald Weber
Mount Holyoke College

SELECTED BOOKS: *Early Piety Recommended* ... (Boston, 1748);

True Religion Delineated: Or, Experimental Religion, as Distinguished from Formality on the One Hand, and Enthusiasm on the Other. Set in Scriptural and Rational Light ... (Boston: Printed & sold by S. Kneeland, 1750; London: T. Ward, 1841);

The Great Evil of Sin, as It Is Committed against God ... (Boston: Printed & sold by S. Kneeland, 1753);

A Letter to the Reverend Author of the Winter-Evening Conversation on Original Sin, from One of his Candid Neighbours ... (Boston: Printed & sold by S. Kneeland, 1758);

Sermons upon the Following Subjects, Viz., The Divinity of Jesus Christ. The Millennium. The Wisdom of God in the Permission of Sin. (Boston: Printed & sold by Edes & Gill and by S. Kneeland, 1758; Northampton, England, 1783);

Theron, Paulinus, and Aspasio ... (Boston: Printed & sold by S. Kneeland, 1759); republished as *Letters and Dialogues, between Theron, Paulinus, and Aspasio* ... (London: Printed for Edward Dilly, 1761);

A Letter to Scripturista ... (New Haven: Printed by Parker & Company, 1760);

A Dialogue on the Christian Sacraments ... (Boston: Printed & sold by S. Kneeland, 1762);

An Essay on the Nature and Glory of the Gospel of Jesus Christ ... (Boston: Printed by S. Kneeland, 1762; London: Sold by James Mathews and J. Buckland & A. Hogg, 1784);

A Sermon Delivered before the General Assembly ... (New London: Printed & sold by Timothy Green, 1762);

A Blow at the Root of the Refined Antinomianism of the Present Age ... (Boston: Printed & sold by S. Kneeland, 1763);

Remarks on the Revd. Mr. Crosswell's Letter to the Rev. Mr. Cumming ... (Boston: Printed & sold by S. Kneeland, 1763);

The Half-Way Covenant, A Dialogue ... (New Haven: Printed & sold by Thomas & Samuel Green, 1769);

The Inconsistence of Renouncing the Half-Way Covenant, and Yet Retaining the Half-Way-Practice. A Dialogue (New Haven: Printed & sold by Thomas & Samuel Green, 1769);

That There Is But One Covenant ... (New Haven: Printed & sold by Thomas & Samuel Green, 1769);

A Careful and Strict Examination of the External Covenant, and of the Principles by which It Is Supported ... (New Haven: Printed & sold by Thomas & Samuel Green, 1770);

The Sacramental Controversy Brought to a Point ... (New Haven: Printed by Thomas & Samuel Green, 1770).

Collection: *The Works of the Rev. Joseph Bellamy*, 3 volumes (New York: Published by Stephen Dodge, printed by J. Seymour, 1811-1812).

Joseph Bellamy was an important figure during the Great Awakening (1740-1742) and one of the architects of the New England theology, which sought to preserve the strict Calvinism linked with the heritage of Jonathan Edwards. According to Harriet Beecher Stowe in *Oldtown Folks* (1869), Bellamy's theology, as expressed in his most important work, *True Religion Delineated* (1750), was the gospel of New England religious culture for more than one-hundred years. In the view of Chandler Robbins, who edited the 1855 edition of Cotton Mather's *Magnalia Christi Americana* ... (1702), Bellamy's "name was almost a household word in our family." (Robbins's father, a member of the "black regiment" of revolutionary preachers—those patriot-ministers who exhorted and inspired the Continental army—studied under Bellamy.) Contemporaneous testaments assert that Bellamy's sermons, delivered "with a prodigious voice, vivid imagination, great flow of language," had no rivals in eighteenth-century America, except those of Jonathan Edwards himself.

Bellamy graduated from Yale in 1735 and served as an itinerant preacher throughout New England before settling in the backwater hamlet of Bethlehem, Connecticut, in 1740. The excesses of the New Light revival style—the fiery zeal and censoriousness of its adherents—soured Bellamy to the Awakening's fruits; he remained in his rural pulpit for fifty years, although in the early 1750s a New York church tried, in vain, to woo him to their flock. (After preaching a few Sundays in New York Bellamy decided, "I am not polite enough for them. I may possibly do to be a minister out in the woods, but am not fit for a city.") Despite his disillusionment in the failure of the Great Awakening, Bellamy established a "school of the prophets" to in-

Title page for Bellamy's influential second book, for the most part a popular restatement of the theology of his mentor Jonathan Edwards (courtesy of the John Carter Brown Library at Brown University)

Title page for Bellamy's 1758 book, which includes his sermon asserting the imminence of the millennium (courtesy of the John Carter Brown Library at Brown University)

struct the rising generation of New Light ministers, many of whom, imbibing Bellamy's theology, would later preach the sacred cause of liberty in defense of the American Revolution from various New England pulpits.

In addition to *True Religion Delineated,* for the most part a popular version of Edwards's *A Treatise Concerning Religious Affections* (1746), Bellamy's major writings also include a sermon on *The Millennium* (first published in *Sermons upon the Following Subjects,* 1758), in which Bellamy employs a kind of evangelical demographics in a proof of the millennium's imminence, and the Connecticut Election Sermon for 1762, preached on the text "Righteousness exalteth a nation; but sin is a reproach to any people (Proverbs 14:34)," which celebrates a nation "united in the same faith," with ministers and people knit together "in the most cordial affection to one another." The discourse, Bellamy's application of the Edwardean doctrine of "true virtue" to social and political ideals, suggests Bellamy's role as expounder, disciple, and defender of his theological master. His writings were the touchstone for those succeeding generations who chose to trace their spiritual and religious lineage to Jonathan Edwards.

References:

Glenn P. Anderson, "Joseph Bellamy: His Life and Work," Ph.D. dissertation, Boston University, 1971;

Michael P. Anderson, "The Pope of Litchfield County: An Intellectual Biography of Joseph Bellamy, 1719-1790," Ph.D. dissertation, Claremont Graduate School, 1980;

James W. Davidson, *The Logic of Millennial Thought* (New Haven: Yale University Press, 1977);

Tryon Edwards, "Memoir of Bellamy," in *The Works of the Rev. Joseph Bellamy,* 3 volumes (New York: Published by Stephen Dodge, printed by J. Seymour, 1811-1812);

Frank H. Foster, *A Genetic History of the New England Theology* (Chicago: University of Chicago Press, 1907);

William B. Sprague, *Annals of the American Pulpit,* volume 1 (New York: Robert Carter, 1857).

Papers:
Hartford Seminary and Yale University have collections of Bellamy's papers.

Robert Bolling
(17 August 1738-21 July 1775)

Charles Bolton

BOOK: *A Memoir of a Portion of the Bolling Family in England and Virginia,* translated by John Robertson, Jr. (Richmond: Privately printed by W. H. Wade, 1868).

Robert Bolling is perhaps more interesting as a phenomenon than as a writer. To say so is not to denigrate his often ground-breaking work; rather it is to recognize that his too-brief life spanned crucial years of American history, during which a national identity was being formed from the materials provided by disparate colonial sources. Similarly, his work moved from traditional, often insipid forms, pale imitations of English and Continental models, to a bold engagement with American materials and language. He never achieved greatness in his poetry, and he was rarely better than adequate, given the rigorous standards he often set for himself. His lyrics were conventional, his humor sometimes forced, his metrics obvious. Yet he produced several effective occasional poems, a number of satirical verses that had important political consequences, and at least one long poem, "Neanthe," that is a masterpiece of humor if not of versification.

Bolling was born in Henrico County, Virginia, into the first ranks of colonial Virginia society, a direct descendant of Pocahontas and her English husband, John Rolfe. He was given every opportunity his family's standing could provide, including several years (1751-1755) in England at John Clarke's well-regarded school at Wakefield, Yorkshire, where he studied in the company of several similarly bred scions of Virginia gentry, including Robert Munford, a playwright, and Theodorick Bland, later a patriot and writer, who would be Bolling's lifelong friend and executor. His sojourn in England affected him deeply: there he met his English relations (he chose to memorialize the connection by adopting the name of their Yorkshire estate, Chellowe, for his plantation), and there he received the excellent classical education that was to provide him with the material for much of his early poetry.

These early poems, which were widely published both in the colonies and in England (indeed, Bolling's poems virtually dominated the poetry columns of the *Imperial Magazine* in London during the 1760s), are the most derivative of Bolling's works. Many are little more than adaptations of lyrics by Tasso, Ariosto, Chiabera, and, notably, Metastasio, whose works, more than other writers, seem to have inspired Bolling to greater originality, the achievement of considerable grace, in his borrowings. Two works from this period are remarkably successful. "The Exile," an occasional poem addressed to Bolling's friend Sir Peyton Skipwith, deserves a place in literary history alongside William Byrd's letter to the Earl of Orrery as a cogent, if comic, statement of the colonial sophisticate's sense of diplacement and alienation when contrasting the charms of England with the barren waste of his Virginia habitation. "On a Finally Happy Lover" is a simple lyric celebrating the successful culmination of Bolling's search for a proper wife, a pursuit which had been documented in a series of published poems praising, in predictable language, the predictable charms of a bevy of Virginia beauties (whose marriages to other men Bolling carefully footnoted on manuscript copies of the relevant poems).

"On a Finally Happy Lover" is significant for the idea of wedded bliss it propounds, a straightforward conception presented in straightforward verse. The poem's sincerity and its charming simplicity set it apart from the conventionality of Bolling's other lyrics of the first half of the 1760s. His wedded bliss was short-lived, however: Mary Burton Bolling died, at the age of sixteen, on 2 May 1764, less than a year after the marriage and three days after the birth of a daughter, also named Mary Burton. Robert Bolling married Susannah Watson, who survived him, a little more than a year later, and fathered four children (a son, Powhatan, and a daughter, Pocahontas Rebecca, testify to their father's pride in his lineage), but his first wife's death nevertheless seems to have had a profound effect on him.

Robert Bolling

Through that time, Bolling's career had followed a predictable course—even his involvement in literature was predictable for a Virginia gentleman, although the degree of his success was not. Upon his return from England, he had read law in the Williamsburg office of Benjamin Waller, himself a poet, but there is no evidence that Bolling ever practiced law or indeed that he was admitted to the bar. After his father died in 1757, Bolling inherited extensive plantations in Chesterfield and Buckingham Counties and began to take his place as a leading landowner in the political life of the colony. He served as his county's representative to several sessions of the House of Burgesses, and was by 1764 distinguished by the courtesy title Colonel, indicating that he commanded the county militia. After his first wife's death in 1764, however, he held only minor political offices at the county level, until the end of his life, when he represented Buckingham County at the July Convention of 1775, a convention that virtually completed the transfer of power from England to the colonial government. Tradition holds that Bolling had refused to stand for election to the July Convention, but that he was elected unanimously by his fellow landholders in Buckingham County.

> A SATIRE on the TIMES.
>
> *J' appelle un chat un chat, et* ROLET *un fripon.*
> BOILEAU.
>
> *I call a cat a cat, and ——‡—— a knave.*
> QUARLES.
>
> WHEN Judas lavish'd laud on honest
>   WAYLES,
>   Men, laughing, thought they heard
>   VERMILIO's tales;
> To him should grateful W—— like praise return,
> Mankind would swear all language was forsworn—
> That wisdom meant *mere folly*, folly *sense*,
> High airs *observance*, meekness *insolence*,
> Applauses *satire*, and invective *praise*,
> Happy for blundering BEN would be such days;
> BEN would be thought a *sage*, meant *blockhead* wise,
> And fond of *truth*, were truth design'd by * LIES.
> Against him Virtue would renounce her rage,
> And read with patience his flagitious page;
> The blameless ‡ NELSONS unreviled live,
> And *he* just tribute to fair virtue give.
> BEN seldom deign'd such tribute *heretofore*,
> But wonders may result from W——'s transform-
>   ing power.
>   O say, THALIA (when that season comes,
> Which weighty Johnson to the grocer dooms,
> And lying Bailey to the seat of sighs)
> What further miracles on earth shall rise?

The beginning of one of Bolling's poems on the Chiswell scandal, as it appeared on page one of the Virginia Gazette, *8 January 1767*

Unlike his political activity, Bolling's writing did not cease after 1764. During the year following his first wife's death, Bolling composed his memoir. It was written in French, and Bolling's manuscript is presumed lost, but a translation made as a childhood exercise by John Robertson, Jr., a collateral descendant, survived and was published in 1868 by the antiquary Thomas Wynne as number four of his series, Historical Documents of the Old Dominion. *A Memoir of a Portion of the Bolling Family in England and Virginia* remains Bolling's only published volume, although two manuscript collections of poetry and short prose, "La Gazzatta di Parnasso" and "Bon Mots," as well as a commonplace book, are extant. Nor does Bolling's political inactivity, in an official capacity, necessarily indicate a lack of political interest and involvement. It is in fact through Bolling's life as a political being that his poetry found new direction and both greater energy and originality during the second half of the 1760s.

The pages of the *Virginia Gazette* became Bolling's primary forum during this period and the political life of his colony his primary source of inspiration, at least for his published poetry. The satirical edge that had distinguished many of the earlier poems found full development as Bolling vented his outrage at the constant infringement of the rights of the individual, and as Bolling increasingly gave voice to his impatience and frustration with the machinery of colonial government in breakneck metrics and humor that bordered on the vicious, he achieved a sort of verse whose originality is virtually unmatched in early American literature. As verse, it is not always successful. As political commentary, it was sometimes almost too successful: Bolling's poems relating to the Chiswell scandal of 1766 (which pitted the cream of Virginia's Loyalist faction against the emerging rebel faction) nearly resulted in Bolling's indictment for libel against the crown, tantamount to a charge of treason, for his charges that the General Court was guilty of showing favoritism to John Chiswell, a member of the gentry who had been charged with murder. Neither Bolling nor the *Virginia Gazette*, which had printed his poems and letters on the controversy, was indicted by the grand jury, however, and a major battle for freedom of the press was won. In addition, Bolling was given the impetus toward further poetry on political themes, resulting in a pair of poems, "Civil Dudgeon" and "A Canzonet," treating the Norfolk smallpox inoculation riots of 1768-1769, which Bolling rightly saw as a rehearsal for revolution, pitting as they did rebel factions against Tory.

Simultaneously, Bolling was writing private poetry which had few readers except perhaps his close friends. Ironically, Bolling achieved his greatest originality in these unpublished poems. Many are nothing more than epigrams, but they are highly polished, if often scatological burlesques of major fixtures of Virginia society of the day. (Landon Carter especially stimulated the flow of poison from Bolling's pen.) Only one major poem resulted, but it is perhaps Bolling's finest, most developed work. "Neanthe" is a long narrative poem, cast as a mock epic, treating the wooing of a sluttish heroine (Neanthe) by a pair of combative swains. Although the versification is sometimes not entirely successful, the poem is nevertheless an astonishing achievement, and a major document in the development of American comic literature.

Toward the end of "Neanthe," the parents of the tragic heroine, a suicide, hire a poet to sing her praises. The resulting poem-within-the-poem is a conventionally dishonest lyric in which the repulsive Neanthe is translated into a paradigm of feminine virtue and beauty. It is impossible not to read into this section of the poem a parody of Bolling's own early work, and it seems entirely possible that "Neanthe" was Bolling's way of turning his back on the derivative strain that hindered his development, an announcement of a new material, a new toughness. Yet nothing else in the canon matches "Neanthe" in ambition or achievement, and, indeed, most of Bolling's published works during his last years deal with his experimentation with the establishment of vineyards in Virginia, an experimentation well documented in essays and verses printed by the *Virginia Gazette*.

It is unlikely that Robert Bolling will ever be ranked with the major writers of the colonial American period. Indeed, he remains as interesting for the life he lived (and the changes that transpired in his identity) as for the product of his pen. Yet it is his writing that documents, infallibly, his movement from Englishman-in-exile to American, and, as a record of that movement, so closely parallel to the history of his time, his works are indispensable.

Reference:
J. A. Leo Lemay, "Robert Bolling and the Bailment of Colonel Chiswell," *Early American Literature*, 6 (Fall 1971): 99-142.

Papers:
The manuscripts for Bolling's "La Gazzatta di Parnasso" and "Bon Mots" are at the Huntington Library in San Marino, California. His commonplace book is at the University of Virginia.

Jonathan Boucher

David Curtis Skaggs
Bowling Green State University

BIRTH: Blencogo, Cumberland, England, 12 March 1738, to James and Anne Barnes Boucher.

MARRIAGES: 2 June 1772 to Eleanor Addison. 15 February 1787 to Mary Elizabeth Foreman. 29 October 1789 to Elizabeth Hodgson James; children: James, Ann, Eleanor Mary Elizabeth, Jane, Barton, Elizabeth, Mary, Jonathan, Jr.

DEATH: Epsom, Surrey, England, 27 April 1804.

BOOKS: *A Letter from a Virginian to the Members of the Congress to be Held in Philadelphia* . . . (New York: Printed by Hugh Gaine, 1774; London: Printed for J. Wilkie, 1774);
A View of the Causes and Consequences of the American Revolution; In Thirteen Discourses, Preached in North America between the Years 1763 and 1775 (London: Printed for G. G. & J. Robinson, 1797; New York: Russell & Russell, 1967);
A Sermon Preached at the Assizes Held at the City of Carlisle, August 12, 1798 (Carlisle, England: Printed for the author by the executors of the late W. Halhead, 1798);
A Sermon Preached at the Assizes Held at Guildford, July the 30th, 1798 . . . (London: J. Plymsell, 1798);
An Address to the Inhabitants of the Parish of Epsom, with a Plan for a Soup-Establishment (Southwork, England: Philanthropic Reform, 1800);
Proposals for Printing by Subscription, in Two Volumes, Quarto: Linguae Anglicanae Veteris Thesaurus; Or, A Glossary of the Ancient English Language . . . (London: Printed by Luke Hansard, 1801-1802);
A Supplement to Dr. Johnson's Dictionary of the English Language: Or, A Glossary of Obsolete and Provincial Words, part 1 (London: Longman, Hurst, Rees & Orme, 1807); enlarged as *Boucher's Glossary of Archaic and Provincial Words. A Supplement to the Dictionaries of the English Language* . . . , parts 1 and 2 edited by Joseph Hunter and Joseph Stevenson (London: Printed for Black, Young & Young, 1832-1833);
Reminiscences of an American Loyalist, 1738-1789 . . . Edited by His Grandson Jonathan Bouchier (Boston & New York: Houghton Mifflin, 1925).

OTHER: William Hutchinson, *The History of the County of Cumberland,* 2 volumes, includes material by Boucher (Carlisle, England: Printed by F. Jollie, 1794);
"Address to the Inhabitants of the County of Cumberland," in volume 1 of *The State of the Poor; or An History of the Labouring Classes in England* . . . , by Frederick Morton Eden, 3 volumes (London: Printed by J. Davis for B. & J. White, 1797).

Possibly the best-known Loyalist of the American Revolution, the Reverend Jonathan Boucher has consistently been depicted as the most reactionary defender of royal prerogative in colonial America. While his reputation as an arch-Tory may not be entirely deserved, Boucher, having developed a reasonably coherent political philosophy based largely upon his adaptation of Robert Filmer's *Patriarcha: The Natural Power of Kings* (1680), was one of the last defenders of the patriarchal theory of governmental origins, the divine right of kings, and the biblical requirement of obedience to constituted authority. This Anglican parson fled his Maryland parish in 1775 and returned to his native England where, as vicar of Epsom, Surrey, he continued to enhance his reputation as an articulate preacher, passable poet, reforming educator, compulsive bibliophile, regional historian, and lexicographer of British and American dialects. No amount of explanation of his thought and actions has rehabilitated Boucher from Vernon Louis Parrington's characterization of him as "the high Tory of the Tory cause in America . . . [whose] militant loyalty to the outworn doctrine of passive submission was a real disservice to the [British] ministry, for it revealed the prerogative in a light peculiarly offensive to American prejudices. What a godsend to the liberals was such a doctrine on the lips of so eminent a divine!" More recent studies have pointed to the Whiggish philosophy of his early writings and have explained that his quest for needed patronage forced him to become a spokesman for proprietary, Anglican, and royal privilege. Others argue that his holistic approach to the social and spiritual worlds was neither original nor unique for eighteenth-century Anglican clergy

Jonathan and Eleanor Boucher, circa 1782; portraits by Daniel Gardner (Mabel Brady Garvan Collection, Yale University Art Gallery)

and that he represented philosophical attitudes more common among the revolutionaries, particularly those who became Federalists, than Boucher's earlier detractors would admit. Moreover, his attitudes toward Indians, Negroes, and religious toleration were far more advanced than those of many of his revolutionary contemporaries. While we now have a complete study of his life, there is not yet a definitive analysis of his political thought nor of his contributions to eighteenth-century literature and lexicography.

The Bouchers of Blencogo, County of Cumberland, England, had once been a family of importance, but support of the roundheads, confiscation of estates, and poor management had resulted in their decline from gentry status to that of artisans. James Boucher (other spellings included Bourchier and Bouchier) was a down-and-out shoemaker and tavernkeeper, who drank most of any profits his alehouse provided. His two daughters by a first marriage were shunted off to distant relatives as domestic servants. His second wife, Anne Barnes, bore four children between 1734 and 1741. Jonathan Boucher, second son and third child of this matrimonial alliance, lived in "a state of penury and hardship as I have never since seen equalled, no, not even in parish almshouses." The price of disloyalty to the Crown was constantly impressed upon James Boucher's two sons, who reinforced this lesson when he sent the two impressionable children to witness the execution of Jacobite rebels at Carlisle.

Despite his parents' straitened circumstances, Jonathan learned to read and write at a local free school and saw the fringes of gentility when he visited an elder half sister who was a domestic servant of a clergyman who summered in Blencogo. Always in search of new opportunities, he briefly taught at age sixteen, learned surveying, and at eighteen became usher at Saint Bees School, whose headmaster, the Reverend John James, would become his lifelong mentor and confidant. When a Whitehaven merchant sought a young man to serve as a tutor to a Virginia planter's family, James recommended twenty-one-year-old Jonathan Boucher for the position.

In April 1759, he arrived at Urbanna on the Rappahannock River, where he quickly aped the self-indulgent colonials. His personal reputation was not so besmirched, however, as to prevent his being recommended for holy orders and the rectorship of Hanover Parish, King George County, Virginia, which finally brought him the gentry status he long sought. (His quick ordination by the Bishop of London in March 1762 demonstrates the lack of academic credentials and theological apprenticeship demanded of colonial Anglican clergy in contrast to English standards.) Early in his rectorship he engaged in the contentious argumentation and vigorous confrontation with accusers that was to characterize his American career. He retained the solid support of his parishioners, but when a more lucrative living became available at St. Mary's Parish in Caroline County, across the Rappahannock River, he accepted the post in 1764. Here he continued a three-fold career as parson, teacher, and planter that characterized his colonial years.

Early in his ministry, Boucher denied the orthodox theology of his faith and for several years questioned the internal logic and the traditional tenets of revealed religion. In this questioning he was not unlike many of his fellow Anglican clergy and laity who recognized that the lack of close episcopal supervision allowed them an independence of thought and spirit denied the Church of England clergy in the Mother Country. His rebelliousness from conventional standards of behavior probably best expressed itself in his affair with Judith Dent Chase, a young Maryland widow who spurned his offers of marriage, but apparently not his bed. Anne Zimmer's detailed study of Boucher's life concludes the young cleric probably fathered twin daughters known as Betty and Catherine Charlotte Strange born to Mrs. Chase in 1767.

About this time Boucher's religious convictions underwent a major transformation. Under the influence of the Reverends James Maury of Virginia and Henry Addison of Maryland, Boucher expanded his intellectual horizons through vigorous reading and the building of a personal library that became one of the largest in the Chesapeake region. By the end of the 1760s, Boucher discovered the necessity of order in society, the positive role that hierarchical structure played in maintaining social stability, and the influence of institutions and tradition in support of natural order. He found the colonial agencies of church and state deficient and in need of vigorous reform.

Particularly under Maury's influence, he began to play a role in the political controversies of the age. He defended the clerical position in the Two-Penny Act controversy, but took a decidedly procolonial stance relative to the Proclamation of 1763, the Stamp Act, the Townshend Duties, and the Vandalia colony project. At the end of his first decade in America, Boucher could be classified as a conservative Whig about to be caught in the vortex of controversy that would lead to independence. On the basis of the attitudes he expressed, one could not determine how he would act when the final crisis came. Most dangerous for his survival in America was his decision to actively participate in political controversy.

Insecure as the impoverished young schoolmaster had been in 1759, by 1770 Boucher was a self-assured and respected rising figure among the Chesapeake gentry. Since St. Mary's Parish and his boarding school provided a solid income, he purchased several slaves and engaged an overseer to manage the parish glebe. He became socially active and might have turned into the archetype carousing Virginia parson had not his intellect, ambition, and discipline turned him toward a more productive path. He could now choose among a variety of new opportunities. He refused appointment as master of the grammar school at the College of William and Mary (a prestigious honor, especially for a nonuniversity graduate), and waited, somewhat impatiently, for Addison and his influential in-laws, the Dulanys, to secure him a lucrative living in the Maryland establishment. His wait was ended in 1770 when Governor Sir Robert Eden offered him the rectorship of Saint Anne's Parish, Annapolis. Here, in what he later described as "the genteelist town in North America," he moved in the channels of privilege and power hitherto forbidden this impoverished child from the English north country.

At thirty-two, Jonathan Boucher could reflect on how industry, eloquence, and outward piety combined with the cultivation of well-placed patrons led to success. But his was a success based upon the support of others and subject to the whims of fortune. Immediately after his induction, he plunged into the political controversies of the age, supporting his patrons, the Dulanys and Eden, against the emerging Country Party leadership of William Paca and Samuel Chase. Most critical in Boucher's alienation from the colonial gentry was his vigorous championship of a colonial bishopric. Already fearing they were overtaxed to support the Anglican establishment, most Marylanders, including churchmen, opposed the resident episcopacy on the grounds of its cost and saw it as the source of potential political power as well as a ministerial conspiracy against American liberties. Boucher's stance eventually forced the rector of the capital city's parish into the center of Maryland politics.

Before he became excessively involved in such controversy, Boucher established a reputation as a patron of the theater, as a budding versifier, and as a student of American dialect. He kept careful notes on the peculiarities of Chesapeake speech patterns, which he eventually incorporated into "Absence, a

Pastoral" based upon Vergil's *Eclogues.* Such literary efforts were typical among clerical contemporaries such as James Sterling, Thomas Cradock, and Thomas Bacon. His poetic efforts, which frequently appeared in the *Maryland Gazette,* brought him to the attention of local gentlemen who formed a literary and social group called the Homony Club. Here future Patriots and Loyalists dined and drank with a conviviality that belied their rivalries in the public world outside.

Boucher's year-and-a-half in Annapolis marked the high point of his American career. Were it not for his politics, one might argue he was a liberal thinker. In vain, he urged baptism, communion, and the rudiments of education for blacks. His educational philosophy (best expressed in letters to George Washington relative to the instruction of his stepson, John Parke Custis, and in a 1773 sermon) combined a quest for the inculcation of Christian morality and Anglican orthodoxy with instruction in "practicable and useful" subjects such as history, oratory, English, natural philosophy, modern languages, commercial training, and agriculture. "Let classical learning still be attended to as it deserves . . . but, let it no longer monopolize all our attention," he argued. If Boucher vigorously opposed the doctrine of majority rule, he argued persuasively for its American political corollary—minority rights, religious toleration, and freedom of speech and press. Few modern civil libertarians would object to the opinion he expressed in a letter to Washington shortly before he fled to England to escape physical abuse from American patriots: "The true plan . . . is for each party to defend his own side as well as he can by fair argument, and also, if possible, to convince his adversary: but everything that savours of, or but approaches to, coercion or compulsion is persecution and tyranny." The anti-Catholic demogoguery expressed in the opposition to the Quebec Act was denounced by Boucher as inimical to the ideals of religious toleration inherent in the Age of Reason. Robert G. Walker has held that merely because "Boucher did not see the necessity of majority rule to the protection of human rights should not obscure the nobility of his championing of the minority."

It was his political contentiousness that forced his departure from America, even though in the fall of 1771 he accepted the lucrative preferment as rector of rural Queen Anne's Parish in Prince George's County, Maryland. He shortly thereafter married thirty-four-year-old Eleanor Addison, niece of his friend Henry Addison. Thus by marriage the poor boy from Cumberland became a member of the planter elite and related to families closely associated with proprietary influence in the colony—the Addisons and the Dulanys. If Boucher's loyalism had not been insured by the tragic lessons of family history and philosophical temperament, it was finally sealed by his family associations. From his pulpit and his plantation library he spoke and wrote in behalf of a series of causes that made him ever more anathema to his parishioners.

The Maryland proprietary and religious establishments required the highest level of local taxation and fees in colonial America. When colonists sought to reduce the income of these public officials, there began political infighting that, probably more than any other factor, separated the eventual Patriots from Loyalists. The Fee Dispute was to His Lordship's Colony what the Two-Penny Act was to Virginia, the Boston Massacre was to Massachusetts, and the *Gaspee* incident was to Rhode Island. Each of these local issues divided the provincial elite, contributed to the elevation of new, more-radical local leadership, and exposed the more moderate- and conservative-minded to ridicule and abuse. Before it was over, Boucher, one of the most outspoken defenders of the status quo in the province, found himself isolated and condemned by the triumphant Country Party Patriots.

Boucher defended high clerical salaries in a series of essays published in the *Maryland Gazette* in 1772-1773. These essays were countered by Paca and Chase, and eventually the validity of the established church's right to tax support came into question. During this dispute, Boucher once again called for an American bishop, a move which brought more denunciations and an honorary M.A. from King's College, New York. In each essay he moved near to a defense of royal authority and narrowed his intellectual and personal options.

In 1774 he wrote *A Letter from a Virginian* defending parliamentary supremacy. This anonymous pamphlet addressed to the delegates at the First Continental Congress argued for a moderate approach in seeking the redress of American grievances and sought accommodation rather than confrontation. None of his ideas was acceptable to the radical elements dominating both Congressional and local politics. Extralegal committees gained control of Maryland's government and charged Boucher with activities inimical to American rights. Undaunted, the parson continued to attack the drift toward independence in letters entitled "Queries

Addressed to the People of Maryland" and "To the Hon[ora]ble the Deputies in Congress from the Southern Provinces." (Although Boucher claimed these were published in New York, no record remains today except in Boucher's *Reminiscences of an American Loyalist*, 1925.)

Driven from his parish and forced to live with Henry Addison, Boucher decided to preach at Queen Anne's on 11 May 1775, a day of public fasting and humiliation proclaimed by the extralegal Maryland Convention. With pistols on the pulpit, he threatened to shoot anyone who opposed him. When an intercolonial fast day in July found him facing two hundred armed men, the redoubtable parson drew his pistol to the head of the ringleader and threatened to "instantly blow his brains out" unless he could leave unharmed.

In August he wrote an embittered farewell letter to George Washington and left America for England. Boucher found his return to his homeland bittersweet. Englishmen were "cold & formal." He discovered himself "fit only for America," where he had "some Character & Note—here, every Body I see eclipses Me." This loss of place in society nearly devastated a man who had so long pursued status. At thirty-eight he began all over again. Without influence, he secured a low-paying curacy and established a small school. In a few years he had more than a dozen young pupils (Governor Eden's son among them).

Soon his prospects improved. A post as an undersecretary for the Society for the Propagation of the Gospel provided modest additional income. Kindness toward an old maid brought him an inheritance worth several hundred pounds a year. Finally, his philological interests led to a totally unexpected reward when in 1784 John Parkhurst, patron of Epsom Parrish, Surrey, and a lexicographer who knew of Boucher only by reputation, appointed him to the vicarship. For nearly two decades Boucher would minister to a flock in the beautiful Epsom Downs countryside. St. Martin's church provided a comfortable living for Boucher.

This moment of personal achievement came at a time of great grief. Eleanor "Nelly" Addison Boucher died on 1 March 1784 and his surrogate father, John James, departed the following New Year's Day. These two deaths mark an important dividing point in Boucher's career—one ended his ties with his impoverished Cumbrian past, the other his ties with his colonial rise to influence and affluence. Then, in October 1786, the Reverend John James, Jr., son of his mentor and the closest thing Boucher had to a son, died of a lingering illness.

Elizabeth Boucher (Gellatly Collection, courtesy of the National Collection of Fine Arts, Smithsonian Institution)

Only twenty-seven, the younger James left a widow and daughter toward whom Boucher had deep affection. Even happy events seemed to lead to personal tragedy. He married Mary Elizabeth Foreman of Epsom in early 1787, and her wealth brought him instant social status hitherto unknown. What was initially thought to be a pregnancy turned from joy into a nightmare when doctors discovered an ovarian tumor that resulted in Mary Elizabeth's death on 14 September 1788.

His "mind shaken and unhinged," he returned to his native Cumbrian hills for solace. With his large inheritance he bought several local properties and reestablished the local prestige of the Boucher name. There also he renewed his acquaintance with twenty-eight-year-old Elizabeth Hodgson James, widow of the younger John James. Their marriage in the fall of 1789 resulted in a growing family that saw eight births in ten years. As Anne Zimmer observes: "The kind of family like he had first glimpsed and envied in the household of John James and Nancy at Saint Bees was now his own."

In the midst of this domestic happiness, Boucher's literary output increased dramatically. He contributed several historical items in William

Hutchinson's *History of the County of Cumberland* (1794), composed his *Reminiscences of an American Loyalist* (not published in full until 1925), wrote his magnum opus *A View of the Causes and Consequences of the American Revolution* (1797), and continued work on his *Glossary of Archaic and Provincial Words* (never completed, but published in part in 1807 and 1832-1833). Boucher's concern for the poor was reflected in his proposals for a "Soup-Establishment" at Epsom and in his "Address to the Inhabitants of the County of Cumberland," printed in *The State of the Poor; or An History of the Labouring Classes in England* (1797) by Frederick Morton Eden (son of Gov. Robert Eden). In addition, two of Boucher's sermons that he preached outside his parish and his proposals for the glossary were published.

Boucher's literary and intellectual renown rests primarily upon his *A View of the Causes and Consequences of the American Revolution*. Dedicated to George Washington, the book consists of a ninety-page preface and thirteen sermons allegedly delivered in America, 1763-1775. These discourses, modeled after those of his Cumberland mentor, John James, reflect the impact of Archbishop John Tillotson upon homiletic style. Tillotson's closely reasoned treatises utilizing biblical rather than the classical illusions of seventeenth-century divines exemplified the customary Anglican and dissenting preaching style until the evangelical tradition epitomized by George Whitefield and John Wesley supplanted it. Boucher followed Tillotson's plain style, his emphasis on moderation, and the philosophy of passive obedience to authority that the archbishop endorsed in his early career. Topically this tradition emphasized sermons dealing with private morality and benevolence, but the addresses printed in *A View of the Causes and Consequences of the American Revolution* are mostly politically oriented. Indeed, they constitute the basis for Boucher's reputation as an uncompromising, archconservative Tory and apostle of the reactionary authoritarian political philosophy of Sir Robert Filmer. Because of this image, Parrington called Boucher the "Tory Priest" whose writing represented "the voice of seventeenth-century Cavalier England, speaking to an alien people" and Richard Gummere labeled him "Toryissimus." However, since World War II, Boucher's reputation has undergone some rehabilitation.

Most recent studies of loyalism find him a profound Loyalist commentator, even if his ideas seem a caricature of royal thought in America. His sermons "On Schisms and Sects" and "On the Toleration of Papists" are now seen by Robert G. Walker as defending minority rights, and his "On American Education" is viewed as a constructive advance from the excessive dependence upon classical languages in the curriculum and as a pragmatic, practical approach to learning. Moreover, his best-known discourse—"On Civil Liberty; Passive Obedience, and Non-Resistance"—has been described by Bernard Bailyn and Michael D. Clark as less reactionary and more typical of traditional thought than previously assumed.

The patriarchalism supported in this sermon is not a mere echo of a seventeenth-century eccentric. Robert Filmer's philosophy of the family as the organizational precursor of the political order, as a symbolic representation of the monarchial state, has an intellectual heritage dating back to Plato and continuing through Richard Hooker. Moreover, it was reinforced in the eighteenth century by the philosophy of the Great Chain of Being with its emphasis on hierarchic gradation. Boucher's em-

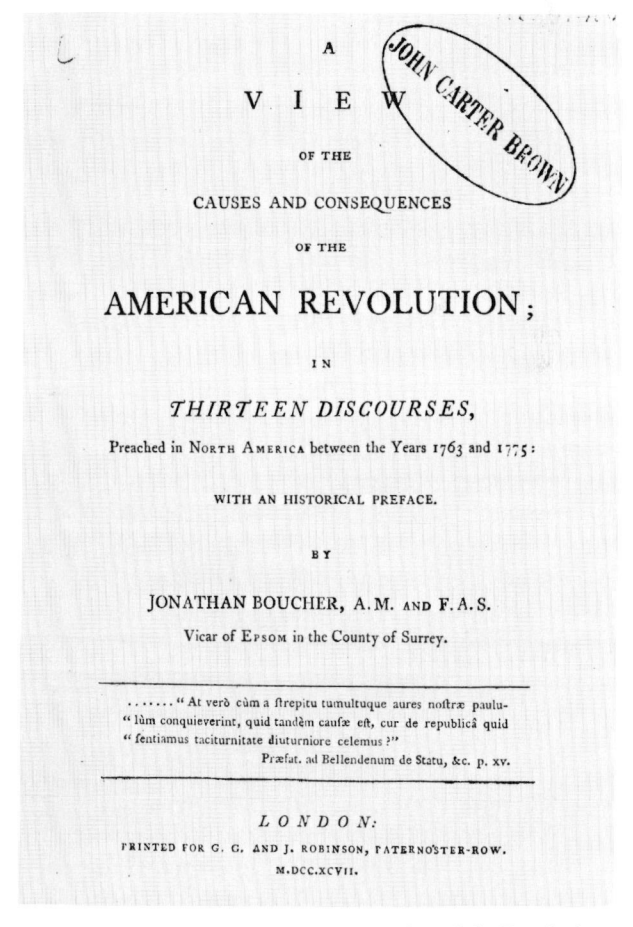

Title page for Boucher's Tory interpretation of the Revolution, which he nonetheless dedicated to his old friend George Washington (courtesy of the John Carter Brown Library at Brown University)

phasis on social station reflects prevailing Anglican notions that each person should labor truly "to do his duty in that state of life" to which God has called him.

Even though Boucher may have composed, as Peter Laslett argues, "the best common-sense defense of Filmer that was ever made," one should not overemphasize the Filmerian portion of his philosophy. Although he accepted the familial origins of government, Boucher rejected Sir Robert's divine-right consequences with a smug comment that Filmer "entertained some very extravagant notions on monarchy, and the sacredness of Kings." Moreover, Boucher went beyond biblical justification to provide historical and anthropological evidence in support of patriarchalism, and it may be argued that Boucher's *A View of the Causes and Consequences of the American Revolution* is more a reflection of his bitterness toward the American Revolution and its "lineal" descendant, the French Revolution, than what he said in the 1770s. Anne Zimmer's biography contends that the texts of the original sermons did not survive the transatlantic voyage and that the thirteen discourses are reconstructions reflecting his later opinions rather than those entertained prior to his departure. There is considerable justification for this position. Even if one accepts their pre-1775 composition, the defense of Filmer is largely in an explanatory footnote of 1797, not part of the sermon text. In that note Boucher acknowledged that only "lately" had he "perused" *Patriarcha*. In fact, Boucher could have made his argument—"The first father was the first king: and . . . it was thus that all government originated; and monarchy is its most ancient form"—without any reference to Sir Robert at all.

Once he established the patriarchal origins of government Boucher proceeded to establish the duty to obey constituted authority: "Obedience to Government is every man's duty, because it is every man's interest: but it is particularly incumbent on Christians, because . . . it is enjoined by the positive commands of God: and therefore, when Christians are disobedient to human ordinances, they are also disobedient to God." "True liberty, then, is a liberty to do every thing that is right, and the being restrained from doing any thing that is wrong."

The great evil advanced by modern political theorists, Boucher found, was their notion "that the whole human race is born equal; and that no man is naturally inferior, or, in any respect, subjected to another." This concept of equality bred contempt for authority, resistance to legitimate laws, political instability, and revolution. During this portion of his argument he employed one of his typical metaphors: "A musical instrument composed of chords, key, or pipes all perfectly equal in size and power might as well be expected to produce harmony as a society composed of members all perfectly equal to be productive of order and peace."

Egalitarianism was not only false, it deceptively contributed to social disharmony which was the bane of political stability. This criticism of egalitarianism appears in other colonial Anglican sermons, for instance those of Thomas Cradock of Baltimore County, and may also be found in many arguments of Patriots, especially during the 1790s. Deeply fearing a recurrence of the upheavals of seventeenth-century England, Boucher and his fellow Loyalists argued that the absence of institutional supports for the natural order of position and subordination left the British Americans without the support beams necessary to hold up the social system. According to Bernard Bailyn, "On Civil Liberty; Passive Obedience, and Non-Resistance" "sums up, as no other essay of the period, the threat to the traditional ordering of human relations implicit in Revolutionary thought." Modern historiography, notably the writings of Bailyn and the "new" social historians, finds Boucher's diagnosis of social and political instability to be essentially correct. What these historians find impossible to accept is the clergyman's prescription of the introduction of more British institutions as the remedy for the problem. Boucher was clearly a man of little faith concerning the efficacy of remedies other than patriarchy, monarchy, and episcopacy for the disease of republicanism he saw flourishing in America. Boucher could not see, Bailyn concludes, that "this defiance, this refusal to truckle, this distrust of all authority, political or social" that appeared in the colonies, "would express human aspirations, not crush them."

If Boucher's antiquated political views represented something incompatible with his day, his lexicographic interests mark an important milestone on the road to philological understanding. Boucher was the first to undertake seriously a glossary of Americanisms and British provincialisms. Undoubtedly the idioms of his native Cumbria prompted his interest in regional language forms. Like many contemporary observers of American linguistic patterns, Boucher felt there were no peculiarities of enunciation, tone, or words that created a true colonial dialect. But he found the Americans "peculiarly addicted to innovation" and hence prone, "in no very distant period," to create a language as independent of England as they were

First page of the manuscript for Boucher's protest over the printer's rejection of the biographical sketch of Sir James Wallace that Boucher had written for William Hutchinson's The History of the County Cumberland. *The printer had shown the sketch to Wallace's son, who was infuriated by it and insisted that his own article about his father be published in its place (Cumbria County Library, Carlisle).*

politically independent, so that their new tongue would become "altogether as unlike English, as the Dutch or Flemish is unlike German, or the Norwegian unlike the Danish, or the Portuguese unlike Spanish."

Professor Allen Walker Read has found Boucher "to be the first commentator of importance ... on the subject of English in America." Boucher's "Absence, a Pastoral" hardly constitutes effective poetry, but it accomplished Boucher's objective "of introducing as many words of speech, . . . prevalent and common in [colonial] Maryland." Here we find many of the Americanisms also noted in Ebenezer Cook's *The Sot-Weed Factor* and Thomas Cradock's "Maryland Eclogues." Among the definitions found in Boucher's notes to this Vergilian imitation and in his glossary are:

> *Buckskins:* natives of Virginia and Maryland are so called, in contradistinction to *outlandish* persons, or natives of any other country. . . .
> *Canoes:* small light boats. . . .
> *A Jacket:* a waistcoat. . . .
> *Squaw:* a wife. . . .
> *Wampum:* strings of shells used for money. . . .

His Irish and American words are far fewer than Boucher desired. The work on the glossary progressed throughout the 1790s, but frequent illness delayed him in the early nineteenth century and he reached only *T* at the time of his death. Portions of Boucher's work were posthumously published, and H. L. Mencken would subsequently credit Boucher as a pioneer in the study of American language.

The last years of the vicar of Epsom's life saw not only domestic happiness but also an increasing reputation and recognition by his contemporaries. He was considered for the Anglican bishoprics of Nova Scotia and Edinburgh and the archdeaconry of Carlisle. He refused a post at the Royal Chapel of Holyrood Castle in Edinburgh. His published sermons at the assizes in Guildford and Carlisle in 1798 reflect his growing conservatism in the face of the French Revolution. Membership in the Edinburgh Society of Antiquarians and the Sterling Literary Society were among the numerous recognitions he received.

Few Loyalists achieved more success in England than Jonathan Boucher. His estates were extensive; his library was more than 10,000 volumes; his scholarly reputation was well known. His family's reputation was assured, and his descendants included writers, public officials, and members of Parliament. Moreover, Boucher is probably the most quoted and most quotable of the Loyalists. His letters, his reminiscences, and, above all, his *A View of the Causes and Consequences of the American Revolution* constitute the High Tory condemnation of the Revolution. A formidable opponent of colonial rebellion, Boucher presented a comprehensive and coherent critique of that event. As anachronistic as his ideas may have been, as much as they failed to comprehend the changing nature of social and political order, Boucher's writings constitute the most detailed analysis of the weaknesses of colonial society written by those driven from America by the cataclysm of the War of American Independence.

Letters:
"Letters of Jonathan Boucher," *Maryland Historical Magazine*, 7 (March 1912): 1-26; 7 (June 1912): 150-165; 7 (September 1912): 286-304; 7 (December 1912): 337-356; 8 (March 1913): 34-50; 8 (June 1913): 168-186; 8 (September 1913): 235-256; 8 (December 1913): 338-352; 9 (March 1914): 54-67; 9 (September 1914): 232-241; 9 (December 1914): 327-336; 10 (March 1915): 25-37; 10 (June 1915): 114-127;
Letters from Jonathan Boucher to George Washington, edited by Worthington Chauncey Ford (Brooklyn, N.Y.: Historical Printing Club, 1899).

Biography:
Anne Y. Zimmer, *Jonathan Boucher: Loyalist in Exile* (Detroit: Wayne State University Press, 1978).

References:
Bernard Bailyn, *The Ideological Origins of the American Revolution* (Cambridge: Harvard University Press, 1967), pp. 314-318;
Carol R. Berkin, "Jonathan Boucher: The Loyalist as Rebel," *Studies in the Social Sciences* (West Georgia State College), 15 (June 1976): 65-78;
Joseph L. Blau, "Jonathan Boucher, Tory," *History*, no. 4 (May 1961): 93-109;
Robert McCluer Calhoon, *The Loyalists in Revolutionary America, 1760-1781* (New York: Harcourt Brace Jovanovich, 1973), pp. 218-233, 536;
Michael D. Clark, "Jonathan Boucher: The Mirror of Reaction," *Huntington Library Quarterly*, 23 (November 1969): 19-32;
Clark, "Jonathan Boucher and the Toleration of Roman Catholics in Maryland," *Maryland His-

torical Magazine, 71 (Summer 1976): 194-204;
Clark, "Jonathan Boucher's *Causes and Consequences,*" in *Loyalist Historians,* volume 1 of *The Colonial Legacy,* edited by Lawrence H. Leder (New York: Harper & Row, 1971), pp. 89-117;
Richard Beale Davis, *Intellectual Life in the Colonial South, 1585-1763,* 3 volumes (Knoxville: University of Tennessee Press, 1978), I: 303-304, 382-384; III: 1395-1396, 1427-1428, 1617-1618;
Philip Evanson, "Jonathan Boucher: The Mind of an American Loyalist," *Maryland Historical Magazine,* 58 (June 1963): 123-136;
Ralph Emmett Fall, "The Rev. Jonathan Boucher, Turbulent Tory (1738-1804)," *Historical Magazine of the Protestant Episcopal Church,* 36 (December 1967): 323-356;
Richard M. Gummere, *The American Mind and the Classical Tradition* (Cambridge: Harvard University Press, 1963), pp. 161-172;
Vernon Louis Parrington, *The Colonial Mind, 1620-1800,* volume 1 of *Main Currents in American Thought* (New York: Harcourt, Brace, 1927), pp. 214-218;
Allen Walker Read, "Boucher's Linguistic Pastoral of Colonial Maryland," *Dialect Notes,* 6 (1933): 353-360;
Read, "British Recognition of American Speech in the Eighteenth Century," *Dialect Notes,* 6 (1933): 313-334;
Moses Coit Tyler, *The Literary History of the American Revolution, 1763-1783,* 2 volumes (New York: Putnam's, 1897), I: 316-328; II: 278-279;
Robert G. Walker, "Jonathan Boucher: Champion of the Minority," *William and Mary Quarterly,* third series, 2 (January 1945): 3-14;
Anne Y. Zimmer and Alfred H. Kelly, "Jonathan Boucher: Constitutional Conservative," *Journal of American History,* 58 (May 1972): 897-922.

Papers:
The Boucher Manuscripts at the East Sussex Record Office in Lewes, England, contain the bulk of Boucher's letters, 1759-1799. Boucher's copy of Hutchinson's *History of the County of Cumberland* containing many annotations, manuscript notes, interleaves, and illustrations is deposited in the Cumbria County Library, Carlisle, England.

John Camm
(1718-1778)

Homer D. Kemp
Tennessee Technological University

BOOKS: *A Single and Distinct View of the Act, Vulgarly entitled Two-Penny Act* . . . (Annapolis: Printed by Jonas Green, 1763);
A Review of the Rector Detected: Or the Colonel Reconnoitered (Williamsburg: Printed by Joseph Royle, 1764);
Critical Remarks on a Letter Ascribed to Common Sense . . . (Williamsburg: Printed by Joseph Royle, 1765);
Sermon Preached . . . at the Funeral of Mr. Nelson (N.p., 1772).

A fierce Tory advocate of the prerogative of the Crown and the established Church, John Camm struggled for more than thirty years against the forces which eventually declared America independent of the Crown and disestablished the Church. As a leader of the Church-and-College party in Virginia, Camm defied the authority of his local vestry, the Board of Visitors of the College of William and Mary, and the colonial legislature in such disputes as the Two-Penny Acts controversies and the American episcopate debates. During his career Camm wrote three lengthy pamphlets, a number of addresses to the King, several dozen essays to the gazettes, and some scattered poetry. One of the most indefatigable letter writers of his generation, his epistolary art reflects the major debates of more than thirty years in Virginia. All in all, Camm made a valuable contribution to American Revolutionary literature by stating cogently the minority viewpoint of Virginia Loyalists.

Born in 1718, in Hornsea, Yorkshire, and educated in the school at nearby Beverley, John

Camm was admitted to Trinity College, Cambridge, on 16 June 1738, and took his B.A. in early 1742. He became the minister of Newport Parish, Isle of Wight County, Virginia, in 1745. From 1749 to 1771, he served on the faculty of the College of William and Mary as professor of divinity and was the minister of York-Hampton Parish, York County.

Camm's great abilities were attested to by friend and foe alike, and his peers elected him to many positions of responsibility throughout his career in Virginia. Even Governor Francis Fauquier, who disliked Camm and alluded in a letter to the Bishop of London to Camm's delight "to raise a Flame and live in it," grudgingly admitted that Camm was a man of abilities. He was a leader in organizing clerical opposition to the Virginia legislature's Two-Penny Acts of 1755 and 1758. Each Anglican clergyman was paid an annual salary of 16,000 pounds of tobacco, which he sold at the prevailing market rate. Short tobacco crops in 1755 and 1758 inflated the price of tobacco, causing the Virginia House of Burgesses to pass temporary acts commuting the year's tobacco salaries into currency at the rate of two pence per pound of tobacco. Clerical opposition to these acts began a debate that occupied the energies of the best minds in Virginia for more than eight years—debates significant far beyond their purely local origins. Most of the significant arguments about Crown prerogatives and colonial autonomy expressed during the Stamp Act crisis and the Revolutionary War were formed earlier during the Two-Penny Acts controversies. Camm was elected to carry the clergy's case to the Privy Council in England in 1758, where he successfully petitioned the King to disallow the Virginia acts. Upon returning to Virginia, Camm was drawn into a heated pamphlet war with two members of the Virginia legislature, Landon Carter and Richard Bland. In addition to his opposition to the Two-Penny Acts, Camm defied the Board of Visitors of the College in their attempts to curb the authority of the president and faculty, was dismissed from his faculty position in 1757, appealed to England, and was reinstated in 1763.

The first two of Camm's three Two-Penny pamphlets are carefully reasoned, unembellished refutations of pamphlets written by Carter and Bland. Camm's *A Single and Distinct View of the Act, Vulgarly entitled Two-Penny Act . . .* (1763) was written in answer to Carter's *A Letter to the Right Reverend Father in God, the Lord B[isho]p of L[ondo]n . . .* (1759) and Bland's *A Letter to the Clergy of Virginia . . .* (1760). *A Review of the Rector Detected . . .* (1764) was written as a retort to Carter's *The Rector Detected . . .* (1764). Both pamphlets prove Camm to be the equal of his opponents in suasory discourse and satire. Unable to accept lay control of the clergy by the vestries and the legislature, Camm saw in the Two-Penny Acts—especially in the impassioned speech of Patrick Henry in the lawsuit of the Reverend James Maury—the seeds of treason and the destruction of all that he considered truly British.

The last and best of Camm's three pamphlets, *Critical Remarks . . .* (1765), has not been properly appreciated as literature. In the context of ideas and in political significance to the Revolution, this last pamphlet in the paper war is only a rather anticlimactic statement of Tory views on Crown prerogatives. As literature, however, the pamphlet is in every way the equal of Richard Bland's *The Colonel Dismounted: Or the Rector Vindicated . . .* (1764), in answer to which it was written and to which it has usually been unfavorably compared. In his essay Camm creates a highly effective piece of satire as he skillfully employs the devices of irony which are found in his models Jonathan Swift and John Dryden and effectively uses the elements of classical discourse to counter his opponents' arguments. Camm skillfully uses a satiric persona, consistently develops an elaborate conceit throughout the pamphlet, and weaves in copious allusions and quotations from dozens of classical and modern sources. A significant amount of thoroughly competent literary criticism is directed at Bland's rhetorical devices, style, logic, and breaches of satiric mask. The pamphlet also contains four pieces of doggerel verse, one more than two hundred lines long, which burlesque Carter, Bland, and Patrick Henry.

During the summer and fall of 1771, Camm became president of William and Mary, rector of Bruton Parish Church in Williamsburg, commissary of the Bishop of London in Virginia, and a member of the Royal Council of Virginia. Just at this point, however, Camm participated in a public debate that was a continuation of his small vocal group of Anglican clergymen's resistance to secular authority. Although the Anglican church was technically the established church in Virginia, its government had never been established on a strong hierarchical basis, and local vestries exercised almost unchecked power. During the period 1770-1772, the clergy supported a move to create an American episcopate, thus raising the ire of the Virginia gentry, who were already upset over excessive Crown prerogatives in America. A literary battle to which Camm lent his vigorous pen was waged in the *Virginia Gazette* in 1771-1774. This episcopate dispute was the deathblow to the established church in America. It is a testament to Camm's public respect that his outspoken Tory views never caused him to be molested even in the height of the episcopate dispute and the Revolution; he did not have to flee with Governor Dunmore, nor did he preach with pistols on his pulpit as did his friend Jonathan Boucher. He died quietly in late 1778.

John Camm was not the great constitutionalist that Richard Bland was, nor was he as accomplished a writer as his contemporaries William Stith and Thomas Jefferson. As literature, however, his essays and pamphlets compare favorably in the mastery of a common tradition of rhetoric and prose style with any written in his generation in Virginia. He represents at its best that portion of Virginia society which looked at the same constitution and laws upon which Richard Bland and Landon Carter wrote and saw there the "rights of Englishmen" in a quite different light.

References:

Edward Lewis Goodwin, *The Colonial Church in Virginia* (Milwaukee: Morehouse, 1927), pp. 329, 340-341, 358;

Jack P. Greene, "A Mirror of Virtue for A Declining Land: John Camm's Funeral Sermon for William Nelson," in *Essays in Early Virginia Literature Honoring Richard Beale Davis,* edited by J. A. Leo Lemay (New York: Burt Franklin, 1977), pp. 181-201;

Homer D. Kemp, "The Pre-Revolutionary Virginia Polemical Essay: The Pistole Fee and the Two-Penny Acts Controversies," Ph.D. dissertation, University of Tennessee, 1972;

Kemp, "The Reverend John Camm: 'To Raise A Flame and Live in It,' " in *Essays in Early Virginia Literature Honoring Richard Beale Davis,* pp. 165-180;

William Wilson Manross, comp., *The Fulham Palace Papers in the Lambeth Palace Library* (Oxford: Clarendon Press, 1965), pp. 158-215.

Landon Carter
(18 August 1710-22 December 1778)

Homer D. Kemp
Tennessee Technological University

BOOKS: *A Letter from a Gentleman in Virginia to the Merchants of Great Britain Trading to that Colony* (London, 1754);

A Letter to a Gentleman in London, from Virginia (Williamsburg: William Hunter, 1759);

A Letter to the Right Reverend Father in God, the Lord B[isho]p of L[ondo]n . . . (Williamsburg, 1759; London, 1760);

The Rector Detected: Being a Just Defense of the Twopenny Act, Against the Artful Misrepresentations of the Reverend John Camm . . . (Williamsburg: Printed by Joseph Royle, 1764);

The Diary of Colonel Landon Carter of Sabine Hall, 1752-1778, edited by Jack P. Greene, 2 volumes (Charlottesville: University Press of Virginia, 1965).

OTHER: " 'Not to be Governed or Taxed, but by . . . our Representatives': Four Essays in Opposition to the Stamp Act by Landon Carter," edited by Jack P. Greene, *Virginia Magazine of History and Biography,* 76 (July 1968): 259-300.

As pamphleteer, essayist, satirist, diarist, scientific writer, poet, and experimental agriculturalist, Landon Carter was perhaps the most prolific author in Virginia during the two decades before the Revolution. He produced at least four major pamphlets, and nearly fifty essays in colonial gazettes and British newspapers have been identified as his. There also exists a considerable body of his satiric verse in the gazettes and in manuscript. His diary is the longest one to survive from colonial Virginia and is for the student of colonial culture one of the most important colonial private journals. One of his essays on the weevil fly won him election to the American Philosophical Society. A man with an obsession for knowledge, Carter amassed a major Southern colonial library, perhaps including a thousand or more titles during his prime years of writing.

Portrait of Landon Carter attributed to Charles Bridges (courtesy of Robert Carter Wellford and Beverley Randolph Wellford)

Carter was born on 18 August 1710, the fourth of five sons of Robert "King" Carter, the third by his second wife Elizabeth Landon Willis. King Carter was one of the wealthiest and most influential men in early eighteenth-century Virginia and the second-generation head of one of the great Virginia dynasties.

Possessing an estate of more than 330,000 acres of land, King Carter was able to leave even his fourth son eight operating plantations. In 1720 Landon was sent to London to attend the excellent classical private school of Solomon Low; he returned to Virginia in 1727 and at least briefly attended the College of William and Mary. His native intelligence and abilities, his wealth, his excellent education, and the fact that he was related by blood or marriage to virtually every important leader in Virginia insured him a prominent place in Virginia society.

In 1752 Carter was elected to the House of Burgesses and remained one of that body's most influential members until 1768. He was a man at the center of everything of importance during the twenty years preceding the Revolution, a man who crystalized the ideals of his society and actively participated in all of the major debates of the period in Virginia. He was also a man who seemed compelled to write down almost everything he thought or experienced. The product of his active public and private life is his diary (which he kept from 1752 until his death), a book that provides the reader with a guide to the minds of the pre-Revolutionary Virginia gentry and to the society which produced those minds. An extremely complex man, Carter was an irascible, moody, introspective, self-conscious, brilliant, independent aristocrat who possessed a passion for knowledge, a profound distrust of human nature, a rigid code of behavior to which he insisted that others measure up, a deep commitment to moderation, an almost uncontrollable temper, an obsession for thoroughness, an unrelenting devotion to public duty, an uncompromising candidness with associates, and an insistence that all things be utilitarian. One quality of the diary which makes it especially important to the student of Southern colonial culture is its very pri-

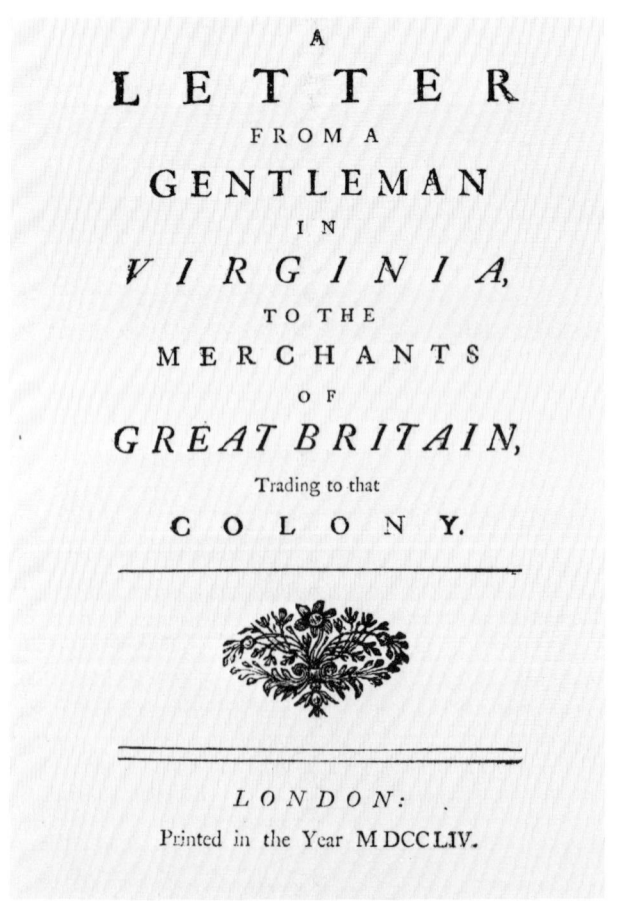

Title page for the first of Carter's pamphlets advocating colonial legislative autonomy in local matters (courtesy of the John Carter Brown Library at Brown University)

Sabine Hall

vate nature; over the years Carter grew as introspective as any of the Puritan diarists and confided more and more intimately in his journal.

From the 1750s until the Revolution, Carter was one of the leading writers in a group which developed in print the ideology and established the tradition of expression adopted in the 1770s by such Revolutionary-era writers as Thomas Jefferson. Carter published pamphlets and essays during the Pistole Fee dispute, the paper-currency act and Two-Penny Acts controversies, the 1760s debate with Britain over such policies as the Stamp Act, and the 1770s discussions of independence. He produced a political polemical canon that, in the words of his diary's editor Jack Greene, "exceeds in quantity that of any other Virginian of his generation and probably reveals more fully than the writings of any other individual the framework of political assumptions and ideas within which his generation of Virginians operated." In addition to their worth as political analyses, Carter's pamphlets, essays, and poetry are important as literature because they reveal him to be a master of satire and irony. As Richard Beale Davis has commented, "perhaps no more effectively reasoned, beautifully phrased, and devastatingly ironic polemical prose was written in the America of the period than the satire of [Richard] Bland and Carter and very close to them in quality is the writing of their antagonist [John] Camm."

At the heart of Carter's many writings is his devotion to the constitution as the guardian of the general welfare of the community. During the early 1750s dispute over Lieutenant-Governor Robert Dinwiddie's fee of one pistole for affixing the royal seal on land patents, Carter wrote *A Letter from a Gentleman in Virginia to the Merchants of Great Britain* (1754) in defense of the colonial legislature's right to establish fees. Again, in *A Letter to a Gentleman in London, from Virginia* (1759), Carter expressed his resentment against British merchants and Crown authorities interfering with local colonial paper currency.

His passionate concern for colonial legislative autonomy in local matters prompted Carter to write *A Letter to the Right Reverend Father in God, the Lord B[isho]p of L[ondo]n* (1759). In this pamphlet Carter vehemently and systematically refutes the charges which the Bishop had made against the Virginia General Assembly in a letter to the Privy Council that secured the disallowance of the 1758 Virginia Two-Penny Act. Short tobacco crops in 1755 and 1758 inflated the price of tobacco, causing the Virginia House of Burgesses to pass temporary acts commuting the year's tobacco salaries into currency at the rate of two pence per pound. Clerical opposition to these acts began a debate that occupied the energies of the best minds in Virginia for more than eight years—debates significant far beyond their purely local origins. Most of the significant arguments about Crown prerogatives and colonial autonomy expressed during the Stamp Act Crisis and the Revolutionary War were formed earlier during the Two-Penny Acts controversies.

The Reverend John Camm's attack on the 1758 Two-Penny Act in *A Single and Distinct View of the Act, Vulgarly entitled Two-Penny Act* (1763) drew a response from Carter in the form of *The Rector Detected* (1764)—a work which again opposes British interference in local affairs. Toward the end of his legislative career Carter wrote four essays opposing the Stamp Act, four essays which represent his whole political philosophy and that of his generation in Virginia.

Never a personally popular man, Carter was respected for his abilities, but his rigid standard of behavior and truculent personality alienated even his closest acquaintances and caused him to be intensely disliked by many. His constituents turned him out of office in 1768, after which Carter withdrew more and more into himself. His diary reveals his bitter disappointment over being denied proper credit for his contributions toward independence, especially over Patrick Henry's being given credit for the first protest against the Stamp Act. After forty-five years of active involvement in the political life of Virginia (sixteen of them in the Burgesses), Carter died a bitter, somewhat paranoid old man on 22 December 1778, but a man who left a much greater mark on his and the following generations of Virginians than he ever realized.

Bibliographies:
Walter Ray Wineman, *The Landon Carter Papers in the University of Virginia Library: A Calendar and Biographical Sketch* (Charlottesville: University Press of Virginia, 1962);

Paul P. Hoffman, *The Carter Family Papers, 1659-1797* (Charlottesville: University of Virginia Library, 1967).

References:
Richard Beale Davis, *Intellectual Life in the Colonial South, 1585-1763*, 3 volumes (Knoxville: University of Tennessee Press, 1978);

Jack P. Greene, Introduction to *The Diary of Colonel Landon Carter of Sabine Hall, 1752-1778*, edited by Greene (Charlottesville: University of Virginia Press, 1965); republished as *Landon Carter: An Inquiry into the Personal Values and Social Imperatives of the Eighteenth-Century Virginia Gentry* (Charlottesville: University Press of Virginia, 1967);

Greene, "Landon Carter and the Pistole Fee Dispute," *William and Mary Quarterly*, third series, 14 (January 1957): 66-69;

Greene, "Landon Carter, Diarist, Essayist and Correspondent," *Manuscripts*, 11 (1959): 35-37, 52;

Homer D. Kemp, "The Pre-Revolutionary Virginia Polemical Essay: The Pistole Fee and the Two-Penny Acts Controversies," Ph.D. dissertation, University of Tennessee, 1972;

J. A. Leo Lemay, *A Calendar of American Poetry in the Colonial Newspapers and Magazines and in the Major English Magazines Through 1765* (Worcester, Mass.: American Antiquarian Society, 1972).

Papers:
The Sabine Hall Collection in the University of Virginia Library includes land documents, correspondence, and diaries of Landon Carter and of his son Robert Wormeley Carter. This collection along with some other Carter manuscripts in other repositories are available in a University of Virginia Library microfilm series. About one-third of Carter's library, including a great deal of Carter's marginalia, remains intact at the family seat, Sabine Hall.

Jonathan Carver
(13 April 1710-31 January 1780)

Daniel E. Williams
Universität Tübingen

BOOKS: *Travels through the Interior Parts of North America in the Years 1766, 1767, and 1768* (London: Printed for the author & sold by J. Walter, 1778); republished as *Three Years Travels through the Interior Parts of North-America . . .* (Philadelphia: Printed & sold by Joseph Crukshank, 1784);

A Treatise on the Culture of the Tobacco Plant . . . (London: Printed for the author & sold by J. Johnson, 1779);

The New Universal Traveller . . ., attributed to Carver but written by others (London: Printed for G. Robinson, 1779);

The Journals of Jonathan Carver and Related Documents, 1766-1770, edited by John Parker (St. Paul: Minnesota Historical Society, 1976).

Jonathan Carver's *Travels through the Interior Parts of North America in the Years 1766, 1767, and 1768* was one of the most popular and most successful American books in the eighteenth and nineteenth centuries. First published in London in 1778, Carver's *Travels* became a best-seller, and over the next one hundred years it was published in nearly sixty editions, including translations in French, German, Dutch, Swedish, and Greek. Its influence was perhaps greater than its popularity Not only was it the first book written by an American to have a large international following, but for more than a century it was cited as a standard authority on the native peoples and places of the upper Great Lakes region. More important, the book touched the imaginations of countless numbers of people, everyone from romantic poets to backwoods pioneers, offering them a unique vision of American wilderness and American promise. Today Carver's *Travels* is one of the least popular of all early exploration narratives, the result of the twentieth-century controversy concerning his use of sources, and it is read neither as literature nor as history. Nevertheless, its previous popularity and influence require attention. At a time when the image of America as a separate national entity was being formed, the book's optimistic faith in the future of America appealed to thousands and was disseminated to tens of thousands.

This portrait was first published as the frontispiece to the 1780 edition of Travels through the Interior Parts of North America.

The Carver controversy involves the man as well as the book, and there remain areas of his life upon which biographers have not agreed. Most, however, have agreed that he was born in 1710 in Weymouth, Massachusetts, and lived there for about eight years until moving with his family to Canterbury, Connecticut. His parents, David and Hannah Dyer Carver, came from good families, and his father was a man of modest wealth and influence, having been elected to several offices in both Weymouth and Canterbury. Carver's specific education is still unknown, but, because of his family's position, he is thought to have received as good an education as was available in the region. Although he is believed by some to have only been an illiterate shoemaker and soldier (and indeed he was both cobbler and militaryman), recent biographers have proven that he was literate, that he taught himself mapmaking and surveying, and that he possibly studied medicine for a short time. In Canterbury in 1746 Carver married Abigail Robbins.

Sometime around 1750, Carver purchased an ensigncy in the local militia and remained in the military until the end of the French and Indian War in 1763. In 1757 he was wounded but survived the famous massacre at Fort William Henry. Two years later he became a lieutenant and was elected selectman of Montague, Massachusetts, where he had recently moved with his family. The following year, 1760, he received the rank of captain. After the war he returned to Montague and to his family but did not remain long, apparently unable or unwilling to return to civilian and domestic life. As an officer in the militia, Carver returned home with neither a pension nor a land grant, but with something he believed far more valuable: a knowledge of the wilderness and a strong belief in its immense potential. In the introduction to his book he wrote, "No sooner was the late war with France concluded . . . than I began to consider (having rendered my country some services during the war) how I might continue still serviceable."

In Boston Carver easily met Maj. Robert Rogers, the popular leader of Roger's Rangers, and was persuaded by Rogers to join his scheme to discover the long-sought Northwest Passage. Rogers, who had recently traveled to England to seek financial support for his project, engaged Carver and two others (James Tute and James Stanley Goddard) to journey west from Fort Mackinac (then called Michillimackinac) exploring the upper Mississippi region and negotiating with the Indians. After receiving a commission and promises for supplies from Rogers, Carver headed west by canoe across Lake Michigan on 3 September 1766. Accompanied by fur traders, Carver first journeyed to present-day Green Bay, and from there he continued westward, crossing Wisconsin to the Mississippi River via the Fox and Wisconsin rivers. He then traveled up the river to the Minneapolis-St. Paul area as far as the Falls of St. Anthony. After entering the Minnesota River, Carver spent the winter in a Sioux village. In the spring, having received neither supplies nor orders from Rogers, he retraced his route down the Mississippi as far as Prairie du Chien, where he met Tute and Goddard.

The three explorers, together with guides and interpreters, next headed north on the Mississippi, then followed the Chippewa, Namekagon, St. Croix, and Bois Brulé rivers, until finally reaching Lake Superior. They proceeded to Grand Portage, hoping there to receive the promised supplies from Rogers, but instead received a letter informing them no supplies would be forthcoming. Although Rogers urged them to continue, they decided to give up their plans for pushing to the Pacific and to return to Mackinac via the north coast of Lake Superior. The party returned in August 1767 only to discover Rogers under suspicion of treason and unable to offer them further support.

After leaving the wilderness Carver experienced a continual series of disappointments. In the autumn orders arrived from Boston for the arrest of Rogers, and Sir William Johnson, his superior, refused to support any of his projects. Not wanting to become involved in the Rogers-Johnson conflict, Carver left Mackinac in the spring of 1768 and traveled to Boston, where he hoped to improve his situation by publishing a journal of his travels and by petitioning General Gage for the wages promised by Rogers. Neither subscribers nor Gage responded as Carver had hoped, and on 22 February 1769, he set sail for London, hoping there to receive reward and recognition. During the last ten years of his life, however, Carver found little of either. He repeatedly petitioned various English authorities for financial support for another expedition and later for an appointment as a western Indian agent. But the English government was more concerned with the question of whether or not it would retain control of its American colonies than with the possibility of opening up the interior. Instead of an expedition and an appointment he received a cash gift of £1,100. But the money soon disappeared, and by 1773 he was again asking for government support, pleading extreme poverty. Despite poverty and a wife still living in America, Carver married a London widow, Mrs. Mary Harris, in 1774. Still hoping for reward and recognition, he spent his last years rewriting his travel journal into a coherent narrative, then with the help of a literary hack added descriptions of the Indians, plants, animals, and natural resources of the Great Lakes region.

Neither hardships nor disappointments are evident in Carver's *Travels*. In fact, his book is entirely optimistic in description and outlook. Hoping to encourage settlement, Carver describes the upper Great Lakes region both as he saw it and as he dreamed of it, offering promises and prophecies as well as descriptions. In his introduction he writes: "But as the seat of empire from time immemorial has been gradually progressive towards the west,

A page from the journal Carver kept during his travels in the Midwest. In the course of preparing his account for publication he revised the journal three times (The British Library).

there is no doubt but that at some future period, mighty kingdoms will emerge from these wildernesses, and stately palaces and solemn temples, with guilded spires reaching the skies, supplant the Indian huts, whose only decorations are the barbarous trophies of their vanquished enemies." In order to fully convince readers of the "mighty kingdoms" in the wilderness, Carver uses a variety of literary strategies intended to appeal to the imagination. His book is by no means a rough travel journal, but a carefully reworked narrative. It is divided into three main sections, and each section contributes to his overall intention of attracting interest. The first section, the actual narrative of his travels, emphasizes the beauty and bounty of the land; difficulties and discomforts are rarely mentioned. The second section, today the most controversial, is a lengthy, encyclopedic description of the Indians, making them seem less terrifying and less barbarous to European readers. And the third section is an exhaustive catalogue of all the plants and animals of the region, complete with their commercial uses. The book concludes with a short appendix in which Carver specifically declares "The probability of the interior parts of North America becoming commercial colonies." In each section Carver skillfully mixes natural description with narration and anecdote. The style is literate and lucid, although in his introduction Carver apologizes for its plainness. But this comment is as much promotion as apology. He asks readers "not to examine it [his style] with too critical an eye . . ." because "his attention has been more employed on giving a just description of a country that promises, in some future period, to be an inexhaustible source of riches to that people who shall be so fortunate as to possess it, than on the stile of composition."

The primary promise Carver offers readers is wealth—the "inexhaustible sources of riches" available in the North American interior. When de-

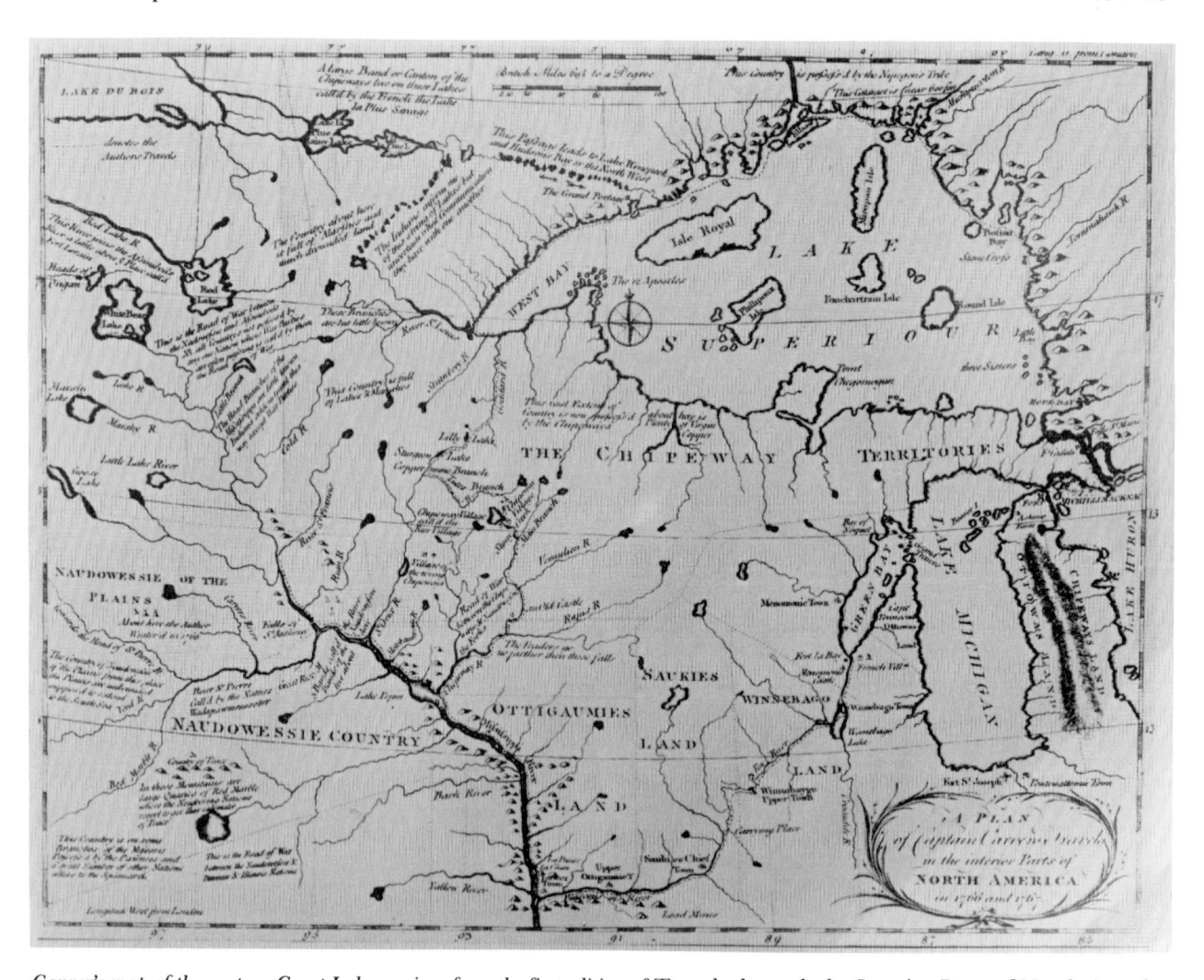

Carver's map of the western Great Lakes region, from the first edition of Travels through the Interior Parts of North America

One Indian tribe told Carver about a snake that was "three fathoms long," almost "as big round as a buffaloe," and had horns, "four feet and claws like a bear," and "somthing like fins on the back." This drawing based on that description is in his third revision of his journal (The British Library).

scribing the Rocky Mountains, which he calls the "Shining Mountains," he repeats the story of Indians who "have gold so plenty among them that they make their most common utensils of it." He then expands upon the theme of future prosperity and progress. "Probably in future ages they [the Rockies] may be found to contain more riches in their bowels, than those of Indostan and Malabar, or that are produced on the golden coast of Guinea; nor will I except the Peruvian mines. To the west of these mountains, when explored by future Columbuses and Raleighs, may be found other lakes, rivers, and countries full fraught with all the necessaries or luxuries of life; and where future generations may find an asylum, whether driven from their country by the ravages of lawless tyrants, or by religious persecution, or reluctantly leaving it to remedy the inconvenience arising from a superabundant increase of inhabitants; whether, I say, impelled by these, or allured by hopes of commercial advantages, there is little doubt but their expectations will be fully gratified in these rich and inexhausted climes." To prove his point, Carver lists a variety of lucrative possibilities. In addition to gold, he mentions copper, fish, fur, timber, trade advantages, and numerous types of fruit and grain.

Carver, however, does not attempt to appeal only to the commercial interests of his readers. He carefully develops the image of the garden, stressing the land's beauty and fertility. Concerning an area of the Mississippi River around Lake Pepin, he writes: "From thence the most beautiful and extensive prospect that imagination can form, opens to your view. Verdant plains, fruitful meadows, numerous islands, and all these abounding with a variety of trees that yield amazing quantities of fruit without care or cultivation; such as the nut tree, the maple which produces sugar, vines loaded with rich grapes, and plumb trees bending under their blooming burdens, but above all, the fine river flowing gently beneath, and reaching as far as the eye can extend, by turns attract your admiration and excite your wonder." After observing the area around the Falls of St. Anthony, Carver states: "a more pleasing and picturesque view cannot, I believe, be found through the universe."

Carver's purpose in publishing was not only to attract attention to the North American interior but also to attract attention to himself. He clearly intended to publish a book which would earn him the reward and recognition he desired. Consequently, he suppressed information about the participation of Tute and Goddard and the inspiration of Rogers. He also included a great deal of information concerning Native Americans which he knew would interest readers and could establish him as an authority on the subject. Unfortunately, at least a third of this material was borrowed from previously published New World narratives, particularly from the accounts of French explorers Louis Hennepin, Louis Lahontan, and Pierre de Charlevoix and from James Adair's *The History of the American Indians* (1775). This discovery of sources led to the decline of Carver's popularity and to the present controversy.

The question of what is and what is not Carver, however, is irrelevant. Throughout the seventeenth and eighteenth centuries unacknowledged compilations were common, especially in New World narratives. More important, Carver, by far more

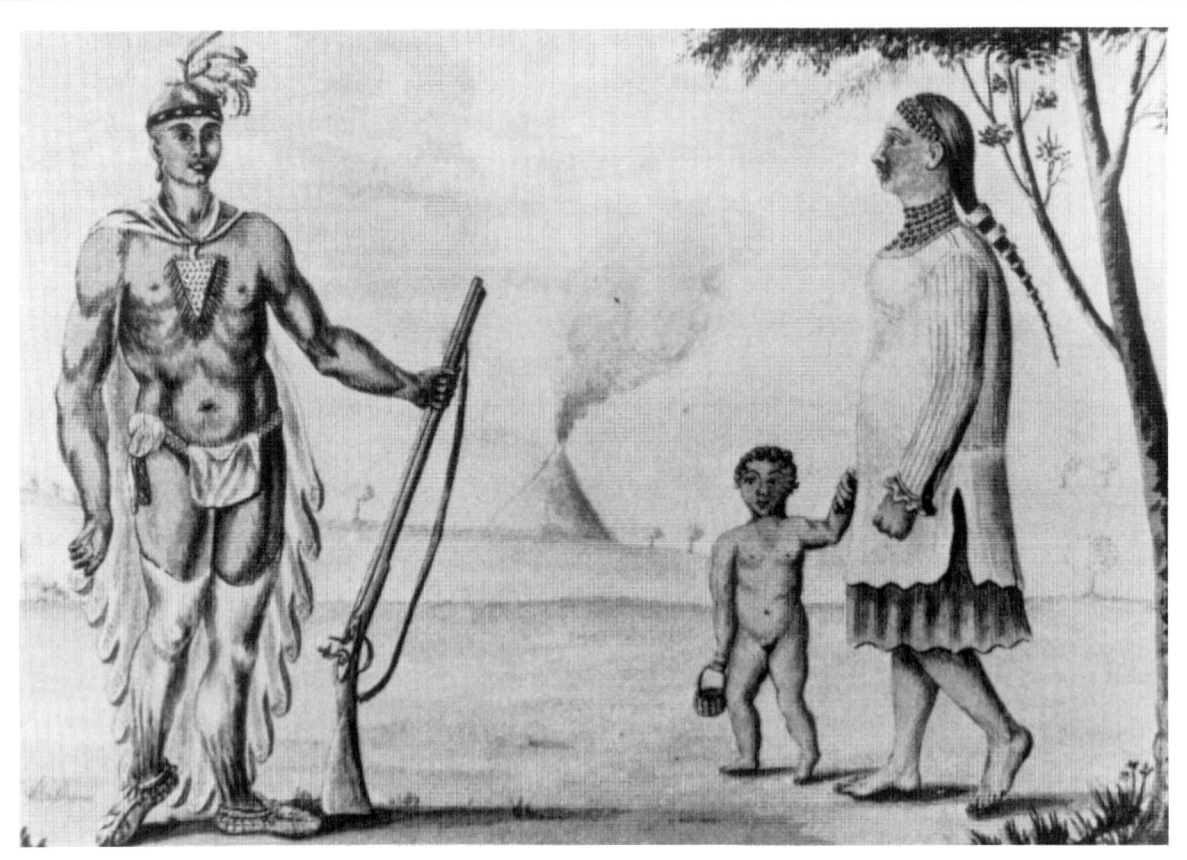

Carver's drawing of an Indian family, from the manuscript for the third revision of his journal (The British Library)

popular than any of his sources, had a greater influence on the European conception of the Indians. Although recognizing their cruelty and treachery in war, his overall image is positive and at times romantic. He praises their wilderness skills, their cleverness, their innocence, their loyalty, and especially their hospitality. In attempting to ease European fears and to further encourage settlement, he states: "I must here observe, that notwithstanding the inhabitants of Europe are apt to entertain horrid ideas of the ferocity of these savages, as they are termed, I received from every tribe of them in the interior parts, the most hospitable and courteous treatment; and am convinced, that till they are contaminated by the example, and spirituous liquors of their more refined neighbors, they retain this friendly and inoffensive conduct towards strangers."

In addition to his promises of wealth, glimpses of wilderness beauty, and exotic Indian descriptions, Carver's narrative skill also gained considerable popularity for him. There are many exciting passages throughout the book, the best-known being Carver's eyewitness account of the massacre at Fort William Henry and his subsequent escape. His description, in fact, is so vivid and detailed that it became one of the principal historical sources about the incident. There are also numerous descriptions of American oddities which attempt to satisfy the European curiosity with the new and the exotic, including stories about a tame rattlesnake which came when it was called and "the most extraordinary animal that the American woods produce": the skunk.

Although the book was immediately well received, Carver gained little from its popularity. The year after its publication he was forced to take a position as a lottery clerk. During this last year of his life he also wrote *A Treatise on the Culture of the Tobacco Plant*. At the same time he was credited with the authorship of *The New Universal Traveller,* a folio which boasted accounts of "all the empires, kingdoms, and states in the known world." Whether he sold his name to the volume's publisher or whether his name was stolen to give the book credibility is not known, but in 1781 his London wife stated that

Carver was not the author. None of these enterprises relieved his immediate difficulties. Early in 1780 Carver died in poverty and was buried in a pauper's grave. He was survived by wives and children on both sides of the Atlantic.

Ironically, after his death Carver did gain the reward and recognition he struggled for during his life. Three days before his death he was treated by Dr. John Coakley Lettsom, who became interested in the man and his *Travels*. After acquiring the publishing rights, Lettsom published an edition in 1781, which was accompanied by a highly sympathetic though inaccurate biography. From the proceeds of this publication and from donations he solicited, Lettsom was able to help Carver's family. His endeavors were instrumental in spreading Carver's reputation and much of the Carver myth.

Carver is important because of the impact his narrative had on the European imagination. Of all the New World narratives published in Europe, Carver's *Travels* is one of the most popular and consequently one of the most influential. Such writers as Schiller, Chateaubriand, Wordsworth, Coleridge, Bryant, and Cooper were all directly influenced. His vision of promise and prosperity awakened many to the possibilities of the interior, and his favorable view of Indians helped to promote the romanticized image of the Noble Savage in Europe. Overall, Carver's influence reveals that American optimism, an essential force in the shaping of the country's culture and society, existed in Europe as well as in America, that at one time Manifest Destiny was an international—and not just a national—ideal. At a time when America was just setting out on its independent course, Carver was influential in gaining European approval.

Bibliographies:
Thomas Lee, "A Bibliography of Carver's Travels," *Wisconsin Historical Society* (1909): 143-183;
"Additional Data," *Wisconsin Historical Society* (1912): 87-123;
John Parker, "A Bibliography of Jonathan Carver's Travels," in *The Journals of Jonathan Carver and Related Documents, 1766-1770*, edited by Parker (St. Paul: Minnesota Historical Society, 1976), pp. 222-231.

References:
Theodore C. Blegen, *Minnesota: A History of the State* (St. Paul: University of Minnesota Press, 1963), pp. 67-70;
E. G. Bourne, "The Travels of Jonathan Carver," *American Historical Review*, 11 (October 1905-July 1906): 287-302;
William Browning, "The Early History of Jonathan Carver," *Wisconsin Magazine of History*, 3 (1919-1920): 291-305;
Louise Phelps Kellog, "The Mission of Jonathan Carver," *Wisconsin Magazine of History*, 12 (1928): 127-145;
Patricia M. Medeiros, "Three Travelers," in *American Literature 1764-1789 The Revolutionary Years*, edited by Everett Emerson (Madison: University of Wisconsin Press, 1977), pp. 195-201;
John Parker, Introduction to *The Journals of Jonathan Carver and Related Documents, 1766-1770*, edited by Parker (St. Paul: Minnesota Historical Society, 1976), pp. 1-56;
Moses Coit Tyler, *The Literary History of the American Revolution 1763-1783* (New York: Putnam's, 1897);
Daniel E. Williams, "Until They Are Contaminated by Their More Refined Neighbors: The Image of the Native American in Carver's *Travels Through the Interior* and It's Influence on the Euro-American Imagination," in *Indians and Europe*, edited by Christian F. Feest (Göttingen: Edition Herodot, forthcoming 1985).

Benjamin Church
(24 August 1734-circa 12 January 1778)

Jeffrey Walker
Oklahoma State University

SELECTED BOOKS: *A Poem Occasioned by the Death of the Honorable Jonathan Law, Esq., Late Governor of Connecticut* (N.p., 1751);

The Choice: A Poem, After the Manner of Mr. Pomfret, as a Young Gentleman (Boston: Printed & sold by Edes & Gill, 1757);

Liberty and Property Vindicated, and the St--pm-n Burnt. A Discourse . . . , as A Friend to the Liberty of His Country (Hartford: Printed by Thomas Green, 1765);

The Times, A Poem, as An American (Boston, 1765);

Elegy on the Death of the Reverend Jonathan Mayhew . . . (Boston: Printed & sold by Edes & Gill, 1766);

An Address to a Provincial Bashaw . . . , as A Son of Liberty (Boston, 1769; London, 1769);

An Elegy to the Infamous Memory of Sr. F— B—, as A Son of Liberty (Boston, 1769);

An Elegy to the Memory of That Pious and Eminent Servant of Jesus Christ the Reverend Mr. George Whitefield . . . (Boston: Printed by Richard Draper, 1770);

An Oration Delivered March Fifth, 1773 (Boston: Printed & sold at the New Printing-Office, 1773).

Benjamin Church

Known by his fellow Harvard graduate Lemuel Howard as "that villain Church" because of his conviction for treason during the American Revolution, Benjamin Church today is better known to historians than to students of literature. Yet Church's literary output, albeit small by most standards, is significant because of its importance in the Revolution and its place in the development of a native American literature.

Born in Newport, Rhode Island, the son of Benjamin and Hannah Dyer Church, Church could trace his genealogy to the first settlers of Boston. With the poets Anne Bradstreet and Edward Johnson, his great-great-grandfather Richard Church traveled to America on John Winthrop's flagship, the *Arbella*, that landed in Massachusetts Bay in 1630. Four generations later, with his great-grandfather, Benjamin Church, the renowned Indian fighter in King Philip's War counted among his ancestors, young Benjamin Church found himself a member of one of Boston's most honored families.

After attending the Boston Latin School, Church entered Harvard College in 1750 along with his Latin School classmate John Hancock and graduated four years later, eighth in a class of twenty. At Harvard, Church rapidly developed a reputation as a wit. His commonplace book, composed of verse written by him and his classmates, reveals the origin of Church's poetic skills, shows the apprentice satirist at work, and exposes those motives that influenced him and that would later make him one of the most feared political propagandists of the Revolutionary scene. Though the poems copied into the commonplace book exhibit little polish, they do demonstrate that Church recognized satire not only as the most popular but also as the principal literary mode by which he could compete for position and honor within the college community. Concerned almost exclusively with satirizing Harvard personalities and events, the verses expose the undergraduates' brushes with sex, alcohol, fisticuffs, and their tutors; and they reveal that name calling, innuendo, and caricature were the principal devices employed to make their objects of satire appear ludicrous. In one especially nasty series of barbs directed at Henry Flynt, tutor for the class of 1754, Church caricatures Flynt as "An ugly monster," one whose "matted Wig of piss-burnt horse-hair made, /Scarce covers half his greasy Head." Calling "His Face a mixture of Deformities," Church concentrates on Flynt's appearance by distorting his features, and in doing so, he exposes his subject's essential ugliness to public view and degrades the tutor by making him appear ridiculous.

In another commonplace book poem, "The Author's Advice," Church continues to attack Flynt by outlining the battle plan for his comrades:

Ye Sons of Honour, Candidates for Fame,
Shake off his yoke, an endless War proclaim:
Vollies of Crackers at his Door explode,
Or thunder down his Stairs vast Logs of Wood.

This poem not only records the actual high jinks committed by Harvard underclassmen but also suggests that as one of the "Sons of Honour, Candidates for Fame," Church learned and practiced the craft that would make him an effective propagandist on the eve of the Revolution. By assuming the voice of the satiric protagonist—the spokesman who sees it his duty to defend those unjustly wronged—and by attacking the reputation of his antagonists through caricature or innuendo, Church was able to damage his subject's credibility. Motivated to write satire because it was the thing to do, he skillfully attacked his antagonists, building in the process a reputation as a responsible and knowledgeable commentator of the time.

An early product of Church's undergraduate verse was a poem begun at Harvard and published in Boston in 1757. Written during a period when Church was studying medicine in Boston, *The Choice* is set squarely in the tradition of the eighteenth century. Unlike the satiric verse written at Harvard, *The Choice* addressed the aristocratic dream of the newly enlightened American: the education and cultivation of the man of leisure. Modeled after John Pomfret's poem of the same name published fifty years earlier in London, Church's *The Choice*, however, provides more than a pastoral version of the American Dream. Church hails not only the aesthetic but also the practical and moral aspects of this daydream. In his opening, Church asks "If youthful Fancy might it's Choice pursue, / And act as natural Reason prompts it to." Church knows that neither he nor his countrymen can yield to the idea that "Inclination could dispose our State, / And human Will . . . govern future Fate." The poem as it develops supports this idea. After introducing the dream of a life of worldly ease, he acknowledges that the new leisure class in America must be educated and cultivated. For the benefit of his audience, he provides a general education reading list "to inform the Mind and mend the Heart." This new American should read to become familiar with the most celebrated writers (Homer, Martial, Plautus, Addison, Milton) and philosophers (Tillotson, Butler, Newton, Locke, Boerhaave), past and present, in order to prepare him for important moral and practical decisions. But Church's poem is not all daydream, nor is it intended as an easy path to success. Beneath the guise of easy dream lies a strong undercurrent of moral and religious awareness, suggesting that "An active State, is Virtue's proper Sphere. /To do, and suffer is our Duty here." While the strong religious emphasis of the seventeenth century had subsided, religious and moral convictions were still expected of a gentleman; thus, it is proper that a poem designed to educate him in the new tastes should also sound the tone of religious devotion. In this respect, Church pays homage to those concerns of the previous century, although his emphasis is most decidedly on the problems confronting the eighteenth-century American. But *The Choice* does more than merely illustrate the taste of Church's age and the poetic techniques of his contemporaries. It also asserts its own individuality by implying that Americans had to establish their own standards for poetry and use the American experience itself as material for their verse.

In the same year *The Choice* was published, Church completed his medical studies and was appointed surgeon on board the *Province Snow Prince* of Wales. Less than five months later, however, he was dismissed from the post just before the vessel was captured by the French. On 8 December he applied for his back pay because he was soon to travel to London to study with Charles Pynchon at the London Medical College. Scarcely a year passed, however, before he wrote to his friend Robert Treat Paine promising to return to Boston and to bring a wife with him. He proved himself accurate in this pronouncement, for soon thereafter he married Sarah Hill, sister of a fellow medical student. In July 1759 he was back in Boston advertising London goods for sale. Never one to conceal his qualifications, Church widely announced his skill at inoculation and soon won the appreciation of the selectmen by becoming most active in giving free service to the poor in time of smallpox epidemics.

Church's medical training and subsequent success solidified his position as a prominent Boston citizen, but he also further sought recognition as a writer. And Francis Bernard's appointment in 1760 as governor of the colonies provided Church with the next opportunity to display his literary skill. With the accession of George III at hand, Bernard suggested that Harvard College follow the example of English universities and compose a volume of poems elegizing the death of the late king and celebrating the arrival of a new one. To that end, a competition was mounted. Any Harvard graduate or undergraduate was encouraged to submit poems to be judged by President Holyoke of Harvard. When the volume finally appeared, it was entitled *Pietas et Gratulatio Collegii Cantabrigiensis Apud Novanglos* (1761) and contained thirty-one poems, two of which were written by Benjamin Church.

Church's first poem celebrated George II's virtue and wisdom. He begins his ode by asking "Are monarchs then such unimportant Things, / That death his dreary triumphs swells with kings?" Church answers by suggesting that "such kings, as George, but take their way / Thro your thick darkness to immortal day." In celebrating the death of George II as something that has swelled the "lustre of the british Crown," he argues that "virtues such as his, are not confin'd / To small domains, they encircle all mankind." For other monarchs, then, Church advises that they should "Learn but to live like George, then die the same."

His second entry, "Where thick embow'ring shades, and clust'ring trees," is one of the best in the volume. A pastoral elegy, the poem begins with Church's invoking the presence of the "pensive Pollio," who in his anguish cries, "George is dead." Church then describes the effect George's death has had upon Nature and mankind. Now "No fost'ring showers . . . refresh the lawn, / No pearly blessings chear the parching dawn." "Darksome horrors" cover the "sad'ning scene," and the ordinary processes of Nature have ceased. Yet by reminding his audience that George's "guide was truth, benevolence his road, / His life, one effort of redundant good," and by cataloguing George's virtues, Church assuages that grief. By the end of the poem when the "full tide of grief his [Pollio's] song suppress'd, / And sighs and tears, instructive, spoke the rest," Church has prepared the colonies for the appearance of "Albion's Guardian": George III. With his arrival, Nature blooms anew, all is well. Church's use of literary tradition to reinforce the rhetorical effect of his poem demonstrates the impact of English verse on mid-eighteenth-century American poetry. But it also illustrates Benjamin Church's own desire to belong to a tradition that was "correct" and "regular" and to display his skill to an audience weaned on the eloquent English style. The poems in *Pietas et Gratulatio* . . . were popular on both sides of the Atlantic, and although Church would regret those impassioned words written for the accession, their appearance in 1761 enhanced his public and literary career.

In 1763 and 1764, however, the Molasses and Sugar Acts were passed, and suddenly the man who had provided Church with an opportunity to publish more poetry was rapidly becoming a villain in the eyes of the colonists. By attempting to enforce unpopular edicts, Francis Bernard emerged as the Whigs' chief whipping boy. Church, buoyed by the excitement of the times, quickly became a major force in the Whig movement and used his skill as a satirist to become an influential propagandist.

In 1765 Church's *Liberty and Property Vindicated, and the St--pm-n Burnt* was published. Purported to have been delivered from a gallows in New London on 22 August 1765, the oration, written in the form of a sermon, presents its readers with an analogy between biblical and current events. For his text, Church uses the story of Moses to construct an analogy between the actions of the people while Moses was on the mountain and the actions of the British government when Lord Bute assumed the power from William Pitt. Asking the question, "Can we find Moses in this evil day which we live in?" Church develops his answer through close analogy. Pitt is like Moses, a man "endow'd with honor, love, truth, and fidelity"; Lord Bute is like Aaron, "For as Aaron led the people into corruption soon after Moses went onto the Mount, So B--e is said to lead the people into mischief (soon after Pitt leaves the helm) by his bad steering"; and Jared Ingersoll, the tax collector, is like the molten calf, a man who "may be said to be like unto a beast by having a beastly disposition." "Corruption," Church concludes, "is at the helm, and our country ship is badly steered."

Church's use of the persona here is skillful, for by using the sermon form and the minister as persona, he appeals both to the the moral and political issues at hand. In effect Church justifies the use of mob action by suggesting that "if any man in this colony, hath for the sake of filthy lucre, misrepresented matters . . . go to such a man, and make him sensible of his error . . . and if he refuses to, use him in such a manner that he will be glad to do anything for a quiet life." The oration is intended, therefore, as a warning to George: end tyranny or be prepared to bear the fury of your subjects.

Despite its merit, *Liberty and Property Vindicated . . .* was not successful because it appealed only to the more educated members of his audience. His later satires, ones in which the antagonists were clearly identifiable and the narrator most clearly the satiric protagonist, are the poems on which Church's reputation as a political firebrand of the Whigs is based. Of these poems, *Elegy on the Death of the Reverend Jonathan Mayhew . . .* (1766), *The Times . . .* (1765), *An Address to a Provincial Bashaw . . .* (1769), and *An Elegy to the Infamous Memory of Sr. F— B—* (1769) are best known and most effective.

In his Mayhew elegy, Church not only eulogizes a leading Boston minister but also celebrates Mayhew's Whig allegiance. After he decries mankind's "awful Conscience" and its inability to find "Virtue's sweet Perfume," Church commemorates the one leader who "never rose more fair, / Nor shone more radiant midst the Files of Heaven." In singing Mayhew's praises, Church exalts him as a model of conduct for the colonies: "Freedom was all his Ardor, all his Bliss, / His Heart turn'd Rebel at that Tho't, a Slave." Not only is Mayhew godlike, but he is also a supporter of liberty. By creating an epic stature for Mayhew, Church has masked his real purpose in the language of the elegy. Here is a man who was not only "divinely good" but also a man whose "earliest Joy was *Liberty.*" Church's technique of calling on his audience, as the minister he eulogizes once called on his congregation, to imitate the great leaders of the past is an effective way of proving that the quest for spiritual peace is not unlike the quest for freedom and independence from Britain. If the traditional elegy was an invitation to exalt and imitate the dead, then Benjamin Church's use of the form was an effort to lend moral force to the necessity of revolution.

Church's other three satires are especially noteworthy because they directly complement the satire he wrote as a Harvard undergraduate. In all three, Church returns to the biting tone he used in castigating his classmates and their tutors. In 1765, however, Church selects Francis Bernard as his target.

In *The Times* Church attacks the attempted passage of the Stamp Act by reminding his readers that the freedoms gained by their forefathers' immigration to America will now be denied by the tax. Singing the praises of his country, Church addresses "Fair Liberty our soul's most darling prize" and asks his audience "was it for this our great forefathers rode; /O'er a vast ocean to this bleak abode!" Having since regretted his praise of George III, Church apologizes for "The paths of error if in youth I trod, /Dress'd a gay idol in the garb of God" and admits that he now weeps "his folly past." Having once said that George's guide was "truth, benevolence his road," he now calls him a "degenerate heir" and warns his countrymen to "dread the curses of your beggar'd heir." To this end, Church addresses all those responsible for the tax and warns that "one general curse must overwhelm them all." Resorting to those tactics he found so successful at Harvard—innuendo, name calling, caricature—he castigates the villains, saving his strongest abuse for Bernard. Church refers to the governor as both "monster" and as "Fop, witling, fav'rite, st--pm-n, tyrant, tool, / Or all of those mighty names in one, thou Fool!" He stamps Bernard as a "vile Pander" and as "traitor," a man who would "Rifle the womb, and on those bowels prey."

Before Church had another chance to personally malign Bernard, another controversy arose requiring his acid pen. In June 1768 when Bernard demanded that the Massachusetts House rescind a resolution which opposed taxation without representation, the measure was defeated—although seventeen members of the House voted to rescind. The seventeen were branded with the name of "rescinders" and treated with contempt by the Whigs. When Paul Revere engraved a caricature of the seventeen entitled "A Warm Place—Hell"—a cartoon showing a pair of monstrous jaws through which Satan was driving the seventeen into the flames with a pitchfork—Benjamin Church wrote the following lines as accompaniment:

On, brave Rescinders! to yon yawning cell,—
Seventeen such miscreants sure will startle hell.
There puny villains damned for petty sin,
On such distinguished scoundrels gaze and grin;
The outdone Devil will resign his sway,—
He never curst his millions in a day.

It was this kind of witty, bombastic verse that made Church one of the favorite sons of Boston, a man who, at least in the public's eye, was quick to reveal the treachery of those men who seemed worthy of no public trust. It is ironic that in the same year he criticized those unworthy men, he built a mansion at Raynham, Massachusetts, which probably created a pecuniary embarrassment that was later to lead to his defection from the cause which in 1768 he vigorously supported. In fact, in 1768 suspicions arose that Church, despite his wife and children, had taken a mistress. The name of this mistress, however, has never been discovered, despite her capture in 1774 when carrying the traitorous letter that would lead to Benjamin Church's conviction for treason.

In 1769, Church resumed his attacks on Bernard. In *An Address to a Provincial Bashaw . . .*, he excoriates the governor for his ineptitude and dishonesty. Church begins his poem by addressing those who have gained the respect of their subjects through kindness, honesty, and character. Unfortunately, Church continues, when "some Miscreant eminently vile, / Springs into place, and blindly arm'd with power / . . . Betrays a keen impatience to devour," the respect that was gained by all those who served their subjects is irreparably damaged. Bernard, the "bashaw," is guilty of this "everlasting Shame." Not only is Bernard responsible for the Stamp act controversy, but he is also to blame for another crisis: the quartering of troops in Boston. A series of rhetorical questions follows, with Church asking Bernard "Where's thy Wisdom? where's thy Pride?" and accusing him of having a "black malignant Heart" whose "savage Favour must be brib'd with blood." Attacking the credibility of Bernard by exposing his basest motives, Church calls him a "parricide" with a "Leprous Heart, Th' infectious Follies of a tainted Sire." It is not surprising that Church's attacks were partially responsible for Bernard's being recalled to England in late 1769, a departure made in such haste that Bernard did not even wait for his family to accompany him.

Benjamin Church, however, was not finished with the former governor. Later that year, in *An Elegy to the Infamous Memory of Sr. F— B—,* Church labels him a "base contaminated Soul / Far worse than Brute in Nature or in Heart!" and charges that Americans have been "Misguided thus by Villainy and Lyes, / Those Seeds of Discord, Hatred and Revenge!" Church's mock elegy is a fitting conclusion to the reign of a man whose "sordid Lust that Concubine of Power" had caused him "to devour / The Life of Freedom, and in triumph ride." Appropriately, he banished Bernard to some place where "Slave-born Mohametans do dwell, / Whose menial Souls in Servitude delight." The doctor's attacks did not go unnoticed in 1769 any more than they had

AN
ADDRESS
TO
A Provincial BASHAW.

O SHAME! where is thy Blufh?

BY A SON OF LIBERTY.

Printed in (the Tyrannic Adminiftration of *St. Francifco*) 1769.

Title page for one of Church's attacks on Governor Francis Bernard (courtesy of the John Carter Brown Library at Brown University)

seventeen years earlier. William Paine, himself a Harvard graduate, responded quite vigorously when he said of Church's efforts: "As to Church's Satire, I would beg to observe, That the man who sets out with a perfect Design of making a Person in Power appear contemptible in the Eyes of the People, without having any Regard to Truth, deserves instead of Thanks, the Curse of ev'ry Man of Sense." Although this attack typified the reactions Church received, Paine's final comments were also typical of the reputation Church had achieved: "Church is a good Poet, but as a Man I detest him as I do ev'ry Partizan. What occasion is there for such inflammatory Pieces? I really pity the malevolence of the Heart that dictated it."

His role as satirist and Whig firebrand now secure, Church continued to praise the virtues of liberty and prosperity. His next venture into propaganda surfaced at his father's instigation. In 1770, the Reverend George Whitefield, one of the major forces in the Great Awakening, died. Known as a champion of individual liberty, Whitefield provided Church with another Mayhew-like figure to eulogize. Church exalts Whitefield as a model Americans should emulate, as one who "brav'd the tempest, try'd the various clime" to "point our view beyond the wreck of time, / And in that prospect, to instruct, and bless." Every loyal colonist should follow the example of Whitefield, who not only stood by but also fought for the principles of liberty.

It is ironic that directly after the appearance of this poem, Benjamin Church's loyalties seemed to be on the verge of wavering. Suspicions were mounting in the Whig camp that Church was on someone's payroll. In a letter to Francis Bernard in 1772 Thomas Hutchinson remarked that "The faction seems to be breaking, The Doctor Church who wrote the Times is now a writer on the side of the Government." Yet at the same time these charges were being discreetly leveled at Church, he was preparing yet another major address to his countrymen. It was Benjamin Church who had been called to examine the body of Crispus Attucks, killed by soldiers in the Boston Massacre of 5 March 1770, and when the third anniversary of the incident was at hand, Church was called upon to present the Massacre Oration. Delivered in the Old South Church, Church's oration was all that the Tories might have feared it would be. Although Church confesses in his opening that "Nothing but a firm attachment to the tottering *liberties* of *America* added to the irresistible importunity of some valued friends, could have induced me (especially with a very short notice) so far to mistake my abilities, as to render the utmost extent of your candor truly indispensable," he proceeds with the vigor of a man who had known all along that this was going to be one of the most important orations of his career. In fact, the crowd that attended the oration was so large that John Hancock, who was acting as moderator, had to be helped through the window of the church so that he might reach the platform.

In his oration Church wastes little time in identifying the issues and in attacking Britain as the source of America's troubles. He particularly criticizes George III as having diverted the true course of democracy and liberty, further describing this breech of government as "crimes acted by a King against the people, [which] are the highest treason *against the highest law among men.*" Arguing in Jeffersonian terms that "When rulers become tyrannts, they cease to be Kings; [and therefore] they can no longer be respected as God's *viceregents*, who violate the laws they were sworn to protect," he

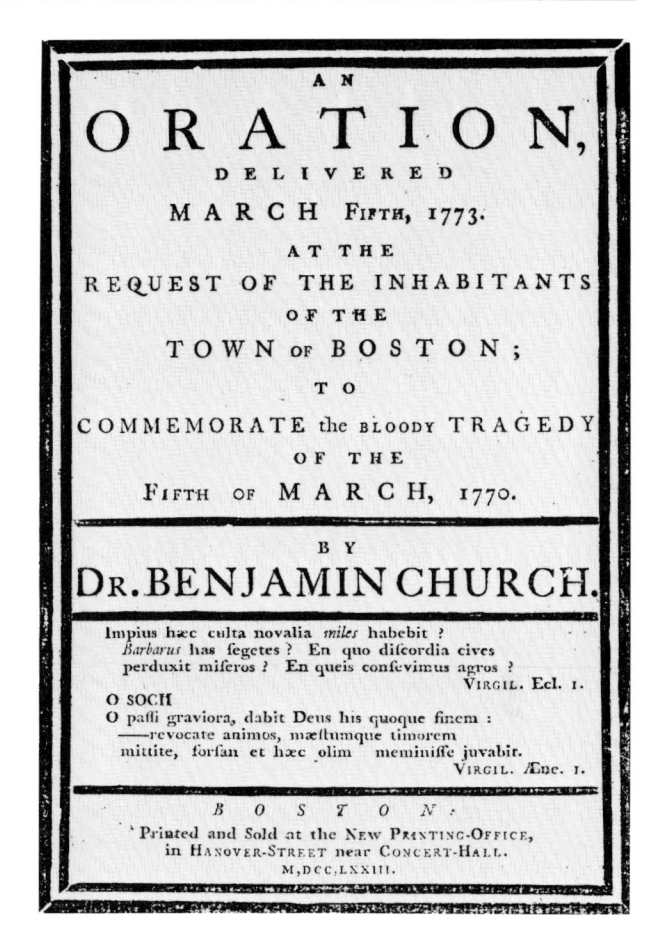

Title page for Church's last Whig political speech, commemorating the third anniversary of the Boston Massacre (courtesy of the John Carter Brown Library at Brown University)

proclaims that the colonists must maintain that "inestimable blessing, Liberty." Church's conclusion is powerful, for by invoking the god of New England—a distinctly different one from the god of old England—as the one "beneath whose wing we shelter all our cares," he again raises the evangelical zeal of his listeners is such a way as to "fire the zeal into manly rage."

Church's massacre oration was the final political speech he would deliver for the Whigs. Despite being named surgeon general of the Continental Hospital in Cambridge, mounting suspicions as to Church's duplicity made him ineffective. Paul Revere "was a constant and critical observer of him" and observed in a letter "that I never thought him a man of principle; and I doubted much in my own mind, whether he was a real whig." Revere's suspicions were confirmed in 1775 when Church was discovered to be in correspondence with General Gage. In a letter sent to his brother-in-law John

A page from one of Church's reports to General Thomas Gage, received by Gage on 24 May 1775 (William L. Clements Library, University of Michigan)

Fleeming, partner in the printing firm of Fleeming and Mein, Boston, Church revealed strategic information he was not authorized to transmit. Carried by his mistress in her silk stocking, the letter was written in code and the translation sealed Church's fate: "I hope this will reach you; three attempts have I made without success; in effecting the last man was discovered in attempting his escape; but fortunately my letter was sewn in the waistband of his breeches; he was confined a few days, during which time you may guess my feelings; but a little art and a little cash, settled the matter." Church was arrested and brought to trial before George Washington.

Church's defense of the letter was argued in typical Church rhetoric. He did not deny writing the letter, but instead argued that his reason was to induce the British into believing that the colonists were much stronger than they appeared to be in order to effect a rapid peace. His explanation was not sufficient to sway the court, however: they found him guilty of criminal correspondence with the enemy. After lengthy appeals, Church was sent to Norwich to await the court's final decision as to his punishment. Finally, in 1778, the General Court voted that "the Sheriff of the County of Suffolk be and hereby is Directed to remove Doct. Church on Board the Sloop *Welcome*, Cpt. James Smitharick Master bound for the Island of Martinique when she is ready for sailing." The ship, however, which sailed shortly thereafter reportedly sank during a storm and Benjamin Church was never heard from again.

The Church legacy, then, ended where it began—on a ship carrying its passengers from a world where they were not wanted to a new one. While Church's treachery may paint him as a man of glib and shallow expression and throw a shadow over his talents, his eagerness to assert his individuality in his poetry and the electrifying quality of his satire provide an illuminating glimpse into the war of letters during the American Revolutionary period. And his contributions included many of the elements that in the new republic of the late-eighteenth century were to help shape a national literary and cultural tradition.

References:

Edwin T. Bowden, "Benjamin Church's *Choice* and American Colonial Poetry," *New England Quarterly*, 32 (June 1959): 174-184;

Allen French, *General Gage's Informers* (Ann Arbor: University of Michigan Press, 1932);

Clifford K. Shipton, *Sibley's Harvard Graduates,* volume 13 (Boston: Massachusetts Historical Society, 1965), pp. 380-398;

Maude B. Vosburgh, "The Disloyalty of Benjamin Church, Jr.," *Publications of the Cambridge Historical Society*, 30 (1935): 69;

Jeffrey Walker, "Benjamin Church's Commonplace Book of Verse: Exemplum for a Political Satirist," *Early American Literature*, 5 (Winter 1980/81): 222-236;

Walker, *The Devil Undone: The Life and Poetry of Benjamin Church, 1734-1778* (New York: Arno, 1982).

Papers:

The United States Revolution Collection of the American Antiquarian Society in Worcester, Massachusetts, contains four letters. The American Manuscript Collection at Houghton Library, Harvard University, contains Church's commonplace book and three miscellaneous documents. The Massachusetts Historical Society in Boston, Massachusetts, has ten miscellaneous documents and three letters.

Thomas Cradock
(circa 8 November 1718-7 May 1770)

David Curtis Skaggs
Bowling Green State University

BOOKS: *Two Sermons. . . . With a Preface Shewing the Author's Reasons for publishing them* (Annapolis: Printed by Jonas Green, 1747);
A Poetical Translation of the Psalms of David. From Buchanan's Latin into English Verse (London: Printed for Mrs. Ann Cradock & sold by R. Ware, 1754); revised as *A New Version of the Psalms of David* (Annapolis: Printed by Jonas Green, 1756);
The Poetic Writings of Thomas Cradock, 1718-1770, edited by David Curtis Skaggs (Newark: University of Delaware Press, 1983).

OTHER: "A Poem Sacred to the Memory of Miss Margaret Lawson, Miss Elizabeth Lawson, Miss Dorothy Lawson and Miss Elizabeth Read," *Maryland Gazette,* 15 March 1753;
"To Thyris," *American Magazine and Monthly Chronicle for the British Colonies,* 1 (September 1758): 605-607;
"Thomas Cradock's Sermon on the Governance of Maryland's Established Church," edited by David Curtis Skaggs, *William and Mary Quarterly,* 27 (October 1970): 629-653;
"Merry Sermon" and "A Poem Sacred to the Memory of Miss Margaret Lawson, Miss Elizabeth Lawson, Miss Dorothy Lawson and Miss Elizabeth Read," *Southern Writing, 1585-1920,* edited by Richard Beale Davis, et al. (New York: Odyssey Press, 1970).

While he was first acclaimed by Richard Beale Davis in 1970 as the author of "perhaps the most courageous sermon of colonial America," Thomas Cradock's modest reputation increased after the 1983 publication of his varied verse. Yet it is probable his best-known work will remain his 1753 "election sermon" before the Maryland General Assembly, in which he described many of his fellow priests of the established church as men "of no Worth, no Learning, no Religion" who have become "Monsters in Wickedness." By publicly discrediting some of his colleagues, Cradock opened the door to a wholesale attack on the religious and proprietary establishments, as well as on the basic social theory of the day, which stressed the stratification of society and the necessary deference one should give to his social and intellectual superiors. Cradock's remedy for clerical irregularities was the creation of an American episcopate, but such a plea for the old order, for the transplantation of European institutions, fell on deaf ears in colonial Maryland.

Born in Staffordshire, Thomas Cradock was the son of Arthur Cradock, a tailor, and his wife, Ann. Thomas lived on the estate of the first Earl Gower until his matriculation at Magdalen Hall,

A
POETICAL TRANSLATION
OF THE
PSALMS
OF
DAVID.
FROM
BUCHANAN'S *Latin* into *English* VERSE.

By the Rev. THOMAS CRADOCK,
Rector of St. *Thomas's* Parish, *Baltimore* County, *Maryland.*

By Permission of the COMPANY OF STATIONERS.

LONDON:
Printed for Mrs. ANN CRADOCK, at *Wells* in *Somersetshire*;
and sold by R. WARE, on *Ludgate-Hill.*
MDCCLIV.

Title page for Cradock's literal translation of George Buchanan's Latin psalter into iambic pentameter couplets (Princeton University Library)

Cradock's church in St. Thomas' Parish

Oxford, in 1737. Although he never took the examinations for a degree, he received ordination in 1743 and immigrated to Maryland the following year. In 1745 he began a quarter-century rectorship of St. Thomas' Parish in western Baltimore County. In 1747, after marrying Catherine Risteau, whose family was part of the local gentry, Cradock established a plantation named Trentham after the Gower-family estate. He lived and taught school there until his death.

Modeling his homiletic style after Archbishop John Tillotson, in most of his more than one hundred surviving sermons Cradock stressed a rational piety which sought the golden mean between enthusiasm and deism. Never concerned with the covenant theology of New England divines, Cradock concentrated on private morality. His extraparochial addresses concerned such broader issues as education (to an audience in Philadelphia), patriotism (before ecumenical groups in south central Pennsylvania), and a "Merry Sermon" against those who believed true Christianity required "a sorrowful countenance, and a sullen Behaviour" (at a St. George's Day celebration in Baltimore). We should, he countered, "all be prudently merry; and reflect on . . . the wholesome Advice in an old *English* Proverb; *Let us take Care to be merry and wise.*" In essence Cradock's preaching joined the traditional creeds and liturgy of the Church of England with a piety and benevolence characteristic of a cultured gentleman of his day.

Cradock's small poetic reputation stemmed from the printing of two slightly different versions of his verse translations of the Psalms and the appearance of some brief verse in the *American Magazine* and the *Maryland Gazette* during his lifetime. The recent publication of the remainder of his poetry should enhance his reputation as an Augustan poet. Employing a neoclassical verse form typical in the England of his youth, the "Maryland Eclogues in Imitation of Virgil's" constitute an incisive commentary on colonial society, manners, and morality. Cradock exploded the pastoral myth of America by filling his wilderness scenes with lost illusion, profanity, intoxication, adultery, irreligion, robbery, and denials of freedom. His five-act, blank-verse "Death of Socrates," a historical drama modeled after Joseph Addison's *Cato* (1713), was one of the first American plays. (It is doubtful that it was ever performed in public.) The object of Cradock's poetry, like the design of his homiletics, was the promulgation of Christian piety and morality. There is little indication he espoused the *translatio studii* motif—the westward migration of the arts—that J. A. Leo Lemay describes as characteristic of colonial Maryland men of letters. Unlike his contemporary, the Reverend James Sterling, Cradock did not foresee America as a future center of learning. His writings praise British ideals and institutions. Thus, in an age when the clergy were at the center of intellectual thought and literary craft, Cradock sought, through his sermons, pietistic verse, satiric lampoons, and drama, to continue on the Chesapeake frontier the values of traditional Anglicanism and the English metropolis.

References:
Ethan Allen, "Sketches of the Colonial Clergy of Maryland: No. I, Rev. Thomas Cradock," *American Church Review*, 7 (July 1854): 302-312;
Richard Beale Davis, "The Intellectual Golden Age in the Chesapeake Bay Country," *Virginia Magazine of History and Biography*, 78 (April 1970): 131-143;
Davis, *Intellectual Life in the Colonial South, 1588-1763*, 3 volumes (Knoxville: University of Tennessee Press, 1978), II: 749-752; III: 1392-1395;
J. A. Leo Lemay, *Men of Letters in Colonial Maryland* (Knoxville: University of Tennessee Press, 1972), pp. 181-182, 190-191;
David Curtis Skaggs, "The Chain of Being in Eighteenth Century Maryland: The Paradox of Thomas Cradock," *Historical Magazine of the Protestant Episcopal Church*, 45 (June 1976): 155-164;
Skaggs, "Thomas Cradock and the Chesapeake Golden Age," *William and Mary Quarterly*, 30 (January 1973): 93-116;
William Jeffrey Welsh, "The Rhetoric of Thomas Cradock, 1744-1770: A Study in the History of Ideas," M.A. thesis, Bowling Green State University, 1977.

Papers:
The Cradock Papers and the Maryland Diocesan Archives at the Maryland Historical Society, Baltimore, contain the bulk of the surviving manuscripts; a few items are located at St. Thomas' Parish, Owings Mills, Maryland.

Charles Crawford
(October 1752-circa 1815)

Robert P. Winston
Dickinson College

SELECTED BOOKS: *A Dissertation on the Phaedon of Plato: Or, Dialogue of the Immortality of the Soul* . . . (London: Printed for the author, 1773);
Sophronia and Hilario, An Elegy . . . (London: Printed for T. Becket, 1774);
The First Canto of the Revolution: An Epic Poem (London: Printed for the author & sold by T. Becket, 1776);
Richmond Hill: A Poem (London: Printed for T. Becket, 1777);
The Christian: A Poem in Four Books (Tunbridge Wells, 1781; Philadelphia: Printed & sold by Joseph Crukshank, 1783); expanded as *The Christian: A Poem in Six Books* (Philadelphia: Printed & sold by Benjamin Johnson, 1794);
A Poem on the Death of Montgomery (Philadelphia: Printed by Robert Aitken?, 1783);
Liberty: A Pindaric Ode (Philadelphia: Printed for the author by Robert Aitken, 1783); republished as *The Progress of Liberty: A Pindaric Ode* (Philadelphia: Printed & sold by Ormrod & Conrad, 1796);
A Poetical Paraphrase on Our Saviour's Sermon on the Mount (Philadelphia: Printed for the author by Robert Aitken, 1783);
Observations upon Negro Slavery . . . (Philadelphia: Printed by J. Crukshank, 1784);
Observations upon the Downfall of Papal Power (Philadelphia: Printed by Joseph Crukshank?, 1785);

George Foxe's Looking Glass for the Jews (1790?);
Observations upon the Revolution in France . . . (Boston: Printed & sold by William Spotswood, 1793);
The Dying Prostitute: A Poem (Philadelphia, 1797);
An Essay upon the Propagation of the Gospel . . . (Philadelphia: Printed by J. Gales, 1799);
An Essay on the Eleventh Chapter of the Revelation of St. John . . . (Philadelphia: Published by Asbury Dickins, printed by H. Maxwell, 1800);
Poems on Several Occasions . . . (London, 1803);
Poems on Various Subjects . . . (London: Printed by R. Taylor for White & Cochran, 1810);
The Poetical Works of Charles, Earl of Crawford and Lindsay, Viscount Garnock (London: C. Cooke, 1814);
Three Letters to the Hebrew Nation (London: Printed by J. Hill for W. Whittemore, 1817).

OTHER: J. P. Brissot de Warville, "An Oration upon the Necessity of Establishing at Paris, A Society to Co-operate with Those of America and London toward the Abolition of the Trade and Slavery of the Negroes," translated by Crawford, in *An Essay on the Impolicy of the African Slave Trade*, by Thomas Clarkson (Philadelphia: Printed by Francis Bailey, 1788).

Charles Crawford was a minor poet and prose writer whose American career covered the last twenty years of the eighteenth century. Born in Antigua, son of Alexander Crawford, a planter, Crawford was educated in England where he attended Queens College, Cambridge, until his expulsion 27 September 1773. His first published work, *A Dissertation on the Phaedon of Plato* (1773), was a pretentious and not very successful denial of the immortality of the soul. He then wrote a sentimental poem on love and honor, *Sophronia and Hilario* (1774), produced the first canto of a projected historical epic, *The First Canto of the Revolution: An Epic Poem* (1776)—which dealt with the reign of James II, including Monmouth's rebellion—and traced the influences of nature upon a young man in *Richmond Hill: A Poem* (1777). Crawford next published *The Christian: A Poem in Four Books* (1781), a work in which he essentially contradicted his earlier view in *A Dissertation on the Phaedon of Plato* and which he would continue to revise and reprint throughout his lifetime.

At about this time, Crawford immigrated to Philadelphia, where in 1783 he published a version of *The Christian* with a preface in which he praised America's religious freedom and to which he appended five miscellaneous poems, including the sentimental poem *The Dying Prostitute; A Poem on the Death of Montgomery; Liberty: A Pindaric Ode*, in which he attacked slavery in the West Indies; and *A Poetical Paraphrase on Our Saviour's Sermon on the Mount*, in which he affirmed Christ as man's saviour. The first of these was published separately in 1797, and the others were printed as separate pamphlets in 1783.

In 1784 Crawford turned to prose and continued to address the evils of slavery with his *Observations upon Negro Slavery;* in this piece he included a long note on Phillis Wheatley's career as a poet to show that blacks were not innately inferior to whites. He continued to work against slavery, translating in 1788 J. P. Brissot de Warville's oration against slavery for the Pennsylvania Society for Promoting the Abolition of Slavery. He also called for greater toleration of the Jews in *Observations upon the Downfall of Papal Power* (1785) and in *George Foxe's Looking Glass for the Jews* (1790?). No copies of this work are extant, and it is known only through an advertisement in a 1790 edition of *Observations upon the Downfall of Papal Power*.

In his last two American works, *An Essay upon the Propagation of the Gospel* (1799) and *An Essay on the Eleventh Chapter of the Revelation of St. John* (1800), Crawford attacked deists for immorality, especially singling out Thomas Paine, who, he said, combined sedition with infidelity; he showed his sympathy for a society organized along clearly defined class lines, praised the notion of a responsible aristocracy, and demonstrated an interest in seeing America governed as a limited monarchy rather than as a democracy or a republic. By 1803 Crawford was back in England, where he generally contented himself with reprinting earlier poems in volumes such as *Poems on Several Occasions* (1803) and *Poems on Various Subjects* (1810). He concluded his career with his *Poetical Works* (1814) and a final, posthumously published work, *Three Letters to the Hebrew Nation* (1817).

References:
Lewis Leary, "Charles Crawford: A Forgotten Poet of Early Pennsylvania," *Pennsylvania Magazine of History and Biography,* 83 (July 1959): 293-306;
Oscar Wegelin, *Early American Poetry* (New York. Peter Smith, 1930), I: 25-26.

Samuel Davies
(3 November 1723-4 February 1761)

Paul W. Harris

SELECTED BOOKS: *A Sermon on Man's Primitive State; and The First Covenant* . . . (Philadelphia: Printed by William Bradford, 1748);

The Impartial Trial, Impartially Tried, and Convicted of Partiality . . . (Williamsburg: Printed by W. Parks, 1748);

The State of Religion among the Protestant Dissenters in Virginia; In a Letter to the Reverend Mr. Joseph Bellamy . . . (Boston: Printed & sold by S. Kneeland, 1751); abridged as *The Substance of a Letter from Mr. Davies . . . to Mr. Bellamy . . . Concerning the State of Religion in Virginia* . . . (Glasgow: Printed for John Orr, 1751); and as *An Account of a Remarkable Work of Grace* . . . (London: Sold by J. Lewis, 1752);

Miscellaneous Poems, Chiefly on Divine Subjects . . . (Williamsburg: Printed & sold by William Hunter, 1752);

A Sermon Preached Before the Reverend Presbytery of New-Castle, October 11, 1752 . . . (Philadelphia: Printed by B. Franklin & D. Hall, 1753);

The Duties Difficulties and Reward of the Faithful Minister . . . (Glasgow: Printed by W. Duncan junior, 1754);

A Sermon Preached at Henrico, 29th April 1753 . . . (Edinburgh: Printed for W. Gray & W. Peter, 1754);

Religion and Patriotism The Constituents of a Good Soldier . . . (Philadelphia: Printed by James Chattin, 1755; London: Printed for J. Buckland, 1756);

Virginia's Danger and Remedy. Two Discourses, Occasioned by the Severe Drought, in Sundry Parts of the Country; And the Defeat of General Braddock (Williamsburg: Printed by William Hunter, 1756; Glasgow: Printed & sold by J. Bryce & D. Paterson, 1756);

The Crisis: or, The Uncertain Doom of Kingdoms at Particular Times, Considered with Reference to Great Britain and Her Colonies in Their Present Circumstance. A Sermon Preached in Hanover, Virginia, Oct. 28, 1756 . . . (London: Printed for J. Buckland, J. Ward, 1757);

Letters from the Rev. Samuel Davies, & c., Shewing the State of Religion (Particularly Among the Negroes) in Virginia . . . (London, 1757);

Portrait of Samuel Davies by James Massalon

The Curse of Cowardice: a Sermon preached to the Militia of Hanover County, in Virginia, at a General muster, May 8, 1758 . . . (London: Printed for J. Buckland, 1758; Woodbridge, N.J.: Printed by James Parker, 1759; Boston: Printed & sold by Z. Fowle & J. Draper, 1759);

The Duty of Christians to propagate their Religion among Heathens, Earnestly recommended to the Masters of Negro Slaves in Virginia . . . (London: Printed by J. Oliver, 1758);

Little Children invited to Jesus Christ: A Sermon preached in Hanover County, Virginia, May 8, 1757 . . . (London: Printed & sold by J. Buckland, 1758; Boston: Printed & sold by Fowle & Draper, 1759);

Religion and Public Spirit. A Valedictory Address to the Senior Class, Delivered in Nassau Hall, September 21, 1760 . . . (New York: Printed & sold by James Parker, 1761);

A Sermon Delivered at Nassau-Hall, January 14, 1761. On the Death of His Late Majesty King George II . . . (New York: Printed & sold by James Parker, 1761);

Sermons on the Most Useful and Important Subjects . . . , 5 volumes (London: Printed for J. Buckland, 1766-1771); enlarged as *Sermons on Important Subjects*, 3 volumes, edited by Thomas Gibbons (London: Printed for T. Vernor, 1792; New York: Printed for T. Allen, 1792); enlarged again, 4 volumes (London: Printed for W. Baynes, 1804-1806; Boston: Printed & published by Lincoln & Edmands, 1810);

The Reverend Samuel Davies Abroad: The Diary of a Journey to England and Scotland, 1753-55, edited by George William Pilcher (Urbana: University of Illinois Press, 1967);

Collected Poems of Samuel Davies, 1723-1761, edited by Richard Beale Davis (Gainesville: Scholars' Facsimiles & Reprints, 1968).

OTHER: Thomas Gibbons, *Hymns Adapted to Divine Worship* . . . , includes sixteen hymns by Davies (London: Printed for J. Buckland, J. Johnson & J. Payne, 1769);

"A Recovered Tract of President Davies: Now First Published" ["Remarks on the Philosophical Works of Lord Bolingbroke"], *Biblical Repertory and Princeton Review*, 9 (1837): 349-364.

Samuel Davies, the principal organizer of Presbyterianism in colonial Virginia, won fame as one of the leading pulpit orators of his day, and his sermons and hymns were frequently reprinted for more than a century after his death.

Davies was born of Welsh parents, David and Martha Davies (or Davis), in New Castle County, Delaware, on 3 November 1723. He was educated at the "log college" at Fagg's Manor, Pennsylvania, one of a number of classical academies created to furnish an educated ministry for the middle colonies. The log-college movement stemmed from the influence of William Tennent, Sr., whose well-known sons included Gilbert Tennent, a revivalist during the Great Awakening. At Fagg's Manor Davies came under the influence of Samuel Blair, a leading minister among the prorevival New Side Presbyterians, then in the process of creating their own organization after the 1741 Presbyterian schism.

A year after his 1746 graduation Davies was ordained to serve the congregations centered around Hanover County, Virginia. A spontaneous awakening had occurred there a few years earlier as a result of dissatisfaction with the Anglican ministry and doctrine, and a series of evangelists had won these congregations over to Presbyterianism preparatory to Davies's settlement. Davies delayed assuming his post until 1748 because of poor health and the death of his first wife, Sarah, but he was soon remarried to Jane Holt, the beloved "Chara" of his poems and the mother of his six children.

In Virginia, Davies faithfully attended a ministry spread over five counties. His great success in building up the nascent Virginia congregations was rooted in a preaching style that was a model of evangelical Calvinism. His manner was solemn but fervent, and his sermons combined clear, reasoned

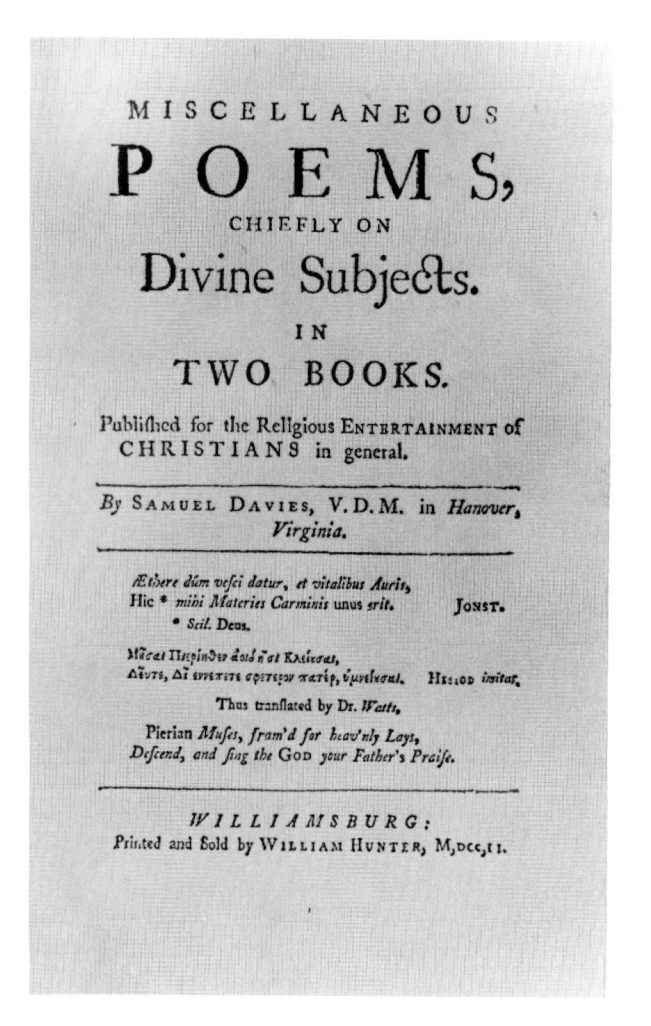

Title page for Davies's misdated 1752 book. In his preface he wrote that he had "frequently thought the Divine Art of Poetry might be made peculiarly subservient to the Interests of Religion and Virtue; and lamented the common Prostitution of the heavenly Muse to the meanest and most wicked Purposes...."

A page from the diary Davies kept while he and Gilbert Tennent were in England seeking funds for the College of New Jersey (Princeton University Library) exposition of doctrine with second-person appeals aimed at awakening his auditors to an immediate and lively concern for their spiritual condition. As dissenters under the established Church of England, the Virginia Presbyterians were repeatedly harassed by the authorities, but Davies's moderation, tact, and skillful leadership made him an effective force in the early struggle for religious toleration. He was also a supporter of early missionary activities to blacks and Indians, and he once estimated that more than a thousand blacks attended his ministry.

The year 1752 saw the publication of Davies's *Miscellaneous Poems, Chiefly on Divine Subjects*. His poems are predominantly meditations in the tradition he shared with Edward Taylor, though Davies's style was cramped by his attempt to force sublime evangelical rhetoric into couplet form. Rhythm and rhetoric were more successfully integrated in his hymnal verse, and Davies has claim to the title of America's first important writer of original hymns.

In 1753 Davies and Gilbert Tennent were appointed to undertake a fund-raising mission to Britain on behalf of the College of New Jersey (later Princeton). The mission was highly successful, and Davies's reputation as a preacher was firmly established among the religious leaders of both England and Scotland. The journey had a twofold significance for Davies's literary legacy: he became friends with Thomas Gibbons, who later assembled and published both his sermons (in *Sermons on the Most Useful and Important Subjects . . .*, 1766-1771) and his hymns (in *Hymns Adapted to Divine Worship . . .*, 1769); and he kept a diary that affords insights into the mind of a typical American evangelical and the character of transatlantic religious relations.

Davies's reputation in America peaked after his return from Britain in 1755, when he preached a series of sermons, several of which were published and widely circulated, in support of the French and Indian War effort. The sermons are excellent examples of the jeremiad form, exhorting his audience to awaken from careless self-indulgence, repent of their sins, and rouse themselves to confront the forces of darkness both within and without. Davies's role as a recruiter for the patriotic cause played an important part in gaining increased toleration for the dissenters in Virginia.

Davies was elected president of the College of New Jersey in 1759. He accepted the post reluctantly and made no major innovations during his eighteen months in the office. His career as an educator was cut short by his death from a sudden illness on 4 February 1761, at age thirty-seven.

References:

Wesley C. Gewehr, *The Great Awakening in Virginia, 1740-1790* (Durham, N.C.: Duke University Press, 1930);

George William Pilcher, *Samuel Davies: Apostle of Dissent in Colonial Virginia* (Knoxville: University of Tennessee Press, 1971).

William Dawson
(1704-20 July 1752)

Homer D. Kemp
Tennessee Technological University

BOOKS: *Poems on Several Occasions . . . by a Gentleman of Virginia* (Williamsburg: Printed & sold by William Parks, 1736);

A Letter from the Reverend Mr. Dawson, Commissary to the Lord Bishop of London, and President of William and Mary College, to the Clergy of Virginia in America (London, 1745).

OTHER: "Epigram," in *Southern Poets: Representative Selections*, edited by Edd W. Parks (New York: American Book Co., 1936), p. 7.

William Dawson—teacher, commissary, councillor, college president—was a man of amiable disposition, highly respected in his own time as an able clergyman and public figure. As a writer he produced thoroughly competent verse and sermons. Born in Cumberland County, England, in 1704, Dawson matriculated at Queen's College, Oxford, on 11 March 1720 at the age of fifteen. After having received his B.A. in 1725 and his M.A. in 1728, Dawson immigrated to Virginia, where he served first as tutor and subsequently as professor of moral

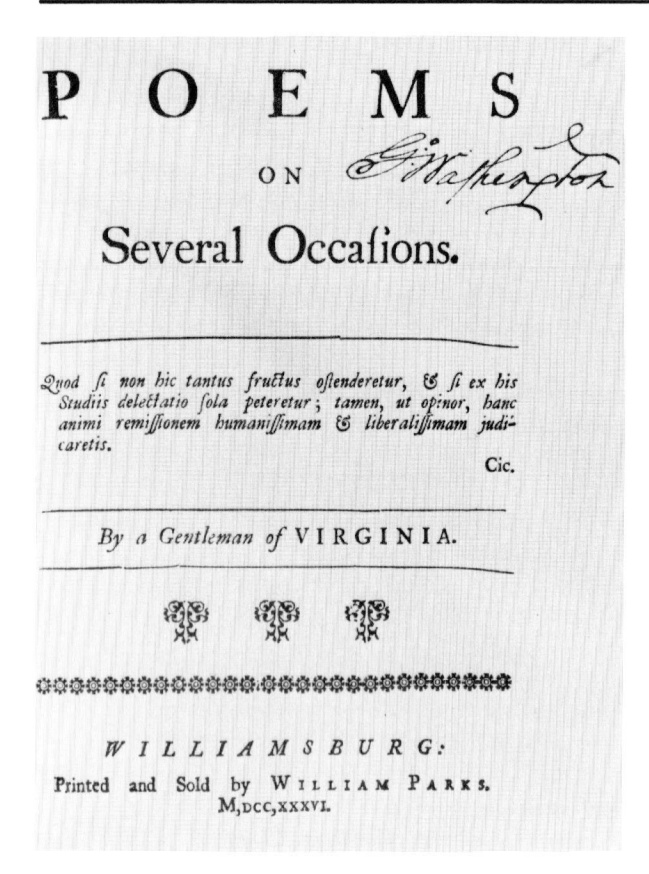

Title page for George Washington's copy of Dawson's book (Boston Athenaeum)

philosophy at the College of William and Mary (1729-1749) and married Mary Stith, sister of historian William Stith. He later (1747) received his D.D. from Oxford by diploma. In addition to his duties at the College of William and Mary, Dawson served several sessions as chaplain of the General Assembly and for many years as rector of the prestigious James City parish.

On 27 October 1736, an advertisement in the *Virginia Gazette* announced the first volume of verse known to have been published in the colony, *Poems on Several Occasions . . . by a Gentleman of Virginia*. The work was to be reprinted in 1920 and 1930, but it remained for Harold Lester Dean in 1937 to identify the "Gentleman of Virginia" as William Dawson. The poems of Dawson's little volume of 1736 are conventional English verse, mostly in the neoclassical pastoral form, with many references to Oxford. It would seem that at the time the poems were written (probably while Dawson was attending Oxford), the poet was a well-read young man, who had read rather thoroughly Milton, the Cavalier poets, Waller, and Pope.

It is felt by several scholars that Dawson anonymously contributed a great deal of verse to the gazettes during his career. One of the poems attributed to Dawson is probably the earliest surviving eighteenth-century formal Virginia elegy, a 148-line tribute to Robert "King" Carter, which appeared in the Philadelphia *American Weekly Mercury* of 14 September 1732 (presumably reprinted from a lost issue of William Park's *Maryland Gazette*). This poem is one of the better colonial elegies written in the pastoral tradition. "To a Lady, On a Screen of Her Working" (*Virginia Gazette,* 10 December 1736) represents well Dawson's poems published in periodicals; it is clearly superior to most of the poems in his earlier collection, probably the result of a greater maturity. In the opening six lines of the poem Dawson flatters the lady's art in comparison with nature:

> A New CREATION charms the ravish'd Sight;
> Delightful Harmony of Shade and Light!
> ART vies with NATURE in a doubtful Strife,
> The finish'd Copy, which and which the Life.
> The Blooming Flow'rs the painted Bow excel;
> The gay Delusion courts, and cheats the Smell.

These lines are followed by twenty-one lines in which all of the specific flowers on the screen are described.

Some readers have assumed that the Virginia William Dawson was the author of *Miscellaneous Poems on Several Occasions,* published by a "Mr. Dawson" in London in 1735. The most recent scholarship would suggest, however, that the earlier London volume was not the work of the Virginia college president. Richard Beale Davis has quite accurately summed up Dawson's place as a poet: "Graceful and competent, all the verses assigned to Dawson suggest a metrist of some ability who had more important things than verse-making to occupy most of his time. They are literally transplanted English verse, but they have significance as indicative of colonial taste and colonial abilities."

Those "more important things" in Dawson's life included his election in 1743 to the offices of Anglican commissary, councillor, and president of the College of William and Mary, posts which he held until his death on 20 July 1752.

References:

George M. Brydon, *Virginia's Mother Church* (Philadelphia: Church Historical Society, 1952), II: 256-268;

Harold L. Dean, "An Identification of the 'Gentleman of Virginia,'" *Papers of the Bibliographical Society of America*, 31 (1937): 10-20;

Jay B. Hubbell, *The South in American Literature, 1607-1900* (Durham: Duke University Press, 1954), pp. 33-35;

J. A. Leo Lemay, *A Calendar of American Poetry in the Colonial Newspapers and Magazines and in the Major English Magazines Through 1765* (Worcester: American Antiquarian Society, 1972);

Ralph L. Rusk, Introduction to *Poems on Several Occasions,* edited by Rusk (New York: Facsimile Text Society, 1930);

Earl Gregg Swem, Introduction to *Poems on Several Occasions,* edited by Swem (New York: Heartman's Historical Series, 1920).

Papers:
The Dawson Papers in the Library of Congress consist of a collection of letters and sermons of William Dawson and his brother Thomas (president of William and Mary, 1755-1761). In addition, the Library of Congress holds the "William and Mary Miscellany," a collection of Latin and English verse probably composed as exercises under William Dawson's direction, which may also include some of his own earlier pieces.

John Dickinson
(8 November 1732-14 February 1808)

Elaine K. Ginsberg
West Virginia University

SELECTED BOOKS: *A Speech, Delivered in the House of Assembly of the Province of Pennsylvania, May 24th, 1764 ... On the Occasion of a Petition, Drawn Up by Order, and Then Under Consideration in the House; Praying His Majesty for a Change of the Government of This Province* (Philadelphia: Printed & sold by William Bradford, 1764; London: Printed for J. Whiston & B. White, 1764);

A Reply to a Piece Called the Speech of Joseph Galloway, Esquire (Philadelphia: Printed & sold by William Bradford, 1764; London: Printed for J. Whiston & B. White, 1765);

Last Tuesday morning Mr. Galloway carried a writing containing some reflections on me, to a printer in this city ... (Philadelphia: Printed by William Bradford, 1764);

The Late Regulations Respecting the British Colonies on the Continent of America, Considered ... (Philadelphia: Printed & sold by William Bradford, 1765; London: Printed for J. Almon, 1765);

An Address to the Committee of Correspondence in Barbados ... (Philadelphia: Printed & sold by William Bradford, 1766);

Letters from a Farmer in Pennsylvania to the Inhabitants of the British Colonies (Philadelphia: Printed by David Hall & William Sellers, 1768; London: Printed by J. Almon, 1768);

An Essay on the Constitutional Power of Great-Britain Over the Colonies in America ... (Philadelphia: Printed & sold by William & Thomas Bradford, 1774); republished as *A New Essay [by the Pennsylvania farmer] on the Constitutional Power of Great Britain over the Colonies in America* (London: Printed for J. Almon, 1774);

The Letters of Fabius, in 1788, on the Federal Constitution; and in 1797 on the Present Situation of Public Affairs (Wilmington: Printed at the office of the *Delaware Gazette*, 1797);

A Caution; or Reflections on the Present Contest Between France and Great Britain (Philadelphia: Printed by Benjamin Franklin Bache, 1798);

The Political Writings of John Dickinson ..., 2 volumes (Wilmington & Baltimore: Printed & sold by Bonsal & Niles, 1801);

An Address on the Past, Present, and Eventual Relations of the United States to France (New York: Printed by T. & J. Swords, 1803).

Collection: *The Writings of John Dickinson,* edited by Paul Leicester Ford (Philadelphia: Historical Society of Pennsylvania, 1895).

PUBLIC DOCUMENT: U.S. Continental Congress, *A Declaration by the Representatives of the United Colonies of North-America, Now Met in General Congress at Philadelphia, Seting* [sic]

Portrait of John Dickinson by Charles Willson Peale (Historical Society of Pennsylvania)

Forth the Causes and Necessity of Their Taking Up Arms (Various imprints, 1775).

John Dickinson is especially known for his *Letters from a Farmer in Pennsylvania* (1768), which were among the most influential and popular writings of the American Revolutionary era.

Dickinson, son of Samuel and Mary Cadwalader Dickinson, was born on the family estate on the eastern shore of Maryland. The family moved in 1740 to Kent County, near Dover, Delaware, where he was educated privately. In 1750 he began studying law in the office of John Moland in Philadelphia. After undertaking further study at the Middle Temple in London from 1753 to 1757, he returned to Philadelphia to practice law. Dickinson kept close ties to his Delaware home, however, and through-

out his life served in public office alternately in Delaware and Pennsylvania. He was elected to the Delaware Assembly in 1759 and became speaker. In 1762 he was elected to represent Philadelphia in the Pennsylvania Assembly, where he and Benjamin Franklin argued opposite sides on such issues as the Quaker proprietary government, taxation, and representation.

As a member of the Pennsylvania Assembly, the Continental Congress, and later the Constitutional Convention, John Dickinson's writing talents were often called upon in drafting messages, resolutions, and letters. He was the chief draftsman of the "Declaration of Rights and Grievances" of the Stamp Act Congress (1765). His first significant publication in the American cause was a pamphlet entitled *The Late Regulations Respecting the British*

THE LATE REGULATIONS RESPECTING THE BRITISH COLONIES ON THE CONTINENT OF AMERICA CONSIDERED;

In a Letter from a Gentleman in PHILADELPHIA to his Friend in LONDON.

Profunt minus recte excogitata; cum alios incitent faltem ad veritatis investigationem. FULB. A BARTOL.

PHILADELPHIA:
Printed and Sold by WILLIAM BRADFORD, at the Corner of Market and Front-Streets. M.DCC.LXV.

Title page for the pamphlet in which Dickinson warned that the surest way for England to force the colonies to declare their independence was to make them "frugal, ingenious, united, and discontented" (courtesy of the John Carter Brown Library at Brown University)

Colonies (1765). The pamphlet uses the epistolary form as a convention: purporting to be "from a Gentleman in Philadelphia to his Friend in London," it argues that London, as well as the colonies, would suffer from the enforcement of the Sugar Act. Dickinson points out the disastrous economic effects of not only this act but of the proposed Stamp Act as well. He warns prophetically: "we can never be made an independent people, except it be by *Great Britain* herself; and the only way for her to do it, is to make us frugal, ingenious, united and discontented." His *An Address to the Committee of Correspondence in Barbados* (1766) replies to the accusation that it is rebellion for the colonies to resist the Stamp Act. In a vigorous and ironic attack, he accuses the committee of ignorance of the source of human rights: "They are created in us by the decrees of Providence, which establish the laws of our nature. They are born with us; exist with us; and cannot be taken from us by any human power, without taking our lives." He defends the resistance to the Stamp Act with eloquent analogies: "If my father, deceived and urged on by bad or weak men, should offer me a draught of poison, and tell me it would be of service to me, should I be undutiful, if, knowing what it is I refuse to drink it? or if inflamed by passion he should aim a dagger at my heart, should I be undutiful, if I refuse to bare my breast for the blow?"

Dickinson's best-known writings, the *Letters from a Farmer in Pennsylvania*, were first printed as a series in the *Pennsylvania Chronicle* beginning 2 December 1767. They were reprinted many times in pamphlet form and in other newspapers and were quoted everywhere. Dickinson's persona is a gentleman farmer, an idealized American who repre-

LETTERS FROM A FARMER IN PENNSYLVANIA, TO THE INHABITANTS OF THE BRITISH COLONIES.

PHILADELPHIA:
Printed by DAVID HALL, and WILLIAM SELLERS.
MDCCLXVIII.

Title page for the series of essays that, until the publication of Thomas Paine's Common Sense *in 1776, was the most widely read political document in the colonies (courtesy of the John Carter Brown Library at Brown University)*

This tribute, printed for Philadelphia bookseller Robert Bell in 1768, is indicative of the esteem in which Dickinson was held after his authorship of Letters from a Farmer in Pennsylvania *was revealed.*

sents the traditional qualities of industry, frugality, and integrity but who is also an educated, rational man. He spends a "good deal" of time in his library and has acquired "a greater knowledge in history, and the laws and constitution" of his country than most men. Dickinson's farmer is, most of all, a peaceful man, who only reluctantly enters the public fray. Thus the credibility of *Letters from a Farmer in Pennsylvania* is enhanced by their attribution to a man who is not personally involved in the conflict. The letters as a whole, despite their original serial publication, appear to be a carefully planned composition following the pattern of a classical oration in five divisions: proem (letter one), narrative (letters two, three, four), argument (letters five, six, seven, eight), remarks (letters nine, ten, eleven), and peroration (letter twelve). The first letter presents the farmer and warns his countrymen of imminent danger. The next three examine the relationship between the colonies and the mother country. Letters five through eight present the grievances of the colonies, and nine through eleven offer further reflections on the subject. The twelfth letter reiterates the warning and urges the necessity of colonial vigilance and unity. The same ideology that Dickinson expresses in his earlier publications undergirds his *Letters from a Farmer in Pennsylvania*: the colonists have an inherent right to be "happy";

they cannot be happy without being free and cannot be free without being secure in their property. Specific issues he addresses include taxation without representation, the right of Parliament to regulate trade, and the distinction between external and internal taxes. The letters are sprinkled with quotations from the classics and from English and European authors. Each letter concludes with a Latin phrase or sentence. Throughout the letters there are rhythmic variations of tone and effective rhetorical devices. So persuasive were the letters that the Tory *Critical Review* in England "accused the Farmer of inciting the colonies to independence."

Dickinson composed his *American Liberty Song* at about the same time he was writing *Letters from a Farmer in Pennsylvania*. The ten stanzas reflect the themes common to most contemporary rhetoric: slavery or freedom, the sufferings of the first settlers in defense of liberty, the penalties of submission, the necessity for union, and the rewards of victory. The song was widely printed as a broadside and soon became one of the most popular of the time. A very different kind of work is Dickinson's *An Essay on the Constitutional Power of Great-Britain* (1774), in which he argues, with ponderous documentation, the legalistic position that "the sovereignty over the colonies must be limited" and that a line must be drawn to set off Parliament's powers from those of the colonial legislatures, thus giving to Parliament the right to regulate commerce and foreign affairs and to the colonial assemblies "exclusive right of internal legislature," including taxation. Dickinson was elected to chair the Philadelphia Committee of Correspondence in 1774 and served as a Pennsylvania representative to the First and Second Continental Congresses (1774-1776). Though he was chief draftsman of *A Declaration by the Representatives of the United Colonies of North-America, Now Met in General Congress at Philadelphia, Seting* [sic] *Forth the Causes and Necessity of Their Taking Up Arms* (6 July 1775), he opposed the Declaration of Independence and refused to sign it, citing the colonies' poor state of preparedness for a war; he believed the colonies lacked foreign allies and internal unity. In July 1776, however, he wrote the first draft of the Articles of Confederation and then left to face the British in northern New Jersey with the First Philadelphia Battalion, which he served as a colonel. Dickinson resigned his commission in September and returned to Delaware, where he later joined the militia as a private and fought at the battle of Brandywine.

In 1781 he was elected President of the Supreme Executive Council of Delaware, and the following year, while still serving as President of Delaware, he was elected to the same position in Pennsylvania. Two months later, he resigned his Delaware presidency. After serving as President of Pennsylvania for three years, he returned to Delaware. As a delegate to the Constitutional Convention (1787) from Delaware, he actively participated in the drafting of the Federal Constitution and defended it in the first of two series of letters that he signed Fabius. In these letters he dropped his pose of gentleman farmer and adopted the tone of elder statesman and philosopher. The nine 1788 Fabius letters answer the various objections to the proposed constitution, contending that "the power of the people pervading the proposed system . . . together with the strong confederation of the states, forms an adequate security against every danger that has been apprehended." The ideas expressed in these letters parallel many of the ideas in Thomas Paine's *The Rights of Man* (1791-1792), a fact made obvious by the many footnotes referring to Paine's work that Dickinson added to the letters when they were collected with the 1797 letters in book form.

During the early 1790s Dickinson chaired the Delaware Constitutional Convention (1791) and was elected to the Delaware Assembly. He resigned from that body in 1793, however, citing poor health. Subsequently, Dickinson became increasingly interested in international relations and objected strenuously to the 1795 treaty that John Jay had negotiated with Britain. An ardent francophile, Dickinson wrote an "Ode to the French Revolution" (1797), sounding the theme "The Cause of France is Freedom's Cause." Three months later he began the publication of fifteen letters, also signed Fabius, defending France, her recent actions, and the pro-French position of the democrats. He reminds Americans that in 1783 Congress expressed the hope that our revolution would set an example to the world; that "example has been followed by the greatest people upon earth." Dickinson calls upon his extensive knowledge of the classics and of history to draw parallels between ancient and modern nations, and finally urges Americans to adhere "to the good old precepts of common sense, and to the sound dispositions of human nature" in remaining loyal to the French, "who first acknowledged our independence, and set the blessed example to others."

John Dickinson published his collected political writings in two volumes in 1801. Taken together, the writings trace the extraordinarily productive career of one of the foremost statesmen and propagandists of the revolutionary and early national periods.

References:
A. Owen Aldridge, "Paine and Dickinson," *Early American Literature,* 11 (Fall 1976): 125-138;
Milton E. Flower, *John Dickinson: Conservative Revolutionary* (Charlottesville: University Press of Virginia, 1983);
David L. Jacobson, *John Dickinson and the Revolution in Pennsylvania 1764-1776* (Berkeley: University of California Press, 1965);
Carl F. Kaestle, "The Public Reaction to John Dickinson's *Farmer's Letters*," *Proceedings of the American Antiquarian Society,* 78, part 2 (1969): 323-353;
Pierre Marambaud, "Dickinson's *Letters from a Farmer in Pennsylvania* as Political Discourse," *Early American Literature,* 12 (Spring 1977): 63-72;
Charles J. Stillé, *The Life and Times of John Dickinson* (Philadelphia: Historical Society of Pennsylvania, 1891).

Papers:
There are important collections of Dickinson's papers at the Library Company of Philadelphia, the Historical Society of Pennsylvania, the Public Archives of the State of Delaware, the Historical Society of Delaware, and the Massachusetts Historical Society.

Nathaniel Evans
(1742-1767)

William D. Andrews
Philadelphia College of Textiles & Science

BOOKS: *Ode on the Late Glorious Successes of His Majesty's Arms, and Present Greatness of the English Nation* (Philadelphia: Printed & sold by William Dunlap, 1762);
An Exercise, Containing a Dialogue and Ode on Peace. Performed at the Public Commencement in the College of Philadelphia, May 17, 1763 . . . , by Evans and Paul Jackson (Philadelphia: Printed by Andrew Steuart, 1764);
The Love of the World Incompatible with the Love of God: A Discourse . . . (Philadelphia: Printed by Henry Miller, 1766);
Poems on Several Occasions . . . (Printed & sold by John Dunlap, 1772).

Because he died at the age of twenty-five, we cannot know whether Nathaniel Evans would have grown toward that mastery of the craft of poetry necessary to qualify him as more than a minor figure in American literature. Based on what he did produce in a short life, we are obliged to regard him as a minor lyricist, of interest not merely for his potential but also for what he reflected of the literary culture of his time. Evans's poetic career illustrates the difficulties attendant upon the emergence of a national literature in advance of a national political state, the struggles—individual and collective—to forge a literary tradition in the British colonies.

Evans was born in Philadelphia in 1742 and entered the first class of the Academy of Philadelphia in 1751. This school, founded by Benjamin Franklin, played a critical role in Evans's life and in the cultural life of eighteenth-century Philadelphia generally. It attracted the sons of the city's merchants and professionals who desired sound, practical education. The entering class included, along with Evans, three young men who achieved individual distinction in Philadelphia's literary and political circles: Thomas Godfrey, playwright; Francis Hopkinson, poet, musician, and politician; Jacob Duché, Anglican priest and essayist. Together these four would-be poets formed a group called the "Swains of the Schuylkill," for the river passing through Philadelphia on the west.

A page from the manuscript for one of the orations on science Evans delivered in 1765 (Archives of the University of Pennsylvania)

Evans and the others rapidly came under the influence of the academy's energetic provost, the Reverend William Smith, who served as mentor to the Swains as well as leader of the school. He intended to establish in the colonies a center of education and the arts that would nourish a generation of artists and writers in the New World. That vision inflamed the Swains, Evans among them, and encouraged their efforts to create a native literature rooted in the larger traditions of Britain. Throughout his brief career Evans pursued Smith's dream.

Evans attended the academy for six years before being recalled by his merchant father, Edward Evans, to an apprenticeship in the family firm. He eventually returned and, though he lacked an A.B. degree, received an A.M. in 1765 from what had by then become the Academy and College of Philadelphia. (The school ultimately evolved into the University of Pennsylvania.) We know little of Evans's life during the years between his attendance at the school except that he continued to engage in versifying. When his friend Thomas Godfrey died in

1763, Evans undertook to collect and edit his work, which appeared in 1765 as *Juvenile Poems on Various Subjects, with the Prince of Parthia, a Tragedy*. The edition is notable largely because it contains the first published text of Godfrey's romantic tragedy.

The principal informing theme of Evans's poetry emerged quite early: the prospect of the new land as a site of art, science, and culture. Inspired directly by Smith, Evans produced in 1758 "Daphnis and Menalcas, A Pastoral Eclogue," which elaborates the concept of a future reign of art in his native land. The piece begins with a lament over the low condition of poetry in the New World:

> SHALL fam'd Arcadia own the tuneful choir,
> And fair Sicilia boast the matchless lyre?
> Shall Gallia's groves resound with heav'nly lays,
> And albion's poets claim immortal bays?
> And this new world ne'er feel the muse's fire;
> No beauties charm us, or no deeds inspire?
> O Pennsylvania! shall no son of thine
> Glow with the raptures of the sacred nine?

The implied answer is that Pennsylvania, too, will soon share in the inspiration of the muse, particularly in the person of young Nathaniel Evans: "Fir'd with the thought, I court the Sylvan muse,/Her magic influence o'er me to diffuse. . . ." Such a prediction was demonstrably self-serving in that it linked the success of the individual poet to the destiny of art in the colonies, a link perfectly consistent with the tradition of personal-social achievement common in the verse of such English writers as Alexander Pope.

Evans enlarged this theme—referred to generically as "the rising glory of America"—in his 1761 "Ode on the Prospect of Peace," which predicts the arrival of the muse of poetry in America following its abandonment of England:

> If thou from Albion's sea-girt shore,
>   Advent'rous muse wilt deign to rove,
> Inclin'd remotest realms t'explore
>   And soothe the savage soul to love;
> Hither wave thy wand'ring pinion,
> Here be fix'd thy last dominion.
>   Warbling in 'Sylvania's grove.

His most complete treatment of the rising glory theme came in 1763 in his "Dialogue and Ode on Peace," written with Paul Jackson for the commencement exercises of the College of Philadelphia. The end of the Seven Years War between England and France, fought extensively in the colonies, where it was called the French and Indian War, suggested to Evans the imminent prospect of American glory:

> This joyful Day in Miniature we've shew'd
> Scenes that enraptur'd *Athens* would have view'd;
> *Science* triumphant! And a Land refin'd,
> Where once rude Ign'rance sway'd th' untutor'd Mind;
> Of uncouth Forms no more the dark Retreat,
> Transform'd to Virtue and the Muse's Seat.

The poem celebrates the arrival in the New World of the muses of civilization while carefully downplaying the related implication that English glory had to decline as America's rose.

In 1765, at the commencement ceremony at which he received his A.M., Evans delivered "Verses, Addressed to the Trustees of the College and Academy of Philadelphia." This piece offered the young poet another opportunity to explore the rising-glory motif, again linked to the effects of education on the eventual creation in the colonies of a native literary tradition.

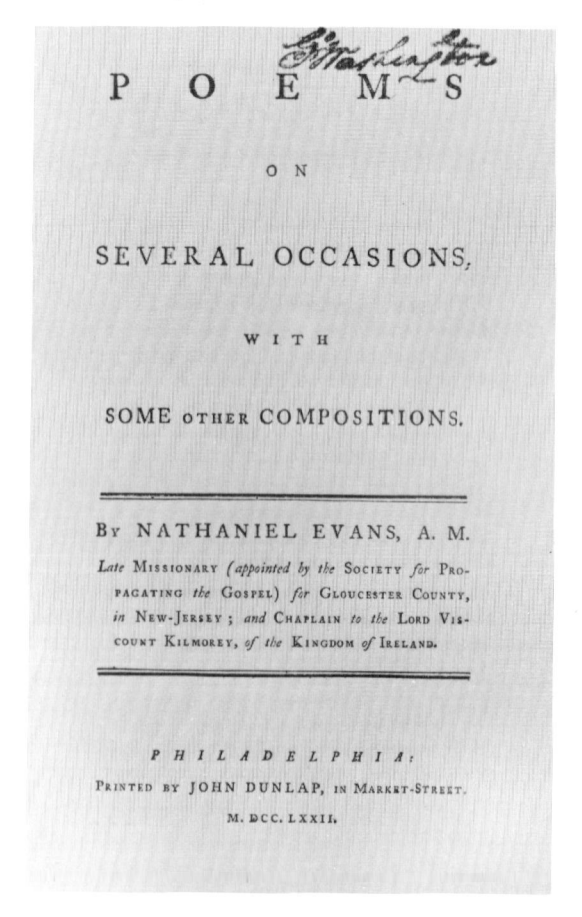

Title page for George Washington's copy of Evans's posthumously published book (Charles Allen Munn Collection, Fordham University Library)

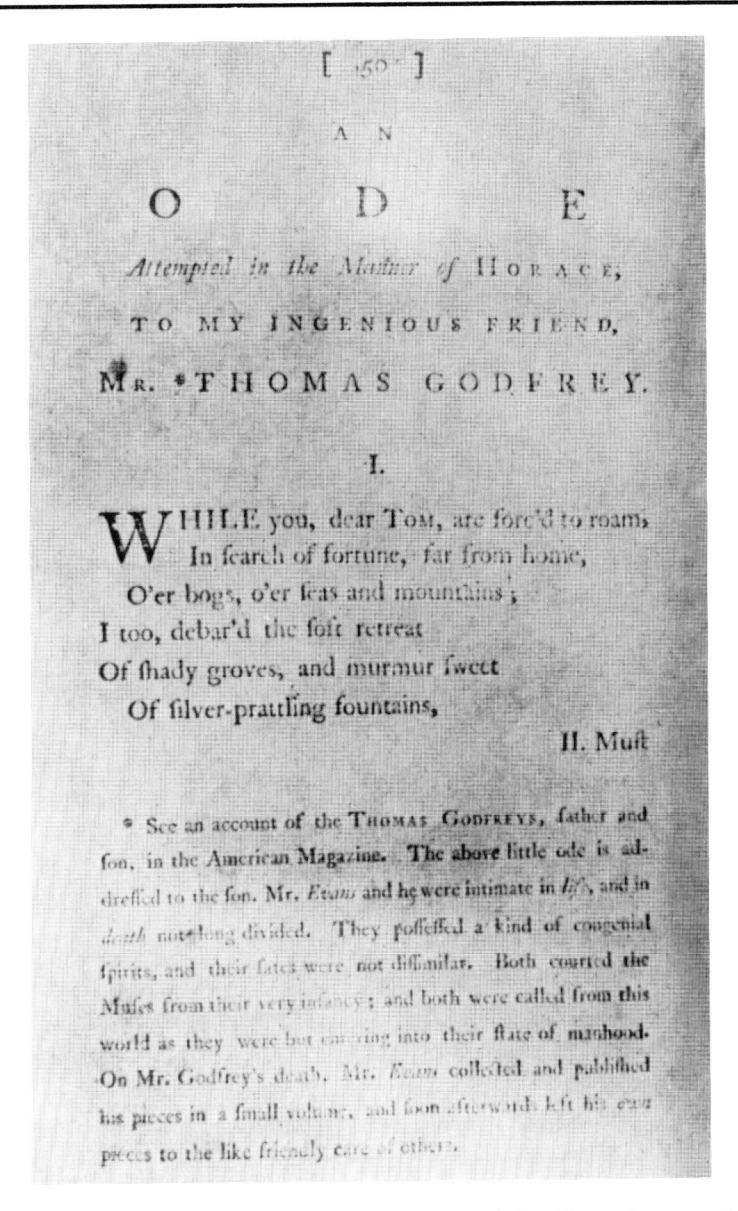

First page for Evans's ode to a friend and fellow poet who had gone to live in North Carolina, as it appears in the posthumously published collection of Evans's poems edited by his mentor William Smith

The next step in Evans's career may seem strange for one who had become such a frequent and eloquent prophet of American glory. At Smith's urging, Evans left for England upon his commencement in 1765. His purpose was to seek further education and specifically to join Smith in the priesthood of the Church of England. We know little of Evans's life abroad. He returned to America as a missionary-priest assigned to Gloucester County, New Jersey, across the Delaware River from Philadelphia. On the return trip he met Elizabeth Graeme, with whom he maintained a correspondence in verse addressing her as Laura, that offered a continuing medium for his efforts to refine his poetic voice.

In the two years following his return from England, Evans's attention was largely directed at lyric versifying, and there is little concern for the rising-glory theme that so absorbed him early in his career. His "Ode. Written at G—Park" is typical of his work during his last years. (Graeme Park was the country seat of Mrs. Graeme and the site of frequent literary/artistic gatherings.) It concludes with these two stanzas:

>   Let *Cheerfulness,* with placid mein,
>   Hold a firm empire o'er thy heart,
>   And sweet *Content* shall ceaseless reign,
>   And never-ending bliss impart.
>
>   Then shall th' immortal Nine unfold
>   What sweets the sylvan scenes can give;
>   In heav'n thy name shall be enroll'd,
>   And others learn like thee to live.

Evans died of tuberculosis in 1767 and was buried at Christ Church, Philadelphia. His mentor William Smith collected and published Evans's work as *Poems on Several Occasions* in 1772. The verse in the volume is conventional and unremarkable. In style and theme it is highly derivative of the English writers Evans and his colonial peers read: Milton, Cowley, Gray, Pope, and Dryden. The occasional pieces—songs, pastorals, and the like—are without distinction even as self-conscious imitations. Evans's achievement as a poet is, rather, in his frequent and mostly successful use of the theme of America's rising glory. He laid a base in verse for a tradition that includes poets, essayists, and novelists, extending from Evans's time into our own. His reputation has always—and justly—been that of a minor poet. But his significance as a typical American writer of the mid-eighteenth century and as a contributor to a literary tradition remains strong.

References:

B. A. Milligan, "An Early American Imitator of Milton," *American Literature,* 1 (1929): 200-206;

Andrew B. Myers, ed., *George Washington's Copy of Poems on Several Occasions by Nathaniel Evans,* facsimile edition (New York: Fordham University Press, 1976);

Edgar L. Pennington, *Nathaniel Evans, A Poet of Colonial America* (Ocala, Fla.: Taylor, 1935).

Papers:

The single manuscript item (of the poem "Oration on Science") known to be held in an archive exists at the Library of the University of Pennsylvania.

Thomas Fitch
(circa 1700-18 July 1774)

O. Glade Hunsaker
Brigham Young University

BOOKS: *Reasons Why the British Colonies in America Should Not Be Charged with Internal Taxes, By Authority of Parliament* . . . (New Haven: Printed by B. Mecom, 1764);

An Explanation of the Say-Brook Platform; Or, The Principles of Consolidated Churches in the Colony of Connecticut . . . (Hartford: Printed by Thomas Green, 1765);

Some Reasons that influenced the Governor to take and the Councillors to administer the Oath required by the Act of Parliament; commonly called the Stamp-act, Humbly submitted to the Consideration of the Publick (Hartford: Printed & sold by Thomas Green, 1766).

Thomas Fitch, best known for his service as a colonial governor of Connecticut, is rightfully respected for his work in revising the Yale College charter and the laws of Connecticut. Born in Norwalk, Connecticut, the son of Thomas and Sarah Fitch, the future governor was graduated from Yale College in 1721. He married Hannah Hall of New Haven on 4 September 1724. Of their ten children, eight lived to adulthood. Having continued his religious studies after his graduation from Yale, Fitch occasionally served as a substitute preacher in Norwalk in 1726, but at the same time he was embarking on the political career to which he would devote himself. He was elected as one of his town's representatives to the sessions of the General Assembly for May 1726, May 1727, May 1729, and May 1730, and he was appointed a justice of the peace annually from 1727 to 1732 and in 1736. In 1754 Fitch succeeded Roger Wolcott as governor of Connecticut and was reelected annually until 1766, when he was defeated by William Pitkin, his deputy governor.

Fitch's numerous letters and essays defending his political positions document the unflinching integrity that ultimately cost him his governorship. Although he opposed the Stamp Act, his loyalty to

Title pages for the pamphlets in which Fitch explained his position on the Stamp Act (courtesy of the John Carter Brown Library at Brown University)

the oath he had given the Crown would not allow him to oppose the King. His style of writing is as disciplined as his attitudes, giving page after page of lucid exposition. Although he is seldom figurative, his writing sustains a grandeur and elegance typical of a governor of the colonial period. Probably Fitch's two most important essays are *Reasons Why the British Colonies in America Should Not Be Charged With Internal Taxes* (1764) and *Some Reasons that influenced the Governor to take and the Councillors to administer the Oath required by the Act of Parliament; commonly called the Stamp-act, Humbly submitted to the Consideration of the Publick* (1766). Neither essay has impassioned argumentation; rather, Fitch uses a subtle yet firm appeal to the virtues of dignity, order, reason, and commitment. In summarizing why he and his councillors defended the Stamp Act despite their personal convictions, Fitch wrote in *Some Reasons that influenced the Governor . . .* , "Upon the whole, then, it may be justly concluded, they [his councillors] were moved from principles of Loyalty to the King, from serious and tender concern for the privileges of the colony; a conscientious Regard to the solemn obligations of their office-oaths; and a just value for their own Interest, Reputation, and Usefulness in Life." Despite his appeal to conscience, the voters resented his having taken the oath to support the Stamp Act and voted him out of office in 1766.

Fitch died in July 1774 after a month's illness. The monument erected in his memory calls him "Eminent and distinguished among mortals for great abilities, large acquirements, and a virtuous character; a clear, strong, sedate mind, and an accurate, extensive acquaintance with law and civil government; a happy talent of presiding, close application and strict fidelity, in the discharge of important trusts, no less than for his employments by the voice of the people in the chief offices of State, and at the head of the Colony."

Letters:
The Fitch Papers: Correspondence and Documents during Thomas Fitch's Governorship of the Colony of Connecticut, 1754-1766, edited by Albert C. Bates, Collections of the Connecticut Historical Society, volumes 17 and 18 (Hartford: Connecticut Historical Society, 1918-1920).

Alexander Garden
(circa 1685-27 September 1756)

Amanda Porterfield
Syracuse University

BOOKS: *Six Letters to the Rev. Mr. George Whitefield* (Charleston: Printed by Lewis Timothy, 1740);

Regeneration, and the Testimony of the Spirit . . . (Charleston: Printed by Peter Timothy, 1740);

Take Heed How Ye Hear . . . (Charleston: Printed by Peter Timothy, 1741);

The Doctrine of Justification according to the Scriptures, and the Articles, and Homilies of the Church of England, Explained and Vindicated . . . (Charleston: Printed by Peter Timothy, 1742);

A Farewell Sermon Preached in the Parish Church of St. Philip, Charles-Town in South-Carolina, Sunday the 31st day of March, 1754 (Charleston: Printed by Peter Timothy, 1754);

A Brief Account of the Deluded Dutartres . . . (New Haven: Printed & sold by James Parker, 1762).

Alexander Garden, an opponent of religious enthusiasm, is known for his arguments with the charismatic instigator of the Great Awakening, George Whitefield. In his office as commissary of the Church of England, Garden represented the ecclesiastical authority of the bishop of London in the Carolinas and Georgia. His censure of Whitefield grew out of the Church's displeasure with its Methodist offspring and with the theologies and practices of the Great Awakening.

Born in Scotland about 1685, Alexander Garden was granted a master's degree and ordained in his land of birth. He came to Charleston in 1719, the same year South Carolina became a royal province. Soon after his arrival, he was elected to the rectorship of St. Philip's parish. The Anglican church in South Carolina had grown during the first two decades of the eighteenth century. Despite yellow fever and hurricanes, a war with the Yemassee Indians, and religious rebellion from Scotch-Irish dissenters, it flourished under the government of the royal province. After Garden was appointed commissary in 1726, church membership and missionary work in his jurisdiction continued to increase. Known for administrative leadership, Garden presided over annual visitations with his clergy with a firm and purposeful hand. Until the Great Awakening began, these annual visitations served to organize the clergy as a unified body of Christian priests and effectively to censure clerical misconduct. After attending one of these sessions in 1737, John Wesley commented approvingly on the "conversation on Christian Righteousness" pursued there.

George Whitefield's opinions of the Anglican clergy were not so approving. He criticized both their theology and their manner of preaching and he even went so far as to publish a letter "Asserting that Archbishop Tillotson knew no more of Christianity than Mahomet." In his journal Whitefield reported that when he visited Charleston in 1740, he "Waited on the Commissary," was first "met with a cool reception," and then with "a great rage" and a threat of suspension. After Whitefield retorted that he would respect a suspension from Alexander Garden as little as he would "a Pope's bull," Garden called him before an ecclesiastical court "to answer to certain articles or interrogatories, which were to be objected and ministered to him concerning the mere health of his soul, and the reformation and correction of his manners and excesses; and chiefly for omitting to use the form of prayer prescribed in the Common Book." Whitefield appeared before Garden's court but refused to recognize its authority.

Garden was incensed at Whitefield not only

for scoffing at Anglican authority and clergy but for theological reasons as well. In *Six letters to the Rev. Mr. George Whitefield* (1740) he argued that Whitefield's identification of Christianity with faith but not good works was illogical, confusing, and dangerous. Garden understood salvation as a gradual process of justification, a growth toward purity and righteousness. He believed that good works were necessary to faith and progress toward salvation. He accused Whitefield of misrepresenting his Anglican doctrine with the "poisonous Insinuation" that Anglican clergy advocated good works as the "meritorious Cause" of salvation. To Garden this twisted representation of Anglican doctrine confused many people and was "destroying the Foundation" of Christianity. In his efforts to clarify the true doctrines of Christianity he attacked the Great Awakening's most eminent theologian, Jonathan Edwards—"poor shatter'd Dr. Edwards, as dogmatical, captious, unfair and confused a writer as any of his Time"—as well as George Whitefield and his "dirty Pamphlets."

Garden's sermons on regeneration depicted Whitefield as a theatrical, manipulative orator. He also objected to Whitefield's view that regeneration was "a sudden instantaneous Work" of the feelings. In Garden's mind, ascribing regeneration to the impulses divested people of responsibility for their beliefs and behavior and left them prey to charismatic demagogues with pretentious claims to Christian authority. Garden quoted Whitefield's statement "it has pleased God to give me a TRUE Knowledge of the Doctrines of Grace," and responded, "choice Armour indeed! Who shall be able to stand before you?" Garden's belief that it was wrong and dangerous to equate powerful impulses with Christian grace was confirmed by his interviews with members of the Dutartres family, who were convicted of murder and incest. The Dutartres, Garden wrote, "were confident they had the Spirit of God Speaking inwardly to their Souls."

Garden was also known for his views about slavery. In his sixth letter to Whitefield, he objected to Whitefield's statements that slaves in the Southern colonies were inhumanly treated and he defended the humanity of the majority of Southern slaveholders. With funds from the Society for Propagating the Gospel, the commissary bought two young slaves and prepared them as teachers for a school for slaves in Charleston. Although it stayed open until 1764, the school failed to meet Garden's expectations as a model for Christian schools for slaves in other parishes.

Garden resigned from the office of commissary in March 1749 and from the rectorship of St. Philip's in June 1754. He then traveled to England, expecting never to return, but his health would not tolerate the harsher climate. He returned to Charleston before the end of 1754 and died there on 27 September 1756. He was buried at St. Philip's in a vault built by the vestry in recognition of his service to the parish.

Title page for the second edition of Garden's letters to the leader of the Great Awakening (courtesy of the John Carter Brown Library at Brown University)

References:

Frederick Dalcho, *The Protestant Episcopal Church in South Carolina, 1670-1820* (Charleston: Charles E. Thayer, 1820);

David Ramsay, *History of South Carolina, From its first settlement in 1670 to the year 1808,* volume 2 (Newberry, S.C.: W. J. Duffle, 1858);

William B. Sprague, "Alexander Garden," in his *Annals of the American Pulpit; or Commemorative Notices of Distinguished American Clergymen of Various Denominations; From the early settlement*

Thomas Godfrey

Frank Shuffelton
University of Rochester

BIRTH: Philadelphia, Pennsylvania, 4 December 1736, to Thomas Godfrey, Sr. (mother's name unknown).

DEATH: Wilmington, North Carolina, 3 August 1763.

BOOKS: *The Court of Fancy* (Philadelphia: Printed & sold by William Dunlap, 1762);
Juvenile Poems on Various Subjects. With the Prince of Parthia, a Tragedy (Philadelphia: Printed by Henry Miller, 1765).

Playgoers of the Southwark Theater in Philadelphia on 24 April 1767 were entertained by a production of a new play, *The Prince of Parthia*, the first play written by a native-born American to receive a professional production. Thomas Godfrey, its author, was not there to receive the congratulations of his friends and neighbors, for he had died nearly four years before, but on the basis of a handful of poems and his play, a surprisingly effective work from a young, provincial author, he has secured his claim to remembrance. Godfrey was born in Philadelphia, the son of Thomas Godfrey, Sr., who had invented the navigator's quadrant and was a member of Benjamin Franklin's Junto. Godfrey senior was a glazier, self-taught and with a propensity for mathematics; legend has it that he discovered the principle of the quadrant while replacing a pane of glass for James Logan and noticing the sun's reflection from his window into a pail of water across the street. When the *American Magazine* printed some of Thomas Godfrey, Jr.'s poems in 1758, it remarked, "Nature seems not to have designed the Father for a greater Mathematician than she has the son for a Poet," and went on to treat both father and son as varieties of natural genius compensating for lack of formal education with intelligence and "pertinacity in acquiring knowledge."

When his father died in 1749, the young Godfrey was apprenticed to a watchmaker, but his precocious talent for verse came to the attention of the energetic provost of the new College, Academy, and Charitable School of Philadelphia (later the University of Pennsylvania), William Smith, who in effect became Godfrey's patron. Smith obtained Godfrey's release from his indenture to the watchmaker, and Godfrey seems to have furthered his education for a period at the Academy and Charitable School, although the records to prove his attendance do not survive. He certainly became the companion of a number of extremely talented young men who were at the School and the College—Benjamin West, Francis Hopkinson, Jacob Duché, and Nathaniel Evans among others. Provost Smith encouraged the artistic ambitions of all these promising students, and the early commencements of his school were distinguished with dramatic performances and original music written for the occasions. He particularly fostered Godfrey, publishing his verse in his *American Magazine,* arranging for the sale and review of *The Court of Fancy* (1762) in England, and using his influence to persuade David Douglass to produce *The Prince of Parthia*. Perhaps even more important to Godfrey were his friendships with his fellow students.

In *Juvenile Poems on Various Subjects* (1765), collected and published after his death, Godfrey was clearly appreciative of the society of cultured young people around him, but he expressed his pleasure in their society by means of the conventional and formalized modes of eighteenth-century pastoral poetry, and the casual reader of his verse might scarcely believe that real men and women stood behind the Sylvias and Damons moving in his universalized and abstracted landscapes. Now and then a glimpse of a more real life peeps out, as in these lines from an untitled poem, which give a hint of the kind of youthful recreation colonial Philadelphians enjoyed:

> How oft together Schuylkil's verdant side
> We've traced, or wantoned in its cooling tide,
> Or soft reclined, where spreading shades were wove,
> With joyful accents fill'd the sounding grove.
> Then all was gay, the sprightly mirth was found,
> And nature bloom'd in vernal beauties round.

The first of the longer efforts in *Juvenile Poems on Various Subjects* is an "Ode on Friendship," written in 1758, and later poems variously pick up this theme: an "Epistle to a Friend; From Fort Henry," where he was stationed with the Pennsylvania militia in 1758, drinking songs such as the "Dithyrambic on Wine," and several pastoral effusions, including the one quoted above, which contrasts the friendship of Hylas (Godfrey himself, apparently) and Alexis (Nathaniel Evans?) to the pains of Damon's love for Delia. Godfrey most often treated friendship in just this way, as an alternative to a more threatening and more sexual, passionate attachment to a woman. In what is probably one of his last poems, written after he had become a merchant's factor in Wilmington, North Carolina, he invited his new circle of friends there to "a pleasant retreat, nigh Cape Fear":

> O Come to Masonborough's grove,
> Ye Nymphs and Swains away,
> Where blooming Innocence and Love,
> And Pleasure crown the day.

Here "Myra, with that scornful air" is banished, for "Tis Virtue shall our songs inspire,/And Mirth without offence." The best of these pastoral exercises have a kind of fragile charm, but they are more important in testifying to the desire of a young American provincial to enter a larger, more cosmopolitan republic of letters, a republic that in the eighteenth century haunted Arcadian groves of the imagination.

The two longest poems in this collection show Godfrey trying to escape the resolutely everyday world of Philadelphia by means of imaginative flights in a somewhat different manner. *The Court of Fancy*, published separately in 1762, and "The Assembly of Birds" have their source in two of Chaucer's dream visions, *The Parlement of Foules* and *House of Fame*, although the immediate inspiration for *The Court of Fancy* is Pope's "Temple of Fame." The poem with which the young Godfrey caught Provost Smith's eye was supposedly entitled "The Temple of Fame," apparently an earlier attempt to imitate Pope's adaptation of Chaucer, and *The Court of Fancy* clearly is another, more sophisticated but highly self-conscious, response to Pope. But where Pope seized upon the ironic possibilities of Chaucer's contrast of the House of Fame and the House of Rumor, Godfrey is more interested in an allegorical contrast between Fancy and Delusion, especially after Fancy has sanctioned the poet to marshal Truth, Beauty, Nature, and Art against such forces of Delusion as Superstition, Affectation, Flattery, and Spleen. If Godfrey's knowledge of Chaucer started with Pope, he did, however return to the original. Pope's inspiration is still primary in *The Court of Fancy*, but Godfrey moved beyond his earlier imitation because, by the time he began this second poem, he had read Chaucer's *House of Fame*,

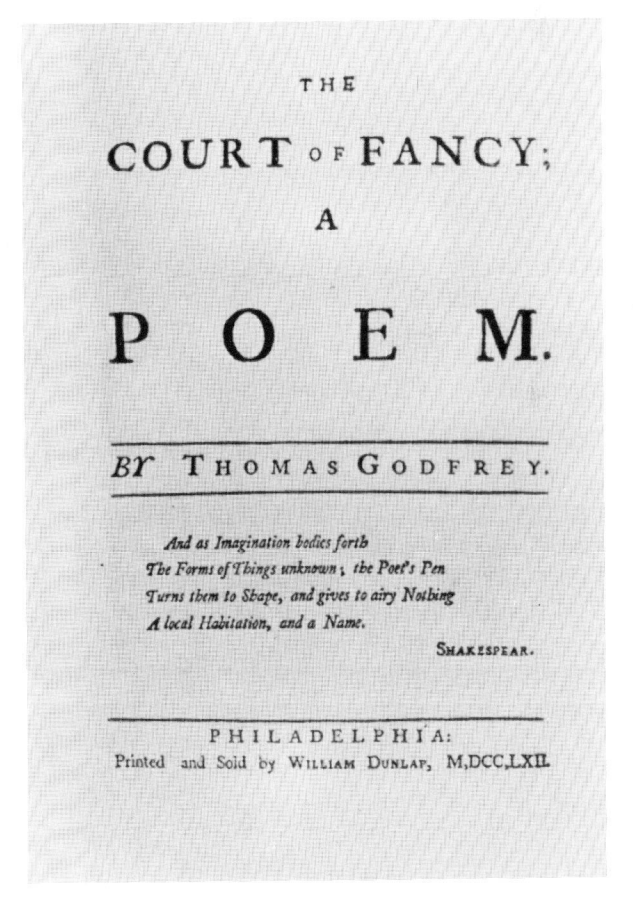

THE

COURT OF FANCY;

A

POEM.

BY THOMAS GODFREY.

And as Imagination bodies forth
The Forms of Things unknown; the Poet's Pen
Turns them to Shape, and gives to airy Nothing
A local Habitation, and a Name.

SHAKESPEAR.

PHILADELPHIA:
Printed and Sold by WILLIAM DUNLAP, M,DCC,LXII.

Title page for Godfrey's first book, in the preface to which he acknowledges "that the Author took the hint of the Transition from the Court of Fancy to that of Delusion, from Chaucer's Poem called the House of Fame . . . ; and that he likewise had Mr. Pope's beautiful Poem on that subject in his eye, at the Time when he compos'd this Piece."

finding in its allegory a way to transform Pope's irony into Whig morality. Apparently his reading of Chaucer encouraged him to try another Chaucerian imitation, and he based "The Assembly of Birds" on *The Parlement of Foules*. "The Assembly of Birds" was left unfinished at his death, but because Godfrey in this poem more obviously kept Chaucer's example in front of him, it has a density of reference missing in much of his other verse. Interestingly enough, since Godfrey begins his imitation at the thirteenth stanza of *The Parlement of Foules* and stops before the courtship of the eagles, he is able to write about imaginary landscapes, visionary escape, and nature without taking on what seems to be for him the disturbing questions about love that Chaucer raises. Godfrey's Chaucerian poems are merely competent, but they do mark him as the first American poet to be influenced by Chaucer, and they signify a willingness, if not the ability, to reach beyond the conventions of eighteenth-century verse.

Godfrey's brief career as a poet spanned the course of the French and Indian War, in which he played a minor role as a lieutenant in the provincial militia posted to a fort on the western frontier, so it is hardly surprising that *Juvenile Poems on Various Subjects* contains a number of verses of patriotic and military themes. The "Epistle to a Friend; from Fort Henry" describes how "darksome forests intercept the sight;/Here fill'd with dread the trembling peasants go" and notices the death of Lord Howe. The use of the word *peasants* indicates that even surrounded by wilderness, he still relied on the conventionalized diction of eighteenth-century poetry to tame an unfamiliar landscape. A pastoral elegy, "To the Memory of General Wolfe," has Damaetas and Lycidas antiphonally mourning "The first of Shepherds, brave *Amintor*'s dead." "Victory. A Poem" and "A Cantata, On Peace. 1763" celebrate the unsuccessful conclusion of the war. "Victory" was published in London in *The Library: or Moral and Critical Magazine for the Year MDCCLXII*, thanks probably to the influence of William Smith. A number of other short lyrics that swell *Juvenile Poems on Various Subjects*—"Dithyrambic on Wine," "The Wish," a perfunctory imitation of Pomfret's "The Choice," "A Night Piece," "A Paraphrase of the First Psalm"—tend to justify the book's titular claim to being a collection of apprentice pieces. But "Amyntor," divided into recitative and airs, and "Cantata, On Peace" seem to have been intended for musical settings, perhaps by Francis Hopkinson, suggesting that Godfrey had a more sophisticated grasp of his art than many contemporary colonial poets.

Godfrey's real accomplishment, however, was his verse tragedy, *The Prince of Parthia,* one of the handful of eighteenth-century American plays to have been staged again in the twentieth century. Just as in his verse Godfrey sought for imaginative control of his situation in transforming conventions, so in his play he turned to historical fable as reflection of the political world he knew. The editor of *Juvenile Poems on Various Subjects,* noting Godfrey's *"licentia poetica"* in dealing with historical facts, apologized, "Such Lapses are not unprecedented among the Poets; and will the more readily admit of an Excuse, when the Voice of History is followed in the Description of Character." Godfrey's play uses historical figures, but ultimately his Parthia is a fiction of his own making, concocted out of literary tradition and the myths of Whig ideology.

The dramatic model for Godfrey's play was Nicholas Rowe's *Tamerlane*, given a Philadelphia production in 1754, and Thomas Clark Pollock has traced his debt to Rowe's play by pointing out the verbal echoes, the similarities of plot, and Rowe's inclusion of Parthian characters. *Tamerlane* was at the time widely viewed as an allegorical eulogy of William III in the guise of Tamerlane and a critique of Louis XIV in the role of Bajazet. Beginning in 1716, it became for sixty years an annual custom to revive *Tamerlane* in London on either 4 November, Williams's birthday, or on 5 November, the anniversary of his landing at Torbay. John Loftis has claimed, "The Frequency with which the play was performed in the first half of the eighteenth century would suggest that it was a chief vehicle by which Whig—and Lockeian—ideas on constitutional theory and religious toleration were disseminated." While the political situation of Godfrey's Philadelphia was very different from that of Rowe's 1701 London, whiggish spectators of *The Prince of Parthia* could still view it in the light of the political conflicts of their time, and like Rowe's play, Godfrey's is not so heavyhandedly allegorical that the dramatic is submerged in the didactic.

The Prince of Parthia demonstrates the evils of despotic power in both the royal family and the kingdom of Parthia. King Artabanus sees himself as if he were a French monarch, one of the "mighty Kings,/whom heav'n delights to favour." His son Vardanes acts "as tho' he were a God," despises both his brother Arsaces and the people, "this many-headed monster multitude," and lives for ambition: "his ambitious soul,/Had it but pow'r to its licen-

> By Authority.
> NEVER PERFORMED BEFORE.
> By the AMERICAN COMPANY,
> At the NEW THEATRE, in Southwark,
> On FRIDAY, the Twenty-Fourth of April, will be presented, A TRAGEDY written by the late ingenious Mr. Thomas Godfrey, of this city, called the
> PRINCE of PARTHIA.
> The PRINCIPAL CHARACTERS by Mr. HALLAM, Mr. DOUGLASS, Mr. WALL, Mr. MORRIS, Mr. ALLYN, Mr. TOMLINSON, Mr. BROADBELT, Mr. GREVILLE, Mrs. DOUGLASS, Mrs. MORRIS, Miss WAINWRIGHT, and Miss CHEER.
> To which will be added, A Ballad Opera called
> The CONTRIVANCES,
> To begin exactly at Seven o'Clock.--Vivant Rex & Regina.

Announcement for the first play by an American to receive a professional production (Pennsylvania Journal, 23 April 1767)

tious wishes, / Would dare dispute with Jove the rule of heav'n." Arsaces, Artabanus's oldest son and the hero of the play, is a successful warrior and the one member of the royal family who is genuinely godlike because of his virtue. The first scene describes his entering the city, fresh from a victory over the Arabians, "Like shining Mars in all the pomp of conquest" as a "prostrate nation" gathers to greet its "bright hope, . . . The Hero friend of humankind." Arsaces has captured Bethas, rebel to the king and father of Evanthe, Arsaces' beloved. When Arsaces asks for mercy for Bethas and permission to marry Evanthe, Artabanus, outraged by resistance to rule and himself desirous of Evanthe, is persuaded by Vardanes and Queen Thermusa, Arsaces' stepmother, that Arsaces plans treachery. Artabanus arrests Arsaces, gives Evanthe to Vardanes, and in turn is murdered by a henchman of Vardanes. In act four Thermusa attempts to kill Arsaces in order to assure the succession to the throne by Vardanes, her son, but she is driven mad by the ghost of Artabanus. In the last act Arsaces kills Vardanes, but his own death is mistakenly reported to Evanthe, who takes poison. Arsaces kills himself when he discovers her corpse, leaving the kingdom to his younger brother, Gotarzes, "a glorious youth."

Conventional wisdom of the age held that unlimited power was dangerous because it was subject only to the will and to the irrational passions; it was, said one of the authors of *Cato's Letters,* "wild and monstrous . . . nor ought it to be entrusted with any mortal man be his intentions ever so upright." The women in *The Prince of Parthia* elicit the passions which subvert the monarchy and lead to the tragic conclusion. Queen Thermusa hates Arsaces for killing her son Vonones, who had rebelled against Artabanus, and she is suspected of manipulating the king "by her will alone. / She rules the realm, her pleasure is a law, / All offices and favours are bestow'd, / As she directs." "The lovely Maid," Evanthe, taken captive in Arsaces' campaign against the Arabians, upsets Thermusa's control of the king's passions, and her presence gives Vardanes, already jealous of the military triumphs of his hated brother, the final incentive he needs to destroy his father and brother in order to seize the throne and the fair captive. Artabanus, Vardanes, and Arsaces become rivals, each in his own fashion, for the favors of Evanthe; Artabanus seeks to obtain her giddy fortune's wheel, / As woman fickle, varying as the wind." He later exults that "The shew of justice gains the changeling croud," but when the soldiers learn "the dreadful tale," they "suddenly, inspir'd with noble rage, / Tore up their ensigns, calling on their leaders / To march them to the city instantly." Immoderate love, fickle as woman, and noble rage justify both the need for government and government itself. If human irrationality demands government, a government which permits the despotic excesses and the conspiracies of the Parthian court in turn demands the "noble rage" which overthrows it in order to restore the state to "virtue's rugged path."

The voice of history that speaks through Godfrey's drama clearly echoes the Whig ideology of the age as described by scholars such as Bernard Bailyn and Caroline Robbins. Godfrey would have found ready to hand a typology of character and situation suitable for his play in contemporary political essays such as William Smith's "Watchman" series, published in the *Pennsylvania Journal* the year before the composition of *The Prince of Parthia*. These essays,

Lewis Hallam, the actor who played Arsaces, Prince of Parthia, in the first professional production of Godfrey's play

through a sort of royal amorous prerogative, Vardanes through Machiavellian schemes and brute force, and Arsaces by means of Virtue, Truth, and a "sympathetic passion." Unregulated in love, the Parthian court is also not restrained by the sort of constitution that protected British subjects from the passions of their monarchs, and the disintegration of the sentimental fabric of fatherly and brotherly love is in turn synonymous with the disintegration of the political fabric of the state. Artabanus's jealousy of the successful Arsaces is manipulated by the schemes of Vardanes, a treasonous conspirator; Arsaces is imprisoned and Artabanus assassinated, but a popular revolt overthrows Vardanes. The progress is clearly from arbitrary will and uncontrolled passion to revolution.

Traditional representatives of will and unreason, the women here represent the ambiguous irrationality—both passion and sentiment—which can either destroy or support rational behavior and the conduct of government. The irrational forces of revenge, envy, and love which variously dominate Thermusa and Evanthe and motivate Artabanus, Vardanes, and Arsaces also define the people at large. Jealous of their loving demonstrations to Arsaces, Vardanes speaks of them slightingly as "This many-headed monster multitude, / Unsteady . . . as

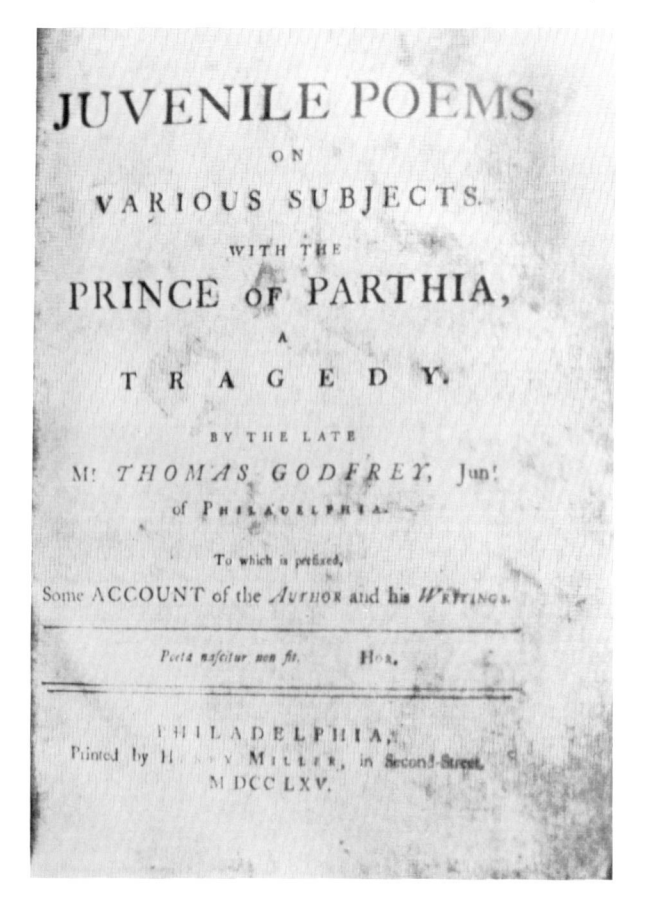

Title page for the posthumously published volume containing Godfrey's verse tragedy, which echoes Whig ideology in its warning about the dangers of unlimited power

aimed at the power of the Quaker oligarchy in the colonial assembly, says Bailyn, "together constitute an exhaustive analysis of the nature of political conspiracy, and anticipate in detail the critical discussion of 'design' that took place during the Revolutionary years." The Watchman warns against "secret Fraud," and "the danger of placing unlimited confidence in any man whatsoever; . . . persons entrusted with power are generally no longer good, than while they are obliged to be so by a strict attention to their conduct." For both Godfrey and Smith's Watchman, absolute monarchs and other unrestrained political agents inhabit a world of suspicion and jealousy; says the Watchman, "If such wicked rulers have only a suspicion of a man, or think him dangerous to their mischievous schemes, it will be full evidence against him." In the face of such a classic Whig model of tyranny, Arsaces's trust in "Virtue, and her fair companion, Truth," is to little avail.

Godfrey's *Prince of Parthia* is not allegory, however, but symbol, a dramatized image collecting and representing his audiences's fears of tyranny, conspiracy, and irrationality while at the same time permitting it to congratulate itself on its British singularity. After seeing or reading this play, Philadelphians fresh from the crisis of the Stamp Act might have told themselves in the words of the Watchman, "But how different is the case among us! . . . should such [men] prevail for a time *above Law* yet, while the constitution remains sound, we may be sure the very act would soon destroy itself, and terminate at length in the utter ruin of the projectors." *The Prince of Parthia* was staged in 1767 not merely because it was the product of a native son, but because, by the standards of eighteenth-century verse tragedy, it was well written, and because it brought together on the stage the deepest political, social, and personal concerns of the time and place. Doomed fathers, corrupt brothers, vengeful mothers, and virtuous sons reverberated in the imaginations of Americans in the decades before the Revolution, and Thomas Godfrey in his one drama spoke to that imagination in ways that his verse never did.

References:

C. Lennart Carlson, "Thomas Godfrey in England," *American Literature,* 7 (October 1935): 302-309;

Archibald Henderson, Introduction to *The Prince of Parthia, A Tragedy, by Thomas Godfrey* (Boston: Little, Brown, 1917), pp. 1-74;

William E. McCarron, Introduction to *A Bicentennial Edition of Thomas Godfrey's The Prince of Parthia* (Colorado Springs: U.S. Air Force Academy, 1976), pp. 1-39;

Walter J. Meserve, *An Emerging Entertainment; The Drama of the American People to 1828* (Bloomington: Indiana University Press, 1977), pp. 47-51;

Thomas Clark Pollock, "Rowe's *Tamerlane* and *The Prince of Parthia,*" *American Literature,* 6 (1934): 158-162;

Frank Shuffleton, "The Voice of History: Thomas Godfrey's *Prince of Parthia* and the American Revolution," *Early American Literature,* 13 (Winter 1978): 12-23;

Henry Bosley Woolf, "Thomas Godfrey: Eighteenth-Century Chaucerian," *American Literature,* 12 (December 1941): 486-490.

Jonas Green
(28 December 1712-11 April 1767)

Robert Micklus
State University of New York at Binghamton

WORKS: Alexander Hamilton, *The History of the Tuesday Club,* includes poems by Green, 3 volumes, edited by Robert Micklus (Williamsburg: Institute of Early American History and Culture, forthcoming 1985).

Jonas Green, "P.P.P.P.P." (purveyor, punster, punchmaker General, printer, and poet of Dr. Alexander Hamilton's Tuesday Club of Annapolis), was known throughout the colonies as public printer of Maryland from 1738 until his death in 1767. During that time he printed the *Maryland Gazette* and published the poetry, essays, and sermons of Maryland's most distinguished men of letters, including the Reverend Thomas Bacon, Henry Callister, the Reverend Thomas Chase, the Reverend Thomas Cradock, the Reverend John Gordon, Dr. Alexander Hamilton, and the Reverend James Sterling. In his own right, Green was one of Maryland's foremost essayists, poets, and humorists.

Like his father before him, Jonas's father, Timothy Green, took up the printing trade in Cambridge, Massachusetts. Shortly after Jonas Green's birth in 1712, Timothy Green moved his family to New London, where he became public printer of Connecticut in 1713. Jonas learned the printing trade from his father. By 1734 he was working for the Boston printing firm of Kneeland and Green (in 1735 he independently printed in Boston the first Hebrew grammar printed in America, *Dickdook leshon gnebreet, A Grammar of the Hebrew Tongue*), and by 1736 he was working for Andrew Bradford in Philadelphia. Green married Anne Catherine Hoof on 25 April 1738, and having been appointed public printer of Maryland, he and his wife moved to Annapolis, borrowing from friends such as Benjamin Franklin to make ends meet. In 1745 he began publishing the *Maryland Gazette*, and for the next twenty years under his guidance the *Gazette* examined—sometimes soberly, often whimsically—the more prominent scientific, political, religious, and literary issues of the day. Among the more humorous literary disputes waged in the *Gazette* was the furious literary battle between the "Annapolis Wits" (Green, Hamilton, and other Tuesday Club members) and the "Baltimore Bards" (Thomas Chase and Thomas Cradock). This great war of wits broke out when "Bard Mevius" (Cradock) circulated some verses he had written on the ladies' charms while viewing them a posteriori in church (instead of listening to Whitefield rant), provoking the Tuesday Club members to pen "An Infallible Receipt to cure the afflicting and epidemical Distempers of Love, and the Poetical Itch" (*Maryland Gazette,* 17 December 1745). As "Theophilus Polypharmacus" Hamilton continued the literary feud in the 4 February 1745/6, issue of the *Gazette,* then delivered the crowning blow against "Bard Bavius" (Chase) in the 18 March 1745/6, issue, posting a reward for the capture of "a dapper-witted, finical Fopling, known by the Name of Bard, alias Bavius," whose "Discourse is entirely excrementitious, and [who] throws out his Sarcasms, as a Scavenger would do Tubs of Sir-Reverence, for his whole Talk and especially his Compositions turn upon B-sh-tt-ng and being B-sh-t, treading upon a T--d, pulling it out of his own Bosom and dropping it into a Lady's, eating and chewing it as one would do a Sugar Plumb. He is a nasty Fellow, for the Sphincter Ani, or Bum Muscle, in him being preternaturally relaxed, he is very apt to bewray himself in Company, and being somewhat foolish, is insensible of his Misbehaviour, and lays all the blame upon others." Among the other more memorable pieces that Green printed in the *Maryland Gazette* were Hamilton's humorous essay on 'the commonplace greeting, "What's News?" (7 January 1746); the speech of the "Honourable Sir William Gooch . . . to the General Assembly" (14 April 1747), which provoked a free-verse parody by Franklin (16 June 1747), and Franklin's "The Speech of Miss Polly Baker" (11 August 1747).

Aside from his duties as editor of the *Maryland Gazette* and public printer, Green was also a first-rate essayist, poet, and humorist. Several of his essays appeared in the *Gazette,* including a piece signed "Philo P.P.P." that he littered with as many Ps as possible (4 September 1751) and his splendid essay on impudence in the 3 May 1753 issue. At least

Alexander Hamilton's caricature of Jonas Green, from the manuscript for The History of the Tuesday Club *(The Milton S. Eisenhower Library, The Johns Hopkins University)*

one poem in the *Gazette*, a "Memorandum for a Seine Hauling, in Severn River," is probably Green's. But the greatest storehouse of Green's wit is Hamilton's 1,900 page mock-epic, *The History of the Tuesday Club*. Green joined the Tuesday Club on 2 February 1747/8. Upon his admission, Hamilton characterized him in *The History of the Tuesday Club* as follows: "This Gentleman is of a middle Stature, inclinable to fat, round faced, small lively eyes, from which, as from two oriental portals, incessantly dart the dawning rays of wit and humor, with a considerable mixture of the amorous leer, in his countenance he wears a constant Smile, having never been once seen to frown; . . . he is a very great admirer, Improver and encourager of wit, humor and drollery, and is fond of that Sort of poetry which is called Doggrell, in which he is himself a very great proficient, and confines his genius chiefly to it, tho sometimes he cannot help emitting some flashes of the true Sublime, in his Club Compositions; . . . in fine, to sum up all he is really a good humored, smooth tempered, merry, jocose, and innofensive companion, a man of the most happy Clubical Genius that ever was known, and a great promoter Improver and encourager of Clubific felicity, for were there 50 Clubs in the place, he'd be a member of every one of them...." For his exceptional knack at doggerel verse, the Tuesday Club members proclaimed Green poet laureate of the club—indeed, of all America—and warned Colley Cibber that even as his star was setting in the East a new star was rising in the West to take his place.

Green took every opportunity to display his extraordinary talents in club, and Hamilton carefully preserved his most memorable performances in *The History of the Tuesday Club*. Especially eloquent was his "Heroic Poem, On the late Tragical Scene acted in the bed chamber, of the Right Honorable Nasifer, Lord president of the ancient and Honorable Tuesday Club," a delightful mock-epic about Lord Jole's (Charles Cole's) miraculous escape from thieves, with the aid of his noble valet de chambre, Don John Charlotto (Cole's servant, John Charlette). After retiring for the night, Jole is rudely awakened by a scoundrel who grips his lordship by the throat, shoves a pistol in his face, and says, "Dam your blood, you old Curmudgeon,/ Tis not for nought, I've scald your Lodging,/ Where is your money? quickly tell,/ Or 'S blood, I'll blow your Soul to hell." The Immortal Jole lets out "many a Lamentable Groan,/ That would have pierc'd a heart of Stone," which arouses his man Don John,

> And peeping slily thro' a breach in
> The Gavel of his Lordship's kitchen,
> He spied a rogue below, expecting,
> Th'event of what within was acting,
> Who seeing John's courageous face,
> In such an unsuspected place,
> Swore "Dam' ye, speak, or make a noise,
> I'll blow your brains out in a trice."
> "Oho! quoth John, and is it so,
> Then faith 'tis time for me to go."
> Then stepping back, he seizd the gun,
> And quickly to the port hole run,
> Where, taking neither aim nor mark,
> He boldly fir'd her in the dark,
> For, as the rusty gun had not,
> Been loaded with or Slug, or Shot,
> He wisely judg'd 'twas all the same,
> To shoot at random as to aim.

Don John's random shot saves the day, frightening off both thieves, and prompting Green to compare him to Hector, Achilles, Hercules, Sampson, and anyone else he can think of. Judging from Green's ludicrous poem, one might never suppose that the event took place; yet Cole's life was actually threatened by two thieves who had been terrorizing the citizens of Annapolis.

Green wrote many such verses for the Tuesday Club, most of them anniversary odes or condolatory verses to the president (who was periodically besieged by fits of indignation or the gout). Cole's refusal to honor the club with his presence inspires Jonathan Grog (Green's persona in *The History of the Tuesday Club*) to pen "The Clubs Lamentation for the Loss of their President," which includes these lamentable stanzas:

> The Birds Lament the general loss,
>   The beasts in Concert groan,
> The little fish pop up their heads
>   And cry alas! he's gone.
> Oft when with beating breasts we cry,
>   O Jole, where art thou, where,
> Eccho, from each resounding hill
>   Replies he is not here.
>
> With each longstanding member round
>   All at this dead of night,
> Hoping they wish, & wishing hope
>   Of Jole to have a Sight,
> Singing they weep, and weeping sing
>   The Loss of Jole away,
> O Lamentable, and forsooth!
>   Alack! and wail a day.

Green wrote or had a hand in writing many other poems for the Tuesday Club, including anniversary odes; the club's "Lugubris Cantus," "Carmen Seculare," and "Carmen Dolorosum"; "The Epicaedion of the Ancient Tuesday Club, on the mournful Indisposition of Nasifer Jole Esqr: their honorable President"; his "Heroic Poem" in three cantos; his "Tragical and Heroic Episode on the Club Tobacco box"; and his "Congratulatory Ode, On the Return of the Honorable Mr President Jole to his Club" and "Congratulatory Pindaric Ode" on Jole's escape from the gout. These humorous verses, coupled with his contributions to the *Maryland Gazette* and publication of that paper for over twenty years, placed Green at the head of Maryland culture and wit.

Reference:

J. A. Leo Lemay, *Men of Letters in Colonial Maryland* (Knoxville: University of Tennessee Press, 1972), pp. 193-212.

Joseph Green
(1706-11 December 1780)

David Robinson
Oregon State University

BOOKS: *Entertainment for a Winter's Evening: Being a Full and True Account of a Very Strange and Wonderful Sight Seen in Boston, on the Twenty-seventh of December, at noon-day . . .*, as the Hon'ble B. B. Esq. (Boston: Printed & sold by G. Rogers, 1750);

The Grand Arcanum Detected; Or a Wonderful Phenomenon Explained, Which Has Baffled the Scrutiny of Many Ages, as Phil Arcanos, Gent., Student in Astrology (Boston, 1755);

An Eclogue Sacred to the Memory of the Rev. Dr. Jonathan Mayhew, Who Departed this Life July 9th, Anno Salutis Humane 1766 . . ., attributed to Green (Boston: Printed by Thomas & John Fleet, 1766).

OTHER: "A Parody on a Hymn by Mather Byles" and "The Poet's Lamentation for the Loss of His Cat," *London Magazine,* 2 (November 1733): 579-580;

"The Disappointed Cooper," in "Joseph Green's Satirical Poem on the Great Awakening," by J. A. Leo Lemay, *Resources for American Literary Study,* 4 (Autumn 1974): 173-183.

Joseph Green, Boston wit and satirical poet, was best known for his humorous verse comments on public figures and events in eighteenth-century New England. A comic epitaph, composed for him by an anonymous friend, captured his reputation for wit:

> Siste Viator, here lies one,
> Whose life was whim, whose soul was pun,
> And if you go too near his hearse
> He'll joke you, both in prose and verse.

Green was born in Boston, and, after he received his A.B. degree from Harvard in 1726, he began a prosperous career in Boston as a merchant and for a time a distiller. While little is known about his personal life, his verse suggests that he was a shrewd social observer with a tendency to wry mockery. His political leanings were Loyalist, and he was strongly enough identified with opposition

Portrait by John Singleton Copley (Museum of Fine Arts, Boston)

to the Revolution that in 1775 he was forced to abandon his home in Boston and flee to England, where he lived the last five years of his life in exile.

Green wrote much of his verse in the then-popular Hudibrastic style of galloping couplets, although his "A Parody on a Hymn by Mather Byles" (*London Magazine,* 1733), the first verse that can be definitely attributed to him, echoes the quatrains of Byles's "A Psalm at Sea," which it burlesques. In his satire, Green turned Byles's praise of the wonders

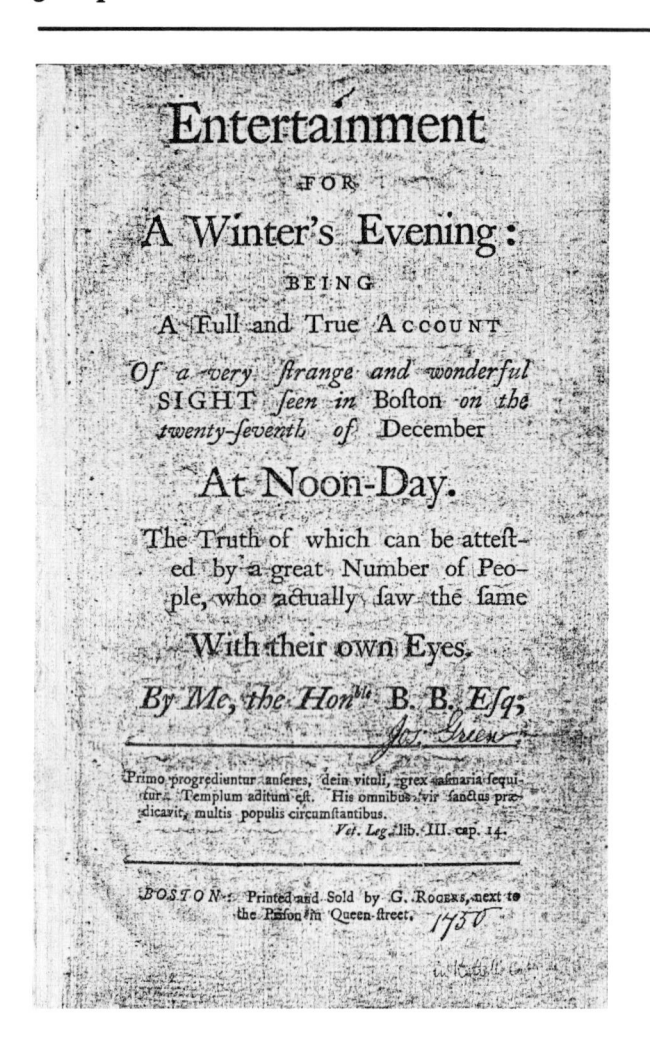

Title page for Green's satire on the Free Masons (courtesy of the Harris Collection of American Poetry and Plays at Brown University)

of the sea into an evocation of seasickness. Green also added a sly reference to rum trading with the Indians, which was part of the purpose of the voyage that Byles had taken with Massachusetts Governor Jonathan Belcher. Byles's motives were innocent, but Green used this aspect of the voyage satirically. The popularity of Green's poem sparked a battle of wits, including an answering parody by Byles, which characterized Green's poem as "doggerell" composed for "his flip-drinking brethren." Probably in response, Green composed "The Poet's Lamentation for the Loss of his Cat," which satirized the fact that Byles called his favorite cat his "muse." In Green's poem, the cat "purr'd in metre" and "mew'd in rhyme." When even she failed to inspire Byles, Green wrote, he "stole a line from *Pope* or *Addison*."

Always keen to comment on current affairs, he satirized the unpopular Governor Belcher, and only recently his satire of the Great Awakening, "The Disappointed Cooper"(written in 1743), has been brought to light by J. A. Leo Lemay. In it, Green satirized one of the leading proponents of the Awakening, Rev. William Cooper, by depicting the "*New Work,* the *Great Work,* the *Good Work*" of the revival as the construction of a huge barrel. In the end, the work collapses because of the ineptness of Cooper at his trade. Perhaps Green's most popular poem was his satire of a meeting and procession of Free Masons, *Entertainment for a Winter's Evening . . .* (1750). Packed with references to particular people, the poem makes fun of the fact that the procession moved from a church to a tavern. Green also wryly comments on the fraternal love which holds the group together with the following remark from the Master of the Lodge, a parson: " 'Tis *Love,* pure *Love* cements the whole,/*Love*—of the *Bottle* and the *Bowl.*" Green followed this poem with a less successful sequel, *The Grand Arcanum Detected . . .* (1755), in which he depicts the masons engaging in a drunken tavern brawl.

Green's poetry is of largely historical interest, and his reputation as "the foremost wit of his day" suggests to the modern reader that wit was at something of a premium in eighteenth-century Boston. Still, Green's work is an important example of opposition to the religious and political trends of the times, and his voice is a reminder that there were demurrers to the mood of those times.

References:

Thomas V. Duggan, "Joseph Green—The Boston Butler," M.A. thesis, Columbia University, 1941;

Samuel Kettell, ed., *Specimens of American Poetry, with Critical and Biographical Notices,* 3 volumes (1829; republished, New York: Blom, 1967), I: 133-139;

Samuel L. Knapp, *Sketches of Eminent Lawyers, Statesmen, and Men of Letters* (Boston: Richardson & Lord, 1821), pp. 129-138;

J. A. Leo Lemay, "Joseph Green's Satirical Poem on the Great Awakening," *Resources for American Literary Study,* 4 (Autumn 1974): 173-183.

Alexander Hamilton
(26 September 1712-13 May 1756)

Robert Micklus
State University of New York at Binghamton

BOOKS: *A Defence of Dr. Thomson's Discourse on the Preparation of the Body for the Small Pox* (Philadelphia: Printed by William Bradford, 1751);

Hamilton's Itinerarium: being a narrative of a Journey from Annapolis, Maryland, through Delaware, Pennsylvania, New York, New Jersey, Connecticut, Rhode Island, Massachusetts and New Hampshire, from May to September, 1744, edited by Albert Bushnell Hart (St. Louis: Printed for private distribution by W. K. Bixby, 1907); republished as *Gentleman's Progress: The Itinerarium of Dr. Alexander Hamilton, 1744*, edited by Carl Bridenbaugh (Chapel Hill: University of North Carolina Press, 1948);

The History of the Tuesday Club, 3 volumes, edited by Robert Micklus (Williamsburg: Institute of Early American History and Culture, forthcoming 1985).

PERIODICAL PUBLICATIONS: "An Infallible Receipt to cure the afflicting and epidemical Distempers of Love, and the Poetical Itch," *Maryland Gazette*, 17 December 1745;

A satire on a poem ("The Baltimore Belles," by Thomas Chase and Thomas Cradock), as Theophilus Polypharmacus, *Maryland Gazette*, 4 February 1745/6;

A mock advertisement for the runaway idiot, Bard Bavius, as Jehoiakim Jerkum, *Maryland Gazette*, 18 March 1745/6;

"What News?," *Maryland Gazette*, 7 January 1746;

A humorous attack against idleness, as Publius Agricola, *Maryland Gazette*, 16 December 1746;

A humorous defense of luxury, as Publius Agricola, *Maryland Gazette*, 23 December 1746;

An essay on the proper objects of ridicule, anonymous, *Maryland Gazette*, 17 February 1748;

A humorous essay on writings that appeared in the *Maryland Gazette*, as Don Francisco de Quevedo Villegas, *Maryland Gazette*, 28 June 1748.

Author of numerous essays, the *Itinerarium* (written in 1744), and *The History of the Tuesday Club* (written in 1755), and guiding genius of colonial Maryland's foremost gentleman's club, the Tuesday Club of Annapolis, Dr. Alexander Hamilton was one of colonial America's most distinguished writers and wits.

Hamilton was born on 26 September 1712 in Edinburgh, where his father, the Reverend William Hamilton, was principal of the University of Edinburgh. Like his oldest brother, Dr. John Hamilton, Alexander Hamilton studied medicine at the University of Edinburgh before leaving for America in 1739 to establish his practice. During his first summer in Maryland, Hamilton became ill, showing signs of the consumption that would eventually cause his death. To escape the muggy Maryland climate, Hamilton at first thought of returning to Great Britain, but he decided instead to set out on a four-month horseback journey with his Negro slave, Dromo, from Annapolis, Maryland, to York, Maine, and back. The trip lasted from 30 May to 27 September 1744 and is vividly related in Hamilton's amusing travel diary, the *Itinerarium*, perhaps the best portrait extant of mid-eighteenth-century colonial American life. In the *Itinerarium* Hamilton colorfully recaptured the scenery, the dialects and colloquialisms, the folk sayings and proverbs, the character types, and the native wit and humor of the regions he visited. Among the more amusing conversations he recorded was a dialogue that passed between him and an "inquisitive rustick"—a type that Hamilton found especially humorous and obnoxious—who traveled with him on the road to Portsmouth, New Hampshire:

> His questions were all stated in the rustick civil stile. "Pray sir, if I may be so bold, where are you going?" "Prithee, friend," says I, "where are you going?" "Why, I go along the road here a little way." "So do I, friend," replied I. "But may I presume, sir, whence do you come?" "And from whence do you come, friend?" says I. "Pardon me, from John Singleton's farm," replied he, "with a bag of oats." "And I come from Maryland," said I, "with a portmanteau and baggage." "Maryland!" said my companion, "where the devil is

Alexander Hamilton's self-caricature, from the manuscript for The History of the Tuesday Club *(The Milton S. Eisenhower Library, The Johns Hopkins University)*

that there place? I have never heard of it. But pray, sir, may I be so free as to ask your name?" "And may I be so bold as to ask yours, friend?" said I. "Mine is Jerry Jacobs, att your service," replied he. I told him that mine was Bombast Huynhym van Helmont, att his service. "A strange name indeed; belike your a Dutchman, sir,—a captain of a ship, belike." "No, friend," says I, "I am a High German alchymist." "Bless us! You don't say so; that's a trade I never heard of; what may you deal in sir?" "I sell air," said I. "Air," said he, "damn it, a strange commodity. I'd thank you for some wholesom air to cure my fevers which have held me these two months."

Soon after Hamilton's return to Annapolis, Jonas Green began publishing the *Maryland Gazette*. Hamilton welcomed the opportunity to indulge the wit that had hitherto been confined to the *Itinerarium* and his letters. First he instigated the mock literary war between the "Annapolis Wits" (Hamilton, Green, and other Tuesday Club members) and the "Baltimore Bards" (Thomas Chase and Thomas Cradock) with pieces for the *Gazette* that included "An Infallible Receipt to cure the afflicting and epidemical Distempers of Love, and the Poetical Itch" (17 December 1745), a humorous piece signed "Theophilus Polypharmacus" (4 February 1745/6), and a mock advertisement for the capture of the runaway idiot "Bard Bavius" (Chase) in the 18 March 1745/6 issue, which describes Bavius's speech as "frothy and incoherent, inclining more to Rhime than Reason, he talks much of the Ladies, whom he stiles Belles, and pretending to aim at Praise, he unhappily slides into Satyr.... His Discourse is entirely excrementitious, and he throws out his Sarcasms, as a Scavenger would do Tubs of Sir-Reverence, for his whole Talk and especially his Compositions turn upon B-sh-tt-ng and being B-sh-t, treading upon a T--d, pulling it out of his own Bosom and dropping it into a Lady's, eating and chewing it as one would do a Sugar Plumb. He is a nasty Fellow, for the Sphincter Ani, or Bum Muscle, in him being preternaturally relaxed, he is very apt to bewray himself in Company, and being somewhat foolish, is insensible of his Misbehaviour, and lays all the blame upon others...."

Hamilton had several other essays published in the *Maryland Gazette*, including his whimsical essay "What News?" (7 January 1746), which satirizes the rustic manners and inquisitiveness of the emerging democratic American; his "Publius Agricola" essays (16 December and 23 December 1746), in which he first attacks and then defends luxury; and his "Quevedo" essay (28 June 1748), which evaluates and satirizes the writings that appeared in the first three years of the *Maryland Gazette*.

But Hamilton will be remembered especially as founder of the Tuesday Club of Annapolis and author of *The History of the Tuesday Club*, a 19,000-page mock epic in prose. The Tuesday Club met in Annapolis from 14 May 1745, when Hamilton organized the club and began keeping its minutes, to 11 February 1756, when it disbanded shortly before his death. During those eleven years almost everyone of importance in the Chesapeake Bay area either joined or visited the Tuesday Club. At its first meeting, the club consisted of only seven members in addition to Hamilton: Witham Marshe (died 1765), secretary to the Maryland Commissioners at the treaty of Lancaster in 1744 with the Six Indian Nations; William Cumming (circa 1696-1752), a Scottish immigrant who had been arrested as a Jacobite rebel and transported to America, where he established himself as a lawyer; the Reverend John Gordon (died 1790), pastor of St. Anne's in Annapolis and later of St. Michael's in Talbot County; William Rogers (1699-1749), clerk of the Prerogative Office in Annapolis; Robert Gordon (circa 1676-1753), an Annapolis merchant, judge of the Provincial court, and commissioner of the Loan Office; John Lomas (died 1757), an Annapolis merchant; and John Bullen (died 1764), captain of the Annapolis Independent Company, alderman, and commissioner of the Paper Currency Office. As the Tuesday Club grew, its membership list expanded to include such men as the Reverend Thomas Bacon (1700?-1768), rector of St. Peter's in Talbot County, a musician, and one of colonial Maryland's most prolific authors; Anthony Bacon, M.P., Thomas Bacon's brother and one of England's wealthiest tycoons; Beale Bordley (1727-1804), a Maryland judge, author, and member of the American Philosophical Society; the Reverend Thomas Cradock (1718-1770), a prominent Maryland clergyman and author; William Fitzhugh (circa 1722-1798), colonel and close friend of George Washington's; Jonas Green (1712-1767), public printer of Maryland, poet, and publisher of the *Maryland Gazette;* John Hesselius (1728-1778), a prolific painter; the Reverend Alexander Malcolm (died 1763), Maryland clergyman, author, and musician; Robert Morris (died 1750), father of the most distinguished merchant of colonial America; the Reverend Archibald Spencer (1698?-1760), minister, physician, and lecturer; the Reverend James Sterling (1701-1763), clergyman, poet, and playwright; and John Wollaston, a prominent eighteenth-century portrait painter from New York to Virginia. The list also includes many of colonial Maryland's most distinguished persons and visitors such as Benjamin Franklin. All comers were welcome except for "those solitary, moaping, morose, humdrum fellows, who evade, shun, run and fly, from all company, hate the Sight of men, as if they were Tygers, bears, Serpents, hobgoblins, Rhinoceroses and Panthers...." " When I see a fellow of this Stamp," Hamilton wrote, "I imagine I behold a black cloud, rising from the dirty blustering South east, saturated with hollow murmuring smouldering blasts, sending before it grumbling, tumbling, jumbling thunder, and infectious puffs of pestiential Steams, darkening the face of the fair day with polluted murky and stiffling vapors, exhalations and damps, saturated, loaded, impregnated and overcharged, with morbific sulphureous atoms, bursting from the mouth of Tartarus it self."

As secretary of the Tuesday Club, Hamilton carefully recorded the club minutes from 1745 until 1756, expanded the minutes into the Tuesday Club "Record Book," and fictionalized the club's proceedings in *The History of the Tuesday Club*. The history is a splendid gauge of the temper of social and literary wit of eighteenth-century America and the finest mock jeremiad in colonial literature.

"Histories founded upon truth, and wrote in a plain, easie and natural Stile," Hamilton soberly announces in the opening pages of *The History of the Tuesday Club,* "are Sirloins of beef plainly dressed, wholesome, hearty and nourishing to a robust and healthy Stomach, but those erected upon fiction, and stuffed with Bombast and fustian phrases, are vapid, windy, unwholsom and adulterated with your damn'd sauces and pickles, fitted only for crazy and luxurious apetites.... The History which I am now about to present ... is none of your vamped up Frenchified pieces of Cookery, it is a solid and serious performance, plain and homely, and withal true, every article thereof, being copied exactly from nature and the life." While Hamilton dutifully establishes his adherence to plainness and truth, his declaration of intent is obviously a ruse, facetiously designed to sidetrack those who might denounce *The History of the Tuesday Club* as the trashy offspring of a luxurious age. Hamilton sought to deflate this kind of oppressive sobriety by presenting in *The History of the Tuesday Club* an exaggerated fictional version of the club's proceedings, stuffed with bombast, doggerel, and assorted absurdities. His inflated, fanciful account of the club's degeneration from primitive simplicity to luxury is designed to help his readers discover the truth in laughter.

The first of the fourteen books that compose *The History of the Tuesday Club* celebrates antiquity and traces the Tuesday Club back to "the ancient and venerable Tuesday (or whin bush) Club of Laneric, in the ancient kingdom of Scotland, which was in its highest Glory, about two centuries before the usurpation of Oliver Cromwel, in the Presidentship of the venerable Congallus de Rutherin." During those halcyon days, the club included "350 Living members," all of whom remembered from oral tradition the heroic deeds of their godlike progenitors, men such as the venerable Fethelmach, "famed for having invented the high relished Dish of Cock-a-leekie, and the comfortable Soup called Dads and Blads." Since Fethelmach's day, the club could boast of such distinguished men as Daniel Hog, treasurer from 1569 to 1574, when he was "expelled the Club, for perpetual sleeping and loud snoring," and Laughlan McLean, master of ceremonies from 1534 to 1552, when he was "deposed for whoring" and succeeded by Jervais Fuckater, who was "killd by an Irishman for excessive farting and belching in Company."

Those were the days of grandeur, the days of heroic frugality and primitive simplicity when the members even enforced a law requiring them to dine on nothing but bread and cheese. "This Law," Hamilton observes, "the ancient and Honorable Tuesday Club of Annapolis at first adopted, in Laudable Imitation of their patrons of the whin bush, but Luxury by degrees crept in among them." Hamilton forebodingly remarks that "Luxury is a destructive thing, and sooner or later fatal to every society or Community that once admits of it; as having a tendency to introduce abject Slavery, by means of its being a promoter of bribery and Corruption." Even the greatest civilizations, he demonstrates, have been consumed by the voracious maw of luxury. "We may thence see & beware of the danger of admitting luxury into any Society, ... and tho' the ancient and honorable Tuesday Club, of Annapolis, be one of the wisest Clubs that ever yet appeared, yet she may see the time, when her constitution will feel the Smart of admitting Luxury."

Hamilton temporarily abandons this ungrateful topic and traces the club's distinguished genealogy from the Whin-Bush Club of Lanneric to the Red-House Club of Annapolis, founded by Mr. George Neilson. A figure of heroic proportions, the great Mr. Neilson has forced many a man to submit "to the prowess of his Invincible Arm," although on one extraordinary occasion "a Gygantic Champion, clapped him in a hamper ... and throwing him headlong into the river, he narrowly escaped a drowning, and after he was dragged out of the water, he remained as mute as a fish, and made no words of the matter." While attending the Royalist Clubs of early Annapolis, Mr. Neilson patiently awaited the right opportunity to establish his own club, meanwhile suffering numerous hardships and abuses "to bring about this laudable Scheme, for clubical liberty; they would call him a hundred abusive names in half an hour, such as lousy scabby scot, poor rascally pedlar, itchified Son of a bitch, Scoundrel, knave, fool, ass, Goose, blockhead, ugly beetle browd, squint eyed, Lenteren Jaw'd, Jacobitish, Skip kennel Scrub, nasty, blewbellied, blanket ars'd, hip-shotten, maggot eaten, round about, Snuff besmeard, flyblown Son of a whore, and conclude all, with the epithet of bloodthirsty traitor and Rebel and No-nation Spawn of vexation." Mr. Neilson

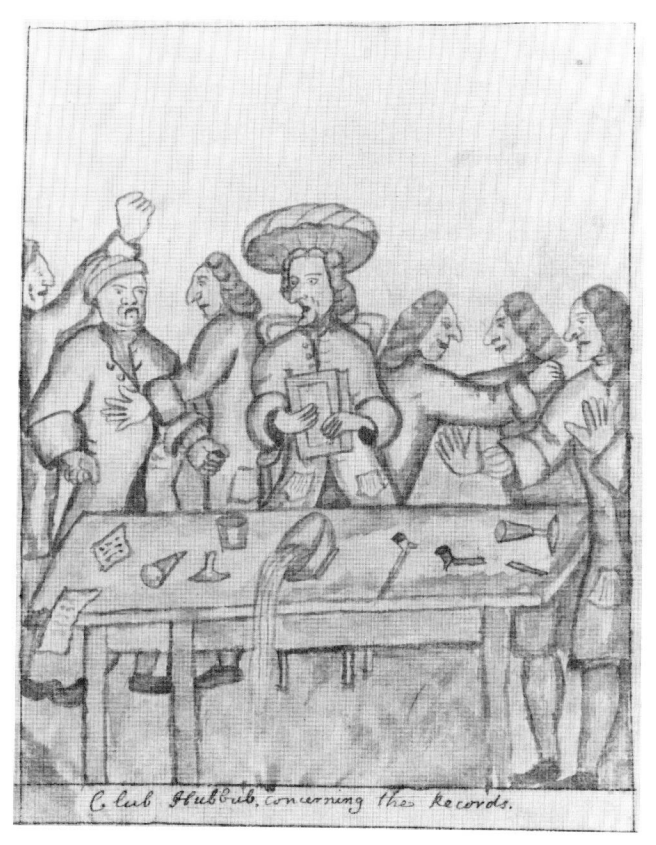

Drawings by Hamilton, from the manuscript for The History of the Tuesday Club *(The Milton S. Eisenhower Library, The Johns Hopkins University)*

swallowed his pride in the face of this rude usage until one night when, "a little warmed with liquor," he heroically revolted against his oppressors. But "his majesties guards at last seized upon Mr. Neilson, . . . stuffed his mouth full of tallow and Candle wick, wrung his nose, . . . and threw him headlong into a puddle." Shortly after Mr. Neilson's ouster, a tremendous schism occurred in the Royalist Clubs, leading to a veritable throng of Neilsonists and enabling him to establish the Red-House Club of Annapolis. Like its Scottish predecessor, the Red-House Club maintained "few and simple" regulations, designed "chiefly to exclude luxury and excess in eatables and drinkables, to prevent wranglings and disputes and all disorders of that Sort, an example worthy the Imitation of all Clubs."

Following the death of the great Mr. Neilson, the Red-House Club disbanded and its place of meeting was converted to a nunnery, but out of its remains sprang the Ugly Club, the immediate progenitor of the Tuesday Club. The Ugly Club upheld the noble tradition of simplicity, for it was "solely upon account of the Slovenliness of the members, . . . their affectation of odd gestures, and the dirtiness and unseemliness of the Club room, that this Society had the name of the Ugly Club." Still, "wrangles, debates and disputes . . . led this Club into parties," and eventually "from a numerous Club, it dwindled to nothing, and at last expired."

Under the guidance of a minor Ugly Club member, Loquacious Scribble (Hamilton's persona), the ancient and honorable Tuesday Club finally gained a firm footing in Annapolis. At their first meeting, on 14 May 1745, the club passed the following laws "with great wisdom and Sagacity":

Law I That the meeting of the Club be weekly, at the members houses, by turns, thro' out the year, upon Tuesday evening.

Law II The Steward for the time being, shall provide a gammon of bacon, or any other one dish of dressed vittles and no more.

Law III No Liquor shall be made, prepared or produced after eleven o clock at night, and every Member shall be at liberty to retire at pleasure.

Law IV No members shall be admitted without the concurring consent, of the whole Club, and after such admission, the member shall serve as Steward next meeting.

Like Law VI (passed later), stating that "such as are batchelor members of the Club may have a Cheese upon one Side board, instead of dress'd vittles," these laws displayed the singular "frugality and moderation" that sustained the club during its earliest days. "How much like the simple frugality of the Golden age was this," Hamilton recalls, "and how different from that luxury and profuseness that prevails in most of our moderen Clubs."

But these days were short-lived. "Happy, O happy had it been for this ancient and honorable Club," Hamilton moans, "had they always kept to this golden mean of frugality and temperance, but the mode soon changed, and Luxury crept in by degrees." In place of the "heroic frugality" that governed the club's first meetings, "Luxury began to peep from behind the Scene, and prepare for her pompous entry upon this Clubical Stage, and . . . this bold actress took one great Stride at her first advance, and proceeded afterwards, with a *grand pas,* to expell Simplicity and plainness from the Club, and to introduce, pomp show and extravagance, her constant pages and attendants, while [Ceremony],her companion and coactor, with the like buskined pride, plaid the part of a momus or mimic, . . . introducing certain fantastical punctillios, forms and modes, by which he so disguised and poisoned the manners and behavior of the long standing members, . . . that they did in no manner seem to be the same persons they were at their first Institution." As they lose touch with their primitive simplicity, the longstanding members gradually display all of the vices associated with luxury during the eighteenth century. Because *luxury* meant extravagance in one's domestic *and* political behavior, it implied not only drunkenness, gluttony, lust, avarice, ceremony, vanity, effeminacy, and affectation, but also ambition, pride, enervation, bribery, corruption, and subjection. The first set of vices, many feared, inevitably led to the second set. In a humorous way, that is precisely what happens in *The History of the Tuesday Club*.

Hamilton's extravagant account of the club's degeneration is learned, witty, and often downright rollicking. As any boon club companion would attest, those dull, drivelling moralizers who moaned about degeneracy and stifled merriment were the bane of society, not simply because they spoiled a good time, but because they failed to recognize how essential a little luxury was to most colonists' mental well-being. To men such as Hamilton, the efforts a society such as the Tuesday Club made to simulate British culture served as a buttress against the jeremiads that deluged the South during the mid-eighteenth century, and the history the good doctor left behind of that club serves as a lasting reminder that the best antidote to Jeremiahs of any age is laughter.

References:

Elaine G. Breslaw, "Dr. Alexander Hamilton and the Enlightenment in Maryland," Ph.D. dissertation, University of Maryland, 1973;

Breslaw, "Wit, Whimsy, and Politics: The Uses of Satire by the Tuesday Club of Annapolis, 1744-1756," *William and Mary Quarterly,* third series, 32 (April 1975): 295-306;

J. A. Leo Lemay, *Men of Letters in Colonial Maryland* (Knoxville: University of Tennessee Press, 1972), pp. 213-256;

Robert Micklus, "Dr. Alexander Hamilton's 'Modest Proposal,'" *Early American Literature,* 16 (Fall 1981): 107-132;

Micklus, "'The History of the Tuesday Club': A Mock-Jeremiad of the Colonial South," *William and Mary Quarterly,* third series, 40 (January 1983): 42-61.

Papers:

The John Work Garrett Library in Baltimore has the minutes of the Tuesday Club and the manuscript for *The History of the Tuesday Club.* The Tuesday Club "Record Book" is at the Maryland Historical Society.

Jupiter Hammon
(17 October 1711-died between 1790 and 1806)

Sondra A. O'Neale
Emory University

BOOKS: *An Essay on the Ten Virgins* (Hartford: Printed by Hudson & Goodwin, 1779);

A Winter Piece: Being a Serious Exhortation, with a Call to the Unconverted: and a Short Contemplation on the Death of Jesus Christ (Hartford, Conn.: Printed by Hudson and Goodwin?, 1782);

An Evening's Improvement: Shewing the Necessity of beholding the Lamb of God, To Which is Added, A Dialogue, Entitled, The Kind Master and Dutiful Servant (Hartford: Printed by Hudson & Goodwin?, circa 1783);

An Address to the Negroes in the State of New-York (New York: Printed by Carroll & Patterson, 1787).

Collection: *America's First Negro Poet: The Complete Work of Jupiter Hammon of Long Island,* edited by Stanley Austin Ramsom, Jr. (Port Washington, N.Y.: Kennikat Press, 1970).

Jupiter Hammon, the first American of African descent to publish poetry and prose in the Western world, was born a slave at the aristocratic Lloyd Manor in Oyster Bay, Long Island, New York, on 17 October 1711. His life spanned the eighteenth century, and his work was forged through arduous indigenous education and set forth in the midst of a classed and autocratic America, which, although teeming with change, still placed the Black slave on the lowest socioeconomic rung and allowed him no opportunity for advancement. A slave's access to education was only tolerated, even on Northern plantations, when literacy would serve the master in some way. Publication was impossible without the master's permission and without broad support from the white community, including authentication of the slave's authorship. Further, colonists greatly resisted any community network among slaves, especially one that extended beyond the borders of local hamlets. Yet Hammon met the challenge of these obstacles to become the first slave in the modern world to publish his works and, even though he was writing about slavery, to reach a vast audience of servants and colonists alike.

Although certainty is impossible because the Lloyds kept scant records of other data pertinent to the slaves' lives, it is probable that Hammon's mother and father arrived with the first shipment of slave imports at the Lloyd estate in the summer of 1687. The second Lloyd son, John Lloyd I, was born in the same year as Jupiter Hammon. Growing up with John and his older brother, Henry (two years their senior), meant that Hammon may have been exposed to some of the educational and cultural training given to the heirs of the estate. In addition, Hammon would have had formal training through the ministers and teachers of the Society for the Propagation of the Gospel (SPG), a missionary arm of the Church of England, which was founded primarily to reach America's African slaves, the native Indians, and any unchurched colonists. The SPG first came to New York in 1705 and to Oyster Bay in 1726.

Family records show that the Lloyds kept only two servants for the life spans of the slaves—one was Hammon and the other a rather militant fellow named "Opium," who, by all indications, was Hammon's father. Nothing is known of Hammon's mother. She was probably sold when the boy was quite young; all other Lloyd slaves were sold or regularly hired out for annual fees. Neither is there evidence that Hammon had a wife or children of his own.

The Lloyd papers do record that Hammon was entrusted with family savings and that he worked as a clerk in the family business. When he was more than seventy, Hammon told a New York audience, "I am . . . able to do almost any kind of business." Obviously, then, the Lloyds allowed Jupiter Hammon to pursue an education so that he could serve in administrative capacities.

In the spring of 1730, when he was about nineteen years old, Jupiter became deathly ill of a goutlike disease. Three years later he purchased a Bible from Henry Lloyd. This purchase was in all probability the beginning of a dramatic religious conversion—one that influenced the young man to become a preacher, a poet, and an essayist, within the limitations of slavery, and to use biblical language to argue against the slave system, again within the subtleties that his slavery demanded. Hammon had to attend church with the Lloyds—both at the Congregational assembly in Huntington, Long Island, the major town near the Oyster Bay community, and at the Anglican church across the bay in Stamford, Connecticut. Although Hammon quotes both Congregational and Anglican preachers in his works, his assumptions are based more on the doctrine of Arminianism—the belief that Christ died for all men and that any man can exercise his free will to choose salvation—rather than on the Calvinist doctrine that a chosen few are predestined. Those colonists who authenticated Hammon's prose and supported his work were the more-liberal Quakers, who by their sustained political activity on Long Island had the most direct bearing on Hammon's ability to publish. The first Quaker church in the colonies was established on Long Island; an early, perhaps the first, antislavery pamphlet was published on Long Island by a Quaker, William Burling, in 1716; and even John Woolman, the great eighteenth-century Quaker abolitionist, twice visited Oyster Bay. The Oyster Bay and Philadelphia Quakers each published Hammon's last prose work posthumously with a dedication, written in language that indicated years of fond association, as well as a guarantee of authorial authenticity. Charles Vertanes, an early Hammon biographer, notes that "Oyster Bay was a hotbed of Quaker abolitionism."

Employing Christian themes that allude to slavery and always addressing a slave audience, Hammon's essays, sermons, and poetry identified Christ with the slave as the servant of God. Hammon frequently used the terms *Saviour* and *Redeemer* in association with God's deliverance of the Israelites from Egypt (making him a potential deliverer for the African slave also) and referred to the Old Testament practice of "redeeming" (that is, buying back the freedom of) Hebrew slaves. Calling slavery and slave-holding Satanic attributes, his writing depended heavily upon the Christian doctrine of final judgment to exonerate the slave and to punish the unjust master; and he also referred to slaves as the *Ethiopians, publicans,* and *Samaritans.* The term *Ethiopian* offered the slave an enhanced self-esteem and national identification; *publican* and *Samaritan* offered the solace of Christ's specific invitation to community pariahs. The poet argued that only faith in God through the conversion experience could simultaneously offer the slave physical, political, and spiritual freedom.

Hammon's first poem, the first work published by a modern writer in the Western hemisphere while the writer was still in slavery, was a broadside entitled *An Evening Thought: Salvation by Christ with Penetential Cries,* which appeared, fittingly, on Christmas Day 1760. Using the four-beats-to-a-line meter so familiar to the Great Awakening and to Negro spiritual a cappella hymns, the twenty-two-stanza poem insists that Christ offers his redemption to "every one" of "every nation" of "all the world" rather than to just a chosen few. When shifting his audience from man to God, the persona becomes an interceding priest who begs God's forgiveness for man's sins and asks that God grant mercy and increase man's love to man.

At the beginning of the Revolutionary War, in 1776, the Lloyd family moved their household to Hartford, Connecticut. Joseph Lloyd was an aberration in the aristocratic family who, since their arrival on the new continent, had been British loyalists. A supporter of the Revolution, he fled to Hartford when British troops overran Long Island.

AN Evening THOUGHT.

SALVATION BY *CHRIST*,

WITH

PENETENTIAL CRIES:

Composed by Jupiter Hammon, a Negro belonging to Mr Lloyd, of Queen's-Village, on Long-Island, the 25th of December, 1760.

SALVATION comes by Jesus Christ alone,
   The only Son of God;
Redemption now to every one,
   That love his holy Word.
Dear Jesus we would fly to Thee,
   And leave off every Sin,
Thy tender Mercy well agree;
   Salvation from our King.
Salvation comes now from the Lord,
   Our victorious King;
His holy Name be well ador'd,
   Salvation surely bring.
Dear Jesus give thy Spirit now,
   Thy Grace to every Nation,
That han't the Lord to whom we bow,
   The Author of Salvation.
Dear Jesus unto Thee we cry,
   Give us thy Preparation;
Turn not away thy tender Eye;
   We seek thy true Salvation.
Salvation comes from God we know,
   The true and only One;
It's well agreed and certain true,
   He gave his only Son.
Lord hear our penetential Cry:
   Salvation from above;
It is the Lord that doth supply,
   With his Redeeming Love.
Dear Jesus by thy precious Blood,
   The World Redemption have:
Salvation comes now from the Lord,
   He being thy captive Slave.
Dear Jesus let the Nations cry,
   And all the People say,
Salvation comes from Christ on high,
   Haste on Tribunal Day.
We cry as Sinners to the Lord,
   Salvation to obtain;
It is firmly fixt his holy Word,
   Ye shall not cry in vain.
Dear Jesus unto Thee we cry,
   And make our Lamentation:
O let our Prayers ascend on high;
   We felt thy Salvation.

Lord turn our dark benighted Souls;
   Give us a true Motion,
And let the Hearts of all the World,
   Make Christ their Salvation.
Ten Thousand Angels cry to Thee,
   Yea louder than the Ocean.
Thou art the Lord, we plainly see;
   Thou art the true Salvation.
Now is the Day, excepted Time;
   The Day of Salvation;
Increase your Faith, do not repine:
   Awake ye every Nation.
Lord unto whom now shall we go,
   Or seek a safe Abode;
Thou hast the Word Salvation too
   The only Son of God.
Ho! every one that hunger hath,
   Or pineth after me,
Salvation be thy leading Staff,
   To set the Sinner free.
Dear Jesus unto Thee we fly;
   Depart, depart from Sin,
Salvation doth at length supply,
   The Glory of our King.
Come ye Blessed of the Lord,
   Salvation gently given;
O turn your Hearts, accept the Word,
   Your Souls are fit for Heaven.
Dear Jesus we now turn to Thee,
   Salvation to obtain;
Our Hearts and Souls do meet again,
   To magnify thy Name.
Come holy Spirit, Heavenly Dove,
   The Object of our Care;
Salvation doth increase our Love;
   Our Hearts hath felt thy fear.
Now Glory be to God on High,
   Salvation high and low;
And thus the Soul on Christ rely,
   To Heaven surely go.
Come Blessed Jesus, Heavenly Dove,
   Accept Repentance here;
Salvation give, with tender Love;
   Let us with Angels share.

FINIS.

The only known copy of the first work by a Negro to be published in colonial America (New-York Historical Society)

Hammon's literary career thrived in Hartford. He published his next five extant works there: a 1778 poem dedicated to eighteenth-century American poet Phillis Wheatley; his first prose work, *A Winter Piece*, which was printed in a pamphlet with "A Poem for Children with Thoughts on Death," in 1782; and a transcription of one of his sermons, *An Evening's Improvement*, published with a lengthy dialogue, "The Kind Master and Dutiful Servant" (publication date unknown).

Structured with Biblical allusions and postscripts, the broadside *An Address to Miss Phillis Wheatly, Ethiopian Poetess, in Boston, who came from Africa at eight years of age, and soon became acquainted with the Gospel of Jesus Christ* reemphasizes Hammon's earlier themes and equates the slaves' ostracism with that of the New Testament Samaritans, who were rejected by the Jews, but to whom Jesus went out of his way to offer salvation and equal inclusion in his "called-out" community. Hammon admonishes Wheatley to be a good example for the young people of the Boston community and to hunger for a deeper relationship with God. "A Poem for Children With Thoughts on Death," written later, continues the didactic theme and introduces Hammon's eschatology of a Day of Judgment that will bring eternal rewards to those who trust in Christ and eternal judgment to those who do not espouse his gospel (or who pay it only lip service).

In his first prose work, *A Winter Piece: Being a Serious Exhortation, with a Call to the Unconverted: and a Short Contemplation on the Death of Jesus Christ*, the aging poet acknowledges that he cannot address the slave audience without the approval and the critical presence of the white slaveholder. He says that the slaveholders may judge him presumptuous because he does not have sufficient education to teach others, but they also suspect that he, as a literate and articulate slave, is imposing ideas upon his less-learned brothers. "I shall endeavor by divine assistance to enlighten the minds of my brethren; for we are a poor despised nation," Hammon argues in rebuttal. He then adds that he must teach the slaves because white masters have neglected their duty to do so.

Final judgment with vindication and eternal reward for those who patiently "behold the Lamb of God" while they endure the injustices of this life is the theme of "a public exhortation" that Hammon later published as *An Evening's Improvement* in which he urges, "We should pray that God would give us grace to love and to fear him, for if we love God, black as we be, and despised as we are, God will love us. 'Then Peter opened his mouth and said, of a truth I perceive that God has no respect to persons. In every nation he that feareth him is accepted of him (Acts 10: 34-35).' "

The theme of judgment continues in Hammon's last extant work, *An Address to the Negroes of the State of New-York*, published one hundred years after the first slave ship bought Hammon's ancestors to the Lloyd plantation. In an urgent summation of his life and work, Hammon pleads that faith in God and God alone is the slave's only weapon against the entrenched institution and that this faith will provide the only absolute freedom. "Our slavery will be at an end, and though ever so mean, low and despised in this world, we shall sit with God in his kingdom, as Kings and Priests, and rejoice for ever and ever."

Undoubtedly, Jupiter Hammon was, when we consider his status as a slave, a rather well-known preacher, essayist, and poet in several parts of New England. His works were published in Boston, Hartford, Philadelphia, and New York. Although

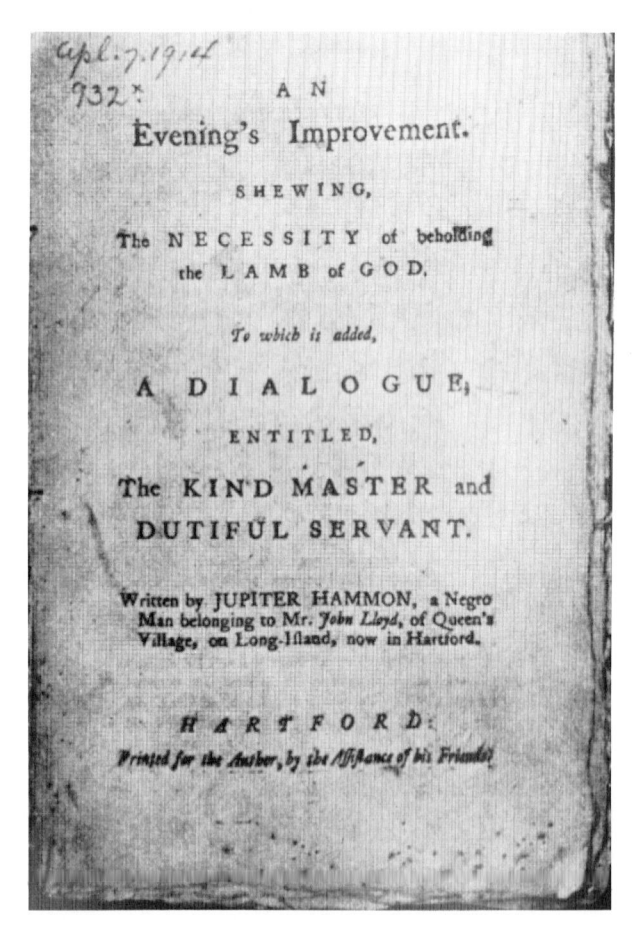

Title page for the sermon in which Hammon promised his fellow slaves, "if we love God, black as we be, and despised as we are, God will love us" (New-York Historical Society)

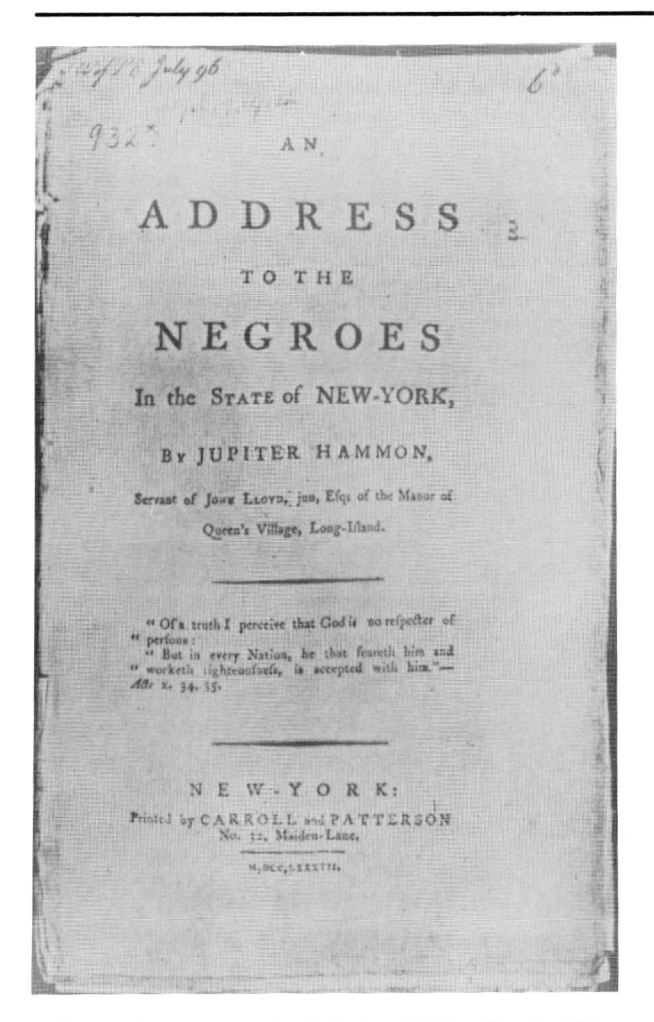

Title page for Hammon's last book, in which he offers the "dying advice, of an old man, who wishes your best good in this world, and in the world to come"

the publications already mentioned are the only ones that have been found, it is known that he published *An Essay on the Ten Virgins* (based on the parable in Matt. 25) in 1779 and that he wrote a set of verses to commemorate the visit of Prince William Henry (later King William IV of Britain) to the Lloyd manor in 1782. Hammon died some time between 1790, when he signed a bill of sale, and 1806, when the Quakers published a memorial to him in their new editions of *An Address to the Negroes in the State of New-York.*

Credit for the discovery that Jupiter Hammon, not Phillis Wheatley, was the first Black American author, goes to literary critic Oscar Wegelin, who suggested in 1904 that he had found a pre-Wheatley poet and published proof of his discovery in 1915.

Because of the historical obscurity of eighteenth-century Northern slavery and because of his necessarily opaque use of Christian apologetics to discuss his opposition to slavery, Hammon's work has been received with suspicion by twentieth-century critics of Black American literature, many of whom feel that he was too much concerned with religion and too little concerned with the plight of the slave. Nevertheless, as scholars continue to study the practice of slavery in that region and that era and Christianity's influence upon the institution of slavery, Hammon's worth as the first black writer, as an effective leader and spokesman of and for the slaves, and as an active participant in the eighteenth-century abolitionist groundswell will assuredly be revealed. That the abolitionist Quakers twice republished his last essay after his death—both as a political tool and as an example of African achievement—is ample evidence of his involvement in that freedom movement.

Biographies:

Oscar Wegelin, "Was Phillis Wheatley America's First Negro poet?" *Literary Collector* (August 1904);

Wegelin, Biography of Hammon, in *Jupiter Hammon: American Negro Poet, Selections from His Writings and a Bibliography,* edited by Wegelin (New York: Printed for C. F. Heartman, 1915);

Charles A. Vertanes, "Jupiter Hammon: Early Negro Poet of Long Island," *Nassau County Historical Journal,* 18 (Winter 1957): 4.

References:

Vernon Loggins, "Critical Analysis of the Works of Jupiter Hammon," in *America's First Negro Poet,* edited by Stanley Austin Ransom, Jr. (Port Washington, N.Y.: Kennikat, 1970), pp. 35-41;

Sondra A. O'Neale, "Jupiter Hammon and his Works: A Discussion of the First Black Preacher to Publish Poems, Sermons, and Essays," *Journal of the Interdenominational Theological Center,* 9 (Spring 1982): 99-113;

Stanley Austin Ransom, Jr., Introduction to *America's First Negro Poet: The Complete Works of Jupiter Hammon of Long Island,* pp. 11-19;

Carolyn Reese, "From Jupiter Hammon to Le Roi Jones," *Changing Education,* 1 (Fall 1966): 30-34;

William H. Robinson, *Early Black American Poets* (Dubuque, Iowa: Wm. C. Brown, 1969).

Papers:
Original copies of Hammon's broadsides, other poetry, and prose are in special collections at the New York Historical Society, the Connecticut Historical Society, the Hartford Public Library, the Providence Public Library, the Massachusetts Historical Society, and the Huntington Public Library in Huntington, New York.

Oliver Hart
(5 July 1723-31 December 1795)

Tony Owens
University of South Carolina

BOOKS: *The Character of a Truly Great Man Delineated, and His Death Deplored as a Public Loss. Occasioned by the Death of the Rev. William Tennent...* (Charleston: Printed by David Bruce, 1777);

Dancing Exploded... (Charleston: Printed by David Bruce, 1778);

An Humble Attempt to Repair the Christian Temple... (Philadelphia: Printed by Robert Aitken, 1785);

A Gospel Church Portrayed... (Trenton: Printed by I. Collins, 1791);

America's Remembrancer, With Respect to Her Blessedness and Duty... (Philadelphia: Printed by T. Dobson, 1791).

OTHER: "Extracts from the Diary of Rev. Oliver Hart from A.D. 1740 to A.D. 1780," edited by William G. Whilden, in *Year Book of the City of Charleston* (1896);

"Oliver Hart's Diary to the Backcountry," edited by J. Glenwood Clayton and Loulie Latimer Owens, *Journal of the South Carolina Baptist Historical Society*, 1 (November 1975): 18-31.

The most influential Baptist minister of revolutionary South Carolina, Oliver Hart represents the union of evangelical religion and political rebellion. Born in Westminster Township, Bucks County, Pennsylvania, to John and Eleanor Crispin Hart, Hart was strongly influenced in his youth by the revivalism of George Whitefield and William and Gilbert Tennent. Though lacking formal education, he acquired a respectable knowledge of the classics, theology, and science. He was ordained in 1747 and moved to Charleston, South Carolina, where he became pastor of the Charleston Baptist Church in 1750. For thirty years Hart dominated the Charleston Baptists, both in the pulpit and within the organization. He founded the first Baptist Association in the South, stressed the value of an educated clergy, and labored for interdenominational cooperation and unified church discipline. In 1769 Hart received an honorary M.A. at the first commencement of Rhode Island College (now Brown University). As revolutionary fervor increased in Charleston during the 1770s, Hart's influence expanded from religion to politics.

Hart's influence among religious dissenters and his reputation as an ardent patriot led to his commission by the Charleston Council of Safety to accompany Henry Drayton and Reverend William Tennent as an emissary to the Carolina backcountry. His three-month mission in 1775 was to garner support for the patriotic cause among the suspicious and often hostile dissenters of the back settlements. One of Hart's diaries, unpublished for over a century, records daily entries from this journey. Written partly in code, this work was eventually published in 1975 in the *Journal of the South Carolina Baptist Historical Society* and offers a valuable record of the political and social turmoil of the backcountry on the eve of the Revolution.

The decade of the 1770s also saw the publication of Hart's best-known sermons. His funeral sermon for the patriot William Tennent (1777) placed Hart firmly among those seeking to disestablish the Anglican church in South Carolina. Characteristic of Hart's evangelical militancy is his 1778 sermon, *Dancing Exploded*, a vigorous attack on the well-known balls and assemblies of Charleston society. Written during the Revolution, the sermon argues that militant times require piety, sobriety, and devotion to the dual causes of religion and

Hart's notes for one of the sermons he delivered in Charleston (South Caroliniana Library, University of South Carolina)

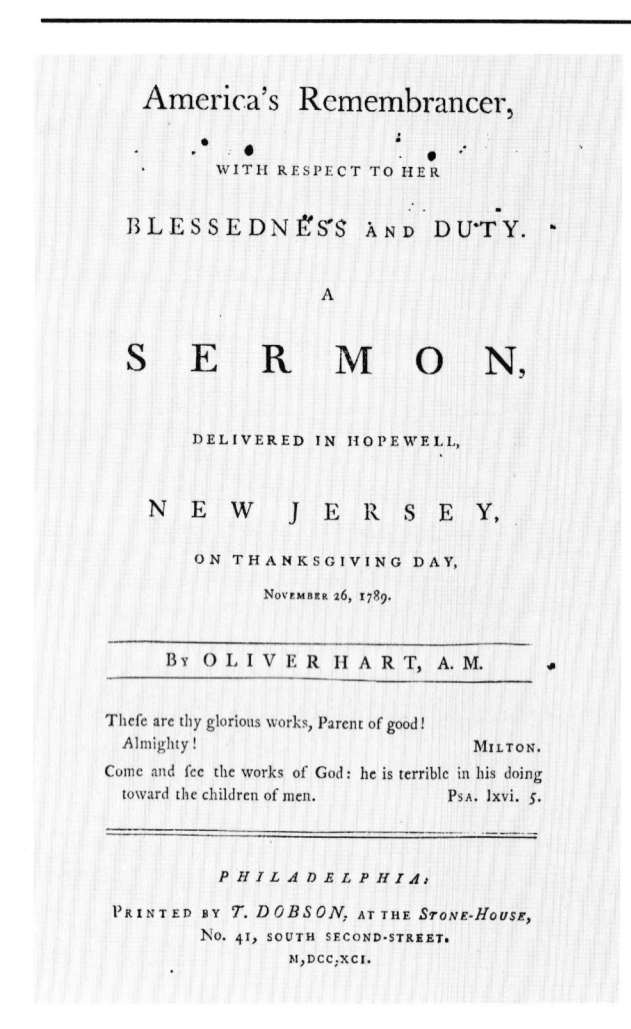

Title page for Hart's sermon commemorating the American Revolution (courtesy of the John Carter Brown Library at Brown University)

liberty. Hart declares war on the "sinful diversions" of society, drawing upon both classical and biblical sources. The sermon is a valuable example of an evangelical appeal for political and spiritual militancy. In an unadorned, direct style, Hart's sermons represent an influencial Southern puritanism in the waning years of the Great Awakening.

With the British conquest of Charleston in 1780, Hart fled north to Hopewell Baptist Church in New Jersey. Hart remained in New Jersey, publishing sermons in Philadelphia and Trenton, until his death in 1795. From this later period comes Hart's *America's Remembrancer,* delivered in 1789 as a public commemoration of the American Revolution. From an evangelical perspective, Hart embellishes the puritan vision of America as the fulfillment of a messianic destiny. For him the Revolution was but the most recent evidence of the providential order of history. Physically and spiritually blessed, the new nation's progress is the inevitable triumph of the divine will. This Christian interpretation of the Revolution contrasts strongly with the more secular, rational views of the American Enlightenment and represents a significant colonial attitude toward the emerging nation.

Oliver Hart epitomizes a large and influential element of colonial society—the crucial role of evangelical dissent in the development of revolutionary attitudes. Theologically, Hart's works exemplify Southern puritanism in its purest form, stressing a militant piety. Combining his religious influence with his patriotism, Hart won many converts to the patriot cause. His sermons and diaries provide a useful account of the critical years before, during, and immediately after the American Revolution.

Biography:
Loulie Latimer Owens, *Oliver Hart* (Greenville, S.C.: South Carolina Baptist Historical Society, 1966).

References:
Richard Beale Davis, *Intellectual Life in the Colonial South* (Knoxville: University of Tennessee Press, 1978), II: 760;

Richard Furman, *Rewards of Grace Conferred on Christ's Faithful People: A Sermon Occasioned by the Decease of the Rev. Oliver Hart . . .* (Charleston: Printed by J. M'Iver, 1796);

Joe M. King, *A History of South Carolina Baptists* (Columbia: Privately printed, 1964), pp. 17-20;

William Rogers, *A Sermon Occasioned by the Death of the Rev. Oliver Hart . . .* (Philadelphia: Printed by Lang & Ustick, 1796);

Leah Townsend, *South Carolina Baptists, 1670-1805* (Florence: Privately printed, 1935), pp. 14-25, 282;

David Wallace, *South Carolina, A Short History, 1520-1948* (Chapel Hill: University of North Carolina Press, 1951), pp. 212-213, 279;

B. W. Whilden, "Rev. Oliver Hart," *Baptist Courier,* 9 (1893): 1-7.

Papers:
The South Caroliniana Library at the University of South Carolina and Furman University Library in Greenville, South Carolina, have collections of Hart's papers.

Samuel Hopkins
(17 September 1721-20 December 1803)

Donald Weber
Mount Holyoke College

BOOKS: *Sin, Thro' Divine Interposition, An Advantage to the Universe; and Yet, This No Excuse for Sin, or Encouragement to It* (Boston: Printed & sold by Daniel and John Kneeland, 1759; Edinburgh: Printed for A. Kincaid & W. Creech, 1773);

The Life of the Late Reverend Mr. Jonathan Edwards (Boston: Printed by S. Kneeland, 1765);

An Enquiry Concerning the Promises of the Gospel . . . (Boston: Printed by W. McAlpine & J. Fleeming, 1765);

The Importance and Necessity of Christians Considering Jesus Christ in the Extent of His High and Glorious Character . . . (Boston: Printed & sold by Kneeland & Adams, 1768);

Two Discourses. I. On The Necessity of the Knowledge of the Law of God, In Order to the Knowledge of Sin. II. A Particular, and Critical Inquiry into the Cause, Nature and Means of the Change in Which Men Are Born of God . . . (Boston: Printed & sold by William M'Alpine, 1768);

The True State and Character of the Unregenerate . . . (New Haven: Printed by Thomas & Samuel Green, 1769);

Animadversions on Mr. Hart's Late Dialogue . . . (New London: Printed by T. Green, 1770);

An Inquiry into the Nature of True Holiness . . . (Newport: Printed by Solomon Southwick, 1773);

A Dialogue, Concerning the Slavery of the Africans . . . (Norwich: Printed by Judah H. Spooner, 1776);

An Inquiry Concering [sic] *the Future State of Those Who Die in Their Sins . . .* (Newport: Printed by Solomon Southwick, 1783);

A Discourse Upon the Slave Trade, and The Slavery of the Africans . . . (Providence: Printed by J. Carter, 1793);

The System of Doctrines . . . (Boston: Printed by Isaiah Thomas & Ebenezer T. Andrews, 1793);

A Treatise on the Millennium . . . (Boston: Printed by Isaiah Thomas & Ebenezer T. Andrews, 1793);

Memoirs of the Life of Mrs. Sarah Osborn . . . (Worcester, Mass.: Printed by Leonard Worcester, 1799);

Engraving by H. W. Smith

Sketches of the Life of the Late Rev. Samuel Hopkins . . ., edited by Stephen West (Hartford: Printed by Hudson & Goodwin, 1805).

Collection: *The Works of Samuel Hopkins . . . With a Memoir of His Life and Character*, 3 volumes, edited by Edwards A. Park (Boston: Doctrinal Tract & Book Society, 1854).

Samuel Hopkins was, along with Joseph Bellamy and Jonathan Edwards, Jr., a major figure in the New Divinity group in American religious history, a theological and social movement which sought, after the death of Jonathan Edwards in 1758, to defend the orthodox tenets of Edwardean Calvinism against the emerging, liberal ethos of eighteenth-century rationalism in metaphysics and philosophy. Hopkins is perhaps best recalled as the first editor and biographer of Jonathan Edwards and as an early Abolitionist who, from his Newport pastorate in the 1770s, decried the evils of slavery to a nation on the threshold of independence.

Hopkins was born in 1721 in the backwater town of Waterbury in western Connecticut, to a family newly risen to some prominence after two generations of farming. His father, Timothy, wanted his firstborn son to become a minister, and from an early age Samuel prepared for a pastoral career. In 1731 he entered Yale, where he met the pious David Brainerd, who spurred Hopkins toward an anxious contemplation of his spiritual condition. Later, Hopkins recalled the first, "astonishing" promptings of the spirit: "At length as I was in my closet one evening, while I was meditating, and in my devotions, a new and wonderful scene opened to my view. I had a sense of the being and presence of God, as I never had before; it being more of a reality, and more affecting and glorious, than I have ever before perceived." But it was not until the revival of religion at Yale, in 1740-1741, when he heard the preaching of Gilbert Tennent and, more important, of Jonathan Edwards (who delivered the commencement sermon on the "distinguishing marks" of true religion), that Hopkins resolved to become a minister. He then "concluded to go and live with Mr. Edwards." Hopkins preached in Edwards's Northampton pulpit (as well as in Bellamy's in Bethlehem), remarking later that "people in general then had a hearing ear"—in contrast perhaps to the deaf ears Hopkins was to encounter after the fires of the Great Awakening had died away.

In 1743 Hopkins received a call to a pastorate in Housatonic (later Great Barrington), from which he could journey to both Edwards and Bellamy for spiritual and intellectual guidance. (Hopkins would eventually be instrumental in securing Edwards the wilderness post in nearby Stockbridge after his congregation dismissed him from his Northampton pulpit in 1750 because of his rigid adherence to strict requirements for church membership.) On the eve of assuming his first pulpit Hopkins confessed in his diary: "I now promise allegiance to the God of Heaven. . . . It is done, am no more my own, but give myself away to God, to be his forever." Hopkins dedicated himself from the beginning to the doctrines of strict Calvinism.

The years in Great Barrington were not without affliction. The threat of Indian attacks made life especially perilous; yet even the constant threat of God's judgment (via the Indians) did not result in converts. "My public performances," Hopkins lamented, "have generally been low." His pulpit style was marked by a monotonous nasality—William Ellery Channing likened Hopkins's voice to the sound of "a cracked bell." Life in Great Barrington increased in fractiousness through the 1760s. By 1762, Hopkins had to contend with both a newly settled Anglican church and (in his view) a lay congregation. Demanding a stricter form of church discipline in his own pastorate, Hopkins tried to remove the practice of the Half-Way Covenant, which allowed the children of the unconverted the rite of baptism (and thus a measure of church standing). The community was outraged at Hopkins's attempt to impose authority, and his ministry was dissolved in a dispute over doctrine and salary.

AN
INQUIRY
INTO THE
NATURE OF
TRUE HOLINESS.
WITH
An APPENDIX;
CONTAINING

An Anſwer to the Rev. Mr. WILLIAM HART's Remarks on Preſident EDWARDS's Diſſertation on the *Nature of true Virtue*: And brief Remarks on ſome Things the Rev. Mr. MATHER has lately publiſhed. Alſo an Anſwer to the Rev. Mr. HEMMENWAY's Vindication, &c.

By SAMUEL HOPKINS, M. A.
Paſtor of the Firſt CONGREGATIONAL CHURCH in NEWPORT.

NEWPORT, Rhode-Iſland:
PRINTED BY SOLOMON SOUTHWICK, IN QUEEN-STREET, M,DCC,LXXIII.

Title page for the work in which Hopkins explained his doctrine of "disinterested benevolence," a notion that led to his passionate opposition to slavery (courtesy of the John Carter Brown Library at Brown University) fered by the English moral philosophers, Hopkins set forth his doctrine of "disinterested benevolence," which he defined as an absolute selflessness leading to social activism. As Hopkins's most recent critic, Joseph A. Conforti, suggests, Hopkins modified ("liberalized") Edwards's aesthetic doctrine of true virtue ("love to being in general")—a reformulation which highlights the iniquities (and inequities) of society. In effect, Hopkins's theology criticized the social ideals of eighteenth-century Newport.

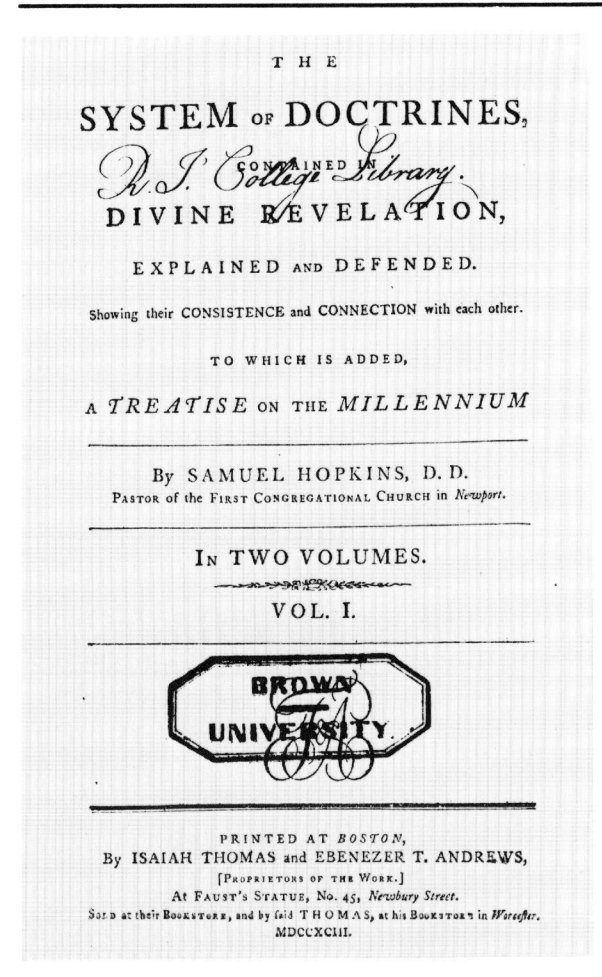

Hopkins's notion of "disinterested benevolence" also led to his passionate antislavery stance. His 1776 *A Dialogue, Concerning the Slavery of the Africans . . . ,* dedicated to the Continental Congress, conflated the opposition to slavery with the signs of spiritual assurance, thus revealing the social dimension of New Divinity metaphysics. Hopkins's magnum opus, his *summa* of the New Divinity, was *The System of Doctrines . . .* (1793), which became the standard text at that citadel of Edwardean Calvinism, Andover Seminary.

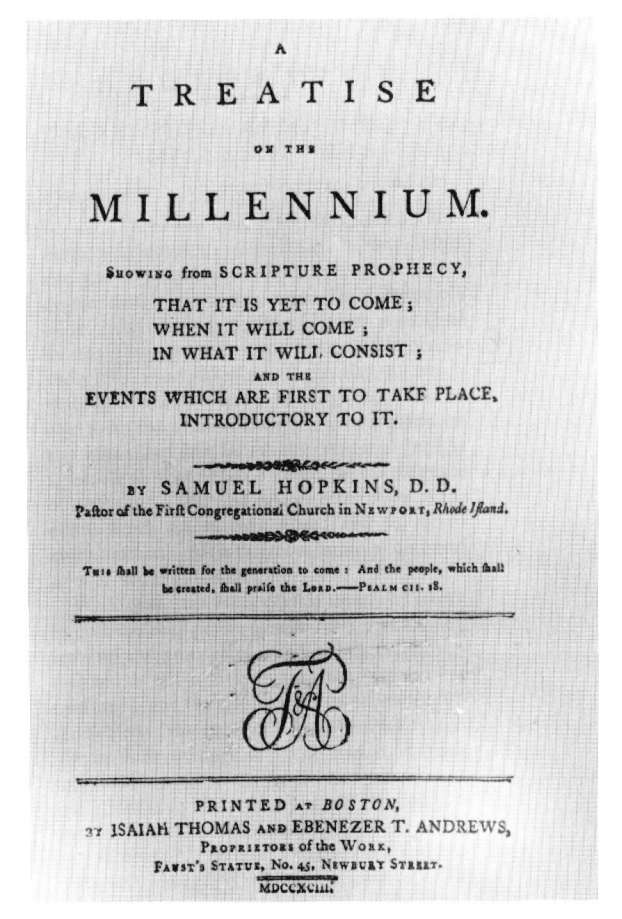

Title page for Hopkins's major summation of the New Divinity (courtesy of the John Carter Brown Library at Brown University)

In 1769, Hopkins received a call to minister to Newport, which he reluctantly accepted.

The removal to Newport signaled Hopkins's arrival as the major spokesman for and defender of the New Divinity. He also became the custodian and editor of the vast piles of Edwards manuscripts (as requested by Edwards's wife, Sarah). Hopkins's 1765 biography of Edwards remains essential, both as a contemporaneous account of Edwards as a figure and for providing the text of the famous *Personal Narrative,* Edwards's spiritual autobiography.

By the early 1770s, Hopkins became embroiled in theological warfare over the question of Edwards's legacy. In response to Old Light William Hart's attack on "Hopkinsian" doctrines (so labeled by their opponents) and Edwards's posthumously published treatise, *The Nature of True Virtue . . .* (1765), Hopkins produced his first major work, *An Inquiry into the Nature of True Holiness . . .* (1773). Against the prevailing theories of self-love prof-

Title page for Hopkins's portrayal of the imminent reign of the saints. William Ellery Channing later observed that the book "has an air of reality, as if written from observation."

A supplement to *The System of Doctrines...* was *A Treatise on the Millennium...* (1793), perhaps Hopkins's most important work. Following in the long tradition of expounders on the millennium in colonial America (notably Increase and Cotton Mather, Edwards and Bellamy), Hopkins portrayed, in a less abstract way than Bellamy (for example) the advances in civilization and technology that would accompany the reign of the saints. The idea of the millennium consumed Hopkins during his later years. Channing, in a memoir of his boyhood pastor, noted that Hopkins "took refuge from the present state of things in the Millennium. The Millennium was his chosen ground.... His book on the subject has an air of reality, as if written from observation." Hopkins died in 1803, after a long and painful decline in the wake of two strokes, perhaps still awaiting the kingdom of God in America.

The image of Hopkins and the New Divinity in general has, from Harriet Beecher Stowe's novel about Hopkins, *The Minister's Wooing* (1859), to Joseph Haroutunian's *Piety versus Moralism* (1932), been viewed as symbolic of the sad movement in American theology from the fervent piety and intellectual rigor of Jonathan Edwards to the abstract metaphysics and deadening moralism of his followers. Never an activist, Hopkins admitted to a "love" of retirement: "I have taken more pleasure *alone*," he acknowledged, "than in any company." Still, as Conforti has argued, the doctrines of New Divinity Calvinism could indeed bring about radical social reform and acts of disinterested, selfless benevolence. Hopkins sought what in his view were the Christian exempla for the self and community, and labored for these ideals, both in his theology and pastoral example.

References:

Joseph A. Conforti, *Samuel Hopkins and the New Divinity Movement* (Grand Rapids: Eerdmans, 1981);

Frank H. Foster, *A Genetic History of the New England Theology* (Chicago: University of Chicago Press, 1907);

Joseph Haroutunian, *Piety versus Moralism: The Passing of the New England Theology* (New York: Holt, 1932).

Papers:

Andover Theological School, Hartford Seminary, and the Historical Society of Pennsylvania have collections of Hopkins's papers.

Francis Hopkinson
(2 October 1737-9 May 1791)

William D. Andrews
Philadelphia College of Textiles & Science

SELECTED BOOKS: *Science, A Poem* (Philadelphia: Printed by William Dunlap, 1762);

A Collection of Psalm Tunes (Philadelphia, 1763);

A Pretty Story Written in the Year of Our Lord 2774, as Peter Grievous (Philadelphia: Printed & sold by John Dunlap, 1774); republished as *The Old Farm and the New Farm* (New York: Dana, 1857);

The Miscellaneous Essays and Occasional Writings of Francis Hopkinson, 3 volumes (Philadelphia: Printed by T. Dobson, 1792).

PERIODICAL PUBLICATIONS: "The Battle of the Kegs," *Pennsylvania Packet*, 4 March 1778;

"A Camp Ballad," *Pennsylvania Gazette*, 4 April 1778;

"Art of Paper War," *Pennsylvania Packet*, 2 August 1786;

"The New Roof," *Pennsylvania Packet*, 29 December 1787.

In his own day Francis Hopkinson enjoyed a reputation substantially in excess of what history has accorded him. This fact is neither surprising nor unjust. Accomplished at music, art, politics, invention, and literature, he achieved distinction in none. Some have concluded that his talents were real but too widely spread; others have assumed

Engraving from a painting by Alonzo Chappel (Henry E. Huntington Library and Art Gallery)

that he lacked depth. It is perhaps fair to say that because he lived in exciting times he allowed himself to be pulled in many directions at once and failed to focus his abundant energies toward depth and achievement in one field. That he was a gentleman amateur in the eighteenth-century tradition, however, is not to be held against him nor allowed to diminish the respect he is owed.

Insofar as there was an establishment in Philadelphia in the first half of the eighteenth century, Hopkinson was a member of it at his birth in 1737. His father, Thomas Hopkinson, an attorney, had been connected with Benjamin Franklin in a number of projects and served as the first president of the American Philosophical Society and secretary of the Library Company, both Franklin-inspired institutions. Francis Hopkinson's mother, Mary Johnson Hopkinson, was the daughter of Baldwin Johnson, a member of a distinguished English family. In 1751 Francis was enrolled in the first class of the Academy of Philadelphia, another Franklin product. Created to offer the sons of Philadelphia merchants and professionals a sound, practical education without the classical orientation of more traditional English and colonial schools, the academy was a nursery for Philadelphia talents. It was later expanded to include a college, and Hopkinson was in its first graduating class in 1757.

While at the Academy and College of Philadelphia, Hopkinson quickly came under the influence of its dynamic provost, the Reverend William Smith, a Scot who entertained dreams of establishing in the colonies a cultural base that would combine the best of the English tradition with the excitement of the new land. Hopkinson's classmates in the first class included the poet Nathaniel Evans, the playwright Thomas Godfrey, and the essayist and preacher Jacob Duché, who later became Hopkinson's brother-in-law. They formed a close but informal group, the Swains of the Schuylkill (named for the river bordering Philadelphia on the west), who met to read verse and discuss the prospects for art and civilization in the colonies.

Hopkinson was active in the social and cultural life of the college and participated in musical and dramatic events with apparent joy and success. In his senior year he appeared in James Thomson and David Mallet's *Alfred, A Masque* (1740), which he helped revise and for which he composed original music. After graduation he retained a deep interest in the school and regularly composed odes about it. In 1762 he published one of these, *Science,* which celebrates the College of Philadelphia for its beneficial effect on the cultural level of the colony. The work depicts "FAIR SCIENCE soft'ning with reforming Hand/ The native Rudeness of a barb'rous Land."

After college Hopkinson moved away from the pattern followed by his fellow swains. He pursued his father's profession, studying law under Benjamin Chew, then attorney general of Pennsylvania, and was admitted to the bar in 1761. In 1763 he obtained a position as collector of customs for the port of Salem, New Jersey; later he operated a store in Philadelphia and generally remained active in the social, political, and commercial life of the city to which his birth and training gave him easy access. Hopkinson's life took an external, public turn consistent with his early experience as a son of the establishment and leading to his later career as a political figure. By 1772—in part because of a tour

Hopkinson's house in Bordentown, New Jersey

of England he made to cultivate political contacts and advance his career, and in part because of his marriage on 1 September 1768, to a well-connected and affluent woman, Ann Borden, daughter of Col. Joseph Borden, the most influential resident of Bordentown, New Jersey—Hopkinson settled into a life of relative prosperity that allowed him the opportunity to pursue his interests in writing and music. Attracted since college to music and drama, he published *A Collection of Psalm Tunes* (1763) and continued to write both music and light verse during the early years of his busy career.

Despite both family ties to the English political establishment and a financial stake in the status quo, in the years of agitation leading to the Revolution Hopkinson quickly became a firm patriot. He attended the Second Continental Congress in June of 1776 as a delegate from New Jersey and signed the Declaration of Independence. During the war he served as chairman of the Navy Board, treasurer of loans, and judge of admiralty. In England he had studied drawing and painting with his old friend from the Academy and College of Philadelphia, the painter Benjamin West, and he developed a reputation as a designer. He helped design the seals for the University of the State of Pennsylvania (one of the names taken by the College of Pennsylvania on its way to becoming the University of Pennsylvania), the seal of New Jersey, and the seal of the American Philosophical Society. He was thus a logical choice to design the flag for the rebel nation, which he did in 1777—perhaps his most symbolic contribution to the cause of independence.

Hopkinson put his pen into the service of the nation as well, producing ballads and satires in verse and prose to inspire his countrymen. In a letter to Benjamin Franklin in 1778, Hopkinson wrote: "I have not Abilities to assist our righteous Cause by personal Prowess & Force of Arms, but I have done it all the Service I could with my Pen—throwing in my mite at Times in Prose & Verse, serious & satirical Essays &ca."

He may have been specifically recalling his best-known writing of the revolutionary period, *A Pretty Story Written in the Year of Our Lord 2774* (1774), published under the pseudonym Peter Grievous. This political allegory was published in Philadelphia during the meeting of the First Continental Congress in 1774 and appeared in a second edition the same year both in Philadelphia and in Williamsburg. It appeared again in 1857 as a plea for national unity as the country headed toward civil war, this time under the title by which it is often known, *The Old Farm and the New Farm.*

The story concerns a "certain Nobleman, who had long possessed a very valuable Farm, and had a great Number of Children and Grandchildren." The Nobleman is of course the king of England, his offspring the colonists. The New Farm, an "immense Tract of wild uncultivated Country at a vast Distance from his Mansion House," is the American colonies. The villain is the Steward (Lord North) who harasses the settlers of the New Farm and enriches himself at their expense. The imposition on the New Farmers of a tax on "Water Gruel" causes one of the settlers, Jack (Massachusetts), to destroy the commodity rather than pay the tax. For this offense his home is padlocked and an Overseer is sent to enforce the laws in the New Farm. These actions parallel colonial resistance to the tax on tea, the imposition of the Boston Port Bill, and the posting of General Gage to establish control in the colonies. *A Pretty Story* ends with uncertainty, as settlers gather, against the Overseer's prohibition, to consider action. Their meeting, of course, suggests the calling of the Continental Congress. Hopkinson clearly expected the Congress to take strong action.

The piece derives from Hopkinson's familiarity with British satirists such as Addison, Steele, and Swift, who remained forceful models for him throughout his literary career. It is modeled directly on John Arbuthnot's *History of John Bull* (1712), a popular political allegory. Hopkinson's piece was a perfectly bald allegory, widely read and readily understood; neither the form nor the theme was subtle or complex. *A Pretty Story* spoke directly to its audience, and the message it carried was simple: the colonies were victims of British political machination and the greed of individual political leaders. Propagandists, as Hopkinson understood, work not with fine knives but with broadaxes. It was a lesson he learned early and applied consistently in his satires and parodies.

Hopkinson's skill as a political propagandist is apparent in another of his popular revolutionary pieces, "The Battle of the Kegs," written in 1778 to satirize the British. The work is based on an amusing incident in the war: Hopkinson's Navy Board commissioned a scheme to float kegs of gunpowder down the Delaware River as mines to sink British ships in the Philadelphia harbor. Because the ships were docked to avoid ice, the kegs exploded harmlessly in the river, missing their mark but engendering panic in the British command in the city. Hopkinson aimed his satire against the British reaction:

> The soldier flew, the sailor too,
>   And scar'd almost to death, sir,
> Wore out their shoes, to spread the news,
>   And ran till out of breath, sir.
>
> . . . .
>
> Some fire cried, which some denied,
>   But said the earth had quaked;
> And girls and boys, with hideous noise,
>   Ran thro' the streets half naked.
>
> Sir William he, snug as a flea,
>   Lay all this time a snoring,
> Nor dream'd of harm as he lay warm,
>   In bed with Mrs. L———g.

Hopkinson wrote a number of ballads designed to be sung by soldiers and generally to boost American morale. In one of these, "A Camp Ballad" (1778), he expressed his faith in the new nation:

Title page for Hopkinson's best-known political allegory (courtesy of the John Carter Brown Library at Brown University)

MAKE room, oh! ye kingdoms in hist'ry renowned
Whose arms have in battle with glory been crown'd,
Make room for America, another great nation,
Arises to claim in your council a station.

Such ephemeral pieces hardly advance Hopkinson's claim on status as a major poet, but they illustrate the interconnection of his literary and musical talents and the ease with which he produced verse for political occasions.

Given both Hopkinson's political involvement and penchant for satire, it is not surprising that he continued to produce verse and prose on later events in American history. His Swiftian "Art of Paper War" (1786), for example, satirizes a local newspaper battle. His best-known later work is "The New Roof," published in the *Pennsylvania Packet* in 1787. In it he used the familiar technique of allegory so successful in *A Pretty Story*, but in this case to advance the cause of the new Federal Constitution (the "new roof") that he so staunchly supported. He produced numerous songs and ballads in support of Federalism in his last years.

Benjamin Rush, scientist, patriot, and friend of Hopkinson, wrote that "the various causes which contributed to the establishment of the independence and federal government of the United States, will not be *fully traced*, unless much is ascribed to the irresistible influence of the *ridicule* which [Hopkinson] poured forth . . . upon the enemies of those great political events." The tag by which Hopkinson is sometimes known—"penman of the Revolution"—accurately captures Rush's meaning. Hopkinson never perceived himself as an artist dedicated to the craft of poetry but rather as a gentleman writer of belles lettres who turned his skills toward subjects of daily interest to produce pleasing if not lasting satire, ballads, and light verse. He is, consequently, remembered as a figure more in American political than literary history. His work is rarely original and seldom fully appreciated outside the context of political or military events. It is not a large body of writing, and it is not a distinguished body, but it is always consistent with Hopkinson the man: talented, public, and personable.

Biography:
George E. Hastings, *The Life and Works of Francis Hopkinson* (Chicago: University of Chicago Press, 1926).

References:
William D. Andrews, "Philip Freneau and Francis Hopkinson," *American Literature, 1764-1789: The Revolutionary Years*, edited by Everett Emerson (Madison: University of Wisconsin Press, 1977), pp. 127-144;

Paul M. Zall, *Comical Spirit of Seventy-Six: The Humor of Francis Hopkinson* (San Marino, Cal.: Huntington Library, 1976).

Papers:
Correspondence, manuscripts, and miscellaneous papers of Hopkinson's reside in the Henry E. Huntington Library, the Library of Congress, the Historical Society of Pennsylvania, and the American Philosophical Society.

Thomas Hutchinson
(9 September 1711-3 June 1780)

Michael P. Kramer
University of California, Davis

BOOKS: *The History of the Colony of Massachusets-Bay, from the first Settlement thereof in 1628. Until Its Incorporation with the Colony of Plimouth, Province of Main, &c., By the Charter of King William and Queen Mary, in 1691* (Boston: Printed by Thomas & John Fleet, 1764; London: Printed for M. Richardson, 1765);

The History of the Province of Massachusetts-Bay, from the Charter of King William and Queen Mary, in 1691, Until the Year 1750 (Boston: Printed by Thomas & John Fleet, 1767; London: Printed by J. Smith for G. Kearsley & W. Davenhill, 1768);

Copy of Letters Sent to Great-Britain, by His Excellency Thomas Hutchinson, the Hon. Andrew Oliver, and several other Persons, born and educated among us . . . (Boston: Printed by Edes & Gill, 1773); republished in *The Letters of Governor Hutchinson and Lieut. Governor Oliver . . . And Remarks Thereon . . .*, edited by Israel Mauduit (London: Printed for J. Wilkie, 1774);

The Speeches of His Excellency Governor Hutchinson, to the General Assembly Of the Massachusetts-Bay . . . (Boston: Printed by Edes & Gill, 1773);

Strictures upon the Declaration of the Congress at Philadelphia, anonymous (London, 1776); edited by M. Freiberg, Old South Leaflets, no. 227 (Boston: Old South Association, 1958);

The History of the Province of Massachusetts Bay from 1750 to June 1774, comprising a Detailed Narrative of the Origin and Early Stages of the American Revolution, edited by John Hutchinson (London: J. Murray, 1828);

The Diary and Letters of His Excellency Thomas Hutchinson . . ., 2 volumes, edited by Peter Orlando Hutchinson (London: Low, Marston, Searle & Rivington, 1883, 1886);

The History of the Colony and Province of Massachusetts Bay, 3 volumes, edited by Lawrence Shaw Mayo (Cambridge: Harvard University Press, 1936).

Thomas Hutchinson, one of the most maligned men in early American history, was the last civilian royal governor of the province of Massachusetts. In the history of American literature, he is known primarily as the author of the valuable, three-volume *History of Massachusetts Bay*. Along with his other, more political works—some published by him, others published without his consent, still others left in manuscript—his writings illuminate the political imagination of an American loyalist in the tumultuous times of the Revolution.

The Hutchinson family had been notable in Massachusetts for four generations before Thomas was born in their Garden Court Street home in Boston. Mistress Anne Hutchinson immigrated to New England in 1634, quickly became the central figure in the Antinomian Controversy that threatened the infant Puritan theocracy, and was banished from the Bay Colony for her dangerously heretical views. Her son Edward, a merchant and representative from Boston, was vocal in his opposition to the Quaker persecutions. Her grandson Elisha, also a merchant, was a member of the Council and a judge of common pleas. His son Thomas, Sr., who was involved in the arrest of Captain Kidd, served on the Council for twenty years. Thomas, Jr., was the son of Thomas and Sara Foster Hutchinson. Receiving his early education at the North Grammar School, he entered Harvard College in 1723, at the age of twelve, and attained a B.A. in 1727 and an M.A. in 1730. After graduation, he entered his father's mercantile business but continued his studies in his spare time, mastering Latin and French and reading heavily in Massachusetts history, including the works of Thomas Prince, Nathaniel Morton, and Cotton Mather. On 16 May 1734 he married Margaret Sanford, to whom he was a devoted husband throughout the eighteen years of their marriage. After her death in 1753, he never remarried.

Thomas Hutchinson followed his father, grandfather, and great-grandfather into public service in 1737, when he was chosen as a Boston selectman and elected to the House of Representatives. He later recalled that his father had warned him, "if you serve your country faithfully you will be reproached & reviled for doing it." He served as a member of the House until 1749 (except in 1739, when he was rejected for his hard-money views) and as speaker from 1746 to 1748. When he failed to be reelected in 1749, again due to popular resentment of his support for hard money over paper currency, he was elected to the Council by the members of the general Court, who reelected him yearly through 1766. In addition to his Council appointment, he was given the offices of probate judge and justice of common pleas for Suffolk County in 1752. Two years later, at the start of the French and Indian War, he represented Massachusetts at the Albany Congress, where he supported Benjamin Franklin's plan of union. In 1758, he became lieutenant-governor, a position he held for thirteen years. When Chief Justice Stephen Sewall died in 1760, Governor Bernard named Hutchinson as Sewall's successor. It was a fateful moment in his career; James Otis, a member of the Superior Court, had expected the position, and when he was passed over in favor of Hutchinson, his son, James Otis, Jr., furiously announced "that he would set the Province in a flame, though he perished in the fire." Although it was accepted practice for a politician to hold several offices simultaneously, Hutchinson soon became a popular symbol of political greed and lust for power. "From so small a spark," he later remarked, "a great fire seems to have been kindled."

During the years that he served the province in his several capacities, Hutchinson began collecting documents relating to Massachusetts history. In 1763, he began writing what became the first volume of his *History of Massachusetts Bay*, covering the years 1628 to 1691. "I think from my beginning the work until I had completed it, which was about twelve months," he wrote to a friend in England, "I never had time to write two sheets at a sitting without avocations by public business." Because of the many interruptions, he claimed, "I found it difficult to keep any plan in my mind" and was forced continually to amend the text with footnotes rather

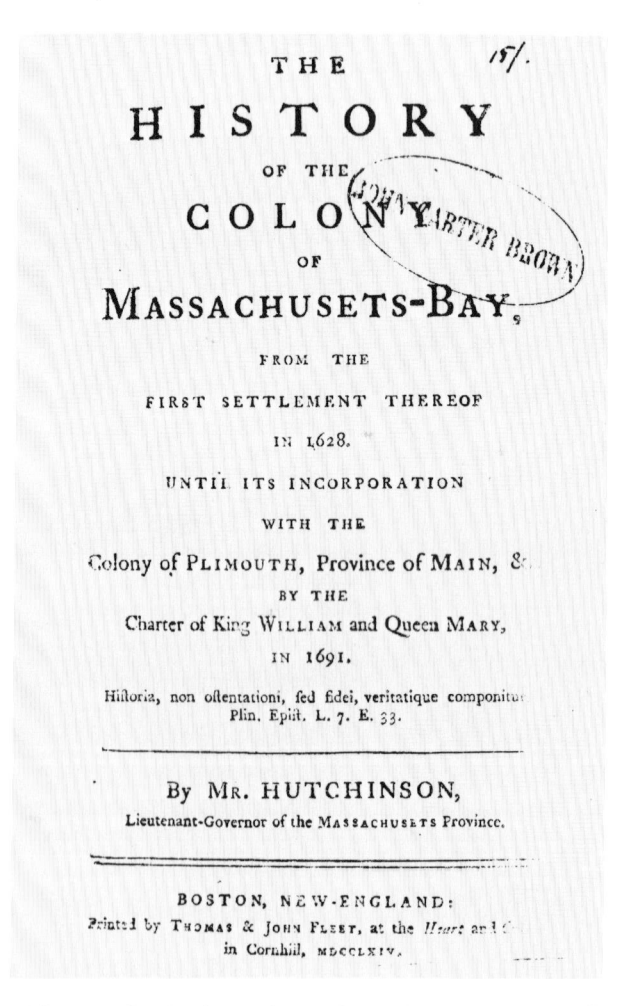

Title page for the first volume of Hutchinson's major work. Although Nathaniel Hawthorne often used the history as a source book, the grandfather in his The Whole History of Grandfather's Chair *(1840) comments that "a duller piece of composition never came from any man's pen" (courtesy of the John Carter Brown Library at Brown University).*

than to revise and rework what he had already written. The style of his history is clear and remarkably dry. (Nathaniel Hawthorne, for whom Hutchinson's history was an invaluable source for his historical tales, once noted through one of his fictional characters that "a duller piece of composition never came from any man's pen.") Hutchinson knew that he had "no talent at painting or describing characters" and was content to "let facts speak for themselves." In the preface he apologized for further "defects" in his "performance"—his predilection for seemingly insignificant details and the "dull and heavy narration" they afford. Still, he was writing chiefly "for the sake of my own countrymen," who "are fond of knowing the minutiae which relate to our ancestors," and felt justified in his attempt "to save them from oblivion."

Hutchinson's unadorned prose is also the history's greatest asset. Through it, the historian achieved a degree of objectivity lost to many of his contemporaries and predecessors. Although he admitted "some difficulty in guarding against every degree of prejudice, in writing the history of my own country," his account of the Puritans is a model of judiciousness. For instance, he wrote of the Quaker persecutions: "That some provision was necessary against these people, so far as they were disturbers of civil peace and order, every one will allow; but such sanguinary laws against particular doctrines or tenets in religion are not to be defended. The most that can be said for our ancestors is, that they tried gentler means at first, which they found utterly ineffectual, and that they followed the example of the authorities in most other states and in most other ages of the world, who, with the like absurdity, have supposed every person could and ought to think as they did, and [with] the like cruelly have punished such as appear to differ from them." Neither vindicating nor condemning his ancestors, Hutchinson evaluated the situation with the eye of a prudent conservative statesman. He discounts both filiopiety and abstract theories of liberty: the Puritans were wrong because their plan was absurd and impractical.

During the early 1760s, when the British Parliament began to enact the revenue measures which eventually brought on the Revolution, Lieutenant-Governor Hutchinson was among those Americans who actively opposed them. But his reasons for opposition were notably different from those of many of his countrymen. He challenged the legality of the writs of assistance, but he retracted his opposition when he discovered that they were being issued in England as well. He disapproved of the Sugar Act—on the grounds that it would have been detrimental to both British and American trade. Never did he claim that Parliament had no right to pass the laws; he simply thought that they were unwise. In 1764, just as the first volume of his history was being published, he wrote an essay on the Stamp Act, which he sent to Richard Jackson, Massachusetts's provincial agent in London, in hopes that it would be used to help persuade Parliament not to enact the law. The tone of the essay is moderate and conciliatory; the arguments are based on legal precedent and history. "I am ... far from imagining the Colonists to be independent of the Parliament," he wrote, "but I consider the Parliament as suspending the exercise of certain powers over the Colonists which would have been in constant exercise if they had remained in the mother Country." Hutchinson's conservative approach did not sit well with the leaders of the opposition, such as Otis, who were raising cries of "no taxation without representation." They appealed to the social contract, going so far as to claim that they were subject to the British government only so long as its rule was salutary. Hutchinson believed "that in the very nature of a Colony it is to remain the appendage of the Mother State." They were ready to resist; he felt bound to comply, appointing his brother-in-law, Andrew Oliver, to the office of stamp distributor. On 26 August 1765, a violent mob attacked his home, forcing the family to flee to the home of their relative the Reverend Samuel Mather. Hutchinson's papers were strewn in the mud of Garden Court Street, among them the manuscript for the second volume of his *History of Massachusetts Bay*. (It was later rescued and returned by family friend Andrew Eliot.) "Such ruin," he wrote to Richard Jackson, "was never seen in America." Despite the setbacks, material and emotional, Hutchinson went on to complete volume two, which was published in 1767, and in 1769 he compiled *A Collection of Original Papers*, the significant documentary sources for his history that had survived the riot.

On 18 March 1766 the Stamp Act was repealed, but it was accompanied by the passage of the Declaratory Act, which reaffirmed, without qualification, Parliament's authority over the colonies. The following year, the Townshend Acts were passed, placing tariffs on certain imported goods, such as glass, paper, and tea. In response, the Massachusetts House issued a circular letter urging all the colonies to resist. Political writers began to produce a literature of opposition: John Dickinson, for one, published his enormously popular *Letters From a Farmer in Pennsylvania . . .* (1768), asserting that the "sacred cause" of liberty "ought to be espoused by every man, on every occasion, to the utmost of his power."

Hutchinson felt the pressing need for "an ingenious writer" to counter the growing influence of the radical pamphleteers who, while defending colonial rights, "would keep the mean between a slavish subjection on the one hand and absolute independence on the other." He began work on such a tract himself, in its final form a dialogue between a "European" Englishman and an "American" Englishman. "America is in a very different state from what it was when I last saw you in England," says the European, and the interlocutors proceed to discuss the troubled state of colonial affairs. Admirably suitable for the expression of his moderate position, the dialogue form allowed Hutchinson to elaborate both sides of the current debates, which he did with skill and probity. "You will say it is our fault," says the American, "we think it is yours." The discussions range from history, both ancient and modern, to law, to the political theories of John Locke. Throughout, Hutchinson kept his personal animosities under tight rein, although at one point he had the American "ready to acknowledge that the most considerate part of the people in America have no great opinion of the virtue of their present leaders," doubting whether any of the leaders "will ever be left executors to any will or entrusted with the guardianship of any children or have the care of any private affairs." In general, however, the dialogue, like the history, is a work distinguished by its evenhandedness, even more so considering the author's own desperate involvement in the issues it discusses. For some reason, Hutchinson made no efforts to have the dialogue published.

Matters went from bad to worse for Hutchinson. The Boston Massacre on 1 March 1770 further enraged the public against royal authority. A year later, he was inaugurated as royal governor although he pleaded with the authorities to appoint "a person of superior power of body and mind." When he named Peter Oliver, his daughter's father-in-law, as Chief Justice and Andrew Oliver, his brother-in-law, as lieutenant-governor, he lay the groundwork for further charges of corruption. On 6 January 1773, amid a controversy over the Crown's assumption of the responsibility for paying the royal governor's salary (thus limiting the colonial legislature's power over him), Hutchinson addressed the General Court. His purpose was once again conservative, "to promote that peace and order, upon which your own happiness and prosperity, as well as his Majesty's service, very much depend." His tone, as always in public, was frank and conciliatory: "I shall be explicit, and treat the subject without reserve," he announced. "I hope you will receive what I have to say upon it, with candor, and, if you shall not agree in sentiments with me, I promise you, with candor, likewise, to receive and consider what you may offer in answer." He argued against colonial attempts to limit Parliamentary authority in words that reverberate with historical irony: "I know of no line that can be drawn between the supreme authority of Parliament and the total independence of the colonies." The speech was soon published by the legislature—along with rebuttals by members of the Court, who were delighted at the opportunity.

That same year, the most critical volume of

COPY

OF

LETTERS

Sent to *Great-Britain*, by his Excellency *Thomas Hutchinson*, the Hon. *Andrew Oliver*, and several other Persons, BORN AND EDUCATED AMONG US.

Which original Letters have been returned to *America*, and laid before the honorable House of Representatives of this Province.

In which (notwithstanding his Excellency's Declaration to the House, that the tendency and Design of them was not to subvert the Constitution, but rather preserve it entire) the judicious Reader will discover the fatal Source of the Confusion and Bloodshed in which this Province especially has been involved, and which threatned total Destruction to the Liberties of all *America*.

BOSTON:

Printed by EDES and GILL, in Queen-Street. 1773.

Title page for the unauthorized publication of the letters in which Hutchinson expressed the belief that order could be restored in the colonies only through the abridgment of liberties (courtesy of the John Carter Brown Library at Brown University)

Hutchinson's career was published, without his authorization and against his will. Since 1768 he had been corresponding wth Thomas Whately, a former member of the British government. There were fourteen letters in all; in them he expressed some of the bitterness he refused to permit in his public writing. After Whately's death, the letters, along with some written by Andrew Oliver and others, came into the possession of Benjamin Franklin, then agent for the Massachusetts legislature, who sent them on to the General Court, who passed judgment on them: "the Tendency and Design of said Letters was to Subvert the Constitution of this Government, and to introduce Arbitrary Power into the Province." Despite Hutchinson's angry, indignant demand that his personal letters be returned to him, they soon found their way into print. One passage was particularly damning: "I never think of the measures necessary for the peace and good order of the colonies without pain: there must be an abridgment of what are called English liberties. I relieve myself by considering that in a remove from the state of nature to the most perfect state of government, there must be a great restraint of natural liberty. I doubt whether it is possible to project a system of government in which a Colony, three thousand miles distant from the parent state, shall enjoy all the liberty of the parent state. I am certain I have never yet seen the projection." Although the passage merely repeats the ideas he had been espousing all along, the bleak tone of the remarks combined with the air of conspiracy that played about the discovery of the letters served to stigmatize Hutchinson as an enemy of liberty and a traitor to his native land. He was burned and hanged in effigy and maligned in newspapers and broadsides throughout the colonies. "It is grievous to be vilified & reproached by so great a part of the people," he wrote to Stephen William, "but the historians of all Centuries and all ages shew that the vulgar or common people are easily led away by artful designing men." There may have been some comfort in these reflections, but Hutchinson's political career was virtually over.

On 13 May 1774, General Gage arrived in Massachusetts to relieve Hutchinson temporarily of his duties. The beleaguered governor sailed for England on 1 June with his son Elisha and his daughter Peggy, arrived at Dover on 29 June, and met with King George III on 1 July. He never returned to America; his property was confiscated. Late in 1775 he wrote an "Account and Defense of Conduct" to vindicate himself against the charges of his old opponents in America as well as his new enemies in England, who charged Hutchinson with fomenting the American rebellion. On 19 January 1776 he delivered the document to Lord Dartmouth to present to the king, but there is no evidence that it was ever read. On 4 July 1776, while his countrymen across the Atlantic were accomplishing what he had long dreaded and fought to prevent, Hutchinson was awarded the honorary degree of Doctor of Civil Law by Oxford University. When the news of American independence reached him he wrote, and published anonymously, *Strictures upon the Declaration of the Congress at Philadelphia*. In it he argued that the colonists' complaints about abuses were simply excuses to instigate rebellion. "I verily believe," he wrote, "if everything had been granted short of absolute independence they would not have been contented, for this was their object from the beginning." He found the glittering generalities of the Declaration hypocritical: how could the Americans in the South "justify the depriving more than an hundred thousand Africans of their rights to liberty and *the pursuit of happiness*, and in some degree to their lives, if these rights are so absolutely inalienable."

With the publication of *Strictures upon the Declaration of Congress at Philadelphia*, the political activities that had occupied him over the last four decades came to a complete halt. He spent his leisure time completing the third volume of his history, which brings the narrative up to the time of his departure for England. He grew homesick: "I prefer the *natale solum* to all other," he admitted to a friend. On 21 September 1777 his daughter Peggy died and Hutchinson was heartbroken. He threw himself into his work, as he confided in his diary: "Sometimes for a week together I write more or less every day, and then neglect it some days together, and fill the time with reading. If I had not found such employment for my thoughts, my troubles would have preyed upon me much more than they have, and I believe been too powerful. I thank God I have never quitted books, and so I have not lost the relish for them." He completed the work on 22 October 1778. He died on 3 June 1780, and was buried in Croyden, England, beside his daughter. The third volume of the history was not published until 1828.

The vicissitudes of Hutchinson's reputation since the Revolution may, if ever charted, form an interesting chapter in the history of American historiography, and perhaps of American political opinion in general. Although he was defended and praised by Tory historians such as Peter Oliver in his *History & Progress of the American Rebellion* (writ-

First page of the diary that Hutchinson began on his return voyage to England ten in 1781 but not published until 1961), Hutchinson was so vilified by his patriot contemporaries and by the Whig historians of the post-Revolutionary period that their image of him remained current in America throughout most of the nineteenth century, most notably in George Bancroft's popular *History of the United States of America from the Discovery of the Continent* (1834-1876). Nathaniel Hawthorne gave a generous, sympathetic account of him in his children's history, *Grandfather's Chair* (1841), but not until James K. Hosmer's 1896 biography was there an attempt to exonerate the royal governor and restore his reputation. In more recent time, Hutchinson has continued to be an object of dispute. In 1951, Clifford Shipton published an adulatory biographical essay; in the 1960s, New Left historians condemned him anew. Only in 1974, when Bernard Bailyn published *The Ordeal of Thomas Hutchinson*, did his ideas and writings, both published and unpublished, receive a systematic, thoroughgoing, and objective (though highly sympathetic) analysis.

Other:

A Collection of Original Papers Relative to the History of the Colony of Massachusetts-Bay, compiled by Hutchinson (Boston: Printed by Thomas & John Fleet, 1769);

"Hutchinson's Essay on Colonial Rights," in "Thomas Hutchinson and the Stamp Act," by Edmund S. Morgan, *New England Quarterly,* 21 (December 1948): 480-492;

"Additions to Thomas Hutchinson's *History of Massachusetts Bay,*" edited by Catherine Barton Mayo, *American Antiquarian Society Proceedings,* new series, 59 (1949): 11-74;

"A Dialogue between an American and a European Englishman (1768)," edited by Bernard Bailyn, *Perspectives in American History,* 9 (1975): 343-410.

References:

Bernard Bailyn, *The Ordeal of Thomas Hutchinson* (Cambridge: Harvard University Press, 1974);

James K. Hosmer, *The Life of Thomas Hutchinson, Royal Governor of the Province of Massachusetts Bay* (Boston & New York: Houghton, Mifflin, 1896; republished, New York: Da Capo Press, 1972);

Edmund S. Morgan, "Thomas Hutchinson and the Stamp Act," *New England Quarterly,* 21 (December 1948): 459-492;

Peter Shaw, "Their Kinsman, Thomas Hutchinson: The Boston Patriots and His Majesty's Royal Governor," *Early American Literature,* 11 (Fall 1976): 183-190;

Clifford Shipton, *Sibley's Harvard Graduates,* volume 8 (Boston: Massachusetts Historical Society, 1951), pp. 149-217.

Papers:

Many of the surviving papers of Thomas Hutchinson are in the Massachusetts Archive at the State House in Boston—some still with the mud prints of the Stamp Act rioters. Another collection is in the Egerton Manuscripts at the British Museum.

John Jay

(12 December 1745-17 May 1829)

Rick W. Sturdevant
U.S. Air Force History Program

BOOKS: *The Charge Delivered by the Hon. John Jay, Chief Justice of the State of New York, to the Grand Jury at the Supreme Court Held at Kingston, in Ulster Country September 9, 1777* (Kingston: Printed by John Holt, 1777);

Letters, Being the Whole of the Correspondence between the Hon. John Jay, Esquire, and Mr. Lewis Littlepage... (New York: Printed & sold by Francis Childs, 1786; revised and enlarged edition, New York: Printed & sold by Ebenezer Oswald, 1786);

An Address to the People of the State of New-York, on the Subject of the Constitution, Agreed upon at Philadelphia, the 17th of September, 1787, as a citizen of New-York (New York: Printed by S. & J. Loudons, 1788);

The Charge of Chief Justice Jay to the Grand Juries on the Eastern Circuit... (Portsmouth: Printed & sold by George Jerry Osborne, Jr., 1790);

A Charge Delivered by the Hon. John Jay, Esq., Chief Justice of the United States, to the Grand Jury of the United States Court, Virginia (Richmond: Printed by Samuel Pleasants, 1793);

Collections: *The Correspondence and Public Papers of John Jay,* 4 volumes, edited by Henry P. Johnston (New York & London: Putnam's, 1890-1893);

The Diary of John Jay during the Peace Negotiations of 1782, edited by Frank Monaghan (New Haven: Bibliographical Press, Yale University, 1934);

Some Conversations of Dr. Franklin and Mr. Jay; being the first publication of a manuscript written by John Jay in Paris during 1783-1784, edited by Monaghan (New Haven: Three Monks Press, 1936);

John Jay: The Making of a Revolutionary, Unpublished Papers, 1745-1780, edited by Richard B. Morris (New York: Harper & Row, 1975);

John Jay: The Winning of the Peace, Unpublished Papers, 1780-1784, edited by Morris (New York: Harper & Row, 1980).

SELECTED PUBLIC DOCUMENTS: U.S. Continental Congress, *To the People of Great Britain*

Portrait by Gilbert Stuart and John Trumbull, circa 1794 (National Portrait Gallery, Smithsonian Institution)

... (Philadelphia: Printed by W. & T. Bradford, 1774; London, 1775);

U.S. Continental Congress, *Lettre Addressé aux Habitans Opprimés de la Province de Québec. De la Part du Congrès Général de l'Amérique Septentrionale Tenu à Philadelphia,* translated by Pierre Eugène du Simitière (Philadelphia: Printed by Fleury Meplet, 1775);

New York (State) Convention of Representatives, *An Address of the Convention of the Representatives of the State of New-York to Their Constituents* (Fishkill: Printed by Samuel Loudon, 1776);

U.S. Continental Congress. *A Circular Letter from the*

Congress of the United States of America to their Constituents (Philadelphia: Printed by David C. Claypoole, 1779).

OTHER: Essays 2, 3, 4, 5, and 64, in *The Federalist: A Collection of Essays, Written in Favour of the New Constitution, As Agreed upon by the Federal Convention,* by Jay, James Madison, and Alexander Hamilton, 2 volumes (New York: Printed & sold by J. & A. McLean, 1788).

As a statesman, diplomat, and jurist, John Jay contributed significantly to the formation of republican order in America. Both his private correspondence and his public communications testify to his staunch integrity and unswerving commitment to the cause of liberty and justice among men. Although peaceful in temperament and reluctant to rush headlong into armed conflict with Great Britain, he consistently opposed absolute parliamentary sovereignty as incompatible with American liberties. A careful survey of Jay's published works, most of them public documents which appeared without acknowledgment of his authorship, establishes him as one of America's foremost political writers.

John Jay, the sixth son of merchant Peter Jay and his wife, Mary Van Cortlandt, was born in New York City on 12 December 1745. His paternal grandfather, Auguste, had come to New York around 1686 as a French Huguenot exile. Peter Jay, who described his son John's disposition as "very grave" and "very reserved," sent John to Calvinist minister Peter Stouppe's school in New Rochelle. The bookish youth graduated with a B.A. from King's College (now Columbia University) in 1764, studied law in Benjamin Kissam's firm, and gained admission to the bar on 26 October 1768. In Kissam's law office Jay first demonstrated an especially lucid literary style—one that would later appear strikingly similar to Alexander Hamilton's. Jay's religious heritage and legal training left their imprint on all that he wrote.

On 28 April 1774, Jay married Sarah Van Brugh Livingston, youngest daughter of politically powerful William Livingston. Six months later, as a delegate to the First Continental Congress, he joined the first rank of republican propagandists by drafting the congress's address, *To the People of Great Britain*. Thomas Jefferson recalled that the reading of Jay's draft evoked "but one sentiment of admiration" among the assembled delegates, and Jefferson labeled it "a production certainly of the finest pen in America . . . the first composition in the English language." Demonstrating Jay's early adherence to the principle that sovereignty rests ultimately with the people rather than the government, the document appealed directly to the people of Great Britain and asked them to prevent Parliamentary ministers from forging additional links in the chain that had enslaved the colonists since 1763. True to Jay's Calvinist upbringing, it roundly condemned the Quebec Act's provision for a Roman Catholic bishop in French Canada. In a rather prophetic anticipation of nineteenth- and twentieth-century opinions on procedural and substantive due process, it argued that the right to trial by jury and the right of the accused to an adequate defense are so fundamental that no earthly power can deny them. Speaking for the congress, he implored the people of Great Britain to, "Permit us to be as free as yourselves, and we shall ever esteem a union with you to be our greatest glory and our greatest happiness." However, in the next pen stroke he asserted, "We will never submit to be hewers of wood or drawers of water for any ministry or nation in the world." This masterful statement of a conciliatory but uncompromising stance provided a rallying point for all but the most outspoken radicals and conservatives in the colonies.

Jay maintained his moderate position during the Second Continental Congress. He drafted in May 1775, *Lettre Addressé aux Habitans Opprimés de la Province de Québec,* which demonstrated a more ecumenical attitude toward Roman Catholicism than that expressed in *To the People of Great Britain* and encouraged Canadian Catholics to join their Protestant neighbors in opposition to British tyranny. In June 1775 his draft of the "Olive Branch Petition"—the final form was largely the work of John Dickinson—disavowed independence and acknowledged Parliament's right to regulate commerce. Into early July 1776 Jay hoped for some settlement short of independence. Then, as a member of New York's Provincial Congress, he drafted the state's resolution endorsing the Declaration of Independence.

When the Continental Army lost Fort Lee and retreated across New Jersey during the waning days of 1776, Jay, on behalf of the New York State Convention of Representatives, and Thomas Paine each wrote pamphlets exhorting their readers to save the revolutionary cause through more vigorous action. *An Address of the Convention of the Representatives of the State of New-York to Their Constituents* evidenced a persuasive method very different from Paine's *The Crisis, Number I*. The convention's address, which bore a much more intellectual approach than Paine's pamphlet, rested its argument on Lockian logic rather than emotional appeal. Jay's clear expression rendered the argument so comprehensible and convincing to a mass audience that the Continental Congress arranged to have the address translated into German, printed, and distributed in German-speaking sections of New Jersey and Pennsylvania, where the British army was likely to penetrate. Countless patriots absorbed the memorable concluding lines: "We believe, and are persuaded, that you will do your duty like men, and cheerfully refer your cause to the great and righteous Judge. If success crown your efforts, all the blessings of Freedom will be your reward. If you fail in the contest, you will be happy with God and Liberty in Heaven." Jay's words were a fitting exhortation for what Paine had described a few days earlier in *The Crisis* as "times that try men's souls."

After serving on the committee which drafted New York's constitution, Jay became the first Chief Justice of the New York Supreme Court in May 1777. On 9 September 1777, he opened the court's first session with a charge to the grand jury at Kingston, Ulster County. Perceiving history as replete with examples of villainous conspiracies and personal vices that undermined constitutional liberties, he encouraged every New Yorker to "diligently read and study the constitution of his country, and teach the rising generation to be free." He believed that a virtuous and vigilant citizenry afforded the only viable safeguard against the collapse of constitutional government.

Jay left the New York bench in December 1778 to assume the presidency of the Continental Congress. On 13 September 1779, that body adopted his draft for *A Circular Letter from the Congress of the United States of America to their Constituents,* which argued that the Articles of Confederation were effective despite less-than-unanimous consent by the states. He reminded his readers that twelve of the thirteen states—all save Maryland—had already consented to the Articles of Confederation and, regardless of Maryland's reluctance, all the states had entered into "perpetual confederation" by approving the Declaration of Independence. His belief that the Union could not be dissolved in favor of restoration of independent, sovereign states proved him an ardent nationalist. Only two weeks after signing the circular letter, Jay became minister plenipotentiary to Spain. He served in Madrid until May 1782, when he went to Paris to serve with John Adams and Benjamin Franklin as a negotiator of the Anglo-American peace. During the first week of October 1782 Jay drew up the initial draft of the Articles of Peace. When he returned to America in July 1784, he served first as the Confederation government's Secretary of Foreign Affairs and then as the new constitutional government's acting secretary of state until Jefferson returned from France in March 1790. Meanwhile, in 1785, he became the first president of the New York Society for Promoting the Manumission of Slaves.

In December 1785 the flamboyant gadfly Lewis Littlepage publicly accused Jay of personal treachery and public conspiracy while on diplomatic service in Europe. Jay, who had sponsored the eighteen-year-old Virginia stranger in Spain, apparently had refused to overlook Littlepage's social misbehavior and financial recklessness. Littlepage sought revenge. To preserve his self-esteem and protect his reputation as a faithful public servant, Jay resorted to publication of his private correspondence with Littlepage from the years in Spain and France. Francis Childs's first edition of *Letters, Being the Whole of the Correspondence between the Hon. John Jay, Esquire, and Mr. Lewis Littlepage,* published during the second week of January 1786, contained so many errors that Jay contracted Eleazar Oswald to print an expanded, revised edition several months later. As he promised in his introduction, the author calmly and methodically arranged the evidence to prove that Littlepage's accusations were a total fabrication.

Jay's best-remembered literary effort may be his collaboration with James Madison and Alexander Hamilton to write *The Federalist*—a series of eighty-five essays designed to promote ratification of the United States Constitution. Due to a lengthy bout with crippling arthritis, Jay contributed only five of the essays: numbers 2, 3, 4, 5, and 64. The four early essays dealt with the importance of a strong, stable union in the maintenance of American peace and freedom. Essay number 2 appeared on 31 October 1787 in New York's *Independent Journal.* Elaborating on themes explored in the circular letter of 1779, Jay reasoned that geographic circumstances, common language, religious customs, and attachment to republican principles of government naturally rendered union more advantageous than independent states or regional confederacies. In essay number 3 he demonstrated his familiarity with literature on international law and military history by arguing that foreign powers were less likely to find "just causes" for war if confronted by an efficient national government, while in essay number 4 he explored the likelihood of "unjust war" if the states appeared weak and dis-

> Having after much Consideration become persuaded that these were Mr. ~~de~~ Rayneval's objects, I mentioned his Journey to Mr Oswald, and after stating to him the first three of those Objects ~~[struck through]~~ I said every thing respecting them, that appeared to me necessary but at the same Time with a greater Degree of Caution than I would have wished, because I well knew it would become the subject of a long Letter to the Ministry — On Reflecting however how necessary it was that Lord Shelburn should know our Sentiments & Resolutions respecting these matters, & how much better they would be conveyed in Conversation than by Letter — and knowing also that Mr. Vaughan was in confidential Correspondence with him, and he was ~~so~~ and always had been strongly attached to the american Cause, I concluded it would be prudent to prevail upon him to go immediately to England —

A page from Jay's 17 November 1782 letter to the Secretary of Foreign Affairs, Robert R. Livingston, on the peace negotiations with England

Jay retired to this house, near Bedford, New York, in 1801.

united in the face of the overwhelming power of England, France, or Spain. Essay number 5 drew an analogy from the history of England and Scotland to suggest the likelihood of divisive wars among regional confederacies if the union of American states was not cemented more effectively. Finally, essay number 64, which appeared on 7 March 1788, defended the treaty-making provisions of the proposed Constitution on the grounds that they made national interest paramount, gave the president authority to negotiate effectively, assured fairness to all states through Senate review, and guaranteed treaties the force of supreme law. In response to objections that corruption might result in treaties serving private rather than public interest, he found it unthinkable "that the president and two thirds of the senate" would "ever be capable of such unworthy conduct." A careful reading of these essays will provide a sense of how diligently Jay labored over phrasing—sometimes producing rare gems but at other points destroying brilliance with cautiously muted expressions.

In *An Address to the People of the State of New-York* (1788), Jay wrote a more emotional, but no less meticulous, appeal for ratification of the United States Constitution. Writing pseudonymously as "a citizen of New-York," he bemoaned the collapse of that union which "was the child of wisdom" blessed by heaven to produce "our political salvation." At a time when people around the world were inspired by America's example, he lamented the political and economic disarray in the republican experiment and urged his fellow New Yorkers to preserve the Union through immediate adoption of the new Constitution. He pointed out that since New York's constitution had no bill of rights, the proposed national Constitution needed none in order to secure the blessings of liberty to posterity. He believed that belaboring the issue would give historians reason to say that something less than the highest motives underlay the formulation of the document. When Benjamin Franklin read the pamphlet, he immediately encouraged Jay to go on public record as its author in order to further bolster the crusade for ratification. George Washington found the copy that Jay sent him so filled with "good sense, forcible observations, temper and moderation" that he passed it on to James Madison and requested several more copies from the author. Noah Webster, reviewing the pamphlet in the April 1788 issue of

American Magazine, remarked, "Several of the observations are new, and all are penned with such moderation of temper, and sound judgment, that they cannot fail to make an impression favorable to the Constitution on minds which are open to conviction."

From March 1789 until June 1795, when he resigned to become governor of New York, Jay served as the first Chief Justice of the United States Supreme Court. His most noteworthy opinion was *Chisholm v. Georgia,* which he delivered on 18 February 1793. Resting his opinion on the principle that state sovereignty and suability are not incompatible, he decided that citizens from one state could sue another state. Only two days after he handed down the decision the Senate entertained a motion to amend the Constitution, and adoption of the Eleventh Amendment effectively reversed Jay's opinion. Later in 1793 he prepared the first draft of the Neutrality Proclamation, and on 22 May of that year he propounded before a Richmond grand jury the controversial doctrine that courts could decide cases involving violation of administrative regulations on neutrality, even in the absence of congressional enabling legislation. In 1794, while still officially on the bench, he traveled to England to negotiate the unpopular treaty bearing his name. Although Jeffersonian Republicans regarded the Jay Treaty as toadying to the English, its contents exhibited Jay's adroitness at balancing the interests of various groups and regions in order to peacefully preserve the new nation's fragile autonomy. Throughout his chief justiceship, Jay's every expression substantiated his ardent federalism.

Between 1795 and 1801 Jay served as governor of New York, and he signed that state's act abolishing slavery. He retired from political life at the end of his second gubernatorial term and participated in efforts to foster the ecumenical spirit encouraged in the 1775 letter to the inhabitants of Quebec. He became president of the Westchester Bible Society in 1818 and of the American Bible Society in 1821. Jay died at his home near Bedford, New York, on 17 May 1829. Privately, he struggled to the end for perfection of his own life through Christian moral decency and rigid self-discipline. Publicly, he never doubted the necessity for eternal vigilance, lest his nation's life degenerate under the influence of political demagogues.

Biographies:

William Jay, *Life of John Jay,* 2 volumes (New York: Harper, 1833);

George Pellew, *John Jay* (Boston & New York: Houghton, Mifflin, 1890);

Frank Monaghan, *John Jay, Defender of Liberty* (New York & Indianapolis: Bobbs-Merrill, 1935).

References:

Jerald A. Combs, *The Jay Treaty: Political Battleground of the Founding Fathers* (Berkeley: University of California Press, 1970);

Gottfried Dietze, *The Federalist, a Classic on Federalism and Free Government* (Baltimore: Johns Hopkins Press, 1960);

Albert Furtwangler, "Strategies of Candor in *The Federalist,*" *Early American Literature,* 14 (Spring 1979): 91-109;

Jon Jay Ide, *The Portraits of John Jay* (New York: New-York Historical Society, 1938);

Richard B. Morris, *John Jay, the Nation, and the Court* (Boston: Boston University Press, 1967);

Morris, *The Peacemakers: The Great Powers and American Independence* (New York: Harper & Row, 1965).

Papers:

John Jay's papers are scattered throughout numerous public and private archives in the United States and Europe. The Jay Papers Project has made an exhaustive effort to obtain originals or photocopies of all extant manuscripts to and from Jay and to place the material in Special Collections, Columbia University Libraries. Among the Jay papers in the New-York Historical Society are his draft of essay 64 in *The Federalist* and his copy of the 1794 treaty with Great Britain. The Library Company of Philadelphia, now housed in the Historical Society of Pennsylvania, has Jay's draft of the "Olive Branch Petition." The Henry E. Huntington Library possesses the letterbook from Jay's Spanish mission. There is also considerable material on Jay's various diplomatic efforts in foreign archives: Archivo Histórico Nacional in Madrid; Archivo General de Indias in Seville; Archivo General de Simancas; British Foreign Office records in the Public Record Office, London; and Archives of the Ministére des Affaires Etrangères, at the Quai d'Orsay, Paris.

Thomas Jefferson

Robert D. Richardson, Jr.
University of Denver

BIRTH: Shadwell, Goochland (now Albemarle) County, Virginia, 13 April 1743, to Peter and Jane Randolph Jefferson.

EDUCATION: William and Mary College, 1760-1762; read law with George Wythe, 1762-1767.

MARRIAGE: 1 January 1772 Martha Wayles Skelton; children: Martha, Jane Randolph, an unnamed son, Mary (or Maria), Lucy Elizabeth, Lucy Elizabeth.

DEATH: Monticello, Virginia, 4 July 1826.

SELECTED BOOKS: *A Summary View of the Rights of British America* . . . (Williamsburg: Printed for Clementina Rind, 1774; London: Printed for G. Kearsly, 1774);
Notes on the State of Virginia . . . (Paris: Privately printed, 1785; London: J. Stockdale, 1787; Philadelphia: Printed & sold by Pritchard & Hall, 1788);
A Manual of Parliamentary Practice For Use in the Senate of the United States (Washington, D.C.: Printed by Samuel Harrison Smith, 1801; enlarged edition, Washington, D.C.: Published by William Cooper/Georgetown: Published by Joseph Milligan, 1812);
The Autobiography of Thomas Jefferson, in volume 1 of *Memoir, Correspondence and Miscellanies from the Papers of Thomas Jefferson*, 4 volumes, edited by Thomas Jefferson Randolph (Charlottesville: F. Carr, 1829); republished as *Memoirs, Correspondence and Private Papers of Thomas Jefferson* (London: Colburn & Bentley, 1829);
An Essay Towards Facilitating Instruction in the Anglo Saxon and Modern Dialects of the English Language . . . (New York: Printed by J. F. Trow for the Trustees of the University of Virginia, 1851);
The Life and Morals of Jesus of Nazareth [English text only] (St. Louis, Chicago & New York: N. D. Thompson, 1902); [Greek, Latin, French, and English texts] (Washington, D.C.: U.S. Government Printing Office, 1904);
The Commonplace Book of Thomas Jefferson, edited by

Portrait of Thomas Jefferson by Charles Willson Peale, 1791 (Independence National Historical Park Collection, Philadelphia)

Gilbert Chinard (Baltimore: Johns Hopkins Press/Paris: Les Presses Universitaires de France, 1926);
The Literary Bible of Thomas Jefferson: His Commonplace Book of Philosophers and Poets, edited by Chinard (Baltimore: Johns Hopkins Press/Paris: Les Presses Universitaires de France, 1928);
Thomas Jefferson's Garden Book, 1766-1824, edited by Edwin Morris Betts (Philadelphia: American Philosophical Society, 1944);
Thomas Jefferson's Farm Book, edited by Betts (Princeton: Princeton University Press, 1953).

Editions and Collections: *The Writings of Thomas*

Jefferson, edited by Paul Leiscester Ford, 10 volumes (New York: Putnam's, 1892-1899);

The Writings of Thomas Jefferson, edited by Andrew A. Lipscomb and Albert Ellery Bergh, 20 volumes (Washington, D.C.: Thomas Jefferson Memorial Association, 1903-1904);

Autobiography, edited by Ford (New York: Putnam's, 1914);

The Declaration of Independence, edited by J. P. Boyd, revised edition (Princeton: Princeton University Press, 1945);

The Papers of Thomas Jefferson, first series, edited by Julian P. Boyd and others, 20 volumes to date (Princeton: Princeton University Press, 1950-); second series, edited by Charles T. Cullen and others, 1 volume to date (Princeton: Princeton University Press, 1983-);

Notes on the State of Virginia, edited by William Peden (Chapel Hill: University of North Carolina Press, 1955).

SELECTED PUBLIC DOCUMENTS: U.S. Declaration of Independence, *In Congress, July 4, 1776. A Declaration by the Representatives of the United States of America, In General Congress Assembled* (Various imprints, 1776);

Virginia. Laws, Statutes, etc., *An Act For Establishing Religious Freedom, Passed in the Assembly of Virginia in the Beginning of the Year 1786* (Paris, 1786; Richmond: Printed by John Dunlap & James Hayes, 1786).

Thomas Jefferson's universally acknowledged importance as a statesman has tended to overshadow his very substantial contributions to American literature. He was the penman of the American Revolution who, more than any other single person, created the characteristic language of the new American experiment in representative democracy. He gave clear, definitive articulation to the concept of natural (as distinguished from civil) rights, to the ideas of both civil and religious liberty, to the concept of minimal government, and to the preference for a rural agricultural citizenry over urban industrialism. Perceiving the need for an educated citizenry if democracy were to work, he advocated an aristocracy of virtue and talent over the "tinsel aristocracy" of inherited wealth and privilege. Jefferson was also an early advocate for the study of Old English, for the acceptance of a changing, adaptive English language, and for the development of a specifically American English. He was a major spokesman in the eighteenth-century revival of the Greek and Roman ethical thought of the Stoic and Epicurean schools, making the ideas and the language of those schools a part of subsequent American values and language. Important as an early writer against a state-established church, he was also a key figure in the late-eighteenth- and early-nineteenth-century revolt against Calvinism, replacing the dogmas of depravity, damnation, and predestination with an enlightenment typology of faith in human nature, and progress through education and free will.

Jefferson's early years were spent at Tuckahoe on the James River, not far from Richmond. His father, Peter Jefferson, was a self-made man. Tradition says he was of Welsh stock. Jefferson's mother was a Virginia Randolph. "They trace their pedigree far back in England and Scotland," Jefferson observed in his autobiography, "to which let everyone ascribe the faith and merit he chooses." At nine, Jefferson attended the school of the Reverend William Douglas, the minister of St. James Parish, Northam, remaining there until 1857, the year his father died. Early the following year Jefferson entered the Reverend James Maury's school in Fredericksville Parish. His admiration for the classics, which dates from this early schooling, was not simply as a discipline of the mind, nor as a help to mastering English. Jefferson's interest in the classics centered, early and late, on the strong arterial tradition of Greek and Roman ethical thought, a tradition which, from the pre-Socratics down to Epicurus, Epictetus, and Marcus Aurelius, was unified in its emphasis on the importance of autarky, or self-rule, as the basis for a virtuous and a happy life.

In March 1760, at the age of sixteen, Jefferson entered the College of William and Mary at Williamsburg, where he was lucky enough to come at once under the influence of Dr. William Small, the only layman on the faculty, the professor of natural philosophy, who also taught ethics, rhetoric, and belles lettres with what Jefferson called a "happy talent of communication." It was Small, said Jefferson, who "probably fixed the destinies of my life.... He, most happily for me, became soon attached to me, and made me his daily companion when not engaged in the school; and from his conversation I got my first views of the expansion of science, and of the system of things in which we are placed." Small introduced Jefferson to Governor Francis Fauquier and George Wythe, the "most noted teacher of law of his generation in Virginia." Jefferson later acknowledged that he owed much to the conversations of this group, in which he heard, he said, "more good sense, more rational and philosophical conversation" than at any other time in his life.

Two years later, in 1762, Small returned to Europe, and the nineteen-year-old Jefferson, still in Williamsburg, began the study of law with Wythe. His education was thus entirely American and entirely local. Indeed Jefferson never thought much of European education. He was, in the fullest sense, a Virginian, born, raised, educated, and formed there. He was twenty-three before he ever made a trip out of the state, on a three-month journey to Annapolis, Philadelphia, and New York. At twenty-four he was admitted to the bar; at twenty-five (in 1768) he was elected to the Virginia Assembly. In the same year he began work on what would be his lifelong home, Monticello. Virginia was as important to Jefferson as Concord was to Thoreau, and Jefferson cannot be fully understood apart from this profoundly local context.

In 1771, when the twenty-eight-year-old Jefferson was reelected to the Virginia Assembly, he took time from his political and legal duties and interests to answer a query from Robert Skipwith about the books one might want for a personal library. On Jefferson's list half the titles are in the "fine arts," and, in turn, the vast majority of these, seventy-four, are in literature, with the emphasis falling heavily on eighteenth-century English. The titles listed under religion are dominated by Epictetus, Marcus Aurelius, Seneca, and Cicero. There are eight titles listed under politics and trade, three under law, twelve under ancient history, eight under modern history, and thirteen under natural philosophy and natural history. Jefferson, called by Gilbert Chinard "the most widely read American of his generation," recognized early the enormous educative power of English literature, much as did Goethe, who was at this time urging the study of English literature in Germany.

From about 1764 to about 1772, Jefferson also compiled a notebook, published only in 1928 as *The Literary Bible of Thomas Jefferson*. Filled with his favorite quotations from Greek, Latin, and English writers, this notebook shows the early Jefferson already absorbed by ideas, particularly ethical ideas, in literature. He clearly valued Homer, Cicero, and others for what they could teach him about how to live. His interest in Cicero, for example, was not in his orations or his oratorical style; it was in Cicero's moral essays, in such things as the argument against physical immortality. From *The Literary Bible* it is clear that the early Jefferson was far more strongly impressed by Greek and Roman ethical thought than by Christianity. If he later called himself a follower of Epicurus, he may be said to have begun as a stoic in the Ciceronian and Senecan tradition.

Jefferson made his first substantial contribution to political literature in 1774. Called *A Summary View of the Rights of British America*, this pamphlet opened a seven-year period of intense productiveness for Jefferson, a period which coincided, not accidentally, with the American Revolution. Jefferson's twenty-three-page pamphlet, which Dumas Malone says "gained wider currency than any other writing of his that was published during the Revolution except the Declaration," was written in response to the English closure of the port of Boston in retaliation for the Boston Tea Party. It is a major articulation of the idea of natural rights, that is, that people have certain rights simply by virtue of being people, rights prior and superior to any rights created by civil law. This pamphlet, an impassioned but clear and forcefully written philosophical preliminary to the more-celebrated Declaration of Independence, also contains Jefferson's early and important grounds for denying the authority of the English Parliament over the colonies. As a young law student and as a landholder, he had early become interested in the legal aspects of how land is held, and in the question of Parliament's legal authority over lands in Virginia and other colonies. He maintained that the colonies stood in relation to England exactly as had Scotland from the accession of James I to the Act of Union; that is, they shared an "executive chief [the king] but no other necessary political connection." This pamphlet, coinciding with the emergence of the revolutionary Committees of Correspondence, brought Jefferson to wide attention as an articulate proponent of freedom and self-government and as one interested not just in Virginia but in making common cause with the older colonies.

Elected in 1775 to the Continental Congress, Jefferson, now thirty-two, arrived in Philadelphia with what John Adams called "a reputation for literature, science and a happy talent of composition." Returning to the second session in 1776, he was appointed to a five-man committee charged with drawing up a formal declaration of independence from Great Britain. Jefferson alone was asked to prepare the first draft. This version underwent heated debate; some changes were made, but the resulting document, passed by Congress 4 July 1776, was almost entirely the work of Jefferson. (The best modern edition of this document is that edited by J. P. Boyd and published in 1945.) The ideas in it owe much to others, but Jefferson was not striving for originality. The Declaration of Inde-

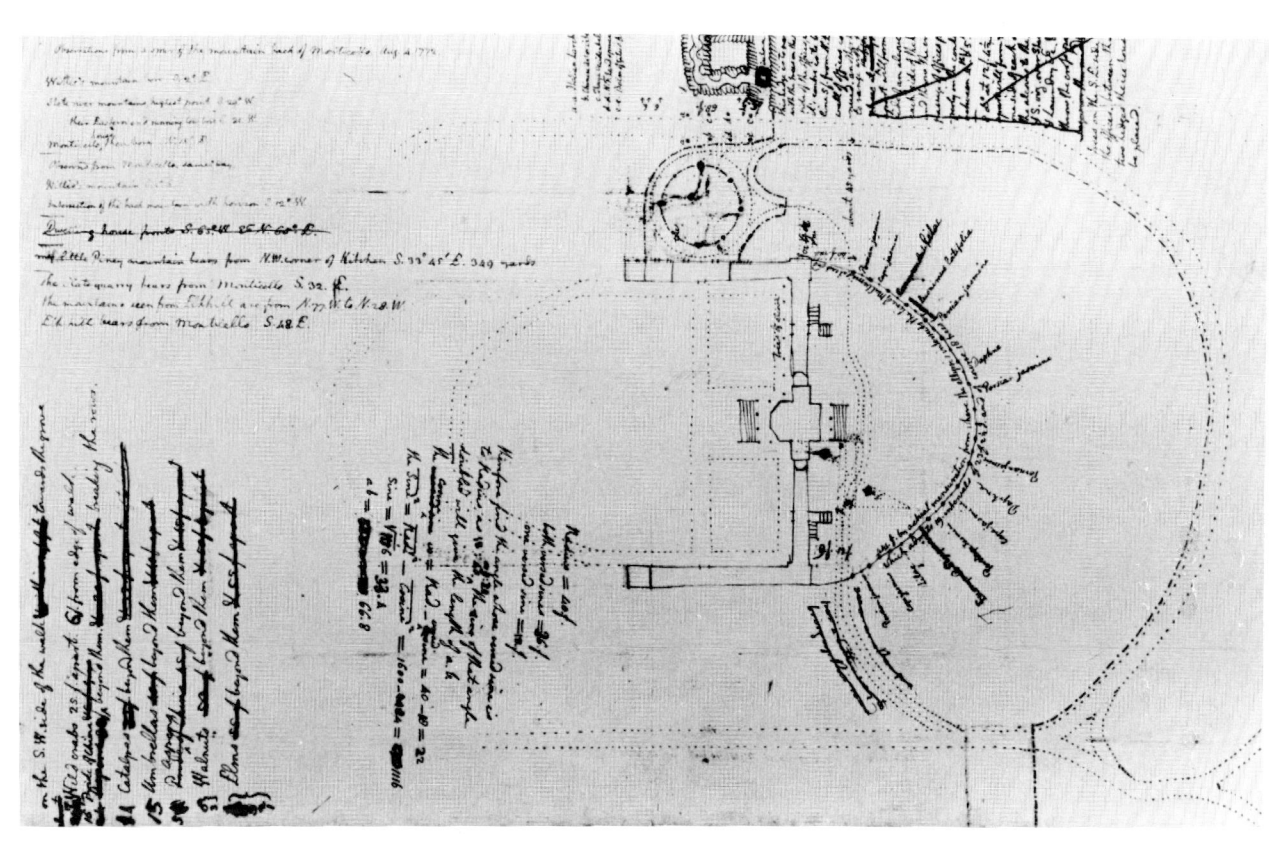

Jefferson's plans for landscaping the mountaintop behind Monticello (Massachusetts Historical Society)

pendence was intended to give plain, emphatic, and above all persuasive expression to a group of generally held ideas about the natural rights belonging to all human beings, the revocable contract that underlies all government, and the right of the people to revolution whenever government becomes destructive of the ends for which it is instituted, namely the individual person's right to life, liberty, and the pursuit of happiness, a formula later adopted by the French for their Declaration of the Rights of Man, but altered there to read "life, liberty and property." Jefferson's style in the declaration also owes much to the eighteenth century that educated him. Though he could write with Baylean wit and irony, especially on religion, and though he could, on occasion, drop into an easy colloquial tone, his style here and in general is marked by what Carl Becker has called an "unimpassioned simplicity of statement." His stylistic virtues are largely those of the Enlightenment. He was no orator; he did not declaim. At his best, Jefferson wrote with persuasive clarity and directness and with a flair for the unimprovable phrase.

Jefferson's lasting achievement in the Declaration of Independence was summed up by Abraham Lincoln, who described Jefferson as "the man who, in the concrete pressure of a struggle for national independence by a single people, had the coolness, forecast, and capacity to introduce into a merely revolutionary document an abstract truth, applicable to all men and all times."

In 1779 Jefferson, then thirty-six, was elected governor of Virginia. As a war governor for the next three years he was adequate if not brilliant, a greater achievement of his first year in that office being his *Act for Establishing Religious Freedom*. Though intended originally only for Virginia and though not passed there until 1786, the act was one of the achievements of his career Jefferson himself most valued. As the central text behind the novel American experiment in separating Church and State, it is as important as the *Declaration of Independence*. "Whereas," Jefferson begins, "Almighty God hath created the mind free; that all attempts to influence it by temporal punishments, or burthens, or by civil incapacitations, tend only to beget habits of hypocrisy and meanness . . . that the impious presumption of legislators and rulers, civil as well as ecclesiastical, who, being themselves but fallible and uninspired men have assumed dominion over the

The portable desk on which Jefferson wrote the Declaration of Independence

faith of others, setting up their own opinions and modes of thinking as the only true and infallible, and as such endeavoring to impose them on others, hath established and maintained false religions over the greatest part of the world and through all time . . ."; the resolution, framed as one long sentence, climbs through twelve reasons mounting to the imperative conclusion: "be it enacted by the general assembly, that no man shall be compelled to frequent or support any religious worship, place or ministry whatsoever. . . ." Based, like the declaration of 1776, on the assumption that people have natural rights, the religious freedom act appeals beyond all institutions, sacred and secular, to recognize the individual conscience as the last, highest court of appeal. Jefferson gives decisive expression here to America's break with the idea of a single state-supported church. In preferring individual conscience to civil or religious authority, Jefferson marks the turn away from the America of Jonathan Edwards toward that of Emerson, Thoreau, and William James.

Toward the close of his busy, war-beset term as governor, and in response to a series of queries put to him by the Marquis de Barbe-Marbois, then Secretary to the French Legation in Philadelphia, Jefferson assembled his *Notes on the State of Virginia* (1785), his only original full-length book. (The best edition of this work is that edited by William Peden and published in 1955.) With little formal unity, *Notes on the State of Virginia* has nevertheless a profound thematic center in Jefferson's love for his native Virginia. The book has been admired as "the most influential scientific book written by an American," and as presenting "more fully than any other treatise of its day what might be called the agenda of the American Enlightenment." In the opening sections, those dedicated to physical description, Jefferson reveals his splendid eye for natural scenery and his romantic sense of the sublime: "The passage of the Potomac through the Blue Ridge is, perhaps, one of the most stupendous scenes in nature. You stand on a very high point of land. On your right comes up the Shenandoah, having ranged along the foot of the mountain an hundred miles to seek a vent. On your left approaches the Potomac, in quest of a passage also. In the moment of their juncture, they rush together

A page from Jefferson's first draft for the Declaration of Independence. The sections in brackets were deleted from the final version (New York Public Library).

against the mountain, rend it asunder, and pass off to the sea." This "full panoramic landscape organized in aesthetic principles," which clearly foreshadows the Hudson River School of painting, was, as Howard Mumford Jones has shown, "the special creation of Thomas Jefferson."

In describing the animals of America, he refutes the assertions of Buffon, the famous French naturalist, that everything common to Europe and America was smaller in America. Much of the vigor of *Notes on the State of Virginia* comes from Jefferson's compositional habit of facing challenges and detractors head on, but without sounding defensive. In the section on laws and government he traces American liberties from the earliest Elizabethan charters with lawyerlike care. In the section on education he describes the College of William and Mary with a sharp eye for its weaknesses and puts forward his idea that an American university ought to have a professorship of ancient Northern languages. On the religious customs of the country, Jefferson, whose bill for religious freedom was not to pass for five more years, was more eloquent and more angry than ever. He insisted that "the legitimate powers of government extend to such acts only as are injurious to others," and he went on in the colloquial style that marks his best writing, especially on the subject of religion, "but it does me no injury for my neighbor to say there are twenty gods, or no God. It neither picks my pocket nor breaks my leg." Yet he was obliged to concede that Virginia still labored under an established church, "a religious slavery under which a people have been willing to remain, who have lavished their lives and fortunes for the establishment of their civil freedom."

By far the least fortunate part of *Notes on the State of Virginia* is Jefferson's account of blacks as inferior to whites, even though he also argued for emancipation, for repatriation, and though he insisted that "it will be right to make great allowances for the difference of condition, of education, of conversation, of the sphere in which they move." On balance, the *Notes on the State of Virginia* is the most remarkable book of its kind between Bradford's *Of Plimmoth Plantation* and Thoreau's *Walden*.

On 6 September 1782, when Jefferson was thirty-nine, his wife Martha died, leaving him with the only two of their children who would survive to maturity—Martha (1772-1836), who was called Patsy, and Mary or Maria (1778-1804), who was called Polly—as well as an infant daughter Lucy Elizabeth, who had been born the previous May and would die in September 1784. The loss affected Jefferson deeply and it was only made worse in that it coincided with the intensification of the war with England and the end of his troubled governorship. Jefferson was a warmly affectionate as well as a deeply private man, but there does not appear to have been any substance to the various rumors begun in 1802 by a notorious scandalmonger named James T. Callender that Jefferson had had liaisons with other women white and black. These rumors persisted, and have figured importantly in such influential accounts as Fawn Brodie's *Thomas Jefferson: An Intimate History* (1974). Jefferson would fall in love with the beautiful Maria Cosway, but that would be some years later, in 1786.

In 1784 Jefferson drew up a "Report of Government for the Western Territories," outlining conditions for the creation of new states. Growing out of Virginia's several-year-old effort to find an acceptable way to cede its territory west of the Ohio, Jefferson's anti-imperialist draft provided that all new states were to be politically equal to the original thirteen, that no person with a hereditary title could become a citizen without forfeiting the title, that any new state would have to remain part of the union "forever," and that there would be no slavery in any new state after 1800. Congress deleted the last two provisions of this far-seeing report, which, had it been passed in its original form, might have prevented the Civil War. The remaining features of Jefferson's report were adopted in the Ordinance of 1784 and again in the Northwest Ordinance of 1787.

This same year, Jefferson was named one of the American Commissioners in Paris, appointed to look after American business interests in Europe, now in disarray because the newly independent nation was no longer part of Britain's trade network. The next year, after only modest success in negotiating commercial treaties, he was appointed to "succeed" Franklin as American Minister to France, since no one, as Jefferson pointed out, could "replace" Benjamin Franklin. Jefferson spent the next four years mostly in Paris. France was edging toward revolution; it was an immensely exciting time. Jefferson knew everyone, and he formed close friendships with Lafayette, La Rochfoucauld, and Condorcet. He traveled, collected furnishings and ideas for Monticello, took notes, bought books, and was "violently smitten" with the Maison Carrée at Nîmes and the Hôtel de Salm in Paris. The architecture of these buildings was reflected later in Jefferson's plans for the state capitol at Richmond and the second Monticello. Jefferson's interests were wide, his taste catholic.

Despite persistent shortages of funds, he loved Paris, as had Franklin, and he revelled in its life. And at the dangerous age of forty-three, he fell completely in love with a witty and beautiful Englishwoman named Maria Cosway. The long letter of 12 October 1786, which he wrote her when she returned to England, is cast as a debate between the head and the heart. As a more or less spontaneous love letter, it is revealing about a seldom seen side of Jefferson. The letter is also an important clue to Jefferson's thinking, in which Neoclassical, Enlightenment and Romantic values coexisted. For Jefferson all three stood for rebellion against the feudal, medieval, Christian past and its ignorance, superstition, and inherited privilege. Technically the debate is not resolved. But no reader can doubt the sincerity of the heart's arguments: "Having performed the last sad office of handing you into your carriage . . . I turned on my heel and walked, more dead than alive, to the opposite door, where my own was awaiting me," Jefferson begins, and nothing in this long letter contradicts this opening impression that Jefferson was deeply in love with Maria Cosway.

Religion too continued to interest him. In Paris he became acquainted with a brilliant circle of deists and skeptics, and he soon was familiar with the new historical school of biblical criticism. His letter of 10 August 1787, to nephew Peter Carr, is a masterfully clear summing up of this rational approach. "Read the Bible, then, as you would read Livy or Tacitus. The facts which are within the ordinary course of nature, you will believe on the authority of the writer, as you do those of the same kind in Livy and Tacitus. The testimony of the writer weighs in their favor, in one scale, and their not being against the laws of nature does not weigh against them. But those facts in the Bible which contradict the laws of nature must be examined with more care. . . ." Jefferson gives examples from the Old and New Testaments, concluding in words that recall Paine and foreshadow Emerson: "you must lay aside all prejudice on both sides, and neither believe or reject anything because any other persons, or descriptions of persons, have rejected or believed it. Your own reason is the only oracle given you by heaven, and you are answerable, not for the rightness, but uprightness of the decision."

In 1789, as the French Revolution was beginning and as Washington was being elected first president of the United States, the forty-six-year-old Jefferson returned to America, where he was appointed secretary of state. Now began the twenty-year period of Jefferson's almost complete immersion in the politics for which his pre-eminently practical imagination was so well suited. From 1789 to 1793 he was secretary of state. After a short hiatus at Monticello, he was vice president from 1797 to 1801, and from 1801 to 1809 he served two terms as president. His administration was noted for the Louisiana Purchase (1803), for the war against the Algerian pirates (1801-1805), American expansion westward, and the prohibition of the importation of slaves (1806). Despite the manifold responsibilities of office, Jefferson maintained his many intellectual and artistic interests. At some point between 1791 and 1802 he translated the first twenty chapters of Constantine Volney's celebrated *Ruins; or Meditations on the Revolution of Empires* (1791). This minor masterpiece of romantic skepticism is a full-scale attack on institutionalized religion; it surveys the major ones, noting the claim of each to possess the only truth. Jefferson's conclusion, now as always, was that it was better to believe nothing than to believe what was not true. Although this greatest figure of the Enlightenment in America was not fond of ignorance, it was, he said, preferable to error.

In 1798 Jefferson began an essay on the Anglo-Saxon—or, as he preferred to think of it, the

Portrait of Jefferson by Rembrandt Peale, 1805
(New-York Historical Society)

Pages from Jefferson's version of the New Testament

39. L'un des malfaiteurs qui étoient crucifiés, l'outrageoit aussi, en disant : Si tu es le Christ, sauve-toi toi-même, et nous aussi.	39 And one of the malefactors, *L.23.* which were hanged, railed on him, saying, If thou be Christ, save thyself and us.
40. Mais l'autre le prenant, lui dit : Ne crains-tu point Dieu, puisque tu es condamné au même suplice.	40 But the other, answering, rebuked him, saying, Dost not thou fear God, seeing thou art in the same condemnation?
41. Et pour nous, *nous le sommes* avec justice; car nous souffrons ce que nos crimes méritent; mais celui-ci n'a fait aucun mal.	41 And we indeed justly; for we receive the due reward of our deeds: but this man hath done nothing amiss.
34. Mais Jésus disoit : Mon père, pardonne-leur : car ils ne savent ce qu'ils font.	34 Then said Jesus, Father, forgive them; for they know not what they do.
25. Or, la Mère de Jésus, et la sœur de sa Mère, Marie, *femme* de Cléopas, et Marie Magdelaine, se tenoient près de sa croix.	25 Now there stood by the cross *J.19* of Jesus, his mother, and his mother's sister, Mary the *wife* of Cleophas, and Mary Magdalene.
26. Jésus donc voyant sa Mère, et près d'elle, le Disciple qu'il aimoit, dit à sa Mère : Femme, voilà ton Fils.	26 When Jesus, therefore, saw his mother, and the disciple standing by whom he loved, he saith unto his mother, Woman, behold thy Son!
27. Puis il dit au Disciple : Voilà ta Mère : Et dès cette heure-là, ce Disciple la prit chez lui.	27 Then saith he to the disciple, Behold thy mother! And from that hour that disciple took her unto his own *home*.
46. Et environ la neuvième heure, Jésus s'écria à haute voix, disant : Eli, Eli, lamma sabachthani? C'est-à-dire, mon Dieu, mon Dieu, pourquoi m'as-tu abandonné!	46 And about the ninth hour, *m.27.* Jesus cried with a loud voice, saying, Eli, Eli, lama sabachthani? that is to say, My God, my God, why hast thou forsaken me?
47. Et quelques-uns de ceux qui étoient présens, ayant ouï cela, disoient : il appelle Elie.	47 Some of them that stood there, when they heard *that*, said, This *man* calleth for Elias.
48. Et aussitôt quelqu'un d'entr'eux courut et prit une éponge, et l'ayant remplie de vinaigre, il la mit au bout d'une canne, et lui en donna à boire.	48 And straightway one of them ran, and took a spunge, and filled *it* with vinegar, and put *it* on a reed, and gave him to drink.
49. Et les autres disoient : attendez, voyons si Elie viendra le délivrer.	49 The rest said, Let be, let us see whether Elias will come to save him.
50. Et Jésus ayant encore crié à haute voix, rendit l'esprit.	50 Jesus, when he had cried again with a loud voice, yielded up the ghost.
55. Il y avoit aussi là plusieurs femmes, qui regardoient de loin, et qui avoient suivi Jésus, depuis la Galilée, en le servant;	55 And many women were there, beholding afar off, which followed Jesus from Galilee, ministering unto him:
56. Entre lesquelles étoient Marie-Magdeleine, et Marie, mère de Jacques et de Joses, et la mère des fils de Zébédée.	56 Among which was Mary Magdalene, and Mary the mother of James and Joses, and the mother of Zebedee's children.

Old English language, the study of which was a lifelong hobby. For twenty-five years he urged its inclusion as a standard subject in school because it was, he insisted, the "basis of our language." Latin, he pointed out, could teach one only about additions and embellishments to English, while the real root of English was Old English. It was, moreover, the old language of common people, while Latin had been known only to a few, usually clerics. Jefferson's radical interest in Old English was not so much literary as it was linguistic and even legal. He had become interested in Anglo-Saxon when, as a young lawyer, he had had to trace English legal terms back to their roots. Yet Jefferson was never anticlassical. He valued Greek and Roman literature more highly than Greek and Roman grammar, which he thought overvalued for teaching young English-speaking people, who, learning Latin but not Old English, were thus cutting themselves off from their own language roots. For these reasons, then, Jefferson argued vigorously "the necessity of making the Anglo-Saxon a regular branch of academic education."

In 1809, aged sixty-six, Jefferson reached the end of his second term as president and retired to Monticello. Here he soon resumed his friendship with John Adams, with whom he had differed on political issues, and began a lengthy, wide-ranging correspondence with him which is one of the great achievements of American letters. Both men had lived extensive public lives at the center of events, and both now enjoyed broad leisure and continuing energy. They discussed a vast array of subjects with verve, wit, and learning. In some ways the letter was Jefferson's ideal form; most of his best writing is either in actual letters or in reports designed to communicate, like letters, carefully defined matters to particular audiences at specific times.

Religion and ethics continued to interest him, and Adams's own eager and informed curiosity about such matters was a fresh encouragement. In 1813 (the same year he wrote an important letter on 16 August to John Waldo defending neologisms and predicting the rise of a specifically American English) Jefferson wrote to Adams on 13 October comparing the ethics of the Old Testament with those of the New, concluding that we need to remove from the New Testament everything except "the very words only of Jesus," leaving out all the miracles and interpretations. The demythologized, miracle-stripped result would be, he thought, "the most sublime and benevolent code of morals which has ever been offered to man." Thus was conceived the celebrated "Jefferson Bible" (usually published as *The Life and Morals of Jesus of Nazareth*), which he prepared, he told Adams, "by cutting verse by verse out of the printed book, and arranging the matter which is evidently his [Jesus's], and which is as easily distinguishable as diamonds in a dunghill. The result is an octavo of forty-six pages, of pure and unsophisticated doctrines, such as were professed and acted on by the *unlettered* Apostles, the Apostolic Fathers, and the Christians of the first century."

But it was education even more than religion that was, in James Bryant Conant's words, "Jefferson's main pre-occupation in the last ten years of his life." In 1817 one of Jefferson's longest-cherished ideas became a reality with the founding of the University of Virginia. Jefferson himself wrote the report setting forth its aim and curricula the following year. He wanted none but the best faculty then available in Europe or America, for he was intent on demonstrating the possibility of building modern, public, secular universities of the highest excellence for the new republic. Actually the founding of the University was only one of Jefferson's four most-important educational ideas. The other parts of his plan for free schools that would form the basis for a new model commonwealth in Virginia were articulated as early as 1779: free elementary schooling for all future citizens, free education of a more-advanced nature for a selected group of poor students (in addition to those who could pay), and university education at public expense to a select few. Though most of his ideas were not adopted during his lifetime, Jefferson was, more than anyone else, the architect of free public education in America.

Philosophically, Jefferson's deepest commitment was now to Epicureanism as he carefully spelled it out in an important letter of 1818: Happiness is the aim of life, virtue is the foundation of happiness. Virtue consists in choosing to live by prudence, temperance, fortitude and justice. Man is a free agent, able to choose good and avoid folly, desire, fear and deceit. Neither Jefferson nor anyone else has ever fully achieved these goals, but his shortcomings do not make his goals unworthy ones. "In the long run," said Thoreau, "men hit only what they aim at."

In 1821, at seventy-seven, Jefferson began an autobiography which, while not a polished or finished memoir, is nevertheless an invaluable Thucydidean account in which the founding of the country far outweighs the role played by Jefferson the man. (The best edition of this work, first published in 1829, is that of Paul Leicester Ford, pub-

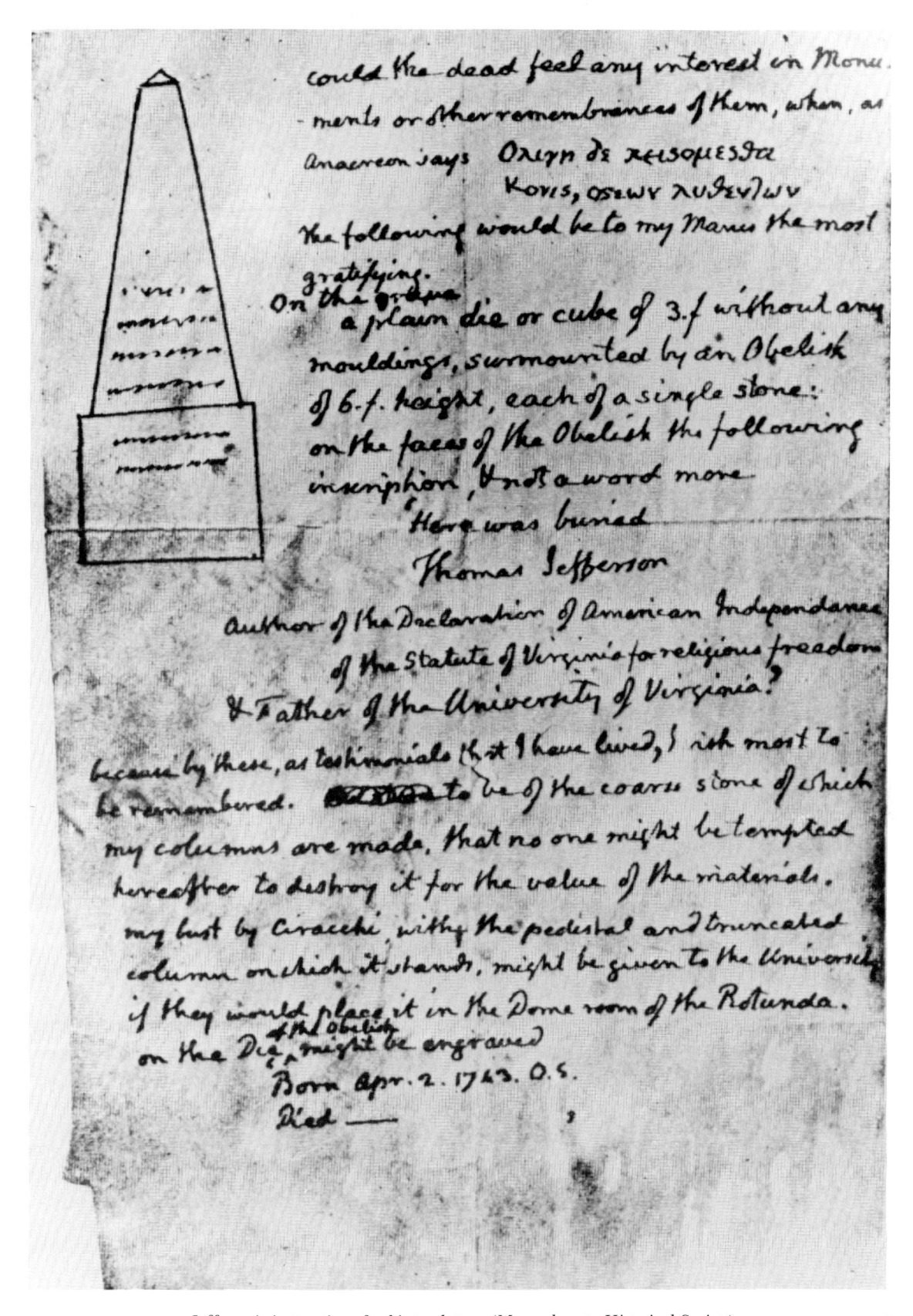

> could the dead feel any interest in Monu-
> ments or other remembrances of them, when, as
> Anacreon says Ὀλίγη δὲ κεισόμεσθα
> κόνις, ὀστέων λυθέντων
> the following would be to my Manes the most
> gratifying.
> On the grave a plain die or cube of 3.f without any
> mouldings, surmounted by an Obelisk
> of 6.f. height, each of a single stone:
> on the faces of the Obelisk the following
> inscription, & not a word more
> "Here was buried
> Thomas Jefferson
> Author of the Declaration of American Independance
> of the Statute of Virginia for religious freedom
> & Father of the University of Virginia."
> because by these, as testimonials that I have lived, I wish most to
> be remembered. to be of the coarse stone of which
> my columns are made, that no one might be tempted
> hereafter to destroy it for the value of the materials.
> my bust by Ciracchi, with the pedestal and truncated
> column on which it stands, might be given to the University
> if they would place it in the Dome room of the Rotunda.
> on the Die of the Obelisk might be engraved
> Born Apr. 2. 1743. O.S.
> Died ———

Jefferson's instructions for his tombstone (Massachusetts Historical Society) lished in 1914.) The autobiography also shows Jefferson's style at its most relaxed and conversational. "We cooked up a resolution," he writes, "appointing the first of June . . . a day of fasting" (to protest against the Stamp Act).

His late letters also bear witness to the culmination of his long-standing quarrel with Calvinism. He attacked the famous five points, the "demoralizing dogmas" of Calvin as he called them in a letter of 26 June 1822, while to Adams he described Calvin as an "atheist" and Calvin's God as "a daemon of malignant spirit," concluding "it would be more pardonable to believe in no God at all, than to blaspheme Him by the atrocious attributes of Calvin." The version of Christianity most compatible with his Stoic and Epicurean convictions, and with what has been called his "conservative materialism," was Unitarianism. He wrote to James Smith on 8 December 1822, "I confidently expect that the present generation will see Unitarianism become the general religion in the United States."

Jefferson's lucidity and strength of mind stayed with him. In 1826 he wrote an important letter in which the distinction between populist Whig and royalist Tory historiography is made with brilliant clarity. "The Whig historians of England," he wrote, "have always gone back to the Saxon period for the true principles of their constitution, while the Tories and Hume, their Coryphaeus, date it from the Norman conquest, and hence conclude that the continual claim by the nation of the good old Saxon laws, and the struggle to recover them, were 'encroachments of the people on the crown, and not usurpations of the crown on the people.' "

For all the clarity of his thought, Jefferson remains a paradoxical figure. He gave us the idea of the West, yet he never went west himself. He distrusted cities, but he loved Paris, and he habitually linked agricultural life with virtue, but overlooked the fact that in the American South, slaves did the labor that made such a life possible. He is one of the great modern spokesmen for individual liberty, yet he held many slaves. He worked to end slavery, but was blind—as even Lincoln was—to any possibility of the compatibility of different races. He was an aristocrat, yet an egalitarian and a democrat. He was a man of property, yet a man of the left. Many of his themes, complete with their undersides and ironies, have become American themes: the West, the land, and the people. But in the end, Jefferson correctly estimated his own major contributions. The driving forces of his life, the "habitual center of his personal energy" had been his belief in freedom from political tyranny, in freedom from religious tyranny, and in the absolute necessity of education for a people who wished to be free. On his grave marker, therefore, he wanted the following "and not a word more" engraved: "Here lies Thomas Jefferson, Author of the Declaration of American Independence, of the Statute of Virginia for Religious Freedom and Father of the University of Virginia." He died on 4 July 1826, on the same day as John Adams, on the fiftieth anniversary of the signing of the Declaration of Independence.

Letters:

Gilbert Chinard, *Jefferson et les Ideologues, d'après sa correspondance inedité avec Destutt de Tracy, Cabanis J.-B. Say et Auguste Comte* (Baltimore: Johns Hopkins Press/Les Presses Universitaires de France, 1925);

The Letters of Lafayette and Jefferson, edited by Chinard (Baltimore: Johns Hopkins Press/Paris: "Les Belles lettres," 1929);

The Correspondence of Jefferson and Du Pont de Nemours, edited by Chinard (Baltimore: Johns Hopkins University Press/Paris: "Les Belles lettres," 1931);

The Adams-Jefferson Letters, 2 volumes, edited by Lester J. Cappon (Chapel Hill: University of North Carolina Press, 1959);

The Family Letters of Thomas Jefferson, edited by Edwin Morris Betts and James Adams Bear, Jr. (Columbia: University of Missouri Press, 1966).

Bibliographies:

E. Millicent Sowerby, *Catalogue of the Library of Thomas Jefferson,* 5 volumes (Washington, D.C.: Library of Congress, 1952-1959);

William B. O'Neal, *Jefferson's Fine Arts Library: His Selections for the University of Virginia Together with His Own Architectural Books* (Charlottesville: University Press of Virginia, 1976).

Biographies:

George Tucker, *The Life of Thomas Jefferson,* 2 volumes (Philadelphia: Carey, Lea & Blanchard, 1837);

Henry S. Randall, *The Life of Thomas Jefferson,* 3 volumes (New York: Derby & Jackson, 1858);

Sarah N. Randolph, *The Domestic Life of Thomas Jefferson* (New York: Harper, 1871);

Gilbert Chinard, *Thomas Jefferson: The Apostle of Americanism* (Boston: Little, Brown, 1929; revised, 1939);

Dumas Malone, *Jefferson and His Times,* 6 volumes: *Jefferson the Virginian* (Boston: Little, Brown,

1948); *Jefferson and the Rights of Man* (Boston: Little, Brown, 1951); *Jefferson and the Ordeal of Liberty* (Boston: Little, Brown, 1962); *Jefferson the President: First Term, 1801-1805* (Boston: Little, Brown, 1970); *Jefferson the President: Second Term, 1805-1809* (Boston: Little, Brown, 1974); *The Sage of Monticello* (Boston: Little, Brown, 1981);

Fawn Brodie, *Thomas Jefferson: An Intimate History* (New York: Norton, 1974);

Virginius Dabney, *The Jefferson Scandals: A Rebuttal* (New York: Dodd, Mead, 1981).

References:

Henry Adams, *History of the United States During the First Administration of Thomas Jefferson*, 2 volumes (New York: Scribners, 1889);

Henry Adams, *History of the United States During the Second Administration of Thomas Jefferson*, 2 volumes (New York: Scribners, 1890);

William Howard Adams, *The Eye of Thomas Jefferson* (Washington, D.C.: National Gallery of Art, 1976);

Charles A. Beard, *Economic Origins of Jeffersonian Democracy* (New York: Macmillan, 1915);

Carl Becker, *The Declaration of Independence: A Study in the History of Political Ideas* (New York: Harcourt, Brace, 1922);

Henry Steele Commager, *Jefferson, Nationalism and the Enlightenment* (New York: Braziller, 1975);

James Bryant Conant, *Thomas Jefferson and the Development of American Public Education* (Berkeley & Los Angeles: University of California Press, 1963);

John Dos Passos, *The Head and Heart of Thomas Jefferson* (Garden City: Doubleday, 1955);

Donald Jackson, *Thomas Jefferson and the Stony Mountains* (Urbana: University of Illinois Press, 1981);

Fiske Kimball, *Thomas Jefferson, Architect* (Cambridge: Privately printed by the Riverside Press, 1916; reprinted, New York: Da Capo, 1968);

Adrienne Koch, *The Philosophy of Thomas Jefferson* (New York: Columbia University Press, 1943);

Vernon L. Parrington, *The Colonial Mind, 1620-1800*, volume 1 of *Main Currents in American Thought* (New York: Harcourt, Brace, 1927);

Howard C. Rice, Jr., *Thomas Jefferson's Paris* (Princeton: Princeton University Press, 1976).

Papers:

There are major collections of Jefferson material at the Library of Congress, the Massachusetts Historical Society, the University of Virginia, the Missouri Historical Society, and the Henry E. Huntington Library.

John Leacock
(21 December 1729-16 November 1802)

Carla Mulford
Villanova University

BOOKS: *The First Book of the American Chronicles of the Times*, 6 pamphlets (Philadelphia: Printed & sold by Benjamin Towne, 1774-1775);

The Fall of British Tyranny; Or, American Liberty Triumphant ... (Philadelphia: Printed by Styner & Cist, 1776).

Only recently has evidence come to light establishing John Leacock, a Philadelphia gold and silversmith, as the author not only of the propaganda play *The Fall of British Tyranny* (1776), but also of a broadside, *A New Song, On the Repeal of the Stamp-Act* (1766), and a pamphlet series, *The First Book of the American Chronicles of the Times* (1774-1775), reprinted several times in Boston, Providence, Salem, and Newbern. Popular in their day, Leacock's works have gone the way of most political propaganda and have become obscured by time and by their author's anonymity. By 1954, however, enough conclusive evidence had accumulated that Francis James Dallett, Jr., could demonstrate Leacock's authorship of *The Fall of British Tyranny*. More recently, J. A. Leo Lemay uncovered an advertisement in the *New York Constitutional Gazette* for 3 July 1776 linking the author of the play to that of *The First Book of the American Chronicles of the Times*.

And Leacock's commonplace book at the American Philosophical Society reveals his authorship of *A New Song, On the Repeal of the Stamp-Act.*

Born on 21 December 1729, John Leacock was one of a family prominent in Philadelphia. His father, John Leacock (1689-1752), was a prosperous pewtersmith and shopkeeper who had come to Philadelphia from Barbados to invest in land and in the earliest iron furnaces in the province. This Leacock married Mary Cash (1694-1765) in 1715 in Christ Church, where he served as a vestryman. Of ten children born to this couple, five reached adulthood. Little is known of their son John Leacock's early years.

Like his two brothers, Leacock was probably apprenticed early to an established gold and silversmith. By the early 1750s he owned his own business in the trade, and his craft seems to have brought in elements of the engraver's and printer's trades, as evidenced by several entries in his commonplace book. His interests in a variety of scientific and cultural concerns were complemented by those of other family members, a printer brother-in-law, David Hall; a lawyer brother-in-law, James Read; and a cousin-in-law, Dr. Benjamin Franklin (Leacock and Franklin's wife, Deborah Read, were second cousins).

Having married Hannah McCally in 1752, Leacock soon began his own family, and upon his father's death late in that year, he gained an inheritance that enabled his moving his trade from Walnut Street to a place (advertised in the *Pennsylvania Gazette*, 29 November 1753) "opposite Mr. Norris's Alley, at the sign of the Golden Cup" on Front Street, the center of Philadelphia gold and silver smithing. By the late 1760s Leacock had evidently gained such prominence that he could retire to the country to take up the pursuits of a farmer. He left his business in Philadelphia in 1767 and bought an estate in Lower Merion, about seven miles from Philadelphia. Interested in agricultural experiments, Leacock there promoted the establishment of a public vineyard, with the help of the American Philosophical Society.

Leacock devoted his leisure time to politics. He could easily receive knowledge of political affairs in the colonies and in London from David Hall, James Read, and Benjamin Franklin. May 1772 found Leacock helping the Philadelphia Sons of Liberty develop a new society, the Society of the Sons of Saint Tammany, commemorating an early chief of the Delawares. Both the Sons of Liberty and the Sons of Saint Tammany concerned themselves with the patriot cause. Leacock's early support of the Whig cause is demonstrated by his support of nonimportation at the time of the Stamp Act and by his broadside ballad denouncing the Stamp Act and praising its repeal, *A New Song, On the Repeal of the Stamp-Act* (1766). Leacock here vilifies George Grenville, John Huske, and John Stuart, third Earl of Bute, comparing in an extended simile the devil's temptation of Eve to his temptation of Grenville, who, in the context of the broadside, reacts with Mephistophilian delight at the devil's attention. Leacock's continued support of the Whig cause is shown in his pamphlet series and in his play.

The First Book of the American Chronicles of the Times (1774-1775) has remained an object of interest and speculation for historians of the Revolution. A propaganda piece in the form of a biblical parody, its six serially published chapters cover events in Boston prior to the Revolution, from the Boston Tea Party to the return to Boston of the Massachusetts delegates to the First Continental Congress. Humorously setting up the political situation from December 1773 to late fall 1774, Leacock's pamphlet series moves from Mordecai the Benjamite's (Benjamin Franklin's) confrontation with a Wedderburnite (Alexander Wedderburn) through Thomas the Gageite's (Thomas Gage's) consternation with the Bostonites led by Jedediah the priest (Samuel Cooper, pastor of Boston's Brattle Street Church), to Thomas's terrifying dream of the Old Boy (Oliver Cromwell) and the triumphant news about the First Continental Congress. Much of the parody's humor derives from its characterizations of the people already mentioned as well as of those who had already reached mythic proportion, such as Phineas (Israel Putnam) and Matherius Cottonius (Cotton Mather). Moreover, the generalized Indian leader Occunneocogeccococacheecacheecadungo and the symbol of the Liberty Tree figure in the humorous ideology of the piece. Humor also arises from the clashing of the actual events described with the manner of their narration, in the style of the Old Testament books Numbers, Kings, and Chronicles, especially. These surface effects work complexly with Leacock's authorial voice. That the patriots are, above all, funny as they make their declarations in millennial terms is precisely Leacock's point. To exaggerate the importance of the patriot cause (Leacock's authorial voice implies) was to undercut its actual importance in fact. Leacock's ironic stance, then, enabled him not only to depict the situation in the patriots' favor but to comment on their behavior as well. Such a complex

Title page for Leacock's patriotic propaganda play (courtesy of the John Carter Brown Library at Brown University)

stance could not be sustained in those turbulent times, however, and Leacock soon chose another form for his patriot message.

Leacock next turned to serious propagandizing in *The Fall of British Tyranny; Or, American Liberty Triumphant* (1776). The play's major propaganda statement, that Bute (the play's Lord Paramount) incited the Revolution to secure power and privileges for himself and his relatives, the Stuarts, is made in the first two acts, which consist primarily of speeches, act one using speeches of America's enemies in England, and act two, those of her supporters. Act three reveals in action the effects of England's coercive measures in America and the tensions arising there between Whig and Tory; and it reports on battles fought. After the highly emotional conclusion of act three in which Clarissa (Joseph Warren's widow) bewails her husband's death, Leacock portrays Lord Kidnapper (John Murray, Earl of Dunmore) in act four as a vicious fool and concludes the act with a display of British backbiting after the battle of Bunker Hill. Act five produces a shift to Canada, where Ethan Allen suffers at the hands of General Prescott, and then to Cambridge, where Washington discusses with Generals Lee and Putnam British atrocities and laments the death of Montgomery. In developing these characters, Leacock effectively manipulates his material to create admiration for the patriots and their English supporters and scorn for the opposition. The admiration and scorn are evident even in his naming of characters. Patriot characters act under their real names while pro-British characters suffer derision in their names, designed to name their "humors" or natures.

By 1779, Leacock was in Easton and Reading, signing bills of credit of the United States. And, having moved back to Philadelphia in 1780, he gained the position of city coroner by 1785. Leacock spent the last decades of his life in social, political, and literary prominence. He died 16 November 1802 and was buried in Christ Church cemetery in the corner near his relative Benjamin Franklin.

References:

Francis James Dallett, Jr., "John Leacock and *The Fall of British Tyranny*," *Pennsylvania Magazine of History and Biography*, 78 (1954); 456-475;

Norman Philbrick, Introduction to *The Fall of British Tyranny*, in *Trumpets Sounding: Propaganda Plays of the American Revolution* (New York: Blom, 1972).

Papers:

Leacock's commonplace book and some family documents (including the Cash-Leacock family Bible) are located at the American Philosophical Society.

William Livingston

(30 November 1723-25 July 1790)

William K. Bottorff
University of Toledo

SELECTED BOOKS: *Philosophic Solitude: Or, the Choice of a Rural Life. A Poem* (New York: Printed by James Parker, 1747);

A Funeral Eulogium, on the Reverend Mr. Aaron Burr, Late President of the College of New-Jersey... (New York: Printed & sold by H. Gaine, 1757);

A Review of the Military Operations in North-America, from the Commencement of the French Hostilities on the Frontiers of Virginia in 1753, to the Surrender of Oswego, on the 14th of August, 1756. Interspersed with Various Observations, Characters, and Anecdotes; Necessary to Give Light into the Conduct of American Affairs in General; And More Especially into the Political Management of Affairs in New-York. In a Letter to a Nobleman (London: Printed for R. & J. Dodsley, 1757; New Haven, 1758);

A Letter to the Right Reverend Father in God, John, Lord Bishop of Landaff; Occasioned by Some Passages in His Lordship's Sermon, On the 20th of February, 1767, in Which the American Colonies Are Loaded With Great and Undeserved Reproach... (New York: Printed for the author & sold by Garrat Noel, 1768; London: Printed for J. Buckland, E. & C. Dilly, and G. Keith, 1768);

America: Or, A Poem on the Settlement of the British Colonies (New Haven: Printed by Thomas & Samuel Green, 1770);

A Soliloquy... (Philadelphia: Printed by John Dunlay, 1770).

OTHER: Elihu Hubbard Smith, ed., *American Poems, Selected and Original*, includes Livingston's *Philosophic Solitude* (Litchfield, Conn.: Printed by Collier & Buel, 1793; reprinted, Gainesville: Scholars' Facsimiles & Reprints, 1966).

Portrait by John Wollaston (Fraunces Tavern Museum, New York)

A member of one of the most illustrious families of his time, William Livingston gained renown as a lawyer, polemic journalist, patriot, politician, and to a lesser extent, as a poet. His was one of the earliest voices against British rule, the satirizing of which earned him a seat in the Continental Congress. He later became the first governor of the State of New Jersey and was a delegate to the Constitutional Convention. His long poem, *Philosophic Solitude*, was the major item included in the first anthology of American poetry, *American Poems, Selected and Original* (1793), edited by Elihu Hubbard Smith.

Livingston, the son of Philip and Catharine Van Brugh Livingston, was born at Albany and remained a New Yorker for almost half a century. He spent a part of his boyhood traveling with an English missionary among the Mohawk Indians, learning the language and ways of the Mohawks. Livingston had every advantage of the privileged classes in the colonies. At Livingston Manor he was prepared for college, and apparently he studied painting until he became convinced his was but a small artistic talent. He entered Yale College at the age of fourteen, graduating in 1741 at the head of his class.

Subsequently he was indentured to a New York lawyer. Finding the study of law under the apprentice-master system distasteful, the headstrong young Livingston wrote a diatribe denouncing the custom, which was published in the *New-York Weekly Post-Box* in 1745. Although this publication led to the breaking of his indenture, he was admitted to the bar in 1748. Meanwhile, he produced further newspaper essays, on a variety of subjects, and fell in love. Not yet launched on a career, Livingston married Susanna French in 1745. Many years and thirteen children later, in 1787, he wrote a letter to his wife remarking how idyllic their marriage had been: "If I were to live to the age of Methusalem, I believe I should not forget a certain flower that I once saw in a certain garden; and however that flower may have since faded, towards the evening of that day, I shall always remember how it bloomed in the morning; nor shall I ever love it the less for the decay which the most beautiful and fragrant flowers are subject to in the course of nature." This poetic conceit, with its reference to the world of nature, was consonant with the other main activity occupying his time and fancy at the time of his marriage: he was writing his only long poem, one of the major verse efforts yet seen in the colonies.

Philosophic Solitude, subtitled *Or, the Choice of a Rural Life,* was first published as a small book in 1747 in New York. The poem is a splendid example of American Augustan verse, with 670 lines in rhymed couplets reminiscent of "tuneful" Pope and "polish'd" Dryden. Another model, echoed in prominent images and allusions, was *Paradise Lost* (Milton is called "great" and "peerless"). Classical and biblical allusions also abound.

Philosophic Solitude is prefaced by "The Argument": "The Subject proposed. Situation of the Author's House. His Frugality in its Furniture. The Beauties of the Country. His Love of Retirement, and Choice of his Friends. A Description of the Morning. Hymn to the Sun. Contemplation of the Heavens. The Existence of God inferr'd from a View of the Beauty and Harmony of the Creation. Morning and Evening Devotion. The Vanity of Riches and Grandeur. The Choice of his Books. Praise of the Marriage State. A Knot of Modern Ladies described. The Author's Exit." The third

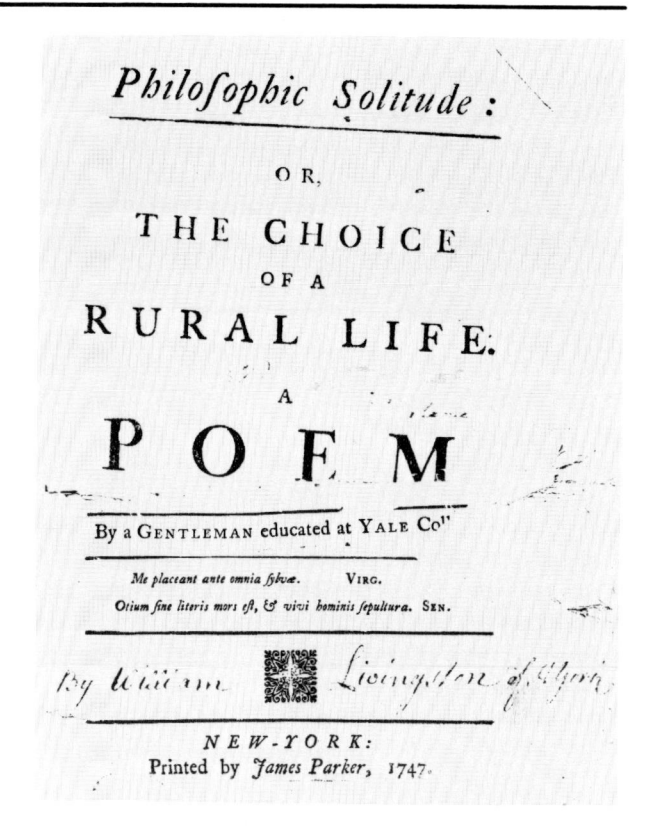

Title page for Livingston's first book, one of the most popular poems in eighteenth-century America (courtesy of the John Carter Brown Library at Brown University)

couplet announces the theme, with typical inversion and rather prosaic diction: "Mine be the pleasure of a rural life,/From noise remote, and ignorant of strife." There follows much flat, stock imagery, as in "unfolding roses," "varied bow'rs," and "industrious bees."

Yet the poem has some real strengths, including such vivid imagery as "Autumn bends beneath the golden grain" and "The trees weep amber." The first of these phrases is sustained by its alliteration and its picture of heavy fruitfulness, the second by its personification of the trees and its suggestion that they are saddened by summer's ending.

The key to the poem though lies in the phrase "philosophic solitude." *Philosophic* is a term of broad dimensions for the poet. It encompasses meditation, male companionship, reading and study, the sharing of woodland delights with his wife, and the achievement of religious insight. All these dimensions are involved in a rhythmic series of complementary passages; things condemned or shunned are balanced by things admired and sought. City ways (noise, confusion, crowds) and the pomp and ceremony of society (fops, painted and overdressed women, courtly obsequies) are to be left behind, to be washed away by nature's garden-like freshness and simplicity.

Nature alone, of course, will not sustain the poet. He also needs human friendship and books to contribute to his sense of well-being. Thus, he expects his cronies to call; he will take with him volumes both entertaining and useful (for "delight" the poets, for "profit" Locke, Cato, Newton). And, most important, his spouse must be with him: "By love directed, I would choose a wife" (as he had in fact recently done), "To improve my bliss, and ease the load of life." His is a quietly gregarious, enlightened, loving, "philosophic" variety of withdrawal indeed.

Philosophic Solitude went through at least five printings during the poet's lifetime, establishing it as one of the most popular eighteenth-century poems in America. Then it was collected by Elihu Hubbard Smith in the first book-length gathering of American poetry, in 1793, where it is the oldest and longest poem included—proof of an almost reverential attachment afforded it and its author as the Enlightenment-Revolutionary era closed. Its theme represented one very early aspect of the American dream, a theme to be variously made manifest as "agrarianism" in Transcendentalism and even in the pastoral regionalism of the early twentieth century.

As for Livingston, he still spoke, in a letter of 1783, of a "relish for that rural life and noiseless retirement for which I have long had an ardent passion." It was a dream he partially realized at the estate of his later years, Liberty Hall, near Elizabethtown, New Jersey. Poetry, however, was not to become his calling: he turned his energies toward prose, and to law and politics.

His chief contribution to the law came in 1752 when, with William Smith, Jr., he compiled the first digest of the laws of the colony of New York. A second volume followed ten years later, revealing Livingston's long involvement in codifying the American legal system. This work, along with his political writings and activities, were to bring him an LL.D. degree from Yale in 1788.

Livingston began his role as a leading—and very early—spokesman for American rights in 1752 when, with his friends Smith and John Morin Scott, he established a weekly newspaper, the *Independent Reflector*. These men became known as the New York Triumvirate, heads of the comparatively liberal political movement beginning in the colonies. The Livingston faction was to control the New York Assembly during the years leading up to the Revolution. At first, however, the editor of the *Reflector* claimed political neutrality while seeking only "the exposure of official abuse, negligence, and corruption in whatever rank they were to be found." The self-styled voice of the people added: "The Reflector is determined to succeed unawed and alike fearless of the humble scoundrel and the eminent villain. The cause he is engaged in is a glorious cause. 'Tis the cause of truth and liberty: what he intends to oppose is superstition, bigotry, priestcraft, tyranny, servitude, public mismanagement, and dishonesty in office. The things he proposes to teach, are the nature and excellence of our constitution, the inestimable value of liberty...."

Under the heading of what Livingston called "priestcraft" came the question of whether Anglicanism would become the established church in New York, as it was in the mother country. Livingston, nominally a Presbyterian but a man with deistical tendencies, fought vigorously and without hypocrisy for the freedom of religion that was ultimately guaranteed by the Constitution. (Separation of church and state he took to be a sacred principle.) He had been named a trustee of Kings College (later Columbia University) in 1751 and opposed Anglican domination over that institution. He spoke out on religious freedom in a series of essays called "The Watch Tower" in the mid-1750s. Finally, in 1768, he produced *A Letter to the Right Reverend Father in God, John, Lord Bishop of Landaff; Occasioned by Some Passages in His Lordship's Sermon On the 20th of February, 1767, in Which the American Colonies Are Loaded With Great and Undeserved Reproach ...*, a strong statement against establishment—and against the English habit of viewing colonials as politically inferior.

Now a spokesman for "the American Colonies," not just for New York, Livingston kept up his political barrage as "The American Whig" in the *New-York Gazette* (circa 1767-1770) and in other columns and essays. He had been elected a member of the New York Assembly in 1758 and had defended the American cause a year earlier in a pamphlet published in London, *A Review of the Military Operations in North-America, from the Commencement of the French Hostilities on the Frontiers of Virginia in 1753, to the Surrender of Oswego, on the 14th of August, 1756. Interspersed with Various Observations, Characters, and Anecdotes; Necessary to Give Light into the Conduct of American Affairs in General; And More Especially into the Political Management of Affairs in New-York ...* (1757). His words were little heeded in England, but the cumulative effect of his American writings was to establish him as one of the first figures leading

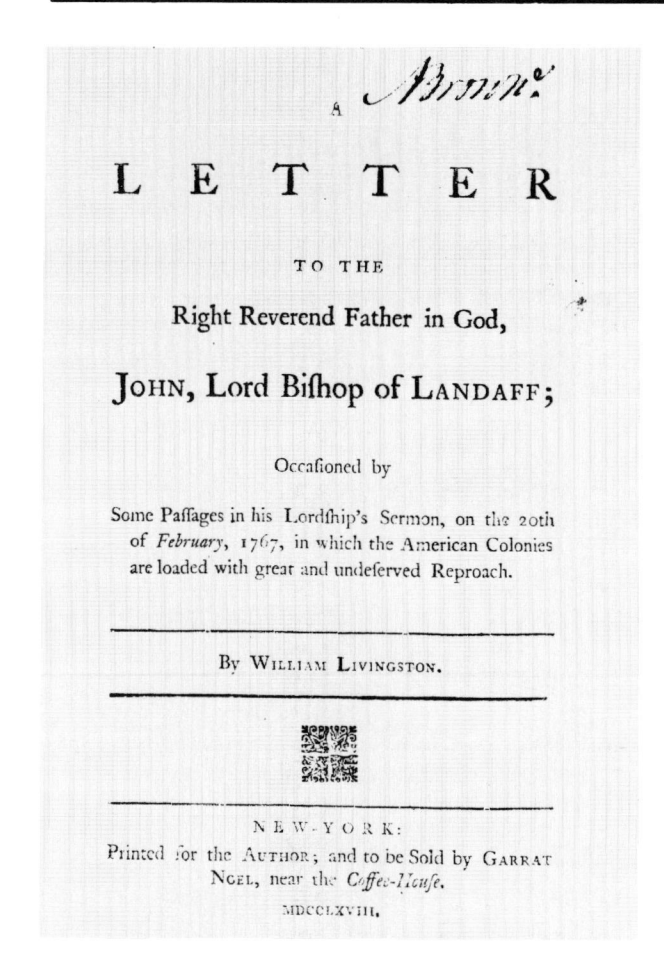

Title page for the pamphlet in which Livingston presents a strong argument for separation of Church and State (courtesy of the John Carter Brown Library at Brown University)

the colonies toward independence.

The nature of government was much on Livingston's mind, and, as he entered the First Continental Congress as a member from New Jersey (he had moved to Elizabethtown in 1772), his words from an *Independent Reflector* essay of 1753 must have echoed in his memory. Of government he had said: "It is an human Establishment, depending upon the free Consent of Mankind, whereby one or more Individuals are elevated above the Rest, and cloathed by them with their united Power, which is to be exercised in an invariable Pursuit of the Welfare of the Community, and in compelling the Practice of Justice, and prohibiting the Contrary." Livingston was a member of both Continental Congresses and of the Committee of Correspondence, and in 1776 he was named brigadier general in command of the New Jersey Militia. He then rose to the exercise of "Power" for "the Welfare" of the people when he was elected first governor of the state of New Jersey in 1776. He was reelected governor annually for the remainder of his life.

Even while holding high public office—and even after the Revolution—Livingston continued his journalistic writings, advocating liberty and justice. Under signatures such as Hortentius, Scipio, and Primitive Whig (these pen names were a matter of conventional usage; they were not intended to hide his identity), his patriotic and satirical prose graced the *New-Jersey Gazette*. Occasionally these pieces took the form of verse, as when he celebrated the figure of Washington.

In 1757, he produced *A Funeral Eulogium, on the Reverend Mr. Aaron Burr, Late President of the College of New-Jersey* ... (the Reverend Mr. Burr, president of what would become Princeton University, was the father of the Aaron Burr who became vice-president under Jefferson and killed Alexander Hamilton in a duel in 1804). In 1778, working again in the old tradition of extolling exemplary figures as public models, he wrote for the *Gazette* his "Ode to General Washington."

The "Ode to General Washington" was one of the earliest pieces of any kind to honor the new nation's military leader. Written in blank verse, a form quite congenial to Livingston's talent (here much influenced by Milton), it sings the general's praises without intensity of emotion, though with great sincerity. This ode was certainly one more piece that kept its author's influence before the public and which helped him to be elected a member of the American Philosophical Society in 1781. Within the society he shared honors with such fellow members as Franklin and Jefferson. His long-held philosophic opposition to slavery resulted, in 1786, in his freeing the only two slaves he held.

One final distinction came to Livingston when he became a member of the Constitutional Convention in May of 1787. In September he proudly signed the new document that would provide Americans with the assurance of a stable government, a government of the kind which the New Jersey governor had hoped and worked for longer than had almost any of his countrymen.

Livingston finally found some measure of philosophic solitude at his estate, Liberty Hall, where he took great delight in gardening and in being with his family. Nevertheless, he continued as governor. He remained a liberal, but one who—with the Revolution over and the Constitution gaining acceptance—might well have evolved into a Federalist had he lived into the period of the formation of the first two great American political parties. He was more Lockian—putting governmental protection of property high on his list of the rulers' responsibilities—than Jeffersonian: Livingston did not advocate any extension of the franchise toward greater democracy. He now longed for stability, not change.

During the period 1788-1790 (that is, to the close of his life) there appeared in Philadelphia's *American Museum* a series of contributions by Livingston. Several of the items had been published before, and they together amounted to something of a coda to his long career of public service and polemic journalism. A prestigious magazine, published in the new nation's capital, the *American Museum* gave one last measure of honor to the author-politician.

William Livingston had the highest of reputations in his lifetime and in the decades following his death. He was revered as a public servant, as a significant essayist, and as an accomplished gentlemen-poet. In recent times, however, he has been generally neglected, especially as a literary figure. He has become one of those "founding fathers" whom Americans have almost completely forgotten.

References:

Dorothy R. Dillon, *The New York Triumvirate: A Study of the Legal and Political Careers of William Livingston, John Morin Scott, William Smith, Jr.* (New York: Columbia University Press, 1949);

Edwin B. Livingston, *The Livingstons of Livingston Manor* (New York: Knickerbocker Press, 1910);

Louis H. Patterson, "Governor William Livingston as Apprentice, Writer and Executive," *Proceedings of the New Jersey Historical Society*, 9 (April 1924): 97-106;

Theodore Sedgwick, Jr., *A Memoir of the Life of William Livingston, Member of Congress in 1774, 1775, and 1776; Delegate to the Federal Convention in 1787, and Governor of the State of New-Jersey from 1776 to 1790, with Extracts from His Correspondence and Notice of Various Members of His Family* (New York: Harper, 1833);

Harold Wesley Thatcher, *The Social Philosophy of William Livingston* (Chicago: University of Chicago Libraries, 1938).

James Maury
(18 April 1718-9 June 1769)

Homer D. Kemp
Tennessee Technological University

BOOK: *To Christians of Every Denomination . . . An Address Enforcing an Inquiry Into . . . the Pretensions of the . . . Anabaptists* (Annapolis: Printed by Anne Catherine Green, 1771).

OTHER: "A Dissertation on Education in the Form of a Letter from James Maury to Robert Jackson, July 17, 1762," edited by Helen Duprey Bullock, *Papers of the Albemarle Historical Society*, 2 (1941/1942): 36-60.

James Maury's name is best known in histories in connection with the Parson's Cause; however, he established in his own day a wide reputation as an exceptionally able, hardworking minister, a thorough and inspiring teacher, a competent essayist, and a deeply spiritual man. From 1752 until his death, Maury conducted what Richard Beale Davis has called "one of the best genuinely private schools in the [colonial] South," whose pupils included Thomas Jefferson, James Madison (Virginia's first bishop and a president of the College of William and Mary), James Monroe, Dabney Carr the elder, and Maury's son James. Maury was one of the most learned classical scholars of his day and at his death left a major colonial Virginia library of some four hundred titles and forty-four pamphlets (probably more than five hundred volumes). In addition, he was the patriarch of a great American family which included his son James, who was United States Consul to Liverpool for many years, and his grandson Matthew Fontaine Maury, the well-known nineteenth-century naval leader and oceanographer.

Maury was born in Dublin, Ireland, on 18 April 1718, into the French Huguenot family of Matthew and Mary Ann Fontaine Maury. In 1719 Matthew Maury settled at Hickory Hill in King William County, Virginia, on a portion of the plantation which his brother-in-law John Fontaine had acquired. Entirely educated in Virginia, young James was guided through a good secondary education by a family deeply committed to education and, probably around 1738, entered the College of William and Mary, where he was made an usher in the grammar school in July 1741.

After his ordination in 1742, the young clergyman returned home to be rector of King William parish and married (11 November 1743) Mary Walker, niece of Dr. Thomas Walker, thus connecting himself to an influential family. In 1752 Maury assumed the rectorship of the frontier Fredericksville parish, near Dr. Walker's plantation in a part of Louisa County which later became Albemarle County. Here Maury's frail health worsened rapidly as he rode a circuit that included three churches and a chapel and tried to provide for a rapidly growing family—with nine children before 1760, and eventually twelve.

During the 1750s Maury began a long career of writing essays and letters. He has been seriously considered, along with the Reverend Samuel Davies, as a possible author of the 1756-1757 Virginia "Centinel" essay series in the *Virginia Gazette*—one of the best-written of Virginia essay series—but the essays are now generally accepted as Davies's. Maury's letters are as valuable as his other writings; most of them are well-written epistolary essays which reveal a man, well informed and perceptive about public affairs, who had a wide knowledge of American geography and a profound concern about western lands and commerce. In one of these letter-essays—to his friend Robert Jackson on 17 July 1762—Maury wrote a pioneer treatise in American educational theory. Jackson had given him an essay on education by the Reverend Jonathan Boucher in which Boucher insisted on a thorough grounding in Greek and Latin as the foundation for all further intellectual acquirements. Maury considers the whole question of what is "useful, practical Knowledge" for a young Virginian and advocates the anticlassical, pragmatic view of education which was to gain ascendancy in America. Although he greatly admired the classics, he felt that, for the bulk of future Virginia gentlemen, those preciously few years of boyhood education should be spent acquiring such basics as English grammar, reading, writing, arithmetic, history, geology, eloquence, and a taste for the best literature in the student's native language. This epistolary dissertation on education is indeed an interesting document when one considers that Maury was an avid classical scholar and that his pupil Thomas Jefferson, who learned his classics under Maury and found enjoyment in them all his life, also opposed the requirement of the classical languages as basic to learning.

It was at Maury's 1 December 1763 trial for damages resulting from the 1758 Two-Penny Act that Patrick Henry made the impassioned speech which brought about his election soon afterward to the House of Burgesses. Short tobacco crops in 1755 and 1758 inflated the price of tobacco, causing the Virginia House of Burgesses to pass temporary acts commuting the year's tobacco salaries into currency at the rate of two pence per pound. Clerical opposition to these acts began a debate that occupied the energies of the best minds in Virginia for more than eight years. The Reverend John Camm was elected to carry the clergy's case to the Privy Council in England, where in 1758 he successfully petitioned the King to disallow the Virginia acts. Maury instituted suit for his original tobacco salary in Hanover County on 1 April 1762; in the December 1763 trial, however, Henry's speech resulted in Maury being awarded one-penny damages. During this period Maury developed a close association and friendship with the Tory John Camm and established a very special lifelong friendship with Jonathan Boucher, the well-known Loyalist clergyman. Even though he agreed with these men wholeheartedly in their opposition to the colonial legislature's usurping the rights of the clergy, his letters concernng the Stamp Act and his other writings indicate that he would have sided with the patriots had he lived to see the Revolution.

Maury's sermons reveal him to be as able a preacher as any colonial Anglican clergyman of his day. He was a deeply spiritual but thoroughly rational theologian who abhorred the excessive enthusiasm of the Great Awakening. A sermon tract entitled *To Christians of Every Denomination . . . An Address Enforcing an Inquiry Into . . . the Pretensions of the . . . Anabaptists,* published posthumously in 1771 but probably written a year or two after 1763, takes to task the itinerant Baptist enthusiast preachers for claiming to be "sent from God" and for intolerantly insisting that those who did not follow them were going to hell. Maury masterfully employs the plain style with its clear, logical organization and his sophisticated and effective skill in suasory discourse.

Although he did not publish a great many works, James Maury was one of the ablest Anglican clergymen in Virginia in both theology and literature. His former pupil Thomas Jefferson remembered Maury respectfully as a "correct classical scholar" and Jonathan Boucher praised his "fine style." As an educator, Maury's influence can surely be seen in the expressions of Jefferson and James Madison. When Maury's letters, sermons, and essays are edited and published, he will be recognized as a highly significant literary figure in his age in Virginia.

References:

Jonathan Boucher, *Reminiscences of an American Loyalist, 1738-1789,* edited by Jonathan Bouchier (New York: Houghton Mifflin, 1925), pp. 60-62;

Richard Beale Davis, *Intellectual Life in the Colonial South, 1585-1763* (Knoxville: University of Tennessee Press, 1978), I: 382-383; II: 552, 740-742; III: 1446;

Jacques Fontaine and others, *Memoirs of a Huguenot Family,* edited and translated by Anne Maury (New York: Putnam's, 1853);

J. A. Leo Lemay, "The Rev. Samuel Davies' Essay Series: The Virginia Centinel, 1756, 1757," in *Essays in Early Virginia Literature Honoring Richard Beale Davis* (New York: Burt Franklin, 1977), pp. 121-163;

Dumas Malone, *Jefferson the Virginian,* volume 1 of *Jefferson and His Time* (Boston: Little, Brown, 1948), pp. 40-46;

William Meade, *Old Churches, Ministers and Families of Virginia* (Philadelphia: J. B. Lippincott, 1857);

Richard L. Morton, *Colonial Virginia* (Chapel Hill: University of North Carolina Press, 1960), II: 576-577, 680-682, 808-812.

Papers:

The bulk of Maury's manuscript sermons and letters were for many years included in the Maury Deposit in Alderman Library of the University of Virginia; however, this collection was broken up. Some of this material may be found in the collections of the American Philosophical Society and Colonial Williamsburg. Some of the manuscripts are as yet unlocated.

Jonathan Mayhew

Michael P. Kramer
University of California, Davis

BIRTH: Chilmark, Martha's Vineyard, 8 October 1720, to Experience and Remember Bourne Mayhew.

EDUCATION: B.A., 1744; M.A., 1747; Harvard College.

MARRIAGE: 11 November 1756 to Elizabeth Clarke; children: Elizabeth, Jonathan, Sarah.

DEATH: Boston, Massachusetts, 9 July 1766.

BOOKS: *Seven Sermons upon the Following Subjects . . .* (Boston: Printed & sold by Rogers & Fowle, 1749; London: Printed for J. Noon, 1750);

A Discourse Concerning Unlimited Submission and Non-Resistance to the Higher Powers . . . (Boston: Printed & sold by D. Fowle, 1750); republished in *The Pillars of Priestcraft and Orthodoxy Shaken,* edited by Richard Baron (London: Printed for R. Griffiths, 1752);

A Sermon Preached at Boston in New-England, May 26, 1751. Occassioned by The much-lamented Death of His Royal Highness Frederick, Prince of Wales . . . (Boston: Printed & sold by Richard Draper, 1751);

A Sermon Preach'd in the Audience of His Excellency William Shirley, Esq.; Captain General, Governor and Commander in Chief . . . (Boston: Printed by Samuel Kneeland, 1754; London: Printed for G. Woodfall, 1755);

Portrait by John Greenwood (Congregational Library)

The Expected Dissolution of all Things, a motive to universal holiness ... (Boston: Printed & sold by Edes & Gill & sold by R. Draper, 1755);

A Discourse on Rev. XV. 3d, 4th. Occasioned by the Earthquakes in November 1755 ... (Boston: Printed & sold by Edes & Gill & sold by R. Draper, 1755);

Sermons Upon the following Subjects, Viz. On hearing the Word ... (Boston: Printed by Richard Draper, 1755; London: Printed for A. Millar, 1756);

Two Discourses Delivered November 23d. 1758. Being the Day appointed by Authority to be Observed as a Day of public Thanksgiving: Relating, more Especially, to the Success of His Majesty's Arms, and those of the King of Prussia, the Last Year ... (Boston: Printed & sold by R. Draper & sold by Edes & Gill, 1758);

Two Discourses Delivered October 25th. 1759. Being the Day appointed by Authority to be observed as A Day of public Thanksgiving, for the Success of His Majesty's Arms, More particularly in the Reduction of Quebec ... (Boston: Printed & sold by Richard Draper and by Edes & Gill and Thomas & John Fleet, 1759; London, 1760);

Two Discourses Delivered October 9, 1760. Being the Day appointed to be observed As a Day of public Thanksgiving For the Success of His Majesty's Arms, more especially In the intire Reduction of Canada ... (Boston: Printed & sold by R. Draper, Edes & Gill, and T. & J. Fleet, 1760; London, 1760);

Practical Discourses Delivered on the Occasion of the Earthquakes in November, 1755 ... (Boston: Printed & sold by R. Draper & by Edes & Gill, 1760);

A Discourse Occasioned by the Death of the Honourable Stephen Sewall, Esq.; Chief-Justice of the Superiour Court of Judicature ... (Boston: Printed by Richard Draper, Edes & Gill, and T. and J. Fleet, 1760);

God's Hand and Providence to be religiously acknowledged in public Calamities ... (Boston: Printed by Richard Draper, Edes & Gill, and Thomas & John Fleet, 1760);

A Discourse Occasioned by the Death of King George II, and the Happy Accession of his Majesty King George III ... (Boston: Printed & sold by Edes & Gill, 1761);

Striving to enter in at the strait Gate explain'd and inculcated ... (Boston: Printed & sold by Richard Draper, Edes & Gill, and Thomas & John Fleet, 1761);

Christian Sobriety: Being Eight Sermons on Titus II.6 ... (Boston: Printed by Richard & Samuel Draper, 1763);

Two Sermons on the Nature, Extent and Perfection of the Divine Goodness ... (Boston: Printed & sold by D. & J. Kneeland, 1763);

Observations on the Charter and Conduct of the Society For the Propagation of the Gospel in Foreign Parts ... (Boston: Printed by Richard & Samuel Draper, Edes & Gill, and Thomas & John Fleet, 1763; London: Printed for W. Nicoll, 1763);

A Defence of the Observations on the Charter and Conduct of the Society for the Propagation of the Gospel in Foreign Parts ... (Boston: Printed & sold by R. & S. Draper, Edes & Gill, and T. & J. Fleet, 1763; London: Printed for W. Nicoll, 1764);

Remarks on an Anonymous Tract ... (Boston: Printed & sold by R. & S. Draper, Edes & Gill, and T. & J. Fleet, 1764; London: Printed for W. Nicoll, 1765);

A Letter of Reproof to Mr. John Cleaveland of Ipswich, Occasioned by a Defamatory Libel Published under His Name . . . (Boston: Printed & sold by R. & S. Draper, Edes & Gill, and T. & J. Fleet, 1764);

Popish Idolatry . . . (Boston: Printed by R. & S. Draper, Edes & Gill, and T. & J. Fleet, 1765);

The Snare Broken. A Thanksgiving Discourse . . . Occasioned by the Repeal of the Stamp-Act (Boston: Printed & sold by R. & S. Draper, Edes & Gill, and T. & J. Fleet, 1766; London: Printed for G. Kearsly, 1766).

OTHER: "Dr. Mayhew's Sermon of January 30, 1750," in *The Pulpit of the American Revolution*, edited by John Wingate Thornton (Boston: Gould/London & New York: Sheldon, 1860), pp. 39-104;

"The Snare Broken," in *The Patriot Preachers of the American Revolution*, edited by Frank Moore (New York: Privately printed, 1860), pp. 7-48;

"A Discourse Concerning Unlimited Submission and Non-Resistance to the Higher Powers," in *Pamphlets of the American Revolution, 1750-1776*, volume 1, edited by Bernard Bailyn (Cambridge: Harvard University Press, 1965), pp. 204-247;

"Jonathan Mayhew's Election Sermon of 1754," in *The Wall and the Garden: Selected Massachusetts Election Sermons, 1670-1775*, edited by A. W. Plumstead (Minneapolis: University of Minnesota Press, 1968), pp. 281-319;

"Jonathan Mayhew's Memorandum," in "Religion and Revolution: Three Biographical Studies," by Bailyn, *Perspectives in American History*, 4 (1970): 140-144.

During the critical years that link the religious eruptions of the Great Awakening to the political rumblings that ushered in the American Revolution, no figure played a more conspicuous role in the intellectual life of New England than the notorious Reverend Jonathan Mayhew. For nearly two decades he assaulted conservative, Calvinist Boston from the liberal redoubt of his West Church pulpit, preaching Arminianism in a style that joined uncompromising rationalism to intense piety. A staunch Congregationalist, he took up the banner of dissension bequeathed to him by his Puritan forebears and launched relentless attacks against the Church of England, sending shock waves through the Anglican establishment from its colonial mission to the cathedral at Canterbury. When the British government sought to tighten its control over the colonies, Mayhew married the emotional force of the Bible to the political authority of the social contract, justifying resistance to civil tyranny as a religious duty. To some of his contemporaries, he was a dangerous heretic and a firebrand; to others, like John Adams, he was a "transcendent genius." Religious historians see him as a forerunner of American Unitarianism; political historians, as a herald of American independence. His place in the literary tradition is secured by his contributions to the conflation of religious and political rhetoric that took place over the course of the Revolutionary period and helped shape the corporate self-image of the American nation.

The Mayhew family sailed to America in the early years of the Great Migration of the 1630s but remained for the next century on the periphery of New England society. In 1641, rather than remain in Massachusetts Bay, Thomas Mayhew, Sr., secured title to Martha's Vineyard and established a feudal manor there, ruling as its governor for almost forty years. Thomas, Jr., who had immigrated with his father, turned aside from his parent's aristocratic ways and dedicated his life to ministering to the island's Indians. He was followed in this spiritual pursuit by his son, John, and his grandson, Experience. Jonathan Mayhew was the sixth child of Experience Mayhew and his second wife, Remember Bourne, who died giving birth to a seventh child before Jonathan's second birthday. By this time the fortune of Thomas, Sr., had dwindled; the family was land poor. Jonathan was raised in the humble, rural environment of Chilmark, Martha's Vineyard, obtaining the rudiments of liberal learning and a modified, pragmatic Calvinism from his missionary father. Because he was the youngest son in the family, the prospect of a college education did not present itself to Jonathan—that being reserved for his older brother Nathan. But after the brother's untimely death in 1733 and after it became apparent to the father that his youngest son had an aptitude and a desire for learning, Experience Mayhew, with the aid of a grant from the government, managed to appropriate enough money to send Jonathan to Harvard in 1740.

That was the year revivalist George Whitefield arrived in Boston and preached before thousands in Harvard Yard. Like many of his fellow students, Jonathan was swept away by the evangelical rhetoric of the Great Awakening. Tutor Henry Flynt recorded in his diary that the young Mayhew, along with schoolmates (and future revolutionaries) Samuel Cooper and James Otis, joined a devotional group which "prayed together Sung Psalms & discoursed together 2 or 3 at a time and read good books." Mayhew fell ill and found in his sickness the benevolent reproach of God. He traveled to Maine and was overcome by the spiritual harvest he witnessed there. He looked toward a redemptive death, for freedom from the "Shackels and Prison" of the "Sensual & Carnal World." With glimmerings of future eloquence, he yearned for a language of pure reverence: "May our souls be more & more inflamed with the love of Christ, and grow warmer and warmer in our Devotions to Him," he wrote to his brother Zachariah on 26 March 1742, "till we arrive at the Regions of Immortal Glory, where we shall never know any Coldness of Affection, and where Hosannas shall never languish on our Tongues; where Glory shall irradiate every Heart, and [a] smile in every Eye, and our Tongues shall ever utter the melting Language of redeeming Love." But by 1747, when he heard Whitefield deliver his farewell sermon on Copp's Hill in Boston, Mayhew's attitude toward the Great Awakening had become radically altered. The sermon, he wrote to his relieved father, "was a very low, confused, puerile, conceited, ill-natur'd, enthusiastick, &c. Performance as ever I heard in my Life." The following year he would formulate a more rational theory of sermonic style, influenced by the writings of John Locke. Linguistic truth, "as it relates to *words* and *propositions*," he wrote, "is nothing but the *right* use of certain arbitrary signs, having a meaning annexed to them by common consent; *i.e.* the using them in such a manner that they shall be conformable to, and expressive of, the real nature and properties of the thing treated of." He would fall back upon this theory of language in the years to come in his attacks upon enthusiasm, false eloquence, and muddled thinking. Still, echoes of the young man's early pietism remained in his writings throughout his career.

Mayhew's undergraduate experience was characterized by wide extremes of behavior and strikingly diverse intellectual pursuits. Reports of his praying and psalm singing are balanced by evidence of rowdiness and illegal drinking. His attraction to Whitefield and his reading of "good books" is matched, and superseded, by his embrace of the works of modern philosophers, theologians, and scientists such as Robert Boyle, Samuel Clarke, Samuel Parker, John Ray, William Wollaston, and John Woodward. Most important, he began to invite the libertarian thought that informed nearly all of his writings. Looking back over his career in his last published work, *The Snare Broken . . .* (1766), Mayhew recalled the doubleness of his early intellectual development: "Having been initiated, in youth, in the doctrines of civil liberty, as they were taught by such men as Plato, Demosthenes, Cicero and other renowned persons among the ancients; and such as [Algernon] Sidney and [John] Milton, [John] Locke and [Benjamin] Hoadley, among the moderns; I liked them; they seemed rational. Having earlier still learnt from the holy scriptures, That wise, brave and vertuous men were always friends to liberty; that God gave the Israelites a King (or absolute Monarch) in his anger, because they had not sense and virtue enough to like a free commonwealth, and to have himself for their King; that the Son of God came down from heaven, to make us 'free indeed'; and that 'where the Spirit of the Lord is, there is liberty'; this made me conclude that freedom was a great blessing." Mayhew emerged from Harvard with his piety still intact, but directed and defined by the philosophy of the Enlightenment.

The future champion of liberty was graduated from Harvard College on Wednesday, 4 July 1744, but not before being reprimanded for his antiauthoritarian behavior after an incident involving a student election. In "a very imprudent manner," he had "made an impertinent recrimination upon some of the imediate Governors of the House they all being present." Nevertheless, the Harvard Overseers voted Mayhew a grant from the Saltonstall foundation to continue study toward the master of arts degree and a career in the ministry. He remained in residence in Cambridge for the next three years and was befriended, and influenced, by the moderately liberal minister Ebenezer Gay. Toward the end of this period, after being rejected by the congregation in Worcester in favor of a revivalist preacher and turning down an offer from the small church in Cohasset, he accepted a position at Boston's new, affluent West Church. Mayhew's tumultuous career was launched.

Not even his ordination was free from controversy. Customarily, ordinations were overseen by a ministerial council from neighboring churches, but the West Church decided to invite from Boston only Benjamin Colman of Brattle Street and Charles Chauncy of the First Church (the only churches, it claimed, to have invited Mayhew to preach). The council was to be completed by Ebenezer Gay of Hingham, Nathaniel Appleton of Cambridge, and the new pastor's father. The ceremony was scheduled for 20 May 1747. But the West Church was already looked upon with suspicion: the previous pastor, William Hooper, had scandalized Boston not long before by defecting to the Anglican Trinity Church. Now, slighting the older (and more strictly Calvinist) Boston divines compounded doubts. Colman, fearing dissension, declined to attend, and Chauncy was restrained by division within his own congregation. When Experience Mayhew was also prevented from arriving, due to delays in transit, the ordination was postponed until 20 June. This time the Boston churches were ignored altogether; the council was composed strictly of ministers from surrounding towns. In his ordination sermon, Gay spoke in militant tones that proved to be prophetic of the new pastor's career: "Be valiant for the Truth against all Opposition from the Lusts of Men, and Powers of Darkness.... So that from the Blood of the uncircumcised Slain, from the Fat of the Mighty, the Bow of *Jonathan* turn not back empty!"

Several days after his ordination, Mayhew completed the requirements for his degree, defending the thesis that faith and reason were compatible. It is reported that, when a classmate, Abraham Williams, challenged the candidate with the assertion that no religion which included the doctrine of original sin could be considered rational, Mayhew boldly parried, "Sir, it is true." (He would later present a wittily pragmatic attitude toward original sin: "Let us therefore mourn and amend our Faults; and not trouble our Consciences about the Sins of Adam. We have Sins enough of our own to bewail, without taking those of others upon ourselves.") Bringing this heretical baggage with him to Boston, Mayhew could hardly have been surprised when few ministers inaugurated exchanges of pulpits with him. Nor could he have wondered why he was never invited to join the Boston Association of Ministers nor asked to deliver a Thursday lecture. All these were matters of course for members of the clergy, but Mayhew did not bend under the pressure of ostracism. On the contrary, he grew more defiant. Beginning in June 1748, he initiated a Thursday lecture series of his own and attracted larger audiences than the regularly scheduled lectures—including, legend has it, a young Paul Revere, whose father whipped him as a consequence. Preaching on the text Luke 12:54-57 (which ends, "Yea, and why even of yourselves judge ye not what is right?"), he spoke of "the *Scribes* and *Pharisees*" who had set themselves up as "infallible guides" and "stigmatized our Lord as an ill man," who, "without any reason or authority, was attempting to discredit certain opinions which they had *received to have and to hold from their forefathers*" and who was introducing "innovations in the old established religion." Few in the audience could have failed to see through this thinly veiled attack upon Mayhew's ministerial colleagues or to feel the sense of Christ-like martyrdom that charged his exegesis. His hearers no doubt would have felt some satisfaction when he berated the ancient Hebrews who had refused "to come and hear [Christ] preach (this being represented to them as dangerous) so that they might know what he had to say for himself."

When the lectures were published in 1749 as *Seven Sermons . . .* , Mayhew's reputation as a religious rebel spread. Not only did the young preacher reject the basic tenets of Calvinism, but, between heresy and invective, he challenged the authority of the established ministry. Mayhew's theology rested upon "The Right and Duty of Private Judgment." Religious authority was invested, not in traditional creeds or in ecclesiastical hierarchies, but in each individual's native ability to distinguish rationally "betwixt Truth and Falsehood, Right and Wrong." Christ himself, *"the author and finisher of our faith,"*

SEVEN
SERMONS
Upon the
Following Subjects;
VIZ.

The Difference betwixt Truth and Falshood, Right and Wrong.
The natural Abilities of Men for discerning these Differences.
The Right and Duty of private Judgment.

Objections considered.
The Love of God.
The Love of our Neighbour.
The first and great Commandment. &c.

Preached
At a LECTURE in the West Meeting-House
In BOSTON,
Begun the first Thursday in *June*, and ended the last Thursday
In *August*, 1748.

By JONATHAN MAYHEW, A. M.
Pastor of the West Church in *Boston*.

BOSTON, N.E.
Printed and Sold by ROGERS and FOWLE in Queen-street.
MDCCXLIX.

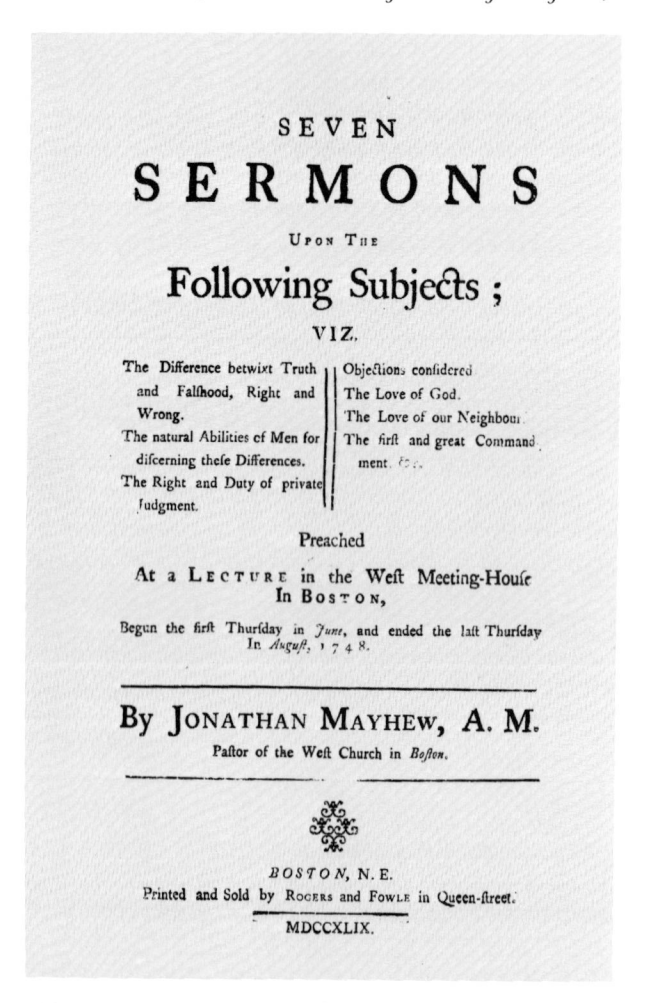

Title page for Mayhew's first book, which not only rejects basic Calvinist tenets but also challenges the authority of the ecclesiastical hierarchy (courtesy of the John Carter Brown Library at Brown University)

never demanded blind obedience from his followers. Indeed, his practice of reasoning with his audience bespeaks "a disclaiming of *authority* properly so called: for it implies, that the arguments are to be judged by the reason of him to whom they are proposed." Truth is determined neither by the prevalence of a religious opinion ("How many votes are necessary to change a great lye into a glorious truth?"), nor by the show of force: "To attempt to *dragoon* men into sound orthodox *Christians*, is as unnatural and fruitless as to *dragoon* them into good *poets, physicians,* or *mathematicians*. A blow with a club may fracture a man's skull; but I suppose he will not think and reason the more clearly for that; though he may possibly believe the more orthodoxly, according to the opinions of some." A true Christian must judge freely; he must bring to religious matters a mind "in *acquilibrio,*" without "old prejudices and prepossessions." Depravity is not a prior spiritual condition but a relinquishing of the "state of *indifferency,*" due to physical, social, or political causes. To accept anything as a matter of faith is to accept slavery; for "to determine any point without reason or proof cannot be to judge *freely,* unless it be in a bad sense of the word."

"Let us all *stand fast,*" Mayhew demands, *"in the liberty wherewith Christ has made us free"*—a liberty, he explains, "from an ignominious slavery to the dictates of men." The psychological liberty Mayhew defends in *Seven Sermons* . . . stood for him as the ultimate justification for his later defense of religious and political liberty, so it is important that it not be misconstrued. Mayhew did not support a radical egalitarianism, neither in regard to society as a whole nor to the church in particular. Although it "is principally on account of our reason that we are said to have been *Created in the image of God,*" not all men are equally rational. "From the most dull and stupid of the human species, there is a continual rise and gradation," Mayhew writes, "there being as great a variety in the intellectual powers of men as in their bodily and active powers." To these natural factors he adds cultural and social distinctions, betraying an underlying ethnocentrism and elitism: "Who will pretend that the natives of *Greenland,* or the *Cape of Good Hope,* enjoy the same, or equal, means of knowledge, with those that are born in the polite and learned nations of *Europe*? Who imagines that one brought up at the plough is as likely to form right notions of things as if he had been educated at a university? Or that a man who has conversed only with ordinary Mechanics, has the same advantages with those who have enjoyed the familiarity of the greatest proficients in literature?" Neither does Mayhew's advocacy of free inquiry imply a philosophical relativism; men are not "at liberty to judge wrong, and to reject the true religion." Rather, they are free only "to judge truly and justly and reject what is wrong." "Truth still remains the same simple, uniform, consistent thing," he insists, "amidst all the various and contrary opinions of mankind concerning it." Nor did Mayhew's enthronement of reason and intellectual freedom preclude practical piety; the essential element of Arminianism was the efficacy of works. While the first four of the *Seven Sermons* . . . deal with religious psychology, the remaining four concern the "Love of God" and the "Love of our Neighbor." "Christianity," after all, "is principally an institution of life and manners." Reason and revelation both make it clear that the "end of our being" is "acting our part in the great *drama* of the world" to which "God himself is a spectator." Mayhew fully believed that the strict exercise of private judgment would sustain, not threaten, social stability and religious morality.

The publication of *Seven Sermons* . . . drew no official response from Boston's Calvinists, although several pseudonymous reviewers expressed the consensus well when they castigated Mayhew for his brazen infidelity. Even Charles Chauncy, who sympathized with Mayhew's views, felt that at times the author's "imagination got the better of his judgment, betraying him into too warm and satyrical expressions." But in England the volume was greeted by liberal dissenters and low-church Anglicans—among them Bishop Benjamin Hoadley—with enthusiastic, if condescending, applause. Finally an American had dared to profess the enlightened Christianity that had been espoused in England for decades. Mayhew's supporters recommended that the book be reprinted in England and managed to secure for him the honorary degree of Doctor of Divinity from the University of Aberdeen. In May 1750, he received a sheepskin diploma confirming his transatlantic reputation.

By this time, however, the Reverend Dr. Mayhew was feeling the aftershocks of his second publication. Several months earlier, as the one hundred first anniversary of the beheading of Charles I on 30 January 1649 approached, Mayhew noted a "strange sort of frenzy" among Boston's Anglicans, preaching "passive obedience, worshipping King Charles I, and cursing dissenters and puritans for murdering him." It had been customary for Anglicans to observe the anniversary as a day of rededication to the theory of the divine right of kings, and the practice set Mayhew's teeth on edge. As much as he had renounced the dogmatism of his

Puritan ancestors, he retained their antipathy to prelacy. Seizing the opportunity, he delivered a series of three sermons on the subject, the last of which was delivered on the Sunday of the anniversary and published soon after as *A Discourse Concerning Unlimited Submission and Non-Resistance to the Higher Powers . . .* (1750).

Preaching on Romans 13:1-8 ("Let every soul be subject unto the higher power...."), Mayhew turns the scriptural justification for the divine rights theory on its head, reading the Apostle Paul's strictures as if he were a disciple of John Locke. Drawing principally from the writings of Bishop Hoadley (he was later to be accused of plagiarism), Mayhew argues that "the true ground and reason of our obligation to be subject to the *higher powers* is the usefulness of magistracy (when properly exercised) to human society and its subserviency to the general welfare." When government fulfills its obligations—whether that government be "monarchical, republican, aristocratical"—an act of disobedience "is not merely a *political* sin but a heinous *offence against God and religion.*" But, Mayhew asks, when a government is tyrannical, when its rules are self-serving, would it not "be more rational to suppose that they [who] did NOT *resist* than they who did would *receive to themselves damnation*"? In such a case "a people (if I may allude to an ancient *fable*) have, like the Hesperian fruit, a DRAGON for their *protector* and *guardian*, nor would they have any reason to mourn if some HERCULES should appear to dispatch him." Such, indeed, was the case with Charles I, and adumbrating the strategy of the Declaration of Independence a quarter century later, Mayhew lists a long train of abuses perpetrated by the Stuart monarch. The Puritan Revolution was a duty, not a crime. Charles was a sinner, not a saint. To reaffirm the divine right of kings, a doctrine "as fabulous and chimerical as transubstantiation or any of the most absurd reveries of ancient or modern visionaries," was, in fact, treasonous; the "justice and legality" of the British monarchy after 1689 rested upon, not divine right, but the right of revolution. If the anniversary is to be celebrated, Mayhew suggests, let it be as "a standing *memento* that *Britons* will not be *slaves.*" In short, he concludes, "let us learn to be *free* and to be *loyal.*" Fifteen years later he would learn firsthand the precariousness of this balance.

Strictly speaking, Mayhew's purpose in *A Discourse Concerning Unlimited Submission and Non-Resistance to the Higher Powers . . .* was not political. His target was not the British government, still a salutary force in American life, but the Anglican

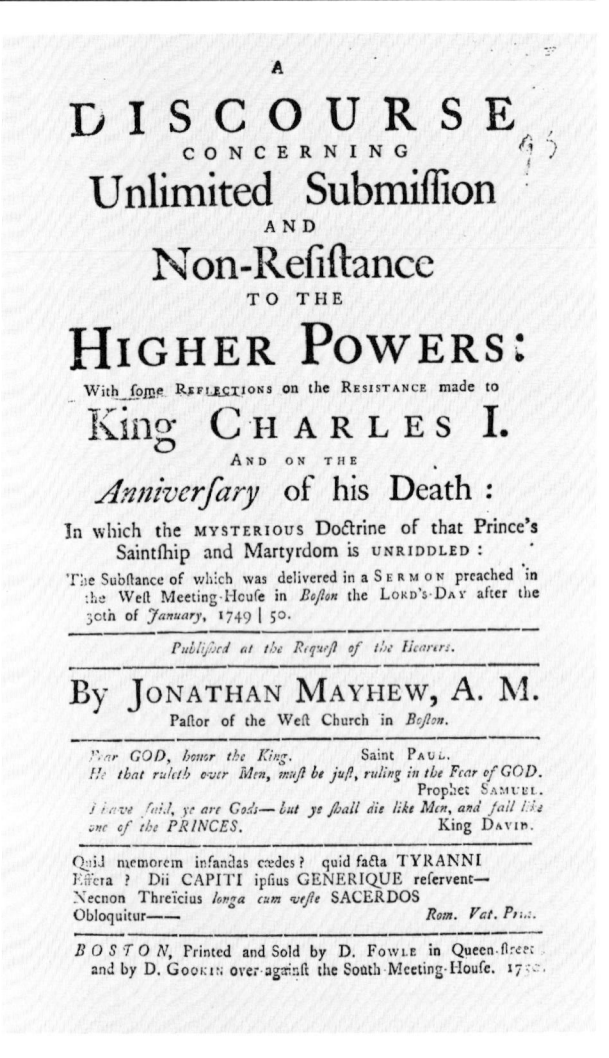

Title page for Mayhew's second book, in which he challenged authority still further by employing a Lockian argument against the divine rights of kings (courtesy of the John Carter Brown Library at Brown University)

ministry, for whom he reserved, in John Adams's opinion, a "wit superior to any in Swift or Franklin." Why had the Church of England canonized Charles I? Surely, "*that church* must be but *poorly stocked* with saints and martyrs which is forced to adopt such enormous sinners into her *calendar* in order to swell the number." In his attempts "to unravel this *mystery of (nonsense* as well as of*) iniquity,*" Mayhew uncovers a century-old conspiracy: "In *plain English,*" he explains, playing upon Charles's links to Rome through his French queen ("a true *daughter* of that true *mother of harlots*"), "there seems to have been an impious bargain struck up betwixt the *scepter* and the *surplice* for enslaving both the *bodies* and *souls* of men." Mayhew's defense of the right and duty of revolution in *A Discourse Concerning Unlimited Submission and Non-Resistance to the Higher Powers . . .* is thus linked to his advocacy of the right and duty of private judgment in *Seven Sermons. . . .* The enemy in each case is the same: "*Tyranny brings* ignorance *and* brutality *along with it. It degrades men from their just rank into the class of brutes. It damps their spirits. It suppresses arts. It extinguishes every spark of noble ardor and generosity in the breast of those who are enslaved by it. It makes naturally strong and great minds feeble and little and triumphs over the ruins of virtue and humanity.*" Whether civil or ecclesiastical, tyranny is ultimately a moral evil; Mayhew could thus with conviction urge "*every lover of God and the Christian religion, to bear a part in opposing this hateful monster.*"

A Discourse Concerning Unlimited Submission and Non-Resistance to the Higher Powers . . . dropped like a bomb on Boston, and its reverberations were felt throughout New England and even in Britain itself, where it was eventually republished in Richard Baron's *The Pillars of Priestcraft and Orthodoxy Shaken* (1752). According to John Adams, the discourse was "read by everybody, celebrated by friends and abused by enemies." The newspapers carried charges and countercharges for the next six months. Critics called Mayhew a "Bully," a "*Don Quixote* in *Religion* and *Politics*," a "wrangling Preacher" who "belch'd out a Flood of Obloquy." Even some of Boston's Congregationalists, whose forebears had supported the Grand Old Cause of the Puritan Revolution and who were the objects of the Anglicans' attacks, recoiled at the minister's "*unmannerly behavior.*" But Mayhew had his supporters, too, including loyal congregant Harrison Gray, who later judged that "altho' there was a considerable quantity of *Mercury* in the Emetick, the stubborn Malady of the patient required it." Over the years, *A Discourse Concerning Unlimited Submission and Non-Resistance to the Higher Powers . . .* has become Mayhew's most famous and widely studied work, a significant document for those who, as John Adams suggested, "really wish to investigate the principles and feelings which produced the Revolution."

Mayhew's fluency in libertarian rhetoric translated itself into challenges to literary convention as well as to political and ecclesiastical authority. Social contract theory transforms his *A Sermon . . . Occassioned by The much-lamented Death of His Royal Highness Frederick, Prince of Wales . . .* (1751) into an antieulogy. He refused on principle to flatter King George II with an encomium to his deceased heir. "Good sense is not entailed with the crown," he preached, "on the elder branch of the male line." If the prince's death were to be lamented, it should be for his reported "abhorrence of popery and arbitrary government," not for his birthright. Similarly, the social contract authorizes his revision of Puritan history in his Election Sermon of 1754. "Our ancestors," he announced to the General Court, "were a religious, brave, and virtuous set of men" (though he admitted they were "not perfect and infallible in all respects"), "whose love of liberty, civil and religious, brought them from their native land into the American desarts." And when Mayhew goes on to dismiss the idea that "we are so far degenerated from the laudable spirit of our ancestors as to despise and abuse what they procured for us at so dear a rate," he repudiates the myth of declension that had informed the genre of the election sermon for the last hundred years. At the same time, when the minister astutely recognizes the growing need for strong intercolonial defenses in the face of French threats of attack, he betrays, for all his literary and ideological progressiveness, the deep-seated cultural prejudice and religious animosity that buttressed his rational politics. In a "restless, roving fancy, or something of a higher nature," he envisions "motley armies of French and painted savages" and "an herd of lazy monks, and Jesuits, and exorcists, and inquisitors." The vision darkens: "What indignity is yonder offered to the matrons! and here to the virgins!" And grows more terrifying: "Do I see all liberty, property, religion, happiness, changed, or rather transubstantiated, into slavery, poverty, superstition, wretchedness!" Ironically, neither Mayhew, nor the legislature, nor Governor Shirley knew that on 28 May, the day before the sermon was delivered, George Washington had engaged the French in battle at Fort Duquesne. The French and Indian War had already begun.

The war years were difficult ones for Boston. Several of Mayhew's most prominent congregants were forced into bankruptcy. But some of the most serious hardships of these years, both financial and psychological, did not result from the war. On 18 November 1755, at 4:30 A.M., the city was hit by a devastating earthquake that destroyed homes and property and left the inhabitants emotionally, let alone physically, shaken. Then, in 1760, the city was ravaged by fires; several hundred families were left homeless. During these years Mayhew displayed a side of his intellectual character too often obscured by his theological and political radicalism. Like many of his colleagues, and like the Mathers, Danforths, and Wigglesworths before them, the rationalist minister saw the earthquakes, the fires, and the early military setbacks as divine admonitions against worldliness and irreligion. In numerous published discourses Mayhew employed a rhetoric in some ways more reminiscent of the fire and brimstone of Jonathan Edwards than of the natural philosophy of the scientists he had read at Harvard. He impressed upon his audience that "God's Hand and Providence [ought] to be religiously acknowledged in public Calamities." The disasters were a frightening reminder of "The Expected Dissolution of all Things" at the end of time and ought, therefore, to be a "motive to universal holiness." To be sure, Mayhew did not abandon his insistence upon a rational approach to religion but saw the purpose of seemingly inexplicable events in God's scheme. "A little reflection upon the operations of our own minds will indeed make it evident," he explained, "that all wonder, surprise, astonishment, at bottom proceed from, and connote ignorance." To inspire awe, God must at times interrupt the orderly operations of nature, "for nothing which we fully understand, ever excites wonder and admiration." True piety can never be the issue of reason. Mayhew's hybrid theology has been called "rational supernaturalism."

In the years immediately following the outbreak of the French and Indian War, Mayhew published nothing of a political nature. But during that period he entered into the most significant political relationship of his career, with the eccentric English libertarian Thomas Hollis. Hollis, having read *A Discourse Concerning Unlimited Submission and Non-Resistance to the Higher Powers . . .* , became convinced that the colonial divine would prove an important American ally, so he began to send him shipments of books—Milton, Sidney, Locke. Thus began a long and fruitful correspondence: Hollis was delighted with Mayhew's later political activities and was instrumental in the British publication of the minister's works. Their letters are an important source in the history of English and American libertarian thought.

The war years witnessed as well the beginning of another important relationship in Mayhew's life. On 11 November 1756 he married twenty-two-year-old Elizabeth Clarke, a noted beauty in Boston, in spite of repeated warnings to her prominent family that they protect her from the dangerous heretic. According to Harrison Gray, "there was never a more happy Match upon Earth." "I need not multiply words," Mayhew wrote his "dear Betsey," "because words, however multiplied, cannot express how much, and how sincerely, I am yours."

On 1 May 1759, their first child, a daughter, was born and named Elizabeth for her mother. By the time the baby was seven months old, British forces had taken Quebec, and the outcome of the war seemed certain. With the dangers of popery removed and the promise of vast territories opening to British settlement, Mayhew could foresee "a grand and flourishing kingdom in these parts of America, peopled by our posterity." On 25 October, he offered a thanksgiving discourse which echoed John Winthrop's 1630 vision of an American "cittie vpon a hill" and reversed the dire predictions of 1754: "Methinks I see mighty cities rising on every hill, and by the side of every commodious port; mighty fleets alternately sailing out and returning, laden with the produce of this, and every other country under heaven; happy fields and villages wherever I turn my eyes, thro' a vastly extended territory; there the pastures cloathed with flocks, and here the vallies covered with corn, while the little hills rejoice on every side! And do I not there behold the savage nations, no longer our enemies, bowing to the knee of Jesus Christ, and with joy confessing him to be 'Lord, to the Glory of God the Father!' Methinks I see religion professed and practised throughout this spacious kingdom, in far and greater purity and perfection, than since the times of the apostles; the Lord being still as a wall of fire round about, and the glory in the midst of her! O happy country! happy kingdom!" With the coming of the Revolution, this "rising glory" motif, with its blend of material and spiritual elements, would become a staple of American rhetoric.

Mayhew was a theological thorn in the side of the Boston clergy throughout his career, but the desperate warnings to the Clarke family before his marriage to Elizabeth Clarke were perhaps more immediately prompted by the publication in 1755 of the prospective suitor's second volume of liberal theology, *Sermons Upon the following Subjects . . .* , known popularly by the title of its opening sermon, *On hearing the Word. . . .* Having already publicly rejected such fundamentals of orthodoxy as the doctrine of original sin in *Seven Sermons . . .* , Mayhew now infuriated the orthodox by trifling with the Athanasian Trinity. His was not a thoroughgoing refutation; he was too much concerned with practical religion to be "bold enough to meddle" with theological metaphysics. But he was certain that the notion of a triune godhead was unscriptural as well as irrational. "The scripture informs us that the *Logos* had a *body* prepared for him, and that he partook of *flesh* and *blood*," he admitted. "But that he took into *personal union* with himself, an human *soul,* my Bible saith not." In any case, whatever "the metaphysical abstract nature, or essence of the Deity," the practical results of the espousal of trinitarian doctrine were enough to recommend its rejection. For its supporters, Mayhew added in the smug tone that irritated his enemies as much as his blasphemous ideas, "contend, and foam, and curse their brethren," making it clear that "they do not love and fear the ONE living and true God as they ought to do."

The attack on the trinitarians was by far the most scandalous of Mayhew's pronouncements in *On hearing the Word . . . ,* and it proved to be the most significant historically as well, gaining for him a reputation as a pioneer of American Unitarianism. But it was literally only a footnote to the text. It was in the margins of the volume, too, that Mayhew offered his views on one of the most profound philosophical questions of his time—the issue of free will. Jonathan Edwards's *A Careful and Strict Enquiry into the Modern Prevailing Notions of that Freedom of the Will* had been published in 1754, and Mayhew apparently felt it necessary, if not to respond fully to the revivalist's cogent challenge to Arminianism, at least to explain in some detail his opposition to it. Edwards's intricate web of abstract arguments, he felt, could not stand up against the simple fact that we "are conscious of, and feel our freedom within us, as truly and certainly as we see or feel corporeal objects without us." Language confirms that we all share this "internal sensation": we commonly use expressions that presuppose free will ("that we can do so, or so; but cannot do another thing") that would otherwise "be quite senseless and unintelligible." Moreover—and this argument was the most salient for Mayhew—the idea of free will formed the basis of "the common moral sense of things, of actions and characters, which all mankind, in all ages, in all countries, have had and have." Clearly "the great author of our being has framed our minds in such a manner, that we naturally connect the idea of liberty with that of demerit, or ill-desert." Without free will there would be no accountability and, hence, no moral government. No amount of casuistry, Mayhew concluded, could change that simple truth.

Mayhew added nothing of consequence to the debate over free will; his long marginal note only restates the arguments which had originally spurred Edwards's formidable treatise. Still, the remarks bolster the framework of liberty he had built in *Seven Sermons . . .* and *A Discourse Concerning Unlimited Submission and Non-Resistance to the Higher Powers . . . ,* reaffirming the position of private judgment in the moral scheme of the universe. They underscore as well Mayhew's primary concerns in *On hearing the Word . . . ,* the inculcations of morality, and, most significantly from a literary point of view, the role of the ministry in light of his rationalist view of religious psychology. He opens the volume with a defense of his sermonic style against the stylish ornamentalism of the Anglicans, the arcane dogmatism of the Old Light Calvinists, and the excessive emotionalism of the revivalists. The search for religious knowledge, he believed, demanded a sort of plain style, an unadorned representation of evidence and argument, because theological views must be open to refutation. His opinions, however controversial, are therefore "not disguised by any kind of artifice: they do not just peep through the mask of studied, equivocal, and ambiguous phrase; nor skulk in the dark, as it were from a consciousness of what they are, and a fear of being detected."

But Mayhew had not turned so far from his early pietism to discount completely the role of the affections in religious life. He denied "that the informing of men's understandings either is or ought to be the sole end of preaching." True piety included "the spirit of devotion, and the religion of the heart," which Mayhew likened to "a fire which will insensibly languish and go to decay, in the damps and mists and impure vapors of the world, if it be not often supplied with fewel from heaven." It is the role of the "word of God which is sometimes like a fire, to melt and inflame the heart, as well as, at others, like a sword to pierce, or a hammer to break it to pieces." Sermons could, and should, be addressed to the heart, as well as the head, as long as they were true, undistorted representations of the Word. In this he concurred with his Puritan predecessors; sermonic language should not call attention to itself. In the dedication to a later volume of sermons, *Christian Sobriety . . .* (1763), Mayhew noted the moral implications of pretentious preaching: "If discourses from the pulpit are adapted only to please the ear and the fancy, like many modern fashionable ones; instead of having a direct tendency to alarm the conscience of a sinner, to warm the heart of a saint, or to enlighten the understandings of any; they serve, in my opinion, to no better purposes, than those of unseasonably amusing the hearers, disgracing the places in which, and the persons by whom they are delivered, as frivolous, conceited declaimers; who seek only the applause of men, by their sounding brass and tinkling symbols; instead of designing to do good, by manifestation of the truth, and commending themselves to every man's conscience in the sight of God."

Over the next decade, Mayhew continued to preach his rational supernaturalism with the bold clarity of logical argument and the driving force of religious passion, as well as the taunting wit of unalloyed self-confidence. "I will not be even *religiously* scolded, nor pitied, nor wept and lamented, out of any principles which I believe upon the authority of Scripture, in the exercise of that small share of reason which God has given," he declared in the preface to *On hearing the Word* . . . . Nor would he "postpone this authority, to that of the good *Fathers* of the Church, even with that of the good *Mothers* added to it." The major theological works which followed—*Striving to enter in at the strait Gate explain'd and inculcated* . . . (1761), *Christian Sobriety* . . . , and *Two Sermons on the Nature, Extent and Perfection of the Divine Goodness* . . . (1763)—continued to antagonize his clerical colleagues. Sometimes they responded publicly with scholarly treatises, but more often with venomous, and anonymous, newspaper attacks. Through it all, Mayhew declined to enter into direct battle with anyone, until John Cleaveland, a mildly infamous revivalist from Ipswich (he had been expelled from Yale), challenged Mayhew's doctrine of the atonement. Mayhew's response, *A Letter of Reproof to Mr. John Cleaveland of Ipswich* . . . (1764), was a contemptuous, vituperative, personal attack that displayed the quickness of his temper as much as the sharpness of his mind.

If Mayhew preferred to avoid outright theological wrangling, leaving his ideas to stand and fall, for the most part, on the strength of rational argument and biblical evidence, he exercised no such restraint when it came to ecclesiastical matters, entering the lists in 1763 against his old opponents, the Anglicans, in what became known as "The Mayhew Controversy." After the British defeat of French forces at Quebec in 1759, when the fears of Catholic ascendancy in North America had been allayed, Congregationalists, Old and New Light alike, grew alarmed at what they felt was a similar threat from within—the rise of the Episcopal church in New England. Institutional support for this rise had come from the Society for the Propagation of the Gospel in Foreign Parts, founded by Anglicans in 1701 with a vaguely worded royal charter, whose goal, as the Congregationalists understood it, was missionary activity among the Indians and black slaves. Instead, the S.P.G. had been establishing missions in New England towns, including one in Cambridge, not far from Harvard College. Fears of an attempt to establish an American episcopate were renewed. When Dr. Ebenezer Miller, rector of the S.P.G.-supported Anglican church in Braintree, died in February 1763, a biting satire in the *Boston Gazette* told of his courageous attempt "to Civilize and Christianize the poor *Natives* and *Africans*" of Braintree, who looked suspiciously like Europeans. In answer to the attack, East Apthorp, the Anglican missionary at Cambridge, Massachusetts, published a short work defending the society, arguing condescendingly that it had indeed been established to "hinder *corruptions* of Christianity" and to cultivate "good manners and a christian life" among the English colonists, and only secondarily to convert the Indians.

Mayhew had for several years been suspicious of the society. The military successes of the British had brought hopes of "the savage nation, no longer our enemies, bowing to the knee of Jesus Christ," but as he noted in his 1760 funeral sermon for Stephen Sewall, it had become apparent that "a certain SOCIETY beyond the sea, had done nothing, or but very little, to this important end." Apthorp's tract brought the resentment of the son of Indian missionaries to the surface, and he responded with *Observations on the Charter and Conduct of the Society For the Propagation of the Gospel in Foreign Parts* (1763). The literary war began.

Many of the charges in Mayhew's observations are literary and linguistic: Apthorp had violated Mayhew's strict rhetorical standards. Beginning with the contractual premise that "the words of the charter itself must determine and limit the sense of the royal *Grantor,* and consequently the legal power conferred on the noble and reverend *Grantees,* the Society," Mayhew finds that Apthorp had consistently either misquoted the charter or had chosen his quotations so selectively as to obscure the document's meaning. Moreover, he had distorted the definitions of significant terms. Anglicans and Congregationalists differed, for the most part, on matters of church practice and polity, not theology (Apthorp and Mayhew were, in fact, both Arminians). Yet he had accused the New England churches of unorthodoxy, when the word *orthodox,* Mayhew claimed, "relates particularly to doctrinal points, or articles of faith, as distinguished from opinions about the best modes of ecclesiastical polity, external order, rites and ceremonies." This meaning was, at least, "the commonly received sense of the word among protestants," he added pointedly, a fact that

Title page for the sermon in which Mayhew once again challenged established authority and initiated a war of words that lasted two years (courtesy of the John Carter Brown Library at Brown University)

Apthorp, "a gentleman so well skilled in Christian philology," could hardly dispute. Indeed, the Anglican had been so much more concerned with style than with content, offering "many specimens of a singular imagination, a florid, rhetorical diction, a brisk, lively way of reasoning, marvellous turns of arguments, surprising hyperboles, and diverse other licenses even in grammar," that the work seems less "*didactic*" than "truly poetical." No literary criticism could have been, from Mayhew's point of view, more damning.

Mayhew's substantive arguments in *Observations on the Charter and Conduct of the Society For the Propagation of the Gospel in Foreign Parts . . .* were aimed at uncovering the insidious designs of the society. Surely their stated motives, as Apthorp expressed them, were nonsense. New Englanders were hardly deficient in religion, or in manners, even if "divers of our Forefathers had somewhat *too long* faces, and a too set, formal air." On the contrary, "the common people in New England, by means of our schools, and the instructions of our 'able, learned, orthodox ministers,' are, and have all along, been philosophers and divines in comparison of the common people in England, of the communion of the church there established." Furthermore, while the sons of the Puritans had no need of missionaries, the Indians clearly had, both for their own spiritual well-being and for the political well-being of the British empire. Spreading the gospel among the tribes that bordered the American colonies would insure their allegiance. The wisdom of this strategy had been underscored by the Jesuit successes that determined the alignments of the French and Indian War. Why, then, would the society spend its money so foolishly, when the fate of the empire was at stake?

Apparently, Mayhew believed, the Anglican Church was up to its old tricks again. In the most powerful prose of the tract, he recalled "what our Forefathers suffered from the mitred, lordly SUCCESSORS *of the fishermen of Galilee.*" To be rescued from the Church's "unholy zeal and oppression, countenanced by sceptr'd tyrants," they had thrown themselves "into the arms of Savages and Barbarians." Had their sacrifices been in vain? Would history repeat itself? Mayhew builds to an emotional crescendo: "Is it not enough, that they persecuted us out of the old world? Will they pursue us into the new to convert us here?—*compassing sea and land to make* US *proselytes,* while they neglect the heathen and heathenish plantations! What other new world remains as a sanctuary for us from their oppressions, in case of need? Where is the COLUMBUS to explore one for, and pilot us to it, before we are consumed in a flood of episcopacy?" The Puritan errand into the wilderness was a unique American legacy: it ran deep in Mayhew's consciousness and exerted an enormous force on his imagination. It surfaced periodically: in 1750, to vindicate "*our forefathers*" in their opposition to Charles I; in 1754, to celebrate the immigrants' "love of liberty, civil and religious"; in 1759, to lend credence to a vision of "a great and flourishing kingdom in these parts of America." But never before had it betrayed the wide psychological wedge history had driven between Britain and her American colonies. To be sure, Mayhew often professed loyalty; the King and parliament were not directly implicated in his charges. Nevertheless, the tremendous weight carried by the pronoun "US" bespeaks the fragility of the Americans' double allegiance to the Puritan fathers and to their father the King. Although he did not intend it, the literary battles of "The Mayhew Controversy" were crucial to what John Adams called "the awakening and revival of American principles and feelings" before the Revolution.

The war of words raged for two years. Mayhew was attacked, often scurrilously, nearly always anonymously, in newspapers and pamphlets. He responded only twice: to Hugh Caner of Boston's King's Chapel and Samuel Johnson of King's College (*A Defence of the Observations on the Charter and Conduct of the Society for the Propagation of the Gospel in Foreign Parts . . .* , 1763) and to Thomas Secker, Archbishop of Canterbury (*Remarks on an Anonymous Tract . . .* , 1764). He may be said to have landed the final blow, indirectly, in the Dudleian lecture he delivered at Harvard in May 1765 on the subject of *Popish Idolatry . . .* (1765). The bulk of the lecture deals with "the doctrine and practice of the church of Rome respecting the worship of the eucharist, saints and angels, pictures and images." But at the close, he clarifies his more immediate concerns: "Detestable as the idolatry of the church of Rome is," Mayhew's "controversy with her is not merely a religious one" but "a defense of our laws, liberties, and civil rights as men, in opposition to the proud claims of and encroachments of ecclesiastical persons, who under the pretext of religion, and saving men's souls, would engross all power and property to themselves, and reduce us to the most abject slaves." If the innuendos were not understood, Mayhew outlined more sharply the links between Canterbury and Rome: "Popery is now making great strides in England; as great, perhaps as it did in the reign either of Charles or James the second: I pray God, things may not at length be brought to as bad a pass! Thousands of weak and wicked Protestants are annually perverted to an impious, horrid system of tyranny over the bodies and souls of men; which less deserves the name of religion, than that of an outrage on the senses, and most valuable rights of men, and a satire upon God. . . . Heaven only knows what the end of these things will be; the prospect is alarming." It was certainly clear to Thomas Hollis what Mayhew was getting at. Thrilled with the lecture, he rushed a copy to the British Museum, over which Archbishop Secker officially presided, "to gall Leviathan." But the war, by then, was over.

Still, New England knew no peace; for just as "The Mayhew Controversy" began to cool down, the Stamp Act crisis began to simmer and quickly boiled over. The fear expressed in Mayhew's Dudleian lecture of popish (and by extension Anglican) usurpation of "power and property" gives some indication of how far the two issues had become connected in the minds of the colonists. When Lord Grenville sought to regain British financial losses during the French and Indian War by taxing the colonies, New Englanders were ready to oppose the measures with religious zeal. Mayhew's declaration in 1750 that resistance to governmental tyranny was a religious duty was to be put into action.

Before the events of 1765, Mayhew's commitment to revolutionary principles was purely theoretical. The reign of George II had been salutary, and, when Mayhew preached on the accession of George III, he could reasonably expect that the status quo would be maintained. Yet the relationship between the royal authorities and their colonial subjects was beginning to deteriorate. When Chief Justice Stephen Sewall died several months earlier (in a funeral sermon, Mayhew had compared Sewall to the biblical judge Samuel, whose authority, he claimed, began prior to, and thus superseded, the authority of the Israelite monarchy established during his tenure), and, when Gov. Francis Bernard named Thomas Hutchinson to replace him as chief justice, James Otis, Jr., Mayhew's former schoolmate and fellow religious enthusiast, declared he would set the province aflame in retribution. Mayhew himself had an encounter with Bernard the following year, although it began much more humorously. When two Indians from Martha's Vineyard brought a petition to Bernard on 17 November 1761, they delivered it, wrapped around two dollars, to a servant, whom the Indians mistook for Bernard himself. The servant immediately took the money. On a visit to the Mayhew house, the Indians told the minister the story, and he related it, in turn, to some friends. When the governor got wind of the incident, he demanded an apology. Mayhew stubbornly refused: "The English government allow'd of great freedom of speech and writing," he responded at one point, and "much greater liberties were taken in Britain with *greater men* than any in America." The feud stretched out over months. Mayhew recorded his version of it in "A circumstantial Narrative," but it was never published. The case was indeed trivial, but it marked Mayhew's first clash with secular authority since his days at Harvard.

The Stamp Tax was to go into effect 1 November 1765. The colonists waited. Lt. Gov. Thomas Hutchinson appointed his brother-in-law Andrew Oliver to collect the revenue, and, though he actually opposed the tax, Hutchinson was thought to be in collusion with British authorities to enslave New England. On 25 August, Mayhew preached a sermon on Galatians 5:12-13: "I would that they were cut off which trouble you. For brethren, ye have been called unto liberty; only use not liberty for an occasion to the flesh, but by love serve one another." On 26 August, an uncontrollable mob ransacked Hutchinson's home, strewing his papers, including the manuscript of his *History of Massachusetts Bay,* in the mud. In his *Origin & Progress of the American Rebellion* (written in 1781, published in 1961), Peter Oliver, Andrew Oliver's brother, claimed that Mayhew's sermon precipitated the attack: the minister had "preached so seditious a Sermon, that some of his Auditors, who were of the Mob . . . could scarce contain themselves going out of the Assembly & beginning their Work." Hutchinson himself later reported that a member of the mob admitted "that he was excited . . . by this sermon, and that he thought he was doing God's service."

Mayhew was appalled by the violence. Immediately, he rushed a letter of condolence to Hutchinson: "God is my witness, that from the bottom of my heart I detest these proceedings; that I am sincerely grieved for them; and have a deep sympathy with you and your distressed family." But he denied that the sermon itself was incendiary, and he refused to accept responsibility for the riot. He admitted that he opposed the Stamp Act and had encouraged his audience to do the same. He remained firm in the belief that he acted upon biblical authority. An outline of the sermon written by him some days after the fact clarified the hermeneutical basis of his political views. He explained the verse "For brethren, ye have been called unto liberty" by listing "the several ac[c]eptations" of the term "liberty":

1. Philosophical liberty, or freedom of choice and action.
2. Gracious liberty, given in regeneration, and consisting in a will or disposition to do good, in opposition to the slavery of [sin].
3. What is commonly called religious liberty; or that natural right which every man has to worship God as he pleases, provided his principles & practices are not prejudicial to others.
4. Liberty, or freedom from the ceremonial law, which law is considered in scripture as a yoke & burthen to those who were under it.
5. That liberty which every man has, in what is commonly called a state of nature, or antecedent to the consideration of his being a member of civil society; consisting in a right to act as he pleases, in opposition to being bound by any human laws; always provided that he violates no law of God, nature, or right reason; which no man is at liberty to do.
6. Civil Liberty. . . .

Mayhew believed that "the apostle considered liberty in general as a great good, or important blessing." As he had been preaching since 1749, all these aspects of liberty were intricately woven together. Physical enslavement, he had explained again and again, would lead to spiritual enslavement, and spiritual to physical. Not to protest taxation without representation was a sin. But political opposition should not be "an occasion to the flesh." He fully expected his audience to understand, as he did, that liberty never meant anarchy and confusion. Clearly, he had misjudged his audience. As he explained to Robert Clarke, an enraged congregant: "it was a very unfortunate time to preach a sermon, the chief aim of which was to show the importance of liberty, when people were before so generally apprehensive of the danger of losing it."

The Stamp Act was repealed on 18 March 1766. Two months later, at the request of his congregation, Mayhew delivered a thanksgiving discourse, entitled *The Snare Broken* ("Our soul is escaped as a bird from the snare of the fowlers; the snare is broken and we are escaped. Our help is in the name of the Lord, who made heaven and earth." Psalms 124:7, 8). New England had known danger before, he admitted. It had "known repeated earthquakes," "seen wide devastations, made by fire," "known times when the French and Savage armies made terrible havok on our frontiers." But it had never before experienced "a season of such universal consternation and anxiety among people of all ranks and ages, in these colonies, as was occasioned by that parliamentary procedure, which threatened us and our posterity with perpetual bondage and slavery." Now that the act had been repealed, the colonies "are reinstated in the enjoyment of their ancient rights and privileges, and a foundation is laid for lasting harmony between Great Britain and them, to their mutual advantage." It was a time to give thanks. True, the authorities had not proclaimed it a day of thanksgiving as they had after the victories over France. So much the better: theirs was a "perfectly voluntary and free-will offering," an exercising of "that liberty, wherewith Christ hath made us free."

The repeal had been a triumph—for

Frontispiece and title page for the London edition of Mayhew's last book. Although his tone was generally conciliatory, he warned that, if "that ugly Hag Slavery, the deformed child of Satan," ever again appeared on American shores, the colonists would rebel again (courtesy of the John Carter Brown Library at Brown University).

Mayhew, for New England, for the colonies in general. But the shadow of 26 August 1765 still hung over the West Church pulpit. The minister made sure roundly to condemn "the riotous and fellonious proceedings of certain *men of Belial,* as they have been justly called, who had the effrontery to cloke their rapacious violence with the pretext of zeal for liberty." Now that the threat to liberty was removed, his immediate aim was "to recommend industry good order, and harmony." Too long had there been "a general dissipation among us" and "a great neglect and stagnation of business." In "the late times of tumult and confusion," the "poor and laboring part of the community" had risen above their stations to protest the stamp tax. But liberty was worthless without social stability: "If one had wings like a dove," Mayhew writes, "it were better to fly away, and remain alone in the wilderness, where he might be at rest, than to live in a society where there is no order, no subordination; but anarchy and confusion reign." His tone is often highly conciliatory. He made certain to dedicate the sermon, not to an American hero, but to William Pitt, the "PATRON OF AMERICA," who had defended the colonists in Parliament. He urged loyalty to the King and to Parliament, and support of "all persons in authority."

But he remained defiant on matters of principle. The colonists had rights, and Parliament had sought to abridge them. He detailed many of the arguments that had been leveled against the stamp tax. Emphatically he declared that if "that ugly Hag *Slavery,* the deformed child of Satan," would again try to invade her shores, America would again repel her. In what would be the final paean to liberty of his career, Mayhew once again reveals that, despite his protestations to the contrary, his loyalty lay firmly on this side of the Atlantic: "Once more then,

Hail! celestial Maid, the daughter of God, and, excepting his son, the first-born of heaven; Welcome to these shores again; welcome to every expanding heart! Long mayest thou reside among us, the delight of the wise, good and brave; the protectress of innocence from wrongs and oppression, the patroness of learning, arts, eloquence, virtue, rational loyalty, religion! And if any miserable people on the continent or isles of Europe, after being weakened by luxury, venality, intestine quarrels, or other vices, should in the rude collisions, or now uncertain revolutions of kingdoms, be driven, in their extremity, to seek a safe retreat from slavery in some far distant climate; let them find, O let them find one in America under thy brooding, sacred wings; where *our* oppressed fathers once found it, and we now enjoy it, by the favor of Him, whose service is the most glorious freedom! Never, O never may He permit thee to forsake us for our unworthiness to enjoy thy enlivening presence! By his high permission, attend us thro' life AND DEATH to the regions of the blessed, thy original abode, there to enjoy forever the 'glorious liberty of the sons of God!' " Mayhew calls this effusion an "odd excursion" and asks his audience's forebearance toward his "enthusiasm." Nevertheless, these were the symbolic underpinnings of Mayhew's thought. History had conspired with myth to give America a special place in God's scheme. Religion and politics had merged in a highly charged language of liberty. The force of the rhetoric was irresistible, not only to Mayhew and his contemporaries, but to generations of future Americans.

Mayhew was a hero in Boston in 1766. Even reconciliation with the clergy seemed a possibility. In April he was invited to attend an ordination at the New South Church. But exactly a month after he had delivered *The Snare Broken*, he suffered a stroke from which he never recovered. He died early on the morning of 9 July 1766. (Had the heretic renounced his sins?, people wondered.) He was forty-five years old. He was survived by his wife and daughter Elizabeth. Two other children, Jonathan and Sarah, had died in infancy during the final two years of his life. One of the great ironies of American history is that Elizabeth's son, Jonathan Mayhew Wainwright, joined the Episcopal church and became Bishop of New York.

The Reverend Dr. Jonathan Mayhew was eulogized by Charles Chauncy, Ebenezer Gay, and John Brown of Cohasset as "a friend to liberty, both civil and religious." Countless tributes appeared, even from former enemies. This threnody is representative:

AH, Mayhew! art thou *forever* gone?
No—I oft have seen the bright descending sun
Leave the blue arch, and threaten endless night;
Yet rise again and bless the world with light!
Thus in thy works shalt thou, for aye revolving, shine,
And prove the hand which formed them was divine;
Till that great day, when night shall be no more,
And tyrants cease to persecute the poor;
When none shall dread the bigot's cruel rod,
But ev'ry upright heart rejoice in God.

John Adams was instrumental in promoting Mayhew's reputation as a proto-Revolutionary, including him among the five most important figures (he was the only minister) in the early years of colonial mobilization. Nineteenth-century historians, such as George Bancroft, who saw the Revolution as the natural outgrowth of American history, looked to Mayhew's pre-Revolutionary rhetoric, especially in *A Discourse Concerning Unlimited Submission and Non-Resistance to the Higher Powers . . .* and *The Snare Broken . . .* , to support their interpretations. In the twentieth century, Clinton Rossiter continued the tradition, depicting Mayhew as one of *Six Characters in Search of a Republic*. Two recent writers have attempted to revise our understanding of Mayhew's politics: Bernard Bailyn has placed him in the broader, transatlantic community of libertarian thinkers, and Alan Heimert has tried to argue that Mayhew's conservative social view actually impeded the coming of the Revolution.

Although Mayhew's contemporaries, and the minister himself, considered his religion as the core of his life and work, only a few later writers deal extensively with it, among them Conrad Wright, who analyzes Mayhew's importance as a forerunner of Unitarianism, and Carl Bridenbaugh, who treats in depth the issue of colonial opposition to episcopacy. Only two writers have dealt comprehensively with Mayhew's career: Alden Bradford, who compiled a valuable selection from Mayhew's writings and letters in his 1838 biography, and Charles Akers, whose 1964 biography remains the only full-length modern treatment of the life and thought of Jonathan Mayhew.

Letters:
Bernard Knollenberg, ed., "Thomas Hollis and Jonathan Mayhew: Their Correspondence, 1759-1766," *Proceedings of the Massachusetts Historical Society,* 69 (1956): 102-193.

Biographies:

Alden Bradford, *Memoir of the Life and Writings of Jonathan Mayhew, D.D.* (Boston: C. C. Little, 1838);

Louis Leonard Tucker, ed., "Memoir of Dr. Jonathan Mayhew, by Harrison Gray [1776]," *Proceedings of the Bostonian Society* (17 January 1961): 26-48;

Clinton Rossiter, "The Life and Mind of Jonathan Mayhew," *William and Mary Quarterly,* third series, 7 (October 1950): 531-558; republished as "Jonathan Mayhew," in his *Six Characters in Search of a Republic* (New York: Harcourt, Brace & World, 1964), pp. 116-149;

Charles W. Akers, *Called Unto Liberty: A Life of Jonathan Mayhew, 1720-1766* (Cambridge: Harvard University Press, 1964);

Bernard Bailyn, "Religion and Revolution: Three Biographical Studies," *Perspectives in American History,* 4 (1970): 111-124.

References:

Bernard Bailyn, *The Ideological Origins of the American Revolution* (Cambridge: Harvard University Press, 1967);

Carl Bridenbaugh, *Mitre and Sceptre: Transatlantic Faiths, Ideas, Personalities, and Politics, 1689-1775* (New York: Oxford University Press, 1962);

Alan Heimert, *Religion and the American Mind: From the Great Awakening to the Revolution* (Cambridge: Harvard University Press, 1966);

Richard James Hooker, "The Mayhew Controversy," *Church History,* 5 (1936): 239-255;

Jean-Pierre Martin, "Jonathan Mayhew: Un théologien de la rébellion," *Revue Française d'Etudes Americaines,* 1 (October 1976): 119-127;

Clifford K. Shipton, *Sibley's Harvard Graduates,* volume 11 (Boston: Massachusetts Historical Society, 1960), pp. 440-472;

Conrad Wright, *The Beginnings of Unitarianism in America* (Boston: Starr King Press, 1955).

Papers:

The bulk of the Mayhew papers are at Boston University. Eight manuscript sermons are in the Henry E. Huntington Library. The Hollis-Mayhew correspondence is at the Massachusetts Historical Society.

John Mercer

(6 February 1704-14 October 1768)

Meta Robinson Braymer
Virginia Commonwealth University

BOOKS: *An Exact Abridgment of The Public Acts of the Assembly, of Virginia, in Force and Use . . .* (Williamsburg: Printed by William Parks, 1737);

A Continuation of the Abridgment of All the Public Acts of Assembly, of Virginia, in Force and Use . . . (Williamsburg: Printed by William Parks, 1739);

An Exact Abridgment of the Public Acts of the Assembly of Virginia in Force and Use. January 1, 1758 (Glasgow: Printed by John Bryce & David Paterson, 1759).

OTHER: " 'The Dinwiddianae' Poems and Prose," in *The Colonial Virginia Satirist,* by Richard Beale Davis (Philadelphia: American Philosophical Society, 1967), pp. 17-42.

A political and legal theorist as well as a belletristic writer, John Mercer was born in Dublin, the namesake of his Anglo-Irish merchant father. Mercer claimed to have attended Trinity College, but since records do not show a graduation date, he apparently never completed a degree. He came to Virginia in 1720 and read his way into a legal profession; in Stafford County he built Marlborough, one of the most elaborate and original houses in colonial America.

For more than forty years, Mercer was a prominent and vocal attorney, who sustained a series of reprimands and reinstatements to the bar. Yet his abridgment of Virginia laws, modeled after Edmund Wingate's abridgment of English statutes

(1655), was indispensable to court justices soon after its publication in 1737. The first digested code printed in Virginia, the work made the laws as intelligible as possible and included punishments and fines for public and private acts from stealing hogs to refusing to baptize children. The abridgment also indicated which laws were obsolete, expired, repealed, or annulled and covered such items as standard weights and measures and descriptions of the architecture of towns and buildings. Mercer added to and altered the work in 1739 and 1759, always with the intent to make the laws more understandable.

Known also as a literary man among his contemporaries, Mercer is the most probable author for the "Dinwiddianae," a series of poems and letters written from 4 November 1754-3 May 1757, satirizing Governor Robert Dinwiddie, General Edward Braddock, and other favorites of the governor. The documents contain poems, prose glossaries, and quasi-dialectal letters dealing with such matters as taxation, settlement of western lands, and the Jacobites.

As a whole, the work documents the widespread literary opposition to the Royalist policies. The satirist at work was clearly conscious of popular forms of satire, including the works of Pope and the Hudibrastic verse of Samuel Butler. In the "Dinwiddianae" the author employs mock heroic, burlesque, pun, and direct invective. The roughness in rhyme and meter may be intentional, the marginal annotations a device to enhance the satire.

Although several candidates for authorship have been suggested, most of the evidence points to Mercer. He would have been familiar with the activities of Dinwiddie since he was frequently in Williamsburg. Mercer is known to have been a writer, and his papers contain poems similar to those in the "Dinwiddianae." Furthermore, although primarily devoted to law books, Mercer's library, one of the largest and finest in colonial America, contained works on the arts and sciences, the classics, divinity, history, and gardening—books the satirist used extensively. Sometimes exhibiting more political than literary merit, the "Dinwiddianae" is representative of the early political resentment of British authority.

Also a successful man of business, Mercer served as secretary and general counsel of the Ohio Company of Virginia, speculating in western lands. Yet he had difficulty securing payment from clients as early as 1745, and after he retired in 1765, he attempted to recoup his fortune by establishing a brewery at Marlborough. The beer was barely drinkable, and Mercer died in debt at his home on 14 October 1768.

Mercer's writings reveal much about the times. His abridgments, as well as his account book (1725-1732) and diary (1 January 1740-31 March 1768), provide information about law practice in the eighteenth century. Parts of his poems compare favorably with those of his British counterparts, and the "Dinwiddianae" reveals much about the wit, the creativity, the artistic and intellectual pursuits of American colonials.

References:

Richard Beale Davis, *The Colonial Virginia Satirist* (Philadelphia: American Philosophical Society, 1967), pp. 15-16;

Helen Hill Miller, "A Portrait of an Irascible Gentleman: John Mercer of Marlborough," *Virginia Cavalcade,* 26 (Autumn 1976): 74-85;

C. Malcolm Watkins, *The Cultural History of Marlborough* (Washington, D.C.: Smithsonian Institution Press, 1968).

Papers:

The "Dinwiddianae" papers are at the Huntington Library. Mercer's account book, diary, letters, and poems are in the Virginia Historical Society and the Virginia State Library.

George Micklejohn
(circa 1717-1818)

Robert W. Hill
Clemson University

BOOK: *On the Important Duty of Subjection to the Civil Powers. A sermon preached before his Excellency William Tryon, Esquire, Governor and Commander in Chief of the Province of North-Carolina, and the Troops Raised to Quell the Late Insurrection, at Hillsborough, in Orange County, on Sunday, September 25, 1768* (New Bern, N.C.: Printed by James Davis, 1768).

Born in Scotland, George Micklejohn was an Anglican minister sent to North Carolina by the Society for the Propagation of the Gospel. Arriving under the gubernatorial aegis of William Tryon in 1766, he was to serve the largest parish in North Carolina, St. Matthew's, at Hillsborough.

Micklejohn tried constantly to serve and placate both the English officials and the increasingly more discontented local citizens. He was apparently respected in both camps. Having spent brief times in "the back settlements," including Rowan County and Brunswick, Micklejohn ingratiated himself with the governor, who had "great expectations from" the minister.

On the other hand, a group of farmers protesting public corruption, the Regulators, who were at the heart of unrest in Micklejohn's region, relied on him as mediator and (sometimes no more than) messenger as they tried to negotiate with the British authorities. This point is most clearly illustrated by events that occurred in May 1768, when Micklejohn, in apparent innocence, set up a meeting at which the officials simply moved in and arrested several people, but there are also stories of his having met with Regulators in jail and having helped them at least enough to have made some Tories distrust him.

Micklejohn's sermon *On the Important Duty of Subjection to the Civil Powers* was delivered on 25 September 1768 by invitation of Governor Tryon, who wanted his troops from Granville and Orange counties to be properly instructed on their suppression of rebels around Hillsborough. Henry Pattillo, a Presbyterian minister, also preached to troops on that day, and, like Micklejohn, he was later thanked by Tryon for his assistance. Micklejohn's sermon, however, was so pleasing to the governor that he instructed the assembly to have copies printed at public cost and personally sent one to the Lord Bishop of London. Micklejohn dedicated the publication to his benefactor.

Clearly outraged at rebellious activities by the group at Hillsborough, Micklejohn raised the hands of Godly authority both to smite and support, hoping that his sermon "should be instrumental in bringing any to a just Sense of the great DUTY inculcated therein, and a religious observance of it for the future." Appalled at the specters of anarchy and the disparate passions of men, Micklejohn cited Paul's epistles to Romans, Titus, and Timothy, as well as the gospel of Matthew, to impress upon his congregation the divine authority lying behind all civil authority. Arguing that "God's viceregents . . . are sometimes unhappily obliged, through the perverseness and wickedness that is in the world, to become *unwilling* avengers," Micklejohn urged peace in the interests of duty to others (such as family) who might be hurt by rebellious disorder, of gratitude to the much-put-upon viceregents, of God's command to obey earthly rulers, of affections for the rebel's own selves ("their own everlasting wellfare"), and in emulation of Christ's obedience to secular laws. Although he never mentioned any details of the Hillsborough uprising, discussing neither motives nor much of the outcome, except to say that the King's men were valorous and humane ("for where one has not fallen, twenty ought to have suffered"), Micklejohn did berate those citizens who failed to remember that they, through their admittedly limited representative government, had had a voice in making the laws they had later denied: "for an *Englishman* to oppose the laws of his country, is an instance of the highest folly and contradiction we can conceive."

Micklejohn was among the British Loyalists captured at Moores Creek Bridge; but the Provincial Congress paroled him on 3 May 1776, to "Perquimons, in that part of said county on the south side of the river," and by August he was opening "Congress by reading prayers in the church at Hillsborough." Although Micklejohn's name does not appear in the 1790 or the 1810 censuses of Virginia or North Carolina, there is some evidence that he eventually moved to Virginia, where he lived out the remainder of his life.

Robert Munford
(circa 1737-1783)

Hugh J. Dawson
University of San Francisco

BOOK: *A Collection of Plays and Poems, by the Late Col. Robert Munford, of Mecklenburg County, in the State of Virginia*, edited by William Munford (Petersburg, Va.: Printed by William Prentis, 1798).

Robert Munford has some claim to being regarded as the first American comic dramatist. While his plays have generally been thought slight, derivative artistic achievements, they nonetheless retain interest for their commentary on the social life and politics of pre-Revolutionary Virginia.

The son of a well-descended but impoverished colonial family, Munford was favored by William Beverley, his uncle and the father of his future wife, with an education in England at the Beverley School and Wakefield Grammar School from 1750 to 1756, whence he returned to acquire legal training in the law office of his cousin Peyton Randolph. Marriage to Anna Beverley in 1760 or early 1761 and the extension of his family's tobacco plantation in the following years made Munford one of the wealthiest landowners in the Virginia that would provide the milieu of his plays. After the formation of Mecklenburg County, he became county lieutenant in 1765 and sat in the Virginia House of Burgesses and General Assembly from 1765 to the outbreak of the Revolution. Although a moderate in the years preceding the break with England, Munford aligned himself with Patrick Henry in signing the anti-Stamp Act resolutions and the Williamsburg Association's 1774 boycott of tea imported from England. Early in the Revolution he became active in the recruitment of colonial troops and rose to the rank of major. His literary legacy—besides his two plays and poems, Munford left an unfinished translation of Ovid's *Metamorphoses*—was dutifully edited and published in 1798 by his son. There is no record that either of the plays was performed in the author's lifetime.

A Virginia election provides the dramatic conflict of *The Candidates*, which was probably written in the early 1770s. When an aristocrat who has served honorably in the House of Burgesses decides against seeking reelection, three self-seeking politicians announce their candidacies to fill the vacancy and to oppose a second honorable patrician officeholder. The farcical electioneering that follows gives clear proof of their unworthiness, and, after the first aristocrat decides to run after all, political virtue is reasserted in the two incumbents' return to office. Munford's comedy offers valuable perspectives on the eighteenth-century politics of deference in America and the Augustan sense of responsibility shown by the best of the colonial patrician class. Although the yeomanry of the electorate are not won over by the candidates bent on their own advancement, Munford suggests fears of what electoral politics might become while indicting those

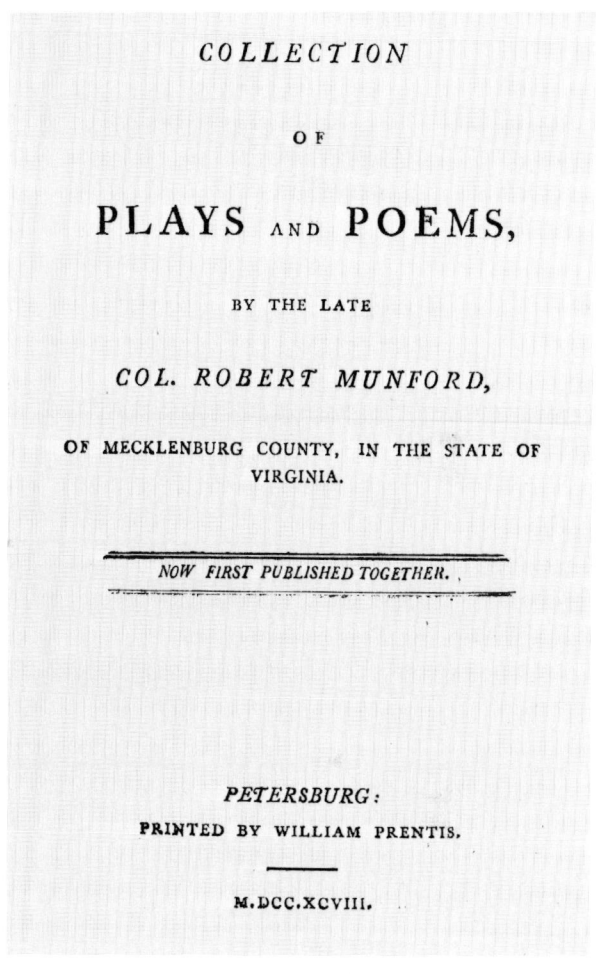

Title page for the posthumously published volume that contains Munford's comedies (courtesy of the John Carter Brown Library at Brown University)

who betray their obligations and the common good in pursuit of selfish ends.

Apparently a work of the late 1770s, *The Patriots* is a comedy rich in variety, integrating farcical, comic, and serious levels of romance. Set in Southside Virginia, it presents a society where suspicion of disloyalty is thought to supply its own proof and where social differences threaten to divide the community. The play caricatures local figures who would have been readily recognized had the play been staged at the time and shows Munford's resentment of the persecution suffered by some of his relatives and friends, especially those who were Scots, who were thought insufficiently loyal in time of revolution. Both the dialogue and plot advance Munford's belief that excessive displays of zeal are false and that genuine patriotism is distinguished by its moderation and quiet confidence.

Munford's handling of farce and comedy and his skill in managing multiple subplots suggest his familiarity with the plays of George Farquhar and other Restoration playwrights popular in Virginia. Read as evidence of social change, the comedies have been thought to reflect the shift of political power in the Virginia Southside toward the small freeholders and the incipient rise of party politics. Considered as statements of political philosophy, they have been found to manifest deeply felt concerns—about the nature of the favored class's civic responsibilities, the electoral abuses to which an unsettled society is especially open, the precariousness of the traditional order when the stays of custom are weakened, and the excesses of partisan fervor that mandate orthodoxies and generate suspicions of dissident minorities—that troubled Munford's circle and that have remained problematic for succeeding generations of Americans.

References:

Rodney Baine, *Robert Munford: America's First Comic Dramatist* (Athens: University of Georgia Press, 1967);

Richard R. Beeman, "Robert Munford and the Political Culture of Frontier Virginia," *Journal of American Studies,* 12 (August 1978): 169-183;

Courtlandt Canby, "Robert Munford's *The Patriots,*" *William and Mary Quarterly,* third series, 6 (July 1949): 437-503;

Jay B. Hubbell and Douglass Adair, "Robert Munford's *The Candidates,*" *William and Mary Quarterly,* third series, 5 (April 1948): 217-257;

Jon Charles Miller, "*A Collection of Plays and Poems, by the Late Col. Robert Munford, of Mecklenburg County, in the State of Virginia:* A Critical Edition," Ph.D. dissertation, University of North Carolina at Chapel Hill, 1979;

Norman Philbrick, Introduction to *The Patriots,* in *Trumpets Sounding: Propaganda Plays of the American Revolution* (New York: Blom, 1972), pp. 257-263;

Charles S. Sydnor, *Gentlemen Freeholders: Political Practices in Washington's Virginia* (Chapel Hill: University of North Carolina Press, 1953).

Papers:

The largest collections of Munford's papers are at the Perkins Library, Duke University, the Huntington Library, and the Virginia Historical Society.

Jonathan Odell

(25 September 1737-25 November 1818)

James C. Gaston

BOOKS: *The American Times . . . ,* as Camillo Querno, in *Cow-chace . . . ,* by John André (New York: Printed by James Rivington, 1780); republished separately (London: Printed for the author & sold by W. Richardson, 1780);

The Loyal Verses of Joseph Stansbury and Doctor Jonathan Odell, edited by Winthrop Sargent (Albany: Munsell, 1860).

Jonathan Odell was a master of Loyalist invective who poured satirical verse into Rivington's New York *Royal Gazette* and other Tory publications throughout the Revolution. A true believer who found no redeeming virtues in his foes, he had little use for half measures. Even when he turned to such auspicious topics (for Loyalists) as the king's birthday or the British victory at Savannah in 1779, Odell rarely forgot entirely about his Yankee enemies or his mission "to poison with the pen / These rats, who nestle in the Lion's den!"

Odell acquired his Loyalist fervor honestly, if somewhat circuitously. He was born in Newark, New Jersey, to Temperance Dickinson Odell, a daughter of Jonathan Dickinson, and John Odell, a descendant of William Odell, who had been among the founders of the Massachusetts colony. Jonathan's maternal grandfather was the first president of the College of New Jersey (now Princeton University), and Jonathan graduated from that school in 1759, before becoming a surgeon in the British army. He was stationed in the West Indies for a time, then left the army and went to England to study for the ministry. He was ordained in January 1767.

Later that year, just as the Townshend Act was stirring old resentments about taxation, he returned to New Jersey as an Anglican missionary to St. Ann's Church in the town of Burlington. In 1771 he also began to practice medicine, and on 6 May 1772 he married Anne De Cou.

While regretting what he viewed as ill-advised British taxes, Odell avoided political debates. Nevertheless, as a minister of the Church of England, he was increasingly suspected of having Loyalist sympathies. In October 1775 he was arrested and interrogated after two of his private letters had been intercepted and found to contain unfavorable statements about Congress. Passions on both sides intensified in the next few months, and on 4 June 1776 he made his Loyalist sympathies public in an ode for the king's birthday.

Odell wrote the "Birthday Ode" to be sung by a group of British officers who had been taken prisoner by General Montgomery and were being held in Burlington. They were allowed to observe the day with an entertainment and dinner on a small island in the Delaware River. The ode itself is undistinguished occasional verse. Eight of its twelve stanzas celebrate "George's happy sway" in conventional phrases that might have come from any of William Whitehead's many birthday odes for George III. However, four stanzas in the center become a commentary on George's American subjects: "Sons of Briton, fierce and blind." That line and others like it were intolerable to American patriots in New Jersey. The people of Burlington threatened Odell in July and chased him from his house and family in December. For a few days he hid near the town. Then on 18 December he made good his escape to New York and the safety of the king's arms.

Staying in New York through the remainder of the war, he made himself indispensable to the British in a variety of roles: translator, chaplain, intermediary in the Benedict Arnold-John André conspiracy, and assistant secretary to commander-in-chief Sir Guy Carleton. He also wrote the satirical poetry on which his reputation now depends.

Perhaps the best known of these poems is his brief "Inscription for a Curious Chamber-Stove, in the Form of an Urn, so Contrived as to Make the Flame Descend, Instead of Rise, from the Fire: Invented by Doctor Franklin" (1776). In it Odell attacks Benjamin Franklin, claiming that the brilliant inventor had inverted his genius to serve mere fame and sedition, just as his famous stove was supposed to have caused its flame to burn downward. This poem appeared in several newspapers and was reprinted in popular magazines, such as the *Gentleman's Magazine,* in England and America.

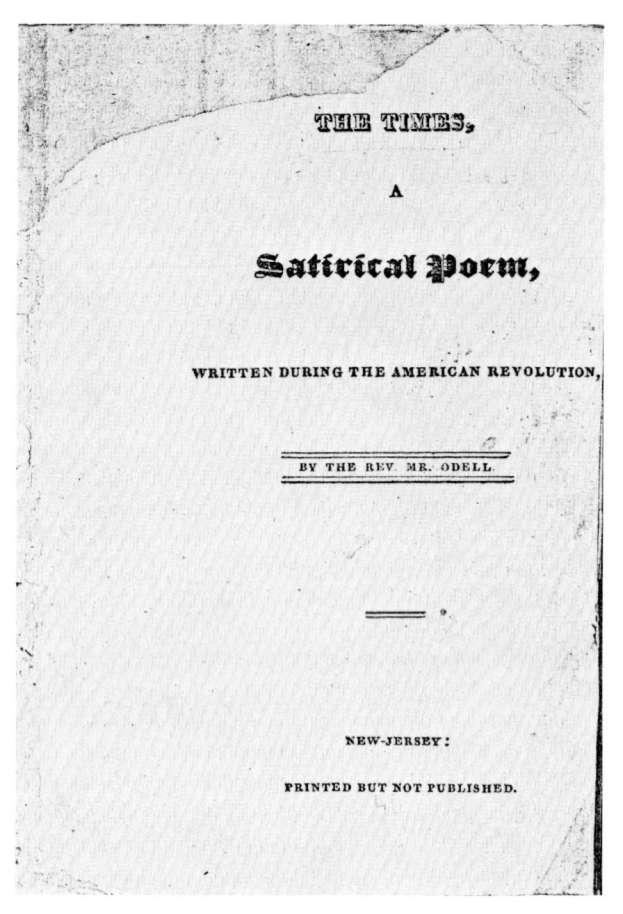

Title page for the first separate American edition of Odell's Tory satire, which portrays John Hancock, George Washington, Thomas Jefferson, and other patriots as "Furies from profoundest hell" (courtesy of the Harris Collection of American Poetry and Plays at Brown University)

"The Feu de Joie," published in the *Royal Gazette* in 1779, recounts the British victory at the Battle of Savannah. Heroic couplets laud the bravery of the British defenders and scorn the follies of the Yankees and their French ally D'Estaing. The poem ends with an invitation to the deluded Americans: "Leave those, whom Justice must at length destroy / Repent, come over, and partake our joy."

The American Times, at 822 lines his longest work, was printed along with John André's "The Cow-Chace" in New York early in 1780. Posing as "Camillo Querno, Chaplain to the Congress," Odell summons "the Furies from profoundest hell" to help explain why the times in America are so bad. When the monsters appear, he recognizes many of them as Hancock, Washington, Jefferson, and numerous other patriots. Personifications of Democracy ("With harlot smiles adorn'd and winning grace") and Taxation ("kindler of the flame") also march by for Querno's disapproval. Finally, "Britannia's guardian angel" comes to pronounce judgment on Britain's ungrateful sons: " 'At length the day of Vengeance is at hand / Th' exterminating Angel takes his stand.' " The angel ends with a hope that America's times will be better when the pollution caused by these rebels has been purged.

The American Times and virtually all of Odell's shorter poems are hotly partisan. He wrote most of them quickly to get them in the newspapers while events were still fresh in his readers' minds. Like Freneau, he favored frankness and vigor over subtlety; much of his poetry surely resembles what Freneau would have written if Freneau had been a Loyalist. Jonathan Odell was an adept writer of caustic, popular verse who served his Loyalist friends well indeed—both Moses Coit Tyler and Vernon Parrington rank him first among Tory satirists—and the British rewarded him after the war with profitable appointments in New Brunswick, Nova Scotia.

References:

Vernon L. Parrington, *The Colonial Mind,* volume 1 of *Main Currents in American Thought* (New York: Harcourt, Brace, 1927), pp. 255-259;

Moses Coit Tyler, *The Literary History of the American Revolution, 1763-1783,* volume 2 (New York & London: Putnam's, 1897) pp. 97-129.

James Otis, Jr.
(5 February 1725-23 May 1783)

Anne Y. Zimmer
Wayne State University

BOOKS: *The Rudiments of Latin Prosody: with a Dissertation on Letters, and the Principles of Harmony, in Poetic and Prosaic Composition* . . . (Boston: Printed & sold by B. Mecom, 1760);

A Vindication of the Conduct of the House of Representatives of the Province of the Massachusetts-Bay . . . (Boston: Printed by Edes & Gill, 1762);

The Rights of the British Colonies Asserted and Proved (Boston: Printed & sold by Edes & Gill, 1764; London: Printed for J. Almon, 1765);

Considerations on Behalf of the Colonists . . . (London: Printed for J. Almon, 1765);

Vindication of the British Colonies, Against the Aspersions of the Halifax Gentleman, in his Letter to a Rhode-Island Friend . . . (Boston: Printed & sold by Edes & Gill, 1765; London: Printed by J. Almon, 1769);

Brief Remarks on the Defence of the Halifax Libel, on the British-American Colonies . . . (Boston: Printed & sold by Edes & Gill, 1765).

James Otis, Jr., was a literary scholar, lawyer, politician, and polemicist of the American Revolution. Born in West Barnstable, Cape Cod, Massachusetts, to James and Mary Allyne Otis, James Otis, Jr., was the fifth generation of Otises in America, the descendant of John Otis (1581-1657), whose roots had been in Glastonbury, Somerset, until 1621 when he moved to Barnstaple in Devon. The family immigrated to Hingham, Massachusetts, in 1630 hoping, like many other settlers in America, to improve their fortune. Although Hingham was a conservative community whose Congregational establishment was the oldest in Massachusetts, there is no evidence that the Otises made a commitment to Puritanism.

Otis family members were notable for sagacity in business dealings, for strong family ties, and for extraordinary fertility. The first three generations of Otises in America produced extremely large families and were unusual in their ability to survive. Fewer than ten percent of grandparents lived to see a grandchild in that day, yet Otis patriarchs presided over a host of children and grandchildren. Through astute marriage alliances, the family

Portrait by Joseph Blackburn

created an effective network of support for Otis interests in trade, politics, and society.

James Otis, Jr., inherited all of the economic and political achievements of preceding generations who had used the fluid structure of colonial politics to displace one elite with one of their own. The family's greatest advances had taken place in periods of war and crisis, particularly during the Seven Years War, when they made enormous profits from supplying the military. Thus James Otis, Jr., launched his career on a firm foundation of family wealth in land, mercantile interests, social position, and political influence. In addition, he was the first of the Otises to have the advantage of a Harvard education. His father considered it a wise investment for the entire family and equated its value with twenty years of his own hard work and striving. Otis entered Harvard in 1739 at age fourteen, graduated with a B.A. in 1743, and was granted an M.A. in 1746.

From 1743 to 1745 Otis lived in Boston with his mother's Allyne relatives, reading extensively in the English classics, in Greek and Roman history, in poetry, and in both ancient and modern political theory. He interrupted his studies when necessary to act as agent for his father on any Boston business. His interest in scholarly work eventually led to the publication of *The Rudiments of Latin Prosody: with a Dissertation on Letters, and the Principles of Harmony, in Poetic and Prosaic Composition* (1760), which was later used as a textbook at Harvard. A similar treatise on Greek prosody remained in manuscript form and was later destroyed.

His Boston literary period ended in 1745 when Otis began his legal studies in West Barnstable with Jeremiah Gridley, a well-known lawyer. At twenty-three he was admitted to the bar at Plymouth, where he practiced until 1750. Rural legal business did not interest him, and, unlike his father, who handled half of all of the cases on the Barnstable docket, he did not get many cases. Two years in Plymouth convinced young Otis that he would prefer the larger arena of Boston with its potential for a diverse and cosmopolitan clientele.

Setting up a practice in Boston posed few problems for Otis. His Harvard degrees and his family and business connections made success almost certain. He was soon accepted as a peer among the ablest of lawyers. His services were in great demand as far away as Halifax, Nova Scotia, where on one occasion he was paid the highest fee recorded in Massachusetts. His rise to distinction rested on his knowledge of common, civil, admiralty, and constitutional law, as well as legal theory, and on his brilliant and dramatic pleading of cases.

Professional success brought other changes in his life. In 1755 he courted and married Ruth Cunningham, the beautiful daughter of a wealthy merchant and heiress to a fortune of £10,000. The following year Governor Thomas Pownall appointed Otis to his first public office, that of justice of the peace for Suffolk. Four years later, in 1760, he became the King's advocate general of the Vice-Admiralty Court at Boston.

Otis's political career began in 1760 over the issue of writs of assistance, and for ten years he was the intellectual leader of Massachusetts politics. His most recent and best biographer, John J. Waters, considers him as close to a genius as any American of his period. He was the first to recognize and explore the challenge to the legislature which lay in the new fiscal policies and imperial demands from Britain. Pitt's order of 1760 for the strict enforcement of the Sugar Act of 1733 (which had been generally evaded) led the royal customs collectors to apply to the Superior Court of Massachusetts for writs of assistance to aid in the search for evidence of violations. The writs were general, or "John Doe" warrants, which permitted sweeping searches without specifying either the location or the goods. Otis, in his official capacity as advocate general of the Vice-Admiralty Court, was expected to argue for the writs. Instead, he resigned from his post because he was opposed to the writs in principle, and with Oxenbridge Thacher he agreed to represent the merchants of Boston and Salem in opposing the writs.

After the hearing on the legality of the writs, which took place in February 1761, Otis became a celebrity. His extensive knowledge allowed him to argue for four or five hours with wit and eloquence, it is said. Insisting that the writs were the "worst instrument of arbitrary power" and destructive to English liberty and the fundamental principles of the constitution, he called them a remnant of the Star Chamber proceedings that had cost one king of England his head and another his throne. General writs would violate the privacy of a man's home, and, furthermore, he argued, acts of Parliament which violated the principles of justice were void.

Otis had enunciated a constitutional principle of revolutionary consequence: the unalterable law of nature took precedence over the survival of the state. This well-known speech put Otis in the forefront of politics. Three months later, in May 1761, he was elected to the General Court from Boston and was reelected almost annually thereafter. Although the writs, in more proper and specific language, were later declared legal, Otis had put Lieutenant Governor Thomas Hutchinson in a defensive position, had harassed the customs and thereby raised the morale of Boston, and had put the question of enforcement into the realm of politics.

In September 1762 Governor Francis Bernard provided yet another forum for Otis. He authorized an expenditure for the sloop *Massachusetts* for reasons of defense, but without prior consent of the House. Otis seized upon Bernard's appropriation of funds as an example of the arbitrary levy of a tax. Working with a committee, Otis prepared an address to Bernard which passed the House by a large majority, although some were dubious about the language. The questionable passage stated that whether citizens were subjects of King George or King Louis either king would be arbitrary if he could levy taxes without Parliament. Bernard objected to the passage and urged its eradication. The House complied, but Otis was dissatisfied. He prepared his first political publication, *A Vindication of the Conduct of the House of Representatives* (1762), in which he developed the principle that representative taxation is a basic requirement of constitutional, limited government, a tenet which became an important source for subsequent arguments against taxation. He also set forth three other important principles which opened new political territory and startled the administration: (1) God made all men naturally equal, and all ideas about superiority are acquired, not innate; (2) kings exist (and plantation governors should exist) for the good of the people, and not the opposite; (3) no government has a right to make hobby horses, asses, and slaves of their subjects. John Adams considered this pamphlet the genesis of the Declaration of Independence, since it contained the arguments employed by some of the most avant-garde supporters of the rights of man.

The Sugar Act of 1764, rather than the Stamp Act, is now generally recognized as the critical juncture in British-American affairs. One of the few Americans who recognized the implications at the time was Thomas Hutchinson; the other was Otis, who was appointed chairman of a committee formed to study the new acts. The committee concluded that the Sugar Act must be repealed, with no further bargaining for lower duties, and that the impending Stamp Act must be opposed on the basis of colonial rights. Otis sent Jasper Mauduit, the colonial agent for Massachusetts in London, a copy of his latest tract to make the position clear.

The Rights of the British Colonies Asserted and Proved (1764) logically extended the objections Otis presented against the writs of assistance in 1761. But in this pamphlet he abandoned his earlier authorities, such as Sir Edward Coke and John Locke, dismissing their assertions that government was based on contract, power, or property. Instead, he posited the "will of God, the author of nature, whose laws never vary," as the origin of government. Government existed for the good of all, he argued, and therefore nature had intended that all men should be free.

Otis now held that equity required American representation since Parliament, while absolute in its power, could not be arbitrary because it was bound by a higher authority, God. Any actions of Parliament against God's natural laws would be contrary to eternal truth, equity, and justice, and thus automatically void. To tax Americans without representation was therefore illegal, and distinctions between internal and external taxes were meaningless. If Parliament could tax trade, he concluded, it could just as well tax lands or anything else.

Belief in the natural rights of the colonists led Otis to consider the natural rights of slaves: "The colonists are by the law of nature free born, as indeed all men are, white and black.... Does it follow that 'tis right to enslave a man because he is black?" Furthermore, Otis declared the slave traffic "the most shocking violation of the law of nature." Otis's conclusions predate the antislavery theorists of the nineteenth century, but unhappily he never offered a formal plan for emancipation, nor did he ever free his own Negro slave.

In another pamphlet, *Considerations on Behalf of the Colonists* (1765), Otis submitted a surprisingly

Title page for the pamphlet that John Adams called the genesis of the Declaration of Independence (courtesy of the John Carter Brown Library at Brown University)

Title page for Otis's second pamphlet asserting the illegality of taxation without representation (courtesy of the John Carter Brown Library at Brown University)

egalitarian political doctrine. As a corollary to the premise that every man was entitled to his life and liberty, so should people be equal in representation. His argument that participation in politics stemmed from human rights, not property rights, swept Locke aside and would bestow a vote even if a man lacked property. This was scarcely less radical than his statements on slavery.

Otis next bewildered his confreres with a new pamphlet, *Vindication of the British Colonies* (1765), which conceded that Parliament had "power, authority, and jurisdiction" over the whole, obviously including the right to tax the colonies internally or externally. The argument in this pamphlet nullified the position he had stated in *The Rights of the British Colonies Asserted and Proved,* and he continued in this reversal of position in *Brief Remarks on the Defence of the Halifax Libel* (1765). Both pamphlets were replies to Loyalist Martin Howard's *Letter from a Gentleman at Halifax* and *Defence of the Letter from a Gentleman at Halifax* (the Rhode Island friend and correspondent of Howard was Governor Stephen Hopkins). His repudiation of the *Rights of the Colonies* may well have been based on his fear that denying the right of Parliament to tax the colonies might prove a justification for revolution. A change of face was not unknown for Otis; he would take an extreme stand, wait for the commendation, then follow it with a moderate remark, according to his most recent biographer, John F. Waters, Jr. But for a scurrilous ditty printed in the *Boston Evening-Post, Vindication of the British Colonies* nearly cost Otis his seat in the assembly. "And Jemmy is a madman, and Jemmy is an ass / And Jemmy has a leaden head, & forehead spread with brass." Since it was written by Samuel Waterhouse, a minor customs official, John Adams thought it convinced many that anyone so unpopular with the administration should be re-elected.

Although *Vindication of the British Colonies* seemed to indicate a shift of position on the part of Otis, it also attacked Soame Jenyn's reasoning in his defense of the Stamp Act, declaring that Jenyn's logic could as easily prove that the "whole globe" was represented in the House of Commons. But Otis's greatest indignation was aimed at the concept that the admission of colonial representation would "defile the purity" and destroy the "beauty and symmetry" of the House of Commons. In addition, he challenged the justice of suppressing colonial manufacturing and the exploitation inherent in the imperial system.

The Stamp Act protest resulted in the Stamp Act Congress (7-25 October 1765), an idea born at the Warren household during conversations with the Warrens and Otises. The Massachusetts House endorsed the plan, and Otis was elected as one of its three delegates to the New York Congress, where he conducted himself moderately.

Clearly, Otis was ambivalent about his position. He had been the champion of Boston's mercantile community with his eloquent defense of their interests during the writs of assistance controversy, and he had retained their approval ever since, but the Stamp Act riots in August 1765 had given him second thoughts. While the crowds echoed expressions in Otis's pamphlets, privately in letters to friends he stated his abhorrence of the attacks on private property and the violence he witnessed.

On one point Otis was consistent: he believed in peaceful resistance. Knowing that some of his colleagues were eager to precipitate a crisis, he was determined to block them. He feared leaving Boston in their hands, he confided to his sister Mercy Otis Warren. The trading interests continued to look to Otis for guidance, knowing his awareness of their dissatisfaction with England's mercantile system and of the hardships imposed by Britain's veto power over colonial laws. Otis also knew that he had the charisma to lead them.

After England's imposition of the Townshend Acts in 1767 resurrected the issue of colonial taxation, Otis organized the people of Boston against the duties the acts imposed. The first recorded opposition, proposing nonimportation, came from a town meeting chaired by Otis, which states a conservative line: "No Mobs and Tumults, let the Person and Properties of our most inveterate Enemies be safe—Save your Money and you save your Country."

The circular letter of 11 February 1768 that Otis and Samuel Adams drafted for the Massachusetts House reflected the dualism of the Otis position. It denied the right of Parliament to tax the colonies, affirmed loyalty, and denied that America sought independence. Otis maintained a moderate approach to ensuing events. He was opposed to offensive measures in the Massachusetts Convention which Samuel Adams convened, and he was not elected one of its officers. He was even more appalled by the stationing of troops in Boston; yet he considered himself above reproach in his loyalty to Britain.

In October 1768 Otis was genuinely aghast when, on a visit to Boston, Thomas Gage refused his invitation to dinner. But he was even more shocked and aggrieved to learn in autumn 1769 that his circular letter was considered seditious by the customs officers, who had so reported in dispatches to London. Otis denounced them as liars in the *Boston Gazette* (4 September 1769), and the following evening in the British Coffee House Otis became involved in a violent quarrel with John Robinson, one of the commissioners. Other officers came to Robinson's aid, the lights were put out, and Otis, severely beaten, suffered a deep saber cut to his head.

Soon after, Otis's mental and physical condition appeared to be deteriorating. By November 1769 he had given up his law practice, and his professional and public career ended. Historians have generally agreed that his decline stemmed from mental illness. The medical records of his family are marked by instances of melancholia and mental instability. Those who had been close to him for the past several years were aware that he was sometimes depressed, emotional, inconsistent, or intemperate. However, it is reasonable to speculate that the injury he suffered in the attack may have inflicted neurological damage that could not have been diagnosed at the time.

The next few years were stressful. He mourned the loss of his leadership role to others, of whom he said, "when the pot boils, the scum rises." More important, the ambiguity of his political position plagued him. He struggled with what, in his mind, were irreconcilables: colonial rights versus loyalty, union versus autonomy. Having set in motion a sequence of events which could lead to separation, he did not want to face the results.

Otis survived for fourteen years after his injury, drifting in and out of sanity. He played no further role, officially, in the Revolution. However, whether he acted rationally or not, he borrowed a musket and took part for a day in the Battle of Bunker Hill. Eight years later, on 23 May 1783, in Andover, Massachusetts, Otis was killed by lightning in his fifty-eighth year.

In the short span of ten years, Otis contributed immeasurably to American politics and history. Possessed of a powerful intellect, a great command of language, and an impressive oratorical style, he used them skillfully to shape the American perception of fundamental law and a vision of independence.

Biographies:

William Tudor, *The Life of James Otis of Massachusetts* (Boston: Wells & Lilly, 1823);

John J. Waters, Jr., *The Otis Family in Provincial and Revolutionary Massachusetts* (Chapel Hill: University of North Carolina, 1968).

References:

Ellen Brennan, "James Otis, Recreant and Patriot," *New England Quarterly*, 12 (December 1939): 691-725;

Louis Hartz, "Otis and Anti-Slavery Doctrine," *New England Quarterly*, 12 (December 1939): 745-747;

Ralph K. Huitt, "The Constitutional Ideas of James Otis," *University of Kansas Law Review*, 2 (December 1953): 152-173;

Richard B. Morris, "Then and there the child Independence was born," *American Heritage*, 13 (February 1982): 36-39, 82-84.

Papers:

Otis's papers are in the Otis Family Manuscripts and the Gay-Otis Papers at Butler Library, Columbia University; the Otis Papers at the Massachusetts Historical Society; and the Suffolk Court Files, Boston.

Thomas Paine

Maureen Goldman
Bentley College

BIRTH: Thetford, Norfolk, England, 29 January 1737, to Joseph and Frances Cocke Pain.

MARRIAGES: 27 September 1759 to Mary Lambert. 26 March 1771 to Elizabeth Ollive.

DEATH: New Rochelle, New York, 8 June 1809.

SELECTED BOOKS: *Common Sense: Addressed to the Inhabitants of America* ... (Philadelphia: Printed & sold by R. Bell, 1776; revised and enlarged edition, Philadelphia: Printed by William Bradford, 1776; expurgated edition, London: Printed for J. Almon, 1776; unexpurgated edition, Edinburgh: Sold by Charles Eliot/Sterling: Sold by William Anderson, 1776);

The American Crisis, numbers 1-4 (Philadelphia: Printed & sold by Styner & Cist, 1776-1777); number 5 (Lancaster: Printed by John Dunlap, 1778); numbers 6-7 (Philadelphia: Printed by John Dunlap, 1778); numbers 8-9 (Philadelphia: Printed by John Dunlap?, 1780); *The Crisis Extraordinary* (Philadelphia: Sold by William Harris, 1780); *The American Crisis,* numbers 10-12 (Philadelphia: Printed by John Dunlap?, 1782); number 13 (Philadelphia, 1783); *A Supernumerary Crisis* (Philadelphia, 1783); *A Supernumerary Crisis* [number 2] (New York, 1783); numbers 2-9, 11, and *The Crisis Extraordinary* republished in *The American Crisis, and a Letter to Sir Guy Carleton* ... (London: Printed & sold by D. I. Eaton, 1796?);

Public Good, Being an Examination into the Claims of Virginia to the Vacant Western Territory and of the Right of the United States to the Same ... (Philadelphia: Printed by John Dunlap, 1780; London: Printed by W. T. Sherwin, 1817);

Letter Addressed to the Abbé Raynal on the Affairs of North America ... (Philadelphia: Printed by Melchior Steiner & sold by Robert Aitken, 1782; London: Printed for C. Dilly, 1782);

Dissertations on Government; The Affairs of the Bank; and Paper-Money (Philadelphia: Printed by Charles Cist & sold by Hall & Sellers, Robert Aitken, and William Pritchard, 1786; London: W. T. Sherman, 1817);

Rights of Man: Being an Answer to Mr. Burke's Attack on the French Revolution (London: Printed for J. Johnson, 1791; Baltimore: Printed & sold by David Graham, 1791);

Rights of Man: Part the Second (London: Printed by J. S. Jordan, 1792; New York: Printed by Hugh Gaine, 1792);

Letter Addressed to the Addressers on the Late Proclamation (London, 1792; New York: Printed by Thomas Greenleaf, 1793; Philadelphia: Printed by H. & P. Rice, 1793);

Portrait by John Wesley Jarvis, circa 1805 (National Gallery of Art)

The Age of Reason: Being an Investigation of True and Fabulous Theology (Paris: Printed by Barrois, 1794; London: Sold by D. I. Eaton, 1794; New York: Printed by T. & J. Swords for J. Fellows, 1794);

The Age of Reason: Part the Second. Being an Investigation of True and of Fabulous Theology (Paris: Printed for the author, 1795; London: Printed for H. D. Symonds, 1795; Philadelphia: Printed by Benjamin Franklin Bache for the author, 1795);

Letter to George Washington, President of the United States of America on Affairs Public and Private (Philadelphia: Printed by Benjamin Franklin Bache, 1796; London: Printed for H. D. Symonds, 1797);

Thomas Payne à la législature et au directoire. Ou la justice agraire opposée à la lor agraire, et aux privilèges agraire (Paris: Ragouleau, 1797); republished as *Agrarian Justice, Opposed to Agrarian Law, and to Agrarian Monopoly...* (London: Printed for T. Williams, 1797; Philadelphia: Printed by R. Folwell for Benjamin Franklin Bache, 1797).

Collections:

The Writings of Thomas Paine, 4 volumes, edited by Moncure Daniel Conway (New York: Putnam's, 1894-1896);

The Complete Writings of Thomas Paine, 2 volumes, edited by Philip S. Foner (New York: Citadel Press, 1945).

"I speak an open and disinterested language, dictated by no passion but that of humanity.... Independence is my happiness, and I view things as they are, without regard to place or person; my country is the world, and my religion is to do good." With these words in the *Rights of Man* II (1792) Thomas Paine, age fifty-five, explained his mission to an eighteenth-century world which viewed him with a mixture of passionate admiration, loathing, and exasperation. At this time he was famous in the Western world for his electrifying defense of American independence in *Common Sense* (1776) and for his essays in *The American Crisis* series (1776-1783), which had kept Americans informed and heartened during the Revolution. Since the American Revolution, he had traveled in England and France, involving himself in the political affairs of both countries, and earning the enmity of the British government for his opposition to monarchy and the favor of the French government for his support of the French Revolution. With the publication of his *Rights of Man* (1791, 1792), he had the respect of liberals everywhere, and, his reputation at its height, he was, for a while at least, one of the most notable "citizens of the world."

Paine's position as a leader of world opinion did not last long. As a consequence of his involvement in the politics of three nations, he was somewhat less than the "disinterested" figure that he claimed to be in *Rights of Man,* and he had many enemies. When in the years 1794 and 1795 he published *The Age of Reason,* attacking the Bible and organized religion, opposition became outspoken. Many of those who had honored him in America for his support of the Revolution now reviled him for his supposed atheism. While he continued to have loyal supporters, he lost his international constituency, and by the end of his life was nearly forgotten. Although his reputation recovered after his death, and he is recognized today as one of the American Revolution's most powerful essayists, many still dislike his radicalism and think of his writing as merely propaganda.

Yet Paine's life and work remain significant. Of plain background, like Benjamin Franklin, Thomas Paine rose to lead revolutions, to influence the political development of three countries, and to express for the common reader as no one else of his time could the ideas of the Enlightenment in politics, economics, and religion. He was a man who captured the ideals of the American Revolution in his writing, tried to spread them throughout the world and then, disappointed, returned finally to America, for him the only real "republic." He was a man, as well, who had an instinctive distrust of authority, "received" opinion, and the status quo, for whom no idea or person was too sacred to question and attack—outspoken, egotistical, and opinionated—the kind of person who is indispensable when revolutions are occurring but too radical and difficult to live with when they are over. Those readers—and there are still many—who take the time to read his work, will find his spirit and the spirit of the American Revolution in his writings. Whether they conclude that he was a militant radical or an idealistic reformer, they will find him readable and provocative, a man whose life and work remain an inspiring part of America's cultural heritage.

Little in Paine's background suggests that he was to become a man of notoriety and "consequence." He was born in modest circumstances in the small rural community of Thetford, England, to parents of Quaker leanings. While his mother, an

Anglican, was the daughter of a local attorney, his father, a Quaker, earned a meager living as a staymaker, and his parents, Paine later observed, "were not able to give me a shilling, beyond what they gave me in education; and to do this they distressed themselves." By his own account, Paine, who was sent to Thetford Grammar School, received "a good moral education and a tolerable stock of useful learning." It was an education that did not include Latin, Greek, or modern languages but did include the sciences. He also acquired the conviction that education is a lifelong process and that "every person of learning is finally his own teacher." Accordingly, he kept abreast of current ideas, most particularly being influenced by the work of the two leading figures of the Enlightenment, Isaac Newton and John Locke. Newton had shown that there were natural laws which governed the universe and which could be understood with the methods of scientific inquiry. Locke had argued that human beings were largely the products of their environments. If they were sound and good, then people would be as well. Both men had emphasized that reason was the key to unlocking the mysteries of human life. These beliefs—in a universal order, in human perfectibility, and in the power of reason—guided Paine throughout his life.

Paine's early adult years (1753-1759) offered him little opportunity to exert his intellectual abilities and were spent in obscurity and near poverty. He was apprenticed to his father's profession as a staymaker, but impatient with that and feeling "raw and adventurous" took a berth on a privateer, *The King of Prussia*. This adventure was not a happy one and Paine, back on land, worked for a while as a staymaker in Sandwich and then as an "exciseman" or customs officer in Lewes. During the years 1759-1772 he married twice. His first wife died within a year of their marriage. He separated, evidently amicably, from his second wife after a shop they operated briefly together went bankrupt. Throughout his second marriage, he had also worked as a customs officer, but he jeopardized this position when, in 1772, he wrote an essay, "The Case of the Officers of the Excise," arguing that the customs officers deserved higher wages. Subsequently he was dismissed from his position. All of his household possessions were sold to pay his bills. It was time, he knew, to find more promising directions for his life.

Unattached, unemployed, and thirty-six years old, Thomas Paine in London in 1773 was ready for new challenges. Well-read, his interest in Newtonian science advanced, and his sensitivity to social injustice already evident, Paine involved himself in the scientific and intellectual life of London. But he knew that for a man of his lowly background horizons were limited. Therefore, when he met Benjamin Franklin and Franklin offered to help him find a place in America, Paine accepted. Shortly thereafter he left for Philadelphia, armed with a letter from Franklin identifying him as "an ingenious, worthy young man," employable as "a clerk, or assistant tutor in a school, or assistant surveyor."

Paine arrived in Philadelphia in November of 1774, and he immediately felt at home in the political turmoil of Revolutionary politics that had been building up in the colonies since the Stamp Act of 1765 and that had reached a fever pitch with the Boston Tea Party in December of 1773, which had resulted in the closing of the port of Boston and garrisoning of the British troops in the city. In a society much more fluid and open than that of England, he made, as he later wrote, "many friends and much reputation." He also found a place to express his liberal and reformist views. He worked as an editor for the *Pennsylvania Magazine*, publishing essays on such subjects as "Reflections on Titles" (against) and on "The Abolition of Slavery" (for).

The issue of American independence, however, aroused Paine's passion. As an English citizen, he had suffered from the closed, privileged political system which had kept him and other workers in England virtually unrepresented in the British government. Moreover, he was a man who was deeply angered by distinctions of class and privilege, especially as they had worked in England to oppress small-business and working-class people like him. Americans, too, had felt the same sense of disenfranchisement. "Taxation without representation is tyranny," James Otis had written as far back as the early 1760s in protest to British colonial policies. Americans also resented the British system of privilege and title which effectively kept them from power. In America, Paine believed, there was a chance of righting the balance and bringing the ordinary citizen into power, if only the country could be made to see the necessity of making the break with Britain.

Stirred by these feelings, Paine published *Common Sense* in January of 1776, calling for independence from Great Britain and making his case with a force of language and a persuasiveness that immediately set the essay apart from the other political writing of the period. While most eighteenth-century political writers used an academic, Latinate style designed to appeal to the educated reader, *Common Sense* is direct and simple, matter of "simple facts, plain arguments, and common sense." His language is emotional as well as reasonable, literally "sensational," appealing to both the feelings and the mind. Americans, trained in the Puritan respect for the direct, "plain" word which touched the heart and brought the individual closer to God, had always respected such warmth of language. Thus, when Paine called the nation to action in *Common Sense,* eloquently asserting that "the sun never shone on a cause of greater worth" and observing that this cause is "the seed time of continental union, faith and honor," he struck a responsive chord.

Paine's arguments in *Common Sense* were also persuasive. Expressed in the form of a sermon, they appealed to America's sense of duty and mission. Thus, in the first section, which, as in the sermon, is a statement of principle, Paine uses analogies from the Newtonian world of immutable natural laws to argue that there is a reasonable social design by which men are meant to live. In this natural society, government exists only when moral virtue is deficient. Its limited role is to protect happiness and security. But, Paine says, monarchies and other tyrannical systems have perverted this natural order, and it is the duty of Americans to set another example. Separation from Britain, therefore, is not merely a little rebellion of obstinate colonies, as the British would have people believe, rather: "The cause of America is in a great measure the cause of all mankind."

Continuing the sermon format, Paine, in the second, or application, section of *Common Sense,* details in heated language the specific injuries that the British have inflicted on Americans and shows that whatever claims Britain might have had as the parent country were forfeited on 19 April 1775, at the Battle of Lexington and Concord, when Britain became an enemy. Even if Americans felt that it was in their interests—which it was not, said Paine—to go back to the old footing with Britain, they could not. One had only to think of the suffering of Boston: "that seat of wretchedness will teach us wisdom, and instruct us forever to renounce a power in whom we can have no trust." Anyone who could shake hands after that affair is "unworthy of the name of husband, father, friend, or lover, and whatever may be your rank or title in life, you have the heart of a coward and the spirit of a sycophant."

In the third, or to use sermon terminology, the reform, section of *Common Sense,* Paine maps out the course of action he thinks Americans should follow. Continuing the themes of duty and mission, he calls on America to declare independence from Britain

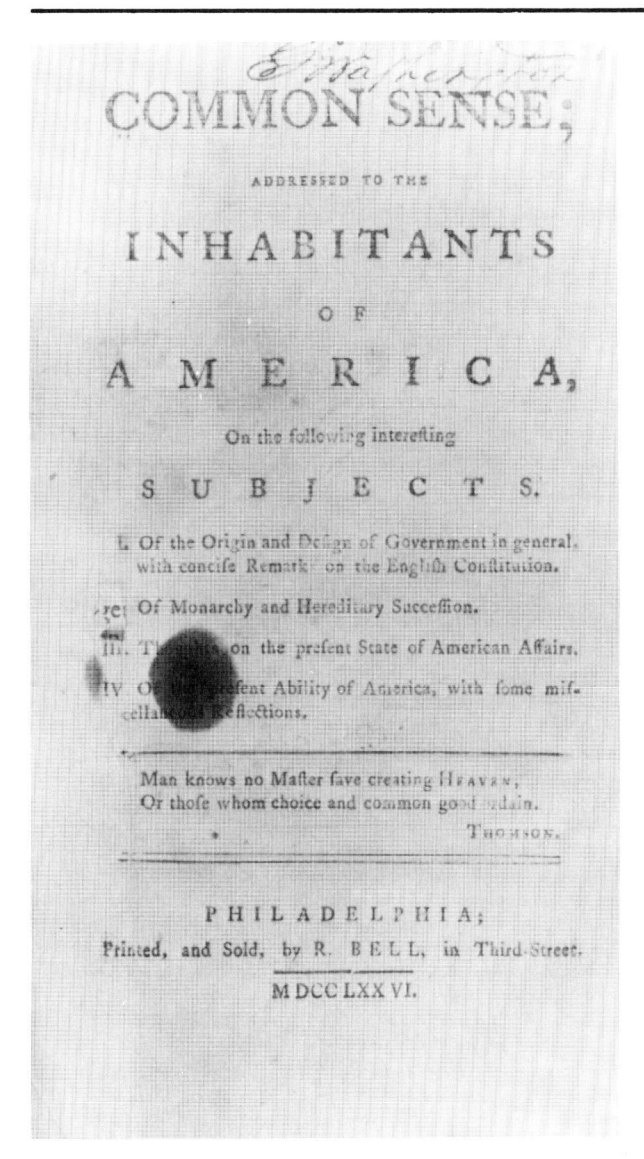

Title page for George Washington's copy of Paine's influential call for American independence: "nothing can settle our affairs so expeditiously as an open and determined DECLARATION FOR INDEPENDENCE" *(Boston Athenaeum)*

intended for the ordinary reader as well as the educated one. Paine's employing this language was no accident. As were most educated men of his day, Paine was familiar with John Locke's arguments in *On Human Understanding* that all men are possessed of a common ability to make meaning which is derived from their ability to "sense" the world around them. Paine believed that this sense, or "reason," common to all people, could be relied upon, when used collectively, to bring about the common good. Therefore, in *Common Sense,* he invites the ordinary reader to judge and take responsibility with him for public affairs, because, he says, they are merely a or risk depriving posterity of its birthright to freedom. Americans, after all, are not simply fighting *against* Britain but *for* a better way of life. Independence will allow the country to shape a new society based on reason, justice, and equality. To this end, the people should authorize a constitutional convention to draw up a document which will guide a future government of the country. This government, which would be republican in form, should be broadly representative and guarantee personal freedom, secure property, and the free exercise of religion. It is, Paine asserts, a unique time in the society, when it is young and fluid enough to shape its own future. "We have it in our power to begin the world over again," he concludes. The nation must pull together and establish its independence from Great Britain.

Blunt, angry, optimistic, and righteous, *Common Sense* unified American sentiment for independence as nothing before it had done. In one year it went through twenty-five editions, amounting to over a hundred thousand copies, and was read or known by virtually every American. It also transformed Paine's life, not only catapulting him to fame and into the forefront of the Revolution, but also causing him to devote his life to writing about and working for reform and revolution wherever he could. As he later wrote, "It was the cause of America that made me an author.... a DECLARATION OF INDEPENDENCE made it impossible for me, feeling as I did, to be silent."

With a conscious sense of mission, therefore, Paine threw himself into the Revolutionary cause. He wrote a number of letters, published in the Pennsylvania newspapers and signed "The Forester," defending the ideas in *Common Sense*. In addition, since *Common Sense* had made him well known both to political leaders and to ordinary citizens, he used his various connections for political purposes. He worked, for example, with politically liberal elements in Pennsylvania, and it was this group which, at the constitutional convention in Pennsylvania, successfully proposed a state governmental system with a unicameral legislature much like that outlined by Paine in *Common Sense*.

With the Declaration of Independence on 4 July Paine, perhaps wishing to set an example, enlisted in the army and was assigned to Gen. Nathaniel Greene as an aide-de-camp. He was on hand during some of the darkest days of the American Revolution. In November the Americans lost Fort Washington in New York, and Washington was forced to make a hazardous retreat across New Jersey, finally stopping outside of Trenton, New Jersey, in December. By this time the regular army was reduced to 2,400 men who were, Washington informed congress, "so thinly clad as to be unfit for service." Paine, who with Greene was encamped with Washington, realized full well the desperate plight not only of Washington's troops but of the American cause. Hoping to alert Americans to the danger, he wrote perhaps the most eloquent essay of his life, beginning with words familiar to this day to most Americans: "These are the times that try men's souls. The summer soldier and the sunshine patriot will, in this crisis, shrink from the service of their country; but he that stands it *now* deserves the love and thanks of man and woman. Tyranny, like hell, is not easily conquered; yet we have this consolation with us, that the harder the conflict, the more glorious the triumph."

Entitled "The American Crisis," this ringing call for "perseverance and fortitude" roused citizen and soldier alike. Americans were moved by its matter-of-fact recounting of the plight of Washington's soldiers, and they were sustained by Paine's belief that the cause could not be lost because it was a just one, and "God Almighty will not give up a people to military destruction." They were strengthened by Paine's firmness of tone and with his assertion that "tis the business of little minds to shrink." The essay not only spurred Americans to relieve the physical distress of the army with supplies and money, but it also bolstered the morale of the soldiers, and some believed that it made them more ready to fight. So impressed was Washington with the essay that he had it read to his troops as an inspiration before he successfully crossed the Delaware into Trenton to defeat the Hessians as they were celebrating Christmas Eve.

The essay also helped Paine to focus his own war efforts. By now well aware of his ability to shape public opinion through his writing, he saw himself as an unofficial spokesman for the war. It was a view probably shared by Congress, which, recognizing the power of what John Adams called his "ready pen," appointed Paine in April of 1777 to a position as a Secretary for Foreign Affairs, an appointment which gave him the flexibility to be both involved in the affairs of the war and free enough to write about them.

In this role as a sort of combined war correspondent, propagandist, and political philosopher, from December 1776 to December 1783, Paine wrote sixteen essays about the war, *The American Crisis*. Varying considerably in tone and subject matter, these essays capture the shifting moods of the war period and demonstrate Paine's ability to

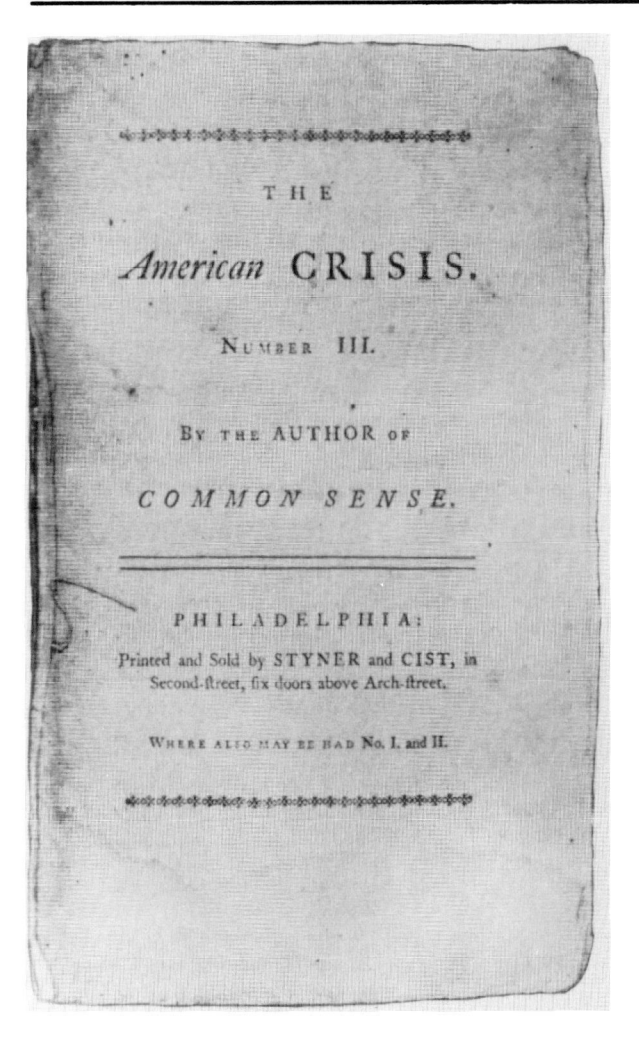

Title page for one of the pamphlets in Paine's series of essays about the American Revolution. In this essay he asserts that those who oppose independence do so out of "avarice, down-right villany, and lust of personal power. There is not such a being in America as a Tory from conscience...."

respond to the country's fears and aspirations. Sometimes, for example, he was reassuring, as after the initial setbacks in 1776 when he wrote: "Wisdom is not the purchase of a day, and it is no wonder that we should err at the first setting off." At other times he was blandly ironic, asserting that "It is remarkable that the whole race of prostitutes in New York were tories." Almost always he is compelling, as when he warns that "those who expect to reap the blessings of freedom, must, like men, undergo the fatigues of supporting it." In the most difficult times Paine could be cool and objective. For example after the surrender of Charleston, South Carolina, to the British in 1780, Paine wrote, "This piece-meal work is not the conquering of a nation"; and, pointing out that the lack of supplies was as much responsible for the American defeat as any other cause, he began, with five hundred dollars of his own money, a "voluntary subscription" to support the Pennsylvania army.

The American Crisis essays, moreover, were not limited to war events, because Paine always kept in view larger political and social issues. Thus, in these essays, he berated the Tories, warned against the temptations of compromise with the British, and addressed the British citizenry telling them of the high cost of the war. Paine also discussed political events, in one essay reviewing his role in the Silas Deane affair in which he had correctly accused the American commissioner to France of profiteering. Finally, as the war was drawing to a close, the essays turned to the problems of keeping the peace, which as Paine, who had popularized the term "The United States of America," well knew, could only last if the colonies acted together. Thus, in number thirteen, which Paine thought would be the last essay, he devoted himself to the issues of union, arguing that it is with "confederated states as with individuals in society; something must be yielded up to make the whole secure.... Our citizenship in the United States is our national character. Our citizenship in any particular state is only our local distinction. By the latter we are known at home, by the former to the world."

Appearing in pamphlet form and reprinted in colonial newspapers, these essays attracted a large and appreciative audience. Taken with *Common Sense,* they established Paine as the leading pamphleteer of the Revolution, a writer who used a remarkable range of tone and language to persuade and inform Americans about a cause for which he felt so passionately. Moreover, the essays have lost none of their vigor with the passage of time, and taken as a group, they constitute one of our most vivid records of the moods as well as the events of the Revolutionary war.

Although *The American Crisis* essays were Paine's most important contribution to the Revolution, he was also during this period involved in the political affairs of both the state of Pennsylvania and the Continental Congress. Here he met with less success than he did in his writing. As a writer his idealism and rhetorical aggressiveness enhanced his positions, especially as, on the whole, they were widely shared by the American public. But, in the give-and-take of politics he found that many issues could not be resolved through recourse to "principle" and argumentation. It was, for example, quite easy for everyone to agree that the common man had rights in the new government, but in translating that ideal into practical legislation, it was clear that many resisted too much leveling. Paine, who favored extending the franchise to anyone who had a stake in the society, therefore was often at odds with more conservative political figures.

Political differences aside, Paine also earned enemies by his methods. Personally direct and tenacious in his opinions, he evidently had a very argumentative nature. It was said that he had "at different times disputed with everybody." Also, acting as a reporter-politician he involved himself in everybody's affairs, and no one knew when he would find his words in print. Thus, while he was correct in his accusations concerning Silas Deane's profiteering, he earned lasting enemies by his insistence on making all of the details of the incident public, including the involvement in American affairs of the French government, thereby embarrassing both the American government and an ally. Likewise, he was appalled, as were most Americans, by the inflation and profiteering of the war and, in his attempts to combat them, he made powerful enemies. In sum he had many of the instincts of the modern-day muckraker, and some politicians, as a consequence, did not feel quite comfortable in his presence.

Nevertheless Paine's accomplishments during the Revolution were considerable and varied. In addition to his day-to-day political activity, he had some notable achievements. At his own expense he accompanied the official emissary Henry Laurens to France, where he and Laurens, together with Benjamin Franklin, secured from the French an aid package of ten thousand livres in silver and military supplies. On his return, probably at the request of the Congress, he wrote six public letters to Rhode Island arguing the right of the federal government to tax that state. These letters were important because they made the case for federal priority in taxing, a fundamental right if the national government was going to succeed. Finally, in a *Letter Addressed to the Abbé Raynal* (1782) Paine answered the Abbé's charges that the American Revolution was no more than a power struggle. Paine's reply, optimistic and idealistic, affirmed the values of the Revolution, asserting that America was the first society to show real social progress but that others would soon follow.

As the war drew to an end, Paine could look back on his contributions with satisfaction, but he was not clear about what to do with his future. Before he could make any plans, however, he was faced with one immediate problem. He was without funds. It had been a matter of principle with him not to take money for his political writing. As he had announced in *The American Crisis,* number two: "What I write is pure nature, and my pen and my soul have ever gone together. My writings I have always given away, reserving only the expense of printing and paper and sometimes not even that." Hoping to be recognized for his war service, Paine petitioned Congress and was awarded three thousand dollars. The state of New York also recognized his work with the gift of a confiscated Tory estate. As a result, Paine was relatively well off and free to pursue his interests.

One of those interests was economics, an area that was directly linked to Paine's political concerns. He thought that just as free political systems fostered personal happiness, so free economic systems fostered prosperity. In these views he was probably influenced by the ideas of Adam Smith, who in his *The Wealth of Nations* (1776) had contended that there were laws of commerce like the laws of nature, which, when allowed to operate freely, worked for the good of mankind. Paine's belief in economic laissez faire was not complete, however, because he believed that it should be modified so that no one would suffer economic hardship: society had a responsibility to look after the poor.

As with many of Paine's political ideas, the translation of his economic theories into practice proved controversial. The Bank of Pennsylvania had come out in support of hard currency, that is, gold or silver, and against the use of paper money. Paine supported the bank in an essay entitled *Dissertations on Government; The Affairs of the Bank; and Paper-Money* (1786). The essay contended that paper money disrupted free markets, was unstable, and therefore, "endangered the rights and property of every man." This position, essentially that of financier Robert Morris and other conservative, wealthy landowners and businessmen, opened Paine up to charges of having sold out his working-class constituency. Although Paine's position on the bank prevailed, he lost the trust of many of his liberal political allies.

Another of Paine's interests was science. As so many others of his age, Paine was a projector; that is, he was fascinated by the possibilities for practical use of the new scientific knowledge. Indeed, he had long shared his ideas with Benjamin Franklin and the noted scientist David Rittenhouse. What most captured his attention was the possibility of designing and building for commercial use a single-arched bridge which he believed would be of "great utility." By the fall of 1786 he had put it on display at the

New York State House, where it was admired but judged too impractical for construction.

With all of this activity, however, Paine was somewhat at loose ends. A man who avowedly wrote to "serve mankind," he had no cause in America compelling enough to arouse his unqualified commitment. An idea of his point of view can be gathered from a story, typical but almost certainly apocryphal, which his biographers tell about a conversation between Franklin and Paine. Franklin is supposed to have remarked, "Where liberty is, there is my country." Paine answered: "Where liberty is not, there is mine." America was now free, but there were other countries, such as France, which were not. Indeed, Paine, as a result of his trip to France during the war, well knew of its political turmoil and the discussions of revolution. Perhaps sensing that he could find an outlet for his talents there, and financially free to travel as a result of his Congressional grant, Paine, taking a model of his bridge with him for exhibition, left for France in the spring of 1787.

For the next few years Paine spent his time in France and also in England as a self-appointed promoter of American interests and "statesman for humanity." (He also promoted his bridge, which was not successful.) Although he held no official post, he was well known throughout the educated classes of Europe and had access to the political leaders of France and England. In France he associated with the Marquis de Lafayette and his political circle and also with Thomas Jefferson, with whom he developed a lifelong friendship based on shared political philosophies. In England he associated with Edmund Burke, whom Paine respected for his support of the American Revolution, and with other liberal political figures.

Gradually Paine became involved in the internal political affairs of both England and France, and he especially welcomed the coming of the French Revolution. Thus, when political events in France took a decisive turn with the storming of the Bastille on 14 July 1789, Paine rejoiced and looked forward to contributing to the cause, writing to Washington that "a share in two revolutions is living to some purpose." He hoped that this revolution would produce results like those in America. When Lafayette gave the key to the Bastille to Paine to be presented to Washington, Paine sent it with a note that it was one of the "fruits of American principles transplanted into Europe."

Paine also hoped that a similar reformation would follow in England, and he spent most of his time from 1790 to 1792 in that country sending information to America about British reactions to events in France and associating with British constitutional-reform groups, where he talked with such forward-looking social thinkers as the political philosopher William Godwin and the women's rights advocate Mary Wollstonecraft. He found however, that his optimistic views about the political upheaval in France were not shared either by most Tories or by Whigs. While Paine saw in the French Revolution a model for change, the British Whigs and Tories alike saw instability and chaos. They feared that the spirit of France might spread to their country. The notable Edmund Burke made this clear in a closely argued, widely read pamphlet, *Reflections on the Revolution in France* (1790), in which he both attacked the French "anarchy" and defended the rights of the aristocracy and monarchy to rule on the basis of tradition and proven ability.

Burke's essay provided Paine with the ideal opportunity to publish his own radically different ideas in the form of a response to Burke. In his reply, he could systematize and synthesize his experiences and thinking about government, and make the definitive answer to the forces of tradition, privilege, and entrenched power which he had so long opposed. He could, as well, demonstrate the superiority of a "reasonable" approach to government to that based on what Paine believed to be superstition, prejudice, and raw power. Finally, he had, in answering Burke's attack, the chance he had been looking for to explain the benefits of the revolutions in America and in France so as to further the cause of enlightened representative government throughout the world.

Part one of Paine's essay *Rights of Man*, published in 1791 with a dedication to George Washington, came as close as was reasonably possible to fulfilling Paine's aims. Opposing Burke's periodic, learned style with his own blunt, straightforward one, Paine set a democratic tone in the very language of the essay. His argumentation was equally direct and assertive as he built on the social thinking of the Enlightenment to make the case for freedom and equality in society and government, and for revolution, if necessary, to bring it about. The essay begins with a direct rejection of Burke's claim to the legitimacy of tradition in government. Rather Paine says, "every age and generation must be free to act for itself *in all cases*," and, "A government is for the living and not for the dead." Moreover, he asserts, one cannot have a better government merely by changing individuals. The methods of government are systematic, and when the system is evil and corrupt, the only solution is a new system. In France, for example, "the original hereditary despotism, resident in the person of the king, divides and subdivides itself into a thousand shapes and forms." Therefore, the French Revolution distinguished from the beginning between person and principles. Indeed, any excessive violence used by the revolutionaries at the Bastille had been learned from the despotic government: one must change governments to change social behavior. In this respect, Paine insists, Burke's pity for aristocrats is misplaced. Burke "pities the plummage but forgets the dying bird."

Drawing on Locke's concepts of social compact and natural rights, Paine developed the logical basis for his assertion that men are entitled to shape their own government. Civil rights, according to Paine, are drawn from natural rights that begin in the natural equality of man. Since God created men in "one degree only" then rights are equal for every individual. When a man agrees to a social compact with other individuals, these rights are not "thrown into the common stock," so that "society *grants* him nothing." Rather, every man is a proprietor in society and draws on the capital as a matter of right. Historically, however, men have been deprived of their rights by force so that a few powerful men can get rich. This action is the origin of monarchical and hereditary governmental systems, whose only reason for existence is the acquisition of wealth.

Men, however, according to Paine, were beginning to see the light of reason. In France, the "soil" of revolution was "fertilized" by such thinkers as Montesquieu, Voltaire, Rousseau, and Abbé Raynal. Moreover, the American Revolution served as a guide to the French: "The American Constitutions were to liberty, what a grammar is to language: they define its parts of speech and practically construct them into syntax." Thus, Paine contended, the American and French Revolutions showed that it is not necessary for men to put up with monarchical and hereditary systems of government. Once men know what a "natural" system of government is, that is a representative, republican form, they will reject other kinds, There will be a "renovation of the natural order of things, a system of principles as universal as truth and the existence of man, and combining moral with political happiness and prosperity." This is, he announced, "An Age of Revolution."

The impact of part one of *Rights of Man* equalled that of *Common Sense* fifteen years earlier. It was widely read in America, England, and France (where it had been translated and published by May). Its reception in each country was markedly different, though. In America it became something of a partisan matter when the pamphlet was published with an endorsement by Secretary of State Jefferson, an event that angered the British government. To those in America who were trying to end differences with England, Jefferson's act was a sign of his tilt toward France and away from England. On balance, however, the book was favorably received in America, where it won to the cause of France many who had up to that point feared the Revolution's possible destabilizing effect on social order. The book was also favorably received in France, where, among the leaders of the Revolution, Paine was regarded as a hero.

In England, however, the reaction to the work was decidedly mixed. Reformers welcomed the book, but many people, and certainly the government, disliked Paine's message. Many must simply have resented having French political activities held up as an example to them. But most genuinely feared the "anarchy" in France and hoped that the French "disease" was not catching. What for Paine was "reasonable," for them was chaotic and dangerous: they preferred the stability of tradition and the gradual evolution of governmental forms to the frightening revolution that Paine seemed to advocate.

Paine was in England for most of the time of this controversy. Although he had spent his years through early adulthood in England and understood its character well, he had little patience with this traditionalism. He had certainly suffered from the closed class system, and, if it had not been for the opportunity of America, he would have probably lived out his years in near obscurity. Moreover, he was aware that the government was uneasy about his activity, writing to a friend: "By what I can find the Government Gentry begin to threaten." Rather than being intimidated by this scrutiny, he was encouraged to believe that perhaps he was making a dent in "John Bull's" armor after all.

With these ideas in mind, Paine wrote *Rights of Man: Part the Second* which he published in England in 1792. This essay was the most politically incendiary piece that Paine had written to date. In sometimes impatient and angry tones, Paine spelled out the practical implications of his thesis that ordinary men have specific rights in government and that monarchical systems had violated them. In this process he looked directly at England as well as at other "aristocratical systems" and said outright that they were illegitimate: through war and terror, "Bands

In this letter to George Washington, Paine refers to the fifty copies of the first part of Rights of Man *that he had sent Washington the previous year and to his difficulties in finding a publisher for part two of the controversial work (Pierpont Morgan Library).*

of robbers" established their hegemony and a system of hereditary government which is nothing more than "barbaric": "Kings succeed each other, not as rationals, but as animals. It signifies not what their mental or moral characters are." In contrast, the representative system "takes society and civilization for its basis; nature, reason and experience for its guide."

Paine goes on to argue in the essay that not only are systems like the British one illegitimate, but they have deprived citizens of essential rights. Evidence is found in the fact that England has no written constitution, no document that is "the property of the nation" and safeguards a people's rights. Therefore, in England "many of the laws are irrational and tyrannical, and the administration of them vague and problematical." Moreover, the government is both expensive and unjust: "What is called the splendor of a throne is no other than the corruption of the state." It is made up of a "band of parasites living in luxurious indolence, out of the public taxes." Finally, and worst of all, the government makes men worse, not better, and contributes to war: "Man, were he not corrupted by governments, is naturally the friend of man, and ... human nature is not of itself vicious." Therefore, when "we see age going to the work-house and youth to the gallows something must be wrong with the system of government."

Rights of Man concludes with a vision of what a good system of government might do for a society, and, here, Paine went beyond anything he had suggested in his earlier writing. In *Common Sense*, for example, he had argued that government had only to be fair and to interfere as little as possible with people's freedom. But in this essay he says that governments are responsible for the society's well-being. Moreover, governments should recognize that people are entitled to a share in the society by using tax revenue to provide direct grants for education and for starting young people off in the world. Work should be available for those who can do it, and for those who cannot, such as the ill or the elderly, there should be public aid. People will know when a government is doing its job: "When it shall be said in any country in the world 'My poor are happy; neither ignorance nor distress is to be found among them; my jails are empty of prisoners, my streets are free of beggars; the aged are not in want, the taxes are not oppressive; the rational world is my friend, because I am a friend of its happiness.'—When these things can be said, then may that country boast of its constitution and its government." The ending of the essay is both a warning and a prophecy: "To use a trite expression, the iron is becoming hot all over Europe. The insulted German and the enslaved Spaniard, the Russ and the Pole are beginning to think. The present age will hereafter merit to be called The Age of Reason, and the present generation will appear to the future as the Adam of the new World."

The most radical and forward-looking of Paine's writings, *Rights of Man: Part the Second* proved the most controversial to date. Showing the influence of Paine's contacts with European reformers and with the social injustices so obvious everywhere in Europe, the essay was directed at working-class people rather than the well-off. In America, where the divisions between the wealthy and the poor were not as pronounced, the book's social proposals aroused little criticism, but in England it was a powerful document for social change. As such, it was welcomed and published by English reforming clubs (200,000 copies of the combined essays were published in England by 1793) and promoted in working-class areas such as Mansfield and Sheffield, where it became a basic document of the English working-class movement. For more-conservative Englishmen, Paine's views represented a threat to order, a "bribe to the poor" and a "plundering" of the rich. To the government, moreover, the essay bordered on sedition, openly attacking as it did the constitutionalism and legitimacy of the British government. (Indeed, even before its appearance the Pitt ministry had evidently tried to suppress the work by intimidating the publisher.) Finally, the government was also undoubtedly worried about the restlessness among the workers that Paine's essay aroused.

Paine, who was satisfied with the controversy about his work, was not intimidated by the government's surveillance. Nor was he surprised when it notified him that he would be tried for "anti-government" activities and when it also issued a proclamation against his "seditious" writings. He responded to the proclamation with *Letter Addressed to the Addressers on the Late Proclamation* (1792), calling for an immediate revolution in England. He also probably looked forward to the further debate about the power of government which would be stirred up by his trial. However, circumstances in France were changing rapidly, and Paine, wanting to be useful, left for France on 12 September 1792. In December his trial went forward without him. He was declared guilty of seditious writing and *Rights of Man* was suppressed. From then on a wanted man in England, Paine never returned to the country of his birth.

These British political cartoons suggest the vehemence with which the English establishment responded to the radical proposals in Rights of Man. *The cartoon on the right, which refers to Paine's apprenticeship as a staymaker, shows Paine lacing Britannia into an uncomfortable French corset (Gimbel Collection, American Philosophical Society).*

In France circumstances were quite different. There Paine's reputation was at its height. His *Rights of Man,* taken together with his American writing and his long support of the French Revolution, made him in French eyes not only "the champion of republican principles," and the foremost speaker for the "good of humankind," but one of the few outsiders who could be admitted to the inner workings of Revolutionary politics. Immediately following his tumultuous welcome, he was voted French citizenship by the Convention and then elected as a representative. Although he did not speak or write French, he immediately became involved with Marquis Jean de Condorcet and others in drawing up a new constitution for which he largely contributed its declaration of rights.

Paine's position on a political pedestal did not last very long, however. In this highly volatile and dramatic political situation Paine was out of his depth. His disputatious nature and characteristic outspokenness, which had been liabilities in American politics, put his life in danger in France. Somewhat naively oblivious to the dangers in the violent struggle and probably determined to go forward despite the personal cost, he plunged right into a heated controversy about what should be done with the royal family, which was then being held under house arrest.

It was a controversy about which Paine had every right to speak. He had earned the right not only because of his proven record as an antimonarchist but also because he had personally been part of the drama that had brought the family to its present condition. Paine had been in Paris in June of 1791 when the king, fearing the antimonarchical course of French affairs, had tried to flee from Paris to a royalist garrison at Metz. Traveling slowly in large carriages, the royal family had little chance of success, and they were stopped at Varennes and returned to Paris. Paine, viewing this act as another example of royal "folly," composed a manifesto calling for the overthrow of the monarchy and the immediate establishment of a republican form of government in France. He and friends of the French Republican Club covered the walls of Paris with it. Thus, as in America, he had been once again among the earliest proponents for republican government. It was from this perspective, then, that

Paine spoke out on the issue of what was to happen to the king. In the convention the more radical Jacobin party wanted the royal family to pay with their lives. The Girondins were, for the most part, more cautious and wanted a lesser punishment. Paine sided with the Girondists, arguing that the monarchy as an institution had to be separated from the people who served as rulers. Louis Capet, as he called Louis XIV, was, Paine believed, a decent man and not personally responsible for an evil system. But, the deputies voted for the death penalty, despite a dramatic plea by Paine to spare the family's lives.

While this debate, from Paine's point of view, had been a matter of principle rather than politics, it was for the French Revolutionaries a highly emotional issue because the king and the excesses of his court were the symbol of the decadence and oppression under which so much of French society had suffered. Robespierre, along with others in the Jacobin party, resented Paine's position on the king and Paine's political activity generally: the feeling seemed to be that he was a quarrelsome idealist whose notions of republicanism were too soft for the harsh needs of the Revolution. Paine for his part was becoming increasingly disillusioned with the course of events, and, when the Girondins were locked out of the convention (and many of them afterward sent to their deaths), he "cursed with hearty good will the authors of that terrible system that had turned the character of the Revolution." Aware that his defense of the king had "fixed a mark on him" he began to think of returning to the United States.

Before Paine could make plans he was arrested on vague charges of being an English foreigner obstructing the Revolution and sent to Luxembourg prison. There he saw fellow prisoners being taken off to the guillotine, and he escaped a similar fate only by chance. He had been in Luxembourg three months when he contracted a fever which lasted six weeks and which destroyed forever his formerly robust health. During this period Robespierre wrote a note to the Convention asking the death penalty for Paine: "To demand that a decree of accusation be passed against Thomas Paine for the interest of America, as well as of France." But the accusation was never executed perhaps, Paine suggested, because of the "impossibility, on account of that illness." Having narrowly escaped death, he remained in prison eighteen months until James Monroe secured his release.

Upon his release from prison, Thomas Paine completed his last major work, *The Age of Reason* (1794, 1795). This work, which he had been writing throughout this stormy period of French politics, explained Paine's deistic beliefs and also attacked the scriptures and organized religion. At first glance a work far removed from Paine's Revolutionary concerns, the essay was, in fact, profoundly political. Paine believed that institutional religions, as opposed to deism, had supported oppressive governments and had done so by frightening people with scripture. This essay, by demonstrating the truth of deism and exposing the false basis for belief in scriptures, was intended to help to break the power of the clergy and to promote religious and political freedom. In addition Paine thought that by arguing for a belief in God, as he did in *The Age of Reason,* he could as well counterbalance a move to atheism in certain segments of French society which in the Revolution had rebelled against both the established church and the monarchy.

Drawing on the philosophical and scientific thinking of the Enlightenment, *The Age of Reason* is the most complete exposition and defense of deism, or natural religion as it was often called, coming out of the period; and, in its blunt, straightforward language, it is the one work which applied the rational, critical methods of the new science to the scriptures in a way that is acceptable to ordinary readers. Part one outlines Paine's beliefs: there are one God, happiness beyond this life, natural equality among men, and a "religious duty" to do justice, love mercy, and endeavor to make one's fellow creatures happy. Any other of the ideas which have served as the foundation of organized religion, Paine contends, have merely been put forward "to terrify and enslave mankind" and to monopolize power and profit. Indeed, religious institutions have operated with political ones in an "adulterous" relationship and, therefore, there has to be a revolution in religion as well as in government.

It is imperative, Paine argues, to distinguish between the work of God in nature and "revelation," by which Paine meant the Bible. Man has only to study God's work in nature to know how to behave justly, but he cannot learn from scripture because it is not the word of God. Scripture, Paine contends, is a human work, merely "a bag of superstitions." For example, "church mythologists" represent "this virtuous and amiable man, Jesus Christ, to be at once both God and Man, and also the Son of God, celestially begotten, on purpose to be sacrificed, because they say that Eve in her longing had eaten an apple." This is "mystery and miracle," Paine says, and not part of true religion. Rather, moral principle speaks universally through nature and reason: "Adam, if there ever were such a man, was created a Deist."

After this outline of his beliefs, part two of *The Age of Reason* examines both the Old and New Testaments for internal evidence of error. In tones quite shrill and impatient, the essay points out chronological and historical "inconsistencies" and passes judgments on various biblical events and figures. For example, Paine says that the Book of Genesis is nothing more than an "anonymous book of stories." The New Testament fares no better. Typical of the tone is Paine's treatment of Luke's account of the immaculate conception: "Notwithstanding which, Joseph afterward marries her, cohabits with her as his wife, and in his turn, rivals the ghost. This is putting the story into intelligible language, and when told in this manner, there is not a priest but must be ashamed to own it."

Paine concludes *The Age of Reason* by contending that all religions, with the exception of the Quakers, who he says really are deists, have been "established by the sword" and have used scripture to keep people in fear of God. The aim has been to gain "power and revenue" for themselves. But, if people would stop diverting themselves with organized religion and pay attention to the power of God as it is manifested in the creation, they would stand in awe of God and regulate their moral lives with "force"; under such circumstances, "truth will finally prevail."

The Age of Reason, designed as it was to demystify religion and to shake people loose from their respectful deference to religious institutions, caused an uproar when it appeared. Believers were horrified when Paine called ministers and priests "blasphemous" and accused them of preaching "obscene doctrines." Throughout the world they reviled Paine as an anti-Christian and an infidel. In America, many who respected his other writings turned away from *The Age of Reason* in horror and distaste. Although there was positive reaction as well—ordinary people everywhere read it and thousands converted to deism—its overall effect was to gain for Paine the inaccurate label of "atheist," a label which effectively obscured his other beliefs and accomplishments.

While *The Age of Reason* was undergoing its stormy public reception, Paine lived with the American minister in Paris, James Monroe, who had not only secured Paine's release from prison but also offered him a home for as long as he needed it. Paine's health was poor and his mood depressed. Part of the problem was psychological and had to do with the circumstances of his imprisonment. He believed that the American government had not done as much as it should have to free him from prison. The minister who had preceded Monroe in France, Gouverneur Morris, had disliked Paine from the days of Pennsylvania politics. When Paine was arrested, Morris had merely inquired of the French about his case and informed them that Paine was indeed an American citizen. What angered Paine, however, was not Morris's passivity, but George Washington's. Why had not his friend the President come to his rescue?

Certainly, Paine had some grounds to be angry, and the reasons for Washington's continued silence toward him have never been clear—although he may simply have decided to let his ministers handle a difficult diplomatic matter. In fact, during the Reign of Terror there probably was little that the Americans could do to help Paine without causing him to be noticed and perhaps further endangering him. It is also true, however, that neither Morris nor Washington did much to reassure Paine of their concern. In his ill health Paine chose to put the worst possible interpretations on their actions and wrote to Washington accusing him of neglect and asking for an explanation. When no response was forthcoming, Paine composed an open letter to Washington questioning the adequacy of his performance during the Revolution, castigating the Jay treaty, which Paine opposed as being too accommodating to the British, and denouncing Washington's behavior toward him. The angry, outspoken tone of the letter is captured in the concluding sentence, in which Paine writes: "And as to you, Sir, treacherous in private friendship ... and a hypocrite in public life, the world will be puzzled to decide whether you are an apostate or an imposter; whether you have abandoned good principle, or whether you ever had any."

Unfortunately for Paine, who in a less depressed mood might have modified these sentiments toward a man he had always held in highest esteem, this open letter found itself right in the middle of a venomous political campaign. John Adams and Thomas Jefferson were candidates to succeed Washington in the Presidency. Washington's position as the father of his country had allowed him to remain above political attacks, but Paine's letter forced him into the Jefferson versus Adams battle. Paine's letter was welcomed by *Aurora* publisher Benjamin Franklin Bache, who was no admirer of Washington and a supporter of Jefferson. Bache believed that a letter attacking policies supported by both Washington and Adams would be good ammunition in the campaign, and he published it both in his newspaper and in pamphlet form.

When the letter appeared in 1796, it was widely read and widely disliked. Washington was America's most respected figure, and Paine's bitter, denigrating tone toward him, regardless of the merits of the case, was resented. This letter, it has been argued, did more to damage Paine's reputation in America than any of his previous writing. Certainly at the time it did not promote Paine's interests; it embarrassed his host Monroe, who was soon recalled from his post, and it left Paine with a legacy of distrust not only in America but also in France. His political power in both countries was substantially diminished, and he was treated with caution even by those Americans who were sympathetic to his political and religious views.

With his health and good humor considerably diminished, Paine remained in France for the next few years. The overthrow of the Jacobins and the end of the Reign of Terror had brought government by the Directory, and many of Paine's political allies were back in positions of power. The government acknowledged his services to the Revolution, and Paine again was involved in French political affairs, although he was never again admitted to the inner circles of power. During this time he wrote a number of essays growing out of his observations of the Directory's government, the most important of which is *Agrarian Justice* published in 1797. This work, which suggested a "ground rent" to finance a system of social security for those over the age of fifty, shows Paine's continued sensitivity to social injustice and his forward-looking attempts to relieve it.

On the whole, however, Paine was not satisfied with his life in France. It had moved far away from the ideals of the Revolution as he saw them, and he wanted to return to America. As he wrote to a friend: "I know of no Republic in the world except America, which is the only country for such men as you and I." A good opportunity to return arrived when Jefferson, now President, sent him a friendly letter inviting him home, and on 1 November 1802, at age sixty-five and after an absence of fifteen years, Paine returned to the United States.

He returned to a country in which he was a well-known but very controversial figure. The near universal admiration in which he had been held before his departure fifteen years earlier was gone, and in its place were partisan responses to his liberal political and religious views. For some he was a "leveller" to be shunned. To others he was a staunch defender of the working man and to be admired. Orthodox believers reviled him for "atheism"; to others he was the hero of religious freedom. Many saw him as a firebrand and an agitator, a threat to stability in government; still others welcomed his attacks on privilege and tradition. With very few was admiration unqualified, and with Paine an old man now, there were few who knew him personally. While Jefferson welcomed him to Washington, Paine found that most political leaders preferred to stay clear of him because of the controversies surrounding him. Despite Jefferson's friendship, Paine had lost his political leverage and was relegated to the outer fringes of political activity.

Without any plans for the future and an old man in ill health, Paine took up residence at his estate in New Rochelle, which had years ago been given him by the state of New York for his Revolutionary activity. Because most of the buildings on the place had burned down, he lived there in a small cottage. Two sons of the Bonneville family, which had helped him in Paris, stayed with him for a while, and he helped to supervise their education, as their mother Madam Bonneville looked after him. In these years he occupied himself with attending meetings of groups interested in deism and with writing letters on political views. Plagued by money problems and ill health, he gradually became less active, spending the last two years of his life as an invalid.

Perhaps most difficult for him in his last years was the obscurity into which he had fallen. His Revolutionary activity, for which he was admired, was long past; and his other writings, while still well known, were not in the forefront of public attention. Well aware of this fact and concerned about his death, Paine asked the Quaker society for a burial plot. The request was denied. Paine had to settle for being buried on his farm, all the while fearing that "the farm will be sold, and they will dig up my bones before they be half rotten."

Paine died on 8 June 1809 and was buried, as planned, on his farm. Only a few people were present, and Madam Bonneville described her feelings on the occasion: "Contemplating who it was, what man it was, that we were committing to an obscure grave on an open and disregarded bit of land, I could not help feeling most acutely. Before the earth was thrown upon the coffin, I, placing myself at the east end of the grave, said to my son Benjamin, 'Stand you there, at the other end, as a witness for grateful America.' Looking round me, and beholding the small group of spectators, I exclaimed as the earth was tumbled into the grave, 'Oh! Mr.

Paine's cottage at his estate in New Rochelle (New-York Historical Society)

Paine! My son stands here as testimony of the gratitude of America, and I, for France.'" Paine, as he feared, did not remain at this quiet spot. In 1819 William Cobbett, intending to build a monument to Paine in England, disinterred his bones. However, the British disapproved of his project, and when Cobbett died, Paine's bones disappeared.

After his death, Paine's reputation continued to languish. While other leaders of the Revolution—Washington, Jefferson, Franklin—were venerated as Revolutionary heroes, Paine was relegated to a relatively minor place. To many he was "irreligious" and "radical" and, therefore, not worth reading. Yet, such responses do not do justice to Paine's contribution to American letters and society. The drama and immediacy of the American Revolution is captured in *The American Crisis* essays as nowhere else. *Common Sense* and *Rights of Man* articulate so much that was central to the purpose of America in the eighteenth century and remains central today: the optimistic belief that people could escape from tradition and form a society based on egalitarian principles; the faith that ordinary citizens could understand and shape social policy and govern themselves; the humanitarian and social conscience that refused to accept injustice and poverty. *The Age of Reason,* too, remains a central document, summing up the tenets of the "rational" deism which underlay so much of eighteenth-century thought and which produced the principles of freedom of religion and separation of Church and State, fundamental to American society. In their commitment to reason, principle, and clarity, Paine's essays remain among the most articulate statements of American values—either in the eighteenth century or today.

Biographies:

Moncure D. Conway, *The Life of Thomas Paine* (New York & London: Putnam's, 1892);

Frank Smith, *Thomas Paine: Liberator* (New York: Stokes, 1938);

Alfred Owen Aldridge, *Man of Reason: The Life of Thomas Paine* (New York: Lippincott, 1959);

Audrey Williamson, *Thomas Paine: His Life, Work and Times* (London: Allen & Unwin, 1973);

David Freeman Hawke, *Paine* (New York: Harper & Row, 1974);

Eric Foner, *Tom Paine and Revolutionary America* (London: Oxford University Press, 1976);

Jerome E. Wilson and William Ricketson, *Thomas Paine* (Boston: Twayne, 1978).

References:
Alfred Owen Aldridge, "Paine and Dickinson," *Early American Literature* (Fall 1976): 125-138;

Aldridge, "The Problem of Thomas Paine," *Studies in Burke and His Time*, 19 (Spring 1978): 127-143;

Aldridge, "The Rights of Man and the Classics," *Eighteenth Century Studies*, 1 (1968): 370-380;

Aldridge, "Thomas Paine and The French Connection," *French-American Review*, 1 (1977): 240-248;

Bernard Bailyn, *The Ideological Origins of the American Revolution* (Cambridge: Harvard University Press, 1969);

Philip Davidson, *Propaganda and the American Revolution, 1763-1783* (Chapel Hill: University of North Carolina Press, 1941);

J. Rodney Fulcher, "Common Sense vs. Plain Truth: Propaganda and Civil Society," *Southern Quarterly*, 15 (October 1976): 57-74;

Jerry Knudsen, "The Rage Around Tom Paine: Newspaper Reactions to His Homecoming in 1802," *New-York Historical Society Quarterly*, 53 (January 1969): 34-63;

Henry F. May, *The Enlightenment in America* (New York: Oxford University Press, 1976);

Perry Miller, "Thomas Paine, Rationalist," *Nation*, 162 (23 February 1946): 228-232;

Franklyn Prochaska, "Thomas Paine's *The Age of Reason* Revisited," *Journal of the History of Ideas*, 33 (October-December 1972): 561-576;

Kenneth Silverman, *A Cultural History of the American Revolution* (New York: Crowell, 1976);

Moses Coit Tyler, *The Literary History of the American Revolution; 1763-1783*, 2 (New York: Putnam's, 1897);

Margaret M. Vanderhaar, "Whitman, Paine and the Religion of Democracy," *Walt Whitman Review*, 16 (March 1970): 14-22.

Papers:
The largest collection of Paine materials is at the American Philosophical Society in Philadelphia.

John Parke
(7 April 1754-11 December 1789)

Maurice J. Bennett
University of Maryland

BOOK: *The Lyric Works of Horace, Translated into English Verse: to Which Are Added, A Number of Original Poems,* as A Native of America (Philadelphia: Printed by Eleazer Oswald, 1786).

OTHER: John Vardill and John Randolph, *Letters from General Washington, To Several of His Friends in the Year 1776; In Which Are Set Forth, A Fairer and Fuller View of American Politicks, than Ever Yet Transpired, Or the Publick could be made acquainted with through any other Channel,* includes Parke's reply to a letter from Jacob Duché (New York: Printed by James Rivington, 1778).

John Parke, American Revolutionary War soldier-poet, was known principally for his *The Lyric Works of Horace, Translated into English Verse: to Which Are Added, A Number of Original Poems* (1786), published under the pseudonym "A Native of America." This volume is distinguished by one of the earliest literary attempts to celebrate the birthday of George Washington, the allegorical *Virginia: A Pastoral Drama, on the Birth-Day of an Illustrious Personage and the Return of Peace, February 11th, 1784.*

Parke was born to Thomas and Ann Parke in Dover, Delaware. His father was a well-to-do hatmaker and frequent officeholder in Kent County, Delaware. John attended Newark Academy, Newark College (later the University of Delaware), and the College of Philadelphia (later the University of Pennsylvania), where he received his A.B. in 1771 and his A.M. in 1775. On the outbreak of hostilities between Great Britain and her American colonies, he abandoned the study of law, which he had pursued for four years with Thomas McKean, to volunteer for service with the Continental Army.

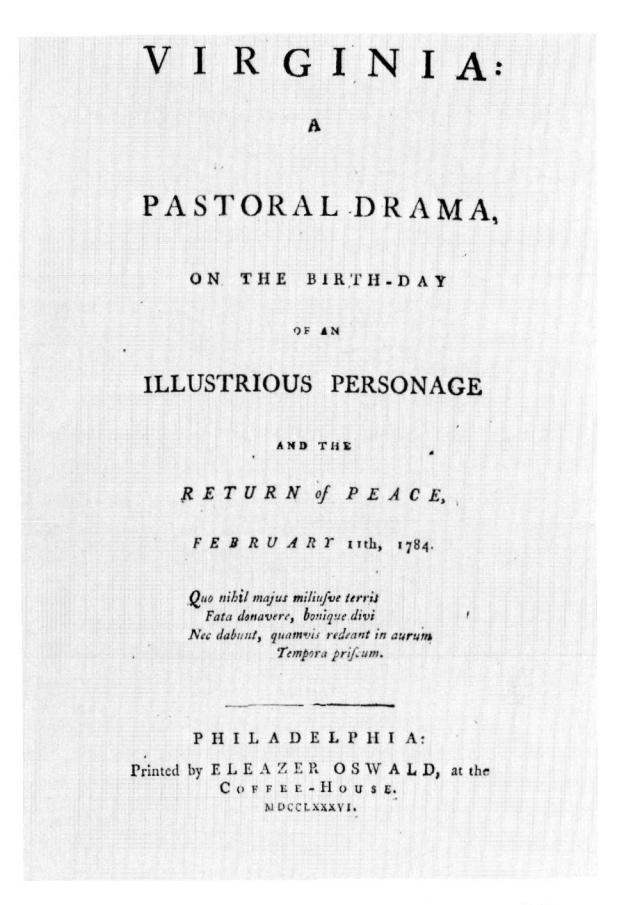

Title page for Parke's book and the interior title page for his allegorical drama, one of the earliest literary celebrations of George Washington's birthday (courtesy of the John Carter Brown Library at Brown University)

On the recommendations of McKean and Caesar Rodney, a member of Delaware's colonial legislature and a representative to the first and second Continental Congresses, he was appointed assistant quartermaster-general on 16 April 1775, and on 29 June 1776, he became a lieutenant-colonel of artificers. He retired from military service on 29 October 1778.

The earliest appearance of Parke's writing in print was a response to a letter addressed to General Washington and published in the Philadelphia papers by the former chaplain to the Continental Congress, Reverend Jacob Duché, calling upon the commander in chief to lend his prestige to a movement for a negotiated resolution of the colonists' differences with the Crown. As a member of Washington's staff with known literary propensities, Parke was entrusted with the reply, which was published along with Duché's original letter as an appendix to the 1778 American edition of a collection of spurious correspondence later attributed to John Vardill and John Randolph, *Letters from General Washington, To Several of His Friends in the Year 1776; In Which Are Set Forth, A Fairer and Fuller View of American Politicks, than Ever Yet Transpired, Or the Publick could be made acquainted with through any other Channel*, originally published in London in 1777. In his letter Parke devotes himself to aspersions on Duché's courage, integrity, and patriotism, but he also indicates the shift in public sentiment from the pique of disgruntled colonists to the sense of separate national identity. "Since the Declaration of Independency," he wrote, "the ground of our contest is materially changed; and it is not rights and privileges for which we now fight, but dominion and empire are the objects of both parties."

The Lyric Works of Horace is little more than an interesting miscellany of translations and paraphrases—of Anacreon, Ovid, and Johann Gesner as well as Horace—after the manner of Pope; a discursive literary biography of Horace; original works by Parke himself; and works by the young British officer John Wilcocks and by the early Pennsylvania poet and translator David French. Including as it does works composed throughout the century, Parke's collection is significant as an index of the primacy of classical learning among eighteenth-century Americans and of the state of their literary culture. The great majority of Parke's own works are addressed to his associates and acquaintances, which run a gamut from Benjamin Franklin, the Marquis de Lafayette, and Admiral Count D'Estaing, to his professors, his orderly, and his friend and printer, Eleazer Oswald. The range and number of persons addressed represents a literary enterprise that is at once nationalistic and commemorative. "To hand down the names and virtues of my fellow citizens to posterity, such as have voluntarily sacrificed their lives on the altar of their country, is the goal of my literary ambition," he claims in the dedication.

Perhaps most significant, Parke's volume is an early item in the progressive exaltation of the figure of Washington as a national icon. The dedication to Washington proclaims, "The whole circle of arts and sciences, is bound to you, by every sacred tie of gratitude and affection. It was your influence that encouraged, and your arms that supported the drooping spirit of learning, through the toils of a long, predatory and unnatural war . . . which would have overturned our liberties, and inveloped [sic] our seminaries of science in the clouds of savage barbarism." In many of his paraphrases of Horace, Parke replaces the original Roman subjects with figures from his contemporary America, thus pointing the Augustan analogy of which his countrymen were so fond. For instance, Horace's ode six, to Agrippa, architect of the naval victory at Actium, is addressed by Parke to Count D'Estaing, "Admiral and Commander of his most Christian Majesty's fleet and army in America," and the more generally ethical ode twenty-four, "Against Misers," is addressed here to "all Speculators, both Civil and Military" who infested the country immediately after the cessation of hostilities. The book's concluding piece, the allegorical drama *Virginia,* adapts the ode describing Augustus's return from Spain to the celebration of Washington's victorious return from Yorktown.

Although Parke and his work have attracted little biographical or critical attention, they testify to the persistence of the attractions of literature under even the harshest social and historical conditions, and his concern with American subjects reflects the inevitable human desire for the imaginative transformation of the familiar.

References:

Joshua Francis Fisher, "Some Account of the Early Poets and Poetry of Pennsylvania," *Memoirs of the Historical Society of Pennsylvania,* 2, part 2 (1830): 53-103;

E. D. Neill, "Notes on American History," no. 8, *New England Historical and Genealogical Register,* 30 (July 1876): 299-301;

George Herbert Ryden, ed., *Letters to and from Caesar Rodney, 1756-1784* (Philadelphia: University of Pennsylvania Press, 1933), p. 62;

John T. Scharf, *History of Delaware,* 2 volumes (Philadelphia: L. J. Richards, 1888), pp. 138, 139, 1046, 1162.

Papers:

The Henry E. Huntington Library, the Library of Congress, the Massachusetts Historical Society, the Pennsylvania Historical Society, and the Beinecke Library at Yale University have letters by Parke.

Benjamin Young Prime
(20 December 1733-31 October 1791)

Michael Robertson
Princeton University

BOOKS: *The Unfortunate Hero; A Pindaric Ode. Occasion'd by the Lamented Fate of Viscount George Augustus Howe* ... (New York: Printed by Parker & Weyman, 1758);
The Patriot Muse, or Poems on Some Principal Events of the Late War ... (London: Printed for John Bird, 1764);
The Fall of Lucifer, An Elegiac Poem on the Infamous Defection of the Late General Arnold (Hartford: Printed by Hudson and Goodwin, 1781);
Columbia's Glory, or British Pride Humbled ... (New York: Printed by Thomas Greenleaf, 1791);
Muscipula sive Cambromyomachia: The Mousetrap, or The Battle of the Welch and the Mice; in Latin and English: With Other Poems, in Different Languages (New York: M. W. Dodd, 1840).

Benjamin Young Prime, physician and writer of patriotic verse, was born Benjamin Youngs Prime (he later dropped the *s* from his middle name) at Huntington, Long Island, the son of Experience Youngs Prime and Ebenezer Prime, a Congregational minister. After graduating in 1751 from the College of New Jersey, then located at Newark, he studied medicine until 1756, when he returned to serve as a tutor at the college, which had moved to Princeton. He left Princeton after one year and returned to Long Island, where, over the next five years, he lived at various times in East Hampton and Huntington while practicing medicine and writing poetry. Yale University awarded Prime an honorary master's degree in 1760, matching the one he had received from the College of New Jersey in 1754.

Prime left for London in 1762 to continue his medical studies. While there he published his first volume of verse, *The Patriot Muse* (1764). Most of the twenty poems in the volume deal with the French and Indian War in verse that is technically adept, fervently patriotic, and equally pious. He celebrates the British as Christian heroes and vilifies the French, in verse forms ranging from the popular ballad to heroic couplets.

Prime wrote his doctoral dissertation while in London, presented it at the University of Leyden, and received the M.D. degree in 1764. He returned to America and settled in New York City shortly before passage of the Stamp Act (1765), an event that started him on his shift from loyal Briton to American nationalist. *An Excellent New Song, For the Sons of Liberty in America,* a broadside written by Prime and published in 1765 or 1766, is a rousing ballad that champions American liberties. By 1770 Prime was so firmly identified with the nationalist cause that he feared arrest by Loyalists. He wrote to a friend, "I myself am threaten'd (by papers thrown into my house) with a Damnation Drubbing and

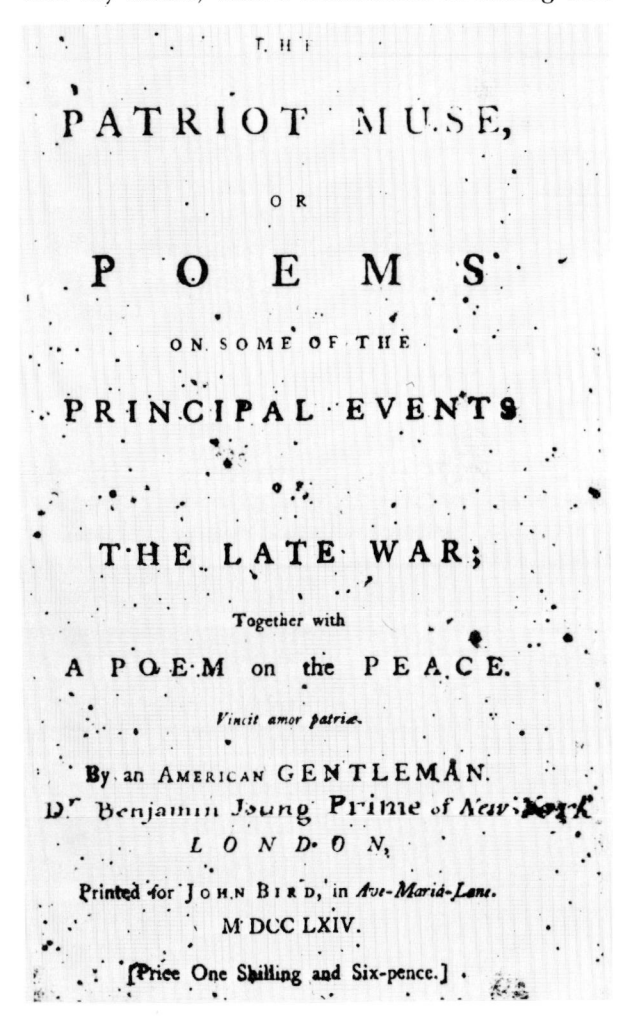

Title page for Prime's collection of poems on the French and Indian War (Library Company of Philadelphia)

Imprisonment, on suspicion of being the Author of the *Watchman* [a series of now untraceable political essays]. So that for 4 or 5 Weeks past I've walk'd the Streets (especially of an Evening) arm'd with either a Sword or Pistols or both." Thomas Jones, Loyalist historian of Revolutionary-era New York, repeated the charge that Prime was author of the *Watchman* papers and characterized him as "a most violent, persecuting republican."

Prime moved back to Huntington two years before the outbreak of the Revolutionary War, and on 18 December 1774 married Mary Wheelwright Greaton, the young widow of an Anglican clergyman. When British troops occupied Long Island early in the war, Prime, his wife, and their year-old son (the first of five children) were forced to flee to Connecticut. They settled first in Wethersfield and later in New Haven, where Prime continued to practice medicine. Prime published only one poem during the war: *The Fall of Lucifer* (1781), on the defection of Benedict Arnold. His major work on the Revolution, *Columbia's Glory, or British Pride Humbled,* was not published until a few weeks before his death in 1791. This 1,441-line poem began as a parody of Prime's earlier poem on the British conquest of Quebec, "Britain's Glory, or Gallic Pride Humbled," published in *The Patriot Muse*. In his post-Revolutionary work he writes:

> The muse for *Britain* sings no more,
> The *British* laurel withers on my brow,
> COLUMBIA only is my country now.

Prime left behind at his death 210 pages of manuscript poetry. His son Nathaniel Scudder Prime edited a brief selection of those poems in 1840, focusing on his father's nontopical verse. The edition consists largely of adept and conventional translations and religious poetry. Though Prime's poetry has not been republished since the nineteenth century, it is valuable for its deft expression of the common patriotic sentiments of the time. Critics have singled out his eulogy for General Washington, which comprises one-fourth of *Columbia's Glory*, as the best of the hundreds of poetic tributes to Washington.

References:

James McLachlan, *Princetonians 1748-1768* (Princeton: Princeton University Press, 1976), pp. 40-44;

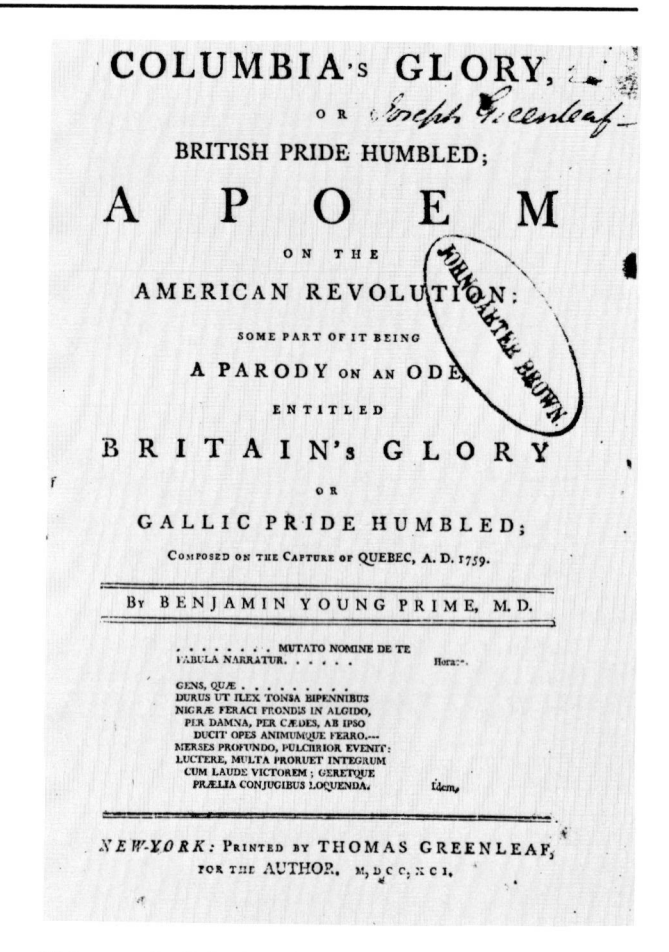

Title page for Prime's major work in praise of the American Revolution. This long poem was conceived as a parody of a pro-British poem he had written during the French and Indian War (courtesy of the John Carter Brown Library at Brown University).

William Bradley Otis, *American Verse: 1625-1807: A History* (New York: Moffat, Yard, 1909), pp. 150-152, 259-260;

Edward D. G. Prime, *Notes Genealogical, Biographical and Bibliographical, of the Prime Family* (Cambridge, Mass.: Wilson, 1888);

E. I. Stevenson, "Four Primes," *New York Genealogical and Biographical Record*, 17 (1886): 197-208;

Charles Webster Wheelock, "Dr. Benjamin Young Prime (1733-1791): American Poet," Ph.D. dissertation, Princeton University, 1967.

Papers:

Benjamin Young Prime's papers and manuscript poetry are at Princeton Theological Seminary.

Samuel Quincy of Georgia

(birth date and death date unknown)

John C. Shields
Illinois State University

BOOK: *Twenty Sermons . . . Preach'd in the Parish of St. Philip, Charles-Town, South-Carolina* (Boston: Printed & sold by John Draper, 1750).

OTHER: "Letter From Mr. Samuel Quincy to the Honourable Edmund Quincy, Esq., Savannah, Oct. 23, 1735," *Collections of the Massachusetts Historical Society*, second series, 2 (1814): 188-189.

During the 1730s, Samuel Quincy, B.A., was not the most popular clergyman in Savannah, Georgia. His later tenure in New England, however, proved much more favorable to him. Indeed the list of subscribers to the 1750 *Twenty Sermons* is impressively long, including the Reverend Samuel Johnson of New York, who requested three copies, as well as others from all parts of the colonies. The learned good sense of Quincy's reasoned responses to the impact of the Great Awakening in the South may help to account for the popularity of these sermons, which are written in a rather fluid form, unlike the more rigid structure of the traditional Puritan sermon.

Little is known of Quincy's life before his arrival in Georgia some time in midsummer 1733. It is known, however, that he was educated in an English university and was ordained on 21 December 1732 by Doctor Waugh, Bishop of Carlisle. Quincy was married, but his wife did not accompany him on his voyage to Georgia, where his charge from the Anglican Society for the Propagation of the Gospel was to replace the Reverend Doctor Henry Herbert, whose poor health had led him to reembark for England within a few weeks of his arrival in Georgia. (He died on the voyage home.)

Quincy's constitution appears not to have been much superior to Herbert's; it was his lack of physical fortitude, he averred before the colony's trustees (among whom were such dignitaries as John Perceval, first Earl of Egmont, and Gen. James E. Oglethorpe), that forced him to leave his congregation unattended for several months in order to journey to New York for his health. Also, according to the best accounts, the populace of Savannah was not disposed to religious discipline, at least not the sort of training Quincy offered. Yet John Perceval recorded in his journal that "Mr. Quincy the Minister does not attend his duty as he ought."

Quincy was soon replaced by John Wesley, the father of modern Methodism, and on 15 March 1736 Quincy left Savannah for South Carolina. It is not known whether Mrs. Quincy ever joined her husband in the New World, but the minister remained there for at least the next fifteen years preaching and traveling about the colonies. At one time he was nearly called to a congregation in Charles Town (present-day Charleston), but the vestry of the parish objected to his low voice. Low voice notwithstanding, sometime in 1742 Quincy was chosen rector of the parish of St. John in Colleton, South Carolina, where he remained until 1745. Following his tenure at Colleton, Quincy accepted a two-year rectorship at Dorchester, South Carolina, after which he was called to Charles Town (the vestry apparently having relented on the matter of his low voice). About 1749 he located at Boston, where his *Twenty Sermons* were published. His whereabouts after 1751 are not now known.

All of the sermons in *Twenty Sermons . . .* were preached in St. Philip's parish, Charles Town, in about 1748. By this time George Whitefield, the voice of the Great Awakening, had already made three of his seven trips to the American Colonies. The calm, rational approach of Quincy's sermons—especially *Christianity a Rational Religion*, the first sermon in *Twenty Sermons*—offers an alternative theological perspective to the fervent emotional enthusiasm which characterized Whitefield's revival meetings and a change from the sense of urgency which predominates Jonathan Edwards's sermons and treatises of the 1740s. An examination of two of the *Twenty Sermons* suggests the probable reason for the book's popularity with opponents of the Great Awakening.

Christianity a Rational Religion may at first suggest the Ramist logic of one of the Puritan Mathers, but Quincy's reasoning actually resembles more closely that employed in other Anglican sermons of his day. He argues that man's reason per-

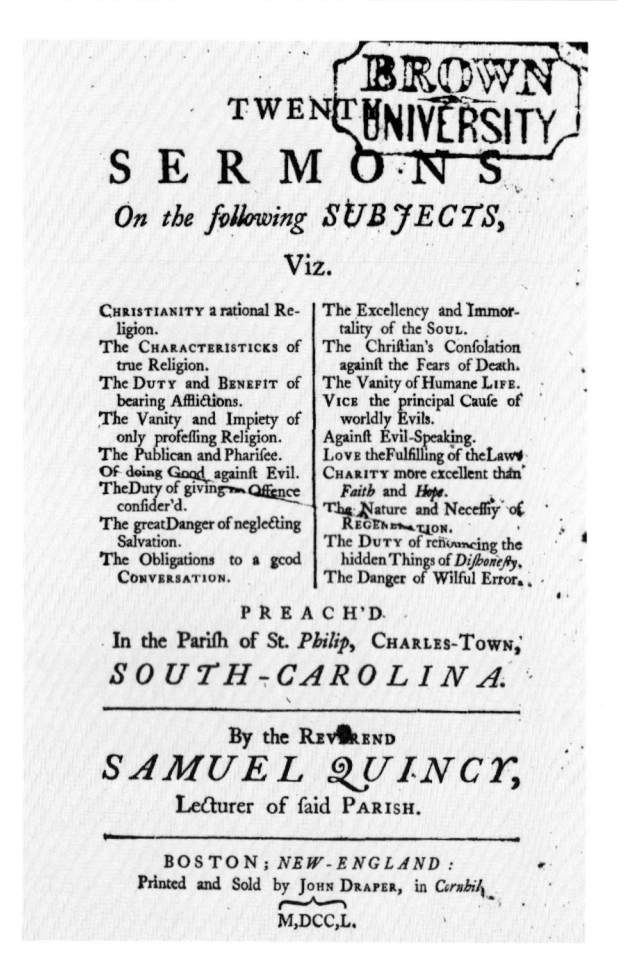

Title page for the only published volume of Quincy's sermons, which are characterized by their rational response to the fervor of the Great Awakening (courtesy of the John Carter Brown Library at Brown University)

mits him to perceive religion and God as realities; if he rejects such reasonings, then he is not merely a skeptic and an atheist, but has degenerated "into a State no better than that of irrational Brutes: For the man who casts off all Sense of God and Religion, confesses himself in no better a Condition." He continues by cautioning that mortal men should "consider well the Reach of our own Capacities," and rely for religious assurances upon that which is "really within the Compass of human Comprehension." For such a venture into questions of the nature of existence and of God "may please our own vain Imaginations with pompous Sounds and magnificent Language." While Quincy's tone is milder than the seventeenth-century Puritans', his faith in man's capacity for independent self-examination shows itself, like theirs, to be small. The lack of regard Quincy exposes here for the faculty of the imagination looks back to the suspicion in which most seventeenth-century Puritans held this faculty. (Edwards tried to reinstate this suspicion in his 1746 *Treatise Concerning Religious Affections*.)

In the twelfth sermon, *The Vanity of Human Life,* Quincy illustrates the validity of his text, "Verily every Man, at his best State, is altogether Vanity" (Psalms 39:5), by appealing to the frailty of the human condition. He maintains that mortal life is "short and uncertain" and that the enjoyments of this life are even of less duration and certainty, therefore promising men no real happiness. Then the minister compares man's short mortality to an "Appearance upon the Stage of this Life" where we "perform a short Part" and then exist on earth no more. Such a stage analogy, although certainly apt, was not typical for the day, even for laymen. Nevertheless, Quincy's theology should not be construed as anything but that of orthodox Anglicanism.

Quincy's greatest role in history was probably his failure to carry out his duties in a manner acceptable to the trustees of the colony of Georgia, whatever the extenuating circumstances, thus creating the opportunity for John Wesley to come to America and to establish ties which would eventually lead to the establishment of Methodism in the United States. Quincy's literary significance is modest, but his sermons enjoyed wide popularity in the colonies during the 1750s, and their calm good sense, although hardly penetrating, offered an alternative theological point of view, which had a measure of appeal to a largely uneducated populace and countered the emotionalism of the Great Awakening.

References:

Harold E. Davis, *The Fledgling Province: Social and Cultural Life in Colonial Georgia, 1733-1776* (Chapel Hill: University of North Carolina Press, 1976), pp. 197, 213-214;

Amos A. Ettinger, *James Edward Oglethorpe: Imperial Idealist* (Oxford: Clarendon Press, 1936), pp. 160-161;

Mills Lane, ed., *General Oglethorpe's Georgia* (Savannah, Ga.: Beehive Press, 1975), I: 129-131 (reprints Quincy's letter of 3 March 1735 to Peter Gordon);

Robert McPherson, ed., *The Journal of the Earl of Egmont* (Athens: University of Georgia Press, 1962);

Edgar L. Pennington, "The Reverend Samuel Quincy, S.P.G. Missionary," *Georgia Historical Quarterly,* 11 (June 1927): 157-165.

Samuel Quincy of Massachusetts
(13 April 1734-9 August 1789)

John C. Shields
Illinois State University

WORKS: *A Monody Inscribed to Benjamin Church, jun. M.D. in Memory of Mr. Edmund Quincy . . .* (Boston, 1768);
Diary of Samuel Quincy, Proceedings of the Massachusetts Historical Society, 19 (1882): 214-223.

Samuel Quincy wrote only one published poem and a diary. The poem, an elegy for his older brother, departs markedly from the Puritan elegiac form, and his diary, written in London in late 1776 and early 1777, during the outbreak of armed resistance in the Colonies, presents an intelligent, discerning, and delightful commentary on the state of the arts in London. The facts that, while he was an undergraduate at Harvard, Quincy was once publicly admonished for having gotten a black slave drunk and that his second wife attributed the aged Quincy's gout to too much dancing testify to this man's determination to enjoy life to the fullest.

Samuel Quincy was born to Josiah and Hannah Sturgis Quincy in Braintree (now known as Quincy), Massachusetts, on 13 April 1734, the second son, among three boys and one girl, Hannah. His older brother, Edmund, took over his father's Boston business in commerce and shipbuilding after the patriarch retired to Braintree. Both Samuel, who remained loyal to the Crown, and his younger brother Josiah, a Revolutionary War patriot, became lawyers. In his diary, John Adams, who was in the class behind Samuel Quincy at Harvard, described the young Samuel as an "easy, social and benevolent companion" and as one who was "not without Genius, Elegance and Taste." Quincy's later experiences in London assuredly bear out Adams's judgment regarding Quincy's sociability.

A year after receiving his B.A. in June 1754 and delivering the valedictory address to his class, Quincy began studying law with Benjamin Prat. He was admitted to the Suffolk bar in 1758, and on 16 June 1761, just as he was establishing his law practice in Boston, he married Hannah Hill. For many years thereafter, as colonial hostilities to British policies increased, Quincy apparently remained sympathetic with the Whig sentiments. He dined at Liberty Tree with the Sons of Liberty and wrote in

Portrait of Samuel Quincy by John Singleton Copley (Museum of Fine Arts, Boston)

glowing terms of Josiah Quincy's participation in Whig politics, praising him in 1768 for having "adopted The Sentiments of Liberty and Freedom with manhood." In *A Monody Inscribed to Benjamin Church, jun. M.D. in Memory of Mr. Edmund Quincy* (1768), the only work by Quincy published during his lifetime, he celebrates Edmund Quincy's "Heart, which late inflam'd with patriot Zeal" and which now, lamentably, can no longer glow "in *Freedom's Cause.*"

Rather than adopting the Puritan, and then standard, form of portraiture (biography: vocation, sanctification, and glorification) followed by an exhortation to the living, which Benjamin Church, to whom Quincy's poem is inscribed, followed for the most part in his 1766 elegy on the Reverend

Jonathan Mayhew, Quincy gave his elegy the much looser structure of a collection of personal memories of his older brother's life. Quincy's inscription to Church apparently acknowledged only his borrowing of Church's iambic-pentameter rhyming *a b a b* from his elegy on Mayhew. While Church clearly prefers "the chaste Muse" and carefully avoids the making of any classical allusions, Quincy invokes the poetic muse of antiquity and refers to Zephyr and Hymen.

The reference to Hymen is particularly appropriate, because Edmund Quincy, who died while traveling in the Caribbean in the hope of improving his waning health, had recorded plans for marriage prior to his embarkation. Quincy deplores his brother's thwarted plans: "The lov'd, scarce known, ere Hymen's bands alli'd, / By wan Disease Life's genial Current froze," and he sensitively describes the bereaved bride-to-be as one to whom "thy Love shall ne'er return, / Nor the fond smile e'er glad thy jocund Heart." The would-be bride does not, of course, mourn alone. Quincy recalls his brother's cheerful participation "at 'the Feast of Reason' circl'd round, / The keen *Remark*, and sensible *Reply*." Here Quincy apparently has in mind the fact that Edmund was especially fond of Jonathan Mayhew, who was an Old Light minister opposed to George Whitefield's enthusiasm, which sparked much of the fervor in the Great Awakening. Edmund Quincy had joined Mayhew's West Church in 1758, and, indeed, the Mayhew circle included many who espoused tenets of the Age of Reason. Significantly, Samuel Quincy closes his poem with two lines which emphasize Mayhew's importance to his brother: "A Star refulgent, bright'ning Meteor glow! / And with thy once lov'd Mayhew, blaze in heav'n."

This poem is not at all a Puritan lament but more closely reflects the pensive, affectionate grief of a cosmopolitan gentleman. It is perhaps Quincy's predilection toward the life of the comfortable cosmopolite which contributed, as much as any real political preference, to his gradual change from sympathies with the coming revolution to loyalty to the British monarchy. In 1770 Samuel Quincy prosecuted Captain Preston and the soldiers who fired on the crowd in the Boston Massacre, while Josiah Quincy, Jr., presented their defense; both brothers, who probably accepted their charges in this trial as challenges of legal principle, reversed their positions in ensuing years, Josiah becoming a fiery patriot of the American cause and Samuel a tepid Loyalist. Phillis Wheatley's poem "To Samuel Quincy, Esq.; a Panegyrick," which is no longer extant, doubtless celebrated Samuel Quincy's role in prosecuting the men who had killed several colonists among whom was Crispus Attucks, the first black to lose his life in America's cause. In March 1771, Quincy accepted appointments from the Crown as a Justice of the Peace and as Solicitor General; as compensation for these two appointments, he drew a salary of £250 a year. Since the revenues for this salary derived from the tea tax, Samuel kept his compensation a secret until after his departure from the colonies.

Just before he sailed for England on 27 May 1775, Samuel wrote his brother-in-law, Henry Hill (with whom Quincy's wife and children remained throughout the war): "if I cannot *serve* my country, which I shall endeavor to the utmost of my power, I will never *betray* it." It is clear from the concerns he expressed throughout the following years that Quincy did, indeed, prefer the colonies as a place of residence and Harvard College as the institution in which to educate his sons. But he did not feel prevented by his country's ills from enjoying the cultures of Paris and London. His London pleasure tours he carefully recorded in his diary, which he kept with imperfect regularity from 9 October 1776 until 30 March 1777. During this six-month period Quincy attended at least eight plays, five operas, and two balls, at many of which the King and Queen put in appearances. In addition, he went to two concerts, two puppet shows, and one art show. And these are only the events he recorded.

Within one two-week period alone, in early 1777, he heard two operas, danced at one ball, and saw an exhibition of "a seventeen feet square, very accurately done" model of Paris. It is especially noteworthy that Quincy does not record merely his attendance at these gala affairs; he also writes down his impressions and critical perceptions of them. Of the operas, one such perception is worth repeating. On the evening of 15 March 1777, he went with a friend to a performance of "the new opera, 'Telemacho,'" most probably the opera by Ferdinando G. Bertoni which had had its premiere in Venice on 26 December 1776. Quincy's attendance at this opera may be of particular interest to historians of the form because he notes that performance of this work included "for the first time on the English stage, singing and dancing at once, after the manner of the French opera at Paris." Quincy was in a position to make such an observation; for in the first entry of his diary, he observes that he had "This day returned ... from my tour to Paris, having just completed it in three weeks."

His entries describing his play attendance are

equally as interesting, since he usually takes pains to list the characters, who played them, and how successfully. On the evening of 6 November 1776, Quincy thoroughly enjoyed a performance of Richard Steele's sentimental comedy *The Conscious Lovers* (1722), which had by then become something of a revered classic. Quincy observes that the parts "of young Bevil by Mr. Lewis, and Indiana by Mrs. Hartley, were admirably executed, insomuch that their Majesties (who were present) and the whole audience were in tears." Concerning the concerts he attended, Quincy takes the same pains to record information, even setting down the instruments and their players, as well as the names of the singers. He twice names Karl Friedrich Abel, called by Percy Scholes the last great player of the gamba or bass viol (which Quincy inaccurately calls "viola de Gamba"), and Johann Christian Bach, eleventh son (eighteenth child) of Johann Sebastian Bach, who at this time was serving the family of George III as music master. During this same six-month period in London, Quincy dined or spent the evening on at least five separate occasions with John Singleton Copley, the American expatriate painter who painted Quincy's portrait.

Although the *Diary* includes entries which explain communications with Mrs. Quincy and give occasional news of the expanding conflict on the American continent, the majority of this six-month record is devoted to what may appear to many to have been an exhausting, almost frenetic attempt to absorb as much culture within as short a time as is humanly possible. Even in the adverse circumstance of not having the comfort of his family, Quincy remained undaunted in his determination to make the best of what must have been an unhappy period. Eventually Quincy was able to secure a position in Antigua as Comptroller of Customs. After having arrived at Antigua in February 1780, however, he soon developed a comfortable law practice, and his position of comptroller fell into relative unimportance. Sometime during or after 1780, Hannah Quincy and the two younger children, Tom and Hannah, joined him in the West Indies, leaving his older son, Samuel, in classes at Harvard. Mrs. Quincy died on 2 November 1782, and, after five years Quincy married a second time, this time to the widow M. A. Chadwell.

Within a month of his death on 9 August 1789, Quincy explained in a letter to his son Samuel his disaffection from the American cause, maintaining that within a republican government rather than a monarchy "people at large feel an overbalance of power in their own favor." As a consequence, continues Quincy, "they will naturally endeavor to ease themselves of all expenses which are not lucrative to them, and retrench the gains of others." This criticism of republican governments has been reiterated often in more recent times. From this commentary, one may well conclude that Quincy was something of an elitist, and his published writings reinforce this interpretation. In his elegy for Edmund Quincy he shows himself sufficiently schooled and well read to produce competent poetry when the occasion demanded, and in his diary, he reveals himself to be an enthusiastic supporter of the arts. Both poem and journal, however, suggest that their author, though attracted to noble causes, was not willing to trade pleasure and comfort for risk of life, limb, or fortune. Even so Quincy's writings are valuable to students of early American literature and aesthetics because of what the poem attests concerning the genre of the elegy and what the diary reveals about the capacity of an American-educated, eighteenth-century gentleman to celebrate the arts.

References:

Clifford K. Shipton, *Biographical Sketches of Those Who Attended Harvard College in the Classes 1751-1755*, volume 13 of *Sibley's Harvard Graduates* (Boston: Massachusetts Historical Society, 1965), pp. 478-488;

James H. Stark, *The Loyalists of Massachusetts* (Boston: Stark, 1910), pp. 364-376.

Papers:

The Massachusetts Historical Society has a collection of letters written by Quincy to his wife and other members of his family from 1758 to 1789.

James Reid
(birth date and death date unknown)

Mark R. Patterson
University of Washington

WORKS: "To My Pen," as Caledoniensis, attributed to Reid, *Virginia Gazette,* 15 September 1768;

"To Caledoniensis from his Pen," attributed to Reid, *Virginia Gazette,* 13 October 1768;

"To my Pen," as Caledoniensis, attributed to Reid, *Virginia Gazette,* 27 October 1768;

"The Lamentation of a Young Lady for the Loss of Her Favourite Bird," as Caledoniensis, attributed to Reid, *Virginia Gazette,* 3 November 1768;

"Epitaph," as Caledoniensis, attributed to Reid, *Virginia Gazette,* 10 November 1768;

"The Sports of Cupid; or, the Fever and Ague of Lovers," as Caledoniensis, attributed to Reid, *Virginia Gazette,* 17 November 1768;

"A Play Upon the words Fire, Ice, Snow," as Caledoniensis, attributed to Reid, *Virginia Gazette,* 17 November 1768;

"A Billet Doux in the Modern Taste," as Caledoniensis, attributed to Reid, *Virginia Gazette,* 1 December 1768;

Essay on Jude, as Caledoniensis, attributed to Reid, *Virginia Gazette,* 15 December 1768;

"Ode on Christmas Day 1768," as Caledoniensis, attributed to Reid, *Virginia Gazette,* 29 December 1768;

Essay on Genesis, as Caledoniensis, attributed to Reid, *Virginia Gazette,* 9 February 1769;

"To Ignorance," as Caledoniensis, attributed to Reid, *Virginia Gazette,* 16 March 1769;

Essay on the Old Testament, as Caledoniensis, attributed to Reid, *Virginia Gazette,* 16 March 1769;

Essay on the misuse of language, as Caledoniensis, attributed to Reid, *Virginia Gazette,* 30 March 1769;

"The Religion of the Bible and Religion of K[ing] W[illiam] County Compared," edited by Richard Beale Davis, *Transactions of the American Philosophical Society,* new series, 57, part 1 (1967): 43-71.

Little is known of James Reid, Virginia poet, essayist, and satirist, save for his activities during the years 1768 and 1769. Undoubtedly born and educated in Scotland, where he was probably an Edinburgh classmate of the Scottish poet Thomas Blacklock, Reid eventually came to write and teach in the literate society of the Tidewater area of Virginia. His writings exhibit a range of reading unusual even for one trained under the Scottish Common Sense thinkers.

The date of Reid's arrival in America is unknown. By September 1768 he appears to have indentured himself to Col. Robert Ruffin, well-known neighbor of the Lees and George Washington in Tidewater Virginia, as a teacher to the Ruffin children. During 1768-1769 Ruffin moved from Dinwiddie to Sweet Hall, and the works signed Caledoniensis and attributed to Reid were first addressed from Mayfield (in the vicinity of Dinwiddie) and then Sweet Hall. Although he never alluded to his particular vocation in his writings, Reid was quick to praise the virtues of pious poverty as he congratulated his own lack of position. This strong Scottish-Presbyterian discipline informs the wit Reid turned against his genial, pleasure-loving neighbors. Yet his Enlightenment upbringing allowed Reid himself to indulge his own fancy in lighter verse.

The serious tone of his later essays and satires is missing in the seven or eight poems addressed from Mayfield and signed Caledoniensis, which appeared in the *Virginia Gazette* from September to December 1768. These light, conventional poems include the witty verse of "To my Pen" and a mock elegy, "The Lamentation of a Young Lady for the Loss of Her Favourite Bird." Following the pattern of other eighteenth-century verses, Reid also wrote a number of amorous poems—including "The Sports of Cupid; or, the Fever and Ague of Lovers" and "A Billet Doux in the Modern Taste"—perhaps designed for a particular young woman. Two final, more solemn poems, "Ode on Christmas Day 1768" and "To Ignorance," are in the more serious tone of Reid's prose works.

In addition to his poems, it is likely that Reid also wrote several essays that appeared in the *Virginia Gazette* in 1768 and 1769, again under the name Caledoniensis. Writing first from Mayfield and then Sweet Hall, Reid exhibits both his erudition and ability to combine the moralizing of his satire with the lighter touch of occasional verse.

On 15 December 1768, he published his first essay, a discussion of Jude, verse 9. Reid handles the question of the fate of Moses by proposing that Moses's body was preserved by being buried in a secret place until Christ's Transfiguration. On 9 February 1769, he contributed a reasonably fashioned argument concerning Genesis 1:26: "Let us make man in our image, after our likeness." Arguing against the deists, Reid explained that God had made man a trinity consisting of spirit, soul, and body. According to Reid, the spirit alone goes to God upon death; the soul remains in Hades until the final judgment. One month later, on 16 March 1769, Reid argued against the view that in the Old Testament there is "not a single text that will prove a future state." The fourth essay published in the *Virginia Gazette* on 30 March is similar in tone and theme to his satire "The Religion of the Bible and the Religion of K[ing] W[illiam] County Compared." Reid takes to task those who misuse language in such slang terms as "hectoring bully" and equates the abuse of language with moral corruption. He concludes that all "are born alike, helpless, naked, poor, ignorant, and weak; and no man deserves the appelation *a Gentleman* until he has done something to merit it." Such moral reasonableness demanded of the true gentleman is the foundation of Reid's ideal society.

The only work bearing Reid's name is the satirical prose piece about the Virginia planters, "The Religion of the Bible and Religion of K[ing] W[illiam] County Compared." Surviving in eighty-four manuscript pages, this work of thirty-four chapters is dated 2 December 1769 but was not published until 1967. Reid displays the range of his erudition throughout, from the French of Fénelon, Voltaire, and Montesquieu to obscure Zoroastrian lore. The work's greatest debt, however, is to eighteenth-century British satire. Its immediate model is Oliver Goldsmith's *The Citizen of the World* (1762), combined with Swiftian satire on the abuse of language.

As in most satires of this period, Reid wishes to emphasize his general moralizing over any particular malice, and he attempts to disarm local criticism by stating in his introduction, "I love Man; but I hate his vices." This conflict between transcendent principles and worldly practice becomes the basis of his entire work. "A man," he continues, "by my rule, must be measured by the greatness or littleness of his Soul, and not of his estate." The greatest vices of the "Ass-queers" (as he called the local esquires) are attendant on their wealth. Reid constantly reminds his readers that wealth is no guarantee of religious piety. He complains that local residents believe if "a King Williamite has Money, Negroes, and Land enough he is a compleat Gentleman." In fact, the satire's main purpose is to show that "Poverty is the school of wisdom." If wealth and human passions destroy man's moral balance, poverty and reason restore it. Among other harmful influences acting on the residents of King William County are the grand jury, worldly enjoyments like dancing, and the confusion of worldly laws and the Bible. In "The Religion of the Bible and Religion of K[ing] W[illiam] County Compared," as in his poems and essays, wit is used to point out the foibles of modern life and to suggest the correct action for the true gentleman.

Reference:

Richard Beale Davis, "James Reid: Colonial Virginia Poet and Moral and Religious Essayist," in his *Literature and Society in Early Virginia (1608-1840)* (Baton Rouge: Louisiana State University Press, 1973), pp. 168-191.

Samuel Seabury
(30 November 1729-25 February 1796)

Arthur Sheps
University of Toronto

BOOKS: *Free Thoughts on the Proceedings of the Continental Congress . . .*, as A. W. Farmer (New York: Printed by James Rivington, 1774; London: Printed for Richardson & Urquhart, 1775);

The Congress Canvassed: Or, an Examination into the Conduct of the Delegates, at Their Grand Convention . . ., as A. W. Farmer (New York: Printed by James Rivington, 1774; London: Printed for Richardson & Urquhart, 1775);

A View of the Controversy between Great-Britain and Her Colonies . . ., as A. W. Farmer (New York: Printed for James Rivington, 1775; London: Printed for Richardson & Urquhart, 1775);

An Alarm to the Legislature of the Province of New-York, Occasioned by the Present Political Disturbances, in North America: Addressed to the Honourable Representatives in General Assembly Convened (New York: Printed for James Rivington, 1775);

A Discourse on Brotherly Love . . . (New York: Printed by Hugh Gaine, 1777);

A Discourse on II Tim. III, 16 . . . (New York: Printed by Hugh Gaine, 1777);

St. Peter's Exhortation to Fear God and Honor the King, Explained and Inculcated: In a Discourse Addressed to His Majesty's Provincial Troops . . . (New York: Printed by H. Gaine, 1777);

A Sermon, Preached Before the Grand Lodge, and the Other Lodges of Ancient Free-masons in New-York . . . (New York: Printed by Robertson, Mills & Hicks, 1783);

Bishop Seabury's Second Charge, to the Clergy of His Diocese . . . (New Haven: Printed by Thomas & Samuel Green, 1786);

A Sermon Delivered Before the Boston Episcopal Charitable Society . . . (Boston: Printed by Thomas & John Fleet, 1788);

The Duty of Considering Our Ways . . . (New Haven: Printed by T. & S. Green, 1789);

An Earnest Persuasive to Frequent Communion . . . (New Haven: Printed by Thomas & Samuel Green, 1789);

An Address to the Ministers and Congregations of the Presbyterian and Independent Persuasions in the United States of America (New Haven: Printed by T. & S. Green, 1790);

A Discourse Delivered in St. John's Church in Portsmouth Newhampshire . . . (Boston: Printed by Isaiah Thomas & Ebenezer T. Andrews for J. Osbourne, 1791);

A Discourse Delivered before the Triennial Convention of the Protestant Episcopal Church in the United States of America . . . (New York: Printed by Hugh Gaine, 1792);

A Discourse Delivered before an Assembly of Free and Accepted Masons . . . (Norwich: Printed by John Trumbull for John Sperry, 1795);

A Discourse Delivered in St. James' Church, in New-London . . . (New London: Printed by Samuel Green, 1795).

Portrait of Samuel Seabury by Thomas Spence Duché, Jr. (Trinity College, Hartford)

Collections: *Discourses on Several Subjects*, 2 volumes

(New York: Printed by T. & J. Swords for J. Rivington, 1793);

Discourses on Several Important Subjects . . . (New York: Printed & sold by T. & J. Swords, 1798);

Letters of a Westchester Farmer, edited by Clarence H. Vance (White Plains: Westchester County Historical Society, 1930).

OTHER: *The Communion-Office, or Order for the Administration of the Holy Eucharist or Supper of the Lord. With Private Devotions . . .* , edited by Seabury (New London: Printed by T. Green, 1786).

Samuel Seabury, colonial Anglican clergyman and first bishop of the Protestant Episcopal church of the United States, was the leading propagandist for the Loyalist cause during the American Revolution. His four tracts published in the winter of 1774-1775, usually known as *Letters of a Westchester Farmer,* were among the best pieces of controversial writing produced by either side of the Revolutionary struggle. Seabury also wrote on behalf of the Anglican interest in a number of colonial controversies before the Revolution. During the War of Independence he helped to organize the Loyalist emigration from New York. However, Seabury remained in the United States, where, as bishop of Connecticut, he promoted high-church principles among Episcopalians by his sermons, writings, and activity.

Seabury was born in Groton, Connecticut, to the Reverend Samuel Seabury, minister to the Congregational church in North Groton, and Abigail Mumford Seabury. A few months after Seabury's birth his father left his ministry, received Anglican ordination, and served as a missionary for the Society for the Propagation of the Gospel, first in New London, Connecticut, and then in Hempstead, Long Island. Seabury, himself, graduated from Yale College with a B.A. in 1748 and was a lay reader for the S.P.G. in Huntington, Long Island, for four years, during which time he also studied and practiced medicine. He then studied medicine at Edinburgh in 1752-1753 and was ordained by the bishop of London at the end of 1753. Seabury returned to America in 1754 as an S.P.G. missionary, serving first at New Brunswick, New Jersey. In the January following his 12 October 1756 marriage to Mary Hicks, he was assigned to Jamaica, Long Island. Later he was given a rectorship at Westchester, New York, and served there from 1767 until the revolutionary war.

Not long after his return from England, Seabury became embroiled in ecclesiastical and political controversy. In New York the Anglican clergy and their opponents from among the other churches quarrelled over two issues during this period: the Anglican funding and control of the proposed King's College (later Columbia University), and the Anglican campaign for a resident American bishop. In 1755 Seabury probably wrote some of the articles in the local papers for the Anglican side of the debate over the college. The second issue, the longstanding question of an American bishop, erupted in the New York press with the publication of Thomas Bradbury Chandler's *Appeal to the Public* (1767) which took a high-church and dogmatic line in calling for an American Anglican bishop. The Presbyterians and independents answered with a series of articles signed The American Whig, and Seabury joined Chandler, Charles Inglis, and perhaps others in a series of rejoinders published in the *New-York Gazette and Weekly Mercury* and signed A Whip for the American Whig. The "Whig" and "Whip" articles appeared in 1767 and 1768 during the aftermath of the Stamp Act. The debate generated public interest throughout America.

Seabury's contributions were witty, but they also revealed a personal sensitivity to insult. Denying Presbyterian accusations that an American bishop would threaten dissenters' liberties, the "Whip" argued that Anglicans were simply trying to satisfy their own ecclesiastical needs and that other groups need not be concerned. However, as secretary of the New York clergy convention in 1766-1767 Seabury prepared its petitions to the S.P.G. and the English hierarchy, and in these he argued that a colonial bishop would be helpful in inculcating the principles of submission in both Church and State, which recent events, including the Stamp Act crisis, showed were under threat. In the context of ecclesiastical struggles Seabury was already formulating the concerns of the Tory mind and the nexus of a Loyalist party before the issue of Loyalism had become acute.

Seabury had nothing further published until after the meeting of the first Continental Congress. But he was personally active in rallying would-be Loyalist opinion throughout New York, and in many places he was able to prevent the election of delegates to Congress or the organization of committees acting under the Congress's authority. Then, in rapid succession from November 1774 to January 1775 he produced the four pamphlets now known as *Letters of a Westchester Farmer*. The first three were signed A. W. Farmer; the fourth was unsigned. Earthy, witty, and biting, they were much feared by the patriots, who seized and burned or tarred and feathered copies in an attempt to stop their distribution. Although the letters do not seem to have enjoyed popularity in New England, they were widely circulated in the middle colonies, and copies were found as far south as Virginia. They were also published in England.

Like most Loyalists, the Westchester Farmer admitted that the colonists had real grievances and that reform of the imperial constitution was necessary. However, he disputed the authority of Congress and the legitimacy of its means of resistance, both of which, he thought, tended toward republicanism and independence for America. Seabury had already detected and feared the same tendency at the time of the Stamp Act. In the ecclesiastical struggles of the 1750s and 1760s he had revealed himself to be a principled Tory already, but the Westchester Farmer's tracts are chiefly pragmatic appeals to the interests of the colonists.

In *Free Thoughts on the Proceedings of the Continental Congress* (1774) Seabury, speaking in the voice of a New York farmer, addressed himself to his fellows. Showing his familiarity with rural idiom and concerns, he appealed to the antiurban prejudices of his readers. Congress, he argued, represented only the grasping merchants who would benefit at the expense of the farmers. The nonimportation, nonexportation, nonconsumption association advocated by Congress should be rejected. Parliament would not be intimidated by such measures, and the result would be more goods to purchase and the loss of markets for rural produce which would never be regained. Thus Seabury argued that the farmers should refuse to be slaves to Congress's tyrannical inspection committees, asserting that they should go about their business as usual and protect their liberties, which were more threatened by Congress than by King or Parliament. He himself would resist the committeemen with a "hiccory cudgel" if necessary, for the proper course for the redress of America's grievances was not Congress's measures but petition and remonstrance only by duly constituted bodies such as the provincial assembly.

In his next pamphlet, *The Congress Canvassed* (1774), Seabury, still employing the voice of a suspicious farmer, tried to appeal to the interests of the merchants of New York City. He complained that the merchants had illegitimately empowered the city's delegates to Congress to speak for the entire province. Congress in any event had no constitutional authority and hence no power to enforce the association, but the merchants, like the farmers,

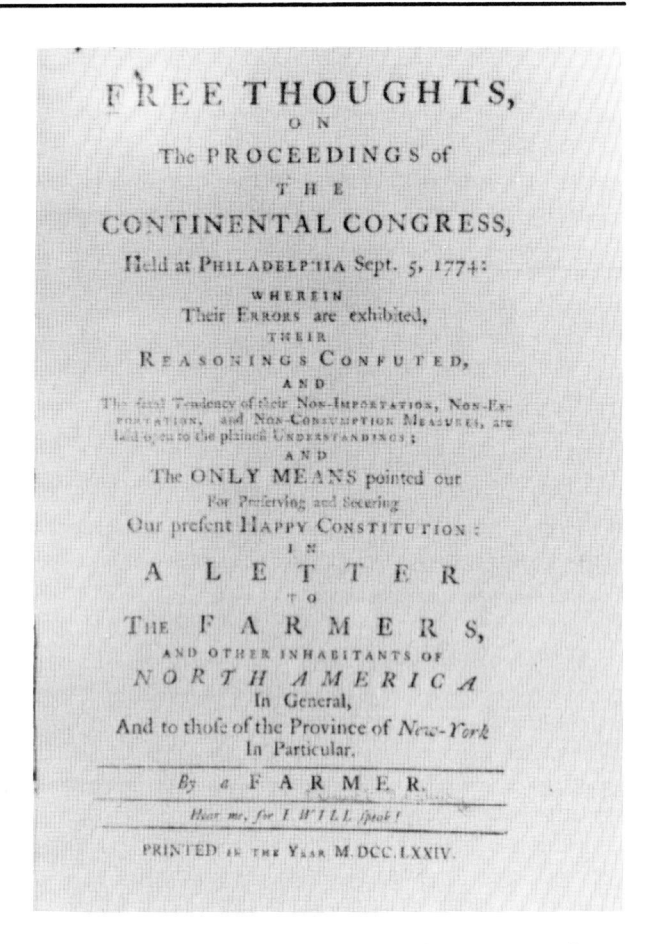

Title page for the first of Seabury's "Westchester Farmer" letters, which presented a Loyalist's perspective on the activities of the Continental Congresses

would also lose control of their own property. Assent to Congressional authority would lead to a grand American Republic in which the interests of New York merchants would be subordinated to those of New England. This pamphlet had little effect on city opinion but the earlier *Free Thoughts* was influential in the countryside where enforcement of the Association was difficult.

The Westchester Farmer's next publication was a reply to the nineteen-year-old Alexander Hamilton's *A Full Vindication of the Measures of Congress* (1774). Seabury's response, *A View of the Controversy between Great-Britain and Her Colonies* (1775), was constrained by the need to answer Hamilton and was not as free ranging or pithy as the earlier works. There is some specific refutation of Hamilton's errors and consideration of the practical dangers and consequences of Congress's actions, but *A View of the Controversy between Great-Britain and Her Colonies* also contains a serious discussion of political and constitutional theory. While Seabury conceded that constitutional reform, including recognition of colonial control over taxation, was necessary, he asserted that the supreme authority of King and Parliament must be acknowledged. Seabury rejected the association or a union of the colonies and took an explicitly Tory view of the need to act through existing and traditional institutions such as colonial assemblies and petitions to Parliament.

The last pamphlet, not signed A. W. Farmer, was addressed to the members of the New York Assembly. *An Alarm to the Legislature of the Province of New-York* asked the assemblymen to seize the initiative and petition Parliament rather than allow the delegates to Congress, who represented only the interests of New York City, to usurp their authority. To adopt the measures of Congress would only lead to rebellion and civil war. Led by its Loyalist members, the Assembly, just as Seabury advised, ignored Congress and petitioned King and Parliament directly.

Seabury was active for the Loyalist cause on several fronts. He personally lobbied assemblymen, organized the largest protest meeting of Loyalists (at White Plains in April 1775) and refused to open his church on Congress-appointed fast days. He was arrested in November 1775 but since his authorship of *Letters of a Westchester Farmer* could not be proved he was released after one month. He returned briefly to Westchester, where he insisted on continuing with the prayers for the Royal family, and the next year he acted as a guide for the British army behind the lines on Long Island. Finally, in November 1776, he sought refuge in New York City, which the British had taken in September. He spent the rest of the war there as physician, chaplain, and champion of the Loyalist cause.

In a published sermon of 1777, *St. Peter's Exhortation to Fear God and Honor the King*, Seabury explicated for the benefit of the British troops the Tory notion that rulers must be obeyed in all things. He was also almost certainly the author of most of the "Brittanicus" essays which appeared in the New York *Royal Gazette* from December 1778 to April 1779. These essays, reminiscent of the tone of the Westchester Farmer, were practical attacks on the French alliance and exposés of the military and financial weakness of Congress. At the same time Seabury prepared a new set of proposals for an episcopal establishment in America. Again he argued that a firm establishment of the Church of England in the colonies would promote political loyalty: submission and orthodoxy in Church and State were intimately connected. Seabury made this same point in his 1783 proposals to the archbishop of York on behalf of a Nova Scotia bishopric, and in his various sets of unpublished proposals for colonial bishops (1767-1783), he revealed a doctrinaire Toryism which was not as evident in the *Letters of a Westchester Farmer*.

Seabury superintended the Loyalist emigration from New York and was about to join it when in 1783 the Anglican clergy of Connecticut elected him as their bishop. The English bishops refused to consecrate him, partly out of political motives, so he received consecration from the nonjuring bishops of the Scottish Episcopal church in Aberdeen in November 1784. He returned to New London, Connecticut, his father's old parish, where he remained until his death in 1796.

Under Seabury the Episcopal church in New England appealed strongly to the Loyalists who had remained in the United States. It was a means of insulating themselves from republican life since that Church had not, like the Congregationalist churches, embodied and advanced the cause of the Revolution. Seabury had originally hoped for a strong relationship between Church and State in defense of the traditional social, political, and religious order. But in the circumstances of republican America Seabury followed the nonjuring Scottish Episcopalians in preferring a more purely spiritual, less Erastian, conception of the church. At the same time he took a high-church line in defending clerical and episcopal authority and in interpreting the liturgy.

The Episcopalians in the states to the south of Connecticut desired a church more cleary sympathetic to republicanism and regarded Seabury's high-church, nonjuring ecclesiastical and liturgical doctrines as evidence of his persistent Toryism. Quarrels between Seabury and the southern Episcopalians prevented a general union of Episcopal churches and agreement on a common prayer book until 1789.

Collections of Seabury's sermons were published in 1793 and, posthumously, in 1798. Their style is crisp and lucid, like that of the Westchester Farmer, but they are drier, more learned and more repetitious. The sermons cover all aspects of the Christian life and emphasize the practices of the primitive catholic church. They are chiefly remarkable for their defence of clerical and episcopal authority and their elaborate eucharistic doctrines. *Discourses on Several Subjects* was republished in 1815 and was in wide circulation among clergy and lay readers in the early nineteenth century. Seabury's high-church doctrines were also promoted by his publication and use of the Scottish Episcopal communion office in 1786 and by his reprinting of Bishop George Innes of Brechin's catechism in 1791. Seabury's communion office, slightly amended, was incorporated into the prayer book of the Protestant Episcopal church, and portions of the Innes catechism were included in Bishop John Henry Hobart's enlarged catechism of 1827.

As a writer Seabury was adept at changing his style to suit his readers. Only Thomas Paine could match him as a polemicist during the Revolution. Seabury was among the earliest to define a Loyalist interest and argument, but after 1783 he wrote only on religious subjects, and here he made a lasting contribution to his church.

References:

W. H. Nelson, *The American Tory* (Oxford: Clarendon Press, 1961);

Bruce E. Steiner, *Samuel Seabury 1729-1796, A Study in the High Church Tradition* (Oberlin: Ohio University Press, 1971).

Papers:

The Samuel Seabury Papers in the General Theological Seminary, New York, contain correspondence, drafts of various proposals, and liturgical notes.

Michael Smith
(1698-circa 1771)

M. Jimmie Killingsworth
New Mexico Institute of Mining and Technology

BOOKS: *A Sermon, Preached in Christ-Church, in Newburn, In North-Carolina . . .* (Newbern: Printed by James Davis, 1756);

Twelve Sermons, Preached upon Several Occasions (London: Sold by H. Turpin, 1770);

Christianity Unmasqued; or, Unavoidable Ignorance Preferable to Corrupt Christianity. A Poem. In Twenty-one Cantos (London: H. Turpin, 1771).

An important exemplar of Anglican preaching in the Carolinas and a skillful and versatile poet, Michael Smith was born in 1698 in County Meath, Ireland, the son of Rev. Robert Smith. Educated at Trinity College, Dublin, he was ordained by the Bishop of London in 1747 and served five years as curate at Hertfordshire. As an Anglican missionary, he brought his family to Prince Frederick's Parish, South Carolina, in 1752. A short time later, his wife and three of his eight children died, after which Smith's behavior became erratic. His parishioners wrote a letter to the Society for the Propagation of the Gospel accusing him of gaming, drinking, philandering, and neglecting his parish duties.

Smith had traveled frequently while still officially a missionary to South Carolina, and in 1756 James Davis, North Carolina's first printer, published Smith's first book, *A Sermon, Preached in Christ-Church, in Newburn, In North-Carolina . . .*, an unassuming discourse in the plain style and on the theme of brotherly love, which is the only published example of Anglican preaching from colonial North Carolina. Seventeen fifty-six was also the year that his angry parishioners in South Carolina closed the doors of the church to him. He moved north, secured his reputation, and even preached before the governor and assembly of North Carolina. The S.P.G. nevertheless responded to the complaints from South Carolina and removed him from his mission in 1759. By 1762 Smith had become chaplain on a British warship, a post he probably gained soon after his dismissal, for in the *South Carolina Gazette* of 26 April-3 May 1760, there had appeared "On the Reduction of Guadalope," Smith's 165-line poem in heroic couplets extolling the glory of William Pitt, first earl of Chatham, and the British military. The poem's diction and meter are admirable, and it probably gained the attention of state dignitaries.

By 1770 the poet-preacher, who had returned to England to become vicar of South Mimms in Hertfordshire, had found a patron in the Earl of Hillsborough. *Twelve Sermons . . .*, dedicated to

Hillsborough and based on what Smith called "Plain Christianity and sound Morality," is a collection of discourses intended for a colonial audience. In the sermons Smith avoids difficult and controversial topics, and with his plain style and unemotional approach, he concentrates on elementary ethical and theological doctrines.

Smith's most interesting and significant literary work is the book-length verse essay, *Christianity Unmasqued* . . . (1771). It is also the last published work of a man who died in obscure circumstances. The dedicatory preface to Hillsborough is of historical interest because in it Smith offers his analysis of the failure of the Anglican mission in America. The calm rationality of this prose preface (Smith fails to comment on his personal difficulties in the Colonies) contrasts sharply with the bitter satire, rasping wit, and occasionally sardonic humor of the first half of the poem. In Hudibrastic (or Swiftian) octosyllabic couplets Smith lashes out at Catholicism and "the enthusiastical sects." In the second half of the poem, Smith's calm tone and measured reason return as he confronts Deism and other enemies of the Church of England. His patriotism and loyalty to Anglicanism never flagged. Though *Christianity Unmasqued* has been relatively neglected by literary scholars, it establishes Michael Smith as one of the most notable poets to emerge from the Southern colonial experience.

References:

Hennig Cohen, *The South Carolina Gazette 1732-1775* (Columbia: University of South Carolina Press, 1953), p. 190;

Richard Beale Davis, *Intellectual Life in the Colonial South, 1585-1763* (Knoxville: University of Tennessee Press, 1978), pp. 604, 754-755, 1491;

M. J. Killingsworth, "The Reverend Michael Smith's Contribution to Colonial Literary History," *Historical Magazine of the Protestant Episcopal Church*, 50 (December 1981): 369-376;

David T. Morgan, Jr., "Scandal in Carolina: The Story of a Capricious Missionary," *North Carolina Historical Review*, 47 (July 1970): 233-243.

William Smith
(27 April 1727-14 May 1803)

William D. Andrews
Philadelphia College of Textiles & Science

SELECTED BOOKS: *Some Thoughts on Education: With Reasons for Erecting a College in This Province, and Fixing the Same at the City of New York* . . . (New York: Printed by J. Parker, 1752);

A General Idea of the College of Mirania: With a Sketch of the Method of Teaching Science and Religion, in Several Classes . . . (New York: Printed by J. Parker & W. Weyman, 1753);

A Poem on Visiting the Academy of Philadelphia, June 1753 . . . (Philadelphia: Printed by Franklin & Hall, 1753);

Personal Affliction and Frequent Reflection upon Human Life, of Great Use to Lead Man to the Remembrance of God. A Sermon, Preach'd on Sunday Sept 1, 1754, in Christ-Church, Philadelphia; Occasioned by the Death of a Beloved Pupil . . . (Philadelphia: Printed & sold by B. Franklin & D. Hall, 1754);

A Brief State of the Province of Pennsylvania, in Which the Conduct of Their Assemblies for Several Years Past is Impartially Examined, and the True Cause of the Continual Encroachments of the French Displayed . . . (London: Printed for R. Griffiths, 1755);

A Sermon Preached in Christ-Church, Philadelphia; Before the Provincial Grand Master, and General Communion of Free and Accepted Masons . . . (Philadelphia: Printed & sold by B. Franklin & D. Hall, 1755; London: Printed for R. Griffiths, 1755);

A Brief View of the Conduct of Pennsylvania, for the Year 1755; So Far as It Affected the General Service of the British Colonies, Particularly the Expedition under the Late General Braddock . . . (London: Printed for R. Griffiths & sold by Mr. Bradford in Philadelphia, 1756);

The Rev. Mr. Smith, Vindicated from the Charge of Perjury (Philadelphia: Printed by William Bradford?, 1756);

A Christian Soldier's Duty; the Lawfulness and Dignity of His Office; and the Importance of the Protestant Cause in the British Colonies. A Sermon, Preached April 5, 1757 . . . (Philadelphia: Printed & sold by J. Chattin, 1757);

A Charge, Delivered May 17, 1757, at the First Anniversary Commencement in the College and Academy of Philadelphia . . . (Philadelphia: Printed by B. Franklin & D. Hall, 1757);

Discourses on Several Public Occasions during the War in America . . . (London: Printed for A. Millar, 1759); enlarged as *Discourses on Public Occasions in America* (London: Printed for A. Millar, 1762);

A Discourse Concerning the Conversion of the Heathen Americans, and the Final Propagation of Christianity and the Sciences to the Ends of the Earth . . . (Philadelphia: Printed by W. Dunlap, 1760; London: Printed for the author, 1762);

The Great Duty of Public Worship and of Erecting and Setting Apart Proper Places for that Purpose . . . (Philadelphia: Printed by W. Dunlap, 1761);

The Last Summons. A Sermon Preached in Christ-Church, Philadelphia on Sunday, January 10, 1762. At the Funeral of the Rev. Robert Jenney . . . (Philadelphia: Printed & sold by A. Steuart, 1762);

An Humble Representation, by William Smith, D.D. and James Jay, M.D. in Behalf of the Lately Erected Colleges of New York and Philadelphia (London, 1762);

Additional Discourses and Essays. Being a Supplement to the First Edition of Discourses on Several Public Occasions during the War in America . . . (London: Printed for A. Millar & R. Griffiths and for G. Keith, 1762);

An Answer to Mr. Franklin's Remarks, On A Late Protest (Philadelphia: Printed & sold by W. Bradford, 1764);

An Historical Account of the Expedition against the Ohio Indians in the Year 1764. Under the Command of Henry Bouquet . . . (Philadelphia: Printed & sold by W. Bradford, 1765; London: Printed for T. Jefferies, 1766);

Some Account of the Charitable Corporation Lately Erected for the Relief of the Widows and Children of Clergymen, in the Communion of the Church of England in America . . . (Philadelphia: Printed by D. Hall & W. Sellers, 1769);

An Oration, Delivered, January 22, 1773, Before the

William Smith, circa 1757; etching by John Sartain, after a portrait by Benjamin West

Patron, Vice-Presidents and Members of the American Philosophical Society . . . (Philadelphia: Printed by John Dunlap, 1773);

An Examination of the Connecticut Claim to Lands in Pennsylvania . . . (Philadelphia: Printed by Joseph Crukshank, 1774);

A Sermon on the Present Situation of American Affairs. Preached in Christ-Church, June 23, 1775 . . . (Philadelphia: Printed & sold by James Humphreys, Jr., 1775; London: Printed for E. & C. Dilly, 1775);

An Oration in Memory of General Montgomery, and of the Officers and Soldiers, Who Fell With Him, December 31, 1775, before Quebec . . . (Philadelphia: Printed by John Dunlap, 1776; London: Printed for J. Almon, 1776);

Plain Truth; Addressed to the Inhabitants of America, Containing Remarks on a Late Pamphlet, Entitled Common Sense . . ., attributed to Smith, as Candidus (Philadelphia: Printed & sold by R. Bell, 1776); enlarged with *Additions to Plain Truth*, attributed to Smith (Philadelphia: Printed & sold by R. Bell, 1776);

A Sermon Preached in Christ-Church, Philadelphia, for

the Benefit of the Poor . . . (Philadelphia: Printed by J. Dunlap, 1779);

An Account of Washington College, in the State of Maryland . . . (Philadelphia: Printed & sold by Joseph Crukshank, 1784);

Oratio Salutatoria, suffr. ampliss. facult. philos. praesido irro celeber Domino Gulielmo Smith, habita in alma Acad. Wash. die decimo quarto Maii, A.D. 1783 (Wilmington: Adams, 1785);

A Sermon Preached in Christ-Church, Philadelphia, on Friday, October 7th, 1785, before the General Convention of the Protestant Episcopal Church, in the States of New-York, New-Jersey, Pennsylvania, Delaware, Maryland, Virginia, and South-Carolina. On occasion of the First Introduction of the Liturgy and Public Service . . . (Philadelphia: Printed & sold by Robert Aitken, 1785);

A Masonic Oration, December 27, 1787, at Northumberland (Philadelphia, 1788);

An Address to the General Assembly of Pennsylvania, In the Case of the Violated Charter, of the College, Academy and Charitable School . . . (Philadelphia: Printed by R. Aitken & son, 1788);

Two Sermons, Delivered in Christ Church, Philadelphia, Before the General Convention of the Protestant Episcopal Church of the States of New York, New Jersey, Pennsylvania, Delaware, Maryland, Virginia, and South Carolina . . . (Philadelphia: Printed by Dobson & Lang, 1789);

A Sermon on Temporal and Spiritual Salvation: Delivered in Christ-Church, Philadelphia, Before the Pennsylvania Society of the Cincinnati (Philadelphia: From the press of T. Dobson, 1790);

Eulogium on Benjamin Franklin, L.L.D. . . . Delivered March 1, 1791 . . . (Philadelphia: Printed by Benjamin Franklin Bache, 1792; London: Printed for T. Cadell, 1792);

A Funeral Address, Delivered in the German Lutheran Church, Lancaster; At the Public Interment of Major-General Mifflin, January 22, 1800 (Lancaster: Printed by W. & R. Dickson, 1800).

Collection: *The Works of William Smith . . .* , 2 volumes (Philadelphia: Published by Hugh Maxwell & William Fry, 1803).

OTHER: *Some Account of the North American Indians; Their Genius, Characters, Customs, and Dispositions, Towards the French and English Nations . . .* , edited by Smith (London: Printed for R. Griffiths, 1754).

William Smith reaped the ambiguous reward of the person who straddles two cultures. Loyal to the literary and political traditions of his native British Isles and a dedicated Anglican, Smith was responsive to the opportunities and challenges of the New World. He wished to establish in the colonies a base of learning and letters that both drew on the British heritage and tapped the resources, energies, and talents of the new land. His efforts appear in retrospect to have been doomed to failure, and there is ample evidence that he never achieved all he intended. Yet even his partial successes are important and deserve both understanding and credit as they reflect the efforts to create a native literary tradition in early America.

Churchman, educator, poet, and promoter of the arts, Smith was an active—and frequently quarrelsome—man, sometimes called by historians a "minor Franklin" in recognition of his wide-ranging interests and prolific schemes. Born in Aberdeen, Scotland, to Thomas and Elizabeth Duncan Smith, he attended the University of Aberdeen from 1743 to 1747 but apparently left without taking a degree. He served as a schoolmaster in rural Scotland until 1751, when his work with the Anglican missionary group, the Society for the Propagation of the Gospel, led him to immigrate to New York to seek a position as a tutor for a Long Island family.

In 1752, Smith published anonymously *Some Thoughts on Education,* his contribution to the pamphlet warfare raging in New York over the establishment of a college. The need for a local institution to serve the needs of the growing population otherwise forced to send their sons north to Harvard or Yale or south to the College of William and Mary was widely felt; but the precise terms for establishing the new college became the subject of political and religious debate between Anglicans and the large Dutch contingent in New York. Both wished to control the school. A compromise was finally reached whereby King's College (now Columbia University) was established in 1754 under Anglican control, but with a provision that the Dutch appoint a professor of theology to represent their Calvinist Reformed principles.

Smith's contribution to the public debate is of considerable interest as an adumbration of a major, lifelong theme in Smith's thinking and writing: the idea of the *translatio studii,* or inevitable westward movement of the muses of civilization, which is often referred to as the theme of "the rising glory of America." This idea found its way into prose and verse throughout the colonies in the eighteenth century, animated the work of the Connecticut Wits at the turn of the century, and must be considered a contributing factor to both literary and political nationalism. To predict, as this idea did, that America, because of its geographic location, would necessarily fall heir to the culture of Europe implied both America's rising glory and Europe's—and especially England's—decline. This concept was troublesome for an Anglophile like Smith and remained a source of intellectual and artistic tension in other expressions of the theme throughout the eighteenth century. Smith faced the dilemma squarely in *Some Thoughts on Education:* "I'm far from thinking it will ever be our Interest, or in our Power, to be independent of *Britain,* while she is able to maintain her own Independency: but should she ever fall into the Way of other Nations, it is not to be supposed that we . . . would contentedly suffer ourselves to be laid in the same Grave with her. . . ." It was in England's best interests, Smith argued, that America be ready to serve as "an Asylum to the noble Gleanings of [England's] brave Sons."

Accompanying the prose polemics of the work is a long poem, "Copy of Verses, Addressed to the Gentlemen of the House of Representatives." This poem, conventional in form and style, is notable chiefly for its core image of the rising glory of America and for Smith's successful sustaining of that theme in polished verse. The piece begins with a versified statement of the rising-glory idea discussed in the prose address: England must decline; the muses of civilization must move west as they always have; and America must therefore be prepared to accept them and create in the New World the last, best outpost of culture. It is, in Smith's rendering, the responsibility of the New York legislature to prepare the ground by planning for a college, a task upon which depends

> No less, perhaps, than whether our *New-World*
> When by the sad Vicissitude of Things
> The *Old* has sunk back to its pristin Sloth
> And *Barbarism* shall be the last Retreat
> Of *Arts,* imperial *Liberty* and *Truth.*

The legislature is thus seen as having the chance to remain loyal to the mother country at the very time it is creating a college in America to receive the remains of culture as they flee England. Smith was quite adept at this sort of rhetorical cleverness. In Smith's vision, repeatedly shaped in physiological and other natural metaphors in "Copy of Verses," the muses of culture will abandon England:

> *Empire* and *Liberty* their radiant Wings
> Expand to quit the sluggish *eastern* World;
> And cross the vast *Atlantic* mediate
> Their Airy Passage to these western Climes,

> In Quest of some Retreat to sojourn safe
> Till Time shall end;—then may we fondly wait
> To hail the glorious Guests on their Approach
> To this *New World;* and woo them first to fix
> Their Reign with us; until again (when we
> Diseas'd and sunk, are ripe for Death) they're call'd
> By Fate to bless a Race of more Desert.

Some Thoughts on Education and its accompanying poem hardly represent great art. Though the verse is solid and controlled, it fails to achieve the strength of conception, reflected through metaphor and form, that would advance it into the higher category of art. Like all of Smith's writing, *Some Thoughts* and "Copy of Verses" are conventional, polished, idea centered, and polemical.

The effects of the work on the parochial debate over higher education in New York are not known, but Smith turned his pen toward education again in 1753, when he published *A General Idea of the College of Mirania.* This work advanced a scheme for the practical education of American youth that Smith patched together from several sources. Unoriginal as it was, Smith cleverly brought it to the attention of Benjamin Franklin, who was then developing a curriculum for the newly founded Academy of Philadelphia. Franklin's intention, described in his *Proposals Relating to the Education of Youth in Pensilvania* (1749), was to create a school offering sound, vocationally oriented education to the sons of Philadelphia merchants and professionals, to whom the classical curriculum of most English and colonial institutions appeared impractical. Franklin was sufficiently impressed by Smith's ideas to invite him to Philadelphia and to offer him, in 1754, the position as provost of the school, which by then was known as the Academy and College of Philadelphia.

For the rest of the decade of the 1750s Smith actively promoted the interests of the new school—and, simultaneously, those of William Smith. The provost envisioned the school as a nursery for the arts and sciences in the New World, and he used his position to advance that cause as well as his own reputation and fortune. He was a close and supportive mentor to the students, especially to a group of would-be writers who styled themselves the "Swains of the Schuylkill": Nathaniel Evans, Thomas Godfrey, and Jacob Duché. He was also instrumental in launching the career of Benjamin West, the native son who ultimately achieved considerable fame in England as a painter and as president of the Royal Academy. As a patron of young writers and artists, Smith always served dual inter-

The Academy and College of Philadelphia

ests: his own as well as those of nascent American culture. In 1757 he established the *American Magazine and Monthly Chronicle of the British Colonies,* published by William Bradford. Although the journal survived only a year (into 1758), it was a useful outlet for the writings of his young protégés and of Smith himself.

Political as well as literary activities occupied him through the 1750s, and Smith's inability to resist a quarrel or pass up a chance to pursue personal fame and power embroiled him in numerous battles. Typical of his personality and his activities during these years was a series of incidents that culminated in his spending four months in jail. In 1757 he supported William Moore, his father-in-law and powerful judge and politician in Chester County, in his running battle with the Pennsylvania assembly. Smith had long been in conflict with the prevailing powers in the assembly, including Franklin, and favored the exclusion of Germans from it, a bold position in a colony with large German settlements. Moore's quarrel with the assembly, which had tried to strip him of his judgeship, gave Smith a chance to rejoin the fray. He assisted Moore in publishing an attack on the assembly in a local newspaper, and as a consequence both Moore and Smith were convicted by the assembly for libel.

Smith spent the months of January through April of 1758 in jail. He conducted college business from his cell and continued to pursue the many land schemes that led to his acquiring extensive tracts of real estate in the Philadelphia area and in central and western Pennsylvania.

When the assembly tried to serve a warrant that would put him back in jail, Smith resolved to go to England to vindicate himself with the proprietary authorities, the Penn family, among whom he had friends. While there in 1758 he also sought contributions for the college and traveled to various universities to promote the provincial institution. During the trip he received honorary degrees from Oxford and the University of Aberdeen.

In the midst of such strife, he continued to develop in his sermons and writing an image of American destiny consistent with his public activities on behalf of education and with its view of the inevitable westward course of civilization. Most of his writing in this vein came in response to the Seven Years War—or French and Indian War, as it was known in the colonies, where the fighting was especially intense. As an Anglican minister, Smith used his pulpit to advance Britain's cause and simultaneously to explore and refine his vision of America's rising glory. Particularly in two

A
DISCOURSE
Concerning the CONVERSION
OF THE
HEATHEN AMERICANS,
AND
The final Propagation of CHRISTIANITY and
the SCIENCES to the Ends of the Earth.

IN TWO PARTS.

PART I. Preached before a voluntary CONVENTION of the EPISCOPAL Clergy of Pennsylvania, and Places adjacent, at Philadelphia, May 2d, 1760; and publifhed at their joint Requeft.

PART II. Preached before the Truftees, Mafters and Scholars of the College and Academy of Philadelphia, at the firft anniverfary Commencement.

By WILLIAM SMITH, D. D.
Provoft of the faid College and Academy.

PHILADELPHIA; Printed by W. DUNLAP,
MDCCLX.

Title page for one of the works in which Smith expressed his convictions about the rising glory of America (courtesy of the John Carter Brown Library at Brown University)

sermons—*An Earnest Exhortation to Religion, Brotherly Love, and Public Spirit* (1755) and *A Christian Soldier's Duty* (1757)—Smith further enlarged and embellished the image of future greatness to be expected in the colonies. In *A Christian Soldier's Duty* he exhorted his audience: "Look round you! behold a country, vast in extent, merciful in its climate, exuberant in its soil, the seat of Plenty, the garden of the Lord! behold it given to us and to our posterity, to propagate Virtue, to cultivate useful Arts, and to spread abroad the pure *evangelical* Religion of Jesus! behold Colonies founded in it! *Protestant* Colonies! *free* Colonies! *British* Colonies! behold them nourishing their Liberty; flourishing in Commerce; the Arts and Sciences planted in them; the GOSPEL *preached*! and in short the seeds of happiness and glory firmly rooted, and growing up among them!"

Many of Smith's themes of relating to the rising glory of America came together in an explicitly religious context in *A Discourse Concerning the Conversion of the Heathen Americans, and the Final Propagation of Christianity and the Sciences to the Ends of the Earth,* published in 1760. Although the themes reappear sporadically throughout his published work and his correspondence thereafter, this discourse marks the last full treatment of the idea in Smith's writing.

Smith traveled to England again in 1762 to seek funds for the college and to further his schemes to support Church of England missionary work among the Indians in New York and Pennsylvania. In 1765 he published *An Historical Account of the Expedition against the Ohio Indians* in which he described Col. Henry Bouquet's successful efforts to subdue hostile Indians, allied with the French, in western Pennsylvania and Ohio. His large land holdings in western Pennsylvania gave Smith a personal stake in the development of the area and the establishment of British power there. This interest is further reflected in his *Examination of the Connecticut Claim to Lands in Pennsylvania* (1774), which attempted to refute that colony's rights to land in Pennsylvania's Wyoming Valley, where not coincidentally Smith also held large tracts.

The events leading to the Revolution caused Smith and many other colonists personal anguish; loyal to the traditions of Britain, he had a large material and emotional stake in the advancement of the colonies that appeared threatened by political and economic policies being pursued in London. In *A Sermon on the Present Situation of American Affairs* (1775), preached to Pennsylvania militiamen in Christ Church, Philadelphia, in 1775, Smith praised America and its prospects in terms reminiscent of his earlier verse and sermon statements on rising glory, yet he stopped short of endorsing separation. His *Oration in Memory of General Montgomery,* published in 1776 at the request of the Continental Congress, expressed his support for the American cause, but his frequently voiced preference for moderation and caution and his known leanings toward British culture made Smith appear lukewarm and kept him from being fully accepted as a supporter of the American cause. In a city where rebel sentiment was strong, Smith was a suspect figure.

Even though he finally proclaimed himself in favor of independence, Smith lost his position at the College of Philadelphia in 1779. He obtained a

Portrait of William Smith by Gilbert Stuart

parish in Maryland and served for a decade as president of the newly established Washington College in Chestertown. He was also elected Bishop of Maryland in 1783, and he described the college in *An Account of Washington College,* published in 1784. But Smith never really accepted estrangement from Philadelphia and petitioned the Pennsylvania assembly to regain his old position. The effort was eventually successful; he returned to Philadelphia in 1789 and resumed his post, but after two years the College of Philadelphia was merged with the University of the State of Pennsylvania to form the University of Pennsylvania, and Smith was left without employment or honor. His final years were private, centering on his real estate ventures, and apparently frustrating. Smith liked the public arena and enjoyed social and political power. When he died in 1803 he was isolated from the institutions and activities that had provided his greatest pleasure and opportunity for service.

One may speculate that the diminution of Smith's literary and sermonic activity after about 1760 and their near cessation after the Revolution can be accounted for by the external fulfillment of the dream of which he had earlier written. In the 1750s America's rising glory was indeed an event to be looked for; by the 1770s the promise was already being fulfilled. To what extent Smith's writings on the subject contributed to the political manifestations of rising glory we can only guess. But it is clear that his influence—both personal and literary—on Philadelphia's young poets helped to establish not only the American convention of looking toward a destined future of national glory but also to the tradition of literary activity among the young that was intended to accomplish that aim. Smith thus stands at the head of a continuing American tradition; and, even though his actual accomplishments in verse and prose may be less than distinguished, that position makes both the man and his work worthy of attention.

Bibliography:
Thomas F. Adams, *Trial Check List of the Writings of William Smith* (Philadelphia: University of Pennsylvania Library, 1950).

Biographies:
Albert Frank Gegenheimer, *William Smith: Educator and Churchman* (Philadelphia: University of Pennsylvania Press, 1843);

Thomas Firth Jones, *A Pair of Lawn Sleeves: A Biog-*

raphy of William Smith (Philadelphia: Chilton, 1972).

Reference:

William D. Andrews, "William Smith and the Rising Glory of America," *Early American Literature*, 8 (1973): 33-43.

Papers:

The chief repository of Smith papers is the Archives and Historical Collection of the Episcopal Church, Austin, Texas. Additional materials are available at the Historical Society of Pennsylvania, the American Philosophical Society, and the Library of the University of Pennsylvania.

Ezra Stiles
(29 November 1727-12 May 1795)

Alasdair Macphail
Connecticut College

BOOKS: *Oratio Funebris pro Exequiis celebrandis Viri perillustris Jonathan Law Armigeri, Coloniae Connecticutensis Gubernatoris* . . . (New London: Printed & sold by Timothy Green, 1751);

A Discourse on the Christian Union . . . (Boston: Printed & sold by Edes & Gill, 1761);

A Discourse On Saving Knowledge: Delivered at the Installment of the Rev. Samuel Hopkins . . . (Newport: Printed & sold by Solomon Southwick, 1770);

To the Public, by Stiles and Samuel Hopkins (Newport, R.I.: Printed by Solomon Southwick, 1776);

Oratio Inauguralis habita in Sacello Collegii Yalensia, quod est Novo-Portu Connecticuttensium, in Nov' Anglis, VIII. Id. Quintil, M.DCC.LXXVIII . . . (Hartford: Printed by Watson & Goodwin, 1778);

The United States elevated to Glory and Honor. A Sermon preached before His Honor Jonathan Trumbull, Esq. L.L.D. Governor and Commander in Chief and the Honorable General Assembly Convened at Hartford, at the Anniversary Election, May 8th, 1783 (New Haven: Printed by Thomas & Samuel Green, 1783);

A Sermon delivered at the Ordination of the Rev. Henry Channing . . . (New London: Printed by T. Green, 1787);

A Funeral Sermon delivered Thursday, July 26, 1787. At the Interment of the Reverend Mr. Chauncey Whittlesey . . . (New Haven: Printed by T. & S. Green, 1787);

A History of Three of the Judges of King Charles I. Major-General Whalley, Major-General Goffe, and Colonel Dixwell . . . (Hartford: Printed by Elisha Babcock, 1794);

The Literary Diary of Ezra Stiles, D.D., LL.D., President of Yale College . . . January 1, 1769-May 6, 1795, edited by Franklin Bowditch Dexter, 3 volumes (New York: Scribners, 1901);

Ezra Stiles and the Jews: Selected Passages from the Literary Diary concerning Jews and Judaism . . . , edited by George A. Kohut (New York: P. Cowen, 1902);

Extracts From The Itineraries And Other Miscellanies of Ezra Stiles, D.D., LL.D. 1755-1794 With A Selection From His Correspondence, edited by Franklin Bowditch Dexter (New Haven: Yale University Press, 1916);

Letters & Papers of Ezra Stiles, President of Yale College, 1778-1795, edited by Isabel M. Calder (New Haven: Yale University Library, 1933);

Plan of a University: A Proposal addressed to the Corporation of Yale College, 3 December, 1777 (New Haven, 1953).

Known to contemporaries as an erudite Congregational minister whose career culminated in the presidency of Yale College from 1778 to 1795, the Reverend Ezra Stiles still tends to be highly esteemed for his intellect. This longstanding reputation is somewhat overblown; originality of thought and insightful productivity were never part of Stiles's accomplishment. His mind was exceptionally far-ranging, but it was more retentive than fertile, more receptive than creative. Its power was harnessed to a form of bookish learning and insatiable empiricism that produced little which lays

Portrait by Samuel King (Yale University Art Gallery. Bequest of Dr. Charles Jenkins Foote, B.A. 1883, M.A. 1890)

claim to modern attention except the copious notes which he took about his daily affairs and the great stir of life around him. His numerous notebooks, diaries, itineraries, accounts, and miscellanea—a sizeable portion of which has been edited and published in the twentieth century—are among the most extensive and informative of private papers to come down from New England during the late-colonial and early-national era: in manuscript, his diary entries for 1769-1795 alone fill fifteen volumes, his Thermometrical Register (1763-1795) fills five others, and by the end of 1788 he notes that he has had bound thirty-one folio or quarter volumes of his assorted jottings, as well as three volumes of letters from other people.

Despite high visibility during his lifetime, Stiles actually had little of consequence published, and his influence was circumscribed. *A History of Three of the Judges of King Charles I* (1794), written late in life, portrays a mind that was more learned than profound, and among his seven published sermons are only two that can be considered truly memorable. Yet even when these limits to his historical stature are acknowledged, there can be no gainsaying the fact that Ezra Stiles was one of the more interesting members of his generation of New Englanders—as can be amply ascertained from the fine biography of him written by Yale historian Edmund S. Morgan.

Born on 29 November 1727 in North Haven,

Connecticut, to the Reverend Isaac Stiles and his first wife, Reverend Edward Taylor's daughter Kezia, who died a few days after her son's birth, Ezra was nursed initially by a loving neighbor; was nurtured later by a vigorous but pliant stepmother; and was influenced finally by his less robust but still domineering father. His father was upwardly mobile in his choice of occupation, and evidently he disdained to honor his own father, whom he looked down on as a simple farmer from Windsor, Connecticut, where members of the Stiles family had numbered among the original settlers back in 1635. In his turn, the Reverend Isaac Stiles was not much respected later in life by his son, who experienced still greater upward mobility and who also lacked the grace to honor a less-distinguished father even though initially he sought the older man's advice when deciding on a career of his own.

Together with the younger children who were born to Esther Hooker Stiles, his stepmother since he was about a year old, the boy evidently smarted under Isaac's domestic tyranny when he was growing up. Then, at the age of fifteen, Ezra's precociousness combined with the family's recent rise in the world to get him admitted to Yale in third place in the class of 1746. This ranking was derived from a complex system that took into consideration both the scholastic ability and the social standing of all the entering freshmen—a prescriptive system which society then took very seriously when assessing the merit of Yale students and alumni, and one which had already marked Ezra's father when it had admitted him to the college only in the next to last place in the class of 1722. The youth soon became condescending toward his father's lesser intellect, and he later confided in his diary that the minister had always "read much, but digested almost nothing. His mind was stored with rich and valuable Ideas, but classed in no Order, like good Books thrown in Confusion in a Library Room."

Indeed, by the time he was a young man Ezra had developed a fixation about the very attributes he deemed lacking in his father's mind—orderliness, classification, and digestion or comprehension. He never outgrew this preoccupation, and it gave a peculiar twist to his priorities, causing him to be more interested in measuring the outer form life takes than in reflecting on its inner mysteries and emotional resonance. That much can be glimpsed, for example, in this shorthand entry from his itineraries, or record of journeys, for 24 May 1760, when, riding from Newport, Rhode Island, on a sightseeing trip that took him to Albany, New York, he heard of his father's death and recorded the day's highlights without even the emphasis that here is added: "Measured the Episc. Chh. at Norwich Landing, 42 by 34. About 70 families at Landing, Presbyt. (Capt. Bushnel. Capt. Tracy, Phin. Holder, Solo. Handleton, Jona. Hall, Saml. Hull, at Landing,—Mr. Griste, Mr. Lancaster, Maj. Bushnel, Wid. Charlton, in Town, Churchmen.) May be 40 Fam. of New Light Separat. in Norwich, Mr. Hide & Mr. Fuller Ministers. New Court House, Norwich, 50 by 28, erected 1760. Mr. Jabez Huntington's Store, 88 by 30, two stories. *Heard of the Death of my Father who died May 14, 1760, AEtat 62 3/4, and in 36th y. of his Ministry.* Arrived at Colchester." Thus ended a relationship that appears to have been cordial during the father's later years but devoid of affection. For his part, as this almost-typical entry shows, Ezra Stiles was a keen observer of material things who busied himself with the outward dimensions of the landscape he inhabited, both natural and manmade, pretty much to the exclusion of such subjective matters as his own feelings and those of others. His was an object-oriented cast of mind.

Stiles stayed on at Yale as a popular college tutor for another ten years after receiving his A.B. degree in 1746, during which time he helped President Thomas Clapp instruct such future literary figures as Timothy Dwight, John Trumbull, and Joel Barlow. Apart from his academic duties and the opportunity to continue studying, which he especially prized, it was a decade of indecision about his future calling. First he joined his father's North Haven church (23 November 1746) and took the initial step toward becoming a minister by obtaining a license to preach in New Haven County (30 May 1749) about the same time that he delivered the valedictory oration for his M.A. degree (15 June 1749). Shortly thereafter he began to grapple with his own mounting skepticism, and then for the next few years (1749-1755) he even flirted with infidelity to his calling to the point where he became apprehensive about his ministerial intentions and prepared, instead, for a career in law. Stiles gained admittance to the New Haven bar on 13 November 1753, but then, having already been sought after by several congregations—including the well-paying Anglicans in both Newport, Rhode Island, and Stratford, Connecticut—he accepted in August 1755 a call to Newport's Second Congregational Church, at an annual salary of sixty-five pounds sterling (plus fuel and a house). As anticipated, Stiles found Newport an "agreeable town" where he could indulge his "love" of preaching, take full advantage of the town's Redwood Library (of which he became librarian in 1756), and realize—at least until the outbreak of Revolutionary War hostilities—his cherished "prospect of Leisure and Books for pursuing Study more than I could expect in the Law."

While his parishioners were raising a house on Clarke Street for their new minister, Stiles began courting Elizabeth Hubbard, of New Haven. A physician's daughter and fellow Congregationalist in full communion, she was, like himself, not given to religious enthusiasm or anything that might disrupt a calm and even walk of life. They were eventually married on 10 February 1757. Thereafter Mrs. Stiles assumed full and competent charge of running the household while he continued serenely to pursue interests which she did not share or understand but about which she was perfectly supportive. She bore eight children between April of 1758 and July of 1769: Betsy, Ezra Jr., Kezia, Emilia, Isaac, Ruth, Mary, and Sarah. All but the last-born child lived to maturity, and five of them survived him. Elizabeth Stiles herself died suddenly in May of 1775. That major disruption, coupled as it had to be the following March with the bereaved family's flight from Newport in the face of a rumored British fleet, brought a temporary end to Stiles's blissful pursuit of both the "Leisure and Books" for studying. The studying continued, of course, but under trying circumstances for quite some time and then finally under the protection of a second solicitous wife, Mary Checkley, a Providence friend's widow whom Stiles married on 17 October 1782 when he was nearly fifty-five and eighteen years her senior. By then Stiles was the president of Yale, surrounded once more by books and possessed of the leisure for study he had always pursued from New Haven, to Newport, and back again by way of Dighton, Massachusetts, and Portsmouth, New Hampshire, where he had served as minister during the war years. And in some ways it was the fame that accrued from one particular sermon which he had allowed to be published early in his Newport career that eventually brought Stiles back to Yale. It helped add a special luster to his reputation for learning and moderation that the Corporation of Yale College found so attractive.

Entitled *A Discourse on the Christian Union*, the sermon was delivered before a convocation of Rhode Island Congregational ministers in 1760 and then was published in Boston the following year at the urging of the Reverend Charles Chauncy. Justly celebrated from the outset for its reconciliatory tone, the address revealed its author at his intellectual and rhetorical best. Arguably it was the finest piece of sustained writing Stiles ever produced: the range of its focus, the force of its argument, and its immediate relevance to a vexing situation throughout New England and elsewhere in English America makes it an illuminating commentary on a troubled era. The text was Philippians 3:16 with the biblical injunction "let us walk by the same Rule." In his application of this text Stiles was, significantly, the first of New England's "Old Light" ministers, or opponents of the Great Awakening of the 1730s and 1740s, to appeal across the bitter schism of twenty-years' duration for a reunification of the divided Congregational denomination. That stance was not so much courageous as it was attuned to the times, and his adroitness in beating other Old Lights to this posture reflected well on the young man. This timeliness is what gave Stiles a following in Congregational circles and thereby launched his career.

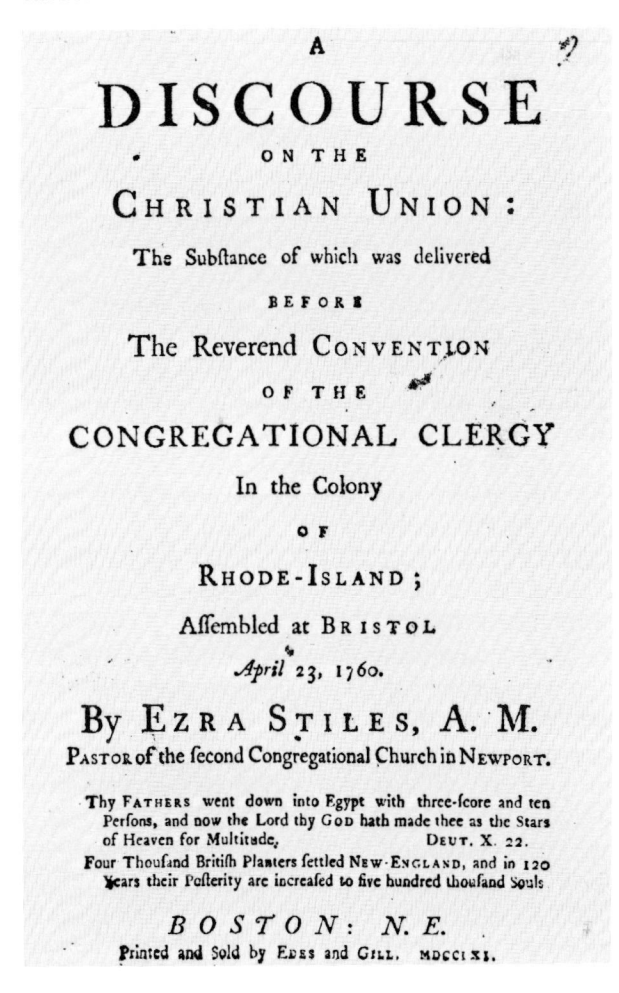

Title page for Stiles's plea for the New Lights and his fellow Old Lights to reunify a Congregational church torn apart by the Great Awakening (courtesy of the John Carter Brown Library at Brown University)

Stiles maintained that all theological differences could be settled "not by appeals to the tenets of parties . . . [or] to the positions of Arminius or Calvin; but by an appeal to the inspired writings" of the Bible itself. He then progressed from this back-to-basics approach to his own learned exegesis and eventually to his faith that the desired restoration of harmony among New England Congregationalists would usher in a new, and larger, unity among all Protestant denominations. His was a stirring vision: "Providence has planted the British America with a variety of sects, which will unavoidably become a mutual balance upon one another. Their temporary collisions . . . will subside in harmony and union, not by the destruction of either, but in the friendly cohabitation of all . . . . [Thus] Resplendent and all-pervading TRUTH will terminate the whole in universal harmony." Stiles projected nothing less than a transatlantic federation of all the Protestant denominations for the sake of harmony itself, for the sake of the countless souls presently deflected from the Protestant camp by the feuding between the denominations, and finally for the sake of civil freedom as it was embodied in the "fundamental principles of *universal liberty*." This sermon was a Protestant manifesto of the first order; a call to Protestant solidarity everywhere and, in America, a call to resist the Anglican hierarchy's age-old attack on religious nonconformity—"Let the grand errand into America never be forgotten," he intoned, evoking the Puritan fathers of American Congregationalism for whom the goal of cohabitation and consortship in the New World had also had universal connotations.

Originality of subject matter was not the distinguishing feature of this sermon. An American Christian union had long since been envisioned in his own generation by such preeminent proponents of the Great Awakening as Jonathan Edwards for the New Light Congregationalists and by Gilbert Tennent for the New Sides Presbyterians. Indeed, the Presbyterians had already been reunited by the time Stiles urged his fellow Old Light ministers to settle their differences with the other Congregationalists and to walk as one with those brethren. As he himself observed approvingly in his sermon, this "wise and happy junction" of the Old-Side Presbyterian Synod of Philadelphia and the New-Side Synod of New York had occurred in 1758. Thus among those Congregational ministers who believed the Great Awakening was more of the Devil's handiwork than God's, Stiles was simply the first openly to hold out the olive branch to those of the other persuasion. And judging from the favorable response on all sides to his suggestion, his timing was perfect.

If that had not been so, he probably would have been given a frosty reception since rhetorical tact was hardly the hallmark of his *Discourse on the Christian Union*. Like his father before him, who had loathed the enthusiasm of the Great Awakening and had suffered aspersions upon his name for daring to oppose its momentum, Stiles let it be known that he still disapproved of the unseemly rash of sudden and suspect conversions that had shattered the New England Way when he was barely in his teens. Said he of "the public mistaken zeal" at that time: "Multitudes were seriously, soberly and solemnly out of their wits." Blunt almost to the point of offensiveness in a sermon that was intended to heal the wounds of discord, Newport's minister used the language Old Lights liked to hear to convey a message of reconciliation, which, in their hearts, they at last were ready to receive. Any New Light whose own ministry or conversion experience was impugned by such rhetoric could at least rejoice in hearing the opposition talk of reunion and could readily join with Stiles in contemplating the prospect of Anglican domination to which he made explicit reference. There, ultimately, lies the genius of this sermon. Its author held before the eyes of a people weary of their own intradenominational backbiting the specter of bishops of the established Church of England scheming tirelessly for the overthrow of true religion everywhere, and especially in New England, where it had taken refuge and had rooted itself most thoroughly. An inherited fear of episcopacy, a pride in the principles of freedom, and a vision of Protestant solidarity all helped fashion an argument on behalf of religious unity in America that appealed to the deepest folk instincts of Stiles's audience.

Thus even though Stiles had nothing new to say as a theologian that might possibly have shed healing light upon the impasse between Old Lights and New, he succeeded brilliantly in suggesting a solution because he understood the emotional and psychological needs of the typical New Englander. What he set in motion among the Old Lights in 1760 others continued in the decade to come. Intramural religious discord did indeed simmer down in New England as the colonists slowly joined hands to defend, as Stiles had urged them, both their "liberty in religion" and their "Free and absolute tenure of land and unburdened property." Of course, like others in 1760, Stiles in no way anticipated the American Revolution. On the contrary, he predicted the brightest of futures for liberty in the colonies on the basis of an elaborate estimation of population growth and sectarian increases which he shared with his audience. By 1860, he asserted, there would be seven million Congregationalists in New England and only 185,000 Anglicans, providing, however, that the Congregationalists did not shortly lose their "precious jewel of religious liberty" and be once more "entangled with that yoke of bondage which our fathers could not, would not, and God grant we may never submit to bear." Since the Congregationalists were already divided into two camps, the burden of his sermon was that Protestant dissenters on both sides of the Atlantic would succumb to the Anglican threat if they did not settle their differences and present a united front. But once that goal had been accomplished, Stiles felt confident in 1760 that America's future would be secure.

Five years later in the throes of the Stamp Act crisis, his confidence was shaken and he was far from certain which side was more in the wrong—England for its arbitrary decision to tax the colonies, or America for its obstruction of legally constituted authority. He allowed privately in a letter to Thomas Hutchinson, the loyal lieutenant governor of Massachusetts, that he had "hoped never to have seen the day when the Colonies should resist the Parent State: nor will I ever take Part in such Resistance." Yet like so many others he did not quite know where to stand on the issues of the day. He attested in this letter to his pride in being an American who was jealous of his liberties, and yet he protested that he would "never be disloyal to my King." Out of these competing loyalties he then fashioned a declaration, with qualifications: "In all parliamentary Resolutions respecting the colonies (except on Religion), so long as the Alternatives are *Submission or Civil War*, I shall not hesitate to chuse and declare for the *first*, till the consequences of the *latter* are less far less tremendous than the Effects of Oppression." A decade later, however, after the events at Lexington and Concord, Stiles became both a refugee from British-occupied Newport and a committed patriot. He also became a dedicated recorder of information pertinent to the conduct of the war. His literary diary and itineraries are filled with information—most of it secondhand—about the numbers of men bearing arms, details of encampments, and accounts of engagements in the field. The bravery of the colonists' response to British advances filled him with still more of the pride in his fellow countrymen that he had begun to know before the war.

Originally, however, Stiles had taken a dim view of what the more active patriots were doing in the late 1760s because, like the enthusiasts of the Great Awakening, they placed in jeopardy the world as he knew it. Thus he had deplored the derring-do of such early radicals as those Newport Sons of Liberty who scuttled and burned the armed sloop *Liberty* at its anchor in 1769. By contrast, he heartily approved of another brand of patriotism—"the whole innocent, cheerful, decent"—that was manifest among local women "of all Denominations, Chh. Quakers, Bapt., Cong., &c" who, on several occasions during the Nonimportation Agreements after the Stamp and Townshend Duties acts, attended "a voluntary Bee or Spinning Match" at his house on Clarke Street—and usually made him a present of their industry. (On one such day his diary records a gift of all "224 fourteen knotted skeins of Linnen" as well as a mound of leftover refreshments: "Ten pounds of Tea more than [was] used, and Gammons, Sugar, Rice &c more than we used.") Stiles took time getting used to the stronger stuff of armed resistance. Then even though his precious union of the Protestant denominations had not materialized by 1776, he became elated over the prospect of a new union of the states.

It was during the public euphoria after Congress had signed the preliminary document which later became the Peace of Paris that ended the war, that Stiles delivered the election sermon of May 1783, the second most impressive bit of his writing published during his lifetime. Elevated to the presidency of Yale College in 1778, he had been further honored with the invitation to address Gov. Jonathan Trumbull and the Connecticut Assembly in the traditional convocation that followed the annual spring elections. *The United States elevated to Glory and Honor* (1783) is one of many prophetic utterances from the period, and even though it is long (ninety-nine pages), rather prosaic in its biblical literalness, and overly erudite for an address to a legislative assembly, the sermon is an interesting document. In it Stiles proclaimed that the grandeur of America was assured since the Lord was on the nation's side. This indubitable fact was made evident by victory over British tyranny and by the many natural advantages which God had bestowed on the land itself and on the people who inhabited it. The matter of population growth, which so interested Stiles the statistician, was just one of many such assurances of America's exceptionality in the divine scheme of things. "This will be a great, a very great nation, nearly equal to half Europe" because, he calculated with an accuracy that has never ceased to impress historians, "it is probable that within a century of our independence the sun will rise on fifty million of inhabitants of the United States." (The actual census figure for 1880 was 50,155,783.) Furthermore, predicted Stiles, "an accelerated multiplication will attend our general propagation, and overspread the whole territory westward for ages."

What he envisioned was a vast continent peopled almost exclusively by white Americans, for in contrast to their rapid increase he believed that "the Indians, as well as the million Africans in America, are decreasing [just] as rapidly." The demographic future for Native Americans and blacks was therefore bleak in his estimate: "Both left to themselves, in this way diminishing, may gradually vanish." Unfortunately it cannot be said that Stiles was disturbed by that anticipated outcome. Previously he had been most responsive to a suggestion by Samuel Hopkins, the neighboring pastor of Newport's First Congregational Church, that manumitted slaves be returned to the Guinea Coast of West Africa accompanied by thirty or forty black ministers to attend to their spiritual needs and those of other Africans. Before Stiles fled town at the advance of the British, he and Hopkins had already selected two of Hopkins's black communicants to be trained for the missionary work involved: Bristol Yamma, a slave, and John Quaumino, a freeman. The two ministers had then solicited funds from the public in a circular, *To The Public*. Hopkins personally contributed £100 toward the purchase of Yamma's freedom and the cost of sending both men to Princeton, where they enrolled late in 1774. By the time the war sabotaged this well-intended scheme, some £500 had been raised and two other black candidates had been identified.

Through that back-to-Africa movement Stiles had vaguely envisioned the lessening, if not the actual demise, of American slavery, an institution which initially had not bothered his conscience and in which he had casually participated as the owner of Newport, a slave whom he had bought and named in 1763, admitted to full communion in his own church in 1775, and did not free until June 1778. Slow to see the evil in slavery, Stiles found moral comfort of sorts in his own dismal forecast for America's black population, and in 1783 he shared it with the state legislators. Through the gradual demise—as he supposed it—of America's black population, "an unrighteous *slavery* may at length, in God's good providence, be abolished, and cease in this land of *liberty*." As callous as it was pious, this hope that slavery would end when there were no more Negroes in America was later proved to be wrong on the very grounds that Stiles used to make his prediction in the first place. His demographic forecast was mistaken partly because of the invention of the cotton gin in 1793, which stimulated the entire plantation economy in ways nobody could have suspected a decade earlier, but primarily because the black population was far more resilient than Stiles had ever realized. Indeed, even during Stiles's lifetime the black population had not been declining at all but was increasing at twenty-five percent or more—sometimes much more—per decade. By 1880 it numbered 6,580,793 in the United States. Scholars who applaud Stiles's accurate calculations about the future of America's white population should note his huge margin of error in predicting what would befall its black counterpart.

It is interesting to note the absence of any real anticipation on Stiles's part of the sort of mechanical wizardry soon to transform the means of production in America and envisioned, significantly enough in the very year of the cotton gin's invention, by his former neighbor, the Reverend Samuel Hopkins, in Hopkins's better-known prophetic tract, *A Treatise on the Millennium* (1793). Stiles had little inclination toward technology beyond what he needed for the study and teaching of astronomy and chemistry. Thus he made no special prediction of the future role of manufacturing or "the mechanic arts," as he called it. Instead, he simply anticipated that America's industrious population would always be "employed, in a just proportion, in agriculture, mechanic arts, commerce, and the literary professions." As to the emerging national debate over which should be given greater attention, commerce or agriculture, he inclined in the safe direction of the North's apparent priority even though some of his suggestions were none too practical in terms of what was feasible in Connecticut. For example, he encouraged "the planting of vineyards and olive yards, and cotton-walks, planting mulberry trees, and the culture of silk; and, I add, establishing manufactories. This last is necessary—far more necessary, indeed, than is thought by many deep politicians."

Although he had little else to say about manufacturing, Stiles did speak enthusiastically about commerce, talking fondly of its transcendent benefits and of the impressive speed with which the United States' shipbuilders launched new vessels. For quite apart from the economic returns of overseas trade, Stiles valued the sea lanes as conduits

First page for the circular in which Stiles and Samuel Hopkins solicited funds for the training of two black men as missionaries to West Africa (courtesy of the John Carter Brown Library at Brown University)

through which the world's store of knowledge would flow to American shores and along which, in return, the United States would express her world-regenerative example. He was therefore at his most lyrical when contemplating how "Navigation will carry the American flag around the globe itself; and display the thirteen stripes and new constellation at Bengal and Canton, on the Indus and Ganges, on the Wang-ha and the Yang-tse-kiang, and with commerce will import the wisdom and literature of the East . . . [which] being here digested and carried to the highest perfection, may reblaze from America to Europe, Asia and Africa, and illumine the world with truth and liberty."

It was, indeed, a grand vision that he had of national glory reflecting itself in time to come, not only on the minds of those who lived within the continental bounds of the United States, but also on the upturned faces of peoples overseas expectantly awaiting truth imported. It was prophetic, too, not in the literal sense of what to date has actually happened but in the mythical and literary sense of what generations of Americans have taken to be their national mission overseas: namely, the exportation of ideological truth and constitutional liberty for the enlightenment of humanity. This idea, variously expressed, is older than the nation itself and was by no means original with Stiles. Just as it can be projected forward from 1783 to the nineteenth-century concept of Manifest Destiny, so can that idea be traced backward from Stiles's day to the Puritans' perception of themselves as a convenanted people with a divine mission to be exemplars of Christian faith and conduct. *The United States elevated to Glory and Honor* was firmly rooted in this cultural tradition, and, like the numerous entries about American Indians in Stiles's literary diary and itineraries, the sermon treats cultural differences with great enthusiasm but with no appreciation of their individual integrity. Akin to others of his time and place, Stiles was no anthropologist. Only fifty-six in 1783 and already competent (or better) in the reading of Arabic, Chaldee, Coptic, French, Hebrew, Latin, Persian, and Syriac, Yale's president can be forgiven for believing that he would be among the foremost of his generation to "digest" the wisdom of the East and carry it, American style, to its "highest perfection." Stiles truly believed in the future perfection of learning that he envisioned, and this reflects the tremendous optimism of his generation as much as the vanity that was his own.

At 5 feet 4½ inches and less than 130 pounds, he was a diminutive clerical dignitary replete with the honorary doctor of theology degree which Benjamin Franklin, who had been urged by Stiles to procure such honors for Americans, had obtained for him from Edinburgh University in 1765. Five years later Stiles happily accepted membership in the newly founded American Academy of Arts and Sciences. Doctor Stiles, as he preferred to be called, relished the limelight as Yale's ceremony-promoting president for seventeen years before a "bilious fever" sent him to the grave at the age of sixty-seven. Even his friendly biographer, Edmund S. Morgan, allows that "the job brought out the worst in him" since "at Yale, in the line of duty, he could give his vanity free rein to magnify the traditions and rituals of which he was now the guardian." Perhaps Morgan is also correct to claim that "happily this was just what the college needed . . . to help bind a highly transitient population into a single community."

His concern for his reputation is apparent in his insistence in 1770-1771, when he engaged Samuel King to paint his portrait, that King include a store of symbols or "Emblems" which, he then recorded in a three-page diary explication of the painting, are essential to the viewer's appreciation because they "are more descriptive of my Mind, than [are] the Effigies of my face." His face is pleasantly interesting and his look is lively, but with so much emphasis placed upon the extraneous forms that surround it, one's eye is quite distracted from contemplating the relation of his features and speculating what they reveal of the man within. Stiles's pose simply overpowers the artist's portraiture. He is seen "sitting in a Green Elbow chair, in a Teaching Attitude, with the right hand on the Breast, and the Left holding a Preaching Bible. Behind & on the left side is a part of a Library—two Shelves of Books . . . by these I denote my Taste for History. . . . On the other Shelf are Newton's Principia, Plato, Watts, Doddridge, Cudworths Intellectual System; & also the New Engld primaeval Divines Hooker, Chauncy, Mather, Cotton. . . . At my Right hand stands a Pillar . . . one Circle . . . one Trajectory around a solar point . . . ." Much about Stiles was planned for effect. Forward yet skillful in cultivating important men on both sides of the Atlantic, which he himself never had occasion to cross, he was wise enough to confine his more egotistical schemes to his notebooks: for example, the various drafts of a constitution for a national fraternity of savants to be known by the immodest title, SOCIETAS ERUDITORIUM STILENSIANA; or the mandate which he laboriously drew up for gatherings of all his descendants in honor of himself, as paterfamilias, and of his wife, as *his* helpmeet, beginning in 1760 and reconvening thereafter every four years until the day of doom 350 years later in 2110 A.D., as he reckoned it.

In its politics, *The United States elevated to Glory and Honor* paid tribute to the Whig ideals dear to the Revolutionary generation and especially to the electoral process that was the mainstay of representative government. Said Stiles: "A well-ordered *Democratical Aristocracy*, standing upon the annual elections of the people, and revocable at pleasure . . . will approve itself the most equitable, liberal, and perfect." That was conventional enough. Indeed, the only utterance in the sermon with which many contemporaries would have disagreed had to do with Stiles's early show of magnanimity toward England, the late and vanquished enemy. "O, England," he began, "how did I once love thee! how did I once glory in thee! how did I once boast of springing from thy bowels! . . . but now, farewell. . . . And yet, even now methinks," he continued in contemplation of some possible danger "to thee from European states . . . in such an exigency, I could leap the Atlantic, not into thy bosom, but to rescue an aged parent from destruction, and then to return on the wings of triumph to this asylum of the world, and rest in the bosom of Liberty." It was a telling insight into the crisis of conscience experienced by countless Americans when they decided to foreswear their inherited loyalty to the Crown in order to swear voluntary allegiance to the United States. Victorious in war but still excluded from the commerce of the British Empire, most Americans felt little goodwill toward the former Mother Country, and some wished her to suffer at the hand of France, traditionally England's foe and only recently America's ally.

Ironically, by the 1790s, when many Americans had come round to Stiles's original position, he had become a Francophile. Whereas others not infrequently were swayed either by economic considerations or the weight of familial sentiment to see Britain in an increasingly favorable light, Yale's president was swayed by the outbreak of the French Revolution to identify the cause of liberty with what was happening in France. Thus his last, longest, and most rambling publication was at odds with the way Americans in general, and New Englanders in particular, were beginning to feel about the leading European powers. By its very subject matter as well as by its tone, it was an anti-British tract: *A History of Three of the Judges of King Charles I* is a celebration of the three military judges (Major-Generals Edward Whalley and William Goffe, and Colonel John Dixwell) who had signed the king's death warrant in 1649 at the end of the English civil war and who then, at the Restoration of the monarchy in 1660, had fled to Puritan New England and eventually found concealment in Connecticut for the remainder of their lives. England, he argued, was too corrupt a land to appreciate those who had tried in vain to protect the people from tyranny itself. Like America, France on the other hand was now the proven home of justice and enlightenment. Then just when Stiles was finishing his treatment of these three regicides, the news of the execution of King Louis XIV early in 1793 crossed the Atlantic. This latest example of regicide deeply disturbed many of Stiles's close associates who had supposed that nothing of the sort could ever take place in France. Their outraged reaction shocked him in turn, for now they claimed that by this single stroke against the life of a king, as well as by the free use of the guillotine in general, France had forfeited her recent—and therefore suspect—claim to be the friend of Liberty. The subsequent desire of many Americans to dissociate their own revolution from whatever bloodthirsty excess was sweeping France was stronger than any concern they might have had for the personal fate of a monarch, but, they as-

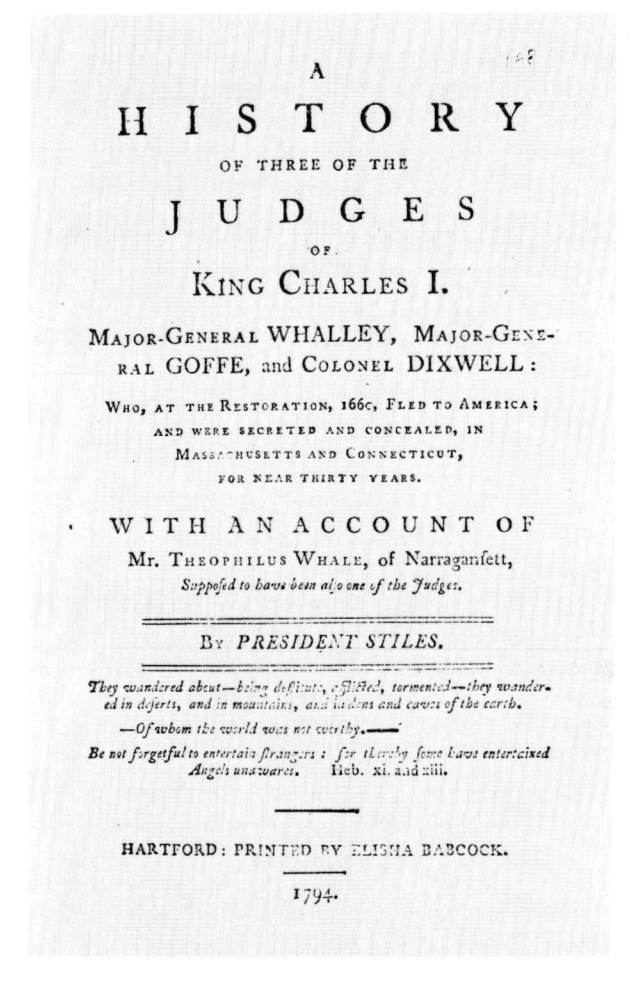

Title page for Stiles's defense of regicide as a legitimate response to tyranny (courtesy of the John Carter Brown Library at Brown University)

serted, regicide was an unconscionable act no matter the circumstances. Stunned by this disavowal of the very action his book implied was morally heroic in the face of tyranny, Stiles appended an ardent defense of tyrannicide and, therefore, of the extreme measures recently taken in France by the radical Jacobin societies.

The Jacobins, he averred, were the salvation of that nation because they were rescuing her from a tyranny that could not otherwise be checked. Excesses were unavoidable, but once France obtained a good and stable government based on popular elections, there would be no cause for more of the same: "The end being answered, and the care of the public consigned into the hands of constitutional government, these societies will spontaneously disappear; nor rise again unless called forth on great occasions worthy of their attention." It would thus be a profound mistake to outlaw such societies in a free country out of fear for what they could set in motion, in unfree lands, when tyranny demanded radical action: "There is no alternative between their right to assemble, and the abolition of liberty. Extinguish this right . . . and the people are slaves." In order to remain free, a free people like the Americans must allow the legal existence of radical factions. But by the same token, so long as they are free, Americans have no cause whatsoever to anticipate that factions of this sort would gain any significant strength.

Noting realistically that "in every state, good or bad, there will always be a number of restless, subtle, crafty, turbulent and ungovernable spirits" who will stir up mischief and discontent, Stiles delivered a ringing testimony to his great faith in the electorate: "Nothing will kill a faction, like the body of a people if consulted . . . let a matter be fairly brought before the people, and they will not only determine it, but will judge and determine right." Stiles was convinced that in America voters would base their decisions "upon information from an abundance of enlightened characters always intermixt among them," an assumption that again testified to Stiles's atypically solid faith, in the 1790s, that American voters would appreciate what was enlightened and act accordingly. He also believed that disgruntled members of society would never want to join a radical faction because they would appreciate that "In elective republics there is another way always open, which will always be effectual for the redress of even real grievances." They would, he said, "Defer and endure till the next election, and then send up men that shall abolish the [offending] law. They will either do it, or bring back reasons which will convince the constituents." Stiles optimistically concluded his discussion of American politics with the observation, "It is therefore next to impossible to suppose a case in an elective republic, wherein resistance can be justified. . . . Because redress may be all times effected in another and more peacable and satisfactory way, without endangering the public tranquility, or disturbing the public order of the general government, and especially without eversion of the constitution."

Tranquillity and order, no less than classification and studying, were always the values Ezra Stiles cherished dearly in private life. So, too, in the life of the new republic. Thus even though he was happy to quote authority and intone "Rebellion to tyrants is obedience to God!," one cannot conclude, as did Morgan, that he latterly harbored Jacobin sentiments. He was an early champion of the American electorate because he supposed it would always listen to the voice of reason and would therefore never waver from casting the enlightened vote. And he championed regicide only because to him, as an American living in a republic wherein there was no king to kill, it was an abstraction buried in the colonists' collective past and remote from the concerns of the American present. Contrary to his idealistic expectations, redress of wrongs—be they political or otherwise—would rarely be as smoothly attained as he imagined. Constituents would not often be so patient as he supposed. Enlightened men would not always be on hand to influence the voters as he assumed. And the appeal of joining some radical "faction" would not invariably be nullified by a conviction that "in [an] elective republic there is another way always open," because by no means all members of society would possess the franchise, and even those who did would not always think it useful. Thus far from being "Yale's Jacobin," President Stiles—for all his abstract faith in the ordinary man—was an instant conservative who helped in this book to conjure up a powerful myth about the operation of America's political system. Few, however, read his tome, and its influence, if any, has yet to be established.

Stiles published *A History of Three of the Judges of King Charles I* in 1794, the year of the Whiskey Insurrection in the United States. He died on 12 May 1795. He called himself an unchanged Son of Liberty, but this was not quite accurate. His love of liberty was genuine always, but he never really approved of the radicalism of the Sons, preferring, instead, to preserve liberty by different means, "the whole innocent, cheerful, decent." He was, indeed, a "gentle" man; someone who was, in his own words, "no politician, but a prophet."

Biography:
Edmund S. Morgan, *The Gentle Puritan: A Life of Ezra Stiles, 1727-1795* (New Haven & London: Yale University Press, 1962).

References:
Richard D. Birdsall, "Ezra Stiles versus the New Divinity Men," *American Quarterly,* 17 (Summer 1965): 248-258;

Carl Bridenbaugh, *Mitre and Sceptre: Transatlantic Faiths, Ideas, Personalities, and Politics 1689-1775* (New York: Oxford University Press, 1962).

Papers:
The Stiles papers are in the archives of Yale University; see the listing of this extensive collection in "A Note on the Stiles Papers," in Edmund S. Morgan, *The Gentle Puritan: A Life of Ezra Stiles, 1727-1795,* pp. 465-472.

William Stith
(1707-19 September 1755)

Homer D. Kemp
Tennessee Technological University

BOOKS: *A Sermon Preached Before the General Assembly* (Williamsburg: Printed by William Parks, 1746);

The History of the First Discovery and Settlement of Virginia . . . (Williamsburg: Printed by William Parks, 1747; London: Printed for S. Birt, 1753);

The Sinfulness and Pernicious Nature of Gaming . . . (Williamsburg: Printed by William Hunter, 1752);

The Nature and Extent of Christ's Redemption . . . (Williamsburg: Printed by William Hunter, 1753).

William Stith—clergyman, teacher, historian, antiquarian, college president—was one of the ablest men of his generation in Virginia. As an antiquarian and a major Southern colonial historian, he made a significant contribution to the tradition of modern historical scholarship; as a pulpiteer, he left three printed sermons which demand respect as both theology and literature.

A native Virginian, Stith was born in 1707, the son of Captain John and Mary Randolph Stith. The Randolph family was one of the most powerful families in Virginia. As the grandson of William and Mary Isham Randolph of Turkey Island ("the Adam and Eve of Virginia"), the nephew of Sir John Randolph (King's Attorney), and the cousin of such men as Richard Bland and Peyton Randolph, the intelligent young Stith had many opportunities available to him. After attending the grammar school at the College of William and Mary, he matriculated at Queen's College, Oxford, on 21 May 1724, taking his B.A. on 27 February 1728 and being ordained on 12 April 1731. He was elected master of the grammar school at William and Mary on 25 October 1731 but stayed there only five years, until he became rector of the affluent Henrico parish. During most of his sixteen years at Henrico parish, Stith was also chaplain to the Virginia House of Burgesses. On 13 July 1738, he married his first cousin Judith Randolph, by whom he had three daughters.

Stith's uncle Sir John Randolph had planned to write a history of Virginia, a project which Stith discussed with both Randolph and his friend William Byrd II of Westover, and after Randolph's death in 1737, Stith took up the project. He had at his disposal not only the books and manuscripts of his uncle's library but also Byrd's library, one of the greatest of Southern colonial book collections, which also included certain quite significant manuscripts. In addition, Stith had access to the partially preserved official records in Williamsburg. The author's plan was to write a comprehensive history of the colony from its beginning through his own day; however, he only managed to complete one rather large volume that covered the period ending in 1624 with the dissolution of the Virginia Company. His *The History of the First Discovery and Settlement of Virginia . . .* appeared in at least two Williamsburg printings in 1747 and in London and Williamsburg editions in 1753.

Stith was the first Virginia historian to attempt to write history for its own purposes based upon detailed, factual reporting from the primary sources. He made a significant contribution to modern historical methodology by using primary sources exclusively, synthesizing them into a single narrative. Despite his insistence upon specific evidence to support his conclusions, however, Stith presents a somewhat one-sided coverage of events, for he depended primarily upon Capt. John Smith's *The Generall Historie of Virginia, New-England, and the Summer Isles* (1624) and the copy of the Virginia Company's Court Records for 1619-1624 that he found in Byrd's library. Smith's *Generall Historie . . .* tells his side of his battles with his opponents, and

THE HISTORY OF THE First DISCOVERY AND SETTLEMENT OF VIRGINIA: BEING An ESSAY towards a General HISTORY of this COLONY.

By WILLIAM STITH. A. M.
Rector of *Henrico* Parish, and one of the Governors of *William* and *Mary* COLLEGE.

Tantæ molis erat *** condere gentem. Virg.

WILLIAMSBURG:
Printed by WILLIAM PARKS, M,DCC,XLVII.

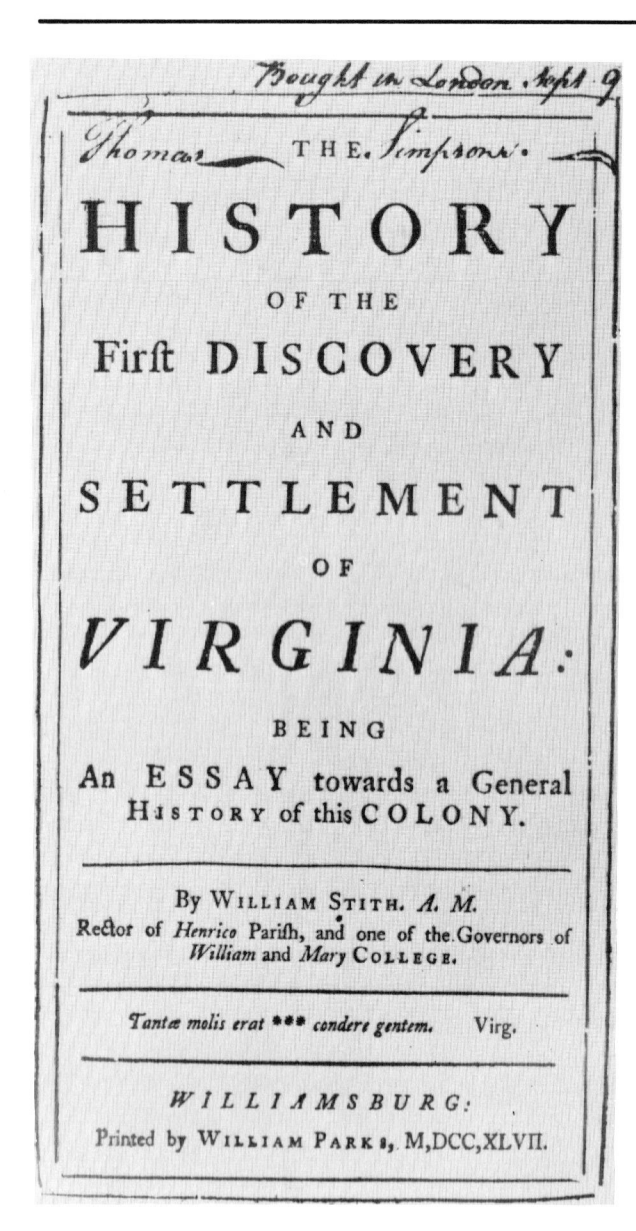

In writing this history of his native colony Stith had access not only to colonial records in Williamsburg but also to the books and manuscripts in the libraries of William Byrd II and Sir John Randolph (University of North Carolina Library, Chapel Hill).

the Virginia Company records relate the Sir Edwin Sandys-Earl of Southampton administration's side of its struggle with King James I.

In addition to the bias of his sources, Stith exhibits the views of an established tradition of Southern colonial historians in his secular New World patriotism (or sectionalism) and his Whiggish interpretation of his colony's early history. Like his contemporary and subsequent American Whig historians, Stith read the principles and concerns of his own time into the events of history. He saw history in terms of politically good men opposing politically evil men, not in terms of God's providence as did the New England historians or in terms of great social or economic forces as have modern historians. Stith, the eighteenth-century Whig champion of individual liberty against Crown prerogative, saw the Virginia Company as representative of the liberty of the people resisting Crown suppression. Building upon John Smith's foundations, Stith employed an eighteenth-century American Whig frame of reference to develop a Virginia mythology which historians after the revolutionary war followed and enlarged upon: the heroic John Smith, champion of the people; "darling" Pocohontas; gracious Sir Edwin Sandys, who insured the liberty of colonials by establishing the House of Burgesses; and the villain King James I, who destroyed the Virginia Company.

Stith's opposition to Crown prerogative embroiled him in the Pistole Fee controversy in 1752, during which time he was credited with coining a toast much used during the heated dispute—"Liberty and Property and No Pistole." This two-year controversy over Lt. Gov. Robert Dinwiddie's personal fee of one pistole for affixing the royal seal on land patents spawned a flurry of writings which proved to be seminal to the arguments and techniques of revolutionary political literature. In 1752 the death of Stith's brother-in-law William Dawson left vacant the traditionally conjoined offices of president of William and Mary, Anglican commissary, and councilor. Gov. Robert Dinwiddie violently opposed Stith as a candidate for the offices because he blamed much of the Pistole Fee opposition upon "an evil spirit" entering the "high priest" Stith. Dinwiddie successfully blocked Stith's appointment as commissary and councilor; in a bitter contest before the Board of Visitors, however, Stith used his family and political connections to win the presidency of the college, a position which he occupied until his untimely death in 1755.

His three extant sermons, delivered before the General Assembly at the official request of the Burgesses, show Stith to be an able pulpit orator. *A Sermon Preached Before the General Assembly* (1746) is a thoroughly competent Whig political sermon which uses the Bible and Roman history to prove that Christian doctrine does not support tyranny. *The Sinfulness and Pernicious Nature of Gaming . . .* (1752) is a pastoral sermon against a major moral problem of his day. *The Nature and Extent of Christ's Redemption . . .* (1753) presents a rather extreme expression of

Christianity as commonsense religion. Stith was accused of liberalism by many fellow Anglicans, and the Presbyterians thought him to be virtually heretical. An allusion in *The Nature and Extent of Christ's Redemption* . . . to New Light Presbyterian minister the Reverend Samuel Davies's *The Impartial Trial, Impartially Tried, and Convicted of Partiality* (1748) prompted Davies to pen an answer in July 1755, entitled "Charity and Truth United." Davies did not publish his pamphlet, however, partially because Stith died in September before Davies was ready to take his piece to the press. Just as his landmark history assures Stith a significant place in the development of modern historical method in America, his sermons demand consideration as thoroughly competent literature in both style and learning.

References:

Richard Beale Davis, *Intellectual Life in the Colonial South, 1585-1763*, 3 volumes (Knoxville: University of Tennessee Press, 1978), pp. 96-102, 737-740;

Morgan P. Robinson, Bibliographical notes and index to *The History of the First Discovery and Settlement of Virginia* (Spartanburg, S.C.: Reprint Co., 1965);

Darrett B. Rutman, Introduction to *The History of the First Discovery and Settlement of Virginia* (New York: Johnson Reprint, 1969);

Thad W. Tate, "William Stith and the Virginia Tradition," *The Colonial Legacy, Volumes III and IV*, edited by Lawrence H. Leder (New York: Harper & Row, 1973), pp. 121-145;

Toshiko Tsuruta, "William Stith, Historian of Colonial Virginia," Ph.D. dissertation, University of Washington, 1957;

Alden T. Vaughan, "The Evolution of Virginia History: Early Historians of the First Colony," *Perspectives on Early American History: Essays in Honor of Richard B. Morris*, edited by Vaughan and George A. Billias (New York: Harper & Row, 1973), pp. 9-39.

Thomas Story
(circa 1670-24 June 1742)

Thomas P. Slaughter
Rutgers University

SELECTED BOOKS: *Reasons Why Those of the People called Quakers Challenged by George Keith to Meet Him at Turners Hall . . . 11 June 1696, Refuse their Appearance at His Peremptory Summons . . .* (London, 1696);

A Word to the Wise of All Perswasions . . . (London: Printed & sold by T. Sowle, 1697);

Thomas Story's Discourse in the Meeting at Horselydown . . . (Horselydown, 1737);

Discourses Delivered in the Publick Assemblies of the People Called Quakers . . . (London: Sold by T. Cooper, 1738); republished as *Four Sermons Preached at the Meeting in White-Hart-Court . . .* (London: Sold by L. Hinde, 1764); republished in part as *Two Discourses, Delivered in the Public Assemblies of People Called Quakers* (Providence: Printed & sold by John Carter, 1769);

Two Sermons on the Following Subjects: VIZ. 1. Salvation by Christ; and the Universality of It Asserted; VIZ. 2. The Nature and Necessity with the Benefit and Advantage of Silence Considered . . . (Leeds: Printed by J. Lister, 1739);

The Means, Nature, Properties and Effects of True Faith Considered . . . (Leeds: Printed by J. Lister, 1740);

To the Saints in Sion, A Song of Praise. Written at Carlisle in Cumberland about Fifty Years Ago . . . (Leeds: Printed by J. Lister, 1740);

A Journal of the Life of Thomas Story . . . (Newcastle upon Tyne: Printed by I. Thompson, 1747); abridged as *The Life of Thomas Story*, abridged by John Kendall (London: Printed & sold by J. Phillips, 1786; Philadelphia: Printed by J. Crukshank, 1805).

Born in Justice Town, near Carlisle, England, Thomas Story was educated at the Carlisle Grammar School and read law under Dr. Richard Gilpin

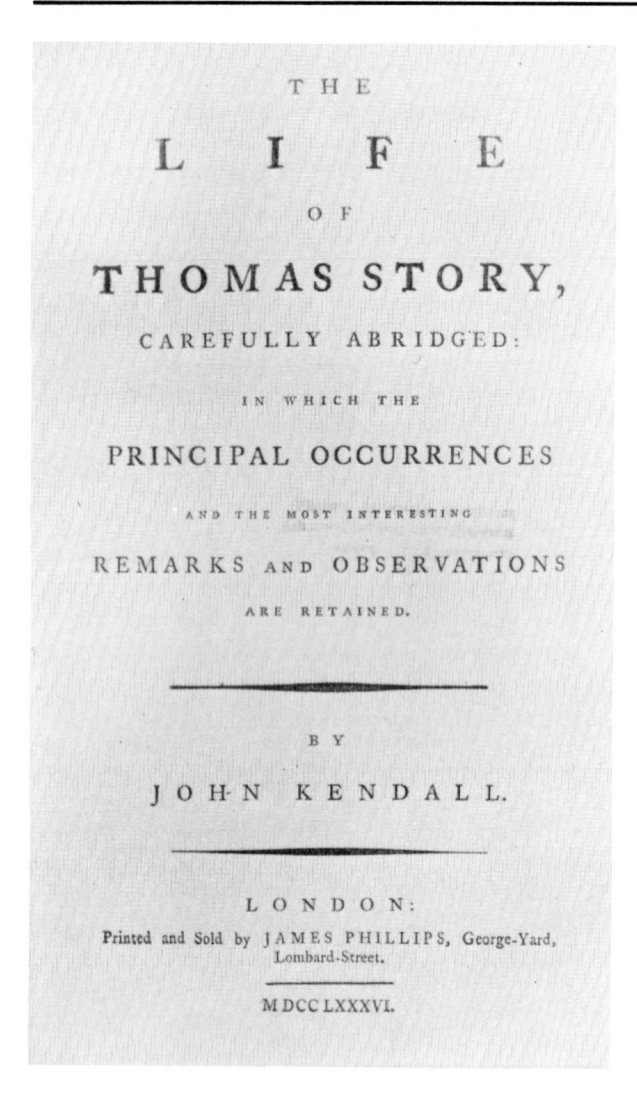

Title page for the abridged edition of Story's journal (Thomas Cooper Library, University of South Carolina)

in Cumberland. Beginning in 1687 he practiced law in Carlisle. At about the same time he began to question the Church of England's rites, especially the practice of christening infants. On 1 April 1689, influenced by the many prominent Quaker families in the area, Story experienced a "conversion" to their beliefs and began to preach in 1693, the same year he met William Penn. When in 1695 Story decided to settle in London, Penn assisted him in finding employment as registrar of the Society of Friends.

Story accompanied Penn to Ireland in 1698. In November of the same year he immigrated to Pennsylvania, ultimately remaining there for sixteen years. He became the first recorder of Philadelphia, a member of the council of state, keeper of the great seal, master of the rolls, and in 1706 was elected mayor of Philadelphia, but declined to serve. He married Ann Shippen (circa 1706), who died about six years later. During this same period Story was accused of unfair and corrupt practices in his capacity as treasurer of the Pennsylvania Land Company, but he was ultimately cleared of criminal conduct by a London court of arbitration. In 1714 Story left Pennsylvania and the New World, apparently for good. During the remaining years of his life he traveled throughout Great Britain and Ireland preaching, debating theology, and bearing witness to his faith.

Story's major literary production was his autobiographical journal, published in full as *A Journal of the Life of Thomas Story* (1747) and in an abridged edition as *The Life of Thomas Story* (1786). In it he details the formative religious experiences of his conversion to the Quaker religion and gives accounts of his experiences preaching in Britain, Europe, and America. Providing fascinating details of his missionary labors and remarkable interviews with people of interest, Story offers important insights to the activities of the Society of Friends during the late seventeenth and early eighteenth centuries and his association with William Penn. The journal is fundamentally oriented toward recording "the tender mercies and judgments of the Lord" and the effects of this relationship upon the course of Story's life. It is a model of the religious autobiographical journal of his time.

Letters:

The Correspondence of James Logan and Thomas Story, 1727-1741, edited by Norman Penney (Philadelphia: Friends' Historical Association, 1927).

Reference:

Doris N. Dalglish, "The First Quaker Poet," in her *People Called Quakers* (London & New York: Oxford University Press, 1938), pp. 33-56.

John Trumbull
(24 April 1750-11 May 1831)

Arthur L. Ford
Lebanon Valley College

SELECTED BOOKS: *An Essay on the Uses and Advantages of the Fine Arts. Delivered at the Public Commencement in New-Haven, September 12th, 1770* (New Haven: Printed by T. & S. Green, 1770);

The Progress of Dulness, Part First: Or the Rare Adventures of Tom Brainless . . . (New Haven: Printed by Thomas & Samuel Green, 1772; corrected, 1773);

The Progress of Dulness, Part Second: Or an Essay on the Life and Character of Dick Hairbrain of Finical Memory . . . (New Haven: Printed by Thomas & Samuel Green, 1773);

The Progress of Dulness, Part Third, and Last: Sometimes Called, The Progress of Coquetry, or the Adventures of Miss Harriet Simper . . . (New Haven: Printed by Thomas & Samuel Green, 1773);

M'Fingal: A Modern Epic Poem. Canto First, or The Town-Meeting (Philadelphia: Printed & sold by William & Thomas Bradford, 1776; London: Printed for J. Almon, 1776);

M'Fingal: A Modern Epic Poem, in Four Cantos (Hartford: Hudson & Goodwin, 1782; London: Printed for J. S. Jordan, 1792);

The Poetical Works of John Trumbull, LL.D., 2 volumes (Hartford: Printed by Lincoln & Stone for Samuel G. Goodrich, 1820).

Portrait of the author by the artist who bore the same name (Yale University Art Gallery)

At the age of eight, John Trumbull wrote a burlesque of his mother's genealogy, a genealogy which his mother prized. According to Trumbull's later account, he "deserved and received a good box on the ears" for his actions. That burlesque reflects two important facets of Trumbull's early life: his precocity and his bent for satire. The precocity—he learned to read at age two and passed the entrance examination to Yale at seven—developed into an imposing erudition. The bent for satire—at times bordering on the indecent in, for instance, "And as when Adam met His Eve"—produced Trumbull's best and most lasting work and elicited considerable personal abuse from those whom he attacked.

Born 24 April 1750 in Westbury parish, Waterbury (now part of Watertown), Connecticut, John Trumbull enjoyed an intellectual boyhood. His father, the Reverend John Trumbull, was, according to Trumbull, a "classical scholar" and a trustee of Yale College. His mother, Sarah Whitman Trumbull, daughter of a clergyman and granddaughter of Reverend Solomon Stoddard, was well-educated. It was she, in fact, who taught young John to read. When she saw the burlesque of her genealogy, however, she must have had second thoughts. Despite his early success in the entrance examination, Trumbull waited until he was thirteen to enter Yale. Upon earning both a Berkeley fellowship and his B.A. degree in 1767, he decided to remain at Yale until 1770 when he received his M.A. degree. During this period, he began to write poetry after the neoclassical models of Pope, Swift, and Butler, and he collaborated with Timothy Dwight on a series of ten Addisonian essays called "The Meddler," published in the *Boston Chronicle* from September 1769 to January 1770, and on "The Correspondent," published in the *Connecticut Journal, and the New-Haven Post-Boy* during 1770 and 1773. His 1770 commencement address, *An Essay on the Uses and Advantages of the Fine Arts,* concluded with the obligatory "Prospect of the Future Glory of America" in heroic couplets. He also wrote between 1769 and 1773 the unpublished "Speculative Essays," primarily composed of commentary on contemporary theological issues in which he urged avoidance of the extremes of skepticism and dogmatism.

After leaving Yale in 1770, Trumbull moved to Wethersfield, where he studied law for two years and probably taught school. He then returned to Yale as a tutor during 1772 and 1773 before passing his bar examination in 1773 and moving to Boston to study law with John Adams. In 1772 he produced the first part of *The Progress of Dulness,* subtitled *Part First: Or the Rare Adventures of Tom Brainless.* In the following year, he published *Part Second: Or an Essay on the Life and Character of Dick Hairbrain of Finical Memory* and *Part Third, and Last: Sometimes Called, The Progress of Coquetry, or the Adventures of Miss Harriet Simper, of the Colony of Connecticut.*

This attack on education was followed in early 1776 by Trumbull's most widely read poem, *M'Fingal. M'Fingal: A Modern Epic Poem. Canto First, or The Town-Meeting* was later divided into two cantos and, in 1782, published with cantos three and four in a new edition. This satire on the British and their supporters represents Trumbull's increasing involvement with politics. He also collaborated with David Humphreys, Joel Barlow, and Lemuel Hopkins on *The Anarchiad,* published in the *New Haven Gazette and the Connecticut Magazine* in 1786-1787. This satiric poem, Trumbull later said, "checked and intimidated the leaders of disorganization and infidel philosophy."

Meanwhile, in 1774 Trumbull had begun practicing law in New Haven, where he married Sarah Hubbard in November 1776. In 1777 the British threat to New Haven forced the Trumbulls to move to Westbury, and in 1781 they settled in Hartford. By 1789 Trumbull's public service began and his poetic production virtually ceased. In that year he was appointed state attorney for the county of Hartford and three years later was elected to represent the town of Hartford in the state legislature. During the second half of the 1790s, poor health forced him to resign from his political offices; however, by 1800 improving health allowed him to resume his position in the General Assembly. When in 1801 he was appointed Judge of the Superior Court of Connecticut, he decided he should remain above partisan politics and gave up completely his interest in satiric political commentary. He was given additional duties as Judge of the Supreme Court of Errors in 1808. From then on Trumbull grew into distinguished old age, publishing his two-volume *The Poetical Works of John Trumbull, LL.D.* in 1820 and reaping the honors accruing to a lifetime of contribution to the young nation's development. He died in Detroit on 11 May 1831, where he had been living with his daughter since 1825.

Trumbull is known primarily as a satiric poet, specifically of two satires, *The Progress of Dulness* and *M'Fingal.* Twentieth-century critics, however, point out Trumbull's sure and efficient use of prose, Alexander Cowie claiming that had Trumbull worked at it he "might have made a permanent reputation as a prose writer" and Victor E. Gimmestad describing his prose as "strong and supple" and "considerably above the level of most political propaganda."

The Revolutionary and post-Revolutionary period in American literature was distinguished for the quality of its prose. One need only mention Franklin, Jefferson, Paine, and the Federalist Papers to suggest the efficiency, effectiveness, and grace of that period's prose style. Perhaps because prose is a more suitable vehicle for expressing abstractions, the most skilled and enduring utterances of the debate over American independence and the course of American life were in the form of nonfiction prose. Even Joel Barlow, whose *Vision of Columbus* impressed Washington as deathless, was a better writer in prose than in poetry. Such too was the case with Trumbull.

As with his poetry, Trumbull wrote his best and most important prose when still a young man. And again as with his poetry, Trumbull's prose reflects the proper neoclassical models of Joseph Addison and Richard Steele as well as the often biting satire of Jonathan Swift.

Trumbull was still a teenager when he and his even younger classmate, Timothy Dwight, published "The Meddler" in 1769 and 1770. Trumbull's contributions, including approximately two-thirds of the ten essays, covered such predictable topics as humor, coquetry, language, the world's sins, and religious pretentiousness, topics he would pursue further in his poetry. The essays are clearly derivative, but they are remarkable as products of two able but young men of colonial America. Gimmestad said of these essays, "They reveal courage, careful observation, youthful ebullience, skill in sentence movement, competence in the use of satire, and acquaintance with Classical and English literature."

Almost immediately following the termination of "The Meddler," Trumbull and Dwight began another series of essays called "The Correspondent," which appeared in two groups separated by almost three years. The first group of eight, all but one by Trumbull, were published during the first half of 1770 and ended when he left New Haven. The topics and tone of "The Correspondent" were more serious than were those of "The Meddler," but Trumbull still employed satire and occasional parody to instruct and castigate. Trumbull also wrote approximately two-thirds of the thirty essays in the second group, published in 1773.

Many of these essays again discussed the standard subjects of the day, but others dealt with serious and even vital issues. Trumbull continued his attack on the religious extremes of the Great Awakening on one hand and the overly rational metaphysicians on the other. He also showed an increasing opposition to England in essays on English colonial laws and the rising patriotic spirit. Finally, these essays gave Trumbull the opportunity to defend himself and his satiric method against attacks engendered by "The Meddler" essays and by *The Progress of Dulness*.

It is, nevertheless, to the verse satires that critics and readers, though few in number, turn continually. *The Progress of Dulness* satirizes what Trumbull saw as the faulty educational practices of his day and the concomitant weak preparation of ministers. Both as a student and later as a tutor at Yale, he saw the results of institutionalized ignorance, and he put that view into a three-part satire describing the education of and the consequences of that education on Tom Brainless, Dick Hairbrain, and Harriet Simper.

Trumbull makes clear in his preface to the first part what he intends to do with Tom Brainless. He promises to describe "a fellow, without any share of genius, or application of study" who can pass through a college "where ignorance wanders unmolested . . . and examinations are dwindled to mere form and ceremony."

In Hudibrastic couplets Trumbull describes Tom's collegiate career: "Four years at college dozed away/In sleep, and slothfulness, and play," and his ecclesiastical preparation: Tom "settles down with earnest zeal/Sermons to study, and to steal." Trumbull aimed to shake up the establishment, and he did. He also aimed to improve education and the preparation of the clergy; instead he received abuse from those whom he attacked.

The second and third parts of *The Progress of Dulness* are less caustic and more generalized. Dick Hairbrain moves from a rustic to a fop. His college days are spent in "the arts of cards and dice," his young manhood in aping foreign ways and getting into debt, his old age in being displaced by younger fops.

Harriet Simper of part three at first seems like an unfair representation of the females of Trumbull's day. Harriet is silly, fashion-crazed, and scheming; but Trumbull points out in his preface to part three that these characteristics result from the neglect of women's education. As Harriet's aunt asks, "And why should girls be learned or wise?/ Books only serve to spoil their eyes." As with Dick, Harriet soon grows old and is quickly outflirted by the other girls. Appropriately, after being rejected by Dick, she marries the Reverend Tom Brainless.

The Progress of Dulness, like *M'Fingal*, reflects Trumbull's familiarity with the neoclassical poets of the eighteenth century. His octosyllabic couplets come from Samuel Butler's *Hudibras* (1663, 1664, 1678), but the poem also shows the influence of Alexander Pope's *The Dunciad* (1728, 1743) as well as the poetry of Jonathan Swift and Charles Churchill.

While *The Progress of Dulness* evoked considerable ire from the orthodox educators and ministers, Trumbull's other well-known satire, *M'Fingal*, produced only praise from American patriots and predictable condemnation from the British and the Loyalists. The first canto, later divided into two cantos, was published at the beginning of the war (1776) and was a conscious attempt to stir the patriots to resistance by ridiculing the British and their followers. M'Fingal is a Scotsman and a Tory as well as the justice of the peace in a small town outside Boston. This canto opposes speeches made by M'Fingal and by Honorius, a Whig patriot, at a town meeting. In the second half of the poem, published in 1782, M'Fingal speaks again against the Whig position at the liberty pole in the center of town, and for his pains he is tarred and feathered. Once free, he goes home to make still one more speech to Tory friends in his cellar. Once more he is interrupted and this time flees to Boston.

M'Fingal is clearly the ridiculous villain of the

Illustrations by E. Tisdale, first published in the 1795 edition of M'Fingal

piece, but Honorius too, despite his Whiggish sentiments, comes out of the debate a bit of a bombastic oaf. No matter what the cause, Trumbull remained a firm foe of posturing and pretentiousness. As he said in a 1775 letter to John Adams, his intent in the poem was "to Expose a number of the principal Villains of the day, to ridicule the high blustering menaces & great expectations of the Tory party, & to burlesque the achievements of our ministerial Heroes, civil, ecclesiastical & military."

M'Fingal remained one of America's most widely read books and Trumbull one of the respected writers long after he gave up belletristic writing completely. Shortly before his death at eighty-one, two writers, commenting on the fledgling American literature, reflected on Trumbull's reputation. Samuel Kettell in *Specimens of American Poetry* (1829) said, "M'Fingal has had a greater celebrity than any other American poem"; and Samuel L. Knapp in *Lectures on American Literature* (1829) added that even in England *M'Fingal* is "at least acknowledged to belong to the first order of satirical poems." In the twentieth century, however, the praise has moderated but it is still there. Alexander Cowie in his *John Trumbull: Connecticut Wit* (1936) asserts that Trumbull's reputation rests secure in *M'Fingal*. Victor E. Gimmestad more cautiously calls Trumbull's work "a solid minor literary achievement."

Once known as the best of the Connecticut

Wits, America's first constellation of writers, Trumbull still remains the best of that group. Both Trumbull and the constellation, however, have dimmed considerably over the past two hundred years.

References:

Alexander Cowie, *John Trumbull: Connecticut Wit* (Chapel Hill: University of North Carolina Press, 1936);

Victor E. Gimmestad, *John Trumbull* (New York: Twayne, 1974);

Leon Howard, *The Connecticut Wits* (Chicago: University of Chicago Press, 1943);

Vernon Louis Parrington, *The Colonial Mind, 1620-1800,* volume 1 of *Main Currents in American Thought* (New York: Harcourt, Brace, 1927);

Parrington, ed., *The Connecticut Wits* (New York: Harcourt, Brace, 1926).

Papers:

The Burton Historical Collection, in the Woodbridge Papers at the Detroit Public Library, contains a number of published and unpublished poetry and prose manuscripts. The Moses Coit Tyler Collection at the Cornell University Library contains the largest group of published and unpublished poetry and prose manuscripts.

Mercy Otis Warren

(25 September 1728-19 October 1814)

Frank Shuffelton
University of Rochester

BOOKS: *The Adulateur. A Tragedy, As it is now acted in Upper Servia* (Boston: Printed & sold at the New Printing-Office, 1773);

The Group, As lately acted, and to be re-acted to the wonder of all superior intelligences, nigh head-quarters at Amboyne (Boston: Printed & sold by Edes & Gill, 1775);

The Blockheads: Or, The Affrighted Officers. A Farce, attributed to Warren (Boston: Printed by John Gill, 1776);

The Motley Assembly, A Farce. Published For the Entertainment Of the Curious, attributed to Warren (Boston: Printed & sold by Nathaniel Coverly, 1779);

Observations on the New Constitution, and on the Federal and State Conventions (Boston, 1788);

Poems, Dramatic and Miscellaneous (Boston: Printed by I. Thomas & E. T. Andrews, 1790);

History of the Rise, Progress and Termination of the American Revolution. Interspersed with Biographical, Political and Moral Observations, 3 volumes (Boston: Printed by Manning & Loring for E. Larkin, 1805).

Mercy Otis Warren is perhaps most widely recognized as the author of several Revolutionary War-era dramatic satires which castigated Thomas Hutchinson and his Massachusetts Loyalist associates, but she also wrote serious drama, poetry, prose, and a history of the Revolution which may be of even more value than her propaganda pieces. When her *Poems, Dramatic and Miscellaneous,* containing her two formal verse tragedies, came out in 1790, Alexander Hamilton wrote to her that "in the career of dramatic composition at least, female genius in the United States has outstripped the Male." And a recent critic, Gerald Weales, in surveying her career, remarks, "The best of Mercy Warren is almost certainly her prose—the *History,* the political pamphlet, the letters," and he goes on to argue that all her work is of interest for its revelation of an "urgent intelligence" and "passionate morality." Because her intelligence and morality were devoted to the cause of freedom during the American Revolution and after, she is one of the most distinctive and forceful voices of her time. She was perhaps the first woman in the United States to aspire to recognition as a writer, as a woman of letters rather than as merely a lady who wrote, and both her situation and her work speak to the difficulties of "female genius" demanding to be taken seriously by a male authority structure.

Born in West Barnstable, Massachusetts, Mercy Otis was the third of the thirteen children of James and Mary Allyne Otis. Her father was a prominent merchant, farmer, and politician who would become a leading figure in the country party opposing the Hutchinsons' and Olivers' control of Massachusetts politics. The most-famous politician from this Cape Cod squirearchy, however, was Mercy Otis's eldest brother, James, who went on to make a name for himself as a patriot propagandist and leader in the years before the Revolution, and her affection and admiration for this brother played a part in her own development as a writer. She received no formal education, but when the Reverend Jonathan Russell, a Barnstable neighbor, tutored James for Harvard, he also provided the young Mercy with books—Pope, Dryden, Raleigh's *History of the World*—and encouragement. Her first view of the world beyond Cape Cod was occasioned by a trip in 1743 to attend her brother's Harvard commencement. Although she was barred by her sex from a Harvard education, her youthful reading was nevertheless shaped in important ways by the expectations and curriculum of eighteenth-century Harvard as she followed in her own way her brother's college progress. When her husband later admired her mind "well-stocked with learning," it was for the most part the learning he himself had learned to respect in his own Harvard education.

On 14 November 1754 she married James Warren, an energetic Plymouth farmer and merchant, a country squirearch with Whig principles like the Otises. Except for eight years after the Revolution, when the Warrens bought and lived on Thomas Hutchinson's former estate in Milton, Plymouth was home for the rest of her life. The marriage was a real love match; Warren's letters to his wife when he was away on political or govern-

James Warren and Mercy Otis Warren, portraits by John Singleton Copley (Museum of Fine Arts, Boston, Bequest of Winslow Warren)

ment business mix news of his doings with expressions of love and concern, and her replies to her "dearest friend" lament his absence and return that love. Her husband not only admired Mercy Warren's learning, he encouraged her writing; when she was low in spirits, he advised her "to sit down and write a Satire on Villains, there are enough of them; if not, take in the Fools, then I am sure you will have enough. I am sure the remedy will succeed and you will feel a laudable pride." Warren's appeal to his wife's self-esteem was discerning, for justifiable pride in her own genuine abilities, in her family, and in her country fueled her creative work. When in 1769 her brother James was savagely beaten in a Boston coffeehouse and subsequently experienced long periods of insanity, she took upon herself the role of the family's propagandist for Whig principle and patriotic sentiment.

She had been writing poetry at least since the early years of her marriage, but her first publication was a satiric verse play, *The Adulateur. A Tragedy, As it is now acted in Upper Servia,* which appeared anonymously and in abbreviated form in March and April 1772 issues of the *Massachusetts Spy.* A memorandum by Warren notes the existence of a volunteer collaborator in the final pamphlet version of 1773: "Before the author thought proper to present another scene to the public, it was taken up and interlaced with productions of an unknown hand. The plagiary swells *The Adulateur* to a considerable pamphlet." The play pits the force of Rapatio, governor of Servia (Thomas Hutchinson), and his Tory cronies against the virtuous indignation of the Patriots led by Brutus (James Otis) and Cassius (Sam Adams). In act one Brutus urges his friends to stand up for their liberty while Rapatio vows "to trample down the choicest of their rights." In the second act Rapatio's "inhuman soldiers," acting on his orders, fill the streets with the blood of citizens, thus implicitly accusing Hutchinson of direct responsibility for the Boston Massacre. In the rather confused scenes of acts three and four Brutus urges the populace to "force a way to freedom," although Rapatio reasserts his control over Servia by means of his glozing speeches, control of the courts, and cunning use of his sycophants, and in the final act Brutus mourns for his country. *The Adulateur* is limited by its basic intention as propaganda; the characters are political cartoons; plot is sketchy at best; and the language plays off the oratorical diction of Whig spellbinders against the conniving whines of Tory rogues. Yet for all these weaknesses the play has an energy and bite that put it above the general run of Revolutionary-era satirical pamphlets.

The Adulateur, as with all of Warren's plays, was never staged, but its focus on the Boston Massacre and the real and imagined political maneuverings around it constitutes a discovery of the dramatic structures of contemporary events. Similarly, when her fragmentary second play, "The Defeat," appeared in the 24 May and 19 July 1773 issues of the *Boston Gazette* with a statement that it had been "lately exhibited," that claim pointed not to a stage presentation but argued for the historicity behind the satirically exaggerated figures of Rapatio and his confederate, Limpit (Andrew Oliver). "The Defeat" was inspired by the publication of incriminating letters written by Hutchinson and Oliver, letters obtained in England by Benjamin Franklin, the colonial agent. In "The Defeat" Rapatio has fallen, fears "the yawning pit . . . where traitors doom'd receive their just rewards," but despite his obvious cowardice still plots with Limpit to save himself, if not the cause, from the anger of "this much injur'd State." "The Defeat," never published separately, is not properly speaking a play but rather a dramatic satire, telling moments in the history of New England tyranny exposed in a form emphasizing their dramatic immediacy.

Warren wrote an epilogue for "The Defeat," but it was not published in the *Gazette*, perhaps because it reveals a broader, more sympathetic view of events than a satirical propagandist could afford to display. "My heart reluctant brands another's fame,/Or stamps an odium on a single name," she said, and in her next satirical play, *The Group*, published both in newspapers and pamphlets in 1775, Warren's satire and characterization are more subtle and complex. Hutchinson/Rapatio has gone to England from whence "He sends a groan across the broad Atlantic,/And with a phiz of Crocodilian stamp,/Can weep, and wreathe. . . ." Left behind are his Tory associates, who now must face the anger of "The people—arm'd—and all resolv'd to die/E're they'll submit." *The Group*, unlike the two previous plays which contrasted virtuous patriots and corrupt Tories, focuses on the anxieties and dissensions within the perilously situated Loyalist party. Hazlerod (Peter Oliver) and Hateall (Timothy Ruggles) continue to bluster, asserting that compassion shall never seize their steadfast breasts "Though blood and carnage spread thro' all the land," but other characters wonder if the game is worth the candle. Crusty Crowbar sees they have been merely Rapatio's "wretched tools" to seal their

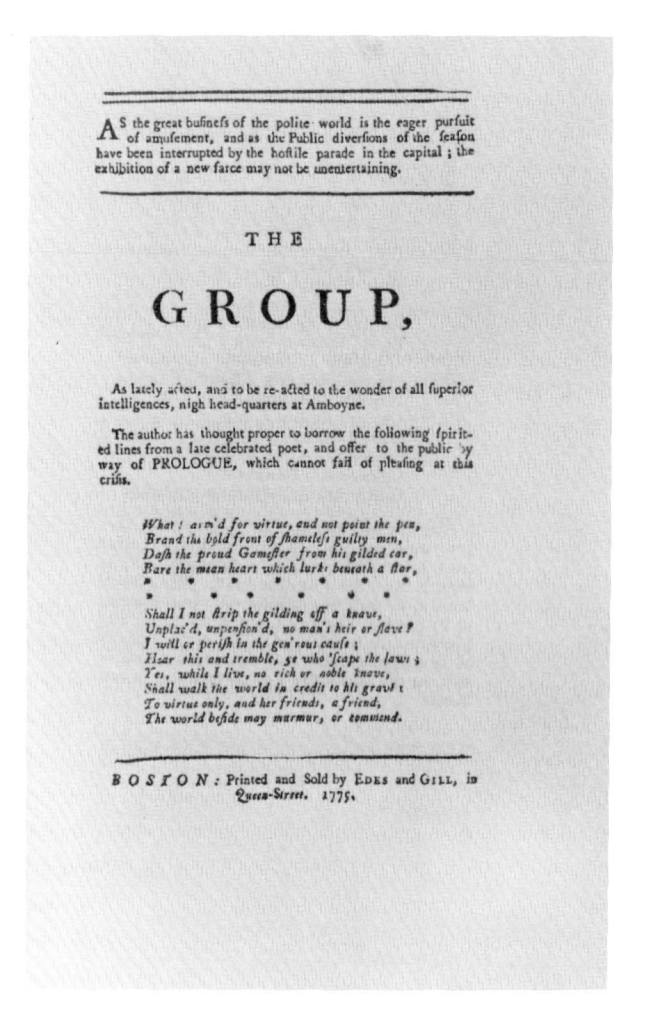

Title page for Warren's third, and best, satiric verse drama

country's ruin, and Simple Sapling notes his wife's call to give it up: "Poor Sylvia weeps,—and urges my return/To rural peace and humble happiness." Yet in the end the moral bankruptcy of the Tory group is complete; Sapling resolves to quarter British troops in his house, and if Sylvia "complains or murmurs at the plan,/Let her solicit charity abroad." The British General Sylla (Gage) feels compassion for "the best subjects that a Brunswick boasts" who "nobly scorn/To wear the fetters of his venal slaves," but the group has no feelings to spare even for their own families. In this play Warren uses the characters' allusions to their wives as a moral barometer of their degeneracy, and the epilogue is delivered by "a Lady nearly connected with one of the principal actors in the group, . . . who in mournful accents accosts them."

The feminine presence in *The Group* signals Warren's increasing recognition that women as well as men had a stake in Revolutionary politics and that they must be prepared to understand and speak for their own interests. Two plays attributed to Warren satirize women who are Tory sympathizers, portraying them as Anglophile provincials enamored of scarlet uniforms and London fashions. Both plays are in prose rather than in the verse of the earlier satires and use racier language than appears in her other works, but they display opinions consonant with hers. *The Blockheads: Or, The Affrighted Officers,* published in Boston in 1776 as a response to the now-lost satire of the Americans *The Blockade of Boston,* attributed to Gen. John Burgoyne, shows British officers cowering before the American threat to fortify Dorchester Hill. When British departure from Boston becomes inevitable, Simple, a friend of the Loyalists, attempts to dissuade his wife and daughter from following the troops, but carried away by their provincial thirst for supposed elegance, they scorn his resurgent American values. In *The Motley Assembly,* printed in Boston in 1779, Esquire Runt plans with Mrs. Flourish, Mrs. Bubble, the Misses Turncoat, and others to stage an assembly which will allow a chance to flirt with the genteel British officers who are in Boston as prisoners of war. When Captain Aid, an American officer, comes to call and proposes to toast General Washington, he is treated superciliously and retires to a coffeehouse where he has the last word, warning lest "dance and song o'er the patriot zeal prevail." The arguments both for and against ascribing these plays to Mrs. Warren are not particularly convincing, and probably the strongest underlying motive for awarding authorship to her is the lack of any other obvious contender. Yet there was the unidentified wit who fleshed out *The Adulateur,* and unlike the earlier satires there is nothing in her papers or letters to suggest responsibility for these two plays. At the end of her life, when the authorship of *The Group* had been ascribed to another, she asked John Adams to stop by the Boston Atheneum to attest to her authorship, but she made no similar attempt to claim these two prose plays. Thus, attribution must remain doubtful.

Regardless of whether she wrote these plays, Warren went on in her next dramatic efforts to give women strong, central roles. In 1790 appeared the first work printed under her own name, *Poems, Dramatic and Miscellaneous,* which contained two formal, five-act verse tragedies. *The Sack of Rome* and *The Ladies of Castile* were written during the years between the end of the Revolution and the ratification of the Constitution, and in various ways they offered lessons in republican virtue and re-

In 1781 the Warrens bought this house in Milton, Massachusetts. Formerly the country house of their political rival Thomas Hutchinson, it had been confiscated, along with his other property in the colonies, early in the Revolution.

publican history to a young nation still trying to define itself. Her preface to *The Sack of Rome* claims "the writer has aimed at moral improvement, by an exhibition of the tumult and misery into which mankind are often plunged by an unwarrantable indulgence of the discordant passions of the human mind." This play, set during the reign of the emperor Valentinian, presents his downfall as a result of his lecherous behavior and political jealousy, and the consequent political destabilization causes the ensuing invasion by the Vandals. Valentinian's wife and daughters, themselves virtuous, are inextricably caught up in the events his unregulated passions set off, and as the play moves toward its conclusion, the focus falls on them, torn between family loyalty to the morally despicable Valentinian and patriotic piety. *The Ladies of Castile* (printed after *The Sack of Rome* in *Poems* but written earlier) puts its women characters in an even more central position. Donna Maria, the wife and sister of patriotic leaders of the Spanish Cortes resisting the oppression of Charles V, demonstrates that her sex is no bar to a sense of political wrong:

> Though weak compassion sinks the female mind,
> And our frail sex dissolve in pity's tears;
> Yet justice' sword can never be resheath'd,
> 'Till Charles is taught to know we will be free.

Yet the revolt fails, Maria is exiled, and as Warren writes in the preface addressed to her son Winslow, "America stands alone."

The years during which the contents of *Poems, Dramatic and Miscellaneous* were being written and assembled were full of personal trials for Mercy Warren and political uncertainty for her country. Her brother James died when struck by lightning; her son James came back from naval duty during the Revolution shattered in mind and body; Winslow, her favorite son, was surely revealing himself as a charming scapegrace; another son, Charles, died of consumption; and the failure of her husband's political career seemed to signal a popular rejection of everything the Otises and Warrens stood for. Her last anonymous publication, *Observations on the New Constitution,* first printed in Boston in 1788, lined her up with her husband on the side of the antifederalists, but, although it was reprinted in Philadelphia, copies sent for distribution in the Albany area were rejected because "the style was too sublime and florid for the common people in this part of the country." *Poems, Dramatic and Miscellaneous* was, with its dedication to George Washington and her own name on the title page, a renewed assertion of her place in the literary and political mainstream of her country. The plays, thoroughly conventional as they were, she felt to be major statements, and she asked John Adams, then minister to Great Britain, to do what he could to have *The Sack of Rome* staged in London. Adams's tactful reply, "Nothing American Sells here," seems not to have injured her authorial pride.

The eighteen poems in the volume reveal Mrs. Warren as a competent versifier with a broad but fairly conventional range of subjects. She warned her son Winslow against the deistic "refinements of a sceptic age" ("To Torrismond"), and she praised Elizabeth Montagu's *Essay on the Writings and Genius of Shakespeare* (1769) for demonstrating that "A sister's hand may wrest a female pen,/ From the bold outrage of imperious men" ("To Mrs. Montagu"). "The Squabble of the Sea Nymphs" is a witty "political sally" requested by John Adams on the occasion of the Boston Tea Party; poems are addressed "To Fidelio, long absent on public Business" (her husband) or "To Honoria, on her Journey to Dover" (Mrs. Hannah Winthrop), while others mourn the deaths of her son Charles and John Winthrop of Harvard College. The poems offer perhaps the clearest demonstration of Mercy Warren's strengths and limitations as a writer; they are intelligent and sometimes witty expositions of sentiments and ideas which are theologically conventional but politically and socially advanced, formally polished but with a tendency to lapse into pomposity or bathos.

There yet remained one more major literary work, the completion and publication in 1805 of her three-volume *History of the Rise, Progress and Termination of the American Revolution. Interspersed with Biographical, Political and Moral Observations.* Warren had peculiar advantages for writing such a work because of the considerable information she derived from her brother, her husband, and such close friends as John and Samuel Adams, and because her thinking about the problems of historiography had been stimulated by her admiration for and acquaintanceship with Catherine Macaulay, the celebrated Whig historian and female intellectual. Begun as early as 1775, the history was completed in the years of the Alien and Sedition Laws and Jefferson's first term, and Warren's purpose was both to preserve a record of "the fortitude and virtue of their ancestors who through difficulties almost insurmountable, planted them in a happy soil" as well as to draw the lineaments of a political morality able to resist the temptations of "ambition and avarice, . . . the leading springs which generally activate the

First page of a letter from John Adams to Mercy Otis Warren (Sotheby Parke Bernet, sale 5187, 23 May 1984)

restless mind." Because her history was ultimately presented as a moral judgment, she could set herself forth as the possessor of "a mind that had not yielded to the assertion, that all political attentions lay out of the road of female life," for "every domestic enjoyment depends on the unimpaired possession of civil and religious liberty." Mercy Warren's history, written over nearly three decades, was shaped by her antifederalist resistance to "arbitrary power," her republican approval of the Jeffersonian revolution of 1800, her inherent feminism, and, below it all, her pride of place and family. American civilization in her view began with the Plymouth Pilgrims—Jamestown being a set of rowdies without a real government—and it was brother James Otis who might "justly claim the honor of laying the foundation of a revolution."

Warren's critical reflections on John Adams led to an epistolary controversy (in which she seems to have come out the better) and a break in the old and deep friendship between the two families. The breach was healed five years after her husband's death in 1808 and in the year before her own death in 1814, but not before Adams could write indignantly to Elbridge Gerry, "History is not the Province of the Ladies." The history found elsewhere a mixed reception, being branded with the party label in some quarters, having its potential market supererogated by the recent appearance of the early volumes of John Marshall's five-volume *The Life of Washington* (1804-1807), and it has undoubtedly gained more serious attention in the twentieth century than it did in the nineteenth. Lester H. Cohen has claimed that among her historian contemporaries "Warren had the most systematic understanding of the relationship between ideology and ethics, the best-developed interpretation of how corruption operated in history, and the clearest insight into the historian's role as a social and political critic." Her poetic and dramatic writing has had a somewhat similar reception; although the Revolutionary-era satires have been remembered, Samuel Kettell's *Specimens of American Poetry* (1829) chose to anthologize only "Simplicity," and then omitted the prologue with its restiveness at "The narrow bounds, prescribed to female life." In Warren's own time a younger poet, Judith Sargent Murray, praised her example as a woman writer—"Yes, honored Lady, to lead the envied way is thine"—but it took the feminist-inspired reexamination of the American literary canon to produce Emily Stipes Watts's assertion that Warren's work is "certainly more valuable and interesting than the poetry of the Connecticut Wits." Warren does not have to stand as the heroine of a party, for she has left behind a body of work that, if caught up in the conventions of its times, still displays a characteristic energy, intelligence, and revolutionary commitment worth serious attention in its own terms.

References:

Katherine Anthony, *First Lady of the Revolution* (Garden City: Doubleday, 1958);

Lester H. Cohen, "Explaining the Revolution: Ideology and Ethics in Mercy Otis Warren's Historical Theory," *William and Mary Quarterly,* third series, 37 (April 1980): 200-218;

Benjamin Franklin V, Introduction to *The Plays and Poems of Mercy Otis Warren* (Delmar, N.Y.: Scholars' Facsimiles, 1980), pp. vii-xxx;

Edmund M. Hayes, "Mercy Otis Warren: *The Defeat,*" *New England Quarterly,* 49 (September 1976): 440-458;

Hayes, "The Private Poems of Mercy Otis Warren," *New England Quarterly,* 54 (June 1981): 199-224;

Maud Macdonald Hutcheson, "Mercy Warren 1728-1814," *William and Mary Quarterly,* third series, 10 (July 1953): 378-401;

Charles H. Lippy, "Independence and Identity: Mercy Otis Warren Interprets the Revolution," *Ohio Journal of Religious Studies,* 4, no. 2 (1976): 66-76;

Walter J. Meserve, *An Emerging Entertainment: The Drama of the American People to 1828* (Bloomington: Indiana University Press, 1977), pp. 64-75;

Arthur H. Quinn, *A History of the American Drama from the Beginnings to the Civil War* (New York: Crofts, 1943), pp. 33-47;

William Raymond Smith, *History as Argument: Three Patriot Historians of the American Revolution* (The Hague: Mouton, 1966), pp. 73-119;

Emily Stipes Watts, *The Poetry of American Women from 1632 to 1945* (Austin: University of Texas Press, 1977), pp. 39-44;

Gerald Weales, "The Quality of Mercy, or Mrs. Warren's Profession," *Georgia Review,* 33 (Winter 1979): 881-894.

Papers:

The Massachusetts Historical Society has a collection of Warren's papers.

George Washington
(22 February 1732-14 December 1799)

David Curtis Skaggs
Bowling Green State University

BOOK: *The Journal of Major George Washington, sent by the Hon. Robert Dinwiddie, Esq.; His Majesty's Lieutenant-Governor and Commander in Chief of Virginia, to the Commandant of the French Forces on Ohio . . .* (Williamsburg: Printed by William Hunter, 1754; London: Printed for T. Jeffreys, 1754).

Editions and Collections: *The Writings of George Washington, 1745-1799,* edited by John C. Fitzpatrick, 39 volumes (Washington, D.C.: Government Printing Office, 1931-1944);

The Diaries of George Washington, edited by Donald Jackson and Dorothy Twohig, 6 volumes (Charlottesville: University Press of Virginia, 1976-1979);

The Papers of George Washington, W. W. Abbot, general editor, 5 volumes to date (Charlottesville: University Press of Virginia, 1981-).

OTHER: Jacob Nicolas Moreau, comp., *Mémoire contenant le précis des faits, avec leurs pièces justificatives pour servir de réponse aux observations envoyées par les ministres d'Angleterre, dans les cours de l'Europe,* includes excerpts from Washington's diary (Paris: Imprime Royal, 1756); republished as *A Memorial Containing a Summary View of Facts with Their Authorities, in Answer to the Observations Sent by the English Ministry to the Courts of Europe* (London, 1757; New York: Printed by Hugh Gaine, 1757).

Portrait by Charles Willson Peale, 1772. This portrait of Washington in his French and Indian War uniform is the only one painted before the American Revolution (courtesy of Washington and Lee University).

Few of his contemporaries wrote more than George Washington. One edition of his writings comprises thirty-nine volumes (and there are four more volumes of diaries), and a new edition of his papers should include one hundred volumes before its completion in the twenty-first century. And yet no important American of the Revolutionary era is more ignored as an author. No one would argue he wrote belles lettres, but neither did Thomas Jefferson. No one would argue that his literary talents involved more than the prose compositions of a planter, general, and statesman, but neither did those of James Madison. No one would argue that his writings reflected intellectual inquiry at the cutting edge of contemporary thought, but neither did Alexander Hamilton's famous essays. Yet all these other men's papers place them in the pantheon of early American literary figures, while Washington is usually omitted. Because his writings are so voluminous, because they usually concern the mundane details of public and private administration, and because they reflect the restraint of a man whose every word demanded attention, no important scholar has analyzed the corpus of Washington's writings with the same scholarly insight that Edmund Wilson provided the Civil War generation in his *Patriotic Gore*. Until such an enterprise is undertaken, early American literature will lack complete analysis.

The outline of Washington's career is well known. Born to a Virginia gentry family slightly below the Byrds, Carters, Lees, and Randolphs in status, he rose to the top rung of influence and affluence through the acquisition of the important skill of surveying, the acquaintance of the influential Fairfax family, the inheritance of the estate of an older half brother, and marriage on 6 January 1759 to Martha Dandridge Custis, a wealthy widow. Before he was thirty he had served as an envoy of the governor of Virginia to French commanders in the Ohio valley, commanded Virginia militiamen in combat during the French and Indian War, accompanied General Edward Braddock on his ill-fated expedition of 1755, published a journal of his western travels, been mentioned at the court of George II, and been elected to the House of Burgesses. He reluctantly joined the Revolutionary movement, commanded the Continental Army through the vicissitudes of war (1775-1783), presided over the federal Constitutional Convention (1787), and became the first President of the United States (1789-1797). For a quarter-century his only rival for American leadership was Benjamin Franklin, and before his death he was a living legend: "First in war, first in peace, and first in the hearts of his countrymen."

The vast body of Washington's writings may be grouped into five categories: diaries, journals, and memoranda; personal and business correspondence; military correspondence; political correspondence; and state papers. The total collection encompasses more than eight thousand documents.

That so much came from the pen of a man

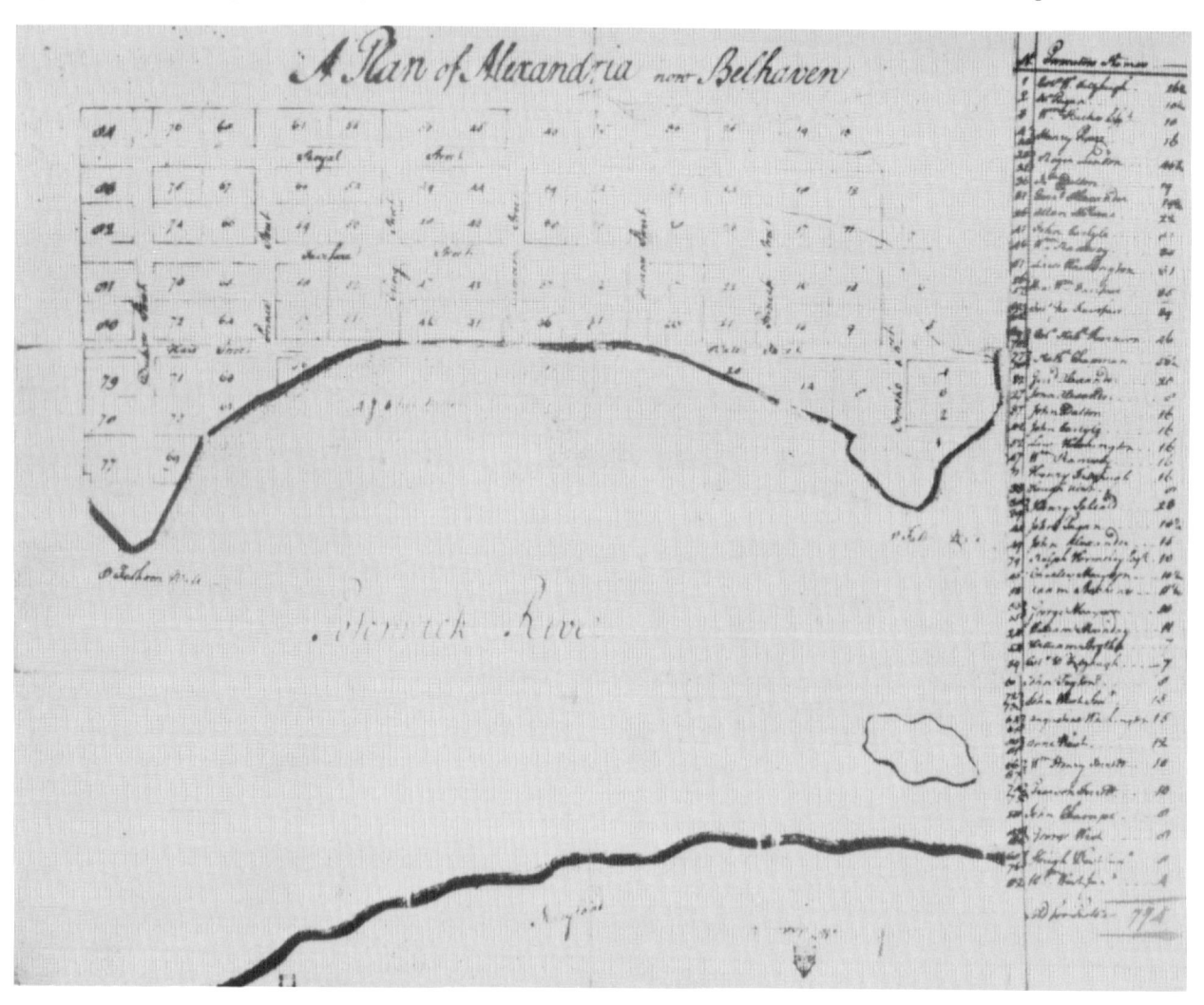

Washington drew these plans at the age of seventeen while he was working for the surveyor whom the General Assembly had hired to lay out the town of Alexandria.

whose formal education was modest is remarkable. His limited schooling ended in his mid-teens, and he spent the rest of his life trying to compensate for the deficiencies in training that contrasted his upbringing with that of many of his gentlemen contemporaries. The best known of his educational exercises is his 110 "Rules of Civility and Decent Behavior" which he transcribed into his copybook. Most of these maxims deal with proper social conduct, not with religious beliefs or the road to salvation. The other ingredients of his formal training involved that of surveying and of organized neatness. Both of these would complement his future military and administrative tasks. With the death of his father in 1743, much of the young man's youth was spent in the company of his older half brothers, particularly that of Lawrence Washington of Mount Vernon. It was at his older brother's side that the young man learned the behavior of a proper gentleman. Schooled in England, commissioned captain in the King's American Regiment which accompanied Admiral Edward Vernon on an ill-fated expedition to Cartagena in 1740-1741, Lawrence Washington was one of the colony's most eligible bachelors when he returned to the Potomac. In 1743 Lawrence married Anne Fairfax, daughter of Colonel William Fairfax, cousin and agent of Thomas Lord Fairfax, the proprietor of the vast tract known as the Northern Neck of Virginia. Young George visited his brother and sister-in-law often, and, through their example and their connections with the Fairfax household at nearby Belvoir, he acquired the polished manners of a gentleman and employment as a surveyor for Fairfax properties in the Shenandoah valley. Before he was nineteen he bought his first 1,500 acres beyond the Blue Ridge, and upon Anne's death in 1761, George inherited Mount Vernon, a gift of his brother who had died in 1752.

Washington's physical condition, western experience, and Fairfax connections made him a likely candidate as Governor Robert Dinwiddie's agent to convey Virginia's disapprobation of the expansion of New France into the upper Ohio valley, to which the Old Dominion had claims. This expedition and the consequent attempt to construct a fort at the Forks of the Ohio resulted in the publication of *The Journal of Major George Washington* (1754), and excerpts of his captured diary were published in Paris as document VIII in *Mémoire contenant les précis des faits...* (Paris, 1756). English translations appeared in London, New York, and Philadelphia in 1757.

Written as memoranda, these journals are typical of the daily accounts of the young

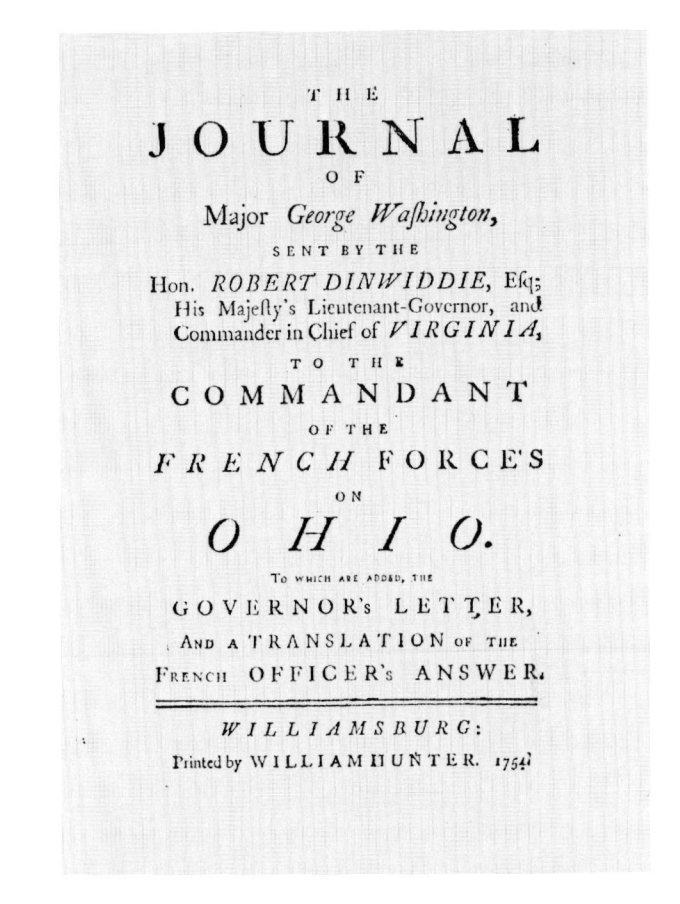

Title page for Washington's account of his journey to the Forks of the Ohio and Fort Le Boeuf. Although its style may be described as straightforward, objective, and even laconic, the journal reveals the depth of Washington's insight into human behavior and the analytic nature of his mind.

Washington. Laconic in style, they illustrate the author's astute insight into personal behavior and his acute analysis of the agricultural potential of the land through which he traveled: "We pass'd over much good Land . . . & through several extensive & very rich Meadows, one of which was near 4 Miles in length, & considerably wide in some Places" (December 1753). A letter describing his first combat demonstrated the romanticism of the young lieutenant colonel: "I heard the bullets whistle, and believe me, there is something charming in the sound."

Washington's prose style continually improved, not only in etymology (he spelled "like a gentleman"), but also in syntax. He was not a man interested in ideas; he was a man of action whose writings are straightforward and objective. His early attempts at flowery prose, such as his well-known love letter to Sally Fairfax, wife of Colonel

Fairfax's son, fall flat and are embarrassing for their awkwardness. More important are the growing self-discipline and attention to detail that the colonial-era letters and diaries convey to the reader.

His election as commander in chief of the Continental Army marked a new phase in Washington's literary career. He now had aides to handle his correspondence, often more than a dozen letters a day; yet one should not mistake an aide's handwriting for an aide's composition. As his noted editor John C. Fitzpatrick wrote, "Washington dominated his correspondence and cannot be denied complete responsibility for it. Sufficient examples are found among the letters of his ability to condense and improve his aides' drafts with simple, more forceful English."

Throughout the thousands of epistles written from his transient headquarters, one finds dozens of maxims about everything from military discipline to romantic advice, from political doctrines to horticultural directions. Among such admonitions are: "be strict in your discipline; that is, to require nothing unreasonable of your officers and men, but see that whatever is required be punctually complied with. Reward and punish every man according to his merit, without partiality or prejudice"; "Three things prompt Men to a regular discharge of their Duty in time of Action: natural bravery, hope of reward, and fear of punishment"; "The foundation of our Empire was not laid in the gloomy age of Ignorance and Superstition, but at an Epocha when the rights of mankind were better understood and more clearly defined, than at any former time.... At this auspicious period, the United States came into existence as a Nation, if their Citizens should not be completely free or happy, the fault will be intirely their own." During the war he kept his diaries only during 1781. He began that year's "Journal of Military transactions" with a lament that eloquently expresses in a series of parallelisms the failures of six years of combat: "Instead of having Magazines filled with provisions, we have a scanty pittance scattered here & there in the different States. Instead of having our Arsenals well supplied with Military Stores, we are poorly provided.... Instead of having the Regiments completed ... scarce any State in the Union has, at this hour an eighth part of its quota and little prospect, that I can see, of ever getting more than half. In a word—instead of having everything in a readiness to take to the field, we have nothing—and instead of having the prospect of a glorious offensive campaign before us, we have a bewildered, and gloomy defensive one."

However often such sentiments may appear platitudinous, they represent clearly his growing assertiveness, his discernment, and his grasp of the situation. His impassive, imperturbable, persistently prosaic tone conveyed the essence of the American cause, a sense of honor, an integrity that surpassed that of his contemporaries. Most important, his writings convey his belief in republican government, that it could succeed in America and that America could provide an example to the world: "To complete the American character, it remains for the citizens of the United States to shew to the world, that the reproach heretofore cast on republican Governments for their want of stability, is without foundation, when that government is the deliberate choice of an enlightened people."

It is this national mission he saw for the American people that is best embodied in his most graceful literary exercises—the state papers. Much of the breadth of vision and felicity of phrase can be found in his wartime letters to Congress. But it is found most commonly after Yorktown when the hectic pace of combat slowed and he had time for contemplative writings. Such papers include his resignation to Congress in 1783, the 1783 circular letter to the states, the first inaugural address of 1789, and the annual messages to Congress. Among the most important and lasting were the Newburgh address of 1783 and the Farewell Address of 1796.

Washington's drawing of the crest for his presidential carriage (Library of Congress)

A letter from Washington to John Jay

Printed-cotton mourning kerchief (New-York Historical Society)

The Newburgh Address is one of the least known important public papers in American history. When his officers threatened to stage a coup d'état to redress their just grievances, Washington spoke to the assembled leaders of the Continental Army and reminded them of their ideals and how an overthrow of the government would mark the ruination of the experiment in republican government. He concluded with phrases that remind modern readers of Sir Winston Churchill: "And let me conjure you, in the name of our common Country, as you value your own sacred honor, as you respect the rights of humanity, and as you regard the Military and National character of America, to express your utmost horror and detestation of the Man who wishes, under any specious pretences, to overturn the liberties of our Country, and who wickedly attempts to open the flood gates of civil discord and deluge our rising Empire in Blood. By thus determining and thus acting, you will pursue the plain and direct road to the attainment of your wishes.... And you will by the dignity of your Conduct, afford occasion for Posterity to say, when speaking of the glorious example you have exhibited to Mankind, 'had this day been wanting, the World had never seen the last stage of perfection to which human nature is capable of attaining.'"

This sense of the judgment of future generations upon his own permeated his leadership of the new nation formed under the Constitution of 1787. When he chose to retire from the presidency, he forwarded to Alexander Hamilton both a copy of a valedictory draft prepared by James Madison in 1792 and his own recommendations relative to foreign policy and domestic politics. Hamilton's redrafted manuscript embodied the form and substance of Washington's proposal but enlarged on many of the president's ideas and introduced new material. Washington felicitously rephrased Hamilton's draft, eschewing the former secretary of the treasury's wordiness for his more restrained syntax. Where Hamilton wrote "Why quit our own ground to stand upon foreign ground?" Washington eliminated the first "ground." Hamilton wrote: "Permanent alliance, intimate connection with any part of the foreign world is to be avoided." Washington rewrote: "Tis our true policy to steer clear of permanent Alliances with any portion of the foreign world." Clearly the commander in chief still successfully revised the prose of his former aide-de-camp. Even so, enough of Hamilton remains to make the document the most prolix of his state papers.

The Farewell Address represents Washington's final legacy to the nation, a political testament with significance well into the twentieth century. As a comprehensive and authoritative statement it pleaded for an ending of domestic political factionalism (obviously ignored), for avoiding partisan conflicts over foreign policy (fitfully observed), and for maintaining an aloofness from the endless wars of European powers (a major force in national diplomacy for over a century).

The literary qualities of Washington's prose are a reflection of his character—dynamic force, prudence, clairvoyance, self-restraint, perseverance, and realistic idealism. Because he lacked the classical training of his contemporaries, his allusions are biblical, or homely, or to contemporary dramatic works such as Joseph Addison's *Cato*. While he inwardly exhibited flashes of extreme passion, he normally wrote with an imperturbability of one accustomed to command. From a boyhood of little formal training, George Washington became a prose writer with a directness and simplicity that commends him to those wishing to understand the rational mind of eighteenth-century America.

Biographies:
Douglas Southall Freeman and others, *George Washington*, 7 volumes (New York: Scribners, 1948-1957);
James Thomas Flexner, *George Washington*, 4 volumes (Boston: Little, Brown, 1965-1972);
John R. Alden, *George Washington: A Biography* (Baton Rouge: Louisiana State University Press, 1984).

References:
Harold W. Bradley, "The Political Thinking of George Washington," *Journal of Southern History*, 11 (November 1955): 469-486;
Gilbert Chinard, *To the Farewell Address: Ideas of Early American Foreign Policy* (Princeton: Princeton University Press, 1961);
Marcus Cunliffe, *George Washington: Man and Monument* (Boston: Little, Brown, 1958);
Edmund S. Morgan, "George Washington: The Aloof American," *Virginia Quarterly Review*, 52 (Summer 1976): 411-436;
Samuel Eliot Morison, "The Young Man Washington," in his *By Land and By Sea* (New York: Knopf, 1953);
Richard B. Morris, "George Washington: Surrogate Father to the Revolutionary Generation," in his *Seven Who Shaped Our Destiny: The Founding Fathers as Revolutionaries* (New York: Harper & Row, 1973);
Saul K. Padover, "The American as Archetype: George Washington (1732-1799)," in his *The Genius of America: Men Whose Ideas Shaped Our Civilization* (New York: McGraw-Hill, 1960);
Victor Hugo Paltsits, *Washington's Farewell Address* (New York: New York Public Library, 1935);
Garry Wills, *Cincinnatus: George Washington and the Enlightenment* (Garden City: Doubleday, 1984).

Papers:
See "Presidential Papers Microfilm: George Washington Papers," 124 reels with printed index (Washington, D.C.: Library of Congress, 1965). This microfilm constitutes the basis for the Abbot edition of *The Papers of George Washington*. By far the largest collection of his papers is in the Library of Congress.

Phillis Wheatley
(circa 1754-5 December 1784)

Sondra A. O'Neale
Emory University

BOOKS: *An Elegiac Poem, on the Death of that Celebrated Divine, and Eminent Servant of Jesus Christ, the Reverend and Learned George Whitefield . . .* (Boston: Printed & sold by Ezekiel Russell & by John Boyles, 1770); republished in *Heaven the Residence of Saints,* by Ebenezer Pemberton (London: Printed for E. & C. Dilly, 1771);

Poems on Various Subjects, Religious and Moral. By Phillis Wheatley, Negro Servant to Mr. John Wheatley of Boston (London: Printed for Archibald Bell & sold in Boston by Cox & Berry, 1773; Philadelphia: Printed by Joseph Crukshank, 1786);

An Elegy, Sacred to the Memory of that Great Divine, The Reverend and Learned Dr. Samuel Cooper (Boston: Printed & sold by E. Russell, 1784);

Liberty and Peace, A Poem (Boston: Printed by Warden & Russell, 1784).

Collections: *Life and Works of Phillis Wheatley. Containing Her Complete Poetical Works, Numerous Letters and a Complete Biography of This Famous Poet of a Century and a Half Ago,* edited by G. Herbert Renfro (Washington, D.C.: A. Jenkins, 1916);

The Poems of Phillis Wheatley, Edited with an Introduction and Notes, edited by Charlotte Ruth Wright (Philadelphia: The Wrights, 1930);

The Poems of Phillis Wheatley, edited by Julian D. Mason, Jr. (Chapel Hill: University of North Carolina Press, 1966).

Although she was an African slave, Phillis Wheatley was one of the best-known poets in prenineteenth-century America. Pampered in the household of prominent Boston commercialist John Wheatley, lionized in New England and England, with presses in both places publishing her poems, and paraded before the new republic's political leadership and the old empire's aristocracy, Phillis was the abolitionists' illustrative testimony that blacks could be both artistic and intellectual. Her name was a household word among literate colonists and her achievements a catalyst for the fledgling antislavery movement.

Phillis was seized from Senegal/Gambia, West Africa, when she was about seven years old. She was transported to the Boston docks with a shipment of "refugee" slaves, who because of age or physical frailty were unsuited for rigorous labor in the West Indian and Southern colonies, the first ports of call after the Atlantic crossing. In the month of August 1761, "in want of a domestic," Susanna Wheatley, wife of prominent Boston tailor John Wheatley, purchased "a slender, frail female child . . . for a trifle" because the captain of the slave ship believed that the waif was terminally ill, and he wanted to gain at least a small profit before she died. A Wheatley relative later reported that the family surmised the girl—who was "of slender frame and evidently suffering from a change of climate," nearly naked, with "no other covering than a quantity of dirty carpet about her"—to be "about seven years old ... from the circumstances of shedding her front teeth."

After discovering the girl's precociousness, the Wheatleys, including their son Nathaniel and their daughter Mary, did not entirely excuse Phillis from her domestic duties but taught her to read and write. Soon she was immersed in the Bible, astronomy, geography, history, British literature (particularly John Milton and Alexander Pope), and the Greek and Latin classics of Vergil, Ovid, Terence, and Homer. In "To the University of Cambridge in New England" (probably the first poem she wrote but not published until 1773) Phillis indicated that despite this exposure, rich and unusual for an American slave, her spirit yearned for the intellectual challenge of a more academic atmosphere.

Although scholars had generally believed that *An Elegiac Poem, on the Death of that Celebrated Divine, and Eminent Servant of Jesus Christ, the Reverend and Learned George Whitefield ...* (1770) was Wheatley's first published poem, Carl Bridenbaugh revealed in 1969 that thirteen-year-old Phillis—after hearing a miraculous saga of survival at sea—wrote "On Messrs. Hussey and Coffin," a poem which was published on 21 December 1767 in the Newport, Rhode Island, *Mercury.* But it was the Whitefield elegy that brought Wheatley national renown. Published as a broadside and a pamphlet in Boston, Newport, and Philadelphia, the poem was published with Ebenezer Pemberton's funeral sermon for Whitefield in London in 1771, bringing her international acclaim.

By the time she was eighteen, Phillis had gathered a collection of twenty-eight poems for which she, with the help of Mrs. Wheatley, ran advertisements for subscribers in Boston newspapers in February 1772. When the colonists were apparently unwilling to support literature by an African, she and the Wheatleys turned in frustration to London for a publisher. Phillis had forwarded the Whitefield poem to Selina Hastings, Countess of Huntingdon, to whom Whitefield had been chaplain. A wealthy supporter of evangelical and abolitionist causes, the countess instructed bookseller Archibald Bell to begin correspondence with Phillis in preparation for the book.

Phillis, suffering from a chronic asthma condition and accompanied by Nathaniel, left for London on 8 May 1771. The now-celebrated poetess was welcomed by several dignitaries: abolitionists' patron the Earl of Dartmouth, poet and activist Baron George Lyttleton, Sir Brook Watson (soon to be the Lord Mayor of London), philanthropist John Thorton, and Benjamin Franklin. While Phillis was recrossing the Atlantic to reach Mrs. Wheatley, who, at the summer's end, had become seriously ill, Bell was circulating the first edition of *Poems on Various Subjects, Religious and Moral* (1773), the first volume of poetry by an American Negro published in modern times.

Poems on Various Subjects revealed that Phillis's favorite poetic form was the couplet, both iambic pentameter and heroic. More than one-third of her canon is composed of elegies, poems on the deaths of noted persons, friends, or even strangers whose loved ones employed the poet. The poems that best demonstrate her abilities and are most often questioned by detractors are those that employ classical themes as well as techniques. In her epyllion "Niobe in Distress for Her Children Slain by Apollo, from Ovid's *Metamorphoses,* Book VI, and from a View of the Painting of Mr. Richard Wilson," she not only

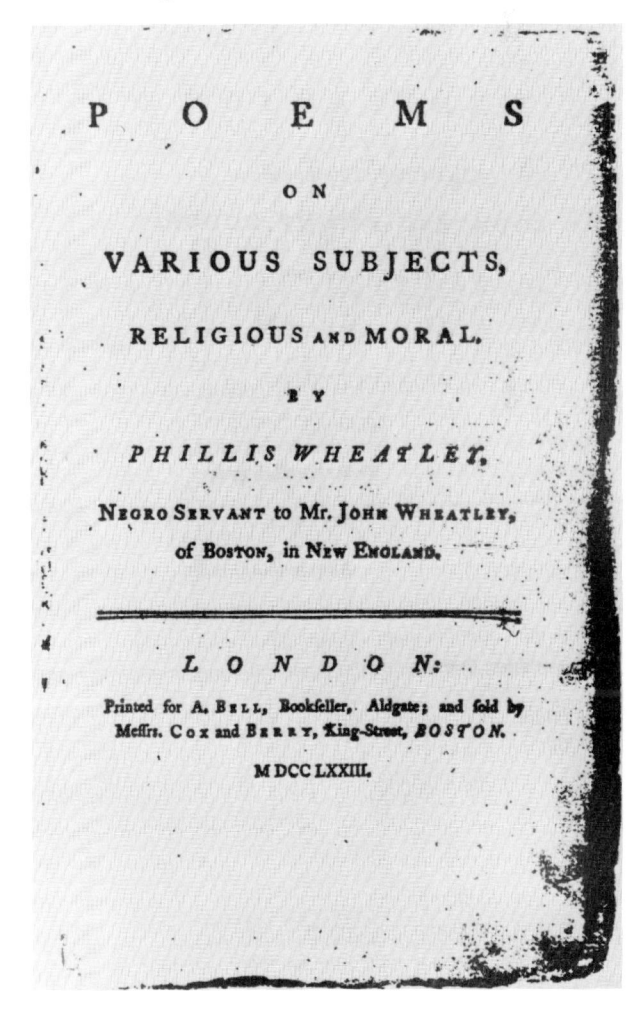

Title page for the first collection of poetry by an American Negro to be published in modern times

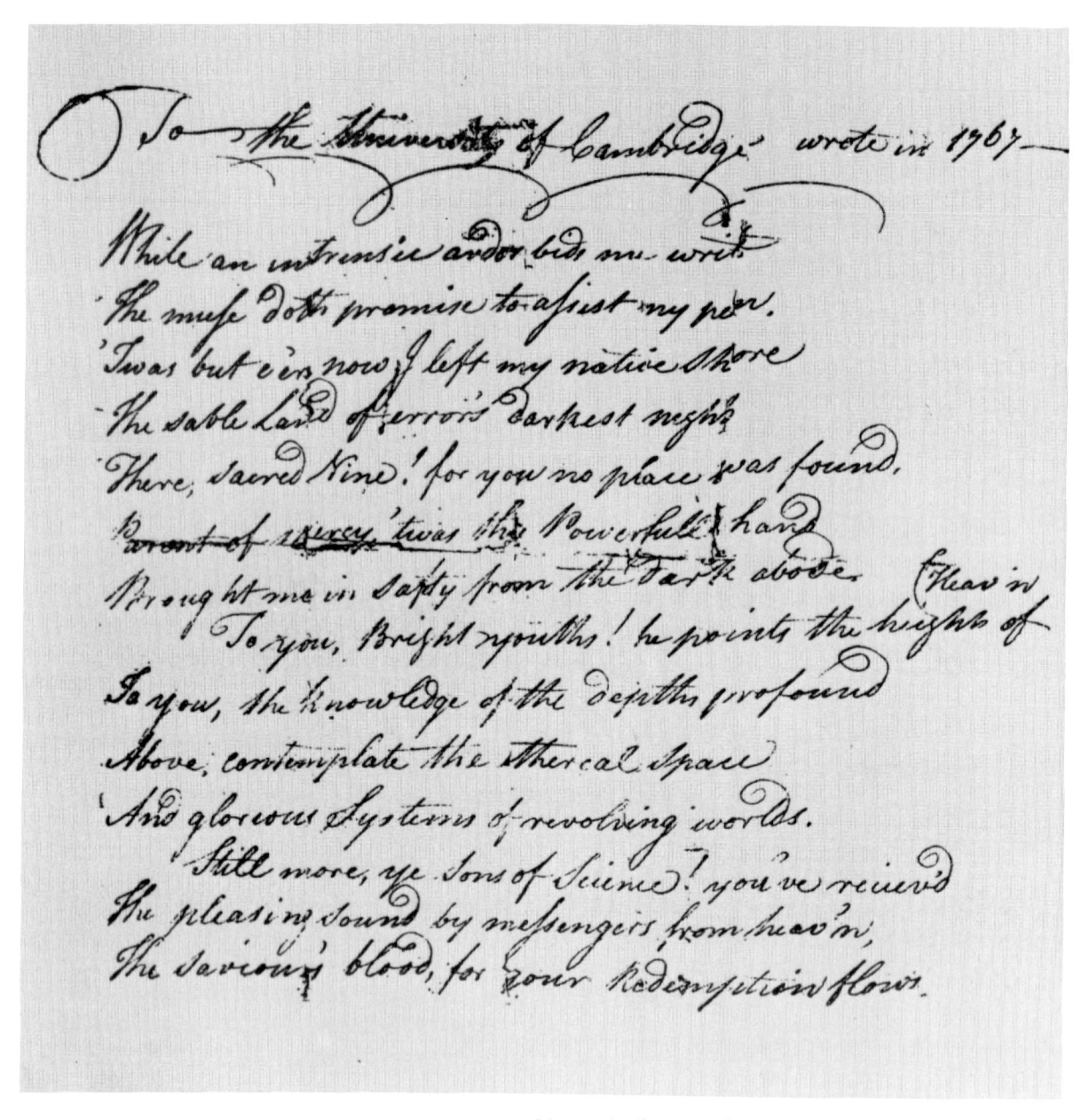

Manuscript for an early poem (American Antiquarian Society)

translates Ovid but adds her own beautiful lines to extend the dramatic imagery. In "To Maecenas" she transforms Horace's ode into a celebration of Christ.

In addition to classical and neoclassical techniques, Wheatley applied biblical symbolism to evangelize and to comment on slavery. For instance, "On Being Brought from Africa to America," the best-known Wheatley poem, chides the Great Awakening audience to remember that Africans must be included in the Christian stream: "Remember, *Christians, Negroes,* black as *Cain,* / May be refin'd and join th' angelic train." The remainder of Wheatley's themes can be classified as celebrations of America. She was the first to applaud this nation as glorious "Columbia" and that in a letter to no less than the first president of the United States, George Washington, with whom she had corresponded and whom she was later privileged to meet. Her love of virgin America as well as her religious fervor is further suggested by the names of those colonial leaders who signed the attestation that appeared in some copies of *Poems on Various Subjects* to authenticate and support her work: Thomas Hutchinson,

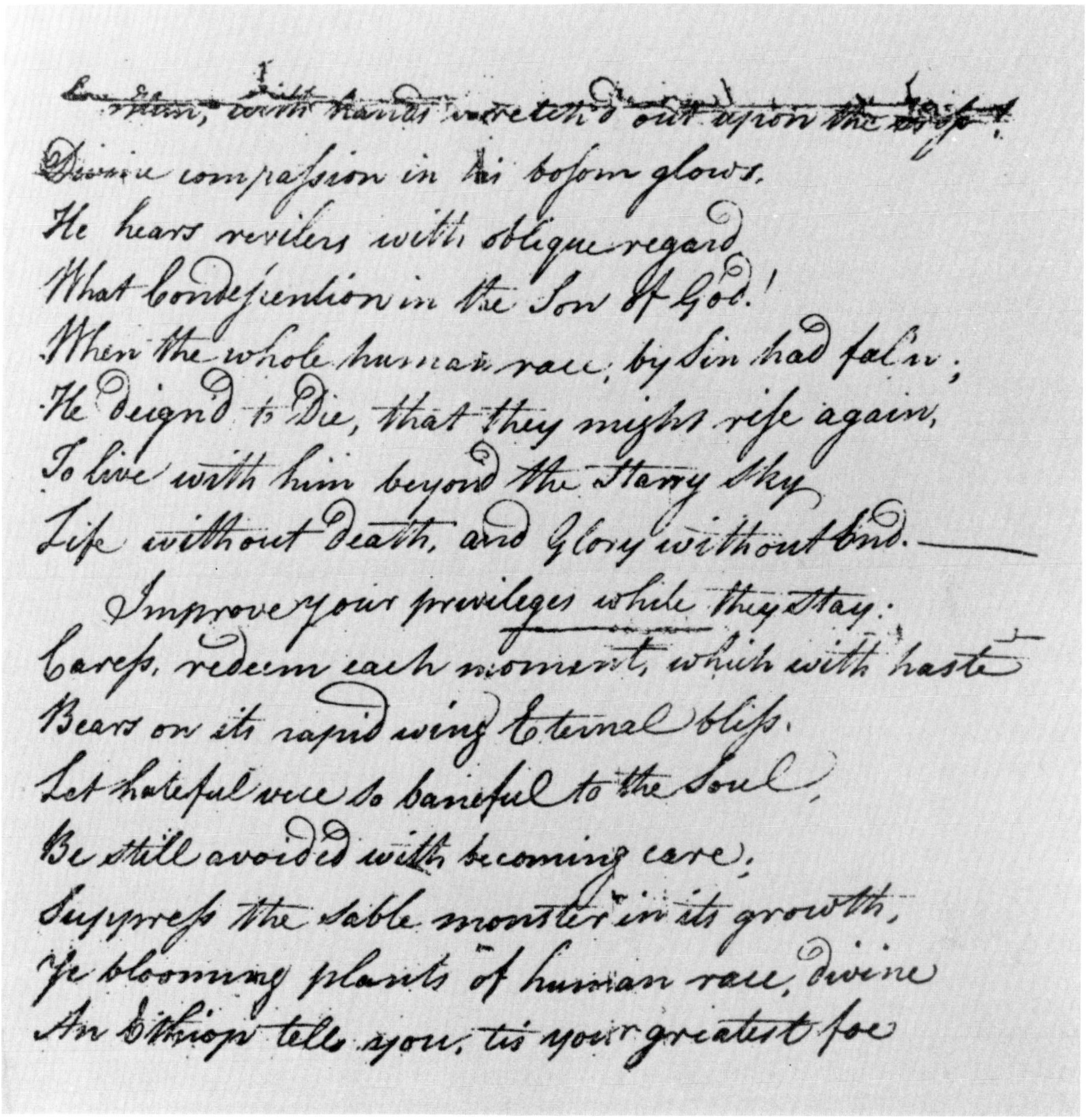
~~Man, with hands stretch'd out upon the Cross!~~
Divine compassion in his bosom glows.
He hears revilers with oblique regard
What Condescention in the Son of God!
When the whole human race, by Sin had fal'n;
He deign'd to Die, that they might rise again,
To live with him beyond the Starry Sky
Life without Death, and Glory without End.—
Improve your privileges while they stay:
Caress, redeem each moment, which with haste
Bears on its rapid wing Eternal bliss.
Let hateful vice so baneful to the Soul,
Be still avoided with becoming care;
Suppress the sable monster in its growth,
Ye blooming plants of human race, divine
An Ethiop tells you, 'tis your greatest foe

governor of Massachusetts; John Hancock; Andrew Oliver, lieutenant governor; James Bowdoin; and Reverend Mather Byles. Another fervent Wheatley supporter was Dr. Benjamin Rush, one of the signers of the Declaration of Independence.

Phillis was manumitted some three months before Mrs. Wheatley died on 3 March 1774. Although many British editorials castigated the Wheatleys for keeping Phillis in slavery while presenting her to London as the African genius, the family had provided an ambiguous haven for the poet. Phillis was kept in a servant's place—a respectable arm's length from the Wheatleys' genteel circles—but she had experienced neither slavery's treacherous demands nor the harsh economic exclusions pervasive in a free-black existence. With the death of her benefactor, Phillis slipped toward this tenuous life. Mary Wheatley and her father died in 1778; Nathaniel, who had married and moved to England, died in 1783. Throughout the lean years of the war and the following depression, the assault of these racial realities was more than her sickly body or aesthetic soul could withstand.

On 1 April 1778, despite the skepticism and

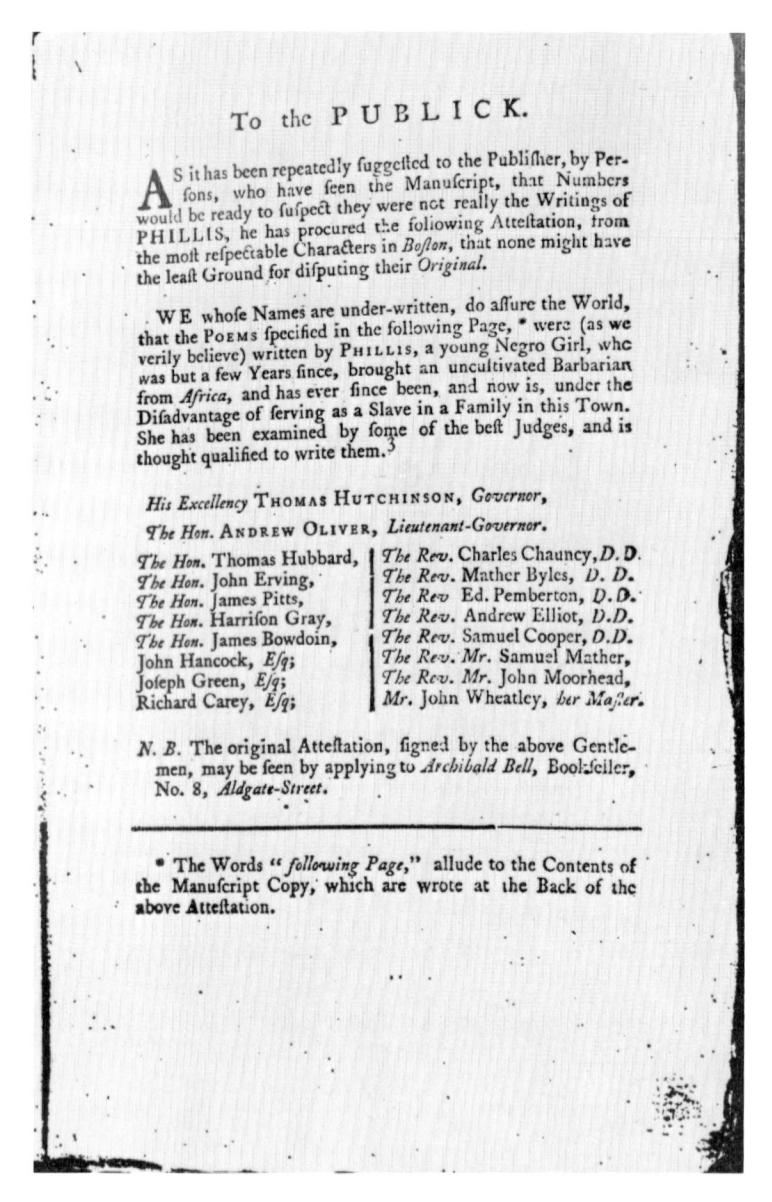

This attestation to the authenticity of Wheatley's writings was first published in a 1773 edition of Poems on Various Subjects

disapproval of some of her closest friends, Phillis married John Peters, whom she had known for some five years. A free black, Peters evidently aspired to entrepreneurial and professional greatness. He is purported in various historical records to have called himself Dr. Peters, to have practiced law (perhaps as a free-lance advocate for hapless blacks), kept a grocery in Court Street, exchanged trade as a baker and a barber, and applied for a liquor license for a bar. Described by Merle A. Richmond as "a man of very handsome person and manners," who "wore a wig, carried a cane, and quite acted out 'the gentleman,'" Peters was also called "a remarkable specimen of his race, being a fluent writer, a ready speaker." Peters's ambitions cast him as "shiftless," arrogant, and proud in the eyes of some reporters, but as a black man in an era that valued only his brawn, Peters's business acumen was simply not salable. Like many others who scattered throughout the Northeast to avoid the fighting during the Revolutionary War, the Peterses moved temporarily from Boston to Wilmington, Massachusetts, shortly after their marriage.

Merle A. Richmond points out that economic conditions in the colonies during and after the war were harsh, particularly for free blacks, who were unprepared to compete with whites in a stringent job market. These societal factors, rather than any refusal to work on Peters's part, were perhaps most responsible for the newfound poverty that Phillis suffered in Wilmington and Boston, after they later returned there. Between 1779 and 1783, the couple had three children (all of whom died as toddlers), and Peters drifted further into penury, often leaving Phillis to fend for herself and the children by working as a charwoman while he dodged creditors and tried to find employment.

During the first six weeks after their return to Boston, Phillis and the children stayed with one of Mrs. Wheatley's nieces in a bombed-out mansion that was converted to a day school after the war. Peters them moved them into an apartment in a rundown section of Boston, where other Wheatley relatives soon found Phillis sick and destitute. As Margaretta Matilda Odell recalls, "Two of her children were dead, and the third was sick unto death. She was herself suffering for want of attention, for many comforts, and that greatest of all comforts in sickness—cleanliness. She was reduced to a condition too loathsome to describe.... In a filthy apartment, in an obscure part of the metropolis, lay dying the mother, and the wasting child. The woman who had stood honored and respected in the presence of the wise and good . . . was numbering the last hours of life in a state of the most abject misery, surrounded by all the emblems of a squalid poverty!"

Yet throughout these lean years, Phillis continued to write and publish her poems and to maintain, though on a much more limited scale, her international correspondence. She also felt that despite the poor economy, her American audience and certainly her evangelical friends would support a second volume of poetry. Between 30 October and 18 December 1779, with at least the partial motive of raising funds for her family, she ran six advertisements soliciting subscribers for "300 pages in Octavo," a volume "Dedicated to the Right Hon. Benjamin Franklin, Esq.: One of the Ambassadors of the United States at the Court of France," that would include thirty-three poems and thirteen letters. As with *Poems on Various Subjects,* however, the American populace would not support one of its most noted poets. (The first American edition of this book was not published until two years after her death.) During the year of her death (1784), she was able to publish, under the name Phillis Peters, a masterful sixty-four-line poem in a pamphlet entitled *Liberty and Peace,* which hailed America as "*Co-lumbia*" victorious over "Britannia Law." Proud of her nation's intense struggle for freedom that, to her, bespoke an eternal spiritual greatness, Phillis ended the poem with a triumphant ring:

Britannia owns her Independent Reign,
Hibernia, Scotia, and the Realms of Spain;
And Great *Germania's* ample Coast admires
The generous Spirit that *Columbia* fires.
Auspicious Heaven shall fill with fav'ring Gales,
Where e'er *Columbia* spreads her swelling Sails:
To every Realm shall *Peace* her Charms display,
And Heavenly *Freedom* spread her gold Ray.

On 2 January of that same year, she published *An Elegy, Sacred to the Memory of that Great Divine, The Reverend and Learned Dr. Samuel Cooper,* just a few days after the death of the Brattle Street church's pastor. And, sadly, in September the "Poetical Essays" section of *The Boston Magazine* carried "To Mr. and Mrs. ————, on the Death of their Infant Son," which probably was a lamentation for the death of one of her own children and which certainly foreshadowed her death three months later.

Phillis Wheatley died, uncared for and alone. As Richmond concludes, with ample evidence, when Phillis expired on 5 December 1784, John Peters was incarcerated, "forced to relieve himself of debt by an imprisonment in the county jail." Their last surviving child died in time to be buried with his mother, and, as Odell recalled, "A grandniece of Phillis' benefactress, passing up Court Street, met the funeral of an adult and a child: a bystander informed her that they were bearing Phillis Wheatley to that silent mansion...."

Recent scholarship shows that Phillis Wheatley wrote perhaps 145 poems (most of which would have been published if the encouragers she begged for had come forth to support the second volume), but this artistic heritage is now lost, probably abandoned during Peters's quest for subsistence after her death. Of the numerous letters she wrote to national and international political and religious leaders, some two dozen notes and letters are extant. As an exhibition of African intelligence, exploitable by members of the enlightenment movement, by evangelical Christians, and by other abolitionists, she was perhaps recognized even more in England and Europe than in America. Early twentieth-century critics of Black American literature were not very kind to Wheatley because of her supposed lack of concern about slavery. Wheatley, however, did have a statement to make about the institution of slavery, and she made it to the most influential segment of eighteenth-century society—the institutional church. Two of the greatest influences on Phillis Wheatley's thought and poetry were the Bible and eighteenth-century evangelical Christianity; but until fairly recently Wheatley's critics did not consider her use of biblical allusion nor its symbolic application as a statement against slavery. She often spoke in explicit biblical language designed to move church members to decisive action. For instance, these bold lines in her poetic eulogy to General David Wooster castigate patriots who confess Christianity yet oppress her people:

> But how presumptuous shall we hope to find
> Divine acceptance with the Almighty mind
> While yet o deed ungenerous they disgrace
> And hold in bondage Afric: blameless race
> Let virtue reign and then accord our prayers
> Be victory ours and generous freedom theirs.

And in an outspoken letter to the Reverend Samson Occom, written after Wheatley was free and published repeatedly in Boston newspapers in 1774, she equates American slaveholding to that of pagan Egypt in ancient times: "Otherwise, perhaps, the Israelites had been less solicitous for their Freedom from Egyptian Slavery: I don't say they would have been contented without it, by no Means, for in every human Breast, God has implanted a Principle, which we call Love of freedom; it is impatient of Oppression, and pants for Deliverance; and by the Leave of our modern Egyptians I will assert that the same Principle lives in us."

In the past ten years, Wheatley scholars have uncovered poems, letters, and more facts about her life and her association with eighteenth-century black abolitionists. They have also charted her notable use of classicism and have explicated the sociological intent of her biblical allusions. All this research and interpretation has proven Wheatley's disdain for the institution of slavery and her use of art to undermine its practice. Before the end of this century the full aesthetic, political, and religious implications of Wheatley's art and even more salient facts about her life and works will surely be known and celebrated by all who study the eighteenth century and by all who revere this woman, a most important poet in the American literary canon.

Letters:
Charles Deane, ed., *Letters of Phillis Wheatley, the Negro-Slave Poet of Boston* (Boston: Privately printed, 1864);
Carter G. Woodson, ed., *The Mind of the Negro as Reflected in Letters Written During the Crisis: 1800-1860* (Washington, D.C., 1926): xvi-xxi.

Bibliography:
William H. Robinson, *Phillis Wheatley: A Bio-Bibliography* (Boston: G. K. Hall, 1981).

Biographies:
Margaretta Matilda Odell, *Memoir and Poems of Phillis Wheatley* (Boston: Light, 1834);
B. B. Thatcher, *Memoir of Phillis Wheatley, A Native African and a Slave* (Boston: G. W. Light/New York: Moore & Payne, 1834);
Benjamin Griffith Brawley, Note on Wheatley, in *Early Negro American Writers: Selections with Biographical and Critical Introductions,* edited by Brawley (Chapel Hill: University of North Carolina Press, 1935), pp. 31-55;
Brawley, *Negro Builders and Heroes* (Chapel Hill: University of North Carolina Press, 1937);
Shirley Graham, *The Story of Phillis Wheatley* (New York: J. Messner, 1949);
Martha Bacon, *Puritan Promenade* (Boston: Houghton Mifflin, 1964);
Sidney Kaplan, "Phillis Wheatley," in *The Black Presence in the Era of the American Revolution, 1770-1800* (Greenwich, Conn.: New York Graphic Society, 1973), pp. 150-170;
Merle A. Richmond, *Bid the Vassal Soar: Interpretive Essays on the Life and Poetry of Phillis Wheatley (ca. 1753-1784) and George Moses Horton (ca. 1799-1883)* (Washington, D.C.: Howard University Press, 1974).

References:
Carl Bridenbaugh, "The First Published Poems of Phillis Wheatley," *New England Quarterly,* 42 (December 1969): 583-584;
Charles F. Heartman, *Phillis Wheatley: A Critical Attempt and a Bibliography of Her Writings* (New York: Printed for the author, 1915);
Mukhtar Ali Isani, "The British Reception of Wheatley's Poems on Various Subjects," *Journal of Negro History,* 66 (Summer 1981): 144-149;
Sarah Dunlap Jackson, "Letters of Phillis Wheatley and Susanna Wheatley," *Journal of Negro History,* 58 (April 1972): 212;
Robert C. Kuncio, "Some Unpublished Poems of Phillis Wheatley," *New England Quarterly,* 43 (June 1970): 287-297;
Thomas Oxley, "Survey of Negro Literature," *Mes-

senger: World's Greatest Negro Monthly, 60 (February 1927): 37-39;

Carole A. Parks, "Phillis Wheatley Comes Home," Black World, 23 (February 1974): 92-97;

Benjamin Quarles, "A Phillis Wheatley Letter," Journal of Negro History, 34 (October 1949): 462-466;

Gregory Rigsby, "Form and Content in Phillis Wheatley's Elegies," CLA Journal, 19 (December 1975): 248-257;

Rigsby, "Phillis Wheatley's Craft as Reflected in Her Revised Elegies," Journal of Negro Education, 47 (Fall 1978): 402-413;

William H. Robinson, Phillis Wheatley in the Black American Beginnings (Detroit: Broadside Press, 1975);

Robinson, "Phillis Wheatley in London," CLA Journal, 21 (December 1977): 187-201;

Robinson, ed., Critical Essays on Phillis Wheatley (Boston: G. K. Hall, 1982);

Charles Scruggs, "Phillis Wheatley and the Poetical Legacy of Eighteenth Century England," Studies in Eighteenth Century Culture, 10 (1981): 279-295;

John C. Shields, "Phillis Wheatley and Mather Byles: A Study in Literary Relationship," CLA Journal, 23 (June 1980): 391-398;

Shields, "Phillis Wheatley's Use of Classicism," American Literature, 52 (March 1980): 97-111;

Kenneth Silverman, "Four New Letters by Phillis Wheatley," Early American Literature, 8 (Winter 1974): 257-271;

Albertha Sistrunk, "Phillis Wheatley: An Eighteenth-Century Black American Poet Revisited," CLA Journal, 23 (June 1980): 391-398.

Papers:
Original manuscripts, letters, and first editions are in collections at the Boston Public Library; Duke University Library; Massachusetts Historical Society; Historical Society of Pennsylvania; Library Company of Philadelphia; American Antiquarian Society; Houghton Library, Harvard University; The Schomburg Collection, New York City; Churchill College, Cambridge; The Scottish Record Office, Edinburgh; Dartmouth College Library; William Salt Library, Staffordshire, England; Cheshunt Foundation, Cambridge University; British Library, London.

John Witherspoon
(5 February 1723-15 November 1794)

Christopher J. MacGowan
College of William and Mary

SELECTED BOOKS: *Ecclesiastical Characteristics: or, the Arcana of Church Policy* (Glasgow, 1753; Philadelphia: Printed by William & Thomas Bradford, 1767);

Essay on the Connection between the Doctrine of Justification by the imputed Righteousness of Christ, and Holiness of Life . . . (Glasgow: Printed by John Bryce & David Paterson, 1756);

A Serious Enquiry into the Nature and Effects of the Stage (Glasgow: Printed by J. Bryce & D. Paterson, 1757; New York: Published by Whiting & Watson, 1812);

The Charge of Sedition and Faction against good Men . . . (Glasgow: Printed by J. Bryce & D. Paterson, 1758; Boston: Printed by Lincoln & Edmands, 1811);

The Absolute Necessity of Salvation through Christ (Edinburgh: Printed for W. Miller, 1758);

Prayer for National Prosperity and for the Revival of Religion inseparably connected (London: Printed for T. Field, 1758);

The Trial of Religious Truth by its Moral Influence (Glasgow: Printed for James Wilkin, 1759);

Seasonable Advice to Young Persons (Glasgow: Printed by Robert Urie, 1762);

A Serious Apology for the Ecclesiastical Characteristics (Edinburgh: Printed by Sands, Murray & Cochran for William Gray, 1763);

A Practical Treatise on Regeneration (London: Printed for Edward & Charles Dilly, 1764);

Essays on Important Subjects, 2 volumes (London: Printed for Edward & Charles Dilly, in the Poultry, 1765);

The History of a Corporation of Servants . . . (Glasgow:

Printed for John Gilmour, 1765);
Practical Discourses on the Leading Truths of the Gospel (Edinburgh: Kincaid & Bell & Gray, 1768; Philadelphia: W. & T. Bradford, 1770);
Sermons on Practical Subjects (Glasgow: Printed by A. Duncan for James Duncan & William Walker, 1768);
Essays and Sermons on Important Subjects . . . , 5 volumes (Edinburgh: Printed for A. Kincaid & J. Bell & W. Gray and for J. Duncan & W. Walker in Glasgow, 1768);
An Inquiry Into the Scripture-Meaning of Charity (Edinburgh: Printed for A. Kincaid, J. Bell & W. Gray, 1768);
The Nature and Extent of Visible Religion (Edinburgh: Printed for Kincaid & Bell, and for W. Gray, 1768);
Address to the Inhabitants of Jamaica, and the West-India Islands, in Behalf of the College of New Jersey (Philadelphia: Printed by William & Thomas Bradford, 1772);
The Dominion of Providence over the Passions of Men A Sermon preached at Princeton, on the 17th of May, 1776. . . . To which is added, An Address to the Natives of Scotland residing in America (Philadelphia: Printed by R. Aitken, 1776; Glasgow, 1777);
An Address to the Natives of Scotland residing in America (London: Printed for Fielding & Walker, 1778);
Essay on Money, as a Medium of Commerce . . . (Philadelphia: Printed by Young, Stewart & McCulloch, 1786);
Christian Magnanimity (Princeton: Printed by James Tod, 1787);
A Sermon on the Religious Education of Children (Elizabethtown, N.J.: Printed by Shepard Kollock, 1789; Paisley: Printed by J. Neilson for G. Caldwell, 1790);
A Series of Letters on Education (New York: Printed by J. Buell for C. Davis, 1797; Bristol: Printed by J. Rose for I. James & sold by W. Button in London, 1798);
Sermons by the late John Witherspoon . . . (Edinburgh: Printed for J. Dickson, J. Fairburn & J. Ogle, 1798);
Lectures on Moral Philosophy and Eloquence (Philadelphia: Printed by & for William W. Woodward, 1810).

Editions and Collections: *The Works of the Rev. John Witherspoon . . .* , 4 volumes (Philadelphia: Printed & published by William W. Woodward, 1800-1801);
The Works of John Witherspoon, 9 volumes (Edinburgh: Printed for Ogle & Aikman, J. Pillans & Sons, J. Ritchie, and J. Turnbull, 1804-1805);
Lectures on Moral Philosophy, edited by Varnum Lansing Collins (Princeton: Princeton University Press, 1912).

Princeton University Library

John Witherspoon achieved major distinction as a church leader, revolutionary statesman, and college president and teacher. A leading Scottish minister, later the spokesman for the American Presbyterian church, he was the only clergyman to sign the Declaration of Independence. As president of the College of New Jersey (later Princeton University), he revitalized the institution, increasing the endowment and student body, while introducing reforms that shifted the college's emphasis from preparation for the ministry to thorough training for civic leadership. In his sermons and writings, as in his political and educational career, he consistently applied his conservative theology and commonsense realism to the pressing issues of the age. He gave those views a voice and a relevance in the critical years around his adopted nation's birth.

Witherspoon was born to James and Anne Walker Witherspoon, in the Scottish village of Gifford—just east of Edinburgh—in Yester parish, where his father was the local minister. At four he could read from the Bible, and could recite much of the New Testament and many of Watt's *Psalms and Hymns*. He graduated with an M.A. from the University of Edinburgh at sixteen and had completed a doctorate in theology by the time he was twenty. Two years later in 1745, he received his first call—to be minister at Beith in Ayrshire. He married Elizabeth Montgomery on 2 September 1748. They eventually had ten children, only five of whom lived to adulthood.

He early became involved in the struggles within the Scottish Church. Under the rising influence of rationalism and natural science, many clergy were lax in enforcing church dogma, regarding sermons as chiefly vehicles of literary expression, while glossing over the topic of innate sin. In addition, this "Moderate" faction favored giving the disposition of church livings to wealthy patrons rather than to the choice of the congregation. Witherspoon led the minority opposing group of "Popularists." This party emphasized the importance of the scriptural texts, insisted upon man's essential depravity, and upheld the right of congregations to find a minister suitable to their particular needs.

Witherspoon's first publication, "Remarks on an Essay on Human Liberty," appeared in 1753 in *Scots Magazine*. His second, *Ecclesiastical Characteristics* (1753), a sharp satire on the Moderate position, won him notice throughout Scotland, England, and America. In this pamphlet which passed through seven different editions and nine reprints, Witherspoon offers thirteen maxims for "a plain and easy Way to attaining to the Character of a Moderate Man." The central tenets of the Moderate position emerge in an "Athenian Creed" from maxim six: worship of "the beauty and comely proportions of Dame Nature," acceptance of the universe as merely "a huge machine, wound up from everlasting by necessity," and a comfortable belief "that there is no ill in the universe, nor any such thing as virtue absolutely considered." Lord Shaftesbury and Francis Hutcheson serve the Moderates as divinities. *Ecclesiastical Characteristics* is Witherspoon's most successful piece of satire—his other two pieces in this vein being heavy-handed in comparison. The 1765 *History of a Corporation of Servants*, allegorical fiction along the lines of *Gulliver's Travels*, has church history as its target—especially the history of the Scottish branch. *Caspipina's Catechism*, written in 1777 but unpublished in Witherspoon's lifetime, is a scathing attack upon the Reverend Jacob Duché, the chaplain to Congress who opportunely switched his allegiance to the British upon their occupation of Philadelphia.

The controversy stirred by *Ecclesiastical Characteristics* proved troublesome when Witherspoon was called to the living at the growing town of Paisley in 1756. But his temperate if unrepentant defense of his purposes before the Synod of Glasgow and Ayr cleared the way for him to accept the position in 1757. While at Paisley he continued at the forefront of Church debate, and a number of his major sermons date from these years. *The Absolute Necessity of Salvation through Christ* (1758), preached before the High Church of Edinburgh, insists upon the essential truths that the Moderates and Rationalists have "softened"—man's unredeemed state, his everlasting misery, and the necessity of Christ's sacrifice to bring redemption. *Prayer for National Prosperity and for the Revival of Religion inseparably connected* (1758) asserts the divine purpose behind the acts of Providence. *The Trial of Religious Truth by its Moral Influence* (1759) argues that the truth of the gospels and the principles of justice can be intuitively apprehended through man's innate conscience. This innate sense of Christian truths is as infallible as the assurance from our external senses that the material world exists, Witherspoon insists; no legal or scholarly training is necessary to grasp these truths—in fact rational argument may even lead to error. The blend of Calvinism and commonsense realism in these sermons is firmly anchored to the scriptural passages on which the sermons are based. Witherspoon's direction is always to insist upon the absolute truth of the text, then to examine its implications, and finally to apply his results to the pressing problems of the day.

Witherspoon's reputation continued to grow. The University of St. Andrews granted him an honorary degree in 1764, and in the following year a London publisher collected his works in three volumes. His reputation was no less on the other side of the Atlantic. When in 1766 the College of New Jersey was searching for a man of solid learning and passionate convictions to serve as its sixth president—a candidate who could also cement the reconciliation between the Old Side and the New Side in the American Presbyterian church—Witherspoon emerged as the ideal figure to fill both roles.

Witherspoon did not assume his post for two

This letter from Witherspoon to Benjamin Rush was one of many Witherspoon exchanged with representatives of the College of New Jersey during the negotiations preceding his accepting the presidency of the college (Princeton University Library).

years. The difficult negotiations involved letters criss-crossing the Atlantic and a flurry of emissaries from the college to Paisley. The correspondence of the various figures involved has been collected in *John Witherspoon Comes to America* (1953).

Once he arrived in New Jersey in 1768, Witherspoon set to work as president with characteristic determination and thoroughness. He substituted his commonsense realism for the Idealism then in vogue at the college, introduced the lecture system, increased enrollment, raised much-needed funds, and broadened the curriculum to include such subjects as moral and natural philosophy, French, history, and geography. The college became a preparation for such professions as the law and medicine, as well as the ministry. Also, against some opposition, he encouraged the students to debate the pressing political questions arising out of the dispute with Britain.

In addition to his duties as president, Witherspoon undertook preaching and pastoral duties at Princeton's Presbyterian church and assumed leadership of the Church in America. In May 1775 he headed a committee of the Synod of New York and Philadelphia that released ministers from the obligation not to use their pulpits to espouse political views. His lifelong involvement in controversy prepared him well to represent church, college, state, and his adopted country in ensuing events.

Witherspoon's first discussion of the independence issue in print is his essay *Thoughts on American Liberty* (1774), which supports the Continental Congress, but his most influential statement came in a sermon preached on 17 May 1776 before the college—*The Dominion of Providence over the Passions of Men*. The subsequent printing ran through four editions in three years, and it was reprinted in Glasgow with notes denouncing the author as a traitor.

The sermon follows Witherspoon's characteristic method. Taking as his text Psalm 76:10., he argues that the wrath of man proves his sinfulness, and that God, through his own wrath and that of men, punishes such sin. While God's own wrath is infinite, He sets limits to the power of man's wrath. When these truths are applied to the circumstances of May 1776, we find the wrath of Britain proving its sinfulness, and the successful resistance of the colonists serving as the vehicle of Providence to curb that wrath. Witherspoon placed the Church firmly on the side of the colonists—insisting that civil liberty is an essential prerequisite for religious liberty.

Witherspoon's political career began with this sermon. Appointed to the Continental Congress, he served from 1776 to 1779, and again from 1780 to 1782. His committee work included membership on the Committee on Foreign Affairs and a number of important appointments to finance committees. His financial expertise is distilled into his *Essay on Money* (1786), which condemns the indiscriminate printing of paper money as the cause of inflation.

The war and his subsequent political activities interrupted a series of essays Witherspoon had been publishing in the *Pennsylvania Magazine*. Their common theme is an attempt to present immutable standards at a time of uncertainty and change. The *Letters on Education*, published in 1775-1776, insist upon the primary role of religion in providing a framework within which to exercise firm parental authority. The *Letters on Marriage* (1775-1776) assert the central place of marriage in "the order of providence, and . . . the constitution of society." With independence approaching, Witherspoon's three *Druid* papers of May, June, and July 1776 discuss the principles of waging war and the circumstances under which rebellion against authority is justifed.

By 1781 Witherspoon could again devote time to writing, and he resumed these *Druid* papers, three of which discuss American English. In the future, he notes, Great Britain may not provide the standards upon which the American language should be judged, but until such a time there are certain local improprieties that should be corrected. Witherspoon's analysis provides the starting point of H. L. Mencken's study of the language more than a century later.

Upon retiring from Congress, Witherspoon sought to restore the college to its prewar prosperity—but inflation had taken a heavy toll on the endowment, and the war had left Nassau Hall and its grounds severely damaged. The fortunes of the Church also needed to be restored. Church membership had diminished, and the ministry had lost much of its influence with the decline of interest in spirituality. In response to these problems, Witherspoon chaired a committee in 1785 to reorganize the American Presbyterian church. The committee's final report shaped what is essentially the form of church government that exists today.

Witherspoon's wife died in Princeton in 1789, at the age of sixty-eight on 30 May. In 1791 he married Ann Dill, the twenty-four-year-old widow of Dr. Armstrong Dill. One of their two daughters died in infancy.

Although blind in the last three years of his life, Witherspoon continued his presidential and ministerial duties. In his funeral oration for Witherspoon the Reverend John Rodgers remembered "he was frequently led into the pulpit, both at home and abroad, during his blindness; and always acquitted himself with his usual accuracy, and frequently, with more than his usual solemnity and animation." But although he remained active in these spheres, his writing career closed in 1791 with an unsigned address "To the Reader" replacing the dedication to King James in American Bibles.

More than half of Witherspoon's works are sermons. They formulate no new theology and are characterized more by their clarity and order than by memorable lines or passages. His essays on various topics exhibit a mind observant of human nature, but the *Essay on Money* and the satires are the works that have received the most favorable comment from scholars in recent years. Yet it is as a teacher and administrator that he has left his greatest mark. Woodrow Wilson considered him Princeton's greatest president. His Calvinism—filtered through his pupil James Madison—has been seen as an influence on the checks and balances of the American Constitution, and the commonsense realism that he brought from Scotland has been claimed as the direct forerunner of nineteenth-century American pragmatism.

Letters:
John Witherspoon Comes to America, edited by Henry L. Butterfield (Princeton: Princeton University Press, 1953).

Biographies:
Varnum Lansing Collins, *President Witherspoon*, 2 volumes (Princeton: Princeton University Press, 1925);

Ashbel Green, *The Life of the Revd. John Witherspoon*, edited by Henry Lyttleton Savage (Princeton: Princeton University Press, 1973);

Martha Lou Lemmon Stohlman, *John Witherspoon: Parson, Politician, Patriot* (Philadelphia: Westminster Press, 1976).

Papers:
Many of Witherspoon's papers were destroyed during the War of Independence. The Library of Congress has a number of papers and letters, and Princeton's Firestone Library holds a series of letters recording Witherspoon's negotiations with the college before taking up his appointment as president.

Charles Woodmason
(circa 1720-death date unknown)

Alan Axelrod
Henry Francis du Pont Winterthur Museum

BOOKS: *A Letter from a Gentleman of South-Carolina, on the Cultivation of Indico* (Charleston, S.C., 1754);

The Carolina Backcountry on the Eve of the Revolution: The Journal and Other Writings of Charles Woodmason, Anglican Itinerant, edited by Richard J. Hooker (Chapel Hill: University of North Carolina Press, 1953);

A Poetical Epistle to Benjamin Franklin, Esq., of Philadelphia on His Experiments and Discoveries in Electricity. Written at Cooper River, South Carolina, in 1753 (Richmond: William Byrd Press, 1954).

An itinerant Anglican minister in the northwest backcountry of pre-Revolutionary South Carolina, Charles Woodmason is remembered for the journal in which he recorded his wilderness experiences. This document, the fruit of a three-year sojourn (1766-1768), during which Woodmason ranged over some 9,000 miles, may be the fullest firsthand description of any American colonial frontier.

Little is known of Woodmason's early life. He was probably born to a gentry family about 1720 somewhere in England, possibly London. He first immigrated to South Carolina—probably in 1752—in order to set up as a merchant and planter, and he prospered for some ten years, attaining posts of civic responsibility in Charleston. During 1753-1755, he also found sufficient leisure to contribute to the *Gentleman's Magazine* (London) four poems (among them a verse topography of South Carolina and "A Poetical Epistle to Benjamin

Franklin, Esq., of Philadelphia on his Experiments and Discoveries in Electricity") and an essay on cultivating indigo and manufacturing it into a dye. The two-part essay, published in the magazine in 1755, was probably based on *A Letter from a Gentleman of South-Carolina, on the Cultivation of Indico*, which Woodmason had published in Charleston the year before.

Suddenly, in 1762, Woodmason's prosperity collapsed, and he seems to have returned to England for a time. Back in Charleston later that year or early the next, Woodmason resumed at least the civic portion of his career, earning several public appointments, but he fell from grace in 1765 when he applied for the position of stamp distributor under the provisions of the notorious Stamp Act. The precipitous turn of public opinion against him may have prompted Woodmason to seek the post of itinerant minister. It is also apparent that Woodmason, a steadfast Anglican, had a genuine concern for the spiritual welfare of the frontier, where a number of enthusiastic religious sects, foremost among them the New Light Baptists, were threatening the scattered backcountry outposts of Anglicanism.

In 1765 Woodmason sailed again for England, seeking ordination. He returned to South Carolina the following year as a minister of the Gospel. The frontier parish to which Woodmason had been assigned, including much of South Carolina north and west of present-day Camden, was, as he described it in his journal, a place of potential prosperity but present poverty, disease, ignorance, and sloth, as well as moral, religious, and political anarchy. As Woodmason depicts them, his backwoods parishioners were neither civilized nor savage, but lost between civilization and savagery.

As much as the journal reveals about the colonial frontier, it suggests even more about Woodmason, who becomes a living symbol of authoritarian sensibility bred to the institutions and conventions of the Old World confronting the moral, religious, and intellectual relativism of the New. Adherent though he was to established law and order, Woodmason in 1767-1768 nevertheless championed the Regulators, a backwoods vigilante movement that rebelled against the Charleston government's ineffectual administration of frontier justice. As spokesman for the group, Woodmason produced a number of letters (published and unpublished), notices, articles, and a petition titled "A Remonstrance Presented to the Commons House of Assembly of South Carolina, by the Upper Inhabitants of the said Province Nov. 1767" that detail the outlawry and rapine endemic to an indifferently governed frontier. His South Carolina experience also produced letters, sermons, and church papers—all unrelated to the Regulator movement—that further document life in the backcountry.

At heart the frontier minister was a British Loyalist, who, amid early stirrings of revolution, returned to England in 1774. The last written record of Charles Woodmason is a 17 November 1776 entry in one of his sermon books, noting that he had preached at a small town near Bristol, England. The date of his death is not known.

References:

Richard J. Hooker, Introduction and bibliographical notes to *The Carolina Backcountry on the Eve of the Revolution: The Journal and Other Writings of Charles Woodmason, Anglican Itinerant* (Chapel Hill: University of North Carolina Press, 1953);

Claude E. Jones, "Charles Woodmason as Poet," *South Carolina History Magazine*, 59 (1958): 189-194.

Papers:

The Library of Congress holds transcripts of the Fulham Palace Manuscripts, which include letters written from backcountry South Carolina to England. The manuscript for Woodmason's journal and three manuscript sermon books are in the library of the New-York Historical Society.

John Woolman

Thomas Werge
University of Notre Dame

BIRTH: Rancocas, Burlington County, New Jersey, 19 October 1720, to Samuel and Elizabeth Burr Woolman.

MARRIAGE: 18 October 1749 to Sarah Ellis; children: Mary, William.

DEATH: York, England, 7 October 1772.

BOOKS: *Some Considerations on the Keeping of Negroes. Recommended to the Professors of Christianity of Every Denomination* (Philadelphia: Printed & sold by James Chattin, 1754);
Considerations on Keeping Negroes; Recommended to the Professors of Christianity, of Every Denomination. Part Second (Philadelphia: Printed by B. Franklin & D. Hall, 1762);
An Extract from John Woolman's Journal in Manuscript, Concerning the Ministry (London, 1763?; Philadelphia, 1770);
Considerations on Pure Wisdom and Human Policy; on Labour; on Schools; and on the Right Use of the Lord's Outward Gifts (Philadelphia: Printed by D. Hall & W. Sellers, 1768);
Considerations on the True Harmony of Mankind; and How It Is to Be Maintained . . . (Philadelphia: Printed by Joseph Crukshank, 1770);
An Epistle to the Quarterly and Monthly Meetings of Friends (Burlington: Printed by Isaac Collins, 1772);
Serious Considerations on Various Subjects of Importance (London: Printed & sold by Mary Hinde, 1773; enlarged edition, New York: Collins, 1805);
The Works of John Woolman. In Two Parts (Philadelphia: Printed by Joseph Crukshank, 1774; London: T. Letchworth, 1775);
A Plea for the Poor or A Word of Remembrance and Caution to the Rich (Dublin: Jackson, 1793).

Editions and Collections: *A Journal of the Life Gospel Labours, and Christian Experiences, of that faithful Minister of Jesus Christ, John Woolman*, edited by John Comly (Philadelphia: Chapman, 1837);
The Journal of John Woolman, edited by John Greenleaf Whittier (Boston: Osgood, 1871);

The only known portrait of Woolman, this sepia drawing is probably the work of his friend Robert Smith III

The Journal and Essays of John Woolman, edited by Amelia Mott Gummere (New York: Macmillan, 1922);
The Journal of John Woolman, edited by Janet Whitney (Chicago: Regnery, 1950);
The Journal of John Woolman and A Plea for the Poor, edited by Frederick B. Tolles (New York: Corinth, 1961);
The Journal and Major Essays of John Woolman, edited by Phillips P. Moulton (New York: Oxford University Press, 1971).

The Quaker faith has long been associated with "practical mysticism" in its thought, teachings, and written and spoken language. Charles Lamb's exhortation to "get the writings of John Woolman by heart" indicates the respect given to his works by later literary figures in England, where several of his essays were first published. In America, John Greenleaf Whittier, William Ellery Channing, Theodore Dreiser, and many others admired, were moved, and were influenced by Woolman's prose, life, and vision. As a "Quaker saint," Woolman's mysticism and quest for salvation resulted in prophetic critiques of the injustices and complacencies of the social order: slavery, war, materialism, and the exploitation of the Indians and the poor. As Dag Hammarskjöld stated in *Markings* (1964), "the road to holiness necessarily passes through the world of action." Yet Woolman's efforts at practical and humanitarian reform remained so deeply rooted in a pietistic and mystical faith, in a waiting attentiveness to the "openings" God revealed to him, that his social and religious visions cannot be separated. (For the Quakers, God instills the inner light, unmediated, into the individual human heart, and hence requires no sacerdotal hierarchy, appointed ministry, sacraments, or formal doctrine). Further, Woolman's vision shares neither in the wild enthusiasm and private ecstasies of one strain in the Quaker tradition and its Anabaptist-related antecedents nor in the deistic and secular tendencies which began to mark its dominant strain in eighteenth-century America. His vision is consistent, unified, and sacramental, and he expresses it, especially in his journal, in a style which is simple, direct, and compelling—the journal, wrote Channing, is "the sweetest and purest autobiography in the language"—and which seeks always, in the phrase Quakers traditionally use to describe the ultimate aim of the oral and written word, "to speak to our condition."

Woolman was the oldest son in a family of thirteen children. His parents, Samuel and Elizabeth Burr Woolman, were deeply religious and respected in local society. Woolman's grandfather, who had immigrated to Burlington County, New Jersey, from Gloucestershire, England, was a proprietor of West Jersey, and Woolman's father was a candidate for the provincial assembly in 1739. Woolman was educated in a neighborhood Quaker school and had no further formal education, but he was a meditative child who, "through the care of my parents . . . was taught to read near as soon as I was capable of it," and he read widely in his father's fine library. Woolman became conversant with and powerfully moved by the Bible and by mystical and Quietist writings—including, it seems, Fenélon's—and such works as Thomas à Kempis's *The Imitation of Christ* came to occupy an important place in his religious imagination and ideals.

Between the ages of sixteen and twenty, Woolman experienced a series of inner conflicts between faith and disbelief, asceticism and worldliness, and piety and self-indulgence. A pattern of illness and recovery, like those of Pascal and Jonathan Edwards, dramatized his suffering, conversion, and sense of vocation. As a young child, Woolman had once killed a mother robin and then, because they would have died without her, had killed her young. His self-awareness, troubled conscience, and remorse came to confirm his belief in the existence of a divine "principle in the human mind" which, despite man's selfishness and perversity, seeks the good of the invisible God and all visible creatures. Woolman was early convinced that "true religion consisted in an inward life" through which we revere God and the created order: "to say we love God as unseen and at the same time exercise cruelty toward the least creature moving by his life, or by life derived from him, was a contradiction in itself." This inward life, wrote Woolman, echoing the imagery of the book of Revelation, is not automatic or purely natural but becomes a "white stone and new name . . . known rightly to such only who have it."

In 1741 Woolman moved to Mount Holly, New Jersey, where he clerked, kept books, and later worked as an apprentice tailor. In 1746 he began an independent trade as a tailor and retailer; in 1749 he married Sarah Ellis of Chesterfield, and a year later—the year of his father's death—their daughter, Mary, was born. (Their son, William, born in 1754, died at the age of three months.) Early in the 1740s, Woolman had experienced a strong and definite calling to a religious vocation. He began to exercise his Quaker ministry by speaking at meetings, by consistently remaining attentive in his inward life to Christ's promptings through the light—"we are bound in the bonds of pure love to stand still and wait upon him"—and by undertaking a series of arduous journeys as an itinerant preacher. During 1746-1748, Woolman journeyed through Pennsylvania, Maryland, Virginia, and North Carolina (3 months and 1,500 miles); New Jersey (3 weeks and 340 miles); Long Island and New England (4 months and 1,650 miles); and New Jersey and Maryland (6 weeks and 550 miles).

Woolman's house in Mount Holly, New Jersey (Historical Society of Pennsylvania)

These journeys, or literal and spiritual pilgrimages, intensified Woolman's commitment to his religious vision and ministry. They also posed dramatic and agonizing difficulties. William Penn's "Holy Experiment" of Pennsylvania had become corrupted by those Quakers, or, as they had come to be called, Friends, who openly pursued wealth, exploited the poor, approved of war and the oppression of the Indians, and held slaves. America itself had lost sight of its original mission and moral purpose and turned a blind eye to its rampant materialism and injustice—and most especially, the injustice of slavery. Woolman later wrote of his first journey to the Southern colonies that he had seen "so many vices and corruptions increased by this [slave] trade and this way of life that it appeared to me as a dark gloominess hanging over the land; and though now many willingly run into it, yet in future the consequences will be grievous to posterity!" With the images of this evil "fixed on my mind," and with the painful awareness that the Society of Friends included slaveowners, Woolman was moved to speak, biblically and prophetically, to the national sin of slavery.

In 1758 Woolman was one of the leaders of the Philadelphia Yearly Meeting, which Whittier later considered "one of the most important religious convocations in the history of the Christian Church" for its attempt to abolish slavery in the Society of Friends. At this meeting, and two years later at the New England Yearly Meeting at Newport, a center of the slave trade, Woolman spoke—as always, according to Quaker practice, only after a long period of silence and meditation—out of passionate conviction. The Philadelphia Meeting adopted the abolitionist resolutions, while Woolman and those who shared his position were less successful at Newport. But among all his experiences throughout the 1750s, including his itinerant preaching ministry, his opposition to war taxation and the draft, his successful attempts to keep the Friends at peace during a time of war in Pennsylvania, his work among the Indians, his decision to withdraw from a business which (to his mind) had become too successful and therefore a vanity and distraction, and the beginning of his composition of the journal, one of the most significant was the publication of *Some Considerations on the Keeping of Negroes*. Part one of this treatise was published in 1754 and part two in 1762.

The two parts of *Some Considerations on the Keeping of Negroes* form a coherent and sustained whole. While Woolman's argument appeals to reason, experience, self-interest, and "the infallible standard: Truth," it rests throughout on a religious and even Christological vision of virtue and love toward God and the creation. It is suggestive of the religious climate of the time that in 1755, in *The Nature of True Virtue*, Jonathan Edwards—many of whose Calvinist doctrines stand in marked contrast to Woolman's presuppositions—argued, with language and sentiment that could easily be Woolman's, that true virtue "most essentially consists in benevolence to being in general.... It is that consent, propensity and union of heart to being in general, which is immediately exercised in a general good will."

Woolman's treatise consistently distinguishes between self-love and the natural affections on the one hand, and, on the other, the real virtue of Christian charity and benevolence. His "considerations" are addressed and *Recommended to the Professors of Christianity of Every Denomination*, according to the subtitle for part one, and while Woolman wrote on this agonizing subject "with reluctance," he moved through a litany of pointed admonitions, all of which presuppose the importance of good and pure intentions. Woolman emphasizes Christ's lordship over all nations, which constitute a single, blood-related family, and His injunction to do good to "the least of these my brethren" and hence to Him. He points to the biblical command to love "the stranger," and, in this instance, especially those "strangers" who have been brought to America by force; and he condemns the idolatry, dehumanization, and desecration of the master-slave relationship as it usurps and parodies the radically democratic freedom, in Christ, which the Bible holds as a central value. Woolman's affirmation of the natural and divine truth that one's color "avails nothing in matters of right and equity" is rooted in his vision of God's familial concern and compassion for his children: "The parent of mankind is gracious. His care is over his smallest creatures, and a multitude of men escape not his notice; and though many of them are trodden down and despised, yet he remembers them."

Although Woolman's tone is intense, and at times even apocalyptic, he deliberately minimizes the language and form of the traditional jeremiad in favor of a more subdued appeal: "To our great Master we stand or fall; to judge or condemn is most suitable to his wisdom and authority. My inclination is to persuade and entreat, and simply give hints of my way of thinking." Unlike several other Friends, notably Benjamin Lay, whose opposition to slavery led them to increasingly strident and wild denunciations and prophecies—Lay, for example, plunged his sword into a hollowed-out Bible filled with red liquid to simulate blood, thus squirting the Friends he was indicting (the Society finally disowned him)—Woolman attempted to persuade rather than to tyrannize, to convert through empathy and entreaty rather than through fear and trembling. Nonetheless, there runs through *Some Considerations on the Keeping of Negroes* an apprehension of divine judgment: "From one age to another the gloom grows thicker and darker, till error gets established by general opinion.... We know not the time when those scales in which mountains are weighed may turn."

Woolman's plea for abolition and conversion necessitates his audience's attentiveness to "the end and event of things." Although his treatise shares in the movements toward reform and more democratic ways of public governance emerging in England, America, and Europe, it is rooted in a sense of ultimate concern. Its political dimensions are shaped by a religious faith and commitment in ways similar to two analogous and interdependent events: Wesley's Methodist movement in England and the Great Awakening in the American colonies. In each instance, the intensity and profundity of social change and conceptions of freedom are inextricably bound up with the religious imagination. For Woolman in *Some Considerations on the Keeping of Negroes*, the possibility of abolishing slavery depends entirely on the awakening of the mind and heart, or, in effect, on the conversion of the will. Slaveowners and those who support slavery explicitly or passively must attend to and act on that principle, placed in the mind, which is "pure and proceeds from God. It is deep and inward, confined to no forms of religion nor excluded from any, where the heart stands in perfect sincerity. In whomsoever this takes root and grows, of what nation soever, they become brethren in the best sense of the expression."

Yet Woolman did not underestimate the depths of the political and economic opposition he faced, nor did he gloss over the power of custom and convenience. For many, he recognized, slaves were mere ciphers and abstractions: "Had we a son or daughter involved in the same case . . . it would alarm us and make us feel their condition without seeking for it. The adversity of an intimate friend will incite our compassion, while others equally good in the like trouble will but little affect us." Ideas long nurtured by habit and custom, even when they violate Christian precepts by assuming human inequality and encouraging physical, social, and psychological cruelty on a mass and national scale, "do not suddenly leave us." Selfishness "clouds the understanding" and hides the path to justice and truth: "A traveller in cloudy weather misseth his way, makes many turns while he is lost, still forms in his mind the bearing and situation of places; and though the ideas are wrong, they fix as fast as if they were right." The heart of Woolman's vision and the persistence with which he expressed it in *Some Considerations on the Keeping of Negroes* and his other writings always recognized the actual human conditions and dilemmas obstructing the way. Like George Fox, however, whose antislavery sentiments influenced the early Quaker position on slavery, Woolman contributed immensely to the beginnings of the abolitionist movement in American religious thought and culture. As Thomas E. Drake has remarked, "The only significant movement against slavery in colonial America took place among the Quakers. They too groped their way slowly, with heart searching, toward the conviction that slavery could not truly be reconciled with their Christian faith."

Part of the reason for Woolman's ability to acknowledge the vexing and sometimes intractable difficulties of the human condition stemmed from his acutely introspective awareness of his own complexities and weaknesses. His decision to give up his business had not been easy or simple: "my natural inclination was toward merchandise, yet I believed Truth required me to live more free from outward cumbers; and there was . . . a strife in my mind between the two." His long, demanding journeys

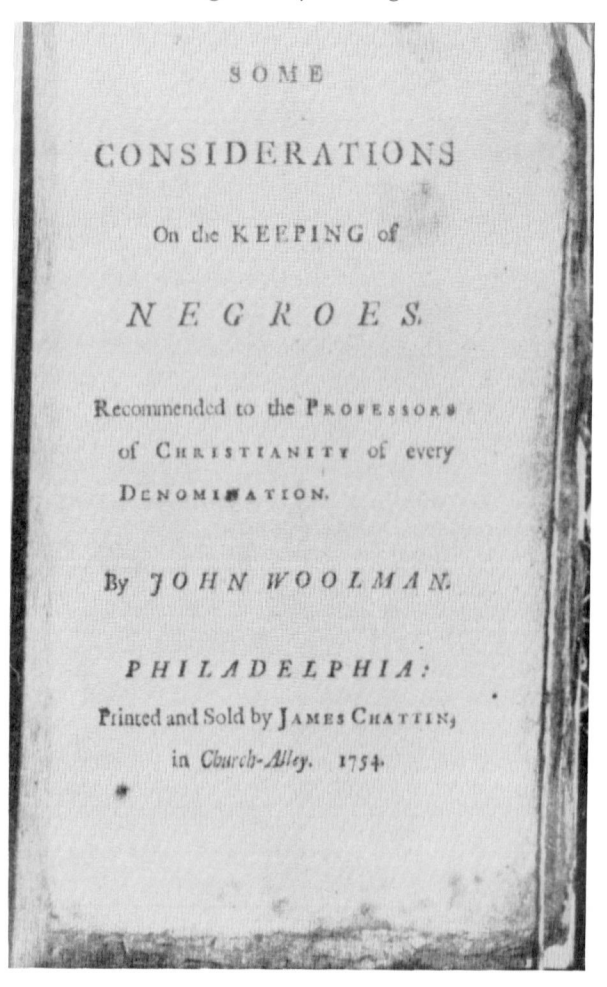

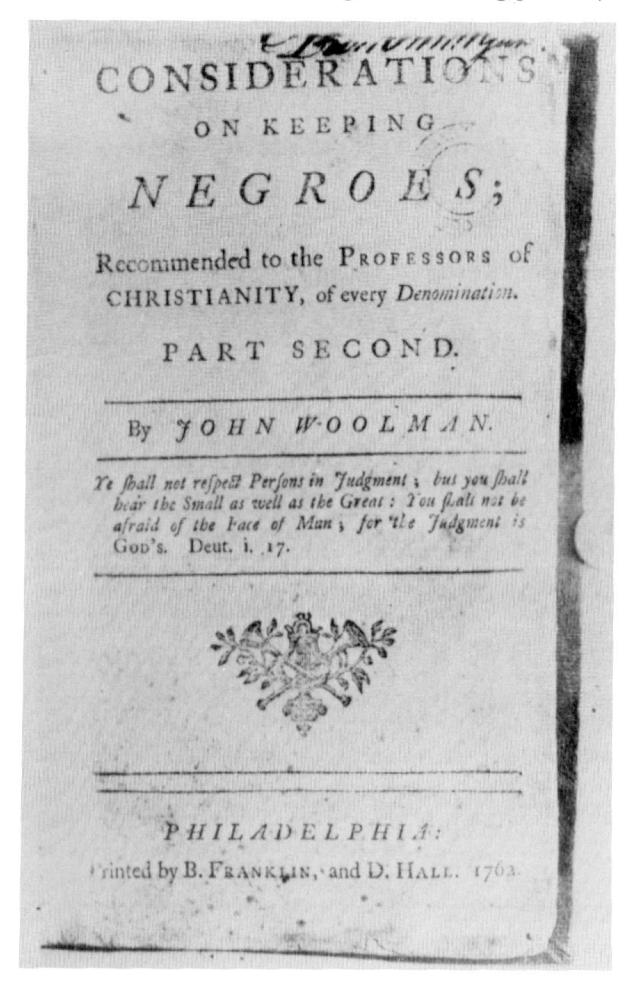

Title pages for Woolman's antislavery pamphlets

kept him from his family and imposed other hardships, yet when he fell ill in 1761 he interpreted his suffering as a divine and necessary chastisement. Feeling "the necessity of further purifying," he later stated, "there was no desire in me for health until the design of my correction [from God] was answered." Woolman responded by seeking even more strenuously after a simple and plain way of life. He decided to wear homespun rather than dyed clothing, to avoid all forms of ostentation, and to continue his journeys and visitations, several of which he undertook not only on foot but alone. In the 1760s Woolman made nine journeys—to Quakers, Indians, and slaveowners—and even considered, at the end of the decade, going to the West Indies as part of his ministry, but he decided to postpone this possible voyage.

Woolman also continued to write. In addition to the second part of his treatise on slavery (1762), Woolman wrote a series of reflections on labor, education, and faith and charity, *Considerations on Pure Wisdom and Human Policy* (1768), in which he emphasizes the importance of inward purity, the sanctification of the spirit, moral justice and harmony, and compassion. The love of money, whether dramatized by the slave trade or by the mad pursuit of wealth in other forms, corrupts the mind and heart and deadens the conscience. In *A Plea for the Poor or A Word of Remembrance and Caution to the Rich,* which Woolman composed during 1763-1764, these emphases and ideas are central to Woolman's vision of a spiritual "economy" and man's perversion of its real treasure: the gift of life and the creation. *A Plea for the Poor* was not published until 1793, and its religious radicalism concerning the poor and laboring classes, slavery, and the economic order has strong affinities with Thomas Paine's *Agrarian Justice* (1797) and other manifestations of a revolutionary political and economic spirit. More than a century after its publication, *A Plea for the Poor* was republished as a tract by the Fabian Society.

In 1664 Henry More, the Cambridge Platonist, referred to "the completeness of the Christian Oeconomy," and in 1725 Louis Dupin used the phrase "the whole Oeconomy of our salvation." Earlier, Calvin had praised "the economy of the divine wisdom, so well ordered and disposed." In *Walden,* Thoreau's chapter on economy seeks to define, or recover, a sense of economy as a divine and moral principle of order and harmony which man might imitate and embody in a life of austere yet bountiful simplicity. Although Thoreau construed the theological dimensions of the word to suit his particular vision and purposes, he clearly echoes this traditional conception.

Woolman's essay *A Plea for the Poor* also seeks to recover a biblical and religious "economy." Christ is man's only real wealth, treasure, object of trust, and vehicle of redemption. Woolman's reflections on creation, business, labor, money, tyranny, slavery, education, and the social and divine orders are linked by a central and recurring thread: man is the steward, not the owner or possessor, of God's creation and creatures, and, therefore, as God "is kind and merciful, we as his creatures, while we live answerable to the design of our creation, we are so far entitled to a convenient subsistence that no man may justly deprive us of it." The true economy of life is divinely ordered, morally apprehended, and realized through a just and merciful benevolence toward others—and especially toward the "stranger," or the poor, the slave, and the dispossessed. Indeed, to labor "for a perfect redemption from this spirit of oppression is the great business of the whole family of Christ Jesus in this world."

Throughout the essay, Woolman presupposes that since man's deepest desire is for God, it cannot be satisfied by earthly possessions. Many of his observations have a pointed and aphoristic quality, as in his assertions that "wealth desired for its own sake obstructs the increase of virtue," that "in the selfish spirit standeth idolatry," and that "the Creator of the earth is the owner of it." His use of biblical allusions is pervasive and always relevant to his major theme, and he occasionally elaborates on a biblical image or similitude when it serves his purpose—as in his commentary on Christ's admonition that it is easier for a camel to pass through a needle's eye than for a rich man to enter the kingdom of God: "as a camel . . . cannot pass through a needle's eye, so a man who trusteth in riches and holds them for the sake of the power and distinction attending them cannot in that spirit enter the kingdom. Now every part of a camel may be so reduced as to pass through a hole as small as a needle's eye, yet such is the bulk of the creature, and the hardness of its bones and teeth, that it could not be completed"—and here Woolman makes fine use of understatement—"without much labour." So man "must cease from that spirit which craves riches," he concludes, "and be reduced into another disposition, before he inherits the kingdom, as effectually as a camel must cease from the form of a camel in passing through the eye of a needle."

Woolman's tone varies according to the particular subject at hand; he admonishes, rebukes, entreats, invites, and witnesses to the object and end

Last page of Woolman's notes on a 1761 interview with a Munsey Indian chief. The additions on the bottom half of the page were made by his wife, Sarah Ellis Woolman (Historical Society of Pennsylvania).

of man's ultimate concern: "The true felicity of man in this life, and that which is to come, is in being inwardly united to the fountain of universal love and bliss." The individual is not a cipher, but a maker of choices whose effect is significant; "as the man whose mind is conformed to universal love hath his trust settled in God and finds a firm foundation to stand on in any changes or revolutions that happen among men, so also the goodness of his conduct tends to spread a kind, benevolent disposition in the world." In the midst of his most vast and universal visions and prophecies, Woolman invokes a specific and referentially concrete image. He imagines a particular slave, an actual child, or a particular commandment's relevance to a real situation. Even in its most visionary and typological form, Woolman's mind acknowledges, as William F. Lynch has said, that "the heart, substance, and center of the human imagination, as of human life, must lie in the particular and limited image or thing. . . . in the single farthing of the Gospel, which was the key to salvation; and in the little sensible things which were the source of insight for St. Thomas." For Woolman, even the tiniest creature is the object of God's love and therefore worthy of man's, as he makes clear when he begins one of his chapters with Matthew 10.29: "Are not two sparrows sold for a farthing, and one of them shall not fall on the ground without your Father." Woolman rejects the radical dualism of Manichaean and other forms of Gnostic thought; the world and its creatures are good, though flawed. He also rejects deism; in his vision, the watchful God is not absent, but omnipresent and compassionate.

In *A Plea for the Poor,* Woolman does not offer a detailed economic system as an alternative to the one whose obvious injustices he decries. Rather, he is prophetic in the traditional sense. He calls a drifting and idolatrous people—an "almost chosen people," as Lincoln would later call Americans—back to their origins as free and purposeful agents created in the image of a God whose watchwords are justice, mercy, and peace. Woolman's political vision once again is inseparable from his vision of redemption, and the order of salvation more central to his preoccupations than a particular economic order narrowly construed. In this work, Woolman insists that the kingdom of God, nurtured in time and space by faith, benevolence, and the guidance of the inner light, must be envisioned as the only enduring basis of, and analogy for, the American social and economic order. Yet his appeal for conversion, even when its tone is most righteous and apocalyptic, does not call for destruction or annihilation but for restoration. His interweaving of indictment and hope echoes John Winthrop, William Penn, Jonathan Edwards, and, here, Cotton Mather, who preached on "the City of God, being Pure Gold; and I bore due Testimonies against the Corruptions of the Market-place . . . and added my Hopes for a city of God, yet to be seen in America."

During the last years of his life, Woolman's personal, spoken, and written ministry continued unabated. He sustained his focus on the individual and national struggles between light and darkness, God and Mammon, and freedom and slavery. In 1770 he suffered a serious attack of pleurisy; one year later, his daughter, Mary, was married to Samuel Comfort; and on 1 May 1772, he embarked on a voyage to England to minister among the Friends and the masses of wretched and displaced poor. He composed, before sailing, *An Epistle to the Quarterly and Monthly Meetings of Friends* (1772). On 8 June, after a rough and difficult voyage, he arrived in London, and on 7 October he died, of smallpox, while working among and ministering to the laboring poor.

Woolman wrote a number of essays during these years, most notably *Considerations on the True Harmony of Mankind* (1770). In 1772, he also composed "Conversations on the True Harmony of Mankind," which remained unpublished until 1837, when it was included in John Comly's edition of the journal. On his voyage to England and during the months after his arrival, he wrote five brief essays—"On Loving Our Neighbors as Ourselves," "On the Slave Trade," "On Trading in Superfluities," "On a Sailor's Life," and "On Silent Worship"—which were collected and published in the year following his death, as *Remarks on Sundry Subjects* with four other works by Woolman in *Serious Considerations on Various Subjects of Importance* (1773). From 1770 to 1772 Woolman also revised his journal, begun some fifteen years earlier, and prepared it for publication.

Edwin Cady rightly describes the *Considerations on the True Harmony of Mankind* as "at once the most learnedly allusive, the most biblical, and the most theological of Woolman's writings." Of its four parts—on serving the Lord in "outward employments," on the example of Christ, on merchandising, and on divine admonitions—the second part, Woolman's delineation of Christ, is the most striking and the most indispensable for an understanding of the journal. In it Woolman clearly affirms Christ's divinity—in contrast to the Deistic, Arminian, and Unitarian strain in so much of En-

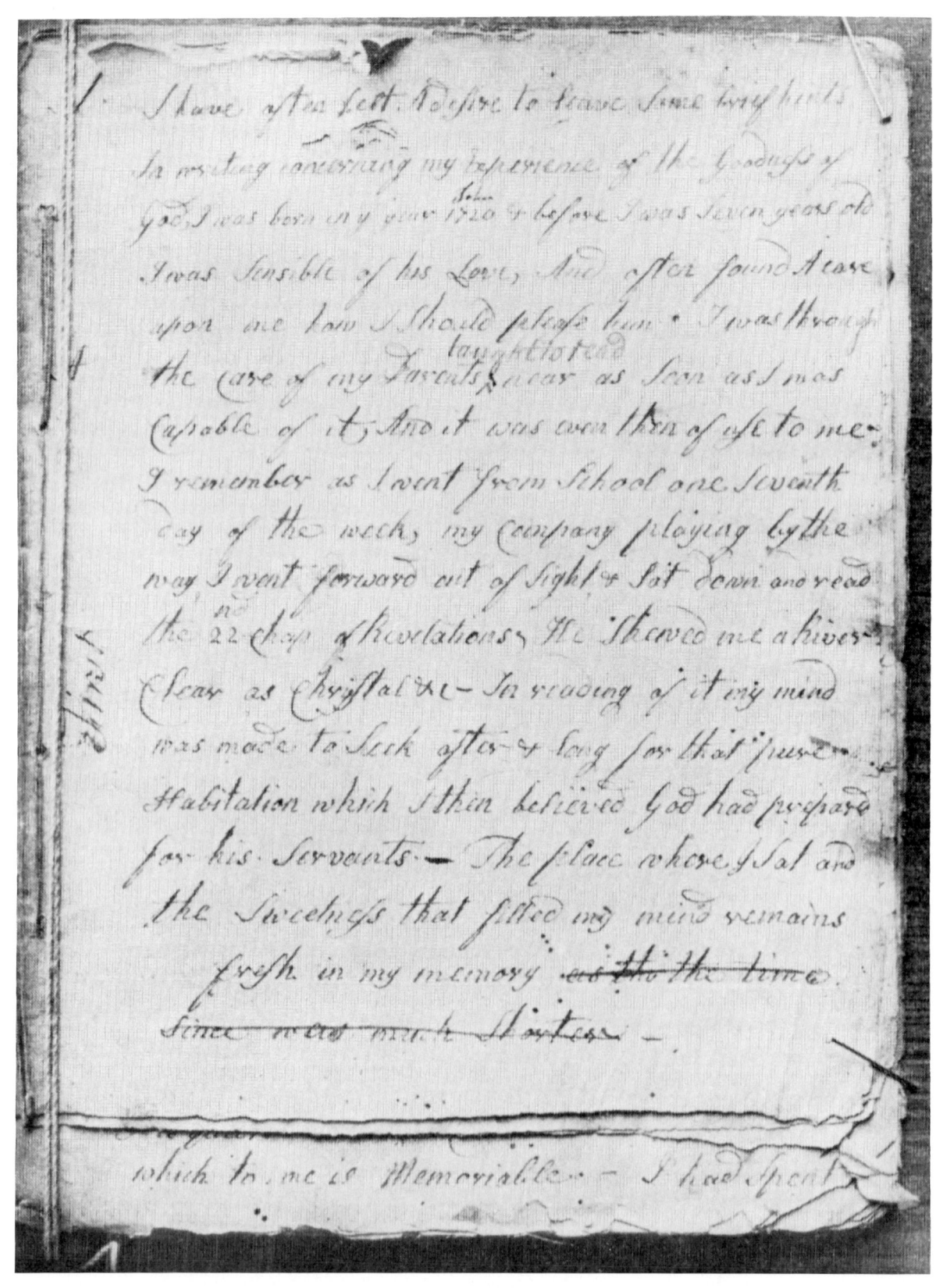

First pages from the journal Woolman began when he was thirty-five (Swarthmore College) and his revised version (Historical Society of Pennsylvania), from which Joseph Crukshank printed the first edition, part one of The Works of John Woolman *(1774)*

I have often felt a motion of Love to leave some hints of my experience of the goodness of God, and pursuant thereto in the 36 year of my age I began this work. — I was born in Northampton in Burlington County in West Jersey in the year of our Lord 1720 and before I was seven years old, I began to be acquainted with the operation of Divine Love.

Through the care of my Parents I was taught to Read near as soon as I was capable of it: and As I went from School one seventh day, ————— I remember while my companions went to play by the way, I went forward out of sight, and seting down I read the twenty second chapter of the Revelations. "He showed me a River of Water clear as Chrystal, proceeding out of the throne of God & of the Lamb &c and in reading it my mind was turned to seek after that pure Habitation, which I then believed God had prepared for his servants. — The place where I sat, and the sweetness that attended my mind remains fresh in my memory. — This and the like gracious Visitations had that effect upon me that when boys used ill language it troubled me, and through the continued Mercies of God I was preserved from it. — The Pious instructions of my Parents were often fresh in my mind when I happened amongst wicked children and was of use to me.

My Parents having a large family of children, used frequently on first days after meeting, to put us to read in the Holy Scriptures or some Religious Books, one after another, the rest seting by without much conversation, which I have often thought was a good practice. — From what I had read, I believed there had been in past ages, people who walked in Uprightness before God in a degree exceeding any that I knew, or heard of, now liveing & the apprehension of there being less Steadiness and firmness, amongst people in this age than in past ages, often troubled me while I was a youth. —

I had a Dream about the ninth year I saw the moon rise

Pages from Woolman's account of his journey to England (Swarthmore College)

[Manuscript facsimile — handwritten journal entry by John Woolman, dated 1772, describing landing at London and attending the yearly meeting of Ministers and Elders. Text partially legible:]

... 1772 Landed at London & went
straitway to the yearly meeting of Ministers and Elders which had been gathered
about, I suppose, half an hour —
In this meeting my mind was humbly
contrite. — Afternoon the meeting
of business opened, which by adjournments
held near a week — In these meetings I
often felt a living concern for the Establishment of Friends in the pure life of Truth
and my heart was enlarged in the meeting
of Ministers, Meeting of business and
in several meetings for publick worship, &
I felt my mind united in true love to the
faithful labourers, now gathered from the
several parts of this Yearly meeting from
various parts.

lightenment thought. Yet he affirms Christ's humanity with equal intensity, and, in the process, rejects the Gnostic view—which had been dominant in some parts of the Quaker and other mystical movements, given their emphasis on the direct and inner experience of God, the irrelevance of history and specific sacraments, the corruption of the natural world, and the conception of Christ as pure spirit—that Christ did not really assume flesh.

In *An Epistle to the Quarterly and Monthly Meetings of Friends* Woolman wrote that Christ "suffered afflictions, in a body of flesh," and in *Considerations on the True Harmony of Mankind* he stresses Christ's willingness to suffer and to be "sorrowful even unto death" in "the same human nature which we have." Woolman's allusions to the Bible, the Church fathers, and various doctrines point to the actuality of Christ's suffering for, and compassion toward, man, and Incarnation as well as the Passion becomes central to Woolman's religious vision and tone of wonder and gratitude: "He who was perfectly happy in himself, moved with infinite love, took not upon him the nature of angels, but our imperfect natures; and therein wrestled with the temptations which attend us in this life; and being the Son of HIM who is greater than earthly princes, yet became a companion to poor, sincere-hearted men." Christ is at once guide and companion, transcendent over and resonant in the human heart, and finitely human as well as supernally divine. For Woolman morality has its source in revelation and in religious truth and experience. They provide the grounds for morality; not the converse. Despite its clear differences from certain tenets of medieval, Reformed, and later Puritan belief, Woolman's faith is part of what Perry Miller calls "the Augustinian strain of piety."

The confessional form of Woolman's journal hearkens back to a long and rich tradition for which St. Augustine's *Confessions* (397-401) is the most seminal prototype. The *Confessions* (1781, 1788) of Rousseau, who died only six years after Woolman, follows this prototype even while it proclaims a wholly good, innocent, and autonomous self whose spiritual journey requires no divine guidance or intervention. But Woolman adheres to the Augustinian insistence on the reality of sin, the perversity of the will, and the wayfarer's need for supernatural grace and conversion. Rousseau's presuppositions about human nature, the individual's radical innocence, and the normative value of the solitary consciousness—rather than of revelation, the Bible, a sovereign God, or the life and tradition of the church—conflict with Augustine's at nearly every turn, except in their assumption that man appears to be and is profoundly unhappy. Yet despite the presence of various "romantic" elements in Quaker thought, Woolman expresses through his journal's form and preoccupations his sympathy with the older vision of sin and salvation.

It is precisely this conflict between the tenets of traditional Christianity and romanticism that defines the philosophical and even psychological starting point for such nineteenth-century American "confessions" as *Walden* (1854) and *The Education of Henry Adams* (1907). In the America of Woolman's time, the Puritan reflectiveness and piety of Edwards's *Personal Narrative* (1765) and the pragmatic utilitarianism of Franklin's *Autobiography* (1791-1798) represent the same conflict, and, far less frequently, convergence. Edwards's inwardness, "ultimate concern," and intensity express a pilgrimage with strong affinities to that of Woolman's journal, while Franklin's "self-made" pilgrimage has about it a deliberately studied ambiguity—he was preserved in it, he says, not by Christ, faith, or revealed truth, but by his own understanding, or "the kind hand of Providence, or some guardian Angel, or accidental favourable Circumstances and Situations, or all together."

The confessional form, whether known strictly as a confession, as a journal, or as a "spiritual autobiography," and always drawing on its medieval antecedents, occupied an important place in the Reformation, in the Puritan movement, and in the Quaker religious and literary tradition in England and America. George Fox set the tone when he described in his journal (1694) the "opening" of his mind by God to the truth "that every Man was enlightened by the Divine Light of Christ, and I saw it shine through all. . . . This I saw in the pure Openings of the Light, without the help of any Man, neither did I then know where to find it in the Scriptures, though afterwards, searching the Scriptures, I found it." Forty Quaker journals, or "memoirs," appeared between 1650 and 1725, while fourteen more were published between 1726 and 1758. Since Woolman was also familiar with the literary forms and styles of important works in the European mystical tradition, it is clear that he wrote and revised the journal, his most sustained work, while aware of, and attentive to, the literary dimensions of spiritual meditation.

Conduct, says Woolman, "is more convincing than language." Yet Woolman uses the "plain style"—favored by Puritans, Quakers, and many later eighteenth-century divines, scientists, and essayists for its simplicity, clarity, and lack of excessive ornamentation—with skill, sophistication, and effectiveness. Woolman subscribed to Thomas Hooker's assertion that the preached word, whether written or spoken, should have for its purpose "not to dazzle, but direct the apprehension of the meanest," or most common, and to Henry Smith's insistence that "to preach simply, is not to preach rudely, nor unlearnedly, nor confusedly, but to preach plainly, that the simplest man may understand what is taught." Inevitably for Woolman, scripture, and especially the Gospels, exemplifies a divinely and humanly effectual language for illuminating the mind and moving the will. Woolman's emphasis on silence—"in true silence strength is renewed, the mind herein is weaned from all things, but as they may be enjoyed in the Divine Will, and a lowliness in outward living, opposite to worldly honour, becomes truly acceptable to us"—while typically Quaker, underscores the power and significance of the uttered word which follows such silence. It also serves to remind the speaker that all speech and exhortation depend on God. Some preachers, says Augustine, "do not realize that it is owing to the gift of God that they by their free will exhort men to undertake to lead a good life, stimulate the sluggish, kindle the frigid, correct the evil, convert people who have turned away from God, and tranquillize rebellious wills."

The unity of the journal revolves around the consistent dialectic between God and the soul and between Woolman's receptivity to grace and denial of it. He dramatizes these relationships and their larger implications in several recurring images and themes: the journey or pilgrimage, whose sacramental dimension is clear; the crucial place of "attentiveness," which enables the soul to be receptive and obedient to God's promptings; the search for and vision of peace, communality, and the kingdom of God; and the conviction that only through a conversion of the will and a turning of the heart to love can deliverance, salvation, and the kingdom be assured. Woolman's doubts, fears, and anguish—over his failings, the slave trade, money lust, war, and all forms of cruelty—pervade the journal as they do his earlier writings, and his apprehension of God's impending judgment remains acute. Yet his hope for an ultimate restoration is also marked. For Woolman especially, as for other Quaker writers, the journal, in Paul Rosenblatt's phrase, was "a way of sacramentalizing a religion with no sacrament"—and also a way of dramatizing the entire created order as sacramental.

In *Considerations on the True Harmony of Mankind,* Woolman notes that scripture often uses the phrase "walking" to represent "our journey through life" and to comprehend "the various affairs and transactions relating to our being in the world." Literally and metaphorically, Woolman's journeys embody and echo the imagery and idea of pilgrimage from its earliest Christian form through John Bunyan's *Pilgrim's Progress* (1678).

As Woolman describes a particularly "difficult road to travel" in the wilderness—replete with mountains, swamps, stones, and rattlesnakes—he reflects that "I had this day often to consider myself as a sojourner in this world, and a belief in the all-sufficiency of God to support his people in their pilgrimage felt comfortable to me, and I was industriously employed to get to a state of perfect resignation." Woolman's landscape is physically and allegorically real. His voyage to England is a "floating pilgrimage," and the vividly realistic conditions of nature during another journey lead to a recollection of Genesis and Eden: "gathering some bushes under an oak we lay down, but the mosquitoes being plenty and the ground damp, I slept but little. Thus lying in the wilderness and looking at the stars, I was led to contemplate the condition of our first parents when they were sent forth from the garden, and considered that they had no house, no tools for business, no garments but what their Creator gave them, no vessels for use, nor any fire to cook roots or herbs. But the Almighty, though they had been disobedient, was a father to them; way opened in the process of time for all the conveniences of life."

It is telling that Woolman is "led" to contemplation and that the purpose of his industrious employment is "perfect resignation." For him, submission to the divine will, not an illusory autonomy or possessiveness, constitutes the good. God remains the initiator, gatherer, and guide, and the soul the respondent.

This pattern is clear in Woolman's consistent use of the passive voice to describe his religious experiences. In the very first memory he recounts—reading, as a child, the description of heaven in the book of Revelation— he writes that his mind "was drawn to seek after that pure habitation" and of "the sweetness that attended my mind." After several "openings," he states, "a universal love to my fellow creatures increased in me." In 1757 Woolman had a powerful mystical experience. As he awakened from sleep, he saw a radiant light: "As I lay still . . . looking upon it, words were spoken to my inward ear . . . as the language of the Holy One spoke in my mind. The words were, 'Certain Evidence of Divine Truth.'" The soul listens to and apprehends, rather than generating or obtaining, the divine light and voice.

The French mystic Simone Weil has insisted that we "cannot take a step toward the heavens. God crosses the universe and comes to us," and we can do nothing "except to wait." Yet this waiting, she argues, constitutes a real expectation and attentiveness, especially since it entails suffering—for "something in our soul has a far more violent repugnance for true attention than the flesh has for bodily fatigue." Woolman's valuing of silence, receptivity, and attentiveness parallels Weil's. As he anticipates a confrontation with slaveowners, for example, he hopes that he "might attend with the singleness of heart to the voice of the True Shepherd and be so supported as to remain unmoved at the faces of men." Throughout his journal, Woolman's attentiveness to and "inward waiting" for the "openings" God initiates provide the foundation for his "outward employments" and social actions. When he is incapable of such attentiveness, Woolman becomes uncertain of the authenticity of his faith and intentions, and, therefore, of the value and purposefulness of his good works and actions.

According to St. Bonaventura (1221-1274), all real journeys in which one seeks to discover the "traces of God" in the world and the path to salvation must be *intra nos, extra nos,* and *supra nos*—within, outside, and above or beyond ourselves. Woolman's attentiveness to the supernal light and voice leads and illuminates his journey within. Yet the inner journey of faith, he insists, must find expression in works and in the self-denial and suffering love such works demand. In moving "outside" himself, whether among the Indians and whites in order to effect reconciliation and peace, among the poor, or among the slaves and slaveowners, Woolman inevitably moves toward the realization of a larger communion in which moral awareness, compassion, and purification are not separate spheres but parts of a single dynamic process: "From an inward purifying, and steadfast abiding under it, springs a lively operative desire for the good of others."

For Woolman, such purification and compassion should typify all believers in Christ no matter what their specific religious commitment. Adhering to Quaker tradition, Woolman's vision of a gathered church is neither institutional nor ecclesiastical, but radically democratic. An experiential faith and genuine empathy with the world's suffering are the keys to Woolman's conception of the kingdom: "The outward modes of worship are various, but wherever men are true ministers of Jesus Christ it is from the operation of his spirit upon their hearts, first purifying them and thus giving them a feeling sense of the conditions of others." God, for Woolman, is a divine and loving parent. By analogy God's creatures at once reflect and express—at least potentially—the same familial trust, reciprocity, and love which characterize the kingdom of God. "Strong desires have attended me," writes Woolman, that God's "family, who are acquainted with the movings of his Holy Spirit, may be so redeemed from the love of money and from that spirit in which men seek honour one of another that in all business by sea or land we may constantly keep in view the coming of his kingdom on earth as it is in heaven, and by faithfully following this safe guide, may show forth examples tending to lead out of that under which the creation groans."

The creation is sacramental. It is marked by Christ's presence and sustained by "the all-sufficiency of him who formed the great deep, and whose care is so extensive that a sparrow falls not without his notice." Yet the creation also "groans," says Woolman, echoing St. Paul, and the sin which constitutes the source of this pain and agony has as its essence the perversity of man's fallen will and rebellious heart. In his self-analysis and analysis of the world, Woolman is consistently aware of the discrepancy between knowing the good and acting on that knowledge. Many of his slaveowners know the concrete torments and suffering slaves experience, know slavery is evil, and know that it cannot honestly be reconciled with faith in Christ. Yet their hearts and wills remain unmoved by the truth they recognize only abstractly and intellectually. For Woolman, St. Paul's cry in Romans 7:15 defines the problem: "for what I would [do], that do I not; but what I hate, that do I."

By locating the source of all travail and unhappiness in the fallen will, Woolman once again finds himself far closer to such a fideistic Christian as Pascal than to Rousseau and other romantic individualists. As Ernst Cassirer points out, "Rousseau's feeling and thinking both rebel against Pascal's hypothesis of an original perversion of the human will. The idea of the fall of man has lost all its force and validity for Rousseau." But for Woolman, man's only salvation lies in the contrite heart and the converted will: "In an entire subjection of our wills the Lord graciously opens a way for his people." Indeed, the climactic and resolving dramatic moment of his journal centers on the subject of Woolman's own will.

As he wrote the journal, in England, Woolman recalled his illness two years earlier, when he was "brought so near the gates of death that I forgot my name." Woolman means this literally, but he also suggests a spiritual resonance which echoes his earlier conviction that the "white stone and new name" of the real believer "is known rightly to such only who have it." Desiring to know "who I was," he immediately sees a gloomy vision of miserable human beings of whom he is part. He then hears a soft and melodious voice, "more pure and harmonious than any voice I had heard with my ears before, and I believed it was the voice of an angel who spake to other angels. The words were, 'John Woolman is dead.'"

Awed by the mystery of these words, Woolman is "carried in spirit" to mines in which the laboring poor blaspheme Christ's name. To Woolman's grief and pain, the poor respond by saying their oppressors are Christians and that Christ must be a "cruel tyrant" to direct their oppression. Still bewildered by the mystery, Woolman lies still, feels "divine power prepare my mouth that I could speak," and says, "'I am crucified with Christ, nevertheless I live; yet not I, but Christ that liveth in me, and the life I now live in the flesh is by faith in the Son of God, who loved me and gave himself for me' [Galatians 2:20]. Then the mystery was opened, and I perceived there was joy in heaven over a sinner who had repented and that language *John Woolman is dead* meant no more than the death of my own will."

Woolman's conception of love, or caritas, demands suffering and sacrifice; only the death and rebirth—the conversion—of the fallen or natural will leads to this radical and universal love. Before he was seven years old, he wrote, he "began to be acquainted with the operations of divine love." While the creation groans under the suffering for which the prototype is the cross, it is also watched over and loved by the "Fountain of Goodness, who gave being to all creatures, and whose love extends to that of caring for the sparrows." So long as the "natural will remains unsubjected," Woolman insists, there also remains "an obstruction against the clearness of divine light operating in us; but when we love God with all our heart and with all our strength, then in this love we love our neighbours as ourselves, and a tenderness of heart is felt toward all people, even such who as to outward circumstances may be to us as the Jews were to the Samaritans." Woolman's emphasis on the common and communal nature of the experience of suffering and love—on "our" heart and journey—again echoes Augustine, who wrote his *Confessions*, as Woolman did his journal, for the "sharers of my joy, and partners in my mortality, my fellow-citizens, and fellow-pilgrims, who are gone before, or are to follow on, companions of my way."

The protagonist of Theodore Dreiser's *The Bulwark* (1946), torn between Quaker precepts and the demands and power of American business, experiences a conversion as his daughter reads to him Woolman's descriptions of humility, community, and love. It is even appropriate to imagine Woolman's radically spiritual presence in the setting of Mailer's apocalyptic tone and vision at the end of *Armies of the Night:* "But if the end of the march [on Washington] took place in the isolation in which these last [Quaker] pacifists suffered naked in freezing cells, and gave up prayers for penance, then who was to say they were not saints? And who was to say that the sins of America were not by their witness a tithe remitted?"

The American literary tradition has deeply religious roots and dimensions. Woolman's journal, says Edwin Cady, belongs to "American scripture." Its influence in the nineteenth century, at times as explicit as it was later on Dreiser and in other instances an implicit but crucial part of the religious imagination in America, was considerable. Howard W. Hintz, in *The Quaker Influence in American Literature* (1940) and Phillips Moulton in a briefer and more recent consideration (1971) discuss the question.

Whittier's introduction to Woolman's life and writings (1871) is valuable for its insights into the political as well as the religious aspects, while Rufus Jones's studies of Woolman and the Quaker tradition to which he, like Whittier, belongs, are indispensable. Janet Whitney's biography (1942) is very useful. Even when the studies of Woolman from the Quaker perspective become hagiographic in tone, they are often illuminating.

Between 1965 and 1971, four important books dealing with Woolman appeared. Edwin Cady's *John Woolman* (1965) is an intense and urgent account which considers Woolman in his own time, his relevance to later literary, cultural, and political movements—including, of course, civil rights—and his importance as a religiously prophetic voice. Daniel B. Shea's *Spiritual Autobiography in Early America* (1968) discusses Woolman's journal in light of this generic literary and spiritual tradition. Paul Rosenblatt's *John Woolman* (1969) provides a succinct analysis of Woolman's writings and several useful literary and religious contexts in which to consider them. In 1971 Phillips Moulton published his carefully researched and immensely helpful edition of *The Journal and Major Essays of John Woolman*.

Even Woolman's most dispassionate critics consider him a compelling figure and the journal a significant work. Since Woolman's language itself seeks to be a witness and testament, it resists a narrowly aesthetic approach and requires an understanding of the divine and human word as an instrument of potential moral persuasion and spiritual regeneraton. Walker Percy suggests that the human being in our time consistently confronts "the need of recovering oneself as neither angel nor organism but as a wayfaring creature somewhere between." If this is so, Woolman's voice should persist with some resonance.

Bibliography:
Amelia Mott Gummere, "Bibliography," in *The Journal and Essays of John Woolman*, edited by Gummere (New York: Macmillan, 1922), pp. 610-630.

Biography:
Janet Whitney, *John Woolman: American Quaker* (Boston: Little, Brown, 1942).

References:
Walter F. Altman, "John Woolman's Reading of the Mystics," *Bulletin of Friends' Historical Association*, 48 (Autumn 1959): 103-115;

Hugh Barbour, *The Quakers in Puritan England* (New Haven: Yale University Press, 1964), pp. 242-259;

Edwin Cady, *John Woolman* (New York: Washington Square Press, 1965);

Henry S. Canby, *Classic Americans* (New York: Harcourt, Brace, 1931), pp. 28-31;

William A. Christian, "Inwardness and Outward Concerns: A Study of John Woolman's Thought," *Quaker History*, 67 (Autumn 1978): 88-104;

Jackson I. Cope, "Seventeenth-Century Quaker Style," *PMLA*, 71 (September 1956): 725-754;

Thomas E. Drake, *Quakers and Slavery in America* (New Haven: Yale University Press, 1950), pp. 51-64, 68-71;

Theodore Dreiser, *The Letters of Theodore Dreiser*, edited by Robert H. Elias, 3 volumes (Philadelphia: University of Pennsylvania Press, 1959), III: 822n, 833, 834;

Dreiser, ed., *The Living Thoughts of Thoreau* (New York: Longmans, Green, 1939);

Gerhard Friedrich, "Theodore Dreiser's Debt to Woolman's *Journal*," *American Quarterly*, 7 (Winter 1955): 385-392;

Howard W. Hintz, *The Quaker Influence in American Literature* (New York: Revell, 1940), pp. 26-33;

Sidney V. James, *A People among Peoples: Quaker Benevolence in Eighteenth-Century America* (Cambridge: Harvard University Press, 1963), pp. 98-100, 131-139, 177-178, 215-222;

Rufus M. Jones, "Evidence of the Influence of Quietism on John Woolman," *Friends Intelligencer*, 105 (Third Month 1948);

Jones and others, eds., *The Quakers in the American Colonies* (New York: Russell & Russell, 1962), pp. 391-400, 401-413;

Ronald A. Knox, *Enthusiasm: A Chapter in the History of Religion* (New York: Oxford University Press, 1950);

Phillips Moulton, "The Influence of the Writings of John Woolman," *Quaker History*, 60 (Spring 1971): 3-13;

Paul Rosenblatt, *John Woolman* (New York: Twayne, 1969);

Daniel B. Shea, *Spiritual Autobiography in Early America* (Princeton: Princeton University Press, 1968), pp. 45-84;

Frederick B. Tolles, *Meeting House and Counting House: The Quaker Merchants of Colonial Philadelphia, 1682-1763* (Chapel Hill: University of North Carolina Press, 1948): pp. 81-133;

John Greenleaf Whittier, Introduction to *The Journal of John Woolman*, edited by Whittier (Boston: Osgood, 1871).

Papers:
Most of Woolman's major extant manuscripts are in the Friends Historical Library, Swarthmore College; Friends Library, London; Manuscript Department, Historical Society of Pennsylvania; Friends Historical Library, Dublin; Quaker Collection, Haverford College Library; Rutgers University Library; Department of Records, Philadelphia Yearly Meeting.

John Joachim Zubly
(27 August 1724-23 July 1781)

Louis P. Masur
Princeton University

SELECTED BOOKS: *Leichenpredigt, Eines Berühmten Geistlichen in Georgien Über Offenbarung vii. 13* (Germantown: Printed by Christoph Saur, 1746);

Eine Leicht-Predig, Welche ein Reformirter Prediger in Savanna in Georgien Gehalten Über die Worte Apoc. 7 Wer sind diese in Weisen Kleidern, &c. (Germantown: Printed by Christoph Saur, 1748);

Eine Predigt Welche ein Schweitzer, ein Reformirter Prediger in Sud Carolina bey Charlestaun gehalten, über die Worte des Propheten Hosea: Sie bekehren sich, aber nicht recht (Germantown: Printed by Christoph Saur, 1749);

Evangelisches Zeugnuss. Vom Elend und Erlosung Der Menschen, in zwey Predigten Abgelegt Und auf hofnung Mehrer Erbauung dem Druck überlassen Vom Johann Joachim Zublin Prediger bey einer englishen gemeinde ohnweil Carles Stade in Sud Carolina (Germantown: Printed by Christoph Saur, 1751);

The Real Christians Hope in Death; or an Account of the Edifying Behavior of Persons of Piety in their Last Moments (Germantown: Printed by Christopher Sower, 1756);

The Stamp-Act Repealed; A Sermon, Preached at the Meeting at Savannah in Georgia, June 25th, 1766 (Savannah: Printed by James Johnston, 1766);

An Humble Enquiry into the Nature of the Dependency of the American Colonies upon the Parliament of Great-Britain, and the Right of Parliament to Lay Taxes on the Said Colonies (Charleston?, 1769); republished as *Great Britain's Right to Tax Her Colonies Placed in the Clearest Light, by a Swiss* (London: J. Delegal, 1774; Philadelphia?, 1785);

A Letter to the Reverend Samuel Frink, A. M. Rector of Christ's Church Parish in Georgia, Relating to Some Fees Demanded of Some of His Dissenting Parishioners (Savannah?: Printed by James Johnston?, 1770?); republished as *Letter to Mr. Frinck. Thoughts on the Day of Judgment* (Philadelphia: Printed by Henry Miller, 1775);

The Wise Shining as the Brightness of the Firmament ... A Funeral Sermon, Preached at Savannah ... November 11, 1770, on the ... death of the Rev. George Whitefield ... (Savannah: Printed & sold by James Johnston & sold in Charleston by John Edwards, 1770); republished as *Funeral Sermon on the Death of the Rev. George Whitefield* (Philadelphia: Printed by Henry Miller, 1770);

An Account of the Remarkable Conversion of Jachiel Hirshel, from the Jewish to the Christian Religion ... (Savannah: Printed by James Johnston, 1770);

The Christian's Gain in Death, Represented in a Funeral Sermon, Preached at Purysbourg, in South-Carolina, Jan. 28, 1770, at the Interment of Mr. Jacob Waldburger (Savannah: Printed by J. Johnston, 1770);

The Nature of that Faith without which It Is Impossible to Please God, Considered in a Sermon on Hebrews XI 6 ... (Savannah: Printed by James Johnston, 1772);

Calm and Respectful Thoughts on the Negative of the Crown on a Speaker Chosen and Presented by the Representatives of the People ... (Savannah?: Printed by James Johnston?, 1772);

The Faithful Minister's Course Finished: A Funeral Sermon ... August the 4th, 1773, in the Meeting at Midway, Georgia, at the Interment of the Rev. John Osgood ... (Savannah: Printed by James Johnston, 1773);

The Law of Liberty. A Sermon on American Affairs, Preached at the Opening of the Provincial Congress of Georgia ... (Philadelphia: Printed by Henry Miller, 1775; London: Printed for J. Almon, 1775);

Eine Kurzgefasste historische Nachricht von den Kämpfen der Schweitzer für die Freyheit [appendix to *The Law of Liberty*] (Philadelphia: Printed by Henry Miller, 1775);

Pious Advice. Sermon on the Faith (Philadelphia: Printed by Henry Miller, 1775).

John Joachim Zubly, minister and political pamphleteer, was born and educated in St. Gall, Switzerland, and, in 1744, ordained at the German Church in London. Shortly thereafter, he immigrated to the British Colonies in North America and arrived in Georgia in 1745. He served in Savannah as assistant to the Reverend Bartholomew Zouberbuhler, a German-Swiss minister, for two years and then moved to Purrysburg, South Carolina, to join his father, David, who had established his own ministry there in 1736. Zubly married Anna Tobler, also a German-Swiss immigrant, in November 1746, and together they had three children, John (who died in 1780), Anne (born in 1756), and David (who died in 1790). Some time after Anna Zubly's death in 1765, Zubly wed Anne Pyne.

In 1760, Zubly returned to Savannah as minister of the Independent Church, a meetinghouse composed chiefly of dissenters from the Church of England. Zubly prospered in Savannah, and he quickly became a prominent land and slave owner as well as a minor officeholder. His ability to preach in German, French, or English helped make him the most influential clergyman in pre-Revolutionary Georgia.

During the crises of the 1760s and 1770s, Zubly's activities helped push Georgia, the youngest and most loyal colony, toward resistance to Parliament. His sermons, which combined religious exegesis with political and constitutional theory, formed a part of the pamphlet literature that articulated an ideology of opposition to Great Britain. Zubly's first political tract, *The Stamp-Act Repealed; A Sermon, Preached at the Meeting at Savannah in Georgia, June 25th, 1766* (1766), gave thanks that "affection and confidence is restored between us and our mother country."

Three years later, with a new series of Parliamentary acts threatening the colonies, Zubly anonymously published *An Humble Enquiry into the Nature of the Dependency of the American Colonies upon the Parliament of Great-Britain . . .* (1769). In his analysis of the conflict with Great Britain he invoked the biblical injunction "a house divided against itself cannot stand." Employing standard Whig-opposition language, Zubly argued that Parliament could not levy taxes because they refused to grant the colonists actual, rather than virtual, representation, thus depriving them of the rights of Englishmen. Moreover, Zubly insisted that Parliament's sovereignty over the colonies extended only to matters of trade.

Describing himself only as a "freeman," Zubly also wrote *Calm and Respectful Thoughts on the Negative of the Crown . . .* (1772), in which he expressed his doubts that the Crown had a constitutional right to reject a speaker of the Georgian Commons House who was chosen by the representatives of the people. By 1774, when Princeton University awarded him an honorary D.D., Zubly's reputation had spread beyond the South.

Zubly's best-known pamphlet was *The Law of Liberty . . .* (1775). In this tract the minister argued that "to restore peace and harmony nothing is necessary than to secure to America the known blessing of the British constitution." He made it clear, however, that independence was not the desired goal of the colonists. "Our interests," Zubly reminded the delegates, "lies in a perpetual connection with our mother country."

As a whole, then, Zubly's political writings belonged to the mainstream of essays in the 1760s and 1770s that explored the issues of taxation, representation, and sovereignty. His were neither the most sophisticated nor most controversial statements of an incipient revolutionary ideology. But as a respected and influential spokesman for this position in the lower South, his writings took on added importance.

The Provincial Congress of Georgia elected Zubly a delegate to the Continental Congress, and he served in Philadelphia from 5 September 1775 through sometime in November. In his diary John Adams described Zubly as "a man of warm and

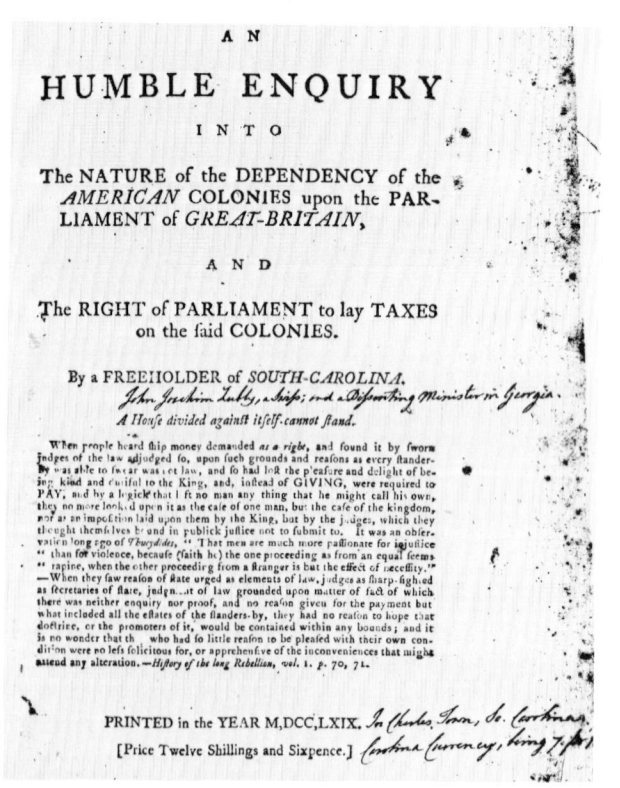

Title page for the pamphlet in which Zubly argued that Great Britain's sovereignty over the American colonies extended only to regulation of trade (courtesy of the John Carter Brown Library at Brown University)

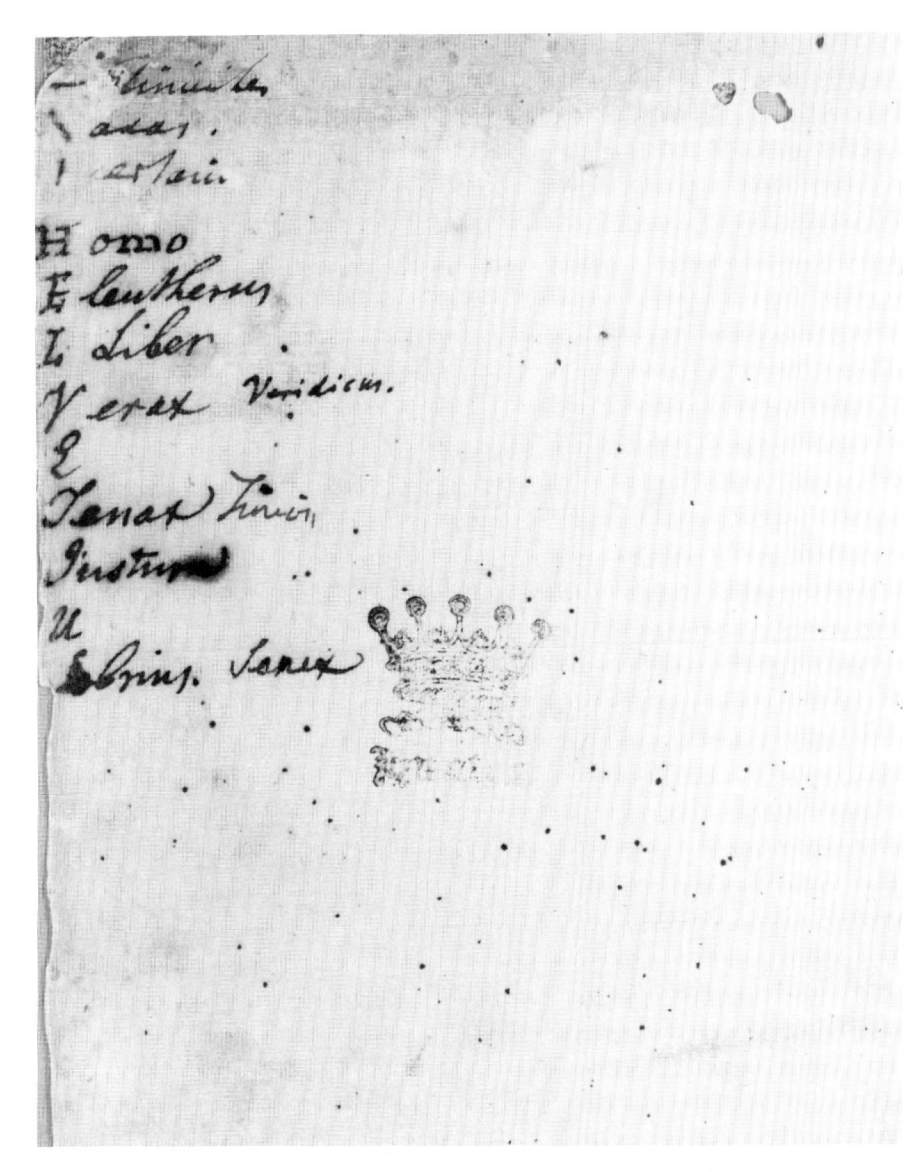

An acrostic on the pseudonym with which Zubly signed his Loyalist essays, from the final page of Zubly's last journal (Georgia Historical Society)

zealous spirit; it is said that he possesses considerable property." Zubly, whose constitutional stand made him a radical prior to 1775, rejected the move to independence that many other delegates were beginning to embrace. Although he recognized in *The Law of Liberty* . . . that "in times of public confusion men of all parties are sometimes carried further than they intended at first setting out," he despised the idea of rebellion or revolution. Zubly maintained the opinion that a republican government was "little better than government of devils."

While still a delegate to Congress, Zubly wrote Sir James Wright, the Royal Governor of Georgia, with news of the proceedings in Philadelphia. After one letter was intercepted, Zubly's position was not only further compromised but Congress adopted a resolution prohibiting any member from divulging its deliberations. Zubly departed for Georgia, and in 1777, after he refused to swear an oath of allegiance to the patriot cause, the Revolutionary government in Georgia confiscated his lands and banished him from the state. After the British reestablished royal government in Georgia in 1779, Zubly returned to Savannah from South Carolina's Black Swamp and resumed his ministerial responsibilities. He also once again took up his quill and, under the pseudonym Helvetius, published a series of essays in the *Royal Georgia Qazette* (July through October 1780). These essays, consummate expressions of Loyalist ideology, denounced the patriots as "desperate and wicked men" engaged in an unjust and unlawful war that mocked human reason, shattered public order, and plunged the country into "blood and flames." Despairing the turn in his fortunes and never comprehending the revolution he had helped wrought, Zubly died in 1781.

References:
Roger A. Martin, "John J. Zubly: Preacher, Planter, and Politician," Ph.D. dissertation, University of Georgia, 1976;

Randall M. Miller, Introduction to *"A Warm & Zealous Spirit": John J. Zubly and the American Revolution, a selection of his writings* (Macon: Mercer University Press, 1982), pp. 1-27;

William E. Pauley, Jr., "Tragic Hero: Loyalist John J. Zubly," *Journal of Presbyterian History*, 54 (Spring 1976): 61-81.

Papers:
Selected papers and journals are located at the Georgia Historical Society, Savannah.

Appendix I

Eighteenth-Century Philosophical Background

The designation "Age of the Enlightenment" describes nearly a century of the most profound philosophical changes in Western culture. The remarkable movement from the holy wars and witch burnings in seventeenth-century Europe to the establishment of republican governments and the spread of religious skepticism by the last third of the eighteenth century stemmed, of course, from complex causes. But the student of Western civilization cannot examine this phenomenal shift for long without recognizing the pervasive importance of the philosophical and scientific works of Bacon, Newton, Descartes, Hobbes, and Locke. These philosophers created new ways of seeing the world and provided texts that were used by others who sought philosophical grounds for social and political change. Enlightenment of the mind of man to the errors of religious superstition, to the potential of reason, to the order of the universe, and to the means for progress in the sciences and the arts—in the eighteenth century, poets, essayists, and men of learning pursued these goals with astonishing energy and optimism.

The impact of these developments upon intellectual life in America in the eighteenth century has been a subject of considerable research and scholarship, represented most recently by the works of Norman Fiering, Henry May, Alfred Aldridge, and Terence Martin. The picture these and earlier studies presents is a complicated one. On the one hand, religious authority remained very strong in the colonies until the decade of the Revolution. Wherever the Calvinist spirit prevailed there was resistance to philosophical change unless new theories could be reconciled with established doctrines. On the other hand, the main figure of the Great Awakening revivals in America, Rev. Jonathan Edwards, was clearly influenced in his own theological and psychological formulations by Locke and Newton. From Edwards's perspective Locke simply provided a more sophisticated way of understanding God's plan for the universe and man's interaction with nature, which was itself only one of the tools through which the creator expressed his divine sovereignty. Yet some of Edwards's critics, ministers and theologians who were disturbed by the emotionalism of the Great Awakening, found in the rationalist ideas of Locke an argument against the perceived pietistic excesses of Edwards and the New Light clergy, and still others, who found Locke's thought tending too much toward the philosophical extreme of materialism, found attractive the idealism of Bishop George Berkeley. There had always been a strain of Platonism in American Puritan thought, articulated most clearly in the vision of the City on a Hill and a New World Zion as a corporate destiny, and Berkeley's well-known poem "Verses by the author on the prospect of Planting Arts and Learning in America," with its theme of *translatio studii* depicting the westward movement of culture to America, appealed to this Platonist strain and served to heighten Berkeley's appeal in the colonies.

With the exception of Edwards, whose influence diminished after the Great Awakening and his untimely death soon after he assumed the presidency of the College of New Jersey (later to become Princeton University), there was no original systematic thinker in America. In such an age of philosophical change, however, young scholars, especially those training for the clergy and the professions, demanded knowledge of current theories and answers to their nagging questions and doubts. For the American colleges in the mid-eighteenth century the solutions to bewildering, philosophical concerns seemed to be best provided by the group of Scottish Realists of what came to be called the commonsense school. The leaders of this group steered a middle course between the idealism of Berkeley and the tendency toward skepticism most fully expressed in the works of David Hume, who was little read in America during this period. The commonsense doctrines, which emphasized "experience and fact interpreted by plain common sense," also reconciled the apparent conflict between natural philosophy and religion simply by arguing that reason could find practical value in both of these existing realities. The clergy who presided over the American colleges in the 1760s and 1770s found the writings of Reid, Kames, and other Scottish thinkers most appealing because they provided a new philosophical legitimization for maintaining religious orthodoxy.

One of the key figures in the transmission of the commonsense precepts to America was Rev. John Witherspoon, who arrived from Scotland to become president of the College of New Jersey in 1768. Following the aesthetic principles of Kames and other commonsense philosophers, Witherspoon established a new curriculum, which stressed the classics, poetry, eloquence, and the arts as disciplines that would improve the moral sense. With these changes Witherspoon started an educational reform that quickly spread to Yale, Harvard, and the College of Philadelphia (later the University of Pennsylvania). The new curriculum was eventually codified in a text by Hugh Blair, *Lectures on Rhetoric and Belles Lettres* (1783). This work increased the dissemination of commonsense thought throughout the American colleges, a process that continued until the middle of the nineteenth century. In 1803 when Samuel Miller composed his small cultural history of America, *A Brief Retrospect of the Eighteenth Century,* he asserted that Witherspoon's arrival in the colonies was a turning-point event in "the advancement of literature and science in our country."

Leading political figures of the Revolution and the New Republic, such as Thomas Jefferson, Benjamin Franklin, James Madison, and George Washington, were deeply influenced by the writings of John Locke and of the commonsense philosophers, and every American writer of the period of the Revolution embraced a notion of the moral value of belles lettres which had been learned at the feet of teachers such as Witherspoon, William Smith, or Ezra Stiles. Because such Americans were so influenced by the European philosophers they read, essays on some of these key figures are included here.

—*Emory Elliott*

John Locke
(29 August 1632-28 October 1704)

David Woolwine
Princeton University

SELECTED BOOKS: *Epistola de tolerantia . . .* (Goudae: Apud J. ab Hoeve, 1689); translated by William Popple as *A Letter Concerning Toleration* (London: Printed for Awnsham Churchill, 1689; Boston: Printed & sold by Rogers & Fowle, 1743);

Two Treatises of Government. In the Former the false Principles and Foundations of Sir Robert Filmir, and his Followers, are detected and overthrown. The latter is an Essay concerning the true Original, Extent and End of Civil-Government (London: Printed for Awnsham Churchill, 1690; second treatise only, Boston: Printed & sold by Edes & Gill, 1773);

An Essay Concerning Human Understanding. In Four Books (London: Printed for Tho. Basset, 1690; republished in part as *An Abridgment of Mr. Locke's Essay Concerning Human Understanding*, abridged by John Wynne (Boston: Printed by Manning & Loring, 1794);

Some Considerations of the Consequences of the Lowering of Interest, and Raising the Value of Money. In a Letter to a Member of Parliament (London: Printed for Awnsham & John Churchill, 1692);

Some Thoughts concerning Education (London: Printed for Awnsham & John Churchill, 1693);

The Reasonableness of Christianity, as deliver'd in the Scriptures (London: Printed for Awnsham & John Churchill, 1695; Boston: Printed by T. B. Wait, 1811).

John Locke

John Locke, as the author of the *Two Treatises of Government* (1690), must be recognized as one of the foremost influences on American revolutionary thought. Although recent scholarship into the origins of the ideology of the American Revolution has uncovered influences other than Locke, nonetheless there can be little doubt that Locke's account of the nature of human society was a central element in the revolutionaries' attempt to formulate a justification for their withdrawal of allegiance to the British crown. Locke's importance as a writer must be recognized in another sense as well, for it is Locke's ideal conception of what a society should be that has come, for better or worse, to be realized in the modern world. Locke's beliefs that the polity should be based on free and rational consent of individuals, that government should be organized for the protection of the rights of the citizen, especially the rights to hold property, to participate in the political process and to exercise freedom of conscience, have become the defining characteristics of Western democracies. For these reasons, both for his influence and for his prescience, Locke must be ranked among the most important thinkers of the modern political tradition.

John Locke was born in 1632 in Wrington, Somersetshire, and spent his boyhood in the nearby town of Somerset, where his father, John Locke, Sr., was a lawyer and clerk to the justices of the peace.

His mother, born Agnes Keene, was the daughter of a tanner. Locke's father fought on the Parliamentary side in the Civil War, and it was his commander, Colonel Alexander Popham, who managed to secure for the young Locke entrance to Westminster School.

Locke went to Christ College, Oxford, in 1652, supported by a scholarship won at Westminster in 1650. It was probably at Oxford that Locke first came into contact with the broadminded and tolerant opinions that were to inform his later religious writings. The dean of Christ College in those years was John Owen who, although a supporter of the Parliamentary cause and former chaplain to Cromwell's armies, was nonetheless a staunch and early advocate of tolerance in religious affairs. After the Restoration Locke remained at Oxford, serving as tutor in Greek and holding various offices at the university. He also served in 1665 as secretary to the British mission to the Elector of Brandenburg. In Cleves, the seat of the elector, Locke first observed full religious tolerance in practice.

After service at Cleves Locke returned to England to take up the study of medicine at Oxford. It was while on a medical errand that Locke first met Sir Anthony Ashley Cooper (later First Lord Shaftesbury). This was an important meeting, both for Locke and for the history of political thought. Soon after this initial meeting Locke accepted an invitation to become secretary and private physician to Shaftesbury.

Lord Shaftesbury had originally served with the King during the Civil War; however, he threw his support to the Parliamentary side in 1644. He was active in the negotiations leading to the restoration of the Stuarts and served in several of Charles II's governments, holding several high offices, including that of Lord Chancellor. However, most important for Locke's career and intellectual development was the fact that Shaftesbury was the key force in the attempt in 1679 to remove the Duke of York, on the basis of his Catholicism, from the succession.

Shaftesbury was also an early capitalist, investing in the African Company and the Bank of England and convincing Locke to invest likewise. It is arguable that Shaftesbury's interest in religious toleration grew out of his belief that such a policy would aid the economic development of England. The third Lord Shaftesbury, Locke's pupil, wrote that his grandfather urged Locke to "turn his thoughts another way.... He put upon him the study of the religious and civil affairs of the nation...." This statement is essentially correct, for we know that it was during this period of service that Locke began several drafts of an "Essay on Toleration," the thoughts of which were to find final expression in *A Letter Concerning Toleration* (1689). It was also in the service of Shaftesbury, then Chancellor of the Exchequer, that Locke acted as adviser in the composition of the *Fundamental Constitutions of Carolina* (1669). Authorship of several anonymous pamphlets written during this period has been attributed to him as well, although Shaftesbury is the most likely author. One such pamphlet, *A Letter from a Person of Quality to his Friends in the Country* (1675), which argued for frequent summoning of Parliaments, is entirely in accord with Shaftesbury's political program.

Finally it was Locke's association with Shaftesbury which led to his own exile in 1683 and to his subsequent return to England in the favor of William of Orange in 1688. Shaftesbury was undoubtedly involved in the Insurrection Plot of 1682, an attempt to place the Duke of Monmouth on the throne. Locke himself may have been one of the conspirators, since it is known that he attended a secret meeting of the plotters on 15 September 1682, along with Shaftesbury and the Earl of Essex. Warrants were issued for Shaftesbury's arrest upon the failure of Monmouth's rebellion, and he fled to Holland, dying there in 1683. Locke soon followed his mentor into exile. For a short period his name was on a list of exiles the Crown was demanding that the Dutch return to England, and at this time he was expelled from Oxford by royal decree.

It is, therefore, in the context of service to Lord Shaftesbury, and in the context of the larger political controversies of the reigns of Charles II and James II that Locke's religious and political works must be understood. For although Locke's works were published upon his return to England, the ideas behind them were formulated during the time when Locke was secretary to Shaftesbury and during the period of exile. *Two Treatises of Government* may have in fact been begun during the years 1679 to 1681, since this was the period of the Exclusion Crisis, and the period in which the works of Robert Filmer, which Locke spends the first essay refuting, were most popular. In *A Letter Concerning Toleration* Locke argues for religious toleration on grounds completely in accord with arguments he later put forth in the *Two Treatises of Government* to support the general liberty of the subject: that is, that men do not have the power to give up their rights to work out their own salvation and therefore that the state can claim no power over their consciences. Locke does not, however, argue for complete religious toleration, inasmuch as, in his view, Catholics should be exempted. The practice of the Catholic faith, although never explicitly discussed in *A Letter Concerning Toleration* is, he implies, contrary to the common good and safety. Catholics may be looked upon, Locke seems to say, as being at war with the non-Catholic polity, since they are taught by their religion not to keep contract with those outside of the faith. The argument, therefore, for the toleration of all sects excepting that of the Church of Rome makes sense if seen as growing out of Shaftesbury and Locke's attempt to bring the largely entrepreneurial class of dissenters into the political fold in England, while at the same time excluding the duke of York and other Catholics from any role in the government.

It is the *Two Treatises of Government* which stand as Locke's primary contribution to political thought. After refuting in the first half of the book the claims put forth by Sir Robert Filmer in the *Patriarchia* (1680) that the rights of kings are unlimited and derived from the absolute paternal dominion given by God to Adam, Locke turns his attention to the "true original, extent and end of civil government." Locke's purpose in the second treatise is to show that all government is derived from the consent of the governed, based as it is upon a contract made by equal and independent individuals. He argues that this contract is made first in a state of nature and is entered into in order to preserve life and certain rights which cannot be best protected in that earlier state. Locke's account of the origin of civil society differs in several important respects from that of the other great social contract theorist of the period, Thomas Hobbes. Locke's individuals enter into contract with each other to set up a civil government; their contract is not primarily, as in Hobbes, with a sovereign. Ultimate sovereignty remains, therefore, with the individuals. Locke's account also differs from Hobbes in that "justice" can be said to exist in the state of nature itself, inasmuch as property rights exist there. Property rights adhere to men in their very being as individuals and as laborers; as Locke argues "Though the earth and all inferior creatures be common to all men, yet every man has a 'property' in his own 'person.' This nobody had a right to but himself. The 'labour' of his body and the 'work' of his hands, we may say, are properly his. Whatsoever, then, he removes out of the state that Nature hath provided and left in it, he hath mixed his labour with it, and joined to it something that is his own, and thereby makes it his property."

The central difference between Hobbes and Locke, therefore (and herein lies Locke's most original contribution to political philosophy), is his conception of property rights. Whereas Hobbes argues that civil government is instituted for the preservation of life alone, and property and justice come into being only afterward, for Locke civil society and property rights exist prior to the establishment of political authority, and civil government is charged with the protection and preservation of more than mere life. Representation in government is also mandated by this conception of property, since it is only by representative government that property may be legitimately disposed of by government, especially in taxation. A civil government which violates any of these several rights may be resisted in Locke's view, not only one which by tyranny or incompetence endangers the lives of its subjects.

In 1690 Locke also published his major philosophical work, *An Essay Concerning Human Understanding*. It was for this work that Locke was best known in the seventeenth and eighteenth centuries, in both England and America. His stature as a political theorist was in part based on the fact that he was the "Great Locke" of *The Essay*. The major purpose of this work, as Locke suggests in its introduction, is a limited one. He did not set out to answer all questions concerning human understanding, but rather to see if he could "find out how far the understanding can extend its view; how far it has faculties to attain certainty, and in what cases it can only judge and guess."

The epistemology of *An Essay Concerning Human Understanding* is a sensationalist one and the first full-fledged sensationalist epistemology put forth in English. Locke's main point is that all men's knowledge is of ideas and relations between ideas, and that these ideas arise by experience. He spends a good part of book one refuting the notion of innate ideas, showing that all ideas which men possess can be reduced to either direct experience or reflection upon the ideas derived from experience. The concept of *idea* is nowhere clearly defined in the book and is used throughout in varying senses, a weakness of which Locke seems to be aware. The final section, book four, deals with the method of obtaining certain knowledge, namely through the process of intuition. This section has been criticized as returning Locke to a position similar to that of the Cartesians and being overly close to the doctrine of innate ideas. But it may be argued in Locke's defense that he differs from Descartes because he consistently maintains that, regardless of the operations performed by the mind, the ideas of which knowledge is constituted are ultimately reducible to sense experience.

Upon his return to England after the removal of James II from the throne, Locke held several minor offices in the governments of William III. Ill health eventually led to his complete retirement from public affairs in 1700. He spent most of these later years at Oates, the home of Sir Francis and Lady Masham, far enough from the London air to escape its ill effects on his health. This period was also one of controversy for Locke, who had sought all his life to avoid controversy by publishing most of his works anonymously. His letter on toleration was especially attacked, forcing him to reply with three more essays on the subject. A minor work on finance was also published during this period (*Some Considerations of the Consequences of the Lowering of Interest, and Raising the Value of Money*, 1692), as well as his *Some Thoughts concerning Education* (1693). It was also the period of the publication of *The Reasonableness of Christianity* (1695), in which Locke lays out his Latitudinarian view (later attacked unfairly as a deist one) that the essence of Christianity is the belief that Christ is the Messiah, that further theological doctrine is unwarranted by scripture, and that Christ's mission was to teach morality. It was at Oates that Locke died on 28 October 1704.

There are essentially two areas of American revolutionary thought where Locke's influence is noticeable; epistemological-theological thought and political thought. It has been argued by some (most notably Conrad Wright and Perry Miller) that the Lockian epistemology, the "new way of ideas," was so widely accepted among learned men, particularly the clergy, that little else was represented in the colonies. Wright has maintained that explicit Lockian assumptions underlie the Arminian and moderate Calvinist Dudleian lectures given at Harvard by such men as President Edward Holyoke and the Reverend John Barnard, and has shown how such assumptions influenced the development of early Unitarian theology in America. Perry Miller has emphasized the influence of Locke's *An Essay Concerning Human Understanding* on Jonathan Edwards, the combatant of Arminianism, especially in Edward's "Notes on the Mind," *A Treatise Concerning Religious Affections* (1746), and *Freedom of the Will* (1754). More recent scholarship, however, tends to maintain that although Edwards undoubtedly read Locke's *An Essay Concerning Human Understanding* at an early age (certainly before the writing of "Notes on the Mind"), he can best be seen as incorporating Locke's sensationalist epistemology when it suits his purposes. Edwards frequently, as in "Notes on the Mind," and *Freedom of the Will*, starts with Lockian notions only to arrive ultimately either at idealist conclusions similar to those of Berkeley or at orthodox Christian ones.

The most ardently debated issue of late concerning Locke's influence in America has been the question of the degree to which Jefferson employed Lockian notions in composing the Declaration of Independence. An earlier generation of scholars, inspired by Carl Becker, had perhaps erred in viewing not only the Declaration but the whole body of American revolutionary writings as merely Locke translated into an American context. Most historians today, however, have come to recognize the influence of the more historical and legal-constitutional commonwealth school in the writings of the period. Some, in fact, have gone so far as to deny any place to Locke's ideas in the development of American revolutionary ideology. Another body of scholarship has also argued that Jefferson was influenced in the writing of the Declaration more by the moral doctrines of the Scottish commonsense philosophers than directly by Locke's political writings.

It cannot be argued that a return to Becker's views is warranted, or even defensible. However, it would appear that an almost total exclusion of Locke's political thought from the American scene by some "republican" and "Scottish Commonsense" revisionists is an extreme reaction to an earlier glorification of Locke. For although there is, as yet, no consensus among historians as to the importance of Locke's ideas for Jefferson, several points are worth noting. First, the presence of a commonwealth ideology in the colonies, represented by Algernon Sidney and James Harrington, does not militate against the concomitant influence of Locke. It appears that frequently Locke's name is mentioned along with these more historically oriented commonwealth writers, as if little or no distinction was made at the time between Locke and the commonwealth school. Second, the influence of the ideas of the Scottish moral philosophers on Jefferson in the writing of the Declaration again does not argue against the concomitant influence of Locke's political notions (particularly that of the social contract). There also remains the question of which Scottish moral philosophy must be seen behind the Declaration. As Daniel Walker Howe has recently argued, Thomas Reid is as good, or better, a candidate than the revisionist's Francis Hutcheson for this role. Given Reid's close agreement with Locke on the origin of moral concepts in sensation and reflection, Jefferson could have been a Lockian in his moral views even if his philosophy were derived from Reid.

Finally the Declaration of Independence itself is clearly a political document, not a moral treatise. To treat it as essentially a moral treatise is to do a grave injustice to the text. It speaks of the "unalienable rights" of life and liberty, which are identical to Locke's unalienable rights preexistent in the state of nature. It speaks clearly of the human institution of government, instituted for the preservation of rights, and of the right to "alter or abolish" the government when it becomes destructive of its proper ends. These are not ideas derived from Scottish moral philosophy, which adopts on the whole a more general and apolitical tone. The appeal in the Declaration is to nature and to the contractual origin of society, for which ideas there can only be one likely source, book two of Locke's *Two Treatises of Government*.

Biographies:
Peter King, *The Life of John Locke*, enlarged edition (London: Colburn & Bentley, 1830);
H. R. Fox Bourne, *The Life of John Locke* (London: King, 1876);
Maurice W. Cranston, *John Locke: A Biography* (London: Longmans, Green, 1957).

References:
Richard I. Aaron, *John Locke* (London: Oxford University Press, 1937);
Carl Becker, *The Declaration of Independence* (New York: Harcourt, Brace, 1922);
Paul Helm, "John Locke and Jonathan Edwards: A Reconsideration," *Journal of the History of Philosophy*, 7 (January 1969): 51-61;
Daniel Walker Howe, "European Sources of Political Ideas in Jeffersonian America," in *The Promise of American History: Progress and Prospects*, edited by Stanley Kutler and Stanley Katz (Baltimore: Johns Hopkins University Press, 1982), pp. 28-44;
Isaac Kramnick, "Republican Revisionism Revisited," *American Historical Review*, 87 (June 1982): 629-664;
Perry Miller, *Jonathan Edwards* (New York: Sloane, 1949);
J. G. A. Pocock and Richard Ashcraft, *John Locke* (Los Angeles: William Andrews Clarke Memorial Library, University of California, 1980);
Conrad Wright, *The Liberal Christians* (Boston: Beacon, 1970).

George Berkeley
(12 March 1685-14 January 1753)

John Holland
Princeton University

SELECTED BOOKS: *An Essay towards a New Theory of Vision* (Dublin: Printed by A. Rhames for J. Pepyat, 1709);

A Treatise concerning the Principles of Human Knowledge . . . (Dublin: Printed by A. Rhames for J. Pepyat, 1710);

Three Dialogues between Hylas and Philonous . . . (London: Printed by G. James for Hy. Clements, 1713);

De Motu . . . (London: J. Tonson, 1721);

An Essay towards Preventing the Ruine of Great Britain (London: Sold by J. Roberts, 1721);

A Proposal for the Better Supplying of Churches in our Foreign Plantations, and for Converting the Savage Americans to Christianity (London: Printed by H. Woodfull, 1724);

Alciphron; or the Minute Philosopher, 2 volumes (London: Printed for J. Tonson, 1732); 1 volume (New Haven: Printed by Sydney for Increase Cooke, 1803);

A Sermon Preached before the Incorporated Society of the Propagation of the Gospel in Foreign Parts at their Anniversary Meeting in the Parish Church of St. Mary-le-Bow on Friday, February 18, 1731 (London: Printed by J. Downing, 1732);

The Theory of Vision, or Visual Language . . . (London: Printed for J. Tonson, 1733);

The Analyst; or, a Discourse Addressed to an Infidel Mathematician . . . (London: Printed for J. Tonson, 1734);

A Defence of Free-Thinking in Mathematics . . . (Dublin: Printed by M. Rhames for R. Gunne, 1735; London: Printed for J. Tonson, 1735);

Siris: A Chain of Philosophical Reflexions and Inquiries Concerning the Virtues of Tar-Water, and Divers Other Subjects Connected Together and Arising One from Another (Dublin: Printed by M. Rhames for R. Gunne, 1744; London: Printed for C. Hitch & C. Davis, 1744);

A Word to the Wise: Or, an Exhortation to the Roman Catholic Clergy of Ireland (Dublin: Printed by G. Faulkner, 1749; Boston: Printed by S. Kneeland, 1750);

A Miscellany Containing Several Tracts on Various Subjects (Dublin: G. Faulkner, 1752; London: Printed for J. & R. Tonson and S. Draper, 1752).

Collection: *The Works of George Berkeley, Bishop of Cloyne*, edited by A. A. Luce and T. E. Jessop, 9 volumes (London: Nelson, 1948-1957).

Bishop Berkeley is undoubtedly more important to the history of philosophy than to American literary and cultural history. Nevertheless, his interest in America and his influence on American thought are noteworthy. He lived for nearly three years in Newport, Rhode Island, where he wrote his attack on skepticism, *Alciphron* (1732). A benefactor of American education, he made significant contributions to the libraries of Yale and Harvard, and he influenced the founders of the institutions which eventually became Columbia University and the University of Pennsylvania. His popular "Verses by the author on the prospect of Planting Arts and Learning in America," which he wrote in 1716 while working on plans for a college in Bermuda and included in *A Miscellany* (1752), provided readers with a vision of the westward movement of civilization in which America supplants a decadent Europe as the seat of culture. Finally, his philosophical system had a modest influence upon eighteenth-century American thinkers.

Born near Kilkenny, Ireland, in 1685, George Berkeley, the son of William Berkeley was sent, eleven years later, to Kilkenny College and, in 1700 at the age of fifteen, to Trinity College, Dublin. In 1707 he received a Master of Arts degree and became a fellow of the college, a position he retained until 1724, when he was appointed dean of Derry. He published his first book, *An Essay towards a New Theory of Vision*, in 1709 and expounded his epistemological theories in his next two works, *A Treatise concerning the Principles of Human Knowledge* (1710) and *Three Dialogues between Hylas and Philonous* (1713). It is upon these two works that his modern reputation rests.

In an argument aimed at rationalists and skeptics and designed to strengthen the forces of religion, Berkeley attacked the concepts John Locke had developed in *An Essay Concerning Human Un-*

George Berkeley, portrait by Van der Bank. The scene in the background reproduces the symbolic frontispiece in Alciphron *(Bibliothèque Nationale)*

derstanding (1690). Locke had argued that although sense experience provides the basis of all knowledge, one does not gain a direct perception of objects. Rather, the senses transmit to the mind ideas, which are not the physical objects themselves but which represent them. Instead of perceiving objects, the mind perceives ideas of objects, and while some of these representations duplicate the originals exactly, many others do not. Locke explained this assertion by distinguishing between the primary and secondary qualities of objects. The primary qualities are absolute and inherent properties—size, shape, weight, place, and movement. Secondary characteristics, on the other hand, are not innate. Qualities such as color, sound, and heat are effects which an object's primary properties produce in beings possessing sense organs. Ideas of the primary properties thus resemble the objects themselves exactly; ideas of secondary qualities exist only relative to the observer.

Berkeley argued that Locke's theory was, in fact, skeptical; if one does not perceive material substances directly, then one can have no certainty that one's ideas actually resemble these objects. He then proceeded to declare invalid Locke's distinction between primary and secondary qualities. First, he argued, primary properties cannot be separated from the secondary: "Extension, figure, and motion, abstracted from all other qualities, are inconceivable." Further, primary properties can be shown to be just as dependent upon the observer as secondary ones. When judging motion, one must apply relative terms, such as *fast* or *slow,* to it. *Shape,* another primary quality, depends upon the position of the observer. For these reasons, it becomes impossible, Berkeley argued, to make a distinction between inherent and merely perceived qualities.

He then discussed the reasons that all such qualities can exist only in connection with the mind. The "absolute existence of unthinking things without any relation to their being perceived . . . seems perfectly unintelligible. Their *esse* is *percipi*." In other words, shape can only refer to something which can be touched or seen, sound to something heard, and color to something seen. Such qualities cannot exist apart from a perceiver. Berkeley tried to prove this contention further by asking the reader to think of something which exists completely unperceived. It is impossible to do so, he says, because, Hylas finally concedes, "As I was thinking of a tree in a solitary place, where no one was present to see it, methought that was to conceive a tree as existing unperceived or unthought of, not considering that I myself conceived it all the while."

Berkeley, however, would have resisted being classed as a purely subjective idealist. He had, after all, attacked Locke because he believed that his predecessor's epistemology left man in a state of almost complete uncertainty. Further, he stated repeatedly that the purpose of his own system was to justify the commonsense belief that we can have direct knowledge of the external world. Sensory qualities exist in relation to a perceiver. If they were not perceived at all, then they would have no existence. Fortunately, God's constant observation of the world ensures the existence of such objects. Describing Berkeley's ideas, T. E. Jessop has written, "Sensory fact is only evidenced by our perceiving; it is constituted by God's." The existence of God guarantees the truth of what one sees and ensures that objects will not cease to exist when one stops perceiving them. Berkeley's epistemological system thus ends as a statement of faith in revealed religion.

In 1713 Berkeley visited England for the first time. While in London he became associated with Joseph Addison, Richard Steele, and Alexander Pope, and was presented at court by Jonathan Swift. From October 1713 to August 1714, and then again from 1716 to 1720, he toured the Continent.

In 1721, his *An Essay towards Preventing the Ruine of Great Britain* was published. Here he castigated his contemporaries for relinquishing their religious values and succumbing to the lures of greed and skepticism. "Other nations have been wicked," Berkeley opined. "But we are the first who have been wicked upon principle." The signs of this condition are plentiful: "Vice and villainy have by degrees grown reputable among us; our infidels have passed for fine gentlemen, and our venal traitors for men of sense, who knew the world. We have made a jest of public spirit, and cancelled all respect for whatever our laws and religion repute sacred. The old English modesty is quite worn off, and instead of blushing for our crimes we are ashamed only of piety and virtue." Because of these failings, Berkeley ominously warned his readers "We have long been preparing for some great catastrophe" which may not lie far in the future, for "the final period of our State approaches."

Yet if Europe has been corrupted, there is hope that America will become the bearer of civilization. He expressed this belief in a poem which he circulated among friends in 1726 but did not publish until 1752, "Verses by the Author on the prospect of Planting Arts and Learning in America." The civilization which is dying out in decadent Europe will eventually be reborn in full glory in America:

> The Muse, disgusted at an age and clime
>   Barren of every glorious theme,
> In distant lands now waits a better time,
>   Producing subjects worthy fame:
>
> In happy climes where from the genial sun
>   And virgin earth such scenes ensue,
> The force of art by nature seems outdone,
>   And fancied beauties by the true:
>
> In happy climes, the seat of innocence,
>   Where nature guides and virtue rules,
> Where man shall not impose for truth and sense
>   The pedantry of courts and schools:
>
> There shall be sung another golden age,
>   The rise of empire and of arts,
> The good and great inspiring epic rage,
>   The wisest heads and noblest hearts.
>
> Not such as Europe breeds in her decay;
>   Such as she bred when fresh and young,
> When heavenly flame did animate her clay,
>   By future poets shall be sung.

This vision of decline and renascence reaches its highest point in the final stanza, in which Berkeley sees history as a vast drama, the final act of which will be an American golden age:

> Westward the course of empire takes its way;
>   The four first acts already past,
> A fifth shall close the drama with the day;
>   Time's noblest offspring is the last.

Unwilling simply to watch the spectacle take its course, Berkeley desired to help it along. In 1722 he conceived a plan for founding a college in Bermuda in order to further the cause of knowledge in the New World. The college would train "pastors of good morals and good learning," he declared in a letter to his friend Sir John Percival. Such a college would teach not only English immigrants but also "a number of young American savages," who would then "become the fittest missionaries for spreading religion, morality, and civil life among their countrymen." He expanded upon these ideas in a pamphlet published in 1724, *A Proposal for the Better Supplying of Churches in our Foreign Plantations, and for Converting the Savage Americans to Christianity.* Here he argued that Bermuda was a better location for the college than any spot on the American continent because conditions were, he had been informed, unfavorable on the mainland. The atmosphere on the continent was one of irreligion and moral corruption, he wrote, and Harvard and Yale could make little headway against this spirit. Bermuda, on the other hand, was inhabited by honest and uncorrupted settlers, blessed with the finest climate in the New World, and far safer than the continent from bands of marauding Indians.

In the next year, 1725, the British government granted Berkeley a charter to establish St. Paul's College on Bermuda and to serve as its president during the first eighteen months of its existence. He then began the job of raising the money required for his venture, a task which became increasingly difficult as evidence that he had overrated the advantages of Bermuda mounted. By 1728 the venture had made so little progress that Berkeley attempted to push his project forward by traveling to America himself. In September 1728, several weeks after his marriage to Anne Forster of Dublin, he sailed not to Bermuda but to Newport, Rhode Island, where he spent the next thirty-three months of his life.

While he was in Newport, his plan fell through, but he became, in numerous instances, a benefactor to budding American institutions. He donated to Trinity Church in Newport the first organ to reach New England. This gift, however, pales when compared with his extensive gifts to Yale and Harvard. He donated 880 volumes—on subjects as varied as agriculture, history, philosophy, and religion—to Yale's library. In 1742, ten years after this gift, the collection was estimated to account for one-third of all books at Yale. To the more-established Harvard, Berkeley sent about 125 volumes, most of which consisted of Latin classics. Berkeley's beneficence to these institutions did not stop with the donation of books. When he had become certain that he would be unable to establish St. Paul's College, he gave to Yale, for the token sum of five shillings, his home in Newport and the ninety-six acres of farmland, woodland, meadow, and orchard which surrounded it. The income derived from this land was to be used to support outstanding students.

His sojourn in America also gave him the opportunity to make, in the person of Samuel Johnson, an Anglican tutor at Yale, one of the few contemporary converts to his philosophical system. Johnson, at the time, was searching for a philosophical system to take the place of the Puritan theories in which he had ceased to believe; therefore, he began an extensive correspondence with the older man in which he tested Berkeley's thought against other systems then prominent. In one series of letters, for example, they discussed the relative merits of immaterialism and deism. Referring to Berkeley's argument that God must exist in order to guarantee the continued presence of objects, Johnson wondered what this conception implied about God's nature. God must constantly act to keep the world in existence, "to stand by it and influence and direct all its motions." The God of the deists, on the other hand, is like a watchmaker who, in creating the world, endows it with the ability to run, from then on, of its own accord, without his constant intervention. Does not, Johnson wondered, the God of the deists seem more powerful than Berkeley's supreme being? Berkeley answered this query first by exposing the faulty metaphor upon which deism operated. When a watchmaker completes one of his clocks, he relies upon forces over which he has no control, such as gravity, to enable the machine to continue working. The "artificer is not the adequate cause of the clock; so that the analogy would not be just to suppose a clock is in respect to its artist what the world is in respect of its creator." Berkeley concluded his reply by asserting that the notion that God acts upon the world should in no way impoverish our view of the deity. "For aught I can see, it is no disparagement to the perfection of God to say that all things necessarily depend on Him . . . and that all nature would shrink to nothing, if not upheld and preserved in being by the same force that first created it." Such exchanges would eventually contribute much to Johnson's formulations in *Elementa Philosophica* (1752).

While living in Newport, Berkeley attacked the forces of skepticism not only in his letters but also in a series of philosophical dialogues, *Alciphron; or the Minute Philosopher*. His targets here are Anthony Ashley Cooper, third earl of Shaftsbury, who, in *Characteristicks of Men, Manners, Opinions, Times* (1711) had laughed at religious orthodoxy and exalted the powers of nature, and Bernard Mandeville, whose *Fable of the Bees* (1714) had argued that people are egoistic rather than altruistic, and that vices should be indulged because they lead to a nation's economic prosperity. These opinions are represented in Berkeley's dialogue by two freethinkers, Lysicles and Alciphron, and refuted by Euphranor, a farmer, and Crito, a village parson. In the face of Alciphron's glorification of nature as against "artificial" religion and government, Euphranor is able to show that these two are universal, and therefore "natural to man, notwithstanding they admit of sundry forms and different degrees of perfection." Then, arguing against Mandeville, Euphranor and Crito demonstrate that vice and freethinking, rather than contributing to the public good, do in fact destroy a society; "a corruption of principles works its ruin more slowly" than open rebellion, "perhaps, but more surely." In the final dialogue, Alciphron argues that grace is "but an empty name," and Crito breaks through a series of abstractions which have shrouded the concept by arguing that grace is God's active demonstration of his love for man. Grace, like faith, is "not an indolent perception, but an operative persuasion of mind" which one can easily grasp when one ceases to look at it as a dead abstraction. When *Alciphron* was published, it immediately drew fire from Mandeville, who complained that in Lysicles and Alciphron, such "Undauntedness in assaulting, and Alacrity in yielding . . . never met in the same Individuals before." On the other hand, the book found a place on the shelves of many, including Jonathan Edwards, who valued defenses of religion.

By March 1731 Berkeley had realized that he would never receive the money to establish the college in Bermuda and, in September of that year, he and his wife left Newport and sailed for Britain. He was appointed bishop of Cloyne in 1734 and fulfilled his duties there for the next eighteen years. In 1744, he published what was, for contemporary readers, his most popular book, *Siris: A Chain of Philosophical Reflexions and Inquiries Concerning the Virtues of Tar-Water, and Divers Other Subjects Connected Together and Arising One from Another,* in which he extolls tar water as a cure for virtually all illnesses. This subject was to obsess him for the rest of his life.

In 1749, Berkeley briefly put aside this new preoccupation in order to advise Johnson about the project of founding King's College (later Columbia University), an institution designed to serve as a focal point for Anglicans in America. Having taken to heart the failure of his design for Bermuda, he suggested that, rather than "applying to England for Charters or Statutes (which might cause great trouble expense and delay)," Johnson and his colleagues should simply go ahead with their plans and "do the business quietly." The faculties should be made up of people from New England for "I am very apprehensive none can be got in Old England (who are willing to go) worth sending." Berkeley suggested further that available funds should be spent not upon buildings but upon faculty, for the "chief concern must be to set out in good method, and introduce from the very first, a good taste into Society." The curriculum should concentrate upon the classics and upon inculcating a concern for morality. Prizes "may prove useful encouragement to the students" and degree requirements should be based upon the systems of Oxford and Cambridge in order to "pave the way for admitting their graduates *ad eundem* in the British universities." When Johnson answered Berkeley's letter, he indicated that these suggestions had been forwarded to Philadelphia, where Benjamin Franklin and others were also planning to establish a college. This correspondence constituted Berkeley's final attempt to further the cause of education in the colonies. He died four years later, in Oxford.

Berkeley's works were read and debated in America through much of the remainder of the century. "Verses by the Author on the prospect of Planting Arts and Learning in America" became popular during the 1750s and 1760s, a time in which concern about America's cultural role was growing. His poem served as a definitive expression of ideas about the westward movement of culture, a concept which had become widespread. Traveling through the mid-Atlantic colonies in 1759, Andrew Burnaby, for example, noted that "an idea strange as it is visionary, has entered into the minds of the generality of mankind, that empire is travelling westward; and everyone is looking forward with eager and impatient expectation to that destined moment. . . ."

Berkeley's philosophical ideas did not fare as well, however; after a brief period in which they found a champion in Samuel Johnson, they quickly fell into disrepute. Johnson's textbook *Elementa Philosophica,* which Benjamin Franklin published in 1752, was dedicated "To the Right Reverend Father in God, George, Lord Bishop of Cloyne, in Ireland," and bore the following acknowledgment of its relation to the Irish philosopher: "Tho' I would not be too much attached to any one author or system; yet whoever is versed in the writings of Bishop Berkeley, will be sensible that I am in a particular manner beholden to that excellent philosophy for several thoughts that occur in the following tract. And I cannot but recommend it to any one that would think with exactness on these subjects, to peruse all the works of that great and good gentleman...." Like Berkeley and Locke, Johnson used the term ideas to refer to the "immediate objects of sense." Ideas "must derive to us from an Almighty, intelligent active cause, exhibiting them to us, impressing our minds with them, or producing them in us"; thus everything which man perceived had "an immediate dependence upon the Deity." As in Berkeley's system, only God's perception of all objects guarantees that they will not, when not observed by other beings, drop out of existence. One "must infer the necessary existence of an eternal mind" in order to understand why unseen objects continue to exist. Indeed, God is "the continual Preserver of all His creatures and consequently . . . the moment he should cease to will the continuance of their existence, they must unavoidably cease and drop into nothing."

Other colonial thinkers of the mid-eighteenth century rejected Berkeley's system unambiguously. After Cadwallader Colden read *De Motu* at the suggestion of Samuel Johnson, he wrote Johnson that "I think that the Doctor has made the greatest collection in this and his other performances, of indistinct and indigested conceptions from the writings of both the ancients and the moderns that I ever met with in any man's performances."

The commonsense philosophy of Thomas Reid eventually displaced Berkeley's immaterialism in most colleges. Disciples of the Scottish philosopher portrayed Berkeley as a fool who, in attempting to deliver Christianity from the assault of the skeptics, had actually paved the way for David Hume's much more thoroughgoing skepticism. John Witherspoon, a Scottish minister who became president of the College of New Jersey in 1768, strove mightily, and in the end, successfully, to extirpate what was left of Berkeley's influence. He succeeded eventually in demonstrating to the disciples of immaterialism that, as he put it in one of the lectures collected in his posthumous *Works* (1800), Berkeley's system was simply "a wild and ridiculous attempt to unsettle the common sense of metaphysical reasoning." By the end of the eighteenth century, serious defenders of Berkeleyan epistemology had virtually disappeared from the American intellectual scene.

Bibliography:
T. E. Jessop, *A Bibliography of George Berkeley*, revised and enlarged edition (The Hague: Martinus Nijhoff, 1973).

Biography:
A. A. Luce, *The Life of George Berkeley, Bishop of Cloyne* (London & New York: Nelson, 1949).

References:
D. M. Armstrong, *Berkeley's Theory of Vision* (Parkville: Melbourne University Press, 1960);

Joseph J. Ellis, *After the Revolution* (New York: Norton, 1979);

Edwin S. Gaustad, *George Berkeley in America* (New Haven: Yale University Press, 1979);

R. H. Popkin, "Berkeley's Influence on American Philosophy," *Hermathena*, 82 (November 1953): 128-141;

John Wild, *George Berkeley* (Cambridge: Harvard University Press, 1936).

Papers:
Berkeley's manuscripts are in the British Library, Trinity College, Dublin, and the National Library of Ireland.

Francis Hutcheson
(8 August 1694-8 August 1746)

Mark Valeri
Princeton University

BOOKS: *An Inquiry into the Original of our Ideas of Beauty and Virtue; In Two Treatises*... (London: Printed for J. Darby, 1725; fourth edition, revised and enlarged, London: D. Midwinter, A. Bettesworth, & C. Hitch/Glasgow: R. Foulis, 1738);

An Essay on the Nature and Conduct of the Passions and Affections. With Illustrations on the Moral Sense (London: J. Darby & T. Browne, 1728);

De naturali hominum Socialitate. Oratio Inauguralis (Glasgow: Typis Academicis, 1730);

Letters Between the late Mr. Gilbert Burnet and Mr. Hutchinson [sic], Concerning the True Foundation of Virtue or Moral Goodness... (London: W. Wilkins, 1735);

Considerations on Patronages. Addressed to the Gentlemen of Scotland... (London: Printed for J. Roberts, 1735);

Philosophiae Morlis Institutio Compendiaria, Ethices et Jurisprudentiae Naturalis Elementa continens, Libri Tres (Glasgow: Typis R. Foulis, 1742); translated into English and published as *A Short Introduction to Moral Philosophy in Three Books, containing the Elements of Ethics and the Law of Nature* (Glasgow: R. Foulis, 1747);

Metaphysicae Synopsis Ontologiam et Pneumatogiam complectens (Glasgow: R. Foulis, 1742); republished as *Synopsis Metaphysicae*... (Glasgow, 1744);

Reflections upon Laughter and Remarks upon the Fable of the Bees (Glasgow: Printed by R. Urie for D. Baxter, 1750);

A System of Moral Philosophy, in Three Books... *Published from the Original Manuscript, by his son, Francis Hutcheson, M.D. To Which is Prefixed Some Account of the Life, Writings, and Character of the Author, by the Reverend William Leechman*, 2 volumes (Glasgow: Printed & sold by R. Foulis/London: A. Millar, T. Longman, 1755);

Logicae Comendium (Glasgow: R. & A. Foulis, 1756).

Collections: *Works*, 6 volumes (Glasgow: R. Foulis, 1769-1774);

Collected Works of Francis Hutcheson: Facsimile Editions Prepared by Bernhard Fabian, 7 volumes (Hildesheim: Georg Olms Verlagsbuchhandlung, 1971).

Francis Hutcheson, moral philosopher, led the attempts of the Scottish Enlightenment to ground moral discourse on the presuppositions of current psychological and epistemological theories—primarily those of John Locke—and to construct an ethical system oriented toward an essentially social, rather than private, view of the ends of moral life. Hutcheson drew together the ideas of Locke, the third Earl of Shaftesbury (1671-1713), Joseph Butler (1692-1752), and the ancient moralists (particularly Cicero and Aristotle) to become the spokesman for the moral-sense philosophy. His theory of aesthetics contributed to neoclassicism, and his ideas of ethics and economics influenced not only his fellow Scots David Hume and Adam Smith but also early British utilitarianism. Hutcheson's writings found attentive audiences in America, in such divergent quarters as the theological ethics of Jonathan Edwards, the liberal religion of William Ellery Channing, and the political ideas of Thomas Jefferson.

Hutcheson was born into a family of Scotch Presbyterians who had immigrated to Ulster at the end of the seventeenth century. His grandfather, a Presbyterian minister, settled in County Down and developed ties to the local aristocracy. John Hutcheson, father of Francis, pastored a Presbyterian congregation in Armagh and was active in Protestant political interests in Ulster. Francis took his early education at dissenting academies near his grandfather's estate. He matriculated at the university in Glasgow in 1711, when the liberal ideals of the Enlightenment began to challenge the prevalence there of Calvinist orthodoxy. After a brief pastorate, which was troubled by quarrels in the Irish Presbytery between conservative Calvinists and proponents of the new learning, he accepted in 1720 an invitation to organize and lead a dissenting academy in Dublin, where he remained until 1729.

While directing the academy Hutcheson entered a circle of aristocratic, liberal dissenters—chiefly James Arbuckle (1700-1746), Robert

Francis Hutcheson, bronze medallion by Selvi after a portrait by I. Gosset (Scottish National Portrait Gallery, Edinburgh)

Molesworth (1656-1725), and Edward Synge (1696-1770)—who introduced him to the ideas of Shaftesbury and to the opposition politics of the commonwealthman, especially James Harrington (1611-1677). From this period on, Hutcheson turned from theology to philosophy. He assumed the goals of forwarding Shaftesbury's ideas without their anti-Christian biases and of fostering religious toleration and social reform.

In Dublin Hutcheson wrote the two books which became the center of his ethical system, *An Inquiry into the Original of our Ideas of Beauty and Virtue* (1725) and *An Essay on the Nature and Conduct of the Passions and Affections. With Illustrations on the Moral Sense* (1728). Hutcheson intended to refute English rational ethics and the pragmatic egoism of Thomas Hobbes and Bernard Mandeville (1670-1733). The English rational moralists, including Richard Cumberland (1632-1718), Samuel Clarke (1675-1729), and William Wollaston (1659-1724), based their ideas on Locke's ethical theories. They argued that moral precepts could be rationally determined as logical extensions of axiomatic moral laws, or truths. Hobbes maintained, on supposedly empirical bases, that all behavior was ultimately based on an instinct of self-interest. Shaftesbury attempted in his *Characteristics of Men, Manners, Opinions, and Times* (1711) to form a more secure basis for social morality. Against the rationalists, he argued that moral judgments originated in a moral sense. This inner instinct, or affection, was much more immediately available—and therefore knowable—than exterior moral laws deduced by reason. Shaftesbury countered the egoism of Hobbes by describing moral sense as a natural sympathy with society. One's natural impulses, or feelings, contained the highest degree of mental pleasure when harmonized to the happiness of the whole of society. Shaftesbury's optimistic view of man and the system of nature inspired not only Pope's *Essay on Man* but also the shrewd and shocking critique of Mandeville, whose *Fable of the Bees or Private Vices Public Benefits* (1714) restated Hobbes's egoism. If virtue meant the subjugation of self-interest, Mandeville reasoned, then human nature was vicious; even the most apparently disinterested acts could be reduced to the motivations of self-love and pride. Benevolence was a sham, and realism demanded that self-interest be accepted as the basis upon which society functioned.

Hutcheson's writings began as a defense of Shaftesbury against Mandeville and included critiques of the rationalist position. Rational morality was vulnerable to epistemological skepticism, which questioned whether a moral axiom conformed to exterior reality. By reducing the essentials of morality to reasoning on abstract principles, rational moralism failed to provide common people with confidence in their own judgments and with the motivation to virtuous action. Hutcheson complained in *An Inquiry into the Original of our Ideas of Beauty and Virtue*, "must a Man have the Reflection of CUMBERLAND, or PUFFENDORF, to admire Generosity, Faith, Humanity, Gratitude? ... Unhappy it would be for *Mankind* if a *Sense* of *Virtue* was of a narrow an extent, as a Capacity for such *Metaphysics*." Egoistic ethics contradicted the social nature of truly moral action by justifying self-interest.

Both the rationalistic and egoistic schools of thought inherently lacked confidence in the abilities of the common person to accurately determine principles of social relations and to virtuously act in corporate life. A moral authority took precedence over individual judgment. For the rationalists, law—whether a political constitution, tacit social contract, or divine revelation—arbitrated social ethics. For the egoists, some kind of social or political sovereign was necessary to constrain self-interest. With Hutcheson's defense of Shaftesbury came an assertion that political life, as a branch of social affairs, could be ordered by the moral sense common to every person.

The specific principles which Hutcheson delineated from the moral sense—religious toleration, the right of violent resistance, and the right to the fruits of one's labor—accorded with the interests of his own social position. Nonconformity remained a political liability in Britain. Westminster refused to grant Irish parliamentary independence and hampered the development of competitive Irish and Scottish economies. Hutcheson complained in his *Considerations on Patronages* (1735) that Scottish patronages were apportioned so as to deter Presbyterianism and native industry in favor of the political interests of Queen Anne's ministry. Throughout his career, Hutcheson linked his moral-sense philosophy to Whiggish politics.

An Inquiry into the Original of our Ideas of Beauty and Virtue begins with the sensationalist assumption that knowledge, even of moral states, is founded upon our sensations. Hutcheson's method, in contrast to moral systems which begin with divine revelation or with Aristotelian conceptions of ethical principles, takes our common experiences as the foundation of ethical reflection. He draws analogies from Locke's discussion of the exterior senses to two other senses—or aspects of our natural constitution upon which objects make an impression and thereby produce ideas. We have ideas of beauty; these are perceived by an internal sense. We also have ideas of virtue; these are perceived by the moral sense.

In the first treatise Hutcheson attempts to demonstrate the reality of the inner sense. Our idea of beauty is a sensation of inner pleasure as we encounter a beautiful object, and this pleasure is itself a judgment that the object perceived is beautiful. Although different combinations of experiences and complex associations of various ideas may result in contradictory aesthetic sensations from any particular object, we can distill from our experiences of the inner sense a uniform pleasure in, or assent to, "Uniformity amidst Variety." Beauty is an equal proportion of uniformity and variety in bodies. Hutcheson displays his neoclassical affinity for geometric simplicity and symmetry in his illustrations of the qualities of beauty. The variety of a hexagon, for example, makes it more beautiful than a square, and the uniformity of a square makes it clearly superior to a rhombus. Nature itself, however, displays the most beauty. It is a system perfectly proportioned: with uniformity among one species of animal and variety between the species, and with spherical planets all pursuing elliptical orbits yet each planet having a different period of axial rotation and length of orbit.

The universality of our aesthetic sense shows both that a nonphysical sense exists and that there is an objective, orderly system reinforcing our inner judgments. The congruence of our tastes with nature (that is, we take pleasure in beauty and beauty exists) commends the idea of a designing cause, God, and strengthens our confidence in this inner sense.

Hutcheson draws his picture of the moral sense, in the second treatise, along the same lines as the inner sense. As we find physical pleasure in certain objects, and a higher "pleasure of the mind" in beauty, so we sense the highest (the most intense and durable) pleasure in virtue. Hutcheson repeatedly turns this moral sense against the theory of egoism.

We have a sense of moral goodness, Hutcheson says, which "denotes our Idea of some Quality apprehended in Actions, which procures Approbation, and Love toward the Actor...." Hutcheson's antiegoistic argument follows from the characteristics of moral sense. We find pleasure particularly in certain inner dispositions or affections. The objects of our moral sense include our own as well as others' motivations, and we most approve of the social affections: of love or benevolence to others without regard to one's own interest. Hutcheson distinguishes between the *pleasure* one receives from observing benevolence in others or in one's self and *interest,* or regard to one's private advantage. Moral pleasure is a sensation passively received. It has little to do with the willing of one's own good. Many apparent acts of benevolence, of course, stem from self-interest; they are not, properly speaking, benevolent. But many acts arise from (that is, are motivated by) the pleasure of benevolence and therefore have as their end the happiness of others. What else could explain our approval of virtue in characters completely removed from any advantage to us, such as those in Shakespeare's plays or Roman history? We are not only capable of making moral determinations apart from self-interest; we cause pain to ourselves and incur the shame of others' moral disapprobation when we do not act from benevolence.

The pleasure one receives from the moral sense links the individual's welfare to that of the whole of society. Nature is so designed that "by intending the *Good* of others, we undesignedly promote our own greatest *private* Good." We may prolong the delight we feel as we observe an act of benevolence by, in turn, acting benevolently. Thus all moral relations are designed to be untied in a system of mutual motivation, in which one's own happiness increases in proportion to the regard one has for the happiness of others.

How do we decide which of two possible actions is most benevolent, if both have some merit? Or how can we deduce a universal moral sense out of the variety of ethical recommendations currently in use? There is a universal principle: "*that Action is best,* which accomplishes the *greatest Happiness* for the *greatest Numbers,* and *that, worst,* which, in *like manner,* occasions *Misery.*" Moral errors arise from a failure to heed this "*universal Determination to Benevolence*"; that is, from a myopic self-interest or from benevolence to particular, small, social groups. Hutcheson then proceeds to develop a moral calculus—similar to that later used by Bentham—which elaborates the principle of social happiness in terms of quantity, quality, and duration. This provides the transition to the final part of *An Inquiry,* in which Hutcheson applies his ethical theory to political issues.

His argument shifts to the issues of obligations and rights, after a preface which discusses the priority of the moral sense over authoritarian moral systems as the means to determine social ethics. The moral sense is far superior to any idea of law which, with a system of rewards and punishments, constrains benevolence through an appeal to self-interest. Hutcheson reminds his readers that the origin of moral ideas is in the "*moral Sense* of *Excellence* in every Appearance, or Evidence of *Benevolence;* and that we have Ideas of *Virtue* and *Vice,* abstractly from any *Law, Human or Divine.*"

Rights, therefore, derive from the principle of public happiness. Actions or powers are rights to the extent that they tend to promote the public good. Hutcheson avoids any conception of individual sovereignty or any notion that rights depend on some kind of implicit social contract. Rights may be seen as perfect or imperfect. Perfect rights are so necessary to the public good that any violation of them justifies immediate and violent defense. Instances of perfect rights are life, the fruits of one's labor, and the power to direct one's actions to the common good. The right to the fruits of one's labor is perfect because society depends on industry and men are most motivated to industry (however lamentably) by the prospect of private gain. Imperfect rights, the violation of which would decrease the amount of happiness but not engender misery, are exemplified by charity to the poor. Although violation of them is vicious, it does not justify forceful defense. Rights may also be described as alienable or unalienable. Unalienable rights, which include the right to life, private moral sentiments, and religion, are not within our power to transfer to another.

Hutcheson refined and enlarged his ethical theory in response to several criticisms of *An Inquiry into the Original of our Ideas of Beauty and Virtue.* Gilbert Burnet (1690-1726) and Samuel Clarke argued that Hutcheson had completely subjectivized moral judgments. Clarke thought that the inquiry's focus on the inner perception of pleasure, rather than on objective and universal truths available to the understanding, put Hutcheson on the side of egoism. In *An Essay on the Nature and Conduct of the Passions and Affections* Hutcheson attempted to distinguish the moral sense from mere passion and thus to leave room for reason in moral judgment.

Much of this new material came from Joseph Butler (1692-1752), who thought that reason balanced the private affections (self-love) and the public affections (benevolence).

Hutcheson organizes his argument upon the distinction between the lower instincts, or passions, and the affections. He also includes a discussion of two senses that were not mentioned in *An Inquiry:* The Public Sense and the Sense of Honor. Passions, whether benevolent or self-interested, are violent inner states which overwhelm reason. Affections, however, are calm and capable of being guided by reason. Thus the best moral sense is calm universal benevolence, which gains from reason an understanding of the moral system. In the fourth editon of *An Inquiry* (1738), *A System of Moral Philosophy* (1755), and *A Short Introduction to Moral Philosophy* (1747; first published in Latin in 1742), Hutcheson enlarged on the relationship between reason and the moral sense. In these later works, he followed his conclusion in *An Essay* that the moral sense alone can perceive the ultimate end, or basic principles, of moral life and motivate truly benevolent action. Reason is an arbiter of moral judgment only in its capability to present to the sense a larger view of the moral system and to recommend the best means to pursue the happiness of that system. As he explains in *A System of Moral Philosophy,* "the ultimate end is settled by some sense, and some determination of will.... Reason can only direct to the means; or compare two ends previously constituted by some other immediate powers.... We improve our *moral taste* by presenting larger systems to our mind, and more extensive affections toward them; and thus finer objects are exhibited to the moral faculty, which it will approve...." After 1726, Hutcheson dropped the detailed equations of his moral calculus and changed the emphasis of his discussion from the sensation of pleasure to the idea of moral approbation and to the function of conscience. In the fourth edition of *An Inquiry,* Hutcheson describes the pleasure of the moral sense not as an immediate sensation but as a complex idea of reflection frequently mixed with the sense of pain. In these shifts of expression he attempts to guard the moral sense from hedonism and to link it to judgments on the objective moral status of actions and affections.

Through these modifications Hutcheson intended to better demonstrate his system's capability of producing objective moral judgments and of nurturing social virtue. Such concerns attended his rise to a position of intellectual and social leadership. In 1730 he accepted the chair of moral philosophy in Glasgow, which had been offered him only after intense opposition by the conservatives among the faculty. He was an extraordinarily popular teacher, lecturing in English (instead of the conventional Latin), making emotional appeals to the students on behalf of virtue, and displaying personal concern for his pupils. He even lectured with great success to the townspeople on the evidences for Christianity. In the early 1730s, moral debate was the center of British intellectual life, and Hutcheson held an important position. Adam Smith and John Witherspoon (future president of the College of New Jersey) sat in his classes. In 1739 David Hume and Hutcheson began a four-year correspondence, which was to result in Hume's complete dependence on the Glasgow professor for his theory of ethics.

Hutcheson's writings in the 1730s and 1740s include much more discussion of political and social policy and of the value of religious devotion. His largest work, *A System of Moral Philosophy,* was a posthumous collection of lectures he gave in Glasgow from 1733 to 1737. It contains much material from *An Inquiry* and *An Essay,* but it shows a heavier dependence on Aristotle and Cicero. The goal of moral life is not only happiness, but also the perfection of moral agents. Thus the moral sense is no longer seen as simply a vehicle to perceive pleasure or pain. It acts as conscience to approve or condemn one's own actions and affections. He also begins to use the term *will* to describe the affections. The moral sense judges the affections on the following scale of excellence, in ascending order: a taste for art and science; a disposition to candor and veracity; passionate, kind affections; calm, kind, affections; and extensive, calm, kind affections.

The second book of *A System of Moral Philosophy* discusses natural law, and the third book examines civil polity. The order is important; Hutcheson grounds fundamental social rights in the system of nature and thereby gives them priority over social convention and political constitutions. His analysis of rights repeats much of the argument in *An Inquiry,* but adds a distinction between natural and adventitious rights. Natural rights presuppose the principle of natural equality and extend perfect rights to all people. Hutcheson then gives a lengthy criticism of slavery. Adventitious rights are to be protected by law, despite the fact that they do not have the moral priority of perfect rights. The right to property is adventitious, because it is the basis for the perfect right to industry. But it is also alienable in that the right to property may be transferred to another for the social good.

Hutcheson's discussion of civil polity, or politics, is based on a reaffirmation of the basic moral principle that "the pleasures or interests of one, or of a few, must always be subordinated to the more extensive interests of great numbers." The moral sense of benevolence is thus turned against all political forms which would violate perfect rights. Hereditary monarchies are unjust because they deprive society of the right of consent. Hutcheson recommends a mixed form of government. But whatever form the civil polity takes, the authority of its leaders depends on the extent to which they evidence virtue and thereby secure the approbation of society. Governments cannot justly claim immunity from this principle on the basis of divine right or tacit social compacts. The author of nature himself has mandated, through the moral sense, the priority of common consent over law and the right to defend with violence our perfect rights. Active resistance is justified—indeed, obligatory—when by intention or action rulers harm the commonweal: "But in all governments . . . the natural end of the trust is acknowledged on all sides to be the prosperity and safety of the whole body. When therefore the power is perverted from this and to the ruin of a people . . . the subjects must have a right of resistance. . . ." The priority of the sense of social happiness over self-serving political policies and laws informs our judgments of imperial-colonial relationships. His conclusions would hearten not only Scots resenting Parliamentary prerogative but also patriots in Boston, Philadelphia, and Virginia: "Nay as the end of political unions is the general good of those thus united, and this good must be subordinated to the more extensive interests of mankind. If the plan of the mother-country is changed by force, or degenerates by degrees from a safe, mild, and gentle limited power, to a severe and absolute one; or if under the same plan of polity, oppressive laws are made with respect to the colonies or provinces; and any colony is so increased in numbers and strength that they are sufficient by themselves for all the good ends of a political union; they are not bound to continue in their subjection, when it is grown so much more burdensome than was expected. Their consent to be subject to a safe and gentle plan of power or laws, imposes no subjection to the dangerous and oppressive ones. Not to mention that all the principles of humanity require that where the retaining of any right or claim is of far less importance to the happiness or safety of one body, then it is dangerous and oppressive to another, the former should quit the claim, or agree to all such restrictions and limitations of it as are necessary for the liberty and happiness of the other. . . . The insisting on old claims and tacit conventions, to extend civil power over distant nations, and form grand unwieldly empires, without regard to the obvious maxims of humanity, has been one great source of human misery."

Many American colonists certainly read these words; by the mid-eighteenth century Hutcheson was among the best known of British moralists. American literati such as James Logan (1674-1751) and Benjamin Franklin owned copies of *An Inquiry* and *An Essay*. Franklin's *Proposals Relating to the Education of Youth in Pensilvania* (1749) recommended Hutcheson's educational theories and ethical ideas. Thomas Brand Hollis (1719-1804) introduced Hutcheson's *A System of Moral Philosophy* to John Adams. After the Pennsylvania presbytery wrote to the Glasgow professor lamenting the pernicious effects which New Light revivalism had upon ministerial learning, Hutcheson agreed to send them qualified candidates and useful books, but he died before fulfilling his promise. *A Short Introduction to Moral Philosophy* (a shorter textbook version of the lectures which formed *A System of Moral Philosophy*, which Hutcheson intended to be a textbook) and *A System of Moral Philosophy* entered the curriculum of moral philosophy in American colleges. In the 1750s and 1760s both works were prescribed at Harvard and used in the divinity course at Yale. At the College of Philadelphia, William Smith (1727-1803) made Hutcheson the central authority on moral philosophy. The schools of the prophets, which were private divinity schools producing most of New England's Calvinist, New Divinity men, used Hutcheson. Joseph Bellamy (1719-1790), the most influential head of such a school, owned and frequently referred to *A System of Moral Philosophy*.

Hutcheson's writings were particularly influential in American religious and political thinking in the second half of the eighteenth century. His own religious ideas bordered on deism. Although he remained loyal to the Presbyterian church, his view of human nature as essentially benevolent and capable of virtue and his elevation of the principle of human happiness above biblical law as the criterion of moral judgment denied the basic tenets of Calvinism. He was tried for heresy in 1740, a minor irritation in his view. He thought that his explanation of the moral sense provided an argument for God's existence and goodness: How else could one explain a system so wonderfully designed to promote benevolence and the happiness of society? How good must the author of nature be, to give us a moral sense which puts in accord our pleasure and the exterior social world! Hutcheson argued earnestly for the moral superiority of religious devotion; God, too, deserved benevolence. *A Short Introduction to Moral Philosophy* contains lengthy hortative passages recommending piety. But Hutcheson's idea of God, who is a "Governing Mind," reflects Ciceronian stoicism more than orthodox Christianity.

Jonathan Edwards and his followers in the New Divinity School, such as Bellamy, Samuel Hopkins (1721-1803), and Nathaniel Emmons (1745-1840), drew upon many of the ideas in Hutcheson's works, while condemning his conclusions on the respective natures of man and God. Norman Fiering has provided a thorough discussion of the extent to which Edwards's aesthetic conception of moral values and sensationalist description of moral and religious knowledge derive from Hutcheson. *The Nature of True Virtue* (1765), in which Edwards mentions Hutcheson, describes virtue in terms of benevolence, beauty in terms of uniformity amidst variety, and moral judgments in terms of an inner sense, or affections. These ideas, Edwards agrees, did prescribe commendable social actions. New Divinity pastors used the principles of social benevolence to attack slavery and to promote the ideals of charity. Edwards, however, argues that benevolence to created beings is a penultimate moral principle. Consent to being-in-general is the ultimate virtue. Since God displays the most amount of being, then love to God, not social happiness, is the summum bonum. The infinite nature of God's being merits God perfect love; human incapacity for such love demonstrates the need for grace. Bellamy and Hopkins realized that the doctrine of eternal punishment could not be reconciled to the humanocentric ideas of happiness. Without judgment Christ's work of atonement was superfluous, and the atonement was inextricably linked to the trinitarian formula. Hutcheson's ideas, however useful for deriving some principles of social ethics, presented an immense threat to Christianity.

The moral-sense philosophy found a friendlier atmosphere in American liberal theology, from the cautious Arminianism of Jonathan Mayhew (1720-1766) and Charles Chauncy (1705-1787) to the proto-Unitarianism of William Ellery Channing (1780-1842). Arminians asserted with the moral-sense doctrine mankind's natural capacity, and thus duty, to form moral judgments and act accordingly. Mayhew's defense of the moral sense in his *Seven Sermons* (1749) restates Hutcheson's: "By virtue of this faculty of [moral sense], moral good and evil, when they are objects to our minds, affect us in a very different manner; the first affording us pleasure, the other pain and uneasiness: And this, as unavoidably as the eye is differently affected with regular and irregular figures in the body; or the ear, with the most grateful harmony, and the most harsh and grating discord...." Channing, while a student at Harvard, eagerly read *A System of Moral Philosophy*. The moral-sense theory buttressed his confidence in mankind's capacity for holiness, and the principle of disinterested benevolence formed the core of his social ethics.

Many colonial social philosophers found in the ideas of benevolence and social happiness a fundamental conception of the potential of the American social order. James Wilson (1742-1798), professor of law at the College of Philadelphia, was greatly influenced by Hutcheson's antirationalist arguments and moral-sense theory. Wilson wrote revolutionary pamphlets, condemned slavery, and became one of the original justices of the Supreme Court. The earliest American publication of Hutcheson's thoughts was part of an antislavery tract compiled by Anthony Benezet, *A Short Account of that Part of Africa Inhabited by the Negroes...* (1762). Hutcheson was quoted in radical pamphlets and patriot newspapers, such as the 13 February 1772 issue of the *Massachusetts Spy*.

Hutcheson's political ideas, particularly those formulated in *A System of Moral Philosophy*, found their way into many of the basic arguments of Thomas Jefferson and other revolutionary writers. It is difficult, however, to distinguish between the influence of Hutcheson and that of other moral-sense theorists. But a comparison of Jefferson's *A Summary View of the Rights of British America* and the Declaration of Independence, or of Hamilton's *Federalist Papers*, with *A System of Moral Philosophy* and *A Short Introduction to Moral Philosophy* reveals several points of contact between Hutcheson and the Americans. Garry Wills argues that Jefferson directly depended on Hutcheson for most of the philosophical, moral, and political positions in his conception of the Declaration of Independence. The Declaration's doctrines of rights, social happiness, and revolution parallel Hutcheson's arguments.

In Britain an influential school of economic, political, and moral theory formed around Hutcheson's students and channeled his ideas into the stream leading to utilitarianism. The Select Club, as this group led by Hume, Adam Smith, Henry Home, Lord Kames (1696-1782), and Adam Ferguson (1723-1816) called itself, continued after

Hutcheson's death in 1746 to build social theory on the moral sense. Toward the end of the eighteenth century, however, many Scottish and American moral philosophers turned away from the moral-sense theory, in large part because of its association with Humean skepticism. The commonsense philosophy of Thomas Reid (1710-1796) and, later, the associationalist school led by Dugald Stewart (1753-1828) became far more popular at Glasgow, Harvard, and Princeton than the ideas of Hutcheson.

The variety of ways in which Hutcheson's influence may be seen in colonial American thought is due in part to the combination of ideas in Hutcheson's moral philosophy. Hutcheson represents a genre of philosophic thought which included Locke, Shaftesbury, Butler, neoclassicism, and deism. To the extent that Americans pursued this genre, they followed interests similar to those of Hutcheson. As the Enlightenment encroached upon Puritanism's territory in America, theological ethics and moral casuistry gave way to moral philosophy. Hutcheson's popularity marked the attempt of eighteenth-century Americans to reformulate the basic principles upon which the republic was to be built.

References:

Norman Fiering, *Jonathan Edwards's Moral Thought and Its British Context* (Chapel Hill: University of North Carolina Press for the Institute of Early American History and Culture, 1981);

Peter Kivy, *The Seventh Sense: A Study of Francis Hutcheson's Aesthetics, and Its Influence in Eighteenth Century Britain* (New York: Burt Franklin, 1976);

David Daiches Raphael, *The Moral Sense* (London: Oxford University Press, 1947);

Caroline Robbins, 'When It Is That Colonies May Turn Independent:' An Analysis of the Environment and Politics of Francis Hutcheson (1694-1746)," *William and Mary Quarterly*, third series, 11 (April 1954): 214-251;

William Robert Scott, *Francis Hutcheson* (Cambridge: Cambridge University Press, 1900);

Garry Wills, *Inventing America: Jefferson's Declaration of Independence* (New York: Random House, 1978).

Thomas Reid
(26 April 1710-7 October 1796)

Susan Mizruchi
Princeton University

SELECTED BOOKS: *An Inquiry into the Human Mind, on the Principles of Common Sense* (Edinburgh: Printed for A. Millar in London and A. Kincaid & J. Bell in Edinburgh, 1764);

Essays on the Intellectual Powers of Man (Edinburgh: J. Bell, 1785; 2 volumes, Philadelphia: Printed by William Young, 1793);

Essays on the Active Powers of Man (Edinburgh: Printed for John Bell and for G. G. J. & J. Robinson in London, 1788);

Analysis of Aristotle's Logic (Edinburgh: Printed for W. Creech, 1806);

Lectures on the Fine Arts, transcribed from the original manuscript by Peter Kivy (The Hague: Martinus Nijhoff, 1973).

Collections: *The Works of Thomas Reid ... With Account of His Life and Writings by Dugald Stewart,* 4 volumes (Charleston: Printed & published by Samuel Etheridge, Jr., 1813-1815);

The Works of Thomas Reid, With Notes, Sectional Heads, and Synoptical Table of Contents by G. N. Wright, 2 volumes (London: Printed for T. Tegg, 1843).

OTHER: "An Essay on Quantity; Occasioned by Reading a Treatise, in which Simple and Compound Ratios Are Applied to Virtue and Merit," *Transactions of the Royal Society,* 45 (1748): 505-520.

Thomas Reid, engraving by W. R. Annin

Thomas Reid, the originator of Scottish commonsense philosophy, is best known for his critique of the British empiricists, particularly Hume. In contrast to the empiricists, who, as Reid observed, shared the assumption that the objects of human knowledge exist only as ideas in the mind, Reid sought to recover the belief in a world independent of human consciousness: that what we perceive has extramental existence and the laws of nature will operate in the future as they have in the past. Though Reid never set foot in America, scholars of recent decades have recognized his impact on important American thinkers of the eighteenth and nineteenth centuries. Reid's admiration for Baconian natural science, which led him to favor inductive observation and commonsense truths over abstract metaphysics, struck a chord in the American Enlightenment. His *Essays on the Intellectual Powers of Man* was printed in Philadelphia in 1793; his works, published in Charleston in 1813-1815, were republished in New York in 1822.

Thomas Reid was born on 26 April 1710 in Kincardineshire, Scotland, a country parish twenty miles from Aberdeen, to Lewis and Margaret Gregory Reid. Reid's paternal ancestors, as well as his maternal ancestors, the Gregorys, were prominent clergymen and intellectuals. His father, the minister of the local parish, entertained a love of letters. After two years at the local parish school, Reid was sent to Aberdeen to attend the grammar school there in preparation for a university education. In October 1722 Reid, in keeping with family tradition, entered Marischal College in Aberdeen, where he came under the influence of George Turnbull, a professor of philosophy. Turnbull, the author of *Principles of Moral Philosophy* (1740), was at the forefront of the philosophical developments of his era. In a philosophical system closely akin to Berkeley's, Turnbull argued for the supremacy of spiritual facts over material ones and referred to what he called the *common sense,* a human faculty which guided man in "all the duties of common life, all our obligations to God and our fellow-men; all that is morally fit and binding."

In his later years Reid related an incident that is revealing of his mature character if not his youthful one. In a letter to William Gregory, an Oxford relative, the sixty-five-year-old Reid recalled, "About the age of fourteen I was almost every night unhappy in my sleep from frightful dreams, sometimes hanging over a dreadful precipice, and just ready to drop down; sometimes pursued for my life.... How long I was plagued with such dreams I do not recollect. I believe it was for a year or two at least...." Describing his efforts to gain control over these nightly plagues, he wrote, "I thought it was worth trying whether it was possible to recollect while I was dreaming that it *was* all a dream, and I was in no danger. Accordingly, I often went to sleep with my mind as strongly impressed as I could with this thought.... After many fruitless endeavors to recollect this when the danger appeared I affected it at last.... After this my dreams were never very uneasy; and in a short time I dreamed not at all.... the fact was that for at least forty years after I dreamt none, to the best of my remembrance...." Reid's sober trust in the powers of human reason over the irrational realm of nightmare seems remarkable in one so young. Of equal interest in this letter is Reid's propensity for self-experiment, a habit which persisted throughout his life and provided the practical foundation for many of his philosophical theories. This dream experiment presages Reid's description, written the year of his death, of the decline of his physical powers, in which he reasons from the infirmity of old age to speculations about reincarnation. Both passages show Reid's belief in intuitive knowledge, the direct apprehension of the external world via the internal senses of man, and his underlying trust in the powers of common sense and reason to overcome the potential disorders of the mysterious unknown.

Following his graduation from college in 1726, Reid was appointed college librarian, an honorific post which he retained for about a year. In 1737 Reid became the pastor at New Machar, a parish ten miles from Aberdeen, where he remained until 1752, and in August 1740 he married his cousin Elizabeth, with whom he shared a long and congenial married life. Five of their nine children survived to adulthood. During his tenure at New Machar Reid spent a good deal of time pursuing scholarly work. In 1748 his first publication, "An Essay on Quantity," appeared in *Transactions of the Royal Society in London.* This early paper, a response to Francis Hutcheson's *Inquiry into the Origin of Our Ideas of Beauty and Virtue* (1725), argues against attempts to apply mathematical principles to qualities that defy quantification, such as beauty and virtue. Probably a more important intellectual event for Reid during this period at New Machar was the 1739 publication of Hume's *Treatise on Human Nature,* which stimulated his thinking about the nature of reality.

In 1752 Reid was appointed professor of philosophy at Kings College in Aberdeen, where his teaching responsibilities included mathematics and physics as well as philosophy and logic, in keeping with an old Scottish tradition that each professor, regardless of his specialty, tutor his students in all of their subjects. At Aberdeen Reid discovered a stimulating and sociable intellectual community. He and some other professors founded the Aberdeen Philosophical Society, which met for almost twenty years. While the interests of the society were chiefly philosophical, most of its members were also conversant with the principles of science, and discussion topics ranged from philosophy, ethics, and natural theology to agriculture, physics, and chemistry. These discussions shaped many significant contributions to Scottish letters, including James Beattie's *Essay on the Nature and Immutability of Truth* (1770), Alexander Gerard's *An Essay on Taste* (1759), George Campbell's *The Philosophy of Rhetoric* (1776), and Reid's *An Inquiry into the Human Mind* (1764). Reid's first book contains in embryo the central themes of his thought. Published in the same year that Reid was appointed successor to Adam Smith as professor of moral philosophy at Glasgow University, *An Inquiry into the Human Mind* is best seen in the light of previous developments in British philosophy. Proceeding from John Locke's theory that one can achieve knowledge of external objects only by means of mental surrogates, ideas or images that represent external objects, George Berkeley had concluded that only another idea can be like an idea and discounted matter entirely, upholding the mind as the sole active agent in the formulation of human knowledge. Finally Hume, in the logical extension of Lockian idealism, argued that ephemerality and change reigned in the realm of mind as well as matter; thus, there is no true permanence or causation, only a flow of ideas held together by convention. Human beings, Hume believed, could not be certain of the existence of other men or even of a substantial self as the product of experience. Reid saw in Hume's views the dissolution of the world, a dangerous threat to the identity of human beings as well as objects. Hume's skepticism undermined Christianity, for it denied the possibility of any order either natural or spiritual as inherent in the world. In answer to Hume Reid offered his theories of common sense, which assumed that empirical knowledge could be understood to be ontologically real.

In *An Inquiry into the Human Mind* Reid outlined the first principles of common sense, which are principles beyond the scope of analysis and explanation, imposed upon us by the "constitution of our nature." These commonsense truths, such as the existence of things outside our immediate perception, personal identity, and the existence of other human beings, are so self-evident, wrote Reid, that only a fool or a madman would deny them. But philosophers, Reid lamented, had insisted on denying the principles which "irresistibly govern the belief and the conduct of all mankind in the common concerns of life." Concerned with reaffirming inductive and unprejudiced guides to human understanding, he asserted: "The language of philosophers, with regard to the original faculties of the mind, is so adapted to the prevailing system, that it cannot fit any other.... Could we but attain a distinct and full history of all that hath past in the mind of a child, from the beginning of life and sensation, till it grows up to the use of reason this would be a treasure of natural history, which would probably give more light into the human faculties, than all the systems of philosophers about them since the beginning of the world. Reflection, the only instrument by which we can discern the powers of the mind, comes too late to observe the progress of nature, in raising them from their infancy to perfection. It must therefore require great caution, and great application of mind, for a man that is grown up in all the prejudices of education, fashioning and philosophy, to unravel his notions and opinions, till he find out the simple and original principles of his constitution of which no account can be given but the will of our Maker." It is significant that Reid assumes the existence of an elemental untrammeled self which can somehow transcend the forces of social conditioning and be recovered by an act of will.

Garry Wills has isolated three themes in Reid's philosophy: "Egalitarian Epistemology," "Humble Empiricism," and "Communitarian Morality." Asserting the equality between the perceptions of the common man and the philosopher, Reid contended that philosophical suppositions must be grounded in the simple perceptions common to all men. The faculties of all human beings, Reid argued, are partial and imperfect; thus men should be humble in the face of God's works, approaching the world with as few predispositions as possible. "If we would know the works of God," Reid declared, "we must consult themselves with attention and humility, without daring to add anything of ours to what they declare...." Most important perhaps, is Reid's application of his commonsense principles to the community of men: man's social relations serve as necessary guides and correctives for his thoughts. Reid referred to a type of metaphysical lunacy which is "apt to seize the patient in solitary and speculative moments; but when he enters into society, common sense recovers her authority." For "without society and the intercourse of kind affection, man is a gloomy, melancholy, and joyless being."

Reid's late works, *Essays on the Intellectual Powers of Man* (1785), and *Essays on the Active Powers of Man* (1788), offer a fuller articulation of the Scottish commonsense philosophy set forth in *An Inquiry into the Human Mind*. Each of the eight essays in *Essays on the Intellectual Powers of Man* is devoted to one of man's intellectual faculties. Demonstrating his commitment to empirical investigation, Reid asserted that through observation one can arrive at knowledge of fundamental laws. Reid's writings are a kind of introspective empiricism: by examining his own mental activities he sought to understand the "human constitution." *Essays on the Active Powers of Man* moves from an exploration of the mental realm of human experience to the moral realm. Herein Reid discusses the miraculous endowments which set man beyond animals. Since man's conscience, which gives him an intuitive sense of right and wrong, is God's gift to man, it can be trusted to lead him to proper actions. Human interest and human duty are complementary, and adherence to reason will always steer men in the direction of virtue. The problem arises in the limitation of man's reasoning power, and in order to undermine the powerful influence of human selfishness God has instilled in man benevolent affections: familial love, compassion, friendship, and sociability. Like his theory of ideas, Reid's moral theory asserts the objectivity of moral truths. These commonsense moral truths consist of the freedom of the will as the basis of human responsibility and moral judgment, and conscience as an innate human faculty. The active human powers incline man toward virtue and happiness.

In 1782 Reid retired from his professorship at Glasgow University in order to devote more time to his scholarship. His final public discourse, a paper on "Muscular Motion" delivered to the Aberdeen Philosophical Society, explores the progressive changes in the human muscles which accompany the aging process. Its conclusion testifies to the spiritual side of this commonsense philosopher. "It is both pleasant and useful to contemplate with gratitude the wisdom and goodness of the Author of our being, in fitting this machine of our body to the various employments and enjoyments of life.... This grand work of nature, like the fruits of the earth, has its maturity, its decay, and its dissolution. Like those also in all its decay it nourishes a principle within which is to be the seed of a future existence. Were the fruit conscious of this, it would drop into the earth with pleasure, in the hope of a happy Resurrection. This hope, by the mercy of God, is given to all good men. It is the consolation of old age, and more than sufficient to make its infirmities sit light." The piece, written in the winter of Reid's final year, reveals the inductive habit of mind seen in all of his writings. With caution and humility Reid moves from observations of himself to speculations about his place in the universe. Secure always is the assurance of the mystery and wonder of all God's creations.

As Daniel Howe has suggested in *The Unitarian Conscience* (1970), Scottish philosophy had a dual legacy in America; on the one hand it served the aims of an expanding dynamic society by accepting material things at face value while discouraging idle theorizing. On the other hand, its belief in the powers of human intuition over abstract laws, of the commonwealth over elite erudition, and its notion of the moral and social nature of man fueled a type of American idealism. This mutuality of concerns arising from the Scottish philosophers, a mixture of commonsense materialism and social idealism, has been traced to the thought of Thomas Jefferson in the Declaration of Independence by Garry Wills, in *Inventing America* (1978), and to the first generation of American writers such as Philip Freneau, Hugh Henry Brackenridge, and Charles Brockden Brown (Emory Elliott, *Revolutionary Writers*, 1982). Scottish commonsense philosophy appeared in America in the 1760s under the auspices of John Witherspoon, the Scottish Presbyterian president of Princeton University. The philosophy was likewise embraced by the Harvard Unitarians at the turn of the eighteenth century. By the time of Emerson's and Thoreau's years at Harvard, the works of the commonsense philosophers were integrated into the school curriculum.

Letters:
"Unpublished Letters of Thomas Reid to Lord Kames, 1762-1782," edited by Ian Simpson Ross, *Texas Studies in Literature and Language*, 7 (Spring 1965): 17-65.

References:
Stephen F. Barker and Tom L. Beauchamp, *Thomas Reid: Critical Interpretations* (Philadelphia: University City Science Center, 1976);

Merrell R. Davis, "Emerson's 'Reason' and the Scottish Philosophers," *New England Quarterly*, 17 (1944): 209-228;

Emory Elliott, *Revolutionary Writers: Literature and Authority in the New Republic, 1725-1810* (New York: Oxford University Press, 1982);

Alexander Campbell Fraser, *Thomas Reid*, Famous Scots Series (Edinburgh & London: Oliphant Anderson, 1898);

Daniel Walker Howe, *The Unitarian Conscience* (Cambridge: Harvard University Press, 1970);

Garry Wills, *Inventing America: Jefferson's Declaration of Independence* (Garden City: Doubleday, 1978).

Henry Home, Lord Kames
(1696-27 December 1782)

Liza Dant
Princeton University

SELECTED BOOKS: *Essays upon Several Subjects in Law* ... (Edinburgh: Printed by R. Fleming & sold by James M'Euen, 1732);

Essays upon Several Subjects concerning British Antiquities ... (Edinburgh: A. Kinkaid, 1747);

Essays on the Principles of Morality and Natural Religion ... (Edinburgh: Printed by R. Fleming for A. Kinkaid & A. Donaldson, 1751);

Historical Law-Tracts ..., 2 volumes (Edinburgh: Printed for A. Millar in London, and for A. Kinkaid & J. Bell in Edinburgh, 1758);

Principles of Equity ... (Edinburgh: Printed by A. Kinkaid for A. Millar in London, and for A. Kinkaid & J. Bell, 1760);

Introduction to the Art of Thinking (Edinburgh: Printed for A. Kinkaid & J. Bell, 1761);

Elements of Criticism ..., 3 volumes (Edinburgh: A. Kinkaid & J. Bell, 1762; 2 volumes, Boston: Printed by Samuel Etheridge for J. White, Thomas & Andrews, W. Spotswood, D. West, W. P. Blake, E. Larkin, and J. West, 1796);

Sketches of the History of Man, 4 volumes (Edinburgh: W. Creech/London: W. Strahan & T. Cadell, 1774); republished in part as *Six Sketches on the History of Man* (Philadelphia: Sold by R. Bell & R. Aitkens, 1776);

The Gentleman Farmer. Being An Attempt to improve Agriculture, By subjecting it to the Test of Rational Principles (Edinburgh: Printed for W. Creech, 1776);

Loose Hints upon Education, chiefly concerning the Culture of the Heart (Edinburgh: J. Bell & J. Murray, 1781).

OTHER: Scotland, Court of Session, *Remarkable Decisions of the Court of Session, from 1716, to 1728*, edited by Kames (Edinburgh: Printed by T. Ruddiman, 1728);

Scotland, Court of Session, *The Decisions of the Court of Session, from Its First Institution to the Present Time. Abridged, and Digested under Proper Heads, in Form of a Dictionary* ..., edited by Kames (Edinburgh: Printed by R. Watkins for himself & A. Kinkaid, 1741);

Scotland, Court of Session, *Remarkable Decisions of the Court of Session, from the Year 1730 to the Year 1752*, edited by Kames (Edinburgh: A. Kinkaid & J. Bell, 1766).

Judging by most assessments of his work, from both his contemporaries and recent commentators, Henry Home, Lord Kames, was not a startlingly original thinker. Samuel Johnson qualified his praise for Kames's venture into literary theory, *Elements of Criticism* (1762): "I do not mean that he has taught us anything: but he has told us old things in a new way." Kames himself, in a rare moment of humility, admitted that he was "not fond of controversy." Yet in his lifetime he managed to stir up a surprising amount of it. His essays and treatises, on everything from Scottish legal history to enlightened agriculture, were read and often rebuked by some of the leading minds of the eighteenth century, including Voltaire, David Hume, and Jonathan Edwards. Recognition of Kames's work was even more striking in America: *Elements of Criticism* quickly became an established part of the curriculum at American colleges, including Princeton and Yale, where his ideas on the social and ethical function of poetry spoke to a rising generation of "American geniuses." And though he is not, like his countryman, Thomas Reid, much studied today by students of philosophy, nevertheless, as an outstanding proponent of the "moral sense" and the "associationist" schools which took root in America in the late-eighteenth and early-nineteenth centuries, he deserves the attention of literary historians.

Henry Home was born in 1696 at Kames in Berwickshire, Scotland. His father, George Home, was a country gentleman and a poor relation of the Earl of Home. As a consequence of his father's genteel impoverishment, Henry Home was largely self-educated, a circumstance in which (like his good friend Benjamin Franklin) he later took some pride. Henry Home received some private instruction in elementary Greek, Latin, physics, and mathematics before going to Edinburgh in 1712 to become apprenticed to a "Writer to the Signet"—a clerk or notary serving the College of Justice. After a few years spent studying civil law, he passed his bar examination in 1722. Practice was slow enough

Henry Home, Lord Kames, portrait by William Miller (The Rt. Hon. the Earl of Stair)

in the next few years that Home devoted his time to legal writings, including his *Remarkable Decisions of the Court of Session, from 1716, to 1728* (1728)—a compilation intending to instruct practicing lawyers by way of "principles" rather than precedents—and his collection of abridged law reports, first published in 1741, which Home continued to update until 1768.

One of Home's protégés, later his biographer, Alexander Fraser Tytler has noted that in Scotland in Home's day, the study of law was usually a private undertaking, the student perusing a few texts on Scottish and Roman law, and attaching himself to one of the more prominent advocates of the day. For Henry Home, this approach was particularly felicitous, since his own method of study was, as Tytler remarks, "not so much to read what had been written or taught upon the subject, as to exercise his mind in earnest and patient investigation: tracing known or acknowledged facts to principles and thence ascending to general laws." Tytler likewise recognized one distinct drawback to Home's method of investigation, which would appear throughout his later life: Home frequently "announced as his own what had before been given to the world by preceding authors" whom he had neglected to read. Nevertheless, whatever Home lacked in thoroughness, he made up for in the sheer eclecticism of his writings, which beside the law tracts, include his *Essays on the Principles of Morality and Natural Religion* (1751); two books on education, *Introduction to the Art of Thinking* (1761) and *Loose Hints upon Education* (1781); a treatise on agriculture, *The Gentleman Farmer* (1776); an anthropological study of the cycles of human development, *Sketches of the History of Man* (1774); as well as the best known of his works, *Elements of Criticism*. In all of these writings, Home evinced the same tendency to adduce a set of illuminating principles from the particulars of each discipline.

Home's first important philosophical work, *Essays on the Principles of Morality and Natural Religion* (1751), allied him with a philosophical movement then taking place in Scotland, which asserted a natural "moral sense" or "common sense" in all men. Home's countrymen and contemporaries Francis Hutcheson (1694-1746), Thomas Reid (1710-1796), and Dugald Stewart (1753-1828) were all a part of this general movement. The proponents of the moral sense and the commonsense schools held that the structure of all human knowledge and reasoning rests on a foundation of undemonstrable, yet irrefutable intuitions. In response to Locke, who believed that the mind holds no more than is perceived by the physical senses, Hutcheson and his followers posited the existence of an "internal" sense (or "moral sense") in all men, which seeks gratification in the sight and performance of benevolent acts. Reid, in his turn, argued that men are equipped with an innate mechanism, their "common sense," which allows them to trust in the reliability of their "simple perception." Both theories, in their ways, were attempting to answer the suspicions which had recently been cast upon human reason—most prominently, by the Scottish skeptic, David Hume (1711-1776), who was just then asserting that there is no rational proof for the existence of the mind as an entity distinct from the particular sensations, sense thoughts, and feelings it contains.

All these ideas were very much in the air that Henry Home was breathing in Edinburgh in the 1740s and 1750s. He was, in fact, a distant relation and close friend to Hume, while he corresponded with Hutcheson. Not surprisingly, one finds echoes and negations of their ideas in the pages of Home's *Essays on the Principles of Morality and Natural Religion*. The greatest part of the book is devoted to Home's discussion of the "moral sense" and its role in determining human behavior. He begins "Of the Foundation and Principles of the Law of Nature" by roundly declaring his allegiance to the empirical method: in moral philosophy, just as in natural philosophy, the truest method of investigation is to try "conclusions by their true touchstone, that of facts and experiments." Nevertheless, the emphasis falls on Home's characteristic principles, the intuited "conclusions," rather than "experiment" or observation. Home goes on to locate the foundation of nature's law in the following unchallenged "reflections": that a being and its actions are connected as are cause and effect (this assertion is a direct refutation of Hume, who denied not only the demonstration of personal identity but also the necessary connection between cause and effect); that, as every species has a common form, so it has a common nature; that actions are good or evil as they conform with or disregard that common nature. "These reflections lead us to the foundation of the laws of our nature. They are to be derived from the common nature of man, of which every person partakes who is not a monster." In fine, from these reflections, Home makes no difficulty to pronounce the presence of a design in human nature: "acting according to nature is acting so as to answer the end of our creation."

The concern with the ends or uses of human behavior is all important in Home's theory of beauty and virtue. Home distinguishes between two types of beauty—the first giving pleasure or delight by its simple existence, and the second, always superior, giving a feeling of pleasure or "approbation" in view of being fitted to an end. Not only objects, but actions also, Home insists, can be fitted to the same criteria. Thus, one peculiar species of beauty or deformity has to do with the intention of an action. The circumstance of intention concerns chiefly human behavior, and good or bad intention figures inevitably in any action we consider "meet" or "unmeet."

Home distinguishes the beauty of action fitted to an end by the name of "moral beauty." But he dismisses any further speculation on what is "meet" or "unmeet" by interjecting the commonsense philosopher's favorite explanation, intuition: "These are simple perceptions, capable of no definition." Instead, man has been granted a special faculty, capable of discerning moral beauty and deformity—the "moral sense," which Home also calls "the voice of God within us which commands our strictest obedience, just as much as when his will is declared by express revelation." Such a doctrine has its affiliation with the Calvinists' belief in irresistible grace; he shares their antirationalist belief that reason cannot effect salvation: "the author of nature has not left our actions to be directed by so weak a principle as reason: and a weak principle it must be to the bulk of mankind, who have little capacity to enter into abstract reasoning; whatever effect it may have upon the learned and contemplative." Yet, he does not hold with the exclusivity of their tenet of an elect few; for him all men have an innate moral sense. This belief suggests the democratic implication of commonsense philosophy—*common* as Garry Wills has pointed out, not meaning *ordinary*, but "a *communal* sense, the shared wisdom of the community."

Thus far, there is little to distinguish Home's "moral beauty" from the precepts of the moral-sense philosophers before him, particularly from Francis Hutcheson's belief in the aesthetic gratification to be derived from acts of benevolence. Yet the moral sense, in Home's view, is not only capable of judging human acts as meet or unmeet, beautiful or deformed, but also as right or wrong. Virtue is not only in our own interest as being pleasing; it is also our "duty" or "obligation" to society. Those actions which fall under the category of duties or obligations are "justice, faith, and truth." Unlike the strictly beautiful gestures of benevolence or generosity, they are so fundamental to the support of society as "to take away all shadow of liberty, and to put us under a necessity of performance." This theory demonstrates Home's quarrel with Hume, who believed that virtues such as justice are not intrinsic to the human heart, but artificial conventions adopted for the good of social life.

Home completed his discussion by considering the several motives which, guided by the moral sense, govern human behavior. In the process, he managed to align himself somewhere between the complete human egoism posited by Hobbes and the benevolence and altruism of Hutcheson. For their single "principles of action," Home substitutes a mixture of motives: self-preservation, self-love, love of justice, veracity, fidelity, gratitude, and, finally, benevolence.

The most controversial section of *Essays on the Principles of Morality and Natural Religion*, at least in Home's time, was the chapter entitled "Of Liberty and Necessity." Here, in an assertion which very nearly lost him his seat on the Scottish Bench, Home argued that the law of necessity governs all motions in the natural world and all actions in the moral world. In answer to the advocates of free will, Home concedes that God permits man a "deceitful" feeling of liberty—which delusion enables him to go about his activities, as if he really were endowed with such freedom. Nevertheless, it is clear from any reflection at all that all human activities are the result of some "principle" or "motive," and that all motives, in turn, can be divided into "desires" and "aversions." From this point, Home worked summarily to dismiss any hint of freedom: "Now, liberty as opposed to moral necessity must signify a power in the mind, of acting without or against motives, that is to say, a power of acting without any view, purpose or design, and even of acting in contradiction to our own desires and aversions, or to the principles of action: which power, besides that no man was ever conscious of it, seems to be an absurdity, altogether inconsistent with a rational nature."

Strangely enough, Home's ideas on necessity were seized by his detractors as evidence of his heretical sympathies with the great Scottish skeptic David Hume, even though one of Hume's most subversive notions was his denial that there is rational proof for causality. Though the two men were close friends, and as Arthur McGuinness remarks, Hume's ethics contained more than a seed of moral sense, Home used his *Essays on the Principles of Morality and Natural Religion* to refute his friend on several points. Not only did Home argue against Hume's theory of justice as an artificial virtue by elevating it to the category of an obligation—the natural right of man to protect what he has acquired by instinct—but in later chapters Home rescued the sacrosanct notions of selfhood (not just a string of fleeting thoughts, feelings, and sensations, as his friend had argued), belief (not reducible to vivid impressions), and the validity of the senses (all else being equal, they are to be trusted). What is important to note about Hume's writings in particular and commonsense philosophy in general—what Terence Martin sees as the force of their attraction for the infant America especially—is their appeal to dogmatism and the certainty of traditional Christian assumptions, just when these assumptions appeared most shaky.

Home managed to survive the barrage of attacks attending publication of his *Essays on the Principles of Morality and Natural Religion* (although he did include a duly modified version of the infamous chapter on liberty and necessity in the book's second edition). In the year following their publication, he was appointed a Lord Ordinary of the Court of Session, Scotland's civil court, and given the judicial title of Lord Kames. He would hold this seat until 1763, when he was advanced to the Scottish Criminal Court, where he would serve until his death in 1782. Throughout his life, Kames seems to have been careful not to let his duties on the bench interfere with his countless other activities, which included his membership in the various philosophical and literary clubs of the day. Among these were the Philosophical Society, of which he was a founding member and eventually vice-president, and the Rankenian Club, a society made up of law and divinity students devoting themselves to legal, philosophical, and aesthetic questions—one of their preoccupations was the state of written English in Scotland and the development of a proper English style.

A perusal of the *Essays on the Principles of Morality and Natural Religion* will prove that Kames was no stranger to polite letters; his ruminations on belles lettres form a steady undercurrent in this book. From the first essay, "Of Our Attachment to Objects of Distress," he is alive to the capacity of art, and particularly literature, to excite the social passions. Hence, the peculiar attraction and value of tragedy: it enables us to exercise and develop our power of sympathy with a regularity not to be found in everyday life: "One thing is evident, that this aptitude of the mind of man to receive impressions from feigned as well as from real objects, contributes to the noblest purposes of life." Later in the *Essays on the Principles of Morality and Natural Religion* he connects the evolution of the moral sense, which each man holds in embryo, with the refinement of taste brought about by the civilizing influences of education and culture: "refinement in taste and manners, operating by communication upon the moral sense, occasions a stronger perception of immorality than what would arise before such refinement."

The principles and faculties which held Kames's attention in these essays continued to occupy him in *Elements of Criticism,* with a slight shift of emphasis: what had begun as an aesthetic approach to ethics became, in 1762, a social and ethical treatment of the arts. And, if the essays allied him with the moral-sense school, the word most often used in conjunction with Kames's aesthetic and psychological theories, as unfolded in *Elements of Criticism,* is *associationism*. Association psychology, as propounded by such writers as David Hume, Adam Smith, Archibald Alison, and Lord Kames, holds that all human knowledge is made up of a train of impressions and ideas which are linked according to certain laws. Beginning with simultaneously occurring sense impressions, we learn to associate one impression with another—likewise, particular objects with particular emotions—until complex ideas are built up. Ideas, then, always occur to the mind in various relations: according to Hume, these were contiguity in time or space, resemblance or contrast, cause and effect. Also implicit in this associationist doctrine, as Emory Elliott has pointed out, are certain social and literary repercussions: since one area of thought is related to another in the social as well as the individual sphere, "an alteration in one area results in parallel changes in other aspects of life.... Thus, it would be reasonable to try to improve the morals and character of a people by raising the level of literary taste through good writing." The theory of associationism, coupled with the theory of the moral sense, could lead to a new degree of moral influence for the poet, whose duty it was to awaken and instruct the tastes of the common man.

The introduction to Kames's *Elements of Criticism* presents just such an argument, for what might be called the domino theory of aesthetics: the repercussions that a developed taste in the arts creates in other spheres of life. For Kames, "Mathematical and metaphysical reasonings have no tendency to improve our knowledge of man; nor are they applicable to the common affairs of life: but a just taste of the fine arts, derived from rational principles, furnishes elegant subjects for conversation, and prepares us for acting in the social state with dignity and propriety." A fine appreciation of the beautiful in literature, painting, architecture, and gardening, Kames continues, prepares us to appreciate beautiful characters or actions. The raison d'etre for this critical excursion once established, Kames goes on to unveil his "design": by first examining the "sensitive branch" of human psychology which responds to beauty, and discovering those objects which it finds naturally agreeable or disagreeable, to formulate "the genuine principles of the fine arts." Happily for readers of this three-volume work, it is in the early chapters on human psychology and the psychological effects of literature, rather than in the sometimes unwieldy applications which follow, that Kames makes his most important contributions to critical theory, both in England and America.

Kames makes his most explicit application of associationist theory in his chapter "Perceptions and Ideas in a train." Here, to the potentially chaotic notion of ideas and perceptions in an endlessly linking chain, Kames adds the assurance of a comforting order: "Every man who attends to his own ideas, will discover order as well as connection in their succession. There is implanted in the breast of every man a principle of order, which governs the arrangement of his perceptions, of his ideas, and of his actions." The principle of order makes men relish its manifestations in art as well as in life: thus, any work of art which models itself on the "natural course" of connected ideas is "so far agreeable," just as any work which destroys that course is disagreeable. Kames's description of the process inevitably invites comparison with Coleridge's later theory of organic unity, though Kames's version is cruder and more doctrinaire: "it is required in every [work of art] that, like an organic system, it have its parts orderly arranged and mutually connected, bearing each of them a relation to the whole, some more intimate, some less, according to their definition: when due regard is paid to these particulars, we have a sense of just composition, and so far are pleased with the performance." In a later chapter on beauty, Kames set out five qualities of natural beauty which the artist should seek to imitate: regularity, simplicity, uniformity, proportion, and order.

His emphasis on what human nature finds "agreeable" or "disagreeable" brings Kames to the subject of emotions, which are roused by actions and objects, including works of art. His simple commonsense formulation is that "we love what is agreeable and hate what is disagreeable" (the quality of agreeability or disagreeability being prior to our feelings of love or hate). He goes on to distinguish between "emotion," which rouses the simple feelings of pleasure and pain, and "passion," which is always accompanied by the "desire" to proceed to action—a distinction which brings to mind his earlier formulation of the two types of beauty in *Essays on the Principles of Morality and Natural Religion*.

Of more immediate relevance to critical theory is Kames's explanation of how literature, wholly reliant upon memory or vicarious experience for its force, manages to excite emotions and passions. Because of its filtered nature, the reading experience could never summon the deepest emotions were it not for the ability to enter a state of mind in which memory and imagination are virtually indistinguishable from reality. Kames calls this state "ideal presence" (it has its affinities with Coleridge's "willing suspension of disbelief," also elicited by imaginative literature). We enter it whenever we recollect or imagine a particular experience so acutely as to form a mental picture of it and to feel the emotions that originally accompanied it— whenever we become "eyewitnesses" to an imagined event. Of course fictions as well as histories and factual accounts have the power to elicit this state of mind (the theory arises in a section entitled "Emotions caused by Fiction"). There are several interesting implications for imaginative literature that follow from the concept of "ideal presence": "history stands upon the same footing with fable: what effect either may have to raise our sympathy, depends on the vivacity of the ideas they raise"; theatrical representation is the most powerful means of producing ideal presence; and poetry which holds to "the order of nature," admitting no supernatural effects or machinery, is most likely to occasion ideal presence. Kames concluded his discussion of ideal presence by drawing the inevitable moral-sense connection between habits of virtue and habits of reading: the moral examples of fiction are more powerful because they are more plentiful than those of history.

The remainder of the *Elements of Criticism* is devoted largely to setting up principles of general aesthetics—notions of beauty, sublimity, grandeur, force, resemblance, congruity—and to rules of poetic composition. Concerning beauty, Kames reiterates his belief, stated in the *Essays on the Principles of Morality and Natural Religion*, that there are two types, "relative" and "intrinsic"—that is, beauty understood in relation to other objects, requiring reflection, and the beauty of a single object viewed apart, requiring only the senses. In general, the artist should seek to emulate the simplicity and order of intrinsic beauty. It is fitting, however, that other aesthetic notions, notably "grandeur" (roused by the sight of large objects) and "sublimity" (the response to elevation) should sometimes violate the canon of order and simplicity. Some of the problems Kames takes up in his chapters on rhetoric are harmony of content and style, the proper uses of the "natural" and "inverted" styles, the use of figures, the importance of vivid imagery. As might be expected, Kames's basic criterion for excellence in writing is that it recreate the associative patterns of human thought and feeling rather than merely adhere to antiquated classical dicta. Kames believed that metaphor is best employed to suggest an agitated state of mind: "similes are not the language of a man in his ordinary state of mind, dispatching his daily and usual work."

Kames concluded his book by reassessing the role of the critic, bringing common sense to bear once again in establishing a "Standard of Taste." Against the axiom "There must be no disputing about taste," he pointed to the universal conviction in "good" and "bad" taste. Just as there is a common nature for every species, so there is a common standard of taste for morals and fine art—that which conforms to the standard being perfect or right, that which deviates from it being wrong or bad. But though the standard of taste is an ideal possible for all men, still the untutored masses commonly fail to recognize it. To ascertain it, then, we must consult the "common sense" of a relatively narrow circle of humanity: those men, like himself, who have "a good natural taste . . . improved by education, reflection, and experience" are alone fit to guide and instruct our aesthetic judgments.

Elements of Criticism, appearing first in 1762, quickly became Kames's best-known work. In particular, the book had a startling success in America, where, as Ian Ross points out, it had run to some thirty editions by 1972. Riding on the wave of a general admiration in American universities for things Scottish—which began with John Witherspoon's introduction of commonsense philosophy at the College of New Jersey (now Princeton University) in 1768—*Elements of Criticism* became one of the standard rhetoric books used at American colleges up until the mid-nineteenth century. Timothy Dwight and Joel Barlow both studied *Elements of Criticism* while at Yale. At Union College in Schenectady in the early nineteenth century an entire course was devoted to Kames's criticism. Among the more illustrious Americans to read and comment on Kames's writings were Jonathan Edwards, who wrote a short critique of Kames's argument for the necessity of human actions—especially of the idea that mankind must be kept ignorant of this necessity—which became an appendix to an early edition of Edwards's *Inquiry into the Freedom of the Will* (1768); Thomas Jefferson, who as a young man found Kames's discussion of the developing moral sense particularly persuasive and quoted him frequently in his commonplace book; and especially Benjamin Franklin, who was not only an avid admirer and disseminator of Kames's writings, but also a close personal friend. Franklin visited his friend at Kames in 1759, and thereafter, they kept up a steady correspondence (in one of his letters to Kames, Franklin even comments—one self-made man to another—on a certain "similarity in our fortunes, and the circumstances of our lives").

Of more profound significance, however, to the literary historian, than the tangible evidence of Kames's influence in America is a consideration of the chord he and his fellow associationists struck in the American reading public, especially in the universities. Robert E. Streeter and Terence Martin have both noted the possibilities which associationist psychology offered to stir feelings of patriotism and build a strong national literature. Since that literary work which roused a train of associated ideas would appear most beautiful, and the raw materials of a given culture (scenery, climate, customs, history) would most readily trigger such associations, there was strong impetus for the writer to turn to his native land as a source of inspiration. Kames's theory, which urged the universal appeal of grand and elevating objects, had special application in America. As Martin notes, "the fact that sublime subjects could be found so specifically and concretely in America caused Americans to investigate the local with increasing intensity as a means of achieving a universal standard of taste."

Moreover, Kames's emphatic belief in the perfectibility of both the moral sense and the sense of taste, along with the poet's (or critic's) capacity to instruct and refine these senses, held a special charm for a class of writers such as the American Revolutionary poets, who were feeling the burden of their obligation as the new moral and spiritual guides to an increasingly secular society. As Emory Elliott has shown, Kames's delicate juggling act, which held the democratic potentiality of moral-sense philosophy poised with the actuality of an intellectual elite, could be an effective check to the apparent threats of materialism and moral degeneracy which followed in the wake of the American Revolution. Indeed long after the Revolution, Kames's ideas would harden into a formula in the numerous articles calling for an American Shiloh or poet of genius: Emerson's poet, for instance, is "isolated among his contemporaries by truth and by his art, but with this consolation in his pursuits, that they will draw all men sooner or later." Whitman's bard, too, speaks for those who cannot speak for themselves: "He is a seer . . . the others are as good as he, only he sees it and they do not." Of course, the finest American writers managed to break well beyond the narrow Kamesian equation of moral habits with the specifically moral example of reading to explore, in all its richness, the possibility of literature not simply to enforce but also to question and to recreate existing moral standards. The *Elements of Criticism* continues to be republished in America, most recently in New York, 1971.

Biographies:

Alexander Fraser Tytler, Lord Woodhouslee, *Memoirs of the Life and Writings of the Honorable Henry Home of Kames* (Edinburgh: W. Creech/London: T. Cadell & W. Davis, 1807);

James Boswell, *Materials for Writing the Life of Lord Kames*, volume 15 of *Private Papers from Malahide Castle*, edited by Geoffrey Scott and Frederick Pottle (Mount Vernon, N.Y.: Rudge, 1928-1934).

References:

Emory Elliott, *Revolutionary Writers, Literature and Authority in the New Republic, 1725-1810* (New York: Oxford University Press, 1982);

Terence Martin, *The Instructed Vision: Scottish Common Sense Philosophy and the Origins of American Fiction*, Indiana University Humanities Series, no. 48 (Bloomington: Indiana University Press, 1961);

Arthur E. McGuinness, *Henry Home, Lord Kames* (New York: Twayne, 1970);

Helen W. Randall, *The Critical Theory of Lord Kames* (Northampton, Mass.: Departments of Modern Languages, Smith College, 1944);

Ian Simpson Ross, *Lord Kames and the Scotland of His Day* (Oxford: Clarendon Press, 1972);

Robert E. Streeter, "Association Psychology and Literary Nationalism in the *North American Review*, 1815-1825," *American Literature*, 17 (November 1945): 243-254;

Garry Wills, *Inventing America: Jefferson's Declaration of Independence* (Garden City: Doubleday, 1978).

Dugald Stewart
(22 November 1753-11 June 1828)

Thomas F. Strychacz
Princeton University

SELECTED BOOKS: *Elements of the Philosophy of the Human Mind* (3 volumes, London: Printed for A. Strahan, and T. Cadell, 1792, 1814, 1827; volume 1, Philadelphia: Printed by William Young, 1793; volume 2, New York: Eastburn, Kirk, 1814; volume 3, Philadelphia: Carey, Lea & Carey, 1827);

Outlines of Moral Philosophy (Edinburgh: Printed for W. Creech & for T. Cadell in London, 1793);

Philosophical Essays (Edinburgh: Printed by George Ramsay & Company & for T. Cadell & W. Davies in London, 1810; Philadelphia: Printed for Anthony Finley / New York: Whiting & Watson, 1811);

Dissertation First: Exhibiting a General View of the Progress of Metaphysical, Ethical, and Political Philosophy, Since the Revival of Letters in Europe (Boston: Wells & Lilly, 1817; Edinburgh, 1821);

The Philosophy of the Active and Moral Powers of Man (Edinburgh: Printed for Adam Black, 1828; Boston: Wells & Lilly, 1828).

Collections: *The Works of Dugald Stewart,* 7 volumes (Cambridge, Mass.: Hilliard & Brown, 1829);

The Collected Works of Dugald Stewart, 11 volumes (Edinburgh: T. Constable, 1854-1860).

During a teaching and writing career of more than forty years at Edinburgh, Dugald Stewart exercised an immense influence on the minds of men in Britain, Europe, and America. That influence did not arise from innovative qualities in Stewart's work, for at few points did he lay claim to any substantial originality; his philosophy merely modified and extended that of Thomas Reid, whom Stewart succeeded as the leading figure in the Scottish school of commonsense philosophy. Stewart's importance lies rather in his role as a teacher, interpreter, and popularizer of the commonsense philosophy. His major works are best described as textbooks of philosophy, some of which became required reading at the most influential American universities and all of which enjoyed great popularity among America's educated readers. Stewart's seminal place in American university curriculums enabled him to reach some of the best young minds in the generations following the Revolutionary War. Although historians have speculated about the extent of Stewart's influence on writers, thinkers, and statesmen of this period, the frequent use of his works by teachers and students makes his full contribution to American culture incalculable. At a time when post-Revolutionary America was generally disposed toward the security offered by the Scottish philosophy, Dugald Stewart came to the forefront as one of the primary exponents of that thought.

Dugald Stewart was born in Edinburgh on 22 November 1753, the son of Reverend Dr. Mathew Stewart, professor of mathematics at the University of Edinburgh. His health as a young boy, according to his memoirist John Veitch, was "feeble and precarious," a fact which may be partly explained by his early devotion to academic learning—as James McCosh comments in *The Scottish Philosophy* (1875), "From his youth he breathed the air of a college." In 1771 and 1772 Stewart studied under Thomas Reid at Glasgow University, two years which provided a frame of reference for Stewart's thought for the rest of his life. In 1772, at his father's request, he returned to Edinburgh to take over his father's chair of mathematics—at the remarkably early age of nineteen. But Stewart's natural inclination was toward philosophy, and in 1785 he was transferred to the chair of moral philosophy at Edinburgh, a position he held until 1810 when ill health forced him to give up teaching. Stewart was thus instrumental in shifting the focus of the commonsense philosophy from Glasgow to Edinburgh.

Dugald Stewart's renown as lecturer in moral philosophy attracted students from England, the Continent, and the United States. He was responsible for educating many of the foremost British statesmen and philosophers of the first half of the nineteenth century. Among the best known of the American contingent was Reverend Dr. Charles Lowell, James Russell Lowell's father. Many testimonies exist to Stewart's power as a lecturer—a capacity which furthered his prominence in the area of Scottish thought. Lord Henry Cockburn, a former student of Stewart's, related a well-known anecdote about the professor's eloquence: "A slight asthmatic tendency made him often clear his throat; and such was my admiration of the whole exhibition, that Marvey Napier told him not long ago that I had said there was eloquence in his very spitting. 'Then,' said he, 'I am glad there was at least one thing in which I had no competitor.'" Other students were more critical. Thomas Chalmers, for instance, wrote in 1801: "I never heard a single discussion of Stewart's which made up one masterly and comprehensive whole.... He almost uniformly avoids every subject which involves any difficult discussion."

Stewart was also careful to avoid arguments which were politically radical in nature. A liberal in economic and political thought, Stewart fell under suspicion of Jacobinism during the French Revolution. Indeed, after 1790 Stewart read his lectures rather than use notes in order to prevent inadvertent political blunders. For Americans of the post-Revolutionary period, Stewart's refusal to enter the political arena increased rather than detracted from his stature. In *The Scottish Enlightenment* (1976), Anand Chitnis makes the general point that "The students he taught were witnessing the questioning of traditional certainties and the collapse of political and social establishments.... Stewart effectively equipped his students with responses to the new age: classical economics, moral seriousness and virtue, industry and sensibility." To the American students, uncertain inheritors of a new and fragile Republic, Stewart's philosophical and moral conservatism was especially valuable.

Stewart's value to a single American—Thomas Jefferson—indicates the importance of Stewart's doctrines to American culture. Jefferson met Stewart in Paris in 1789, and the two men remained friends thereafter. Indeed, when Jefferson became involved in the founding of the University of Virginia and needed several "supereminent professors" from Edinburgh and surrounding institutions, he turned to Dugald Stewart in 1824 for aid. Jefferson, of course, was heavily influenced by the commonsense philosophy before Stewart produced his first writings, but Stewart must be credited with completing the influence of Scottish thought that Thomas Reid and others began. Jefferson called Stewart "a great man, and among the most honest living," and found in Stewart a major source of agreement for his own ideas. In a letter to John Adams in 1820, for instance, Jefferson wrote: "When once we quit the basis of sensation, all is in the wind. To talk of *immaterial* existences, is to talk of *nothings*. To say that the human soul, angels, God, are immaterial, is to say, they are *nothings*, or that there is no God, no angels, no soul. I cannot reason otherwise: but I believe I am supported in my creed of materialism by the Lockes, the Tracys and the Stewarts." Jefferson's concern with "materialism"—and in particular his desire to relate his pragmatism to moral and theological problems—compares closely with Stewart's application of self-evident truths to the worlds of phenomena and theology.

Dugald Stewart's most pervasive influence on American culture, however, resulted from the use of his works as set texts in American universities and as general philosophical works in private homes. An immediate indication of Stewart's popularity can be gained from the fact that *Elements of the Philosophy of the Human Mind* (1793) went through six printings in America before 1864, and *The Philosophy of the Active and Moral Powers of Man* (1828) through nine editions before 1866. Princeton University, where the commonsense philosophy was introduced by John Witherspoon in 1768, was responsible for disseminating Stewart's thought throughout the fields of art, religion, and education. Clergy trained at the

Princeton Theological Seminary, for instance, carried Stewart's doctrines throughout the United States as an integral part of American Protestantism. Thus rooted in the spread of Protestantism, Stewart's doctrines extended their influence far beyond the range of his actual works.

In the area of education, Princeton and Yale together supplied fifty-eight presidents to seventy-five colleges before 1840. And Princeton University's interpretations of the Scottish philosophy dominated the periodicals of literary criticism which were based in Philadelphia during the early nineteenth century. At the same time, the highly popular *Edinburgh Review* and *Quarterly Review*, each working out of a context of Scottish realism, complemented Princeton's powerful influence—in fact, Dugald Stewart personally educated the founding editors of the *Edinburgh Review*. Under the presidency of James McCosh (1868-1888), Princeton University became one of the last major advocates of the commonsense philosophy at a time when the more radical philosophies of Kant and Darwin, among others, were undermining the importance of the Scottish school.

Stewart's first major work, and the most important from the point of view of its influence on early American literature, was *Elements of the Philosophy of the Human Mind*. In this work Stewart discusses several theories of perception before stressing the commonsense philosophy as put forward by Thomas Reid—that is, the mind receives not simply the images and ideas of external objects, as skeptics such as Berkeley and Hume claimed, but external objects themselves. Stewart moves next to a discussion of the various powers of the mind which affect human perception, such as memory, imagination, and association. At the beginning of the second volume, Stewart suggests the term "the fundamental laws of human belief"—that is, self-evident axioms of human existence—as a more precise formulation than Reid's rather ambiguous "common sense." Stewart proceeds to discuss the centrality of "reason" in interpreting human life, and stresses the importance of the inductive method of inquiry. By the inductive method Stewart means an intuitive grasp of the "fundamental laws of human belief" before philosophical inquiry takes place; thus that inquiry must be founded on what everyone accepts as common sense. Stewart himself claimed that his purpose was "by vindicating the principles of Human Knowledge against the attacks of modern Sceptics, to lay a solid foundation for a rational system of logic."

Elements of the Philosophy of the Human Mind became a set text in the Harvard curriculum, and it is here that Stewart's formative influence on the early development of American literature can be seen most clearly. As Leon Howard comments in *Victorian Knight-Errant* (1852), his study of James Russell Lowell, Stewart was "the author who served as the very keystone of the philosophical arch through which all Harvard students from Emerson to Lowell were obliged to pass." While it is impossible to define with any precision the extent of Stewart's influence on the major writers to pass beneath that arch—Emerson, Thoreau, and Lowell—there are several interesting analogies between the writings of Stewart and the works of these American romantics.

The empathy Ralph Waldo Emerson felt at Harvard toward Stewart's theories suggests that Stewart is important not only for the development of Emerson's ideas, but through him the growth of American transcendentalism. Emerson made a close study of *Elements of the Philosophy of the Human Mind* at Harvard and, outside the course, went further to analyze *Outlines of Moral Philosophy* (1793; the publication of five months of Stewart's lectures at the University of Edinburgh).

From these two works, one can trace a number of ideas and patterns of thought which clearly stimulated and shaped Emerson's later thinking. In *Elements of the Philosophy of the Human Mind* Stewart held that the power of reason was divided into the two faculties of rationality and intuition, of which the most important was man's intuitive mode of knowledge. And in his theory of the imagination—at one of the few points where he departed radically from Reid's doctrines—Stewart suggested that the mind creates as well as perceives, implying the existence of multiple factors in man's apprehension of the beautiful. In *Outlines of Moral Philosophy* Stewart applied his theories specifically to the subject of morality. He postulated the existence of a "moral sense," an innate faculty of mind which intuits the distinction between right and wrong. The doctrines of English and German philosophers are more obviously relevant to Emerson's transcendentalism, yet Stewart's emphasis on intuitive perception comes closer to transcendentalism than the overall conservatism of his philosophical position might at first suggest. Emerson's stress on the essential goodness of man and the universe builds further on the Enlightenment-based optimism of Stewart's thought. In fact, as a doctrine of assurance peculiarly suited to the American psyche in the first half of the nineteenth century, Stewart's philosophy is surpassed only by Emerson's complete acceptance of the beneficence and morality of nature, and of man's ability to communicate with it.

Emerson's concern with individuality and the importance of self-reliance may also have much to do with Stewart's thought. Stewart, following Thomas Reid, posits the existence of an intuitive sense "common" to all people; his philosophy assumes that each person has the ability to develop this inborn faculty. Stewart does in fact distinguish between the "vulgar" classes and those people (such as philosophers) who use their intellectual powers to the full. But his notion of fundamental laws underlying the mental powers of all people suggests a kind of "democracy" latent in the universe—a doctrine eagerly seized on by a culture vocal in its support of democracy, yet also, because of its fear of anarchy, seeking a firm sense of authority.

Emerson's belief in the individual's ability to respond to universal forces, and belief in a universal "moral sense," arises naturally out of Stewart's Enlightenment thought. Nevertheless, the difference between the two thinkers is not merely one of emphasis. Stewart's work places the individual firmly within the social order; indeed, he ended his teaching career with the socially oriented subject of political economy. In contrast, Emerson consistently refuses to be limited to the everyday world of observable objects. His concern is with the individual's private perception of the universal mind beyond the immediately apprehended world of nature and social systems.

In many ways, the work of Henry Thoreau suggests a closer parallel than Emerson's to aspects of Stewart's thought. Although Thoreau did not become a convert to transcendentalism until his senior year at Harvard, he had been heavily influenced by the Scottish philosophy during his junior year through reading *Elements of the Philosophy of the Human Mind*, and by the fact that Edward T. Channing and other instructors at Harvard were partisans of the Scottish philosophers. Several hints from Thoreau's undergraduate days suggest the value of Dugald Stewart to the American's later work. In a book review written in 1836, for instance, Thoreau at one point refers to Stewart's theory of the "association of ideas," expressed in chapter five of *Elements of the Philosophy of the Human Mind*. Thoreau's use of association as a thematic and structuring principle in his work (as evidenced by the spring-thaw section of *Walden*) suggests the possible relevance of Stewart as an influence on Thoreau's ideas.

In a brief topic book which Thoreau prepared at Harvard in 1835, he made two suggestive comments on *Elements of the Philosophy of the Human Mind:* "Value of a systematic plan of," and "none of the mental powers should be neglected." The latter statement in particular hints at a link between the encyclopedic quality of Stewart's work and the desire of Thoreau to attain a measure of universality or comprehensiveness. Like most of the writers of the American Renaissance, Stewart sees the various categories of human experience as an integrated whole, rather than as a series of independent parts. An interesting comment by the Scot in a letter of 1788 shows just how closely Dugald Stewart foreshadowed the ability of later American writers to cross with great effect the boundaries of human knowledge: "Tomorrow I proceed to Pneumatics, and am just now employed in premeditating two lectures—the one on the Air-Pump, and the other on the Immortality of the Soul." The first comment Thoreau made in his topic book also seems of radical importance when one considers his concern in *Walden* with all manners of systems—natural, social, economic, and verbal.

Finally, Thoreau's insistence on detailing the observable phenomena of everyday life indicates, perhaps, a closer empathy with Stewart's philosophy of "materialism" than Emerson maintained. The first chapter of *Walden* ("Economy"), for instance, is a pragmatic, "commonsense" (if highly individualized) approach to transcendentalism. In important respects Stewart's articulation of the commensense philosophy in *Elements of the Philosophy of the Human Mind* provides a context for the meeting of intuition and practicality in Thoreau's work. In terms of conscious influence, Thoreau soon completely rejected Dugald Stewart and the Scottish philosophy. For example, in an 1838 letter, which concerns one of Helen Thoreau's female pupils who wished to study philosophy, Thoreau advises: "But if she wishes to know how poor an apology for a mental philosophy men have tacked together, synthetically or analytically, in these latter days—how they have squeezed the infinite mind into a compass that would not nonplus a surveyor of Eastern lands . . . why let her read Locke, or Stewart, or Brown." Nevertheless, despite Thoreau's vehement repudiation of Stewart, it seems clear from some of the patterns of Thoreau's work that he was at least stimulated at Harvard by Stewart's theories and methodology.

Stewart's influence on James Russell Lowell is less certain, partly because Lowell's thought is less cogent than either Emerson's or Thoreau's. Later in Lowell's life, claims Leon Howard in *Victorian Knight-Errant,* "The philosophy of Dugald Stewart was the intellectual Elmwood into which Lowell was to relax . . . when he was through with youthful adventuring." As a youthful adventurer, Lowell seems to have been attracted by Stewart's theory of the existence of innate ideas and a correlative submission to spontaneous impulses. Lowell never mentioned Dugald Stewart after leaving Harvard, but in 1854, faced with delivering a number of lectures to the Lowell Institute on art and literature, Lowell may have turned again directly to *Elements of the Philosophy of the Human Mind* for inspiration. Lowell's lectures reflect Stewart's general approach to aesthetics, in particular his theories on the nature of the imagination and the fancy.

In 1816, the first supplemental volumes to the fourth and fifth editions of the *Encyclopaedia Britannica*—a work which had a pervasive effect on American culture—began to appear in America. Stewart edited the supplement and provided an important work of his own (published separately in Boston in 1817 and in Edinburgh in 1821): *Dissertation First: Exhibiting a General View of the Progress of Metaphysical, Ethical, and Political Philosophy, Since the Revival of Letters in Europe*. The scope of this dissertation in the fields of both history and philosophy, and its appearance in the authoritative *Encyclopaedia Britannica*, made it an influential work of scholarship in the young American Republic. The dissertation strengthened the cultural ties between America and Scotland which contributed to the warm reception of Stewart's work in the first place. Although James McCosh, in *The Scottish Philosophy*, criticizes Stewart at times for his unoriginality, he praises this dissertation as "upon the whole, the best dissertation which ever appeared in a philosophical serial. As a history of modern philosophy, it has not been superseded, and, I believe, never will be set aside."

McCosh may have been overly sanguine about the future of Stewart's dissertation, even though accurate in his evaluation of its importance to its time. Nevertheless, McCosh's claim, some fifty years after Stewart's death, that the future of American philosophy lies in the natural sciences reflects the general influence of the pragmatic Enlightenment philosophy of which Dugald Stewart was a vital part. Stewart did not by himself create the pragmatic or optimistic facets of the American mind; still, works such as *Elements of the Philosophy of the Human Mind, Outlines of Moral Philosophy* and the dissertation became important because they suited so well the temper and needs of the early post-Revolutionary period, and in turn helped to shape that temper. Stewart's philosophy of the mind was one factor in the development of a science of the mind; his clear, analytic methodology a factor in the development of scientific method. Thus McCosh's advocacy of a philosophy of realism and science is both an acute observation of American trends, and a recognition of the importance of the philosophy which helped form the very trends he observed.

Dugald Stewart died on 11 June 1828 after an illness lasting several years (he suffered a paralyzing stroke in 1822), which he spent at his residence of Kinneil House, near Edinburgh, revising and preparing his notes for publication. One of his last works, published in the year of his death, was *The Philosophy of the Active and Moral Powers of Man*. The work merely expands the contents of Stewart's earlier *Outlines of Moral Philosophy*, but its appearance is nevertheless significant. Stewart made the section on natural religion in this work deliberately large, in response to his fear that a great many students were in danger from atheist and skeptical thought. This emphasis on natural religion merely underscores the total effect of his body of work. Stewart's is a philosophy of assurance. His empirical method, combined with a belief in the average man's ability to possess "fundamental laws," appealed to the pragmatic and democratic aspects of the early Republic—an appeal which the great popularity of *The Philosophy of the Active and Moral Powers of Man* again reflects. And his emphasis on the intuitive apprehension of a benevolent God connects him with both American Protestantism and the more confident reaches of transcendentalism. Without ever being a truly original thinker, Dugald Stewart's influence on American culture through his pupils and the readers of his major works remains important. At a time when America turned to the conservative and positivistic doctrines of the Scottish school, Dugald Stewart distinguished himself as the clearest and most comprehensive exponent of that philosophy.

References:

William Charvat, *The Origins of American Critical Thought 1810-1835* (Philadelphia: University of Pennsylvania Press, 1936);

Anand Chitnis, *The Scottish Enlightenment* (Totawa, N.J.: Rowman & Littlefield, 1976);

Merrel R. Davis, "Emerson's 'Reason' and the Scottish Philosophers," *New England Quarterly*, 17 (June 1944): 209-228;

Leon Howard, *Victorian Knight-Errant: A Study of the Early Literary Career of James Russell Lowell* (Berkeley & Los Angeles: University of California Press, 1952);

Joseph J. Kwiat, "Thoreau's Philosophical Apprenticeship," *New England Quarterly,* 18 (March 1945): 51-69;

Terence Martin, *The Instructed Vision: Scottish Common Sense Philosophy and the Origins of American Fiction* (Bloomington: Indiana University Press, 1961);

James McCosh, *The Scottish Philosophy* (New York: Carter, 1875);

John Veitch, "Memoir of Dugald Stewart," in *The Collected Works of Dugald Stewart,* volume 10 (Edinburgh: Constable, 1854-1860);

Garry Wills, *Inventing America: Jefferson's Declaration of Independence* (Garden City: Doubleday, 1968).

Papers:
Only two manuscript items relating to Dugald Stewart are known to exist in American archives: correspondence of Dugald Stewart with Francis Walker Gilmer in the University of Virginia library; and a pupil's verbatim accounts of Stewart's lecture courses, held by Columbia University.

Appendix II

Eighteenth-Century Aesthetic Theories

Too often students and general readers of American literature have the impression that little if no attention was paid to the creation or appreciation of serious imaginative literature in America before the time of Emerson in the 1830s. Unfortunately, this misunderstanding is too often furthered by anthologies that contain only snippets of eighteenth-century American writing and no examples of the considerable number of works about literature produced in the decades stretching between the giant figures of Jonathan Edwards and Emerson. The following excerpts from works by Hugh Blair, John Witherspoon, and William Smith exemplify the energy and the thought given to aesthetic issues in the colonies before the Revolution.

Because it was so widely used as a text in American colleges well into the nineteenth century, Hugh Blair's *Lectures on Rhetoric and Belles Lettres* (1783) remains an important work for students of American literature. Though Blair was not himself an original thinker, he was recognized as a great teacher and articulator of the commonsense theories on taste, style, and eloquence current in Scotland and America in the late eighteenth century. From 1759 to 1783 he presented his lectures at Edinburgh, and in 1762 King George III appointed him the first holder of the distinguished Regius Professorship of Rhetoric and Belles Lettres. Ordained a Presbyterian minister in 1743, Blair also served as the pastor of a fashionable Edinburgh church. Like his Edinburgh classmate John Witherspoon, Blair saw no conflict between the purposes of religion and aims of literature and the arts. In teaching young people how to write well and how to appreciate good literature, Blair hoped to raise the general level of taste and manners in the society and thereby improve morals and advance the purposes of religion. Because corruption of language, morals, and religion were likely to be the result of the same moral deficiency, one way to reform an individual or a society was to improve one area of human activity with the expectation that the others would also benefit. Thus, he approached the subjects of style, taste, and beauty in the arts with the same systematic determination and fervor that a good Puritan or Presbyterian preacher would expound upon a text of scripture or a doctrine of theology.

In America Blair's former classmate also expounded his own interpretations of the commonsense doctrines in a series of lectures on moral philosophy and eloquence. Because Witherspoon's published lectures did not become textbooks in other colleges, his writings on these subjects have not been as frequently reprinted and are today fairly rare. One of the most interesting works about literature that Witherspoon produced was his lecture on the effects of stage plays. During and just after the Revolution, plays were very popular in America, and Witherspoon, who was in every other way a strong supporter of literature and the arts, was moved to speak and write against the theater. Though on the surface this action may seem to be simply yet another Puritan's attack upon theatrical entertainment, the reasons that Witherspoon advances in his argument are more complex. Basically, he supports the drama as a literary expression that has attained a level of artistic excellence in the classics and in Shakespeare. Because he recognizes the tremendous power of the visual and verbal elements of the drama to move the passions, he sees the genre as having great potential for improving morals and society. What disturbs him is that the kinds of plays being performed in his time seem designed to appeal to the basest aspects of human nature; therefore, the people who attend the plays, the prostitutes and other undesirables who frequent the theaters, and the actors who perform in this environment all contribute to the degradation of society. If he could be confident that this situation could be reversed and the drama could again be used for the improvement of morals and taste, he says, he would not oppose the presentation of stage plays, but he believes such a reversal now to be impossible.

The excerpts from Witherspoon's "Lectures on Eloquence" illustrate another dimension of his thought. In charging his students with the responsibility for improving their writing styles and oratorical delivery, Witherspoon not only presents precise and careful definitions of all the functions and dimensions of language and style, he also conveys a sense of mission. It is the writer's duty, he argues, to advance his own art to the highest degree of perfection possible in order that he might thereby raise his audience's level of taste. To achieve this worthy end, the author must be a virtuous person who labors by study and imitation to learn the proper forms and to acquire the grace through which he may express his own genius. If he is deficient in genius, education, or moral discipline, he will fail as a writer or orator and will have only himself, not his critics or audience, to blame.

The utopian spirit in America in the eighteenth century was especially vital. The goal of creating an ideal republic, of blending the sublime beauty of the classics with perfection in morals and religion in the arts, and of building colleges and curriculums that would advance the progress of civilization in America—such dreams inspired many of the makers and shapers of the new nation even before 1776. One utopian scheme that became a reality was William Smith's plan for the establishment of a new college that would not follow the traditional English model and would integrate the study of the English language, poetry, and the arts with the sciences of agriculture, physics, and biology. In 1753 Smith published a short book, *A General Idea of the College of Mirania*, which depicted an imaginary land with a college modeled upon Smith's educational philosophy. It was Smith's aim to get the attention of the New York legislature, which was in the process of planning the province's first college. After New York ignored his ideas and organized King's College (later Columbia University) upon the English model, Smith sent a copy of his book to Benjamin Franklin, who was making plans to establish a college in Philadelphia. Impressed by Smith's proposal, Franklin paved the way for Smith to become the first provost of the College of Philadelphia, where he was able to make his dream a reality. One of the most remarkable innovations of Smith's plan was its classifying the study of religion as a minor subject to be taken up on Sunday evenings. Though a clergyman himself, Smith believed that the study of rhetoric and poetry were more important to the advancement of morals and the forming of good men than the study of theology. The excerpts presented here illustrate Smith's faith in the progress of culture in America and the value of literature and criticism to that end.

—*Emory Elliott*

Hugh Blair

Excerpts from *Lectures on Rhetoric and Belles Lettres* (1783)

"Lecture 1: Introduction"

One of the most distinguished privileges which Providence has conferred upon mankind, is the power of communicating their thoughts to one another. Destitute of this power, Reason would be a solitary, and, in some measure, an unavailing principle. Speech is the great instrument by which man becomes beneficial to man: and it is to the intercourse and transmission of thought, by means of speech, that we are chiefly indebted for the improvement of thought itself. Small are the advances which a single unassisted individual can make towards perfecting any of his powers. What we call human reason, is not the effort or ability of one, so much as it is the result of the reason of many, arising from lights mutually communicated, in consequence of discourse and writing.

It is obvious, then, that writing and discourse are objects intitled to the highest attention. Whether the influence of the speaker, or the entertainment of the hearer, be consulted; whether utility or pleasure be the principal aim in view, we are prompted, by the strongest motives, to study how we may communicate our thoughts to one another with most advantage. Accordingly we find, that in almost every nation, as soon as language had extended itself beyond that scanty communication which was requisite for the supply of men's necessities, the improvement of discourse began to attract regard. In the language even of rude uncultivated tribes, we can trace some attention to the grace and force of those expressions which they used, when they sought to persuade or to affect. They were early sensible of a beauty in discourse, and endeavoured to give it certain decorations which experience had taught them it was capable of receiving, long before the study of those decorations was formed into a regular art.

But, among nations in a civilized state, no art has been cultivated with more care, than that of language, style, and composition. The attention paid to it may, indeed, be assumed as one mark of the progress of society towards its most improved period. For, according as society improves and flourishes, men acquire more influence over one another by means of reasoning and discourse; and in proportion as that influence is felt to enlarge, it must follow, as a natural consequence, that they will bestow more care upon the methods of expressing their conceptions with propriety and eloquence. Hence we find, that in all the polished nations of Europe, this study has been treated as highly important, and has possessed a considerable place in every plan of liberal education.

Indeed, when the arts of speech and writing are mentioned, I am sensible that prejudices against them are apt to rise in the minds of many. A sort of art is immediately thought of, that is ostentatious and deceitful; the minute and trifling study of words alone; the pomp of expression; the studied fallacies of rhetoric; ornament substituted in the room of use. We need not wonder, that under such imputations, all study of discourse as an art, should have suffered in the opinion of men of understanding: and I am far from denying, that rhetoric and criticism have sometimes been so managed as to tend to the corruption, rather than to the improvement, of good taste and true eloquence. But sure it is equally possible to apply the principles of reason and good sense to this art, as to any other that is cultivated among men. If the following Lectures have any merit, it will consist in an endeavour to substitute the application of these principles in the place of artificial and scholastic rhetoric; in an endeavour to explode false ornament, to direct attention more towards substance than show, to recommend good sense as the foundation of all good composition, and simplicity as essential to all true ornament.

When entering on the subject, I may be allowed, on this occasion, to suggest a few thoughts concerning the importance and advantages of such studies, and the rank they are intitled to possess in academical education.[1] I am under no temptation, for this purpose, of extolling their importance at the

---

1. The Author was the first who read Lectures on this subject in the University of Edinburgh. He began with reading them in a private character in the year 1759. In the following year he was chosen Professor of Rhetoric by the Magistrates and Town-council of Edinburgh: and, in 1762, his Majesty was pleased to erect and endow a Profession of Rhetoric and Belles Lettres in that University; and the Author was appointed the first Regius Professor.

expence of any other department of science. On the contrary, the study of Rhetoric and Belles Lettres supposes and requires a proper acquaintance with the rest of the liberal arts. It embraces them all within its circle, and recommends them to the highest regard. The first care of all such as wish either to write with reputation, or to speak in public so as to command attention, must be, to extend their knowledge; to lay in a rich store of ideas relating to those subjects of which the occasions of life may call them to discourse or to write. Hence, among the ancients, it was a fundamental principle, and frequently inculcated, "Quod omnibus disciplinis et artibus debet esse instructus orator"; that the orator ought to be an accomplished scholar, and conversant in every part of learning. It is indeed impossible to contrive an art, and very pernicious it were if it could be contrived, which should give the stamp of merit to any composition rich or splendid in expression, but barren or erroneous in thought. They are the wretched attempts towards an art of this kind which have so often disgraced oratory, and debased it below its true standard. The graces of composition have been employed to disguise or to supply the want of matter; and the temporary applause of the ignorant has been courted, instead of the lasting approbation of the discerning. But such imposture can never maintain its ground long. Knowledge and science must furnish the materials that form the body and substance of any valuable composition. Rhetoric serves to add the polish, and we know that none but firm and solid bodies can be polished well.

Of those who peruse the following Lectures, some, by the profession to which they addict themselves, or in consequence of their prevailing inclination, may have the view of being employed in composition, or in public speaking. Others, without any prospect of this kind, may wish only to improve their taste with respect to writing and discourse, and to acquire principles which will enable them to judge for themselves in that part of literature called the Belles Lettres.

With respect to the former, such as may have occasion to communicate their sentiments to the Public, it is abundantly clear that some preparation of study is requisite for the end which they have in view. To speak or to write perspicuously and agreeably, with purity, with grace and strength, are attainments of the utmost consequence to all who purpose, either by speech or writing, to address the Public. For without being master of those attainments, no man can do justice to his own conceptions; but how rich soever he may be in knowledge and in good sense, will be able to avail himself less of those treasures, than such as possess not half his store, but who can display what they possess with more propriety. Neither are these attainments of that kind for which we are indebted to nature merely. Nature has, indeed, conferred upon some a very favourable distinction in this respect, beyond others. But in these, as in most other talents she bestows, she has left much to be wrought out by every man's own industry. So conspicuous have been the effects of study and improvement in every part of eloquence; such remarkable examples have appeared of persons surmounting, by their diligence, the disadvantages of the most untoward nature, that among the learned it has long been a contested, and remains still an undecided point, whether nature or art confer most towards excelling in writing and discourse.

With respect to the manner in which art can most effectually furnish assistance for such a purpose, there may be diversity of opinions. I by no means pretend to say that mere rhetorical rules, how just soever, are sufficient to form an orator. Supposing natural genius to be favourable, more by a great deal will depend upon private application and study, than upon any system of instruction that is capable of being publicly communicated. But at the same time, though rules and instructions cannot do all that is requisite, they may, however, do much that is of real use. They cannot, it is true, inspire genius; but they can direct and assist it. They cannot remedy barrenness; but they may correct redundancy. They point out proper models for imitation. They bring into view the chief beauties that ought to be studied, and the principal faults that ought to be avoided; and thereby tend to enlighten taste, and to lead genius from unnatural deviations, into its proper channel. What would not avail for the production of great excellencies, may at least serve to prevent the commission of considerable errors.

All that regards the study of eloquence and composition, merits the higher attention upon this account, that it is intimately connected with the improvement of our intellectual powers. For I must be allowed to say, that when we are employed, after a proper manner, in the study of composition, we are cultivating reason itself. True rhetoric and sound logic are very nearly allied. The study of arranging and expressing our thoughts with propriety, teaches to think, as well as to speak, accurately. By putting our sentiments into words, we always conceive them more distinctly. Every one who has the slightest acquaintance with composition knows, that when he expresses himself ill on any subject, when his arrangement becomes loose, and his sentences turn feeble, the defects of his style can, almost on every occasion, be traced back to his indistinct conception of the subject: so close is the connection between thoughts and the words in which they are clothed.

The study of composition, important in itself at all times, has acquired additional importance from the taste and manners of the present age. It is an age wherein improvements, in every part of science, have been prosecuted with ardour. To all the liberal arts much attention has been paid; and to none more than to the beauty of language, and the grace and elegance of every kind of writing. The public ear is become refined. It will not easily bear what is slovenly and incorrect. Every author must aspire to some merit in expression, as well as in sentiment, if he would not incur the danger of being neglected and despised.

I will not deny that the love of minute elegance, and attention to inferior ornaments of composition, may at present have engrossed too great a degree of the public regard. It is indeed my opinion, that we lean to this extreme; often more careful of polishing style, than of storing it with thought. Yet hence arises a new reason for the study of just and proper composition. If it be requisite not to be deficient in elegance or ornament in times when they are in such high estimation, it is still more requisite to attain the power of distinguishing false ornament from true, in order to prevent our being carried away by that torrent of false and frivolous taste, which never fails, when it is prevalent, to sweep along with it the raw and the ignorant. They who have never studied eloquence in its principles, nor have been trained to attend to the genuine and manly beauties of good writing, are always ready to be caught by the mere glare of language; and when they come to speak in public, or to compose, have no other standard on which to form themselves, except what chances to be fashionable and popular, how corrupted soever, or erroneous, that may be.

But as there are many who have no such objects as either composition or public speaking in view, let us next consider what advantages may be derived by them, from such studies as form the subject of these Lectures. To them, rhetoric is not so much a practical art as a speculative science; and the same instructions which assist others in composing, will assist them in judging of, and relishing, the beauties of composition. Whatever enables genius to execute well, will enable taste to criticise justly.

When we name criticising, prejudices may perhaps arise, of the same kind with those which I mentioned before with respect to rhetoric. As rhetoric has been sometimes thought to signify nothing more than the scholastic study of words, and phrases, and tropes, so criticism has been considered as merely the art of finding faults; as the frigid application of certain technical terms, by means of which persons are taught to cavil and censure in a learned manner. But this is the criticism of pedants only. True criticism is a liberal and humane art. It is the offspring of good sense and refined taste. It aims at acquiring a just discernment of the real merit of authors. It promotes a lively relish of their beauties, while it preserves us from that blind and implicit veneration which would confound their beauties and faults in our esteem. It teaches us, in a word, to admire and to blame with judgment, and not to follow the crowd blindly.

In an age when works of genius and literature are so frequently the subjects of discourse, when every one erects himself into a judge, and when we can hardly mingle in polite society without bearing some share in such discussions; studies of this kind, it is not to be doubted, will appear to derive part of their importance from the use to which they may be applied in furnishing materials for those fashionable topics of discourse, and thereby enabling us to support a proper rank in social life.

But I should be sorry if we could not rest the merit of such studies on somewhat of solid and intrinsical use independent of appearance and show. The exercise of taste and of sound criticism, is in truth one of the most improving employments of the understanding. To apply the principles of good sense to composition and discourse; to examine what is beautiful, and why it is so; to employ ourselves in distinguishing accurately between the specious and the solid, between affected and natural ornament, must certainly improve us not a little in the most valuable part of all philosophy, the philosophy of human nature. For such disquisitions are very intimately connected with the knowledge of ourselves. They necessarily lead us to reflect on the operations of the imagination, and the movements of the heart; and increase our acquaintance with some of the most refined feelings which belong to our frame.

Logical and Ethical disquisitions move in a higher sphere; and are conversant with objects of a more severe kind; the progress of the understanding in its search after knowledge, and the direction of the will in the proper pursuit of good. In these they point out to man the improvement of his nature as an intelligent being; and his duties as the subject of moral obligation. Belles Lettres and criticism chiefly consider him as a Being endowed with those powers of taste and imagination, which were intended to embellish his mind, and to supply him with rational and useful entertainment. They open a field of investigation peculiar to themselves. All that relates to beauty, harmony, grandeur, and elegance; all that can sooth the mind, gratify the fancy, or move the affections, belongs to their province. They present human nature under a different aspect from that which it assumes to the view of other sciences. They bring to light various springs of action which without their aid might have passed unobserved; and which, though of a delicate nature, frequently exert a powerful influence on several departments of human life.

Such studies have also this peculiar advantage, that they exercise our reason without fatiguing it. They lead to enquiries acute, but not painful; profound, but not dry nor abstruse. They strew flowers in the path of science; and while they keep the mind bent, in some degree, and active, they relieve it at the same time from that more toilsome labour to which it must submit in the acquisition of necessary erudition, or the investigation of abstract truth.

The cultivation of taste is farther recommended by the happy effects which it naturally tends to produce on human life. The most busy man, in the most active sphere, cannot be always occupied by business. Men of serious professions cannot always be on the stretch of serious thought. Neither can the most gay and flourishing situations of fortune afford any man the power of filling all his hours with pleasure. Life must always languish in the hands of the idle. It will frequently languish even in the hands of the busy, if they have not some employment subsidiary to that which forms their main pursuit. How then shall these vacant spaces, those unemployed intervals, which, more or less, occur in the life of every one, be filled up? How can we contrive to dispose of them in any way that shall be more agreeable in itself, or more consonant to the dignity of the human mind, than in the entertainments of taste, and the study of polite literature? He who is so happy as to have acquired a relish for these, has always at hand an innocent and irreproachable amusement for his leisure hours, to save him from the danger of many a pernicious passion. He is not in hazard of being a burden to himself. He is not obliged to fly to low company, or to court the riot of loose pleasures, in order to cure the tediousness of existence.

Providence seems plainly to have pointed out this useful purpose to which the pleasures of taste may be applied, by interposing them in a middle station between the pleasures of sense, and those of pure intellect. We were not designed to grovel always among objects so low as the former; nor are we capable of dwelling constantly in so high a region as the latter. The pleasures of taste refresh the mind after the toils of the intellect, and the labours of abstract study; and they gradually raise it above the attachments of sense, and prepare it for the enjoyments of virtue.

So consonant is this to experience, that in the education of youth, no object has in every age appeared more important to wise men, than to tincture them early with a relish for the entertainments of taste. The transition is commonly made with ease from these to the discharge of the higher and more important duties of life. Good hopes may be entertained of those whose minds have this liberal and elegant turn. Many virtues may be grafted upon it. Whereas to be entirely devoid of relish for eloquence, poetry, or any of the fine arts, is justly constructed to be an unpromising symptom of youth; and raises suspicions of their being prone to low gratifications, or destined to drudge in the more vulgar and illiberal pursuits of life.

There are indeed few good dispositions of any kind with which the improvement of taste is not more or less connected. A cultivated taste increases sensibility to all the tender and humane passions, by giving them frequent exercise; while it tends to weaken the more violent and fierce emotions.

——Ingenuas didicisse fideliter artes
Emollit mores, nec sinit esse feros.[2]

The elevated sentiments and high examples which poetry, eloquence and history are often bringing under our view, naturally tend to nourish in our minds publick spirit, the love of glory, contempt of external fortune, and the admiration of what is truly illustrious and great.

I will not go so far as to say that the improvement of taste and of virtue is the same; or that they may always be expected to coexist in an equal degree. More powerful correctives than taste can apply, are necessary for reforming the corrupt propensities which too frequently prevail among mankind. Elegant speculations are sometimes found to float on the surface of the mind, while bad passions possess the interior regions of the heart. At the same time this cannot but be admitted, that the exercise of taste is, in its native tendency, moral and purifying. From reading the most admired pro-

2. These polished arts have humaniz'd mankind,
Soften'd the rude, and calm'd the boist'rous mind.

ductions of genius, whether in poetry or prose, almost every one rises with some good impressions left on his mind; and though these may not always be durable, they are at least to be ranked among the means of disposing the heart to virtue. One thing is certain, and I shall hereafter have occasion to illustrate it more fully, that without possessing the virtuous affections in a strong degree, no man can attain eminence in the sublime parts of eloquence. He must feel what a good man feels, if he expects greatly to move or to interest mankind. They are the ardent sentiments of honour, virtue, magnanimity, and publick spirit, that only can kindle that fire of genius, and call up into the mind those high ideas, which attract the admiration of ages; and if this spirit be necessary to produce the most distinguished efforts of eloquence, it must be necessary also to our relishing them with proper taste and feeling.

On these general topics I shall dwell no longer; but proceed directly to the consideration of the subjects which are to employ the following Lectures. They divide themselves into five parts. First, some introductory dissertations on the nature of taste, and upon the sources of its pleasures. Secondly, the consideration of language: Thirdly, of style: Fourthly, of eloquence properly so called, or publick speaking in its different kinds. Lastly, a critical examination of the most distinguished species of composition, both in prose and verse.

From "Lecture 3: Criticism.—Genius.—Pleasures of Taste.—Sublimity in Objects."

Taste, Criticism, and Genius, are words currently employed, without distinct ideas annexed to them. In beginning a course of Lectures where such words must often occur, it is necessary to ascertain their meaning with some precision. Having in the last Lecture treated of Taste, I proceed to explain the nature and foundation of Criticism. True Criticism is the application of Taste and of good sense to the several fine arts. The object which it proposes is, to distinguish what is beautiful and what is faulty in every performance; from particular instances to ascend to general principles; and so to form rules or conclusions concerning the several kinds of beauty in works of Genius.

The rules of Criticism are not formed by any induction, *à priori*, as it is called; that is, they are not formed by a train of abstract reasoning, independent of facts and observations. Criticism is an art founded wholly on experience; on the observation of such beauties as have come nearest to the standard which I before established: that is, of such beauties as have been found to please mankind most generally. For example; Aristotle's rules concerning the unity of action in dramatic and epic composition, were not rules first discovered by logical reasoning, and then applied to poetry; but they were drawn from the practice of Homer and Sophocles: they were founded upon observing the superior pleasure which we receive from the relation of an action which is one and entire, beyond what we receive from the relation of scattered and unconnected facts. Such observations taking their rise at first from feeling and experience, were found on examination to be so consonant to reason, and to the principles of human nature, as to pass into established rules, and to be conveniently applied for judging of the excellency of any performance. This is the most natural account of the origin of Criticism.

A masterly genius, it is true, will of himself, untaught, compose in such a manner as shall be agreeable to the most material rules of Criticism; for as these rules are founded in nature, nature will often suggest them in practice. Homer, it is more than probable, was acquainted with no systems of the art of poetry. Guided by genius alone, he composed in verse a regular story, which all posterity has admired. But this is no argument against the usefulness of Criticism as an art. For as no human genius is perfect, there is no writer but may receive assistance from critical observations upon the beauties and faults of those who have gone before him. No observations or rules can indeed supply the defect of genius, or inspire it where it is wanting. But they may often direct it into its proper channel; they may correct its extravagancies, and point out to it the most just and proper imitation of nature. Critical rules are designed chiefly to shew the faults that ought to be avoided. To nature we must be indebted for the production of eminent beauties.

From what has been said, we are enabled to form a judgment concerning those complaints which it has long been fashionable for petty authors to make against Critics and Criticism. Critics have been represented as the great abridgers of the native liberty of genius; as the imposers of unnatural shackles and bonds upon writers, from whose cruel persecution they must fly to the Public, and implore its protection. Such supplicatory prefaces are not calculated to give very favourable ideas of the genius of the author. For every good writer will be pleased to have his work examined by the principles of sound understanding, and true Taste. The declamations against Criticism commonly proceed upon this supposition, that Critics are such as judge by rule, not by feeling; which is so far from being true, that they who judge after this manner are pedants, not Critics. For all the rules of genuine Criticism I have shewn to be ultimately founded on feeling; and Taste and Feeling are necessary to guide us in the application of these rules to every particular instance. As there is nothing in which all sorts of persons more readily affect to be judges than in works of Taste, there is no doubt that the number of incompetent Critics will always be great. But this affords no more foundation for a general invective against Criticism, than the number of bad philosophers or reasoners affords against reason and philosophy.

An objection more plausible may be formed against Criticism, from the applause that some performances have received from the Public, which, when accurately considered, are found to contradict the rules established by Criticism. Now, according to the principles laid down in the last Lecture, the Public is the supreme judge to whom the last appeal must be made in every work of Taste; as the standard of Taste is founded on the sentiments that are natural and common to all men. But with respect to this we are to observe, that the sense of the Public is often too hastily judged of. The genuine public Taste does not always appear in the first applause given upon the publication of any new work. There are both a great vulgar and a small, apt to be catched and dazzled by very superficial beauties, the admiration of which in a little time passes away: and sometimes a writer may acquire great temporary reputation merely by his compliance with the passions or prejudices, with the party-spirit or superstitious notions, that may chance to rule for a time almost a whole nation. In such cases, though the Public may seem to praise, true Criticism may with reason condemn; and it will in progress of time gain the ascendant: for the judgment of true Criticism, and the voice of the Public, when once become unprejudiced and dispassionate, will ever coincide at last.

Instances, I admit, there are, of some works that contain gross transgressions of the laws of Criticism, acquiring, nevertheless, a general, and even a lasting admiration. Such are the plays of Shakespeare, which, considered as dramatic poems, are irregular in the highest degree. But then we are to remark, that they have gained the public admiration, not by their being irregular, not by their transgressions of the rules of art, but in spite of such transgressions. They possess other beauties which are conformable to just rules; and the force of these beauties has been so great as to overpower all censure, and to give the Public a degree of satisfaction superior to the disgust arising from their blemishes. Shakespeare pleases, not by his bringing the transactions of many years into one play; not by his grotesque mixtures of Tragedy and Comedy in one piece, nor by the strained thoughts, and affected witticisms, which he sometimes employs. These we consider as blemishes, and impute them to the grossness of the age in which he lived. But he pleases by his animated and masterly representations of characters, by the liveliness of his descriptions, the force of his sentiments, and his possessing, beyond all writers, the natural language of passion: Beauties which true Criticism no less teaches us to place in the highest rank, than nature teaches us to feel. ———This much it may suffice to have said concerning the origin, office, and importance of Criticism.

I proceed next to explain the meaning of another term, which there will be frequent occasion to employ in these Lectures; that is, *Genius*.

Taste and Genius are two words frequently joined together; and therefore, by inaccurate thinkers, confounded. They signify however two quite different things. The difference between them can be clearly pointed out; and it is of importance to remember it. Taste consists in the power of judging: Genius, in the power of executing. One may have a considerable degree of Taste in Poetry, Eloquence, or any of the fine arts, who has little or hardly any Genius for composition or execution in any of these arts: But Genius cannot be found without including Taste also. Genius, therefore, deserves to be considered as a higher power of the mind than Taste. Genius always imports something inventive or creative; which does not rest in mere sensibility to beauty where it is perceived, but which can, moreover, produce new beauties, and exhibit them in such a manner as strongly to impress the minds of others. Refined Taste forms a good critic; but Genius is farther necessary to form the poet, or the orator.

It is proper also to observe, that Genius is a word, which, in common acceptation, extends much farther than to the objects of Taste. It is used to signify that talent or aptitude which we receive from nature, for excelling in any one thing whatever. Thus we speak of a Genius for mathematics, as well as a Genius for poetry; of a Genius for war, for politics, or for any mechanical employment.

This talent or aptitude for excelling in some one particular, is, I have said, what we receive from nature. By art and study, no doubt, it may be greatly improved; but by them alone it cannot be acquired. As Genius is a higher faculty than Taste, it is ever, according to the usual frugality of nature, more limited in the sphere of its operations. It is not uncommon to meet with persons who have an excellent Taste in several of the polite arts, such as music, poetry, painting, and eloquence, altogether: But, to find one who is an excellent performer in all these arts, is much more rare; or rather, indeed, such an one is not to be looked for. A sort of Universal Genius, or one who is equally and indifferently turned towards several different professions and arts, is not likely to excel in any. Although there may be some few exceptions, yet in general it holds, that when the bent of the mind is wholly directed towards some one object, exclusive, in a manner, of others, there is the fairest prospect of eminence in that, whatever it be. The rays must converge to a point, in order to glow intensely. This remark I here chuse to make, on account of its great importance to young people; in leading them to examine with care, and to pursue with ardour, the current and pointing of nature towards those exertions of Genius in which they are most likely to excel.

A Genius for any of the fine arts, as I before observed, always supposes Taste; and it is clear, that the improvement of Taste will serve both to forward and to correct the operations of Genius. In proportion as the Taste of a poet, or orator, becomes more refined with respect to the beauties of composition, it will certainly assist him to produce the more finished beauties in his work. Genius, however, in a Poet or Orator, may sometimes exist in a higher degree than Taste; that is, Genius may be bold and strong, when Taste is neither very delicate, nor very correct. This is often the case in the infancy of arts; a period, when Genius frequently exerts itself with great vigour, and executes with much warmth; while Taste, which requires experience, and improves by slower degrees, hath not yet attained its full growth. Homer and Shakespear are proofs of what I now assert; in whose admirable writings are found instances of rudeness and indelicacy, which the more refined Taste of later writers, who had far inferior Genius to them, would have taught them to avoid. As all human perfection is limited, this may very probably be the law of our nature, that it is not given to one man to execute with vigour and fire, and, at the same time, to attend to all the lesser and more refined graces that belong to the exact perfection of his work: While, on the other hand, a thorough Taste for those inferior graces, is, for the most part, accompanied with a diminution of sublimity and force.

Having thus explained the nature of Taste, the nature and importance of Criticism, and the distinction between Taste and Genius; I am now to enter on considering the sources of the Pleasures of Taste. Here opens a very extensive field; no less than all the pleasures of the imagination, as they are commonly called, whether afforded us by natural objects, or by the imitations and descriptions of them. But it is not necessary to the purpose of my Lectures, that all these should be examined fully; the pleasure which we receive from discourse, or writing, being the main object of them. All that I purpose is, to give some opening into the Pleasures of Taste in general; and to insist, more particularly, upon Sublimity and Beauty.

We are far from having yet attained to any system concerning this subject. Mr. Addison was the first who attempted a regular enquiry, in his Essay on the Pleasures of the Imagination, published in the sixth volume of the Spectator. He has reduced these Pleasures under three heads; Beauty, Grandeur, and Novelty. His speculations on this subject, if not exceedingly profound, are, however, very beautiful and entertaining; and he has the merit of having opened a tract, which was before unbeaten. The advances made since his time in this curious part of philosophical Criticism, are not very considerable; though some ingenious writers have pursued the subject. This is owing, doubtless, to that thinness and subtility which are found to be properties of all the feelings of Taste. They are engaging objects; but when we would lay firm hold of them, and subject them to a regular discussion, they are always ready to elude our grasp. It is difficult to make a full enumeration of the several objects that give pleasure to Taste; it is more difficult to define all those which have been discovered, and to reduce them under proper classes; and, when we would go farther, and investigate the efficient causes of the pleasure which we receive from such objects, here, above all, we find ourselves at a loss. For instance; we all learn by experience, that certain figures of bodies appear to us more beautiful than others. On enquiring farther, we find that the regularity of some figures, and the graceful variety of others, are the foundation of the beauty which we discern in them; but when we attempt to go a step beyond this, and enquire what is the cause of regularity and variety producing in our minds the sensation of

Beauty, any reason we can assign is extremely imperfect. Those first principles of internal sensation, nature seems to have covered with an impenetrable veil.

It is some comfort, however, that although the efficient cause be obscure, the final cause of those sensations lies in many cases more open: And, in entering on this subject, we cannot avoid taking notice of the strong impression which the powers of Taste and Imagination are calculated to give us of the benignity of our Creator. By endowing us with such powers, he hath widely enlarged the sphere of the pleasures of human life; and those, too, of a kind the most pure and innocent. The necessary purposes of life might have been abundantly answered, though our senses of seeing and hearing had only served to distinguish external objects, without conveying to us any of those refined and delicate sensations of Beauty and Grandeur, with which we are now so much delighted. This additional embellishment and glory, which, for promoting our entertainment, the Author of nature hath poured forth upon his works, is one striking testimony, among many others, of benevolence and goodness. This thought, which Mr. Addison first started, Dr. Akenside, in his Poem on the Pleasures of the Imagination, has happily pursued.

> ———--Not content
> With every food of life to nourish man,
> By kind illusions of the wondering sense,
> Thou mak'st all nature, Beauty to his eye,
> Or Music to his ear.—

I shall begin with considering the Pleasure which arises from Sublimity or Grandeur, of which I propose to treat at some length; both, as this has a character more precise and distinctly marked, than any other, of the Pleasures of the Imagination, and as it coincides more directly with our main subject. For the greater distinctness I shall, first, treat of the Grandeur or Sublimity of external objects themselves, which will employ the rest of this Lecture; and, afterwards, of the description of such objects, or, of what is called the Sublime in Writing, which shall be the subject of a following Lecture. I distinguish these two things from one another, the Grandeur of the objects themselves when they are presented to the eye, and the description of that Grandeur in discourse or writing; though most Critics, inaccurately I think, blend them together; and I consider Grandeur and Sublimity as terms synonymous, or nearly so. If there be any distinction between them, it arises from Sublimity's expressing Grandeur in its highest degree.[1]

It is not easy to describe, in words, the precise impression which great and sublime objects make upon us, when we behold them; but every one has a conception of it. It consists in a kind of admiration and expansion of the mind; it raises the mind much above its ordinary state; and fills it with a degree of wonder and astonishment, which it cannot well express. The emotion is certainly delightful; but it is altogether of the serious kind: a degree of awfulness and solemnity, even approaching to severity, commonly attends it when at its height; very distinguishable from the more gay and brisk emotion raised by beautiful objects.

The simplest form of external Grandeur appears in the vast and boundless prospects presented to us by nature; such as wide extended plains, to which the eye can see no limits; the firmament of Heaven; or the boundless expanse of the Ocean. All vastness produces the impression of Sublimity. It is to be remarked, however, that space, extended in length, makes not so strong an impression as height or depth. Though a boundless plain be a grand object, yet a high mountain, to which we look up, or an awful precipice or tower whence we look down on the objects which lie below, is still more so. The excessive Grandeur of the firmament arises from its height, joined to its boundless extent; and that of the ocean, not from its extent alone, but from the perpetual motion and irresistible force of that mass of waters. Wherever space is concerned, it is clear, that amplitude or greatness of extent, in one dimension or other, is necessary to Grandeur. Remove all bounds from any object, and you presently render it sublime. Hence infinite space, endless numbers, and eternal duration, fill the mind with great ideas.

From this some have imagined, that vastness, or amplitude of extent, is the foundation of all Sublimity. But I cannot be of this opinion, because many objects appear sublime which have no relation to space at all. Such, for instance, is great loudness of sound. The burst of thunder or of cannon, the roaring of winds, the shouting of multitudes, the sound of vast cataracts of water, are all incontestibly grand objects. "I heard the voice of a great multitude, as the sound of many waters, and of mighty thunderings, saying Allelujah." In general we may observe, that great power and force exerted, always raise sublime ideas: and perhaps the most copious source of these is derived from this quarter. Hence

---

1. See a Philosophical Inquiry into the Origin of our Ideas of the Sublime and Beautiful. Dr. Gerard on Taste, Section II. Elements of Criticism, Chap. IV.

the grandeur of earthquakes and burning mountains; of great conflagrations; of the stormy ocean, and overflowing waters; of tempests of wind; of thunder and lightning; and of all the uncommon violence of the elements. Nothing is more sublime than mighty power and strength. A stream that runs within its banks, is a beautiful object; but when it rushes down with the impetuosity and noise of a torrent, it presently becomes a sublime one. From lions, and other animals of strength, are drawn sublime comparisons in poets. A race horse is looked upon with pleasure; but it is the war-horse, "whose neck is clothed with thunder," that carries grandeur in its idea. The engagement of two great armies, as it is the highest exertion of human might, combines a variety of sources of the Sublime; and has accordingly been always considered as one of the most striking and magnificent spectacles that can be either presented to the eye, or exhibited to the imagination in description....

From "Lecture 37: Philosophical Writing.—Dialogue.—Epistolary Writing.—Fictitious History."

As History is both a very dignified species of Composition, and, by the regular form which it assumes, falls directly under the laws of Criticism, I discoursed of it fully in the two preceding Lectures. The remaining species of Composition, in Prose, afford less room for critical observation.

Philosophical Writing, for instance, will not lead us into any long discussion. As the professed object of Philosophy is to convey instruction, and as they who study it are supposed to do so for instruction, not for entertainment, the Style, the form, and dress, of such Writings, are less material objects. They are objects, however, that must not be wholly neglected. He who attempts to instruct mankind, without studying, at the same time, to engage their attention, and to interest them in his subject by his manner of exhibiting it, is not likely to prove successful. The same truths, and reasonings, delivered in a dry and cold manner, or with a proper measure of elegance and beauty, will make different impressions on the minds of men.

....

There remains to be treated of, another species of Composition in prose, which comprehends a very numerous, though, in general, a very insignificant class of Writings, known by the name of Romances and Novels. These may, at first view, seem too insignificant, to deserve that any particular notice should be taken of them. But I cannot be of this opinion. Mr. Fletcher of Salton, in one of his Tracts, quotes it as the saying of a wise man, that give him the making of all the ballads of a nation, he would allow any one that pleased to make their laws. The saying was founded on reflection and good sense, and applies to the subject now before us. For any kind of Writing, how trifling soever in appearance, that obtains a general currency, and especially that early preoccupies the imagination of the youth of both sexes, must demand particular attention. Its influence is likely to be considerable, both on the morals, and taste of a nation.

In fact, fictitious histories might be employed for very useful purposes. They furnish one of the best channels for conveying instruction, for painting human life and manners, for showing the errors into which we are betrayed by our passions, for rendering virtue amiable and vice odious. The effect of well contrived stories, towards accomplishing these purposes, is stronger than any effect that can be produced by simple and naked instruction; and hence we find, that the wisest men in all ages, have more or less employed fables and fictions, as the vehicles of knowledge. These have ever been the basis of both Epic and Dramatic Poetry. It is not, therefore, the nature of this sort of Writing considered in itself, but the faulty manner of its execution, that can expose it to any contempt. Lord Bacon takes notice of our taste for fictitious history, as a proof of the greatness and dignity of the human mind. He observes very ingeniously, that the objects of this world, and the common train of affairs which we behold going on in it, do not fill the mind, nor give it entire satisfaction. We seek for something that shall expand the mind in a greater degree: we seek for more heroic and illustrious deeds, for more diversified and surprising events, for a more splendid order of things, a more regular and just distribution of rewards and punishments than what we find here: because we meet not with these in true history, we have recourse to fictitious. We create worlds according to our fancy, in order to gratify our capacious desires: "Accomodando," says that great philosopher, "Rerum simulachra ad animi desideria, non submittendo animum rebus, quod ratio facit, et historia."[1] Let us then, since the subject wants neither dignity nor use, make a few observations on the rise and progress of Fictitious History,

[1] "Accommodating the appearances of things to the desires of the mind, not bringing down the mind, as history and philosophy do, to the course of events."

and the different forms it has assumed in different countries.

In all countries we find its origin very antient. The genius of the Eastern nations, in particular, was from the earliest times much turned towards invention, and the love of fiction. Their Divinity, their Philosophy, and their Politics, were clothed in fables and parables. The Indians, the Persians, and Arabians, were all famous for their tales. The "Arabian Night's Entertainments" are the production of a romantic invention, but of a rich and amusing imagination; exhibiting a singular and curious display of manners and characters, and beautified with a very humane morality. Among the ancient Greeks, we hear of the Ionian and Milesian Tales; but they are now perished, and, from any account that we have of them, appear to have been of the loose and wanton kind. Some fictitious histories yet remain, that were composed during the decline of the Roman Empire, by Apuleius, Achilles Tatius, and Heliodorus bishop of Trica, in the 4th century; but none of them are considerable enough to merit particular criticism.

During the dark ages, this sort of writing assumed a new and very singular form, and for a long while made a great figure in the world. The martial spirit of those nations, among whom the feudal government prevailed; the establishment of single combat, as an allowed method of deciding causes both of justice and honour; the appointment of champions in the cause of women, who could not maintain their own rights by the sword; together with the institution of military tournaments, in which different kingdoms vied with one another, gave rise, in those times, to that marvellous system of chivalry, which is one of the most singular appearances in the history of mankind. Upon this were founded those romances of knight-errantry, which carried an ideal chivalry, to a still more extravagant height than it had risen in fact. There was displayed in them a new and very wonderful sort of world, hardly bearing any resemblance to the world in which we dwell. Not only knights setting forth to redress all manner of wrongs, but in every page magicians, dragons, and giants, invulnerable men, winged horses, enchanted armour, and enchanted castles; adventures absolutely incredible, yet suited to the gross ignorance of these ages, and to the legends, and superstitious notions concerning magic and necromancy, which then prevailed. This merit they had, of being writings of the highly moral and heroic kind. Their knights were patterns, not of courage merely, but of religion, generosity, courtesy, and fidelity; and the heroines were no less distinguished for modesty, delicacy, and the utmost dignity of manners.

These were the first compositions that received the name of Romances. The origin of this name is traced, by Mr. Huet the learned bishop of Avranche, to the provencal Troubadoures, a sort of story-tellers and bards in the county of Provençe, where there subsisted some remains of literature and poetry. The language which prevailed in that country was a mixture of Latin and Gallic, called the Roman or Romance Language; and their stories being written in that language, hence it is said the name of Romance, which we now apply to all fictitious Composition.

The earliest of those Romances is that which goes under the name of Turpin, the archbishop of Rheims, written in the 11th century. The subject is, the Atchievements of Charlemagne and his peers, or Paladins, in driving the Saracens out of France and part of Spain; the same subject which Ariosto has taken for his celebrated poem of Orlando Furioso, which is truly a Chivalry Romance, as extravagant as any of the rest, but partly heroic, and partly comic, embellished with the highest graces of poetry. The Romance of Turpin was followed by Amadis de Gaul, and many more of the same stamp. The Crusades both furnished new matter, and increased the spirit for such Writings; the Christians against the Saracens made the common groundwork of them; and from the 11th to the 16th century, they continued to bewitch all Europe. In Spain, where the taste for this sort of writing had been most greedily caught, the ingenious Cervantes, in the beginning of the last century, contributed greatly to explode it; and the abolition of tournaments, the prohibition of single combat, the disbelief of magic and enchantments, and the change in general of manners throughout Europe, began to give a new turn to fictitious Composition.

Then appeared the Astraea of D'urfè, the Grand Cyrus, the Clelia and Cleopatra of Mad. Scuderi, the Arcadia of Sir Philip Sidney, and other grave and stately Compositions in the same style. These may be considered as forming the second stage of Romance Writing. The heroism and the gallantry, the moral and virtuous turn of the chivalry romance, were still preserved; but the dragons, the necromancers, and the enchanted castles, were banished, and some small resemblance to human nature was introduced. Still, however, there was too much of the marvellous in them to please an age which now aspired to refinement. The characters were discerned to be strained; the style to be swoln; the adventures incredible: the books themselves were voluminous and tedious.

Hence, this sort of Composition soon assumed a third form, and from magnificent Heroic Romance, dwindled down to the Familiar Novel. These novels, both in France and England, during the age of Lewis XIV. and King Charles II. were in general of a trifling nature, without the appearance of moral tendency, or useful instruction. Since that time, however, somewhat better has been attempted, and a degree of reformation introduced into the spirit of Novel Writing. Imitations of life and character have been made their principal object. Relations have been professed to be given of the behaviour of persons in particular interesting situations, such as may actually occur in life; by means of which, what is laudable or defective in character and in conduct, may be pointed out, and placed in an useful light. Upon this plan, the French have produced some compositions of considerable merit. Gil Blas, by Le Sage, is a book full of good sense, and instructive knowledge of the world. The works of Marivaux, especially his Marianne, discover great refinement of thought, great penetration into human nature, and paint, with a very delicate pencil, some of the nicest shades and features in the distinction of characters. The Nouvelle Heloise of Rousseau is a production of a very singular kind; in many of the events which are related, improbable and unnatural; in some of the details tedious, and for some of the scenes which are described justly blameable; but withal, for the power of eloquence, for tenderness of sentiment, for ardour of passion, entitled to rank among the highest productions of Fictitious History.

In this kind of Writing we are, it must be confessed, in Great Britain, inferior to the French. We neither relate so agreeably, nor draw characters with so much delicacy; yet we are not without some performances which discover the strength of the British genius. No fiction, in any language, was ever better supported than the Adventures of Robinson Crusoe. While it is carried on with that appearance of truth and simplicity, which takes a strong hold of the imagination of all Readers, it suggests, at the same time, very useful instruction; by showing how much the native powers of man may be exerted for surmounting the difficulties of any external situation. Mr. Fielding's Novels are highly distinguished for their humour; a humour which, if not of the most refined and delicate kind, is original, and peculiar to himself. The characters which he draws are lively and natural, and marked with the strokes of a bold pencil. The general scope of his stories is favourable to humanity and goodness of heart; and in Tom Jones, his greatest work, the artful conduct of the fable, and the subserviency of all the incidents to the winding up of the whole, deserve much praise. The most moral of all our novel Writers is Richardson, the Author of Clarissa, a Writer of excellent intentions, and of very considerable capacity and genius; did he not possess the unfortunate talent of spinning out pieces of amusement into an immeasurable length. The trivial performances which daily appear in public under the title of Lives, Adventures, and Histories, by anonymous Authors, if they be often innocent, yet are most commonly insipid; and, though in the general it ought to be admitted that Characteristical Novels, formed upon Nature and upon Life, without extravagance, and without licentiousness, might furnish an agreeable and useful entertainment to the mind; yet according as these Writings have been, for the most part, conducted, it must also be confessed, that they oftener tend to dissipation and idleness, than to any good purpose. Let us now therefore make our retreat from these regions of fiction.

Reprinted from *Lectures on Rhetoric and Belles Lettres*, 2 volumes (London: Printed for W. Strahan, for T. Cadell & for W. Creech in Edinburgh, 1783).

John Witherspoon

Excerpts from *The Works of the Rev. John Witherspoon* (1800-1801)

From "A Serious Inquiry into the Nature and Effects of the Stage"

The reader will probably conjecture, and therefore I do readily acknowledge, that what gave occasion both to the writing, and publishing the ensuing treatise, was the new tragedy of Douglas, lately acted in the theatre at Edinburgh. This, universal uncontradicted fame says, is the work of a minister of the church of Scotland. One of that character and office employing his time in writing for the stage, every one will allow, is a very new and extraordinary event. In one respect neither author nor actors have suffered any thing from this circumstance: for doubtless, it contributed its share in procuring that run upon the representation, which continued for several days. Natural curiosity prompted many to make trial, whether there was any difference between a play wrote by a clergyman, and one of another author. And a concern for the fate of such a person excited the zeal and diligence of friends, to do all in their power to procure a full house, that the bold adventurer might be treated with respect and honor.

Some resolutions of the presbytery of Edinburgh seem to threaten, that public notice will be taken of this author and his associates, by their superiors in the church. Whether this will be carried on, and, if it be, whether they will be approved or censured; and if the last, to what degree, I pretend not to foretel. But one thing is certain, that it hath been, and will be, the subject of much thought and conversation among the laity of all ranks, and that it must have a very great influence upon the state of religion among us, in this part of the nation. That this influence will be for the better, though I resolve to examine the subject with all impartiality, I confess I see little ground to hope. There is no doubt that it will be condemned by the great plurality of those who go by the appellation of the stricter sort. With them, it will bring a great reproach upon the church of Scotland, as containing one minister who writes for the stage, and many who think it no crime to attend the representation. It is true, no other consequences are to be apprehended from their displeasure, than the weakest of them being provoked to unchristian resentment, or tempted to draw rash and general conclusions from the conduct of a few to the character of the whole, or perhaps some of them separating from the established church, none of which effects of late have been much either feared or shunned. However, even on this account, it were to be wished, either that it had never happened, or that it could be shewn, to the conviction of unprejudiced minds, that it was a just and commendable action.

But, to be sure, the chief danger is, that in case it be really a bad thing, it must give great offence, in the Scripture sense of that word, to those who are most apt to take it, viz. such as have least religion, or none at all. An offence is a stumbling-block over which the weak and unstedfast are in danger of falling; that is to say, It emboldens them to commit, and hardens them in the practice of, sin. Now, if the stage is unlawful or dangerous to a Christian, those who are by inclination so addicted to it that it is already difficult to convince them of their error, must be greatly confirmed in this error, by the example and countenance of such as call themselves ministers of Christ. It has accordingly already occasioned more discourse among the gay part of the world, in defence or commendation of the stage, than past perhaps for some years preceding this event.

Nothing therefore can be more seasonable at this time, or necessary for the public good, than a careful and accurate discussion of this question. Whether supporting and encouraging stage-plays, by writing, acting, or attending them, is consistent, or inconsistent, with the character of a Christian? It is to no purpose to confine the inquiry to this, Whether a minister is not appearing in an improper light, and misapplying his time and talents when he dedicates them to the service of the stage? That point would probably be given up by most, and those who would deny it do not merit a confutation. But if the matter is rested here, it will be considered only as a smaller misdemeanor, and though treated, or even condemned as such, it will still have the bad effect (upon supposition of theatrical amusements being wrong and sinful) of greatly promoting them, though we seem to be already as much given to them as even worldly considerations will allow.

The self-denying apologies common with authors, of their being sensible of their unfitness for the talk they undertake, their doing it to stir up a better hand, and so on, I wholly pass, having never read any of them with approbation. Prudence is good, and I would not willingly lose sight of it, but zeal and concern for the glory of God, and faithfulness to the souls of others, are duties equally necessary in their place, but much more rare. How far I am sensible of my own unfitness for treating this subject, and of the reputation that is risked by attempting it, the world is not obliged to believe upon my own testimony; but in whatever degree it be, it is greatly overbalanced at present, by a view of the declining state of religion among us, the prevalence of national sins and the danger of desolating judgments.

It is some discouragement in this attempt, that it is very uncertain whether many of those, for whose sakes it is chiefly intended, and who stand most in need of information upon the subject, will take the pains to look into it. Such a levity of spirit prevails in this age, that very few persons of fashion will read or consider any thing that is written in a grave or serious style. Whoever will look into the monthly catalogues of books, published in Britain for some years past, may be convinced of this at one glance. What an immense proportion do romances, under the titles of lives, adventures, memoirs, histories, &c. bear to any other sort of production in this age? Perhaps therefore it may be thought that it would have been more proper to have gratified the public taste, by raising up some allegorical structure, and handling this subject in the way of wit and humor; especially as it seems to be a modern principle, that ridicule is the test of truth, and as there seems to be so large a fund for mirth, in the character of a stage-playing priest. But, though I deny not the lawfulness of using ridicule in some cases, or even its propriety here, yet I am far from thinking it is the test of truth. It seems to be more proper for correction than for instruction; and though it may be fit enough to whip an offender, it is not unusual, nor unsuitable, first to expostulate a little with him, and shew him that he deserves it. Besides, every man's talent is not equally fit for it, and indeed, now the matter seems to have been carried beyond a jest, and to require a very serious consideration.

There is also, besides some discouragement, a real difficulty in entering on this disquisition. It will be hard to know in what manner to reason, or on what principles to build. It were easy to show the unlawfulness of stage-plays, by such arguments as would appear conclusive to those who already hate both them and their supporters: but it is not so easy to make it appear to those who chiefly frequent them, because they will both applaud and justify some of the very things that others look upon as the worst effects of the practice, and will deny the very principles on which they are condemned. The truth is, it is our having different views of the nature of religion, that causes different opinions upon this subject. For many ages there was no debate upon it at all. There were players, but they did not pretend to be Christians themselves, and they had neither countenance nor support from any who did. Whereas now, there are abundance of advocates for the lawfulness, some for the usefulness, of plays; not that the stage is become more pure, but that Christians are become less so, and have lowered the standard or measure requisite to attain and preserve that character.

But there is still another difficulty, that whoever undertakes to write against plays, though the provocation is given by what they are, is yet always called upon to attack them, not as they are, but as they might be. A writer on this subject is actually reduced to the necessity of fighting with a shadow, of maintaining a combat with an ideal or imaginary sort of drama, which never yet existed, but which the defenders of the cause form by way of supposition, and which shall appear, in fact, in that happy future age, which shall see, what these gentlemen are pleased to style, a well regulated stage. However little support may seem to be given by this to a vicious and corrupted stage there is no attender of plays but, when he hears this chimera defended, imagines it is his own cause that is espoused, and with great composure and self-satisfaction, continues his practice. A conduct not less absurd, than if one who was expressly assured a certain dish of meat before him was poisoned, should answer thus, All meat is not poisoned, and therefore I may eat this with safety.

It is very plain, that were men but seriously disposed, and without prejudice desiring the knowledge of their duty, it would not be necessary, in order to show the unlawfulness of the stage, as it now is, to combat it in its imaginary reformed state. Such a reformation, were not men by the prevalence of vicious and corrupt affections, in love with it, even in its present condition, would have been long ago given up as a hopeless and visionary project, and the whole trade or employment detested, on account of the abuses that had always adhered to it. But since all advocates for the stage have and do still defend it in this manner, by forming an idea of it separate from its evil qualities; since they defend it so far with success, that many who would otherwise abstain, do, upon this very account, allow themselves in attending the theatre sometimes, to their own hurt and that of others; and, as I am convinced on the most mature deliberation, that the reason why there never was a well regulated stage, in fact, is because it cannot be, the nature of the thing not admitting of it. I will endeavor to shew, that PUBLIC THEATRICAL REPRESENTATIONS, either tragedy or comedy, are, in their general nature or in their best possible state, unlawful, contrary to the purity of our religion; and that writing, acting, or attending them, is inconsistent with the character of a Christian. If this be done with success, it will give great weight to the reflections which shall be added upon the aggravation of the crime, considering the circumstances that at present attend the practice.

But, though I have thus far complied with the unreasonable terms imposed by the advocates for this amusement, they must not proceed to any higher demand, nor expect, because they have prevailed, to have plays considered in the way that they themselves desire, that therefore the same thing must be done by religion, and that it must be lowered down to the descriptions they are sometimes pleased to give of it. I will by no means attack plays upon the principles of modern relaxed morality. In that case, to be sure, it would be a lost cause. If some late writers on the subject of morals be permitted to determine what are the ingredients that must enter into the composition of a good man, that good man, it is agreed, may much more probably be found in the play-house than in any other place. But what belongs to the character of a Christian must be taken from the holy Scriptures, the word of the living God. Notwithstanding therefore, that through the great degeneracy of the age, and very culpable relaxation of discipline, not a few continue to be called Christians, who are a reproach to the name, and support and countenance one another in many practices contrary to the purity of the Christian profession, I shall beg leave still to recur to the unerring standard, and consider, not what many nominal Christians are, but what every real Christian ought to be.

In so doing I think I shall reason justly; and at the same time it is my resolution, not only to speak the sense, but, as often as possible, the very language and phrases of the Scripture, and of our pious fathers. These are either become venerable to me for their antiquity, or they are much fitter for expressing the truths of the gospel, and delineating the character and duty of a disciple of Christ, than any that have been invented in latter times. As the growth or decay of vegetable nature is often so gradual as to be insensible; so in the moral world, verbal alterations, which are counted as nothing, do often introduce real changes, which are firmly established before their approach is so much as suspected. Were the style, not only of some modern essays, but of some modern sermons, to be introduced upon this subject, it would greatly weaken the argument, though no other alteration should be made. Should we every where put virtue for holiness, honor, or even moral sense for conscience, improvement of the heart for sanctification, the opposition between such things and theatrical entertainments would not appear half so sensible.

By taking up the argument in the light now proposed, I am saved, in a great measure, from the repetition of what has been written by other authors on the subject. But let it be remembered, that they have clearly and copiously shewn the corruption and impurity of the stage, and its adherents, since its first institution, and that both in the heathen and Christian world. They have made it undeniably appear, that it was opposed and condemned by the best and wisest men, both heathens and Christians in every age.[1] Its very defenders do all pretend to blame the abuse of it. They do indeed alledge that this abuse is not essential to it, but may be separated from it; however, all of them, so far as I have seen,

---

1. Particularly at Athens, where it first had its birth, both tragedy and comedy were soon abolished by public authority; and among the Romans, though this and other public shows were permitted in a certain degree, yet so cautious were that wise people of suffering them to be frequent, that they did not permit any public theatre, when occasionally erected, to continue above a certain number of days. Even that erected by M. Scaurus, which is said to have cost so immense a sum as a million sterling, was speedily taken down. Pompey the Great was the first who had power and credit enough to get a theatre continued.

The opinion of Seneca may be seen in the following passage:—"Nihil est tam damnosum bonis moribus, quam in aliquo spectaculo desidere. Tunc enim per voluptatem facilius vitia surrepunt."

As to the primitive Christians, see Constit. Apost. lib. 8. cap. 32. where actors and stage-players are enumerated among those who are not to be admitted to baptism. Many different councils appoint that they shall renounce their arts before they be admitted, and if they return to them shall be excommunicated. Te Tullian de Spectaculis, cap. 22. observes, That the heathens themselves marked them with infamy, and excluded them from all honors and dignity. To the same purpose see Aug. de Civ. Dei. lib. 2. cap. 14. "Actores poeticarum fabularum removent a societate civitatis—ab honoribus omnibus repellunt homines scenicos."

The opinion of moderns is well known, few Christian writers of any eminence having failed to pronounce sentence against the stage.

represent this separation as only possible or future; they never attempt to assign any aera in which it could be defended as it then was, or could be affirmed to be more profitable than hurtful. Some writers do mention a few particular plays of which they give their approbation. But these have never yet, in any age or place, amounted to such a number, as to keep one society of players in constant employment, without a mixture of many more that are confessedly pernicious. The only reason of bringing this in view at present when it is not to be insisted on, is, that it ought to procure a fair and candid hearing to this attempt to prove, That the stage, after the greatest improvement of which it is capable, is still inconsistent with the purity of the Christian profession. It is a strong presumptive evidence in favor of this assertion, that, after so many years trial, such improvement has never actually taken place.

It is perhaps also proper here to obviate a pretence, in which the advocates of the stage greatly glory, that there is no express prohibition of it to be found in scripture. I think a countryman of our own[2] has given good reasons to believe, that the apostle Paul, in his epistle to the Ephesians, chap. v. ver. 4. by "filthiness, foolish talking and jesting," intended to prohibit the plays that were then in use. He also thinks it probable, that the word [Komois], used in more places than one, and translated "revelling," points at the same thing. Whether his conjectures are just or not, it is very certain that these, and many other passages, forbid the abuses of the stage; and if these abuses be inseparable from it, as there is reason to believe, there needed no other prohibition of them to every Christian. Nay, if they never had been separated from it till that time, it was sufficient; and it would be idle to expect that the scripture should determine this problematical point, Whether they would ever be so in any after age. To ask that there should be produced a prohibition of the stage, as a stage, universally, is to prescribe to the Holy Ghost, and to require that the scripture should not only forbid sin, but every form in which the restless and changeable dispositions of men shall think fit to be guilty of it, and every name by which they shall think proper to call it. I do not find in scripture any express prohibition of masquerades, routs and drums; and yet I have not the least doubt, that the assemblies called by these names, are contrary to the will of God, and as bad, if not worse, than the common and ordinary entertainments of the stage.

In order to make this inquiry as exact and accurate as possible, and that the strength or weakness of the arguments on either side, may be clearly perceived, it will be proper to state distinctly, what we understand by the stage, or stage-plays, when it is affirmed, that in their most improved and best regulated state, they are unlawful to Christians. This is the more necessary, that there is a great indistinctness and ambiguity in the langauge used by those who, in writing or conversation, undertake to defend it. They analyze and divide it into parts, and take sometimes one part, sometimes another, as will best suit their purpose. They ask, What there can be unlawful in the stage abstractedly considered? Comedy is exposing the folly of vice, and pointing out the ridiculous part of every character. And is not this commendable? Is not ridicule a noble means of discountenancing vice? And is not the use of it warranted by the satire and irony that is to be found in the holy scriptures? Tragedy, they say, is promoting the same end in a way more grave and solemn. It is a moral lecture, or a moral picture, in which virtue appears to great advantage. What is history itself, but representing the characters of men as they actually were, and plays represent them as they may be. In their perfection, plays are as like history and nature, as the poet's art and actor's skill can make them. Is it then the circumstance of their being written in dialogue, that renders them criminal? Who will pretend that? Is it that they are publicly repeated or acted over? Will any one pretend, that it is a crime to personate a character in any case, even where no deceit is intended? Then farewel parables, figures of speech, and the whole oratorial art. Is it a sin to look upon the representation? Then it must be a sin to look upon the world, which is the original, of which plays are the copy.

This is the way which those who appear in defence of the stage ordinarily take, and it is little better than if one should say, What is a stage-play? It is nothing else abstractedly considered but a company of men and women talking together; Where is the harm in that? What hinders them from talking piously and profitably, as well as wickedly or hurtfully? But, rejecting this method of reasoning as unjust and inconclusive, let it be observed, that those who plead for the lawfulness of the stage in any country, however well regulated, plead for what implies, not by accident, but essentially and of necessity the following things. (1.) Such a number of plays as will furnish an habitual course of representations, with such changes as the love of variety in human nature necessarily requires. (2.) These plays of such a kind, as to procure an audience of

2. The late Mr. Anderson.

voluntary spectators, who are able and willing to pay for being so entertained. (3.) A company of hired players, who have this as their only business and occupation, that they may give themselves wholly to it, and be expert in the performance. (4.) The representation must be so frequent as the profits may defray the expence of the apparatus, and maintain those who follow this business. They must also be maintained in that measure of luxury, or elegance, if you please, which their way of life, and the thoughts to which they are accustomed must make them desire and require. It is a thing impracticable to maintain a player at the same expence as you may maintain a peasant.

Now all these things do, and must enter into the idea of a well regulated stage; and, if any defend it without supposing this, he hath no adversary that I know of. Without these there may be poets, or there may be plays, but there cannot be a playhouse. It is in vain then to go about to show, that there have been an instance or two, or may be, of treatises wrote in the form of plays that are unexceptionable. It were easy to shew very great faults in some of those most universally applauded, but this is unnecessary. I believe it is very possible to write a treatise in the form of a dialogue, in which the general rules of the drama are observed, which shall be as wholly and serious, as any sermon that ever was preached or printed. Neither is there any apparent impossibility in getting different persons to assume the different characters, and rehearse it in society. But it may be safely affirmed, that if all plays were of that kind, and human nature to continue in its present state, the doors of the play-house would shut of their own accord, because nobody would demand access;[3] unless there were an act of parliament to force attendance, and even in that case, as much pains would probably be taken to evade the law obliging to attend, as are now taken to evade those that command us to abstain. The fair and plain state of this question then is, Whether it is possible or practicable, in the present state of human nature, to have the above system of things under so good a regulation, as to make the erecting and countenancing the stage agreeable to the will of God, and consistent with the purity of the Christian profession.

And here let us consider a little, what is the primary, and immediate intention of the stage, whether it be for amusement and recreation, or for instruction to make men wise and good. Perhaps, indeed the greatest part will choose to compound these two purposes together, and say it is for both: for amusement immediately, and for improvement ultimately, that it instructs by pleasing, and reforms by stealth. The patrons of a well regulated stage have it no doubt in their power to profess any of these ends in it they please, if it is equally capable of them all; and therefore in one part or other of this discourse, it must be considered in every one of these lights. But as it is of moment, because of some of the arguments to be afterwards produced, let the reader be pleased to consider, how far recreation and amusement enter into the nature of the stage, and are, not only immediately and primarily, but chiefly and ultimately intended by it.

If the general nature of it, or the end proposed from it when well regulated, can be any way determined from its first institution, and the subsequent practice, it seems plainly to point at amusement. The earliest productions of that kind that are now extant, are evidently incapable of any other use, and hardly even of that to a person of any taste or judgment.[4] They usually accompanied the feasts of the ancients in the houses of the rich and opulent,[5] and were particularly used in times of public rejoicing. They have indeed generally been considered, in all ages, as intended for entertainment. A modern author of high rank and reputation,[6] who would not willingly hurt the cause, considers them in this light, and this alone, and represents their improvement, not as lying in their having a greater moral tendency, but in the perfection of the poet's

---

3. This furnishes an easy answer to what is remarked by some in favor of plays, that several eminent Christians have endeavored to supplant bad plays by writing good ones; as Gregory Nazienzen a father of the church, and a person of great piety, and our countryman Buchanan. But did ever these plays come into repute? Were they formerly, or are they now acted upon the stage? the fate of their works proves that these good men judged wrong in attempting to reform the stage, and that the great majority of Christians acted more wisely who were for laying it wholly aside.

4. This is confessed by a defender of the stage, who says, "Such of the comedies before his (that is Menander's) time, as have been preserved to us, are generally very poor pieces, not so much ludicrous as ridiculous, even a mountebank's merry andrew would be hissed, now a days, for such puerilities as we see abounding in Aristophanes." Rem. on Anderson's Positions concerning the unlawfulness of stage-plays, page 8th.

5. Plut. de Glor. Athens & Sympos. lib. 7. quest. 8. "As for the new comedy, it is so necessary an ingredient of all public entertainments, that so to speak, one may as well make a feast without wine, as without Menander."

6. Shaftsbury.

art, and the refinement of the taste of the audience. It is only of late that men have begun to dignify them with a higher title. Formerly they were ever considered as an indulgence of pleasure, and an article of luxury, but now they are exalted into schools of virtue, and represented as bulwarks against vice. It is probable, most readers will be apt to smile when they hear them so called, and to say to their defenders, This is but overdoing, preserve them to us as innocent amusements, and we shall not much contend for their usefulness. It is indeed but an evidence of the distress of the cause, for their advocates only take up this plea when they are unable to answer the arguments against them upon any other footing. It may also appear that they are designed for amusement, if we consider who have been the persons in all ages who have attended them, viz. the rich, the young, and the gay, those who live in pleasure, and the very business of whose lives is amusement.

But not to insist on these circumstances, I think it is plain from the nature of the thing, that the immediate intention of plays is to please, whatever effects may be pretended to flow afterwards, or by accident, from this pleasure. They consist in an exact imitation of nature, and the conformity of the personated to real characters. This is the great aim, and the great perfection, both of the poet and of the actors. Now this imitation, of itself, gives great pleasure to the spectator, whether the actions represented are good or bad. And, in itself considered, it gives only pleasure; for the beauty of the imitation, as such, hath no moral influence, nor any connection with morality, but what it may derive in a distant way from the nature of the actions which the poet or actors choose to represent, or the spectators are willing to see. Every person who thinks impartially, may be from this convinced, that to please, or attempt to do so, is essential to the stage, and its first, or rather its main design; how far it pollutes or purifies is accidental, and must depend upon the skill and honesty of its regulators and managers.

Having thus prepared the way, the following arguments are humbly offered to the consideration of every serious person, to shew, that a public theatre is inconsistent with the purity of the Christian profession: which if they do not to all appear to be each of them singly conclusive, will I hope, when taken together, sufficiently evince the truth of the proposition.

In the first place, If it be considered as an amusement, it is improper, and not such as any Christian may lawfully use. Here we must begin by laying it down as a fundamental principle, that all men are bound supremely to love, and habitually to serve God; that is to say, to take his law as the rule, and his glory as the end, not of one, but of all their actions. No man, at any time or place is, nor can be, absolved from this obligation. Every real Christian lives under an habitual sense of it. I know this expression, aiming, at the glory of God, is called a cant phrase, and is despised and derided by worldly men. It were easy however, to vindicate it from reason; but it will suffice, to all those for whose use this discourse is intended, to say, It is a truth taught and repeated in the sacred oracles, that all things were made for, that all things shall finally tend to, and therefore, that all intelligent creatures should supremely and uniformly aim at the glory of God.

Now, we glorify God by cultivating holy dispositions, and doing pious and useful actions. Recreation is an intermission of duty, and is only necessary because of our weakness; it must be some action indifferent in its nature, which becomes lawful and useful from its tendency to refresh the mind, and invigorate it for duties of more importance. The use of recreation is precisely the same as the use of sleep; though they differ in this, that there is but one way in which sleep becomes sinful, viz. by excess, whereas there are ten thousand ways in which recreations become sinful. It is needless to produce passages of Scripture to verify the above assertion concerning our obligation to glorify God. It is the language of the whole, and is particularly applied to indifferent actions by the apostle Paul, I Cor. x. 13. "Whether therefore ye eat or drink, or whatsoever ye do, do all to the glory of God."

If there were on the minds of men in general, a just sense of this their obligation, stage-plays, nay, and a thousand other amusements now in use, would never have been heard of. The truth is, the need of amusement is much less than people commonly apprehend, and, where it is not necessary, it must be sinful. Those who stand in need of recreation may be divided into two sorts, such as are employed in bodily labor, and such as have their spirits often exhausted by study and application of mind. As to the first of these, a mere cessation from labor is sufficient for refreshment, and indeed of itself gives great pleasure, unless when the appetites are inflamed and iritated by frequent sensual gratifications; and then they are importunately craved, and become necessary to fill the intervals of work. Of this sort very few are able to afford so expensive a recreation as the stage. And even as to the other, viz. those whose spirits are exhausted by application of mind, only a very small number of them will chuse the diversion of the stage, for this very good reason, that social converse and bodily exercise, will answer the purpose much better. Indeed, if we consider the just and legitimate end of recreations, and compare it with the persons who most frequently engage in them, we shall find, that ninety-nine of every hundred are such as do not need recreation at all. Perhaps their time lies heavy upon their hands, and they feel an uneasiness and impatience under their present state; but this is not from work, but from idleness, and from the emptiness and unsatisfying nature of the enjoyments, which they chase with so much eagerness, one after another, vainly seeking from them that good which they do not contain, and that satisfaction which they cannot impart.

From this I think it undeniably appears, that if no body were to attend the stage, but such as really needed recreation or amusement, upon Christian principles, and of these such only as were able to pay for it, and of these only such as did themselves chuse it, there is not a place this day in the world so large as to afford a daily audience. It will be immediately objected, This argument, make as much of it as you please, is not compleat, for it hinders not but that some, however few, may attend in a proper manner, and with warrantable views. But let it be remembered, that I attack not a play singly as a play, nor one person for being a witness to a thing of that nature, but the stage as a system containing all the branches I have enumerated above. This cannot subsist without a full audience, and frequent attendance; and therefore is, by its constitution, a constant and powerful invitation to sin, and cannot be maintained but by the commission of it. Perhaps some will still object, that this argument is too finely spun, that it seems to demand perfection, and to find fault with every practice, in which there is a probability that sin will be committed. That, if this holds, we should no more contribute to the establishment of churches than play-houses, because we have a moral certainty, that no congregation ever will meet together on earth, but much sin will be committed, both by minister and people. But there is a great difference between a commanded duty which is attended with sin by defect, and what is no where commanded, which necessarily invites to sin by its nature, and is in substance sinful to the great majority of those who attend it.

But further, the stage is an improper, that is to say, an unlawful recreation to all without exception, because it consumes too much time. This is a circumstance which, however little impression it may make upon those who find their time often a burden, will appear of the greatest moment to every serious Christian. In proportion as any man improves in holiness of heart, he increases in usefulness of life, and acquires a deeper and stronger sense of the worth and value of time. To spend an hour unprofitably, appears to such a person a greater crime, than to many the commission of gross sin. And, indeed it ought to appear very heinous in the eyes of those who believe the representation given by our Lord Jesus Christ, of his own procedure at the day of judgment, "Cast ye the UNPROFITABLE servant into utter darkness, where there shall be weeping and wailing, and gnashing of teeth." Matt. xxv. 30. Mark this, ye lovers of pleasure, ye sons of gaiety and mirth, who imagine you are sent into the world for no higher end than your own entertainment; and who, if you are free from, or able any how to palliate your grosser sins, never once reflect on the heavy account against you of wasted time.

Though there were no other objection against the stage as a recreation, but this one, it is surely faulty. If recreations are only lawful because necessary, they must cease to be lawful when they are no longer necessary. The length and duration of regular comedy and tragedy is already fixed and settled by rules of long standing; and, I suppose, whatever other circumstance may be confessed to need reformation, all men of taste will agree, that these shall continue as they are. Now I leave to all who know how much time the preparation for such a public appearance, and the necessary attendance, must take up, to judge, whether it is not too much to be given to mere recreation.

This holds particularly in the case of recreation of mind, between which and bodily exercise there is a very great difference. For bodily exercise in some cases, for example, when the health requires it, may be continued for a long time, only for this reason, that it may have effects lasting in proportion to the time spent in it. But giving the mind to pleasure by way of recreation must be short, or it is certainly hurtful; it gives men a habit of idleness and trifling, and makes them averse from returning to any thing that requires serious application. So true is this, and so applicable to the present case, that I could almost rest the whole argument upon it, that no man, who has made the trial, can deliberately and with a good conscience affirm, that attending plays has added strength to his mind, and warmth to his affections, in the duties of devotion; that it has made him more able and willing to exert his intellectual powers in the graver and more important offices of the Christian life; nay, or even made him more diligent and active in the business of civil life. On the contrary, it is commonly to such length as to produce a satiety and weariness of itself, and to require rest and refreshment to recruit the exhausted spirits, a thing quite absurd and self-contradictory in what is called a recreation.

But the stage is not merely an unprofitable consumption of time, it is further improper as a recreation, because it agitates the passions too violently, and interests too deeply, so as, in some cases, to bring people into a real, while they behold an imaginary distress. Keeping in view the end of recreations, will enable us to judge rightly of this. It is to refresh and invigorate the mind.—Therefore when, instead of rest, which is properly called relaxation of mind, recreations are used, their excellence consists in their being, not only a pleasant, but an easy exercise of the intellectual powers. Whatever is difficult, and either requires or causes a strong application of mind, is contrary to their intention. Now it is plain, that dramatic representations fix the attention so very deeply, and interest the affections so very strongly, that, in a little time, they fatigue the mind themselves, and however eagerly are they desired and followed, there are many serious and useful occupations, in which men will continue longer, without exhausting the spirits, than in attending the theatre.

Indeed, in this respect they are wholly contrary to what should be the view of every Christian. He ought to set bounds to, and endeavor to moderate his passions as much as possible, instead of voluntarily and unnecessarily exciting them. The human passions, since the fall, are all of them but too strong; and are not sinful on account of their weakness, but their excess and misapplication. This is so generally true, that it hardly admits of an exception; unless it might be counted an exception, that some vicious passions, when they gain an ascendancy, extinguish others which oppose their gratification. For, though religion is consistent throughout, there are many vices, which are mutually repugnant to, and destructive of, each other. But this exception has little or no effect upon the present argument.

Now the great care of every Christian, is to keep his passions and affections within due bounds, and to direct them to their proper objects. With respect to the first of these, the chief influence of theatrical representations upon the spectator, is to strengthen the passions by indulgence; for there they are all exhibited in a lively manner, and such as is most fit to communicate the impression. As to directing them to their proper objects, it will be afterwards shown, that the stage has rather the contrary effect; in the mean time, it is sufficient to observe, that it may be done much more effectually, and much more safely another way.

This tendency of plays to interest the affections, shows their impropriety as a recreation on another account. It shows that they must be exceeding liable to abuse by excess, even supposing them in a certain degree to be innocent. It is certain there is no life more unworthy of a man, hardly any more criminal in a Christian, than a life of perpetual amusement, a life where no valuable purpose is pursued, but the intellectual faculties wholly employed in purchasing and indulging sensual gratifications. It is also certain, that all of us are by nature too much inclined thus to live to ourselves, and not to God. Therefore, where recreations are necessary, a watchful Christian will particularly beware of those that are insnaring, and, by being too grateful and delicious, ready to lead to excess. This discriminating care and caution, is just as much the duty of a Christian, as any that can be named. Though it is immediately conversant only about the temptations and incitements to sin, and not the actual commission of it, it becomes a duty directly binding, both from the command of God, and the necessity of the thing itself. "Watch and pray, that ye enter not into temptation," Mat. xxvi. 41. says our Saviour to all his disciples; and elsewhere, "What I say unto you, I say unto all, Watch," Mark xiii. 37. And the apostle Paul to the same purpose, "See then that ye walk circumspectly, not as fools, but as wise, redeeming the time because the days are evil," Eph. v. 15.

If we consider the light in which the Scripture sets our present situation, and the account there given of the weakness of human resolution, the same thing will evidently appear to be our duty. It is impossible that we can resist the slightest temptation, but by the assistance of divine grace. Now how can this be expected, if we put our constancy to unnecessary trials, not only contrary to reason, and a prudent regard to our own safety, but in the face of an express command of God to be watchful. "Lord, lead us not into temptation," is a petition which we are taught to offer up, by him who knew what was in man. But how much do those act in opposition to this, and even in comtempt of it, who make temptations to themselves. And are not stage-plays temptations of the strongest kind, in which the mind is softened with pleasure, and the affections powerfully excited? How little reason is there to hope that men in the use of them will keep within the bounds of moderation? If any expect, in such circumstances, to be preserved by divine power, they are guilty of the sin, which is in Scripture called "tempting God."

It is this very circumstance, a liableness to abuse by excess, that renders many other amusements also ordinarily unlawful to Christians, though, perhaps, in their general nature, they cannot be shown to be criminal. Thus it is not easy to refute the reasonings, by which ingenious men endeavor to show that games of hazard are not in themselves sinful; but by their enticing, insnaring nature, and the excess which almost inseparably accompanies them, there can be no difficulty in pronouncing them highly dangerous, lawful to very few persons, and in very few cases. And, if they were as public in their nature as plays, if they required the concurrence of as many operators, and as great a number of persons to join in them, I could have little scruple in affirming, that, in every possible case, they would be sinful.

The preceding considerations are greatly confirmed by the following, That when plays are chosen as a recreation, for which they are so exceedingly improper, it is always in opposition to other methods of recreation, which are perfectly fit for the purpose, and not liable to any of these objections. Where recreations are necessary, if there were only one sort to be had, some inconveniences could not be so strong an argument against the use of them. But where there are different kinds, to prefer those which are less, to those which are more fit, must needs be sinful. Such a tenderness and circumspection is indeed, in this age, so rare and unusual, that I am afraid, it will be almost impossible to fix a sense of its importance upon the mind of the reader; or, if it be done, in any measure for a time, the example of a corrupt world, who are altogether void of it, will immediately efface the impression. But however few may "have ears to hear it," the thing is certain, that as the progress of his sanctification is the supreme desire and care of every Christian, so he is continually liable to be seduced by temptation, and infected by example; and therefore, from a distrust of his own resolution, will not voluntarily and unnecessarily prefer a dangerous to a safe amusement. To prefer a very difficult and doubtful means of attaining any worldly end, to one sure and easy; to prefer a clumsy improper instrument, to one perfectly fit for any piece of work, would be reckoned no small evidence of folly in the affairs of civil life. If one in sickness should chuse a medicine of a very questionable nature, of very dangerous and uncertain operation, when he had equal access to one intirely safe, of approved reputation and superior efficacy, it would be esteemed next to madness. Is there not then a real conformity between the cases? Is not a like care to be taken of our souls as of our bodies? Nay, is not the obligation so much the stronger, by how much the one is of greater value than the other? The different conduct of men, and their different fate in this respect, is well described by the wise man, "Happy is the man that feareth alway, but he that hardeneth his heart shall fall into mischief," Prov. xxviii. 14....

From "Lectures on Eloquence"

Lecture 1

We are now to enter on the study of eloquence, or as perhaps it ought to be called, from the manner in which you will find it treated, Composition, Taste, and Criticism.

Eloquence is undoubtedly a very noble art, and when possessed in a high degree, has been I think in all ages, one of the most admired and envied talents. It has not only been admired in all ages, but if I am not mistaken, among all ranks. Its power is universally felt, and therefore probably the talent more universally esteemed, than either genius or improvement in several other kinds of human excellence. Military skill, and political wisdom, have their admirers, but far inferior in number to those who admire, envy, or would wish to imitate him that has the power of persuasion.

Plato in his republic, or idea of a well regulated state, has banished orators, under pretence, that their power over the minds of men, is dangerous and liable to abuse. Some moderns have adopted the same sentiments.

Sir Thomas More in his Utopia I believe, (though I am not certain) has embraced it. But this is a manner of thinking and reasoning altogether superficial. It would militate equally against all cultivation of the mind, and indeed against every human excellence, natural and acquired. They are, and have been, and may be abused by men of vicious dispositions. But how shall this be prevented? It is impossible. How shall it be counteracted? Only by assisting the good in the cultivation of their powers, and then the same weapons will be used in defence of truth and virtue, with much greater advantage, than they can be in support of falsehood and vice. Learning in general possessed by a bad man is unspeakably pernicious, and that very thing has sometimes made, weak people speak against learning but it is just as absurd as if in the confines of a country exposed to hostile inroads, the inhabitants should say, we will build no forts for protection, because if the enemy get into possession of them, they will become the means of anoyance, we will use no arms for defence; for if the enemy take them from us, they will be turned against us.

Perhaps it may be proper to take notice of what the apostle Paul says in his first epistle to the Corinthians, in several places, particularly from the beginning of the 2d chapter "and I brethren," &c. and in the 4th chap. 11 verse, "And my speech, and my preaching was not," &c. I have mentioned this to prevent any of you mistaking or being prejudiced against the subject, and shall observe upon it, that the meaning of the apostle in this and other similar passages is fully comprehended in one or more of the following particulars (1) That he came not to the Corinthians with an artful delusive eloquence, such as the sophists of these days made use of, to varnish over their foolish sentiments. (2) That he came not to show his skill in speaking for and against any thing, as many of them did not to discover or communicate truth, but to display their own talents. (3) That the truths he had to communicate needed no ornaments to set them off, and were not by any means adapted to the proud spirit of the world, and, (4) that he would use the greatest self denial, and not by any means attempt to recommend himself as a man of ability and learning, but content himself with the humble and simple doctrine of the cross. And the truth is, after the highest improvement in the art of speaking, there must be the greatest reserve and self denial in the use of it, otherwise it will defeat its own purpose. Rhetoricians do usually give it among the very precepts of the art to appear to be in earnest, and to have the subject or the interest of the audience at heart, and not their own fame; and this can never be attained to so great perfection as when there is the humility of a true disciple, and the disinterested zeal of a faithful minister of Christ. That this is not contrary to the most diligent application for the improvement of our powers is manifest in itself, and appears from the many exhortations of the same apostle to his young disciples, Timothy and Titus, 1 Tim. iv. 13. "till I come give attendance," &c. and v. 15. "meditate," &c.

I know not whether any apology is necessary for my undertaking to speak on this subject or the manner of treating it. Some may expect that discourses on eloquence should be distinguished examples of the art of which they treat. Such may just be pleased to observe, that a cool, plain, and simple manner of speaking, is necessary in teaching this, as well as every other art. No doubt, a justness and precision of expression, will be of great benefit in these discourses, but there will be no need of that high and complete polish that might be expected in what is prepared for publication. Nor would the same brevity and conciseness, be any advantage to discourses once delivered, that would be reckoned a beauty in what is in every body's hands, and therefore may be often read.

Before entering on the strict and methodical discussion of the subject, I have commonly begun the course by two or three preliminary discourses, containing such general observations as may be most intelligible, and may serve to prepare the way for what shall be afterwards introduced.

The subject of the first preliminary discourse, shall be the following question; whether does art or nature, contribute most to the production of a complete orator?

This is a question often asked, and many things have been said upon it; yet to discuss it as a matter of controversy, and adduce the arguments on each side, in order to a decision in favor of the one, and prejudice of the other, I take to be of very little consequence, or rather improper and absurd. It seems to be just as if one should propose an inquiry, whether the soil, the climate, or the culture, contributes most to the production of the crop? Therefore, instead of treating the question as if one side of it were true, and the other false, I shall make a few observations on the mutual influence of nature and art, in order to your forming just apprehensions of the subject, and to direct you in your future conduct and studies.

1. Some degree of natural capacity is evidently necessary to the instruction or study of this art, in order to produce any effect. A skilful laborer may subdue a very stubborn, or meliorate a very poor soil; but when there is no soil at all, as on a bare and sollid rock, his labor would be impossible or fruitless. There must therefore doubtless be some capacity, in general, and even some turn for this very branch of knowledge. In this sense it is true of every other art as well as oratory, a man must be born to it.

There are some so destitute of oratorical powers, that nothing can possibly be made of them. It will be strange however, if this is not easily discovered by themselves, and if it does not make the study as unpleasant as it is difficult, so that they will speedily give it over. I have known some examples, but very few, of ministers, whose principal defect was mere barrenness of invention. This is exceedingly rare, because the far greatest number of bad speakers have enough to say, such as it is, and generally the more absurd and incoherent, the greater the abundance.

When speaking on this observation, I must make one remark, that a total want of capacity for one branch of science, is not inconsistent even with a great capacity for another. We sometimes see great mathematicians who make miserable orators. Nay it is reckoned by some of the best judges that this study is unfriendly to oratory. The definite precision of mathematical ideas, which may all be ultimately referred to mensuration, seems to be contrary to the freedom and boldness of imagination, in which the strength of oratory lies. There are, however, exceptions to this in fact. Dr. Clark and Dr. Barrow, two of the most eminent mathematicians of the last age, were also eminent orators, that is to say, the first was a very accurate writer, the other a very fervent preacher.

I have only further to observe, that many have thought academical teaching not to be favorable to oratory; that is to say, those who are accustomed to the cool dispassionate manner of speaking, usual and necessary in the instruction of youth, frequently lose a good deal of that fire and impetuosity which they might naturally possess, and which is of so much importance in speaking to a large and promiscuous assembly.

2. To make what is called a complete orator, very great natural powers are necessary, and great cultivation too. The truth is, when we speak of a complete orator, we generally form an idea of perfection superior to any thing that ever existed, by assembling together all the excellencies of every kind that have been seen in different persons, or that we are able from what we have seen to form an imagination of. We can easily enumerate many of these, for example, great penetration of mind—great literature and extensive knowledge—a strong and lively imagination reined in by a correctness of judgment, a rich invention, and retentive memory, tenderness and sensibility of affection, an acquaintance with the world, and a thorough knowledge of the human heart. To these we must add all external perfections, an open countenance, a graceful carriage, a clear articulate strong melodious voice. There is not one of these but is capable of great improvement by application and study, as well as by much practice. In all the great orators of whom we read, there appears to have been an union of natural talents and acquired skill, Pericles, Demosthenes, Cicero, Hortensius. To these you may add all the speakers mentioned by Cicero and Quintilian, taking their talents and performances to have been as related by these authors.

3. Perhaps the most extraordinary appearances in this, as well as in other branches, have been from nature wholly, or but with little study. These spontaneous productions are as so many prodigies. It is commonly believed that the orators and sages at the first formation of society, were more powerful in their elocution than in more polished times. This, however, I am apt to think is in some degree founded on a mistake. There might be more extraordinary effects of eloquence, because the ignorant or superstitious herd were then more easily moved, but this was as much owing to the state of the audience as the power of the speakers. The same fire that would burn a heap of dry brush, would not make any impression upon a heap of green logs. It might also be owing to another circumstance, which I shall have occasion afterwards to explain more fully, the narrowness of language and the use of figures, which have so great an effect upon the imagination.

But allowing very great force to uncultivated prodigies of genius in every kind, I am apt to think it is less powerful, comparatively speaking, in oratory than in poetry. It has been an old saying, Poeta nascitur & non fit. There are two reasons why the poetry of nature, without art, seems to be so much admired. 1. That in such a poet a strong unbounded fancy must be the prevailing character, and this is what chiefly captivates the mind. It must be a very strong inward impulse that induces a man to become a poet without example, and without instruction. 2. It is found in fact that the knowledge of the rules of art some how cramps and deters the mind, and restrains that boldness, or happy extravagance, that gives such general delight. It is an observation of an ingenious author, that in no polished nation after the rules of criticism were fully settled and generally understood, was there ever any great work of genius produced. This, however, must be understood chiefly of what are called the higher species of poetry, epic poetry and tragedy, and for the reasons just now given it must be so in them. Homer is the great poet of nature, and it is generally thought that there is greater fire in him than in Virgil, just because he lived at a time when the rules of writing were unknown. The same thing is said of Shakespeare, of our own country, and perhaps the late discovered poems of Ossian may be considered as another example. After all, perhaps the comparison made between the effects of nature and art, is at bottom wrong, and that they produce beauties of different kinds—A wild uncultivated forest, a vast precipice or steep cataract or waterfall, is supposed to be an object more august and striking, than any ornaments produced by human skill. The order and symmetry however, of architecture and gardening are highly pleasing, and ought not properly to be compared with the other, as pleasing the imagination in a different degree, so much as in a different kind.

The effects of the poetry of nature, therefore in one view are very great, and continue to be so in all ages, because they touch the soul in one way, which continues to be universally felt: but I doubt much whether eloquence ever arrived at much excellence, without considerable study, or at least previous patterns, on which to form. The first great poets were before all criticism, and before even the polishing of human manners; but the first great orators appeared in improved, civilized states, and were the consequence of the knowledge of mankind, and the study of the human heart.

4. When persons are meanly qualified in point of natural capacity for any art, it is not very proper to attempt to instruct them in it. It is not only difficult to instruct those who have a radical incapacity for any study, but sometimes they are much the worse for application, just as fine clothes and a courtly dress upon a clown renders him unspeakably ridiculous. Some who are utterly void of taste for speaking, after long study, and sometimes even by great literature, become more obscure, more tedious, and more given to swelling and bombast than the most uncultivated person in the world. The want of a fund of good sense and genuine taste, makes ignorant persons fools, and scholars pedants. A plain man will tell you of taking a purge or a dose of physic, and you neither mistake him nor laugh at him. A quack of a physician will tell you of a mucilagenous decoction, to smooth the acid particles, and carry off the acrimonious matter that corrodes and irritates the internal coats of the stomach.

5. In the middle regions of genius, there are often to be found those who reap the greatest benefit from education and study. They improve their powers by exercise, and it is surprising to think what advances are to be made by the force of resolution and application. I might give you many examples of this in the annals of literature; but the one most suited to our purpose is, that Demosthenes himself, is said at first to have labored under almost insuperable difficulties: it is said he could not even pronounce at first, all the letters of the Greek alphabet, particularly the letter R, the first letter of his art, as the critics have called it.

Persons of the middle degrees of capacity, do also, perhaps generally, fill the most useful and important stations in human life. A very great genius, is often like a very fine flower, to be wondered at, but of little service either for food or medicine. A very great genius is also often accompanied with certain irregularities, so that we only consider with regret, what he might have been, if the lively sallies of his imagination had been reined in a little, and kept under the direction of sober judgment.

On the whole, you may plainly perceive what great encouragement there is for diligence in your studies, and be persuaded to attend to the instructions to be given you on this subject in particular, with assiduity and care.

Lecture 2

In this, which as the former, I consider as a preliminary discourse, I will endeavor to give you some general rules, which as they belong equally to all sorts of writing, would not come in so properly under the divisions of the subject.

1. Study and imitate the greatest examples. Get the most approved authors for composition, read them often and with care. Imitation is what commonly gives us our first ideas upon any subject. It is by example that ambition is kindled, and youth prompted to excel. It is by remarks upon actual productions, that criticism itself is formed. Men were not first taught by masters to speak, either in oratory or poesy; but they first felt the impulse, and did as they could, and their reflection and observation, by making the comparison, found out what was best. And after the existence of precepts, it is by examples that precepts are made plain and intelligible. An acquaintance with authors, will also be the best mean of determining what is your own turn and capacity, for you will probably most relish those writers and that manner, that you are best able to imitate.

For this purpose, let the best authors be chosen, ancient and modern. A controversy has often risen among critics and men of letters, upon the preference being due to ancient or modern writers. This question was debated in professo, in the last age, and some very great men engaged in it. The famous M. Fenelon, arch-bishop of Cambray, has written a treatise upon it, called the Wars of the poets; and Dean Swift wrote his account of the battle of the books in St. James library, on the same subject. I reckon it is wrong to be opinionative in such a controversy, and very easy to push it to excess on both sides. No doubt the few remains of remote antiquity, have survived the wrecks of time, in a great measure by their excellence itself, and therefore will always be considered as standards. And as they are chiefly works of imagination that have been so preserved, and true taste is the same in all ages, they must deserve real esteem, and this will be somewhat augmented, by the veneration felt for their antiquity itself. Homer is the first and great pattern of writing, to whom the highest commendations have been given in every age. Horace says, Vos exemplaria Greca (meaning chiefly Homer) nocturna versate manu, versate diurna; and Mr. Pope says, "Be Homer's works your study and delight, Read him by day, and meditate by night."

Now the beauties of Homer we are easily capable of perceiving, though perhaps not his faults. The beauty of a description, the force of a similitude, we can plainly see; but whether he always adhered to truth and nature, we cannot tell, because we have no other way of knowing the manners and customs of his times but from what he has written.

The powers of mankind, however, are certainly the same in all ages, but change of circumstances may create diversity in the appearance and productions of genius. These circumstances tend to produce excellence of different kinds. The boldness, and almost excessive flights of imagination in uncultivated times, give way to beauties of a different nature, to order, judgment and precision. A masterly judgment will endeavor to understand the reasons on both sides. It is certain, however, that there are great and excellent patterns to form upon both ancient and modern. And it is very proper for young persons to read authors, after they have heard criticisms and remarks made upon them. These criticisms you may take at first either from books or conversation. Try if you can observe the genius, or peculiar and characteristic turn of an author, not only his excellencies, but wherein they are peculiar to him, and different from those of others. Cicero is flowing, fervent, ornate—Somewhat vain and ostentatious, but masterly in his way. Demosthenes is simple, close, nervous, rapid and irresistible. Livy has a bewitching knack of telling a story, he is so expressive and descriptive, that one cannot help being pleased with it, even after several times reading.

Sallust excels in giving characters, which he strikes off in single epithets, or very concise remarks, Tacitus is chiefly remarkable for judicious and sagacious observations on human life; and Xenophon is superior to almost every author in dignity, elegance, and sweetness in the narration.

Of modern authors in our own language, Mr. Addison is a noble pattern of elegance, dignity and simplicity. Swift in his political pieces, writes with great strength and force, and is perhaps a pattern of style, which has scarcely been exceeded since his time. Harvey in his meditations has a great deal of very lively and animated description, but it is so highly ornamented, that it is somewhat dangerous in the imitation. Dr. Robertson in his history, has as just a mixture of strength and elegance, as any other author I know in the English language. I cannot help here cautioning you against one modern author of some eminence, Johnson the author of the Rambler. He is so stiff and abstracted in his manner and such a lover of hard words, that he is the worst pattern for young persons that can be named.

It has been given sometimes as a rule, to form one's self upon a particular author, who may be most agreeable to a student's taste, and perhaps congenial (if I may speak so,) to his capacity. It is pretty common to fall into this without design, by a natural propensity. It is said that Demosthenes wrote over the history of Thucedides eight times, that he might the more effectually form himself to his style and manner. I cannot say I would recommend this, it seems to be too much honor to give to any one person. I would not be guilty of idolatry of any kind. A comprehensive knowledge of many authors, or at least a considerable number of the best, is certainly far preferable. If there be any advantage in particular imitation it is that it is the easiest way of coming to a fixed or formed style. One will soon run into an imitation of an author with whom he is much conversant, and of whom he is a great admirer, and in this view, to some persons of moderate capacity, it may not be an improper method. But persons of real and original genius, should be rather above such a practice, as it will certainly make them fall short of what they would otherwise attain.

To this we may add, that particular imitation is liable to several very great dangers. (1) It leads to servility of imitation. Such person often may be said to borrow the piece, instead of imitating the pattern. When a servile imitation is perceived, which it always will be, it is certain to be despised. Even a manner ever so excellent, if merely a copy, brings no credit to a speaker. And if a writer retail the very sentiments and language of another, it is considered as an absurdity. (2) Servile imitation leads to copying defects. There neither is, nor ever was any speaker or writer free from defects or blemishes of some kind. Yet servile imitators never fail to copy the defects as well as beauties. I should suppose that any one who made Cicero his particular model, would very probably transfuse a proportion of his vanity and ostentation, and probably more of that than of his fire.

But of all sorts of imitation the most dangerous is the imitation of living speakers, and yet to this young scholars are most prone, sometimes by design, and sometimes quite insensibly. It is attended in the highest degree with the disadvantage of copying defects. In living speakers, there are not only peculiarities of style and blemishes in composition to copy, but in looks, tone and gesture. It is a matter of constant experience, that imitators catch the blemishes easiest, and retain them longest. And it is to be observed, that defects, when they are natural and undesigned, appear very inconsiderable; but when they are copied and adopted voluntarily, we cannot help despising the folly and absurdity of one that judges so ill. Further, when defects are occasional and undesigned, they are generally inconsiderable; but when they are copied they are commonly aggravated and overcharged, and so appear quite monstrous. This must be so; for even the very best manner looks silly in the imitator, although just and graceful in the original.

2. An excellent general rule is to accustom yourselves early and much to composition, and exercise in pronunciation. Practice is necessary in order to learn any thing to perfection. There is something to be learned from practice, which no instruction can impart. It is so in every other art as well as in this—mathematics, geometry and in navigation; after you have learned the theory in the most perfect manner, there is still a nameless something, which nothing but experience can bestow. You must not wait till you are masters of the rules of art before you begin to put them in practice. Exercise must go hand in hand with instruction, that the one may give meaning, force and direction to the other. I do not mean that you should be fond of entering very soon upon real life, but that you should be assiduous in preparatory exercises. This is a rule given by Cicero in his book De Oratore, which he reckons of great importance—*Scribendum quam plurimum,* and he declares it to have been his own practice.

Since we are upon private exercises of composition, it may perhaps give you a clearer view of the matter to mention some of the various ways in which it may be separately tried. It may be tried in translation, perhaps it may be best to try it first here. Translation will accustom you to attend to the various idioms of language, and to understand the genius of your own language: for when translating you will speedily find that to render out of any one language into another, ad verbum, would be very sorry composition. It may be tried also in narration. This I think should be the next step to translation, to learn to give a naked account of facts with simplicity and precision. This, also, though certainly in itself more obvious and easier than some other kinds, yet it is by no means so easy as some imagine. Imitation of a particular passage, or composition of some author, by writing upon something quite similar, may perhaps be the next in order. To understand what this is you need only look into an admirable example of it in poetry, Mr. Pope's imitation of a satire in Horace, beginning Qui virtus & quanta, &c. After this comes description, painting scenes, or drawing characters. Then argumentation: And, lastly, persuasion. I believe it would be a great improvement of the laudable practice in this college of daily orations, if they were chosen with more judgment, and better suited to the performers. Almost all the pieces we have delivered to us are of the last or highest kind, warm passionate declamations. It is no wonder that some should perform these ill, who have never tried the plainer manner of simple narration. Supposing a student to have tried all these ways of composition for his own improvement, would he not be by that means sensible in what way he is most able to excel, as also having made trial of them separately, he is more able to vary his diction, and give compass to his discourse upon a general subject. These are like an analysis or simple division of composition; and as persons read best who have been first taught to resolve words into syllables, and syllables into letters, so the easiest and completest way of any to composition is to begin it in this order.

In such exercises let me by all means recommend to you, early to acquire, and always to preserve a certain patience and resolution of mind, which will enable you to apply with vigor, not only for a time, but to review and correct your pieces, and bring them to some degree of perfection, and your taste to some degree of accuracy. To explain this a little, there are three things equally contrary to it, and perhaps equally prejudicial. (1.) Mere weakness and want of courage, which finding one attempt unsuccessful, will hardly be brought to make another. When a young person first goes to exercise himself in composition, he finds the thing so uncouth and difficult, that he is apt to consider it as altogether impossible. (2.) There is a fault contrary to this, a vanity of mind, which is so pleased with any thing it does as neither to see its own faults, nor be willing to hear them. There are some who, from the beginning of life, think it a great pity that any of their productions should be blotted or erased. It is not to be supposed that they will make great progress in knowledge or taste. (3.) There is another sort perhaps distinct from both, who are of a loose, desultory disposition, so unstaid that they cannot spend long enough time upon any thing to do it well, or sometimes even to bring it to a conclusion. They will begin an essay upon a subject, but are presently out of conceit with it, and therefore will do it very carelessly, or before it is finished must away to another, which struck their fancy more lately.

That steady application which I have recommended some of the ancients were very remarkable for. Some of them indeed seemed to carry it to an excess. They would sometimes spend as much time in polishing an epigram, or little trifling panegyric, as might have been sufficient for the production of a work of extensive utility. However, this is not the most common error; running over a great deal in a superficial way is the bane of composition. Horace, with his usual elegance, ridicules this disposition, when he says, *Detur nobus locus,* &c. and somewhere else he brings in a vain-glorious poet, boasting how many verses he had made, or could make, when standing upon one foot.

Lecture 6

We now proceed to consider eloquence as divided into its three great kinds—the sublime, the simple, and the mixed. This is very unhappily expressed by Ward, who divides style into the low, the middle, and the sublime. Low is a word which in its first and, literal sense, signifies situation, and when applied metaphorically, never is in any instance used in a good sense, but always signifies what is either unhappy, or base and contemptible, as we say a man's or a state's finances are low. We say a man is in a low state of health. We say he is guilty of low, mean practices. A low, mean, paltry style. It was therefore conveying a very wrong idea to make *low* one of the different kinds of style. You may observe that I have introduced this distinction in a manner somewhat different from him, and some other authors. They consider it as a division of style. I choose rather to say there are three different great kinds into which eloquence and composition may be divided. The reason is I believe, the word *style* which was used both by the Greeks and Romans, but especially the latter, has like many others gradually changed its meaning. At first it signified the manner of writing in general, and is even sometimes used so still, but more commonly now in English it is confined to the diction. Nothing is more common than to say sublimity in sentiments and style, so as to distinguish the one from the other. I am sensible that even in this confined sense there is a sublimity, simplicity, and mediocrity in language itself, which will naturally enough fall to be explained, but it is better upon the whole to consider them as different kinds of eloquence for several reasons.

Sublimity in writing consists with all styles, and particularly many of the highest and most admired examples of sublimity are in the utmost simplicity of style. Sometimes they are so far from losing by it, that they owe a great part of their beauty and their force to it. That remarkable example of sublimity in the Scripture, is wholly in the simple style. "Let there be light, and there was light." There are also many others in Scripture, "The gods of the Gentiles are vanity and lies,"—"I am that I am."

Some of the other kinds also, even the simplest, do sometimes admit great force of expression, though more rarely, and there is a great danger in the simple manner of writing by admitting lofty expressions to swell into bombast. The mixed kind frequently admits of sublimity of style, and indeed is called mixed, as consisting, as it were, alternately of the one and the other, or being made up of a proportion of each.

The sublime kind of writing chiefly belongs to the following subjects: epic poetry, tragedy, orations on great subjects, and then particularly the peroration. Nothing can be too great for these subjects, and unless they are treated with sublimity, they are not treated suitably. The simple kind of writing belongs to scientific writing, epistolary writing, essay and dialogue, and to the whole inferior species of poetry, pastorals, epigrams, epitaphs, &c. The mixed kind belongs to history, system, and controversy. The first sort must be always sublime in sentiment or language, or both. The second may be often sublime in sentiment: sometimes, but very rarely in language. The mixed admits of both sorts with full propriety, and may be often sublime both in sentiment and language.

Let us now consider these three great kinds of composition, separately, in the order in which I have named them.

1. Of the sublime manner of writing—This is very difficult to describe or treat of, in a critical manner. It is very remarkable, that all writers on this subject, not excepting those of the greatest judgment, accuracy and precision, when they come to explain it, have used nothing but metaphorical expressions. It is however certain in general, that metaphor should be kept as much as possible out of definition or explication. These all

agreeing therefore in this circumstance, seems to show that sublimity is a single or simple idea, that cannot be resolved, divided or analysed, and that a taste for it, is in a good measure, a feeling of nature. The critics tell us, that sublimity is that which surprises, ravishes, transports: these are words frequently applied to its effects upon the hearers, and greatness, loftiness, majesty, are ascribed to the sentiments, to the character, to the person. An oration, or the sublime parts of a poem, have been compared to the voice of thunder, or penetration of lightning, to the impetuosity of a torrent; this last, is one of the best metaphorical expressions for sublimity in eloquence, because it carries in it, not only the idea of great force, but of carrying away every thing with it that opposes or lies in its way. That may be said to be sublime, that has an irresistible influence on the hearers, and when examined, carries in it the idea of great power and abilities in the speaker: yet even this is not sufficient, it has the character of greatness, as distinct from that of beauty, sweetness or use. Burke, on the sublime, has endeavored to show that sublimity and beauty, though generally united in our apprehensions, are distinct qualities, and to be traced to a different source. Of sublimity in particular, he says it is always allied to such things as raise the passion of terror: but of this I will speak more fully upon a head I have reserved for that purpose; in which I propose to inquire into the first principles of taste or approbation common to this and all other arts.

Longinus mentions no less than five different sources of the sublime. (1) Greatness or elevation of mind. (2) Pathos or passion. (3) Figure. (4) Nobleness of language. (5) Composition or arrangement of words. But though the last two of these are of considerable moment, and greatly contribute to augment the force as well as beauty of a discourse, I do not think they are of that nature, as to be considered upon the same footing with the other three. Therefore leaving what is to be said upon them to the next head, when it will properly occur, I shall consider the others in their order.

1. Greatness or elevation of mind—This is the first and radical source of sublimity indeed. It is quite impossible for a man to attain to sublimity of composition, unless his soul is great, and his conceptions noble: and on the other hand, he that possesses these, can hardly express himself meanly. Longinus gives it as an advice, that a man should accustom his mind to great thought. But if you ask me what are great thoughts, I confess myself unable to explain it, and unless the feeling is natural, I am afraid it is impossible to impart it; yet it seems to be pretty generally understood. It is common to say such a man has a great soul, or such another has a mean or little soul. A great soul aspires in its hopes; is not easily terrified by enemies or discouraged by difficulties. It is worth while to consider a little the effect of a man's outward circumstances. The mind to be sure, cannot be wholly made by any circumstances. Sentiments and state are different things. Many a great mind has been in narrow circumstances, and many a little rascal has been a king; yet education and manner have a sensible effect upon men in general. I imagine I have observed, that when persons of great rank, have been at the same time, men of real genius, they have generally excelled in majesty and dignity of sentiments and language. This was an advantage generally enjoyed by the ancients whose writings remain to us; having but their own language to study, and being early introduced into public life, and even into the conduct of the greatest affairs, they were led into nobleness of sentiment. Xenophon, Demosthenes, Cicero, Caesar, were all of them great statesmen, and two of them great generals, as well as writers. In modern times, there is a more compleat partition of employments, so that the statesman, general and scholar, are seldom found united in the same person; yet I think it appears in fact, that when statesmen are also scholars, they make upon the whole, greater orators and nobler writers, than those who are scholars merely, though of the greatest capacity. In every station however, this remark has place, that it is of importance to sublimity in writing, to endeavor to acquire a large and liberal manner of thinking. Whilst I am making use of this language, I would caution you against thinking that pride and vanity of mind, are at all allied to greatness, in this respect. There is a set of men called free-thinkers, who are pleased to arrogate to themselves, a large and liberal manner of thinking, and the generality of them, are as little creatures, as any on the face of the earth. Mr. Addison compares them to a fly lighting upon a great building, and perceiving the small interstices between the stones, cries out of vast chasms and irregularities, which is wholly owing to the extreme littleness of his sight, that is not able to see the dignity and grandeur of the whole building.

When I am upon this subject of greatness and elevation of thought as one source of the sublime, you will naturally expect that I should give some examples to illustrate it. I shall begin with some out of the scriptures, where indeed there is the greatest number, and these the noblest that can well be conceived. "I am God alone, and besides me there is no saviour—Who is this that darkeneth counsel by words without knowledge?—Who will set the briars and thorns against me in battle," &c. See also two passages inimitably grand—Isa. 40.12—and v. 21, and onwards.

To mention some of the sayings in heathen antiquity—Alexander's saying to Parmenio is certainly of the great kind, yet perhaps with a considerable mixture of pride as well as greatness. Parmenio told him if he were Alexander he would act in a certain manner. Answer. So would I if I were Parmenio. That of Porus, the Indian king, to Alexander however, was much greater. When he was Alexander's prisoner, and was asked by that prince how he expected to be treated? He answered, Like a king. Caesar's famous saying of veni, vidi, vici, has often been quoted as a concise and noble description of the rapidity of his conquests; yet I confess I think it very dubious; it has not only an air of improper vanity, but looks like an intended and silly play upon the words, and what we call alliteration. They are three words of the same length, the same tense, and the same beginning and ending. Cicero, in one of his orations, I believe in that for Marcellus, has a very noble compliment to Caesar, when he says the gods had given nothing to men so great as a disposition to shew mercy. But of all great sayings on record there is none that ever made such an impression upon me as that of Ayliffe to king James the IIId. He had been detected in some of the plots, &c. The king said to him, Mr. Ayliffe, don't you know 'tis in my power to pardon you? Yes (says he) I know it is in your power, but it is not in your nature!

It is necessary to put you in mind in reading books of criticism, that when examples of greatness of sentiment are produced from Homer and the other ancient writers, that all circumstances must be taken in, in order to form a just opinion concerning them. We must remember his times, and the general belief of his countrymen with regard to theology, and many other subjects. There must be a probability to make a thing natural, otherwise it is not great or noble, but extravagant. Homer in describing the goddess Discord, says, her feet were upon the earth, and her head was covered with the clouds. He makes Pluto look up and affirm, that Neptune would open hell itself, and make the light to shine into that dark abode. There are some of these that appear to me suspicious even in Homer himself; such as when he makes Jupiter brag that if all the other gods were to hang at the bottom of a chain, and earth and sea, and all along with them, he would toss them all up as easily as a ball. However it was with regard to him, who was taught to believe in Jupiter sitting upon Mount Olympus, or quaffing Nector in the council of the gods, modern and Christian writers and speakers should be careful to avoid any thing that is extravagant and ridiculous, or even such allusions to the heathen theology as could only be proper to those who believed in it.

There is the more reason to insist upon this, that as grandeur and sublimity is commonly a great object of ambition, particularly with young persons, they are very ready to degenerate into bombast. You ought always to remember that the language ought to be no higher than the subject, or the part of the subject that is then immediately handled. See an example of the different ways of a simple and a turgid writer, upon the very same sentiment where the Roman empire was extended to the western coast of Spain, Sextus Rufus simply tells it thus—Hispanius per Decimum Brutum obtenuimus et usque ad Gades et oceanum pervenimus. Florus, taking a more lofty flight, says—Decimus Brutus aliquanto totius, &c.

I have only further to observe, that in sublime descriptions great care should be taken that they be all of a piece, and nothing unsuitable brought into view. Longinus justly blamed the poet Hesiod, that after he had said every thing he could to render the goddess of darkness terrible, he adds, that a stinking humor ran from her nose—a circumstance highly disgusting, but no way terrible.

Lecture 7
I come now to the second source of the sublime, which is pathos, more commonly called in English the pathetic, that is, the power of moving the passions. This is a very important part of the subject: a power over the passions is of the utmost consequence to a poet, and it is all in all to an orator. This every one will perceive if he only recollects what influence passion or sentiment has upon reason, or, in other words, inclination upon the practical judgment. He that possesses this power in a high degree has the highest capacity of usefulness, and is likewise able to do the greatest mischief. Sublime sentiments and language may be formed upon any subject, and they touch the heart with a sense of sympathy or approbation; but to move the passions of others so as to incline their choice, or to alter their purpose, is particularly the design of eloquence.

The chief passions eloquence is intended to work upon are, rage, terror, pity, and perhaps desire in general, though occasionally he may have occasion to introduce every affection. In a heroic poem every affection may be said to take its turn;

but the different species of oratory, or the different objects and subjects of it, may be said to divide the passions. A speaker in political or deliberative assemblies may be said to have it in view to excite the passion of rage; he may naturally desire to incense his hearers against their enemies, foreign and domestic, representing the first as terrible and dangerous, to excite aversion and hatred, and the other as weak or worthless, to excite contempt. An example of this you have in the great subject of Demosthene's orations, Philip, king of Macedon—another in Cicero's discourses against Cataline and Anthony. Pity is the chief passion attempted to be raised at the bar, unless in criminal causes, where indignation against villainy of every kind is the part of the accuser. Terror and its attendants belong very much to a speaker in the pulpit; rage he has nothing to do with but in an improper sense, to raise a strong and steady, but uniform indignation, against evil. But even this a speaker from the pulpit should endeavor to convert into compassion for the folly and wretchedness of the guilty person. Pity seems to be the single object in tragedy.

One talent of great moment towards raising the passions is a strong and clear imagination and descriptive manner of speaking, to paint scenes and objects strongly, and set them before the eyes of the hearers. To select such circumstances as will have the most powerful effect, and to dwell only upon these. We have not any where in English a finer example of the pathetic, and the choice and use of circumstances, than the speech which Shakespeare has made for Anthony in the tragedy of Caesar. It appears from the history that Anthony did successfully raise the fury of the Romans against those who killed Caesar, and I think he could hardly select better images and language than those we have in the English poet.

But yesterday, &c.

1. To raising the passions with success much penetration and knowledge of human nature is necessary. Without this every attempt must fail. In confirmation of this remark, though there are persons much better fitted for it by nature than others, the most powerful in raising the passions have generally been those who have had much acquaintance with mankind and practice in life. Recluse students and professed scholars will be able to discover truth, and to defend it, or to write moral precepts with clearness and beauty; but they are seldom equal for the tender and pathetic to those who have been much in what is called the *world*—by a well known use of that word though almost peculiar to the English language. There is perhaps a double reason for persons well versed in the ways of men having the greatest power upon the passions. They not only know others better, and therefore how to touch them, but their own hearts it is likely have been agitated by more passions than those whose lives have been more calm and even.

2. To raising the passions of others, it is necessary the orator or writer should feel what he would communicate. This is so well known a rule, that I am almost ashamed to mention it, or the trite quotation commonly attending it; "Si vis me flere dolendum est primum ipsi tibi." You may as well kindle a fire with a piece of ice, as raise the passions of others while your own are still. I suppose the reason of this, if we would critically examine it, is, that we believe the thing to be a pretence or imposition altogether, if we see that he who wishes us to be moved by what he says, is notwithstanding himself unmoved. The offence is even something more than barely negative in some cases. If we hear a man speaking with coldness and indifference, where we think he ought to be deeply interested, we feel a certain disappointment, and are filled with displeasure; as if an advocate was pleading for a person accused of a capital crime, if he should appear with an air of indifference and unconcern, let his language and composition be what they will, it is always faultless or disgusting: or let a minister when speaking on the weighty subject of eternity, show any levity in his carriage, it must weaken the force of the most moving truths; whereas, when we see the speaker wholly engaged and possessed by his subject, feeling every passion he wishes to communicate, we give ourselves up to him without reserve, and are formed after his very temper by receiving his instructions.

3. It is a direction nearly allied to this, a man should never attempt to raise the passions of his hearers higher than the subject plainly merits it. There are some subjects, that if we are able, are of such moment as to deserve all the zeal and fire we can possibly bestow on them, of which we may say, as Dr. Young, "Passion is reason, transport, temper here." A lawyer for his client, whom he believes to be innocent; a patriot for his country, which he believes to be in danger: but above all, a minister for his people's everlasting welfare, may speak with as much force and vehemence, as his temper and frame are susceptible of; but in many other cases it is easy to transcend the bounds of reason, and make the language more lofty than the theme. We meet often, for example, with raised and labored encomiums in dedications, a species of writing the most difficult to succeed in, of any almost, that can

be named. The person honored by this mark of the author's esteem, is very seldom placed in the same rank by the public, that he is by him. Besides, though he were really meritorious, it seldom comes fairly up to the representation: the truth is, to correspond to the picture, he should be almost the only meritorious person of the age or place in which he lives. Now, considering how cold a compliment this is to all the rest, and particularly to those who read it, there is little wonder that such rhapsodies are treated with contempt. I have often thought the same thing of funeral panegyrics: when a man dies, whose name perhaps, was hardly ever heard of before, we have a splendid character of him in the newspapers, where the prejudice of relations or the partiality of friendship do just what they please. I remember at the death of a person whom I shall not name, who was it must be confessed, not inconsiderable for literature, but otherwise had not much that was either great or amiable about him, an elegiac poem was published, which began with this line, "Whence this astonishment in every face." Had the thing been really true, and the public had been deeply affected with the loss, the introduction had been not inelegant; but on such a pompous expression, when the reader recollected that he had seen no marks of public astonishment, it could not but tempt him to smile.

4. Another important remark to be made here, is, that a writer or speaker in attempting the pathetic, should consider his own natural turn, as well as the subject. Some are naturally of a less warm and glowing imagination, and in themselves susceptible of a less degree of passion than others; these should take care not to attempt a flight that they cannot finish, or enter upon such sentiments and language as they will probably sink as it were, and fall away from, in a little time. Such should substitute gravity and solemnity, instead of fire, and only attempt to make their discourse clear to the understanding, and convincing to the conscience: perhaps, this is in general the best way in serious discourses and moral writings; because, though it may not produce so strong or ardent emotions, it often leaves a deeper and more lasting impression.

OF FIGURATIVE SPEECH

It is common to meet with this expression; "The tropes and figures of rhetoric." This expression is not just; the terms are neither synonimous, nor are they two distinct species of one genus—Figure is the general expression; a trope is one of the figures, but there are many more. Every trope is a figure, but every figure is not a trope: perhaps we may say a trope is an expedient to render language more extensive and copious, and may be used in tranquility; whereas, a figure is the effect of passion. This distinction however, cannot be universally maintained; for tropes are oftentimes the effect of passion as well as of the narrowness of language. Figures may be defined any departure from the plain direct manner of expression, and particularly such as are suggested by the passions, and differ on that account, from the way in which we would have spoken, if in a state of perfect tranquility. Tropes are a species of figures, in which a word or phrase is made use of in a sense different from its first and proper signification, as "The Lord is a sun and shield"; where the words "sun and shield," are used tropically. There are several different tropes.

1 Metonomy—This is a very general kind of trope, comprehending under it several others; the meaning of it is a change of name, or one name for another: this may be done several ways: (1) The cause may be put for the effect, or the effect for the cause: as when we say, cold death; because death makes cold: Old age kept him behind, that is, made him weak, &c. (2) The author for his works. (3) The thing containing, for the thing contained: as drink the cup, that is, the liquor in the cup. (4) A part is taken for the whole, or the whole for a part; as my roof for my house; my house is on fire, when only a small part of it burns—This is called synechdoche. (5) A general term for a particular; a hundred reasons may be given, that is, many reasons may be given. (6) A proper name for a characteristic name, as he is a Nero for a cruel man, or a Sardanapulus for a voluptuous monarch. All these and many more are metonemies.

2 Metaphor—this might as well have been the general term, as trope; for it also signifies change of expression: it is a species of trope, by which any term is applied in a sense different from its natural import, as when we say a tide of pleasure, to express the impetuosity of pleasure: when the heavens are said to be over our heads as brass, and the earth under our feet as iron.

3 Allegory—This is continuing the metaphor, and extending it by a variety of expressions of the same kind, as the Lord is my shepherd, he maketh me to lie down in green pastures—he maketh me to feed beside the still waters.

4 Irony—In using words directly contrary to their meaning; as, "No doubt you are the people and wisdom shall die with you."

5 Hyperbole—When things are carried be-

yond their truth, to express our sentiments more strongly, as "Swifter than the wind, whiter than snow."

6 Catachresis—is the first trope of all, when words are used in an opposite, and sometimes in an impossible sense, as when chains and shackles are called bracelets of iron.

FIGURES

Figures cannot be fully enumerated, because they are without number; and each figure may be used several different ways. (1) Exclamation—This is nothing else than a way of expressing admiration or lamentation, as Oh! Alas! Heavens! &c. used by persons much moved. (2) Doubt—This is frequently the expression of a doubtful mind, in suspense what to do. This is described by Virgil, in the distress of Dido, when Eneas left her; "Shall I go to the neighboring kings whom I have so often despised?" Sometimes it is a beautiful figure, and obliges persons to take notice of it, and sometimes of what they would otherwise have omitted: "Who is this that cometh from Edom?" (3) Epanorthosis—This is a correction or improvement of what has been said: "You are not truly the son of a goddess, nay you must have sucked a tygress." (4) Pleonasm—This is a redundancy, as "I have heard it with my ears, he spake it with his mouth." (5) Similitude—This is comparing one thing with another, as "he shall be like a tree planted" &c. (6) Distribution—This consists of a particular enumeration of several correspondent images: "Their throat is an open sepulchre, their tongues have used deceit." (7) Prosopopei—When, persons dead or absent, or different from the speaker, are brought in speaking, as Cicero supposes his country or Italy, and all the public saying to him, "Marius Tullius what are you doing?" (8) Apostrophe—When persons dead or absent, or any inanimate things are spoken to, as Cicero says, "O! vos, or hear O! Heavens, and give ear O! earth." (9) Communication—When a speaker calls upon his hearers to say what advice they would give, or what they would have done different from what he or the person whom he defends has done; What could you have done in this case? What should I do now? (10) Interrogation—Putting a thing home to the readers, as "What fruit had you then in those things of which you are now ashamed?"

Lecture 8

I have now gone through the account given in the systems of the tropes and figures of rhetoric by which you will sufficiently understand the meaning of both. The proper applications however of them is a matter of much greater moment and of much greater difficulty. I will make a few remarks before I close the subject in addition to what hath been already interspersed through the different parts of it.

1. Perhaps it will not be improper to consider what is the purpose intended by figures. I have introduced them here as a means of giving sublimity to a discourse, but may there not be some little analysis and resolution of that purpose, may we not inquire what are the particular effects of figures? Are the effects of figures in general, and of all figures, the same? It is certain that figurative speech is very powerful in raising the passions, And probably different figures are proper to express or excite different passions; admiration, desire, pity, hatred, rage, or disdain. This appears from the explication of figures formerly given. But besides this, we may observe that there are some effects of figures that seem to be wholly unconnected with passion, of these I shall mention three; ornament, explication, conviction. Sometimes figure is made use of merely for ornament. Of this Rollin gives us an example in which an author says, "The king, to give an eternal mark of the esteem and friendship with which he honored a great general gave an illustrious place to his glorious ashes amidst those masters of the earth, who preserve on the magnificence of their tombs an image of the lustre of their thrones." Under this head may be reckoned all the examples of the use of figures to raise things that are mean and low in themselves to some degree of dignity by the phraseology, or to give a greater dignity to any thing than the simple idea or the proper name would convey, as if one should say, looking round the scene and observing the bounteous gifts of Providence for the support of innumerable creatures, instead of the grass and corn every where growing in abundance. Perhaps also under the same head may be reckoned, the clothing in other terms any thing that might be supposed disagreeable or disgusting, as when Cicero confesses that the servants of Milo killed Clodius, he does not say interficerunt but he says, "They did that which every good man would wish his servants to do in like circumstances." I shall only observe, that the greatest delicacy and judgment imaginable is necessary in the use of figures with this view, because they are very apt to degenerate into bombast. Young persons in their first compositions and especially when they have a good deal of ancient literature fresh in their heads, are very apt to be faulty in this particular. A com-

mon word or sentiment which any body might use, and every body would understand, they think mean and below them, and therefore they have recourse to unnecessary figures, and hard or learned phrases. Instead of walking about the fields they perambulate them, they do not discover a thing, but recognize it. Johnson the author of the Rambler is the most faulty this way, of any writer of character. A little play of wit, or a few strokes of railery, he calls *a reciprocation of smartness.*

Another use of figures is for explication, to make a thing more clearly conceived. This in general may be said to be the use of the similitude, only I think when figures are used for illustration it is as much to assist the imagination as the judgment, and to make the impression which was before real and just very strong. For example when Solomon says, "Let a bear robbed of her whelps meet a man rather than a fool in his folly." "If you bray a fool in a mortar he will return to his folly," "The foolish man walketh by the way, and he saith to every one that he is a fool."

A third use of figures may be said, although improperly, to be for conviction, or to make us more readily or more fully yield to the truth, as when to support what we have said, that persons of sound judgment are reserved in speech, we add, deep waters move without noise—or that men in eminent stations are exposed to observation and censure. "A city that is set on a hill cannot be hid." In all such cases therefore it is certain that a similitude is not an argument, yet the analogy of nature seems to carry in it a good deal of evidence, and adds to the impression made upon the mind.

2. A second remark is, that figures of every kind should come naturally, and never be sought for. The design of explaining the several kinds of figures is not to teach you to make them, but to correct them. Arguments and illustrations we must endeavor to invent, but figures never. If they do not flow spontaneous, they are always forced. If a man having proceeded too far in a subject, bethinks himself, that he will here introduce a similitude, or an allegory, or a prosopeia, &c. He will either miss of it altogether, or he will produce something vastly more jejune and insipid than it is possible for any man to make without figures. It puts me in mind of the ridiculous chasms that some persons bring themselves to in conversation, when they offer to bring a similitude which has not yet occurred to them. They will say "He raged, and raved, and roared just like—I don't know what." Figures should be the native expression of passions or conceptions already felt, as they are the means of raising passions in those to whom you speak. They should therefore be posterior in point of time, to the feelings of the speaker, although prior to those of the hearers. The great purposes therefore of criticism on this part of the subject is to prune the luxuriancies of nature, and see that the figures be just and natural.

3. I have already in speaking upon the tropes, had occasion to give some rules as to the use of them, particularly as to the propriety and consistency of them. But there are some things to be observed further for explaining them. There are two characters frequently given to tropes, especially to metaphors which deserve to be considered. The one is strength, the other is boldness. These are by no means the same. That is a strong metaphor or image that gives us a very lively impression of the thing represented. As that of the wise man, "A stone is heavy, and the sand is weighty, but a fools wrath is heavier than them both." A bold image or metaphor is that which upon the whole is just and strong, but is considerably removed from common observation, and would not easily or readily have occurred to another. It is also called a bold image when the resemblance is but in one single point. There is not any where to be seen a collection of bolder images, than in the book of Job, particularly in the description of the war-horse, among which in particular the following seems to excell, "Hast thou clothed his neck with thunder." To liken the mane of a horse to thunder, would not have occurred to every one; neither in idea does the resemblance hold but in one particular, that the flowing and waving of the mane is like the sheets and forked flakes of lightning.

Lecture 9

I now come to consider the simple manner of writing. If I could explain this fully so as to make every one clearly to understand it, and at the same time incline you to admire and study it, I should think a very difficult and important point was gained. It is exceedingly difficult to bring young persons especially to a taste for the simple way of writing. They are apt to think it of little moment, not so much the object of ambition as an exercise of self-denial, to say a thing plainly when they might have said it nobly. I would observe therefore, in the very beginning, it is a mistake to consider simplicity and sublimity as universally opposite, for on the contrary there is not only a great excellence in some performances which we may call wholly of the simple kind; such as a story told or an epistle written with all the beauty of simplicity, but in the most sublime and animated compositions, some of the greatest sentiments derive their beauty from being clothed in simple language. Simplicity is even as necessary to some parts of an oration, as it is to the whole of some kinds of composition. Let the subject be ever so great and interesting, it is prudent, decent, necessary, to begin the discourse in a cool and dispassionate manner. That man who should begin an oration with the same boldness of figure and the same high pitch of voice that would be proper towards the close of it, would commit one of the greatest faults against propriety, and I think would wholly prevent its effect upon the hearers.

But how shall we explain the simple manner of writing? It is, say many authors, that which is likest to and least removed from the language of common life. It must be therefore easy and obvious, few or no figures in the expression, nothing obscure in the sentiments or involved in the method. Long sentences are contrary to it, words either difficult or uncommon are inconsistent with it. Cicero and Horace have both said, and all critics have said after them, it is that which when men hear they think that they themselves could only have said the same, or that it is just a kind of expression of their own thoughts. They generally remark further, that it is what seems to be easy, but yet is not; as Horace says, ut sibi queris speret idem, &c. We may further observe, that what is truly simple always carries in it the idea of being easy in its production, as well as in imitation, and indeed the one of these seems necessarily to suppose the other. Whatever seems to be the effect of study and much invention, cannot be simple. It is finely exemplified in the introduction of Anthony's speech in Shakespeare: I am no orator as Brutus is, &c. Rollin has given us an admirable example of a story told with a beautiful simplicity from Cicero's offices. There is an example also in Livy's account of the battle of the Horatii & Curiatii, only with a little more force of expression, as the importance and solemnity of the subject seemed to require it. But it requires a very masterly knowledge of the Latin language to perceive the beauties fully that are pointed at by Rollin in the first instance, or might easily be mentioned in the last. There is no author in our language who excels more in simplicity than Addison—The Spectator in general indeed, but especially the papers written by him, excel in this quality. Ease and elegance are happily joined in them, and nature itself, as it were, seems to speak in them. If some of the later periodical writers have equalled, or even excelled them in force or elegance, not one has ever come up to them in simplicity.

The subjects or the species of writing in which simplicity chiefly shines, are narration, dialogue, epistolary writing, essay writing, and all the lighter species of poetry, as odes, songs, epigrams, eligies and such like. The ancients were remarkable for a love and admiration of simplicity, and some of them remain to us as eminent examples of its excellence. Xenophon in his institution of Cyrus, is particularly remarkable for a sweet and dignified simplicity. He uses neither language nor ideas that are difficult and far-fetched. In the smaller compositions of the ancients, as odes, epigrams, &c. they were at prodigious pains to polish them, and make them quite easy and natural. They placed their great glory in bestowing much art, and at the same time making it to appear quite easy and artless, according to the saying now grown into a proverb, *artis est celare artem*. The beauty of simplicity may not appear at first sight, or be at all perceived by persons of a vitiated taste, but all persons of good judgment immediately, and the bulk of mankind in time, are charmed with what is quite easy and yet truly accurate and elegant.

It ought to be carefully observed that simplicity is quite a different thing from lowness and meanness, and the great art of a writer is to preserve the one without degenerating into the other. It is the easiest thing in the world to speak or write vulgarisms, but a person of true taste will carefully avoid every thing of that kind. For example, one who would write simply, and as near the language of plain people in ordinary discourse as possible, would yet avoid every absurdity or barbarism that obtains a place in common conversation, as to say, "This here table, and that there candle." It is also quite contrary to simplicity to adopt the quaint expressions or cant phrases that are the children of fashion and obtain for a little, or in some particular places and not in others. The Spectator attacked with great spirit and propriety several of those that were introduced into conversation and writing in his time, such as *mob, rip, pos, bite, bamboosle*, and several others. Most of them he fairly defeated, but one or two of them got the better of him, and are now freely introduced into the language, such as *mob*. Johnson also has put bamboosle in his Dictionary, which he calls indeed a low word. Arbuthnot is his authority, but it was plainly used by him in the way of ridicule, and therefore it should either not have been in the Dictionary at all, or such an authority should not have been given for it. It is exceedingly difficult and requires an excellent judgment to be able to descend to great simplicity, and yet to keep out every low expression or idea. I do not think it is easy to be a thorough judge of pure diction in any language but our own, and not even in that without a good deal of the knowledge of human life, and a thorough acquaintance with the best authors. Writers and speakers of little judgment are apt by times to go into extremes, to swell too much on the one hand, and to fall into what is vulgar and offensive on the other.

When speaking on simplicity, I observe that there is a simplicity in the taste and composition of a whole discourse, different from simplicity of sentiment and language in the particular parts. This will incline a man to avoid all unnecessary ornament, particularly the ornaments of fashion and the peculiar dress or mode of the times. We say in architecture that a building is in a simple style, when it has not great a multiplicity of ornaments, or is not loaded with beauties, so to speak. It is very remarkable that books written in the same age will differ very much one from another in this respect; and those which have least of the ornaments then in vogue, continue in reputation when the others are grown ridiculous. I will give you an instance of this. A small religious treatise, Scougal's Life of God in the soul of man, which is written with great simplicity, and yet dignity, and may now be read with pleasure and approbation by persons of the best taste; while most of the other writers of his age and country, are ridiculous, or hardly intelligible.

Perhaps it may help us to form right notions of simplicity, to consider what are the opposites, or the greatest enemies to it. (1) One is abstraction of sentiment, or too great refinement of any kind: of this the greatest example in an author of merit, is the writer of the Rambler; almost every page of his writings, furnishes us with instances of departure from simplicity, partly in the sentiment, and partly in the diction.

(2) Another, is allegory, and especially far-fetched allusions, as in the example which the Spectator gives of a poet, who speaks of Bacchus' cast coat: this is little better than a riddle, and even those who discern it, will take a little time to reflect, that according to the heathen mythology, Bacchus was the god of wine; wine is kept in casks, and therefore an empty cask, or at least an useless one, may be called Bacchus' cast coat.

(3) A third enemy to simplicity, is an affectation of learning: This spoils simplicity many ways; it introduces terms of art, which cannot be understood, but by those who are adepts in a particular branch. Such persons have been long exposed to ridicule under the name of pedants. Sometimes indeed, the word pedantry has been in a manner confined to those addicted to classic literature, and who intermix every thing they say, with scraps taken from the learned languages; but this is quite improper, for lawyers, physicians, dunces or schoolmasters are equally ridiculous, when they fill their discourse with words drawn from their particular art.

(4) The only other enemy to simplicity I shall mention, is an ambition to excel. This perhaps, should not have been so much divided from the rest, as made the great principle from which the rest proceed. Nothing more certainly renders a man ridiculous, than an over forwardness to display his excellence; he is not content with plain things, and particularly with such things as every body might say, because these would not distinguish him.

On the whole, as I observed on sublimity, that one of the best and surest ways to attain it was to think nobly, so the best way to write simply, is to think simply, to avoid all affectation, to attempt to form your manner of thinking to a noble self-denial. A man little solicitous about what people think of him, or rather having his attention fixed upon quite another purpose, viz. giving information, or producing conviction, will only attain to a simple manner of writing, and indeed he will write best in all respects.

As to the mixed state or manner of writing, as it consists of the mixture of the other two, I shall not need to say any thing by way of explaining it, but only make a remark or two, of the use and application of it. The mixed kind of writing chiefly consists of history and controversy. The great quality necessary to execute it properly, is soundness of judgment, to determine on what subjects, and on what parts of subjects it is proper to write with simplicity, and on what with force—One would wish not to go beyond, but just to gratify a reader's inclination in this respect.

There are many cases in history, where the greatest sublimity both of sentiments and language, is both admitted and required, particularly all the beauty and all the force that can be admitted into description, is of importance in history. Those who will read in Robertson's history of Scotland, the account he gives of the astonishment, terror and indignation that appeared in the English court, when news was brought of the massacre at Paris, or in the same author, the account of the execution of Mary queen of Scots, will see the force and sublimity of description. The difference between sublimity of sentiment and language in an historian, and in a poet or orator, seems to me to resemble the difference between the fire of a managed horse, when reined in by the rider, and marching with a firm and stately pace, and the same when straining every nerve, in the eager contention in a race. We shall enter a little into this matter, if we consider the different images that are made use of in the different arts. In poetry we say a beautiful, striking, shining metaphor, fervent, glowing imagery. In oratory we say warm, animated, irresistible. In history we use the words force, nobleness, dignity and majesty, particularly those last attributes, of dignity and majesty. Herodotus has been often called the father of history, though I confess I apprehend he has obtained this title, chiefly because of his antiquity, and his being the first that ever gave any thing of a regular history; but though he has some things august enough, yet he has admitted so many incredible stories, and even peculiarities into his work, as very much detracts from its dignity; we must indeed impute a good deal of this to the age in which he lived, and the impossibility of their distinguishing truth from falsehood, so well as those of later ages, who have had the advantage of all past experience.

History indeed, is not only of the mixed kind of writing, so as to admit sometimes sublimity, and sometimes simplicity, but those styles should be really blended together, in every part of it. The most noble and animated sentiments, characters or descriptions in history, should yet be clothed with such a gravity and decency of garb, so to speak, as to give an air of simplicity to the whole. It is an advantage to a poem, that the author says but little in his own person, but makes the characters speak and say all; and in an orator it is an advantage, when he can carry the hearers off from himself to his subject; but above all, an historian should not so much as wish to shine, but with the coolness of a philosopher, and the impartiality of a judge should set the actors and transactions before the reader.

Controversy is another subject of the mixed kind, which ought to be in general written with simplicity, yet will sometimes admit of the ornaments of eloquence: of this I shall speak a little more afterwards, and therefore shall now only add, that controversy differs from history, in that it sometimes admits of passion and warmth, when there seems to be a sufficient foundation laid for it, a controversial writer will endeavor to interest his reader, and excite either contempt or indignation against his adversary.

After having given you this view of the three great kinds of writing, or as they are sometimes called different styles, it may not be amiss to observe, that there are distinctions of style, which it is proper that an able writer should observe, that do not range themselves, at least not fully and properly, under these three heads, but may be said to run through all the kinds of eloquence.

Many eminent authors have said, that the climates have some effect upon the style; that in the warmer countries the style is more animated, and the figures more bold and glowing: and nothing is more common, than to ascribe a peculiarity of style, and that particularly elevated and full of metaphor, to the orientals, as it belonged to that part of the globe; but if I am not mistaken, both this and other things, such as courage, that have been attributed to the climate, belong either not to the climate at all, or in a small measure, and are rather owing to the state of society and manners of men. We have before had occasion to see that all narrow languages are figured. In a state, where there are few or no abstract ideas, how should there be abstract terms. If any body will read the poem of Fingal, which appears to have been composed on the bleak hills of the north of Scotland, he will find as many figures and as bold, as in any thing composed in Arabia or Persia. The state of society then, is what gives a particular color to the style, and by this the styles of different ages and countries are distinguished—that the climate does but little, may be seen just by comparing ancient and modern Italy; what difference between the strength and force of the ancient Latin tongue, and the present Italian language, in the expression of sentiments; it must therefore vary with sentiments and manners; and what difference between the stern and inflexible bravery of a free ancient Roman, and the effeminate softness of a modern Italian; yet they breathed the same air, and were nursed by the same soil. I will just go a little off from the subject to say, that a very late author, (Lord Kaime) seems to think that the courage of mankind is governed by the climates: he says that the northern climates produce hardened constitutions, and bold and firm minds; that invasions have been made from north to south; but I apprehend, he may be mistaken here both in his facts, and the reasons of them—Invasions have not always been made from north to south; for the Roman arms penetrated very far to the north of their territory; the first great conquerors of the east, in Egypt and Babylon, carried their arms to the north: and where the conquest ran the other way, it was owing to other circumstances; and Dean Swift says much nearer the truth, it was from poverty to plenty.

The design of this digression is to show, that not only the circumstances that appear in a language, but several others that have also been attributed to climate, owe very little to it, but to the state of mankind and the progress of society. The maxim of that great modern writer, Montesquieu, which he applies to population, is also true of language—That natural causes are not by far so powerful as moral causes. Allowing, therefore, as some have affirmed that the northern climates may give a roughness and hardness to the accent and pronunciation, I believe it is all that we can expect from climate; the distinction of styles and composition must come from another original.

Lecture 10

Having in a great measure rejected the supposition of the style in writing being affected by the climate, and shown that it rather takes its colour from the state of society, and the sentiments and manners of men, it follows that all the great distinctions that take place in manners will have a correspondent effect upon language spoken or written. When the manners of a people are little polished, there is a plainness or a roughness in the style. Absolute monarchies, and the obsequious subjection introduced at the courts of princes, occasions a pompous swelling and compliment to be in request different from the boldness and sometimes ferocity of republican states.

Seneca in remarking upon the Roman language, says, Genus dicendi mutatur publicos mores, &c. This he exemplifies in the Roman language, which was short and dry in the earliest ages, afterwards become elegant and ornate, and at last loose and diffuse.

The style of an age also is sometimes formed by some one or more eminent persons, who, having obtained reputation, every thing peculiar to them is admired and copied, and carried much into excess. Seneca has remarked this also, that commonly one author obtains the palm, and becomes the model, and all copy him. Haec vitia unuis aliquis inducit. And he gives a very good example of it, of which we may now judge in Sallust. He also very properly observes, that all the faults that arise from imitation become worse in the imitator than in the example. Thus reproving the fault just now mentioned in our ancestors.

It is remarkable that Seneca himself was another example of the same thing. His manner of writing, which is peculiar, came to be the standard of the age. His manner has been called by critics, point and antithesis. A short sentence containing a strong sentiment, or a beautiful one, as it were like a maxim by itself. For an example or two of this; to express the destruction of Lyons he says, Logdunum quod ostandebatur, &c. That Lyons, which was formerly shown, is now sought. And on the same subject—Una nox, &c. There was but one night between a great city and none. Quid est eques Romanus, &c. What! is a Roman knight a freed man or slave! names generated by ambition or oppression.

The fault of this sententious manner of writing does not lie in the particulars being blameable, but in the repetition and uniformity becoming tedious—when every paragraph is stuffed with sentences and bright sayings, generally having the same tune, it wearies the ear. The most remarkable book in the English language for putting continual smartness sentence and antithesis for elegance, is the Gentleman Instructed. I shall read you one paragraph—The misfortune of one breathes vigor into the others: They carry on manfully the attack—Their heads run round with the glasses. Their tongues ride post. Their wits are jaded. Their reason is distanced. Brutes could not talk better, nor men worse. Like skippers in a storm, they rather hallowed than spoke. Scarce one heard his neighbor, and not one understood him; so that noise stood for sense, and every one passed for a virtuoso, because all played the fool to extravagance.

I shall not enlarge much farther upon the difference of style arising from the character of an age, as in the ages before the reformation, called the times of chivalry, when military prowess was the great thing in request—their gallantry and heroism were to be seen in every writer.—At the time of the reformation and the revival of learning, their citations of the ancient writers and allusions to the classic phrases distinguished every author. In the age of the civil wars in England, of which religion was so much the cause, allusions to singular expressions, and theological opinions, are every where to be met with, of which the great Milton is an example.

But there is another distinction of styles, which is chiefly personal, and will distinguish one author from another, in the same age, and perhaps of the same or nearly the same abilities. There are several different epithets given to style in our language, which I shall mention in a certain order, which I suppose will contribute something to explain the meaning of them. We call a style, simple or plain, smooth, sweet, concise, elegant, ornate, just, nervous, chaste, severe. These are all different epithets which will each of them convey to a nice critical ear, something different, though I confess it is not easy to define them clearly or explain them fully. Plainness and simplicity is when the author does not seem to have had any thing in view, but to be understood, and that by persons of the weakest understanding. That ought to be in view in many writings, and indeed perspicuity will be found to be a character of many styles, when there are other great qualities, but we call that plain and simple, where there is no discovery of literature, and no attempt at the pathetic. Scougal's Life of God in the soul of man, and Dr. Evans' Sermons, are admirable patterns of this manner. (2) I would call that a smooth style, when the utmost care had been taken to measure the periods, and to consult the ear on the structure of the sentence; for this I know no author more remarkable than Hervey, in his Meditations. (3) Sweetness seems to me to differ from the former only in that the subjects and the images are generally of a pleasing or soothing nature, such as may particularly be seen in Mrs. Rowe's Letters; perhaps also in a more modern composition by a lady, Lady Mary W. Montague's Letters. And indeed when female authors have excelled, they generally do excell in sweetness. (4) The next is conciseness. This is easily understood, it is just as much brevity as is consistent with perspicuity. It is a beauty in every writing when other qualities are not hurt by it. But it is peculiarly proper for critical or scientific writing, because there we do not so much expect or want to know the author's sentiments, but as soon as possible to learn the facts, to understand them fully, and range them methodically. There are many more authors who excell in this respect in the French, than in the English language. Not only the scientific writings, but even political and moral writings are drawn up by them with great conciseness. There cannot be greater conciseness than in Montesquieu's Spirit of Laws. Brown's Estimate of the manners and principles of the times, seems to be an imitation of that author, in his manner. In essay writing, David Hume seems to have as happily joined conciseness and perspicuity as most of our English writers. Some pious writers have been as successful this way as most of our nation; such as Mason's Sayings, and Mason on Self-knowledge. (5) A style is called elegant when it is formed by the principles of true taste, and much pains is taken to use the best and purest expressions that the language will afford. It is very common to join together ease and elegance. The great patterns we have of these are Addison and Tillotson. Seed's Sermons too may be mentioned here, as very much excelling in both these qualities; so also does David Hume. The other Hume, author of the Elements of Criticism, though a very good judge of writing, seems in point of style to be very defective himself. If he has any talent it is conciseness and plainness; but he is at the same time often abrupt and harsh. (6) An ornate style may be said to be something more than elegant, introducing into a composition all the beauties of language, where they can find a place with propriety. I mentioned before, that Hervey's style in his Meditations, was exceedingly smooth and flowing. I may add it has also the qualities of elegant and ornate. That style is elegant which is correct and free from faults; that is ornate which abounds with beauties. (7) The next character of style, is that it is just. By this I understand, a particular attention to the truth and meaning of every expression. Justness is frequently joined with, or otherwise expressed by precision; so that (if I may speak so) together with a taste which will relish and produce an elegance of language, there is a judgment and accuracy which will abide the scrutiny of philosophy and criticism. Many well turned periods and showy expressions will be found defective here. This justness of style is scarcely ever found without clearness of understanding, so that it appears in accuracy of method, in the whole discourse as well as in the style of particular parts. Dr. Samuel Clark was a great example of this. He was one of those few mathematicians who were good writers, and while he did not love the life and fervor of the orator, preserved the precision of the natural philosopher. (8) Nervous or strong is the next character of style, and this implies that in which the author does not wholly neglect, elegance and precision. But he is much more attentive to dignity and force. A style that is very strong and nervous, might often receive a little additional polish by a few more epithets or copulatives, but cannot descend to such minuteness. It is a fine expression of Richard Baxter, upon style, "May I speak plainly and pertinently, and somewhat nervously, I have my purpose." Baxter was a great example of a nervous style, with great neglect of elegance, and Dean Swift is an illustrious example of the same sort of diction, with a very considerable attention to elegance. Both the one and the other seem to write in the fullness of their hearts, and to me without scruple those terms are commonly best that first present themselves to a fertile invention and warm imagination, without waiting to choose in their room those that might be more smooth or sonorous but less emphatic. (9) Chastity of style I think stands particularly opposed to any embellishments that are not natural, and necessary. Nay, we generally mean by a very chaste writer, one who does not admit even all the ornaments that he might, and what ornaments he does admit are always of the most decent kind, and the most properly executed. (10) Severity of style has this title only, by way of comparison. That is a severe style which has propriety, elegance and force, but seems rather to be above and to disdain the ornaments which every body else would approve, and the greatest part of readers would desire.

Lecture 16

I am now to conclude the discourses upon this subject by an inquiry into the general principles of taste and criticism. In the former discourses we have kept close to the arts of writing and speaking, and have attempted to describe the various kinds of composition, their characters, distinctions, beauties, blemishes, the means of attaining skill in them, and the uses to which they should be applied. But is it not proper to consider the alliance, if there be any such, between this and other arts? This will serve greatly to improve and perfect our judgment and taste. It was very early observed, that there was a relation between the different arts and some common principles, that determine their excellence. Cicero mentions this in the introduction of his oration for Archias the poet. Etenim omnes artes quae ad humanitatem pertinent, habent quaedam inter se continentur.

These arts, which Cicero says, Ad humanitatem pertinent, are called by the moderns the fine arts. This is to distinguish them from those commonly called the mechanic arts, making the utensils and conveniences of common life. And yet even these may be included, as taste and elegance, or the want of it may plainly be discerned in every production of human skill. However, those called the fine arts are the following: Poetry, oratory, music, painting, sculpture, architecture. It must be allowed that, though these arts have some common principles of excellence, there are some persons who have a strong inclination after, and even a capacity of performing in some of them, and not in others. There are good orators who are no musicians, or perhaps who have very little taste for the beauties of architecture. Yet commonly complete critics, and those who have a well formed taste, are able to perceive the beauty of the whole, and the relation of one to another. It is remarkable that the expressions in composition are frequently borrowed from one art and applied to another. We say a smooth, polished style, as well as a polished surface; and we say a building is sweet or elegant, as well as an oration. We say the notes in music are bold and swelling, or warm and animated.

One of our modern authors on eloquence, has thought fit to take exception at the use of the word *taste,* as being of late invention, and as implying nothing but what is carried in judgment and genius. But I apprehend that the application of it, though it should be admitted to be modern, is perfectly just. It came to us from the French. The *bon gout* among them was applied first to classic elegance, and from thence to all the other arts. And as a sense of the beauty of the arts is certainly a thing often distinct from judgment, as well as from erudition; the term seems not only to be allowable, but well chosen. We find persons who can reason very strongly upon many subjects, who yet are incapable of elegance in composition, and indeed of receiving much delight from the other fine arts. Nay, we find persons of uncommon acuteness in mathematics and natural philosophy, who yet are incapable of attaining to a fine taste.

It has been sometimes said, that taste is arbitrary. Some will have it, that there is no such thing as a standard of taste or any method of improving it. It is a kind of common proverb with many, that there is no disputing about taste. That it is of this intellectual as of natural taste, according as the palate or organs are differently formed, what gives an agreeable relish to one, gives a disagreeable one to another. They say that the modes of taste are temporary and variable—that different nations, climates, governments, and ages, have different ways of speaking and writing, and a different turn in all the arts—that chance or particular persons will be able to give a turn to the mode in all these. Even so great a man as Dr. Warburton has embraced this sentiment, and to those who attack the Scriptures as not being a complete model of eloquence he answers there is no fixed standard of eloquence. That eloquence is one thing in Arabia, another in Greece, and another in England, for this reason he condemns those who after the example of Mr. Blackwell in his sacred classics, vindicates the Scriptures from objections of this kind, or produce instances of their sublimity and beauty. But though I have shown you in some of the former discourses, that the style and manner in vogue will receive some tincture and be liable to some variation from all the particulars mentioned, yet there is certainly a real beauty or deformity in nature, independent of these partial changes which when properly explained and examples of it exhibited, will obtain more universal approbation, and retain it longer than the others. The poetry and oratory of the ancients and their painting and statuary, are instances and proofs of this. It may also appear from what I mentioned to you formerly, that those compositions which have most simplicity and such excellencies as are most solid, with fewest of the casual ornaments of fashion, and the peculiarities of their own age please, when their contemporaries are lost in oblivion. The same thing holds with pieces of furniture that are elegant but plain. Such have the beauties of nature, and that belong to every age. But to show this more fully even the remarks upon natural taste is not true in such a sense as to weaken what has been said. For though it is certain that persons used to the coarsest kind of food which they have often eat with relish, may show at first an aversion to the delicacies of cookery, yet after a person has been a little accustomed to that kind of preparation of victuals in which regard is had to the mixtures that are most proper to gratify the palate will not easily return to his slovenly provision. But though there were less in this remark, it seems plain that there is a taste in the fine arts, and a real foundation for it in nature.

But supposing that there is a foundation in nature for taste and criticism, there is another question that arises, viz. Can we tell what it is? Can we reach the original principles which govern this matter? Can we say not only that such and such things please us, but why they do so? Can we go any further than we have already done, as to composition? Some have refused that we can with certainty reach the source of this subject. When the cause is asked, why one person, one thing, or one composition is more excellent than another, they say it is an immediate and simple perception, a je ne scais quoi, as the French say, which phrase seems to have taken its rise from the circumstance which often occurs, that in a house, a garden, a statue or painting, or even in a person's countenance and carriage, you perceive something agreeable upon the whole, and yet cannot suddenly tell wherein it lies, the parts are not better proportioned perhaps, nor the features better formed than in another, and yet there is something in the composition of the whole that gives the most exquisite delight.

Others however, and the far greatest number, have thought it proper to go a great deal further, and to inquire into human nature, its perceptions and powers, and endeavor to trace out the principles of taste, which apply in general to all the fine arts, or in greater or less proportion to each of them, for some apply more to one than to others. As for example, if the sense of harmony is an original perception it applies chiefly to music, and remotely to the pronunciation of an orator, and still more remotely to the composition of an orator. These powers or perceptions in human nature have been generally called the powers of imagination. Mr. Hutchinson calls them reflex senses, finer internal sensations; and upon examination we shall find that besides the internal senses, there are certain finer perceptions, which we are capable of, which may be said to take their rise from outward objects, and to suppose the external sensation, but yet to be additions to, and truly distinct from it. As for example, I see a beautiful person. My eye immediately perceives colour, and shape variously disposed; but I have further a sense of beauty in the whole. I hear the sound of musical instruments; my ear receives the noise; every body's ear who is not deaf does the same. If I have a sense of harmony I take a pleasure in the composition of the sounds. The way to examine the principles of taste is to consider which of these perceptions are simple, immediate, and original; which of them are dependant upon others, and how they may be combined and compounded, and afford delight by such composition.

This is an extensive subject, and it is difficult to treat it concisely, and yet plainly; and indeed after all the pains I can take there will be reason to apprehend some obscurity will remain to persons not used to such kind of disquisitions. The way I shall take is to state to you critically or historically the way in which this matter hath been treated by some of the most celebrated writers. The Spectator, written by Mr. Addison, on the pleasures of the imagination, reduces the sources of delight or approbation to three great classes, novelty, greatness, and beauty. He says, that such is our desire after novelty, that all things that were before unknown are from this circumstance recommended to us, and that we receive a delight in the discovery and contemplation of what we never saw before, except such objects as are painful to the organs of sight. That children run from one play thing to another, not because it is better, but new; that it is the same case with men, and that authors in particular are at great pains to have something new and striking in their manner, which is the more difficult to be attained that they must make use of known words, and that their ideas too must be such as are easily intelligible. There is something here that would require a good deal of explication. I do not think that any object is, properly speaking, painful to the organs of sight, except too much light; but we do not consider this as a fault in the object, but feel it as a weakness in ourselves. And further, if there be such a thing as beauty, one would think that if beauty be agreeable it must have a contrary, which is ugliness, and that must be disagreeable. As to greatness, this has been always considered as a source of admiration. The most ancient critics observe, that we do not admire a small rivulet, but the Danube, the Nile, the ocean. This I will afterwards consider. As to beauty, it has been considered as of all other things most inconceivable, and therefore made a first and immediate perception.

Others have taken beauty and grace as the general terms, including every thing that pleases us. Thus we say a beautiful poem, statue, landscape. Thus also we say a sublime and beautiful sentiment. Thus they have taken in under it novelty and greatness, and every other agreeable quality. Many eminent critics have acted in this manner, particularly the ancients. Longinus, on the Sublime, introduces several things which do not belong to it, as distinguished from beauty. Taking beauty as the general object of approbation or source of delight, and as applicable to all the fine arts, it has been variously analysed.

A French writer, Crousaz Traité de Beau, analyses beauty under the following principles: Variety, unity, regularity, order, proportion. Variety is the first. This seems to be related to, or perhaps in some respects the same with novelty, which was formerly mentioned. It is certain that a dead uniformity cannot produce beauty in any sort of performance, poems, oration, statue, picture, building. Unity is, as it were, the bound and restraint of variety. Things must be connected as well as various, and if they are not connected, the variety is nothing but confusion. Regularity is the similarity of the correspondent parts; order is the easy gradation from one to another, and proportion in the suitableness of each part to the whole, and to every other part. I think it cannot be denied that all these have their influence in producing beauty.

One of the most celebrated pieces upon this subject is the famous painter, Hogarth's Analysis of Beauty. He first produced his system in a sort of enigma, drawing one curved line, with the title of the line of beauty, and another with a double wave, which he called the line of grace. He afterwards published his Analysis of Beauty, which he resolves into the following principles: Fitness, variety, uniformity, simplicity, intricacy and quantity. The first principle is fitness, under which he shows that we always conceive of a thing as intended for some use, and therefore there must be a correspondence or suitableness to the use, otherwise whatever be its appearance we reject it as not beautiful. He instances in sailors, who, whenever there is a ship that sails well, they call her a beauty. The same thing will apply perfectly to all kinds of writing: for whatever fine sentiments and noble expression be in any composition, if they are not suited to the reason and subject, we say with Horace, Sed nunc, non erat hic locus. Variety and uniformity must be compounded together, and as he has made no mention of order and proportion, it is to be supposed that by variety he meant that which changes in a gradual and insensible manner; for variety without order is undistinguishable and a heap of confusion. Simplicity means that which is easy, and which the eye travels over and examines without difficulty; and intricacy is that which requires some exercise and attention to follow it; these two must limit one another. In representing beauty as a visible figure, he observes, that a straight line has the least beauty; that which has a wave or easy declination one way begins to be beautiful; that which has a double wave has still greater grace. The truth is, if these two things do not destroy the one the other, simplicity and intricacy improve and beautify one another. Mr. Hogarth observes, that ringlets of hair waving in the wind have been an expression of grace and elegance in every age, nation and language; which is just a contrasted wave, first, that of the curls, and this again rendered a little more intricate by the motion of the breeze. If one would have a view of this principle as exhibited in a single kind, let him look at the flourishes with which the masters of the pen adorn their pieces, and he will see that if they are easy and gradual in their flexions, and just as intricate as the eye can follow without confusion, any thing less than that is less beautiful, and any thing more destroys the beauty by disorder. I might show you how this principle applies to all the arts, but shall only mention composition, where the simplicity must be combined refinement, and when the combination is just there results the most perfect elegance. Mr. Hogarth adds quantity; that a thing having the other qualities, pleases in proportion as it is great; as, we say, a magnificent building, where the proportions are truly observed, but every part is large.

I have only to observe, that Mr. Hogarth has very well illustrated the principles of beauty, but at the same time he seems to have introduced two, which belong to other sources of delight, viz. fitness and quantity, as will be shown afterwards.

It is to be observed, that in the enumeration of the principles of beauty, there are to be found in some authors things not only different but opposite. A French author, not many years ago, to the principles mentioned by others, adds strength, which he illustrates in this manner. He considers it as a principle of grace and beauty in motion, and says that every thing that we do with great difficulty, and that seems to require our utmost effort is seen with uneasiness, and not with pleasure. For this reason he says the motions of young people in general are more graceful that those of old, and agreeably to this we join the word *ease* to gracefulness as explicatory—a graceful, easy carriage. With this explication it seems abundantly proper to admit the remark. On the other hand, there are some who have made comparative weakness a principle of beauty, and say that the more light and slender any thing is, unless it be remarkably weak, it is the more beautiful, and that things remarkably strong rather belong to another class. Thus we say, a fine, tender, delicate shape—and on the contrary we say, a strong, coarse, robust make—a strong, coarse, masculine woman. Perhaps we may reconcile these two, and say they are both principles, because there should be just as much of each as is suitable to the thing in question, that a person may have either too strong or too weak a frame for being esteemed beautiful—that a pillar or dome may be too delicate to be durable, or too strong and bulky to be elegant.

Again: many writers as you have seen, make greatness a principle of beauty; yet there are others who make littleness one of the constituents of beauty. Those who do so, tell us that *little* is a term of endearment, in every nation and language yet known; that it is the language of the vulgar, and therefore the undesigned expression of nature. They instance the diminutive appellations which are always used in fondling—filiolus, filiola, have more affection, than filius and filia—my dear little creature—it is a pretty little thing. To enumerate these different appearances, some, particularly Bourke on the Sublime, affirms that the ideas of sublimity and beauty, are ideas of a class radically different; that the first, sublimity, ultimately arises from the passion of terror, and the other from that of love and light; he with a good deal of ingenuity resolves all the sources of the sublime, into what is either terrible, or allied to this passion, exciting it either immediately in some degree, or by association. It is however uncertain, whether we should reduce what we receive so much delight from, to a passion, which in itself, or in its purity, so to speak, is painful: this objection he endeavors to remove, by showing that the exercise of all our passions in a moderate degree, is a source of pleasure; but perhaps, we may distinguish the ideas of sublime and beautiful, without having recourse to the passion of terror at all, by saying that there is an affection suited to the greatness of objects, without considering them as terrible, and that is, veneration: nay, perhaps we may go a little further, and say that veneration is the affection truly correspondent to greatness, in innocent creatures, which becomes terror in the guilty. I cannot go through the particulars of Bourke's theory. He seems rightly to divide the ideas of sublime and beautiful; by the union of which, some have made one thing, others directly its contrary to belong to beauty. One thing remarkable in Bourke's Essay, is that he denies proportion to be any of the causes of beauty, which yet almost every other writer, has enumerated among them; and what he says of the infinitely various proportion in plants and animals, seems to be much in support of his opinion: yet in works of art, proportion seems of much moment, and it is difficult to say to what source to refer it. I view a building, and if the parts are not in a regular proportion, it offends my eye, even though I could suppose that the disproportion was voluntary, in order to obtain some great convenience.

I should be inclined to think, that there are a considerable number of simple principles or internal sensations, that contribute each its part, in forming our taste, and are capable of being variously combined, and by this combination are apt to be confounded one with another. One of the most distinct and complete enumerations, we have in Gerard's Essay on Taste, and is as follows; A sense of novelty, sublimity, beauty, imitation, harmony, ridicule and virtue. I cannot go through all these in order, but shall make a few remarks, and show where the division is just or defective. His distinguishing all these from one another, is certainly just; but there are some things that he introduces under wrong heads; fitness, for example, he introduces under the head of beauty; and this seems rather a source of approbation distinct in itself, as also proportion, if that is not included in fitness. Perhaps a more complete enumeration than any of them, may be given thus, novelty, sublimity, beauty, proportion, imitation, harmony, ridicule, utility and virtue.

We shall now proceed to those we have not spoken of before; imitation certainly gives great pleasure to the mind and that of itself even independent of the object imitated. An exceedingly well imitated resemblance of any object, of that which is indifferent or even disagreeable in itself, gives the highest pleasure, either from the act of comparison as some say, or from its suggesting the ideal of skill and ingenuity in the imitator. The arts of painting and statuary, derive their excellence from the perfection of imitation, and it is even thought that poetry and oratory may be considered in the same light, only that the first imitates form and passions, by the means of form, and the other imitates actions and affections by language as the instrument.

Harmony is the most distinct and separate of all the internal senses that have been mentioned; it is concerned only in sound, and therefore must be but remotely applicable to the writer and speaker. What is remarkable, that although harmony may be said to be of much importance in speaking, there are many examples of the most excellent speakers, that yet have no musical ear at all, and I think the instances of those who have a remarkably delicate musical ear, and at the same time are agreeable speakers, are not many.

The sense of ridicule is not very easily explained, but it is easily understood when spoken of, because it is universally felt. It differs in this from most other of our constitutional powers, that there is scarcely any man, who is not sensible of the ridiculous, or may be made easily sensible of it; and yet the number of good performers in the art of ridiculing others, or in wit and humor, is but very small. The multitude who cannot follow speculative reasoning, and are hard to be moved by eloquence, are all struck with works of humor. Most people are apt to think they can do something in the way of humor; and yet we have many who render themselves ridiculous by the attempt.

As to a sense of virtue, my mentioning it, is by no means from my joining with those who would place moral approbation entirely on the same footing with the internal senses, that are the foundation of taste. Hutchinson and Shaftsbury incline very much this way; on the contrary I think we are evidently sensible that the morality of actions is a thing of a different species, and arises from the sense of a law, and obligation of a superior nature: yet I have mentioned it here, because there is certainly a relation or connecting tie between the sentiments of the one kind, and of the other. The beauties of nature, we are sensible, are greatly heightened, by adding to their delightful appearance, a reflection on their utility, and the benevolent intention of their author. In persons capable of morality, as in human nature, we consider fine features and an elegant carriage, as indications of the moral disposition or the mental powers; and as the whole of the sources of delight mentioned above, may be combined in a greater or lesser degree, as novelty, sublimity, beauty, &c. so the governing principle which ought to direct the application of the whole, is what gives them their highest excellence, and indeed only is their true perfection. The gratification even of our internal senses, are highly improved, when united with taste and elegance. As the most delicious food when served up with neatness and order, accompanied with politeness of manners, and seasoned with sprightly conversation: in the same manner, the fine arts themselves, acquire a double beauty and higher relish, when they are inseparably connected with, and made subservient to purity of manners. An admirable poem, or an eloquent discourse, or a fine picture, would be still more excellent, if the subject of them were interesting and valuable, and when any of them are perverted to impious or wicked purposes, they are just objects of detestation.

After having thus attempted the analysis of the principles of taste and elegance, I would observe, that as nature seems to delight in producing many great and different effects from simple causes, perhaps we may find an ultimate principle that governs all these. A French author has written a treatise called the Theory of agreeable Sensations, in which he says that the great principle is, whatever exercises our faculties, without fatiguing them, gives pleasure; and that this principle may be applied to our bodily form, and to the constitution of our mind, to objects of external sensation, to objects of taste, and even to our moral conduct. It may no doubt be carried through the whole of criticism, and we may say this states the bounds between variety and uniformity, simplicity and intricacy, order, proportion and harmony.

Neither would it be difficult to show that this principle may be applied to morality, and that an infinitely wise and gracious God had so ordered matters, that the moderate exercise of all our powers, should produce at once, virtue and happiness, and that the least transgression of the one must prove of necessity an injury to the other.

You may see from the preceding remarks, that the foundation is laid for taste in our natures; yet is there great room for improvement and cultivation; by investigating the grounds of approbation; by comparing one thing with another; by studying the best examples; and by reflection and judgment, men may correct and refine their taste upon the whole, or upon particular confined subjects.

Carrying taste to a finical nicety in any one branch, is a thing not only undesireable, but contemptible; the reason of which may be easily seen: when a person applies his attention so much to a matter of no great moment, it occasions a necessary neglect of other things of much greater value. After you pass a certain point, attachment to a particular pursuit is useless, and then it proceeds to be hurtful, and at last contemptible.

William Smith

Excerpts from *A General Idea of the College of Mirania* (1753)

"Verses Spoken at the Opening of the College of Mirania"

It comes! at last, the *promis'd* AERA comes!
Now *Gospel-Truth* shall dissipate the Glooms
Of *Pagan-Error;* and, in copious Streams,
O'er this dark *Hemisphere,* shed *saving Beams!*
For, lo! her azure Wing bright SCIENCE spreads,
And soft-approaches to these *new-found-Shades;*
Exultant, stretching forth her hallow'd Hands
To plant her *Laurels* in serener Lands!
Each *Muse* around *Her* strikes the warbling String;
And, mid *Her* Train, *Peace, Justice, Freedom sing---*
---A GODDESS comes!—they sing and rend the Air—
A GODDESS comes! to welcome *Her* prepare!
Woods, Brooks, Gales, Fountains, long unknown to Fame,
At length, as conscious of your future Claim,
Prepare to nurse the *Philosophic-Thought*;
To swell the *serious*, or the *sportive* Note!
Prepare, ye *Woods!* to yield the *Sage* your Shade;
And wave ambrosial Verdures o'er his Head!
Ye *Brooks!* prepare to prompt the *Poet*'s Strains;
And softly murmur back his amorous Pains!
Haste, O ye *Gales!* your spicy Sweets impart;
In *Music* breathe *Them* to th' exulting Heart!
Ye *Fountains!* haste, th' *inspiring Wave* to roll;
And give *Castalian-Draughts* to lave the Soul.

    'Tis done!—Woods, Brooks, Gales, Fountains, all, obey;
And say with general Voice—or seem to say—
—Hail, *Heaven-descended!* holy SCIENCE, hail!
Thrice-welcome to these Climes; here ever dwell,
With Shade and Silence, far from dire Alarms;
The Trumpet's horrid Clang, and Din of Arms!
To Thee we offer every softer Seat;
Each sunny Lawn; or sylvan sweet Retreat;
Each Flower-verg'd Stream; each Amber-dropping Grove;[1]

Each Vale of *Pleasure;* and each Bower of *Love:*
Where *youthful Nature,* with stupendous Scenes,
Lifts all the *Powers;* and all the *Frame* serenes.
O then! here fix,—(*Earth, Water, Air* invite!)
And bid a NEW-BRITANNIA spring to Light!—
    Smit-deep, I antedate the *Golden Days;*
And strive to paint them in sublimer Lays!
Behold! on Periods, Periods brightening rise!
On *Worthies, Worthies* croud before mine Eyes;
See! other BACONS, NEWTONS, LOCKES appear;
And to the Skies our Laureat-Honors rear.
See! mid undying *Greens,* they lie inspir'd,
On mossy Beds, by heavenly Visions fir'd:
Aloft they soar, on *Contemplation*'s Wing,
O'er Worlds and Worlds--and reach th' ETERNAL KING.
Awak'd by other *Suns,* and kindling strong
With purest Ardors for celestial *Song,*
Lo! other POPES and SPENCERS glad-resound
The *rural Lay* to Shepherds dancing round;
Find other *Twit'nams* in each bowery Wood;
And other *Mullas* in each sylvan Flood.
Lo! the wild INDIAN, soften'd by their Song,
Emerging from his *Arbors,* bounds along
The green *Savannah* patient of the *Lore*
Of *Dove-ey'd Wisdom*—and is *rude* no more.
Hark! even his *Babes* MESSIAH's Praise proclaim;
Or fondly learn to lisp JEHOVAH's Name!
    O SCIENCE! onward thus thy Reign extend
O'er Realms yet unexplor'd till Time shall end;
Till *Death-like Ignorance* forsake the Ball,
And *Life-endearing Knowlege* cover all;
Till wounded *Slavery* seek her native Hell,
In triple Bonds eternally to dwell!
Not trackless Desarts shall thy Progress stay;
Rocks, Mountains, Floods, before Thee must give Way:
Sequester'd Vales, at thy Approach, shall sing;
And with the Voice of cheerful Labor ring.
Where *Wolves* now howl, shall polish'd *Villas* rise;
And towery *Cities* grow into the Skies.—
"Earth's distant Ends our Glory shall behold;
And the NEW-World launch forth to seek the OLD."[2]

---

1. *Amber*, in this Place, is a general Name for Gums, Resins and all odorous vegetable Juices, exsuding from Trees, Shrubs & Herbs.

2. These two Lines from *Pope*'s Windsor-Forest, 399.

From "College; or Five Learned Classes"

Third Class

The Master of this Class is call'd *Professor of Philosophy*. The Day is divided between the Studies of Ethics and Physics: Under the latter, the *Miranians* comprehend Natural History; Mechanic, or corpuscular Philosophy, and experimental Philosophy; for the Illustration of which, they are provided with a complete Apparatus. With Regard to Ethics, they seem to think that a full, yet compendious, System, calculated by some sound Philosopher, for Youth at Colleges, is a Book still wanted. They own, that the *English* excell in detach'd Pieces on all moral Subjects; but these, say they, are only the—*disjecta membra Ethices.*—No one Author has handled the Subject of Ethics, in all its Ramifications, with a View to the Information of Youth: And 'tis dangerous as well as difficult, to learn Morals from different Authors, most of whom clash with one another; or had their peculiar Notions to propagate, and favorite Systems to erect.—In this Class, at present, they read the Philosoph. Books of *Plato* and *Cicero,* in their Originals, with *Locke, Hutchinson, &c.* the Professor, taking Care to guard the Youth against every Thing in which these Authors stand singular.—But they have a Method peculiar almost to themselves, of teaching Morals, upon which they lay the greatest Stress, and that is by historical Facts; of which I shall speak by and by.—The private Reading of such Books as *Derham, Nettleton,* on Virtue and Happiness, *&c.* are recommended for the greater Improvement of the Youth in the Studies of this Class; the Professor, from Time to Time, satisfying himself, by proper Questions, what Advantage they reap from such Books: I do not mention *Keil, Gravesand, Newton*'s Princip. *&c.* because classical Books; and suppos'd in the Study of natural Philosophy.—

Fourth Class

The Master of this Class is styled *Professor of Rhetoric and Poetry*. As it is in this and the following Class, continued *Evander,* that my Countrymen bring all that has been before taught, home to the Business of Life, and are more singular in their Method; I must beg to be something more particular in the Account of them. A great Stock of Learning, without knowing how to make it useful in the Conduct of Life, is of little Significancy. You may observe, that what has chiefly been aim'd at, in the foregoing Classes, is to teach Youth to *think well,* that is, closely and justly. When this is attain'd, it is a noble Basis; but wou'd, however, be useless without its Superstructure; without teaching them to call forth, and avail themselves of, their Thoughts, in *writing, speaking, acting* and *living well*. To make Youth Masters of the first two, *viz.* writing and speaking well, which are the Business of this Class, nothing contributes so much as being capable to relish what has been well written or spoken by others: Hence the proper Studies of this Class, are Rhetoric and Poetry, from which arise Criticism and Composition.

I shall speak first of Rhetoric, as it is the first Study. The Professor begins with giving the Students a general Notion of the Precepts and different Kinds of *Rhetoric,* from *Tully* and *Quintilian;* then proceeds to made them read *Tully*'s Oration for *Milo,* leisurely in its Original; applying, as they go along, the Precepts of Oratory; and making them apprehend its Plan, Series, Delicacy of Address; the Strength and Disposition of the Proofs; the Justness of the Tropes and Figures; the Beauty of the Imagery and Painting; the Harmony and Fullness of the Periods; the Pomp and Purity of the Diction; and, in fine, that Grandeur of Thought; that astonishing Sublime; that Torrent of Eloquence; which, moving, warming, seizing the Soul, sweeps all irresistably down before it.—After this, *Demosthenes*'s Harangue for *Ctesiphon,* which *Tully* calls the Model of perfect Eloquence, is read in its Original, and explain'd in the same Manner.

These two celebrated Orations, thus explain'd and apprehended, are judged sufficient to give Youth a right Idea of Oratory, and fix its Precepts in their Mind, which is not to be done so much by reading many Orations, as by studying a Few thoroughly: And therefore, only three more Orations, one in Greek, one in Latin, and one in English, are read in the School through the whole Year. These are successively handled thus: In the Evening the Professor prescribes a certain Portion of the Oration, and appoints the Students to write out their Observations upon its Conformity to the Laws of Rhetoric; the Plan, Thoughts, *&c.* by Way of Criticism; this they bring with them next Day to the Class or School, when the Part prescrib'd is read over, and this Criticism of theirs examin'd and corrected. A new Portion, as before, is prescrib'd against next Meeting, till in this Manner they have finish'd the whole three Orations.

In the same Manner is Poetry study'd, which is, indeed, rather the same than a different Study; Poetry being nothing else but the eldest Daughter of Eloquence. The Arrangement of the Fable in the

One corresponds to the Plan and Series of the Other. Tropes and Figures they have in common: And where, in the Peculiarity of her Dress, and the more frequent Use of Epithets, &c. *Poetry* affects to differ, the Youth are not unacquainted with it; as they have been made to observe it in reading the Classic-Poets. The Rules, Nature and Design of the several Kinds of Poetry, are, in the first Place explain'd; then, as in the Study of Rhetoric, they privately write a Piece of Criticism upon them, beginning with the lesser Kinds, as the Ode, Elegy, Satyr, &c. proceeding to the Drama, Pastoral and Epopaea. All these Criticisms are carefully revis'd and corrected by the Professor, which is all the public Business of the Class. The Reading of *Aristotle*'s Poetry, and the best French and English Critics is allow'd, and even recommended, to assist and direct the Judgment of Youth in this Exercise.

Here I interrupted *Evander*, by telling him, that I thought this Study alone, might require half the Year. No, replied he; They don't spend above eight Weeks on the Study of all the Kinds of Poetry. This is owing chiefly to the placing the Study of Poetry after Philosophy and Rhetoric, which makes it extreme easy: And partly to the Age of the Youth, they being now, at least, in their 18th Year, and capable of greater Application; partly to the Delight they take in the Study, and partly to their having read most of the different Kinds of Poems, when learning Languages, which renders the Review of them pleasant, in order to apply the Rules of Criticism.—About a Fortnight is enough for all the lesser Poems; the same Space of Time serves for the Drama and Pastoral, (which all but the English Critics examine by the Laws of the Drama) and lastly, about a Month serves for the Epopaea.—

The Remainder of the Year, which is about six Months, is spent in composing and delivering Orations; and 'tis no Wonder, that this Exercise is attended with great Success, when defer'd to this its proper Season. Philosophy, Rhetoric and Poetry, being sufficiently tasted and admir'd; the Youth must be animated, in their Compositions, to imitate those bright Models that gave them so much Pleasure in the Reading. The Study of Poetry, in particular, teaches them a certain Elevation of Thought; makes them give lively Descriptions, with Strength, Variety, Copiousness and Harmony of Style; and diffuse a Delicacy over every Thing they compose.—They begin first with smaller Essays on proper Subjects; thence proceed to frame Orations according to the Precepts, and on the Models, of perfect Eloquence: These the Professor corrects, carefully pointing out where the Subject wou'd have requir'd more Conciseness; where more Copiousness; where the figurative Style, and Graces of Speech; where the Plain and Simple; where they ought to have ris'n; where fallen; where they have given Conceit instead of Wit; the forc'd and far-fetch'd, instead of the easy and natural; Bombast and Swelling, instead of the Sublime and Florid. Thus to correct one Oration and hear another (that has been corrected before) deliver'd, with proper Grace and Action, is all the Business of the Class at one Meeting or Diet. Of this the Youth have their Turns, so that when the Class consists of twenty Students, each of them, in their Turns, compose and deliver an Oration once in ten Days.[1] And as they must all be present at the correcting and delivering two Orations each Day, they profit as much by the Faults or Beauties found in the Compositions of their School-Fellows, as by their own.—

In correcting the Compositions of Youth, however, the Professor is sensible, that great Judgment and Art is requir'd: Always remembring that they are Youth, he is greatly careful not to discourage them by too much Severity. If ever he seems displeas'd at any Thing, it is when he discovers a Sort of Stiffness, Precision and Judgment in their Pieces above their Years, which he considers as a certain Sign of Coldness and Sterility; while, on the other Hand, Redundancy of Thought, and sprightly Sallies of Imagination, share his distinguish'd Indulgence. These he calls the blooming Shoots of Genius; and, tho' exuberant, thinks they are no more to be lopp'd off at an improper Season, or in an unskilful Manner, than the luxuriant Growth of a thriving young Tree. It is dangerous for any Hand, but that of Time, to reduce these wholly within their proper Bounds.

I'm persuaded, you will think it no Objection against the Study of Rhetoric, that it has often been prostituted to the vilest Purposes. What is there that may not be abus'd by *bad Men*? But in the Possession of a *good Man* (and such my Countrymen are careful to form all their Youth) Eloquence is the most glorious Gift of Nature. It makes Him the Sanctuary of the Unfortunate; the Protector of the Weak; the Support and Praise of the Good; and the eternal Terror and Controul of the Bad. We must often address to the Passions wou'd we reach the Heart. And till we can lay Body aside, and resolve ourselves

1. When we allow but ten Days to compose an Oration, besides attending the Duties of the Class; we must suppose their Pieces short.

into pure Spirit, 'tis proud unmeaning Jargon, to say we can relish naked unornamented Truth; or be ravish'd with the plain unaffected Beauties of Virtue.—The *Miranians* don't, however, propose to make Orators and Poets of their Youth, by these Studies. They are sensible both the Orator and Poet must be born, not made. But, say they, those to whom Nature has given a Genius for Composition, either in Poetry or Prose, will be thus put in the Method of improving that Genius to the greatest Advantage; and those who have no such Genius, will, however, be enabled, by these Studies to write elegantly, or at least correctly, in the epistolary Way, and on the common and most important Concerns in Life.

Unless the Taste is thus form'd, and Youth taught to be sound Critics, on the Beauties of those celebrated Pieces that have challeng'd the Admiration of all Mankind, and stood the Test of Time; unless they can discover wherein those Beauties consist;---what is Learning?—Nay, without this Taste, or Relish for the Pleasures of Imagination; what is Life itself?[2] Nature has given the Rudiments of it to every Man: But if we compare the Man who has perfectly cultivated it, with him who has not, they seem almost of a different Species. To the latter are entirely lost, the *Gay,* the *Tender,* the *Easy,* the *Natural,* the *Sublime,* the *Marvellous,* and all the nameless *Graces* of a finish'd Piece!—Shou'd Solitude, shou'd Want of Business, shou'd Misfortunes of any Kind, force such a Man to seek Relief from Books, alas! he finds them—"But formal Dullness, tedious Friends!"—He may read; but he will be as unconscious of the masterly and delicate Strokes of what he reads, as the Mountain is of the Ore lodg'd in its cavern'd Side. A stupid Sort of Admiration is the highest Pleasure he is capable of receiving.— While, on the Contrary, the Man who has been taught to take the full Gust of the generous Pleasures arising from the Contemplation of *Beauty, Order, Harmony, Design, Symmetry* of *Parts,* and *Conformity* to *Truth* and *Nature,* finds, within Himself, an unexhaustable Fund of the most noble and rational Amusement. No Moment of Time.—I speak it feelingly, said *Evander,*—No Moment of Time needs hang heavy on his Hands. No Situation, no Circumstances, neither at home or abroad;[3] neither in Youth nor old Age; neither in Prosperity nor Adversity; but can be render'd more agreeable, while he can taste the intellectual Joys of his darling Studies. Suppose then Youth shou'd reap no other Advantage from the Studies in this Class, but the Power of filling up those vacant Hours to Advantage, which those, who want such a Taste, usually spend in trifling Visits, Cards, Hunting or Drinking-Matches, and other hurtful Pleasures; we have Reason to think a few Months properly spent in forming this Taste, a very essential Part of Education; and the Master that neglects this in Education, may well expect to earn the bitterest Curses of those he deprives of such a solid Joy, in all Conditions of Life. But further, the *Miranians* say, that this Taste for polite Letters, not only teaches us to write well, and renders Life comfortable to ourselves, but also contributes highly to the Cement of Society, and the Tranquility of the State. They don't hesitate to affirm, that they think it almost impossible for a Man that has a Taste for the imitative Arts, and can feel the noble Charms of Rhetoric, Poetry, Painting, Music, Sculpture, &c.—to be a boisterous Subject, an undutiful Son, a rough Husband, an unnatural Parent, a cruel Master, a treacherous Friend, or in any Shape a bad Man. These Studies enlarge the Mind, refine and exalt the Understanding, improve the Temper, soften the Manners, serene the Passions, cherish Reflection, and lead on that charming Langour of Soul, that philosophic Melancholy, which, most of all, disposes to Love, Friendship, and every tender Emotion.—To conclude this Article, (which, as it treated my favorite Studies, I have,

---

2. In Support of *Evander's* Sentiments in this Paragraph, suffer me to quote the following beautiful Verses from Dr. *Armstrong's* Epistle on Benevolence.

" *'Tis chiefly* Taste, *or blunt, or gross, or fine,*
Makes Life insipid, bestial or divine.
Better be born with Taste to little Rent,
Than the dull *Monarch of a Continent.—*
Without fine Nerves and Bosom justly warm'd,
An Eye, an Ear, a Fancy to be charm'd;
In vain, majestic Wren *expands the Dome;*
Blank as pale Stucco RUBENS *lines the Room;*
Lost are the Raptures of bold Handel's *Strain;*
Great Tully *storms, sweet* Virgil *sings in vain.*
The beauteous Forms of Nature are effac'd;
Tempe's soft Charms, the raging watry Waste,
Each greatly-wild, each sweet romantic Scene,
Unheeded rises and almost unseen.
Yet there are Joys with some of better Clay,
To sooth the Toils of Life's embarrass'd Way."

3. *Haec Studia adolescentiam alunt, Senectutem oblectant; secundas res ornant, Adversis Perfugium & Solatium prebent: Delectant Domi, non impediunt foris; pernoctant Nobiscum, peregrinantur, rusticantur.* Cic.

perhaps, tired you with) it appears to me that the Studies, in this and the next Class, are those we must chiefly cultivate, wou'd we be good Men and good Citizens.—*Si Patriae volumus, si Nobis vivere chari.*—And all the Studies in the former Classes seem of little other Value but as they prepare for these.

Reprinted from *A General Idea of the College of Mirania* (New York: Printed & sold by J. Parker & W. Weyman, 1753).

Supplementary Reading List

Addison, Daniel Dulany. *The Clergy in American Life and Letters*. New York & London: Macmillan, 1900.

Ahlstrom, Sydney E. *A Religious History of the American People*. New Haven & London: Yale University Press, 1972.

Aldridge, Alfred Owen, ed. *The Ibero-American Enlightenment*. Urbana: University of Illinois Press, 1971.

Arieli, Yehoshua. *Individualism and Nationalism in American Ideology*. Cambridge: Harvard University Press, 1964.

Bailyn, Bernard. *Education in the Forming of American Society*. Chapel Hill: University of North Carolina Press, 1960.

Bailyn. "Political Experience and Enlightenment Ideas in Eighteenth Century America," *American Historical Review*, 67 (January 1962): 339-351.

Bailyn and John Clive. "England's Cultural Provinces: Scotland and America," third series, 11 (April 1954): 200-213.

Baldwin, Alice M. *The New England Clergy and the American Revolution*. Durham: Duke University Press, 1928.

Baritz, Loren. *City on a Hill, A History of Ideas and Myths in America*. New York: Wiley, 1964.

Bercovitch, Sacvan. *The American Jeremiad*. Madison: University of Wisconsin Press, 1978.

Bercovitch. *The Puritan Origins of the American Self*. New Haven: Yale University Press, 1975.

Berens, John F. *Providence and Patriotism in Early America*. Charlottesville: University Press of Virginia, 1978.

Boorstin, Daniel. *The Americans: The Colonial Experience*. New York: Random House, 1958.

Bridenbaugh, Carl. *Mitre and Sceptre: Transatlantic Faiths, Ideas, Personalities and Politics, 1689-1775*. New York: Oxford University Press, 1962.

Brumm, Ursula. *American Thought and Religious Typology*, translated by John Hooglund. New Brunswick: Rutgers University Press, 1970.

Bushman, Richard L. *From Puritan to Yankee: Character and the Social Order in Connecticut*. Cambridge: Harvard University Press, 1967.

Butt, John Everett. *The Mid-Eighteenth Century*. Edited and completed by Geoffrey Carnall. Volume 8 of *The Oxford History of English Literature*. Oxford: Clarendon Press/New York: Oxford University Press, 1979.

Cherry, Conrad. *Nature and Religious Imagination: From Edwards to Bushnell*. Philadelphia: Fortress, 1980.

Colbourn, Trevor H. *The Lamp of Experience: Whig History and the Intellectual Origins of the American Revolution*. Chapel Hill: University of North Carolina Press, 1965.

Cowing, Cedric B. *The Great Awakening and the American Revolution: Colonial Thought in the 18th Century.* Chicago: Rand-McNally, 1971.

Crowley, J. E. *This Sheba, Self: The Conceptualization of Economic Life in Eighteenth-Century America.* Baltimore: Johns Hopkins University Press, 1974.

Davidson, Philip. *Propaganda and the American Revolution.* Chapel Hill: University of North Carolina Press, 1941.

Davies, Horton. *Worship and Theology in England*, volume 3: *From Watts and Wesley to Maurice, 1690-1850.* Princeton: Princeton University Press, 1961.

Davis, Richard Beale. "The Colonial Virginia Satirist: Mid-Eighteenth Century Commentaries on Politics, Religion, and Society." *Transactions of the American Philosophical Society,* new series, 57 (March 1967): 5-74.

Davis. *Intellectual Life in the Colonial South, 1585-1763*, 3 volumes. Knoxville: University of Tennessee Press, 1978.

Davis. *Intellectual Life of Jefferson's Virginia, 1790-1830.* Chapel Hill: University of North Carolina Press, 1964.

Downey, James. *The Eighteenth Century Pulpit: A Study of the Sermons of Butler, Berkeley, Secker, Sterne, Whitefield, and Wesley.* Oxford: Oxford University Press, 1969.

Elliott, Emory. "The Development of the Puritan Sermon and Elegy: 1660-1750," *Early American Literature,* 15 (Fall 1980): 151-164.

Elliott. *Revolutionary Writers: Literature and Authority in the New Republic.* New York: Oxford University Press, 1982.

Elliott, ed. *Puritan Influences in American Literature.* Urbana: University of Illinois, 1979.

Emerson, Everett H. *Puritanism in America, 1620-1750.* Boston: Twayne, 1977.

Emerson, ed. *American Literature, 1764-1789.* Madison: University of Wisconsin Press, 1977.

Emerson, ed. *Major Writers of Early American Literature.* Madison: University of Wisconsin Press, 1972.

Fritz, Paul Samuel, and David Williams, eds. *The Triumph of Culture: 18th Century Perspectives.* Toronto: A. M. Hakkert, 1972.

Gay, Peter. *The Enlightenment: An Interpretation,* 2 volumes. New York: Knopf, 1966.

Gilmore, Michael T., ed. *Early American Literature: A Collection of Critical Essays.* Englewood Cliffs, N.J.: Prentice-Hall, 1980.

Gipson, Lawrence Henry. *The Coming of the Revolution, 1763-1775.* New York: Harper, 1954.

Granger, Bruce. *American Essay Serials from Franklin to Irving.* Knoxville: University of Tennessee Press, 1978.

Granger. *Political Satire in the American Revolution, 1763-1783.* New York: Cornell University Press, 1960.

Greene, Jack P. "Search for Identity: An Interpretation of the Meaning of Selected Patterns of Social Response in Eighteenth-Century America," *Journal of Social History,* 3 (Spring 1970): 189-220.

Haroutunian, Joseph. *Piety Versus Moralism: The Passing of the New England Theology.* New York: Holt, 1932.

Heimert, Alan E. "Puritanism, the Wilderness, and the Frontier," *New England Quarterly,* 26 (September 1953): 361-382.

Hofstader, Richard. *America at 1750: A Social Portrait.* New York: Knopf, 1971.

Howell, Wilbur Samuel. *Eighteenth-Century British Logic and Rhetoric.* Princeton: Princeton University Press, 1971.

Israel, Calvin, ed. *Discoveries & Considerations: Essays on Early American Literature & Aesthetics: Presented to Harold Jantz.* Albany: State University of New York Press, 1976.

Jantz, Harold S. *The First Century of New England Verse.* Worcester, Mass.: American Antiquarian Society, 1944.

Kagle, Steven E. *American Diary Literature: 1620-1799.* Boston: Twayne, 1979.

Kammen, Michael G. *People of Paradox: An Inquiry Concerning the Origins of American Civilization.* New York: Knopf, 1972.

Ketcham, Ralph L. *From Colony to Country: The Revolution in American Thought, 1750-1820.* New York: Macmillan, 1974.

Koch, Adrienne. *Power, Morals and the Founding Fathers.* Ithaca: Great Seal Books, 1961.

Koch, ed. *The American Enlightenment: The Shaping of the American Experiment and a Free Society.* New York: Braziller, 1965.

Lemay, J. A. Leo. *Man of Letters in Colonial Maryland.* Knoxville: University of Tennessee Press, 1972.

Levin, David. *In Defense of Historical Literature.* New York: Hill & Wang, 1967.

Lowance, Mason I., Jr. *The Language of Canaan: Metaphor and Symbol in New England from the Puritans to the Transcendentalists.* Cambridge & London: Harvard University Press, 1980.

Lynen, John F. *The Design of the Present: Essays on Time and Form in American Literature.* New Haven: Yale University Press, 1969.

Miller, Perry. *Errand into the Wilderness.* Cambridge: Harvard University Press, 1956.

Moore, Frank. *Diary of the American Revolution. From Newspapers and Original Documents,* 2 volumes. New York: Scribners/London: Low, 1860.

Morgan, Edmund S., ed. *Puritan Political Ideas, 1558-1794.* Indianapolis: Bobbs-Merrill, 1965.

Nash, Gary B. *Class and Society in Early America.* Englewood Cliffs, N.J.: Prentice-Hall, 1970.

Nash. *The Urban Crucible: Social Change, Political Consciousness, and the Origins of the American Revolution.* Cambridge: Harvard University Press, 1979.

Needham, H. A., ed. *Taste and Criticism in the Eighteenth Century: A Selection of Texts Illustrating the Evolution of Taste and the Development of Critical Theory.* London: Harrap, 1952.

Nye, Russel B. *American Literary History: 1607-1830*. New York: Knopf, 1970.

Plumstead, A. W., ed. *The Wall and the Garden: The Massachusetts Election Sermons, 1670-1775*. Minneapolis: University of Minnesota Press, 1968.

Robbins, Caroline. *The Eighteenth-Century Commonwealthman: Studies in the Transmission, Development, and Circumstance of English Liberal Thought from the Restoration of Charles II until the War with the Thirteen Colonies*. Cambridge: Harvard University Press, 1959.

Seelye, John. *Prophetic Waters: The River in Early American Life and Literature*. New York: Oxford University Press, 1977.

Shea, Daniel B., Jr. *Spiritual Autobiography in Early America*. Princeton: Princeton University Press, 1968.

Silverman, Kenneth, ed. *Colonial American Poetry*. New York: Hafner, 1968.

Slotkin, Richard S. *Regeneration through Violence: The Mythology of the American Frontier, 1600-1860*. Middletown, Conn.: Wesleyan University Press, 1973.

Sprague, William B. *Annals of the American Pulpit*, 9 volumes. New York: Carter, 1857-1869.

Stein, Roger B. *Seascape and the American Imagination*. New York: Crown, 1975.

Strout, Cushing. *The New Heavens and New Earth: Political Religion in America*. New York: Harper & Row, 1973.

Tichi, Cecilia. *New World, New Earth: Environmental Reform in American Literature from the Puritans through Whitman*. New Haven: Yale University Press, 1979.

Tyler, Moses Coit. *A History of American Literature: 1607-1765*. New York: Putnam's, 1878.

Watts, Emily Stipes. *The Poetry of American Women from 1632 to 1945*. Austin: University of Texas Press, 1977.

Wood, Gordon S. "Rhetoric and Reality in the American Revolution," *William and Mary Quarterly*, third series, 23 (January 1966): 3-32;

Wright, Louis B. *The Cultural Life of the American Colonies: 1607-1763*. New York: Harper, 1957.

Wright. *Culture on the Moving Frontier*. Bloomington: University of Indiana Press, 1955.

Wright, Thomas G. *Literary Culture in Early New England, 1620-1730*. New Haven: Yale University Press, 1920.

Ziff, Larzer. *Puritanism in America: New Culture in a New World*. New York: Viking, 1973.

Zuckerman, Michael. "The Fabrication of Identity in Early America," *William and Mary Quarterly*, third series, 34 (April 1977): 183-214.

Contributors

William D. Andrews — Philadelphia College of Textiles & Science
Alan Axelrod — Henry Francis du Pont Winterthur Museum
Maurice J. Bennett — University of Maryland
Charles Bolton — Cincinnati, Ohio
William K. Bottorff — University of Toledo
Meta Robinson Braymer — Virginia Commonwealth University
Liza Dant — Princeton University
Hugh J. Dawson — University of San Francisco
Arthur L. Ford — Lebanon Valley College
James C. Gaston — Annandale, Virginia
Elaine K. Ginsberg — West Virginia University
Maureen Goldman — Bentley College
Paul W. Harris — Ann Arbor, Michigan
Robert W. Hill — Clemson University
John Holland — Princeton University
O. Glade Hunsaker — Brigham Young University
Steven E. Kagle — Illinois State University
Homer D. Kemp — Tennessee Technological University
M. Jimmie Killingsworth — New Mexico Institute of Mining and Technology
Michael P. Kramer — University of California, Davis
Lewis Leary — University of North Carolina
Christopher J. MacGowan — College of William and Mary
Alasdair Macphail — Connecticut College
Louis P. Masur — Princeton University
Robert Micklus — State University of New York at Binghamton
Susan Mizruchi — Princeton University
Carla Mulford — Villanova University
Sondra A. O'Neale — Emory University
Tony Owens — University of South Carolina
Mark R. Patterson — University of Washington
Amanda Porterfield — Syracuse University
Robert D. Richardson, Jr. — University of Denver
Michael Robertson — Princeton University
David Robinson — Oregon State University
William J. Scheick — University of Texas at Austin
Arthur Sheps — University of Toronto
John C. Shields — Illinois State University
Frank Shuffelton — University of Rochester
David Curtis Skaggs — Bowling Green State University
Thomas P. Slaughter — Rutgers University
Martha Strom — Princeton University
Thomas F. Strychacz — Princeton University
Rick W. Sturdevant — U.S. Air Force History Program
Mark Valeri — Princeton University
Jeffrey Walker — Oklahoma State University
Donald Weber — Mount Holyoke College
Thomas Werge — University of Notre Dame

Contributors

Daniel E. Williams	*Universität Tübingen*
Robert P. Winston	*Dickinson College*
David Woolwine	*Princeton University*
Anne Y. Zimmer	*Wayne State University*

Cumulative Index

Dictionary of Literary Biography, Volumes 1-31
Dictionary of Literary Biography Yearbook, 1980-1983
Dictionary of Literary Biography Documentary Series, Volumes 1-4

Cumulative Index

DLB before number: *Dictionary of Literary Biography*, Volumes 1-31
Y before number: *Dictionary of Literary Biography Yearbook*, 1980-1983
DS before number: *Dictionary of Literary Biography Documentary Series*, Volumes 1-4

A

Abbot, Willis J. 1863-1934 ....DLB29
Abbott, Jacob 1803-1879 ....DLB1
Abbott, Robert S. 1868-1940 ....DLB29
Abercrombie, Lascelles 1881-1938 ....DLB19
Abse, Dannie 1923- DLB27
Adair, James 1709?-1783? DLB30
Adamic, Louis 1898-1951 ....DLB9
Adams, Douglas 1952- Y83
Adams, Franklin P. 1881-1960 ....DLB29
Adams, Henry 1838-1918 ....DLB12
Adams, James Truslow 1878-1949 ....DLB17
Adams, John 1734-1826 ....DLB31
Adams, Samuel 1722-1803 ....DLB31
Ade, George 1866-1944 ....DLB11, 25
Adeler, Max (see Clark, Charles Heber)
AE 1869-1935 ....DLB19
Agassiz, Jean Louis Rodolphe 1807-1873 ....DLB1
Agee, James 1909-1955 ....DLB2, 26
Aiken, Conrad 1889-1973 ....DLB9
Ainsworth, William Harrison 1805-1882 ....DLB21
Akins, Zoë 1886-1958 ....DLB26
Albee, Edward 1928- DLB7
Alcott, Amos Bronson 1799-1888 ....DLB1
Alcott, Louisa May 1832-1888 ....DLB1
Alcott, William Andrus 1798-1859 ....DLB1
Aldington, Richard 1892-1962 ....DLB20
Aldis, Dorothy 1896-1966 ....DLB22
Aldiss, Brian W. 1925- DLB14
Alexander, James 1691-1756 ....DLB24
Algren, Nelson 1909-1981 ....DLB9; Y81, 82
Alldritt, Keith 1935- DLB14
Allen, Ethan 1738-1789 ....DLB31

Allen, Hervey 1889-1949 ....DLB9
Allen, James 1739-1808 ....DLB31
Allen, Jay Presson 1922- DLB26
Josiah Allen's Wife (see Holly, Marietta)
Allott, Kenneth 1912-1973 ....DLB20
Allston, Washington 1779-1843 ....DLB1
Alsop, George 1636-post 1673 ....DLB24
Alvarez, A. 1929- DLB14
Ames, Mary Clemmer 1831-1884 ....DLB23
Amis, Kingsley 1922- DLB15, 27
Amis, Martin 1949- DLB14
Ammons, A. R. 1926- DLB5
Anderson, Margaret 1886-1973 ....DLB4
Anderson, Maxwell 1888-1959 ....DLB7
Anderson, Paul Y. 1893-1938 ....DLB29
Anderson, Poul 1926- DLB8
Anderson, Robert 1917- DLB7
Anderson, Sherwood 1876-1941 ....DLB4, 9; DS1
Andrews, Charles M. 1863-1943 ....DLB17
Anhalt, Edward 1914- DLB26
Anthony, Piers 1934- DLB8
Archer, William 1856-1924 ....DLB10
Arden, John 1930- DLB13
Arensberg, Ann 1937- Y82
Arnow, Harriette Simpson 1908- DLB6
Arp, Bill (see Smith, Charles Henry)
Arthur, Timothy Shay 1809-1885 ....DLB3
Asch, Nathan 1902-1964 ....DLB4, 28
Ashbery, John 1927- DLB5; Y81
Asher, Sandy 1942- Y83
Ashton, Winifred (see Dane, Clemence)
Asimov, Isaac 1920- DLB8
Atherton, Gertrude 1857-1948 ....DLB9
Atkins, Josiah circa 1755-1781 ....DLB31

Auchincloss, Louis 1917- DLB2; Y80
Auden, W. H. 1907-1973............................DLB10, 20
Austin, Mary 1868-1934.............................DLB9
Ayckbourn, Alan 1939- DLB13

B

Bacon, Delia 1811-1859.............................DLB1
Bacon, Thomas circa 1700-1768.....................DLB31
Bagnold, Enid 1889-1981...........................DLB13
Bailey, Paul 1937- DLB14
Baillie, Hugh 1890-1966 ....DLB29
Bailyn, Bernard 1922- DLB17
Bainbridge, Beryl 1933- DLB14
Bald, Wambly 1902- DLB4
Balderston, John 1889-1954 ....DLB26
Baldwin, James 1924- DLB2, 7
Baldwin, Joseph Glover 1815-1864.................DLB3, 11
Ballard, J. G. 1930- DLB14
Bancroft, George 1800-1891 ....DLB1, 30
Bangs, John Kendrick 1862-1922....................DLB11
Banville, John 1945- DLB14
Baraka, Amiri 1934- DLB5, 7, 16
Barber, John Warner 1798-1885.....................DLB30
Barbour, Ralph Henry 1870-1944...................DLB22
Barker, A. L. 1918- DLB14
Barker, George 1913- DLB20
Barker, Harley Granville 1877-1946 ....DLB10
Barker, Howard 1946- DLB13
Barks, Coleman 1937- DLB5
Barnard, John 1681-1770 ....DLB24
Barnes, Djuna 1892-1982 ....DLB4, 9
Barnes, Margaret Ayer 1886-1967 ....DLB9
Barnes, Peter 1931- DLB13
Barney, Natalie 1876-1972.........................DLB4
Barrie, James M. 1860-1937 ....DLB10
Barry, Philip 1896-1949 ....DLB7
Barstow, Stan 1928- DLB14
Barth, John 1930- DLB2
Barthelme, Donald 1931- DLB2; Y80

Bartlett, John 1820-1905..........................DLB1
Bartol, Cyrus Augustus 1813-1900.................DLB1
Bartram, John 1699-1777 ....DLB31
Bass, T. J. 1932- Y81
Bassett, John Spencer 1867-1928 ....DLB17
Bassler, Thomas Joseph (see Bass, T. J.)
Baum, L. Frank 1856-1919..........................DLB22
Baumbach, Jonathan 1933- Y80
Bawden, Nina 1925- DLB14
Bax, Clifford 1886-1962...........................DLB10
Beach, Sylvia 1887-1962...........................DLB4
Beagle, Peter S. 1939- Y80
Beal, M. F. 1937- Y81
Beale, Howard K. 1899-1959........................DLB17
Beard, Charles A. 1874-1948.......................DLB17
Beattie, Ann 1947- Y82
Becker, Carl 1873-1945............................DLB17
Beckett, Samuel 1906- DLB13, 15
Beecher, Catharine Esther 1800-1878...............DLB1
Beecher, Henry Ward 1813-1887.....................DLB3
Behan, Brendan 1923-1964 ....DLB13
Behrman, S. N. 1893-1973 ....DLB7
Belasco, David 1853-1931 ....DLB7
Belitt, Ben 1911- DLB5
Belknap, Jeremy 1744-1798.........................DLB30
Bell, Marvin 1937- DLB5
Bellamy, Edward 1850-1898 ....DLB12
Bellamy, Joseph 1719-1790.........................DLB31
Belloc, Hilaire 1870-1953.........................DLB19
Bellow, Saul 1915- DLB2, 28; DS3; Y82
Bemelmans, Ludwig 1898-1962.......................DLB22
Bemis, Samuel Flagg 1891-1973.....................DLB17
Benchley, Robert 1889-1945 ....DLB11
Benedictus, David 1938- DLB14
Benedikt, Michael 1935- DLB5
Benét, Stephen Vincent 1898-1943..................DLB4
Benford, Gregory 1941- Y82
Benjamin, Park 1809-1864..........................DLB3
Bennett, Arnold 1867-1931 ....DLB10
Bennett, James Gordon, Jr. 1841-1918..........DLB23

Berg, Stephen 1934-	DLB5
Berger, John 1926-	DLB14
Berger, Meyer 1898-1959	DLB29
Berger, Thomas 1924-	DLB2; Y80
Berrigan, Daniel 1921-	DLB5
Berrigan, Ted 1934-	DLB5
Berry, Wendell 1934-	DLB5, 6
Bessie, Alvah 1904-	DLB26
Bester, Alfred 1913-	DLB8
Betjeman, John 1906-	DLB20
Betts, Doris 1932-	Y82
Beveridge, Albert J. 1862-1927	DLB17
Beverley, Robert circa 1673-1722	DLB24, 30
Bierce, Ambrose 1842-1914?	DLB11, 12, 23
Biggle, Lloyd, Jr. 1923-	DLB8
Biglow, Hosea (see Lowell, James Russell)	
Billings, Josh (see Shaw, Henry Wheeler)	
Binyon, Laurence 1869-1943	DLB19
Bird, William 1888-1963	DLB4
Bishop, Elizabeth 1911-1979	DLB5
Bishop, John Peale 1892-1944	DLB4, 9
Black, Winifred 1863-1936	DLB25
Blackamore, Arthur 1679-?	DLB24
Blackburn, Paul 1926-1971	Y81; DLB16
Blackburn, Thomas 1916-1977	DLB27
Blackmore, R. D. 1825-1900	DLB18
Blackwood, Caroline 1931-	DLB14
Blair, James circa 1655-1743	DLB24
Bledsoe, Albert Taylor 1809-1877	DLB3
Blish, James 1921-1975	DLB8
Block, Rudolph (see Lessing, Bruno)	
Blunden, Edmund 1896-1974	DLB20
Blunt, Wilfrid Scawen 1840-1922	DLB19
Bly, Nellie (see Cochrane, Elizabeth)	
Bly, Robert 1926-	DLB5
Bodenheim, Maxwell 1892-1954	DLB9
Boer, Charles 1939-	DLB5
Bogarde, Dirk 1921-	DLB14
Bolling, Robert 1738-1775	DLB31
Bolt, Robert 1924-	DLB13
Bolton, Herbert E. 1870-1953	DLB17
Bond, Edward 1934-	DLB13
Boorstin, Daniel J. 1914-	DLB17
Booth, Philip 1925-	Y82
Borrow, George 1803-1881	DLB21
Botta, Anne C. Lynch 1815-1891	DLB3
Bottomley, Gordon 1874-1948	DLB10
Bottoms, David 1949-	Y83
Bottrall, Ronald 1906-	DLB20
Boucher, Anthony 1911-1968	DLB8
Boucher, Jonathan 1738-1804	DLB31
Bourjaily, Vance 1922-	DLB2
Bova, Ben 1932-	Y81
Bovard, Oliver K. 1872-1945	DLB25
Bowen, Elizabeth 1899-1973	DLB15
Bowen, Francis 1811-1890	DLB1
Bowen, John 1924-	DLB13
Bowers, Claude G. 1878-1958	DLB17
Bowers, Edgar 1924-	DLB5
Bowles, Paul 1910-	DLB5, 6
Boyd, James 1888-1944	DLB9
Boyd, John 1919-	DLB8
Boyd, Thomas 1898-1935	DLB9
Boyesen, Hjalmar Hjorth 1848-1895	DLB12
Boyle, Kay 1902-	DLB4, 9
Brackett, Charles 1892-1969	DLB26
Brackett, Leigh 1915-1978	DLB8, 26
Brackenridge, Hugh Henry 1748-1816	DLB11
Bradbury, Malcolm 1932-	DLB14
Bradbury, Ray 1920-	DLB2, 8
Braddon, Mary Elizabeth 1835-1915	DLB18
Bradford, Gamaliel 1863-1932	DLB17
Bradford, William 1590-1657	DLB24, 30
Bradley, Marion Zimmer 1930-	DLB8
Bradley, William Aspenwall 1878-1939	DLB4
Bradstreet, Anne 1612 or 1613-1672	DLB24
Bragg, Melvyn 1939-	DLB14
Braine, John 1922-	DLB15
Brautigan, Richard 1935-	DLB2, 5; Y80
Bray, Thomas 1656-1730	DLB24

Bremser, Bonnie 1939- DLB16
Bremser, Ray 1934- DLB16
Brenton, Howard 1942- DLB13
Bridges, Robert 1844-1930 .....DLB19
Bridie, James 1888-1951 .....DLB10
Briggs, Charles Frederick 1804-1877 .....DLB3
Brighouse, Harold 1882-1958 .....DLB10
Brisbane, Albert 1809-1890 .....DLB3
Brisbane, Arthur 1864-1936 .....DLB25
Brodhead, John R. 1814-1873 .....DLB30
Bromfield, Louis 1896-1956 .....DLB4, 9
Broner, E. M. 1930- DLB28
Brontë, Anne 1820-1849 .....DLB21
Brontë, Charlotte 1816-1855 .....DLB21
Brontë, Emily 1818-1848 .....DLB21
Brooke, Rupert 1887-1915 .....DLB19
Brooke-Rose, Christine 1926- DLB14
Brooks, Charles Timothy 1813-1883 .....DLB1
Brooks, Gwendolyn 1917- DLB5
Brooks, Jeremy 1926- DLB14
Brooks, Mel 1926- DLB26
Brophy, Brigid 1929- DLB14
Brossard, Chandler 1922- DLB16
Brother Antoninus (see Everson, William)
Brougham, John 1810-1880 .....DLB11
Broughton, James 1913- DLB5
Broughton, Rhoda 1840-1920 .....DLB18
Broun, Heywood 1888-1939 .....DLB29
Brown, Bob 1886-1959 .....DLB4
Brown, Christy 1932-1981 .....DLB14
Brown, Dee 1908- Y80
Brown, Fredric 1906-1972 .....DLB8
Brown, George Mackay 1921- DLB14, 27
Brown, Harry 1917- DLB26
Brown, Margaret Wise 1910-1952 .....DLB22
Brown, Oliver Madox 1855-1874 .....DLB21
Brown, William Wells 1813-1884 .....DLB3
Browne, Charles Farrar 1834-1867 .....DLB11
Browne, Wynyard 1911-1964 .....DLB13
Brownson, Orestes Augustus 1803-1876 .....DLB1

Bruckman, Clyde 1894-1955 .....DLB26
Bryant, William Cullen 1794-1878 .....DLB3
Buchanan, Robert 1841-1901 .....DLB18
Buchman, Sidney 1902-1975 .....DLB26
Buck, Pearl S. 1892-1973 .....DLB9
Buckley, William F., Jr. 1925- Y80
Buckner, Robert 1906- DLB26
Budd, Thomas ?-1698 .....DLB24
Budrys, A. J. 1931- DLB8
Buechner, Frederick 1926- Y80
Bukowski, Charles 1920- DLB5
Bullins, Ed 1935- DLB7
Bulwer-Lytton, Edward (also Edward Bulwer) 1803-1873 .....DLB21
Bumpus, Jerry 1937- Y81
Bunting, Basil 1900- DLB20
Burgess, Anthony 1917- DLB14
Burgess, Gelett 1866-1951 .....DLB11
Burgess, Thornton W. 1874-1965 .....DLB22
Burnett, W. R. 1899- DLB9
Burns, Alan 1929- DLB14
Burroughs, Edgar Rice 1875-1950 .....DLB8
Burroughs, William S., Jr. 1947-1981 .....DLB16
Burroughs, William Seward 1914- DLB2, 8, 16; Y81
Burroway, Janet 1936- DLB6
Burton, Virginia Lee 1909-1968 .....DLB22
Busch, Frederick 1941- DLB6
Butler, Samuel 1835-1902 .....DLB18
Byatt, A. S. 1936- DLB14
Byles, Mather 1707-1788 .....DLB24
Byrd, William II 1674-1744 .....DLB24
Byrne, John Keyes (see Leonard, Hugh)

C

Cabell, James Branch 1879-1958 .....DLB9
Cable, George Washington 1844-1925 .....DLB12
Cahan, Abraham 1860-1951 .....DLB9, 25, 28
Caldwell, Erskine 1903- DLB9

Calhoun, John C. 1782-1850 ....DLB3
Calisher, Hortense 1911- DLB2
Calmer, Edgar 1907- DLB4
Calvert, George Henry 1803-1889 ....DLB1
Camm, John 1718-1778 ....DLB31
Campbell, John W., Jr. 1910-1971 ....DLB8
Campbell, Roy 1901-1957 ....DLB20
Cannan, Gilbert 1884-1955 ....DLB10
Cannell, Kathleen 1891-1974 ....DLB4
Cantwell, Robert 1908-1978 ....DLB9
Capen, Joseph 1658-1725 ....DLB24
Capote, Truman 1924- DLB2; Y80
Carroll, Gladys Hasty 1904- DLB9
Carroll, Lewis 1832-1898 ....DLB18
Carroll, Paul 1927- DLB16
Carroll, Paul Vincent 1900-1968 ....DLB10
Carruth, Hayden 1921- DLB5
Carter, Angela 1940- DLB14
Carter, Landon 1710-1778 ....DLB31
Carter, Lin 1930- Y81
Caruthers, William Alexander 1802-1846 ....DLB3
Carver, Jonathan 1710-1780 ....DLB31
Cary, Joyce 1888-1957 ....DLB15
Casey, Juanita 1925- DLB14
Casey, Michael 1947- DLB5
Cassady, Carolyn 1923- DLB16
Cassady, Neal 1926-1968 ....DLB16
Cassill, R. V. 1919- DLB6
Cather, Willa 1873-1947 ....DLB9; DS1
Catton, Bruce 1899-1978 ....DLB17
Causley, Charles 1917- DLB27
Caute, David 1936- DLB14
Challans, Eileen Mary (see Renault, Mary)
Chalmers, George 1742-1825 ....DLB30
Chamberlain, Samuel S. 1851-1916 ....DLB25
Chamberlin, William Henry 1897-1969 ....DLB29
Chambers, Charles Haddon 1860-1921 ....DLB10
Chandler, Harry 1864-1944 ....DLB29
Channing, Edward 1856-1931 ....DLB17
Channing, Edward Tyrrell 1790-1856 ....DLB1

Channing, William Ellery 1780-1842 ....DLB1
Channing, William Ellery II 1817-1901 ....DLB1
Channing, William Henry 1810-1884 ....DLB1
Chappell, Fred 1936- DLB6
Charles, Gerda 1914- DLB14
Charyn, Jerome 1937- Y83
Chase, Borden 1900-1971 ....DLB26
Chauncy, Charles 1705-1787 ....DLB24
Chayefsky, Paddy 1923-1981 ....DLB7; Y81
Cheever, Ezekiel 1615-1708 ....DLB24
Cheever, John 1912-1982 ....DLB2; Y80, 82
Cheever, Susan 1943- Y82
Cheney, Ednah Dow (Littlehale) 1824-1904 .....DLB1
Cherry, Kelly 1940- Y83
Cherryh, C. J. 1942- Y80
Chesnutt, Charles Waddell 1858-1932 ....DLB12
Chesterton, G. K. 1874-1936 ....DLB10, 19
Child, Francis James 1825-1896 ....DLB1
Child, Lydia Maria 1802-1880 ....DLB1
Childress, Alice 1920- DLB7
Childs, George W. 1829-1894 ....DLB23
Chivers, Thomas Holley 1809-1858 ....DLB3
Chopin, Kate 1851-1904 ....DLB12
Christie, Agatha 1890-1976 ....DLB13
Church, Benjamin 1734-1778 ....DLB31
Churchill, Caryl 1938- DLB13
Ciardi, John 1916- DLB5
Clapper, Raymond 1892-1944 ....DLB29
Clark, Charles Heber 1841-1915 ....DLB11
Clark, Eleanor 1913- DLB6
Clark, Lewis Gaylord 1808-1873 ....DLB3
Clark, Walter Van Tilburg 1909-1971 ....DLB9
Clarke, Austin 1896-1974 ....DLB10, 20
Clarke, James Freeman 1810-1888 ....DLB1
Clausen, Andy 1943- DLB16
Clemens, Samuel Langhorne 1835-1910
....DLB11, 12, 23
Clement, Hal 1922- DLB8
Clemo, Jack 1916- DLB27
Clifton, Lucille 1936- DLB5

Coates, Robert M. 1897-1973	DLB4, 9
Coatsworth, Elizabeth 1893-	DLB22
Cobb, Frank I. 1869-1923	DLB25
Cobb, Irvin S. 1876-1944	DLB11, 25
Cochran, Thomas C. 1902-	DLB17
Cochrane, Elizabeth 1867-1922	DLB25
Cockerill, John A. 1845-1896	DLB23
Cohen, Arthur A. 1928-	DLB28
Colden, Cadwallader 1688-1776	DLB24, 30
Cole, Barry 1936-	DLB14
Colegate, Isabel 1931-	DLB14
Coleman, Emily Holmes 1899-1974	DLB4
Coleridge, Mary 1861-1907	DLB19
Collins, Mortimer 1827-1876	DLB21
Collins, Wilkie 1824-1889	DLB18
Colman, Benjamin 1673-1747	DLB24
Colum, Padraic 1881-1972	DLB19
Colwin, Laurie 1944-	Y80
Commager, Henry Steele 1902-	DLB17
Connell, Evan S., Jr. 1924-	DLB2; Y81
Connelly, Marc 1890-	DLB7; Y80
Conquest, Robert 1917-	DLB27
Conrad, Joseph 1857-1924	DLB10
Conroy, Jack 1899-	Y81
Conroy, Pat 1945-	DLB6
Conway, Moncure Daniel 1832-1907	DLB1
Cook, Ebenezer circa 1667-circa 1732	DLB24
Cooke, John Esten 1830-1886	DLB3
Cooke, Philip Pendleton 1816-1850	DLB3
Cooke, Rose Terry 1827-1892	DLB12
Cooper, Giles 1918-1966	DLB13
Cooper, James Fenimore 1789-1851	DLB3
Cooper, Kent 1880-1965	DLB29
Coover, Robert 1932-	DLB2; Y81
Coppel, Alfred 1921-	Y83
Corman, Cid 1924-	DLB5
Corn, Alfred 1943-	Y80
Corrington, John William 1932-	DLB6
Corso, Gregory 1930-	DLB5, 16
Costain, Thomas B. 1885-1965	DLB9
Cotton, John 1584-1652	DLB24

Coward, Noel 1899-1973	DLB10
Cowles, Gardner 1861-1946	DLB29
Cowley, Malcolm 1898-	DLB4; Y81
Coxe, Louis 1918-	DLB5
Cozzens, James Gould 1903-1978	DLB9; DS2
Craddock, Charles Egbert (see Murfree, Mary N.)	
Cradock, Thomas 1718-1770	DLB31
Cranch, Christopher Pearse 1813-1892	DLB1
Crane, Hart 1899-1932	DLB4
Crane, Stephen 1871-1900	DLB12
Craven, Avery 1885-1980	DLB17
Crawford, Charles 1752-circa 1815	DLB31
Crayon, Geoffrey (see Irving, Washington)	
Creel, George 1876-1953	DLB25
Creeley, Robert 1926-	DLB5, 16
Creelman, James 1859-1915	DLB23
Cregan, David 1931-	DLB13
Crews, Harry 1935-	DLB6
Crichton, Michael 1942-	Y81
Cristofer, Michael 1946-	DLB7
Crockett, David 1786-1836	DLB3, 11
Croly, Jane Cunningham 1829-1901	DLB23
Crosby, Caresse 1892-1970 and Crosby, Harry 1898-1929	DLB4
Crothers, Rachel 1878-1958	DLB7
Crowley, John 1942-	Y82
Crowley, Mart 1935-	DLB7
Croy, Homer 1883-1965	DLB4
Cullen, Countee 1903-1946	DLB4
Cummings, E. E. 1894-1962	DLB4
Cummings, Ray 1887-1957	DLB8
Cunningham, J. V. 1911-	DLB5
Cuomo, George 1929-	Y80
Cuppy, Will 1884-1949	DLB11
Curti, Merle E. 1897-	DLB17
Curtis, George William 1824-1892	DLB1

D

Dall, Caroline Wells (Healey) 1822-1912	DLB1
Daly, T. A. 1871-1948	DLB11

D'Alton, Louis 1900-1951 ....DLB10

Dana, Charles A. 1819-1897........................DLB3, 23

Dana, Richard Henry, Jr. 1815-1882 ....DLB1

Dane, Clemence 1887-1965...............................DLB10

Danforth, John 1660-1730................................DLB24

Danforth, Samuel I 1626-1674.........................DLB24

Danforth, Samuel II 1666-1727.......................DLB24

Daniels, Josephus 1862-1948 ....DLB29

Daryush, Elizabeth 1887-1977 ....DLB20

d'Aulaire, Edgar Parin 1898- and
d'Aulaire, Ingri 1904- DLB22

Daves, Delmer 1904-1977 ....DLB26

Davidson, Avram 1923- DLB8

Davidson, John 1857-1909...............................DLB19

Davidson, Lionel 1922- DLB14

Davie, Donald 1922- DLB27

Davies, Samuel 1723-1761................................DLB31

Davies, W. H. 1871-1940.................................DLB19

Daviot, Gordon 1896-1952..............................DLB10

Davis, Charles A. 1795-1867.............................DLB11

Davis, Clyde Brion 1894-1962 ....DLB9

Davis, H. L. 1894-1960......................................DLB9

Davis, Margaret Thomson 1926- DLB14

Davis, Ossie 1917- DLB7

Davis, Richard Harding 1864-1916............DLB12, 23

Davison, Peter 1928- DLB5

Dawson, William 1704-1752...........................DLB31

Day, Clarence 1874-1935..................................DLB11

Day, Dorothy 1897-1980..................................DLB29

Day Lewis, C. 1904-1972.........................DLB15, 20

Deal, Borden 1922- DLB6

de Angeli, Marguerite 1889- DLB22

De Bow, James D. B. 1820-1867 ....DLB3

de Camp, L. Sprague 1907- DLB8

De Forest, John William 1826-1906..............DLB12

de Graff, Robert 1895-1981..................................Y81

de la Mare, Walter 1873-1956........................DLB19

Delaney, Shelagh 1939- DLB13

Delany, Samuel R. 1942- DLB8

Delbanco, Nicholas 1942- DLB6

DeLillo, Don 1936- DLB6

Dell, Floyd 1887-1969 ....DLB9

del Rey, Lester 1915- DLB8

Dennis, Nigel 1912- DLB13, 15

Denton, Daniel circa 1626-1703 ....DLB24

Derby, George Horatio 1823-1861.................DLB11

Derleth, August 1909-1971...............................DLB9

DeVoto, Bernard 1897-1955.............................DLB9

De Vries, Peter 1910- DLB6; Y82

de Young, M. H. 1849-1925.............................DLB25

Diamond, I. A. L. 1920- DLB26

Dick, Philip K. 1928- DLB8

Dickens, Charles 1812-1870............................DLB21

Dickey, James 1923- DLB5; Y82

Dickey, William 1928- DLB5

Dickinson, Emily 1830-1886.............................DLB1

Dickinson, John 1732-1808..............................DLB31

Dickinson, Jonathan 1688-1747......................DLB24

Dickinson, Patric 1914- DLB27

Dickson, Gordon R. 1923- DLB8

Didion, Joan 1934- DLB2; Y81

Di Donato, Pietro 1911- DLB9

Dillard, Annie 1945- Y80

Dillard, R. H. W. 1937- DLB5

Diogenes, Jr. (see Brougham, John)

DiPrima, Diane 1934- DLB5, 16

Disch, Thomas M. 1940- DLB8

Disney, Walt 1901-1966...................................DLB22

Disraeli, Benjamin 1804-1881.........................DLB21

Dix, Dorothea Lynde 1802-1887.......................DLB1

Dix, Dorothy (see Gilmer, Elizabeth Meriwether)

Dixon, Richard Watson 1833-1900..................DLB19

Doctorow, E. L. 1931- DLB2, 28; Y80

Dodd, William E. 1869-1940...........................DLB17

Dodgson, Charles Lutwidge (see Carroll, Lewis)

Doesticks, Q. K. Philander, P. B. (see Thomson,
Mortimer)

Donald, David H. 1920- DLB17

Donnelly, Ignatius 1831-1901.........................DLB12

Donleavy, J. P. 1926- DLB6

Doolittle, Hilda 1886-1961................................DLB4

Dorn, Edward 1929- DLB5

Dorr, Rheta Childe 1866-1948 ....DLB25
Dos Passos, John 1896-1970...............DLB4, 9; DS1
Doughty, Charles M. 1843-1926......................DLB19
Douglas, Keith 1920-1944...............................DLB27
Douglass, Frederick 1817?-1895 ....DLB1
Douglass, William circa 1691-1752..................DLB24
Downing, J., Major (see Davis, Charles A.)
Downing, Major Jack (see Smith, Seba)
Dowson, Ernest 1867-1900................................DLB19
Doyle, Arthur Conan 1859-1930......................DLB18
Doyle, Kirby 1932- DLB16
Drabble, Margaret 1939- DLB14
Draper, John W. 1811-1882 ....DLB30
Draper, Lyman C. 1815-1891 ....DLB30
Dreiser, Theodore 1871-1945............DLB9, 12; DS1
Drinkwater, John 1882-1937.....................DLB10, 19
Duffy, Maureen 1933- DLB14
Dugan, Alan 1923- DLB5
Dukes, Ashley 1885-1959..................................DLB10
Duncan, Robert 1919- DLB5, 16
Duncan, Ronald 1914-1982...............................DLB13
Dunlap, William 1766-1839 ....DLB30
Dunne, Finley Peter 1867-1936.................DLB11, 23
Dunne, John Gregory 1932- Y80
Dunne, Philip 1908- DLB26
Dunning, Ralph Cheever 1878-1930..................DLB4
Dunning, William A. 1857-1922......................DLB17
Plunkett, Edward John Moreton Drax,
  Lord Dunsany 1878-1957.............................DLB10
Duranty, Walter 1884-1957...............................DLB29
Durrell, Lawrence 1912- DLB15, 27
Duyckinck, Evert A. 1816-1878..........................DLB3
Duyckinck, George L. 1823-1863.......................DLB3
Dwight, John Sullivan 1813-1893......................DLB1
Dyer, Charles 1928- DLB13
Dylan, Bob 1941- DLB16

E

Eager, Edward 1911-1964.................................DLB22
Eastlake, William 1917- DLB6

Edgar, David 1948- DLB13
Edmonds, Walter D. 1903- DLB9
Edwards, Jonathan 1703-1758..........................DLB24
Effinger, George Alec 1947- DLB8
Eggleston, Edward 1837-1902..........................DLB12
Eigner, Larry 1927- DLB5
Eklund, Gordon 1945- Y83
Elder, Lonne, III 1931- DLB7
Eliot, George 1819-1880...................................DLB21
Eliot, John 1604-1690..DLB24
Eliot, T. S. 1888-1965 ....DLB7, 10
Elkin, Stanley 1930- DLB2, 28; Y80
Ellet, Elizabeth F. 1818?-1877..........................DLB30
Elliott, Janice 1931- DLB14
Elliott, William 1788-1863..................................DLB3
Ellison, Harlan 1934- DLB8
Ellison, Ralph 1914- DLB2
Emerson, Ralph Waldo 1803-1882....................DLB1
Empson, William 1906- DLB20
Enright, D. J. 1920- DLB27
Enright, Elizabeth 1909-1968............................DLB22
Epstein, Julius 1909-   and
  Epstein, Philip 1909-1952.............................DLB26
Erskine, John 1879-1951.....................................DLB9
Ervine, St. John Greer 1883-1971....................DLB10
Eshleman, Clayton 1935- DLB5
Estes, Eleanor 1906- DLB22
Ets, Marie Hall 1893- DLB22
Evans, Mary Ann (see George Eliot)
Evans, Nathaniel 1742-1767..............................DLB31
Everett, Edward 1794-1865................................DLB1
Everson, William 1912- DLB5, 16
Ewing, Juliana Horatia 1841-1885 ....DLB21
Exley, Frederick 1929- Y81

F

Fairfax, Beatrice (see Manning, Marie)
Fancher, Betsy 1928- Y83
Fante, John 1909-1983 ....Y83
Farley, Walter 1920- DLB22

Farmer, Philip José 1918-	DLB8
Farrell, J. G. 1935-1979	DLB14
Farrell, James T. 1904-1979	DLB4, 9; DS2
Fast, Howard 1914-	DLB9
Faulkner, William 1897-1962	DLB9, 11; DS2
Faust, Irvin 1924-	DLB2, 28; Y80
Fearing, Kenneth 1902-1961	DLB9
Federman, Raymond 1928-	Y80
Feiffer, Jules 1929-	DLB7
Feinstein, Elaine 1930-	DLB14
Felton, Cornelius Conway 1807-1862	DLB1
Ferber, Edna 1885-1968	DLB9, 28
Ferlinghetti, Lawrence 1919-	DLB5, 16
Fiedler, Leslie 1917-	DLB28
Field, Eugene 1850-1895	DLB23
Field, Rachel 1894-1942	DLB9, 22
Fields, James Thomas 1817-1881	DLB1
Figes, Eva 1932-	DLB14
Finney, Jack 1911-	DLB8
Finney, Walter Braden (see Finney, Jack)	
Firmin, Giles 1615-1697	DLB24
Fisher, Dorothy Canfield 1879-1958	DLB9
Fisher, Vardis 1895-1968	DLB9
Fiske, John 1608-1677	DLB24
Fitch, Thomas circa 1700-1774	DLB31
Fitch, William Clyde 1865-1909	DLB7
Fitzgerald, F. Scott 1896-1940	DLB4, 9; Y81; DS1
Fitzgerald, Penelope 1916-	DLB14
Fitzgerald, Robert 1910-	Y80
Fitzgerald, Thomas 1819-1891	DLB23
Fitzhugh, William circa 1651-1701	DLB24
Flanagan, Thomas 1923-	Y80
Flanner, Janet 1892-1978	DLB4
Flavin, Martin 1883-1967	DLB9
Flecker, James Elroy 1884-1915	DLB10, 19
Fleeson, Doris 1901-1970	DLB29
Fletcher, John Gould 1886-1950	DLB4
Flint, F. S. 1885-1960	DLB19
Follen, Eliza Lee (Cabot) 1787-1860	DLB1
Follett, Ken 1949-	Y81
Foote, Horton 1916-	DLB26
Foote, Shelby 1916-	DLB2, 17
Forbes, Ester 1891-1967	DLB22
Force, Peter 1790-1868	DLB30
Forché, Carolyn 1950-	DLB5
Ford, Charles Henri 1913-	DLB4
Ford, Corey 1902-1969	DLB11
Ford, Jesse Hill 1928-	DLB6
Foreman, Carl 1914-1984	DLB26
Fornés, María Irene 1930-	DLB7
Fortune, T. Thomas 1856-1928	DLB23
Foster, John 1648-1681	DLB24
Foster, Michael 1904-1956	DLB9
Fowles, John 1926-	DLB14
Fox, John, Jr. 1862 or 1863-1919	DLB9
Fox, William Price 1926-	DLB2; Y81
Fraenkel, Michael 1896-1957	DLB4
France, Richard 1938-	DLB7
Francis, Convers 1795-1863	DLB1
Frank, Waldo 1889-1967	DLB9
Franklin, Benjamin 1706-1790	DLB24
Frantz, Ralph Jules 1902-	DLB4
Fraser, G. S. 1915-1980	DLB27
Frayn, Michael 1933-	DLB13, 14
Frederic, Harold 1856-1898	DLB12, 23
Freeman, Douglas Southall 1886-1953	DLB17
Freeman, Legh Richmond 1842-1915	DLB23
Freeman, Mary Wilkins 1852-1930	DLB12
Friedman, Bruce Jay 1930-	DLB2, 28
Friel, Brian 1929-	DLB13
Friend, Krebs 1895?-1967?	DLB4
Frothingham, Octavius Brooks 1822-1895	DLB1
Froude, James Anthony 1818-1894	DLB18
Fry, Christopher 1907-	DLB13
Fuchs, Daniel 1909-	DLB9, 26, 28
Fuller, Henry Blake 1857-1929	DLB12
Fuller, Roy 1912-	DLB15, 20
Fuller, Samuel 1912-	DLB26
Fuller, Sarah Margaret, Marchesa D'Ossoli 1810-1850	DLB1
Furness, William Henry 1802-1896	DLB1
Furthman, Jules 1888-1966	DLB26

G

Gaddis, William 1922- DLB2
Gág, Wanda 1893-1946...................................DLB22
Gaines, Ernest J. 1933- DLB2; Y80
Gale, Zona 1874-1938......................................DLB9
Gallico, Paul 1897-1976...................................DLB9
Galsworthy, John 1867-1933..........................DLB10
Galvin, Brendan 1938- DLB5
Gannett, Frank E. 1876-1957.........................DLB29
Gardam, Jane 1928- DLB14
Garden, Alexander circa 1685-1756...............DLB31
Gardner, John 1933-1982........................DLB2; Y82
Garis, Howard R. 1873-1962..........................DLB22
Garland, Hamlin 1860-1940..........................DLB12
Garraty, John A. 1920- DLB17
Garrett, George 1929- DLB2, 5; Y83
Garrison, William Lloyd 1805-1879.................DLB1
Gascoyne, David 1916- DLB20
Gaskell, Elizabeth Cleghorn 1810-1865............DLB21
Gass, William 1924- DLB2
Gates, Doris 1901- DLB22
Gay, Ebenezer 1696-1787..............................DLB24
Gayarré, Charles E. A. 1805-1895..................DLB30
Geddes, Virgil 1897- DLB4
Gelber, Jack 1932- DLB7
Gellhorn, Martha 1908- Y82
Gems, Pam 1925- DLB13
Genovese, Eugene D. 1930- DLB17
Gent, Peter 1942- Y82
George, Henry 1839-1897..............................DLB23
Gernsback, Hugo 1884-1967...........................DLB8
Gerrold, David 1944- DLB8
Geston, Mark S. 1946- DLB8
Gibbons, Floyd 1887-1939.............................DLB25
Gibson, Wilfrid 1878-1962.............................DLB19
Gibson, William 1914- DLB7
Gillespie, A. Lincoln, Jr. 1895-1950...............DLB4
Gilliam, Florence ?-?...DLB4
Gilliatt, Penelope 1932- DLB14
Gillott, Jacky 1939-1980................................DLB14

Gilman, Caroline H. 1794-1888.........................DLB3
Gilmer, Elizabeth Meriwether 1861-1951 ....DLB29
Gilroy, Frank D. 1925- DLB7
Ginsberg, Allen 1926- DLB5, 16
Giovanni, Nikki 1943- DLB5
Gipson, Lawrence Henry 1880-1971................DLB17
Gissing, George 1857-1903 ....DLB18
Glanville, Brian 1931- DLB15
Glasgow, Ellen 1873-1945............................DLB9, 12
Glaspell, Susan 1882-1948 ....DLB7, 9
Glass, Montague 1877-1934..........................DLB11
Gluck, Louise 1943- DLB5
Goddard, Morrill 1865-1937..........................DLB25
Godfrey, Thomas 1736-1763 ....DLB31
Godwin, Gail 1937- DLB6
Godwin, Parke 1816-1904..............................DLB3
Gogarty, Oliver St. John 1878-1957 ....DLB15, 19
Gold, Herbert 1924- DLB2; Y81
Gold, Michael 1893-1967..........................DLB9, 28
Goldberg, Dick 1947- DLB7
Golding, William 1911- DLB15
Goodrich, Frances 1891- and
  Hackett, Albert 1900- DLB26
Goodrich, Samuel Griswold 1793-1860.............DLB1
Goodwin, Stephen 1943- Y82
Gookin, Daniel 1612-1687.............................DLB24
Gordon, Caroline 1895-1981.............DLB4, 9; Y81
Gordon, Giles 1940- DLB14
Gordon, Mary 1949- DLB6; Y81
Gordone, Charles 1925- DLB7
Goyen, William 1915-1983...................DLB2; Y83
Grady, Henry W. 1850-1889 ....DLB23
Graham, W. S. 1918- DLB20
Gramatky, Hardie 1907- DLB22
Granich, Irwin (see Gold, Michael)
Grant, Harry J. 1881-1963.............................DLB29
Grant, James Edward 1905-1966...................DLB26
Grasty, Charles H. 1863-1924.......................DLB25
Grau, Shirley Ann 1929- DLB2
Graves, John 1920- Y83
Graves, Robert 1895- DLB20

Gray, Asa 1810-1888 ....DLB1
Gray, Simon 1936- DLB13
Grayson, William J. 1788-1863 ....DLB3
Greeley, Horace 1811-1872 ....DLB3
Green, Gerald 1922- DLB28
Green, Henry 1905-1973 ....DLB15
Green, Jonas 1712-1767 ....DLB31
Green, Joseph 1706-1780 ....DLB31
Green, Julien 1900- DLB4
Green, Paul 1894-1981 ....DLB7, 9; Y81
Greene, Asa 1789-1838 ....DLB11
Greene, Graham 1904- DLB13, 15
Greenhow, Robert 1800-1854 ....DLB30
Greenough, Horatio 1805-1852 ....DLB1
Greenwood, Walter 1903-1974 ....DLB10
Greer, Ben 1948- DLB6
Persse, Isabella Augusta,
 Lady Gregory 1852-1932 ....DLB10
Grey, Zane 1872-1939 ....DLB9
Griffiths, Trevor 1935- DLB13
Grigson, Geoffrey 1905- DLB27
Griswold, Rufus 1815-1857 ....DLB3
Gross, Milt 1895-1953 ....DLB11
Grubb, Davis 1919-1980 ....DLB6
Gruelle, Johnny 1880-1938 ....DLB22
Guare, John 1938- DLB7
Guest, Barbara 1920- DLB5
Guiterman, Arthur 1871-1943 ....DLB11
Gunn, James E. 1923- DLB8
Gunn, Neil M. 1891-1973 ....DLB15
Gunn, Thom 1929- DLB27
Guthrie, A. B., Jr. 1901- DLB6
Guthrie, Ramon 1896-1973 ....DLB4
Gwynne, Erskine 1898-1948 ....DLB4
Gysin, Brion 1916- DLB16

H

H. D. (see Doolittle, Hilda)
Hailey, Arthur 1920- Y82
Haines, John 1924- DLB5

Haldeman, Joe 1943- DLB8
Hale, Edward Everett 1822-1909 ....DLB1
Hale, Nancy 1908- Y80
Hale, Sara Josepha (Buell) 1788-1879 ....DLB1
Haliburton, Thomas Chandler 1796-1865 .....DLB11
Hall, Donald 1928- DLB5
Halleck, Fitz-Greene 1790-1867 ....DLB3
Halper, Albert 1904- DLB9
Halstead, Murat 1829-1908 ....DLB23
Hamburger, Michael 1924- DLB27
Hamilton, Alexander 1712-1756 ....DLB31
Hamilton, Cicely 1872-1952 ....DLB10
Hamilton, Edmond 1904-1977 ....DLB8
Hamilton, Patrick 1904-1962 ....DLB10
Hammon, Jupiter 1711- died between
 1790 and 1806 ....DLB31
Hammond, John ?-1663 ....DLB24
Hamner, Earl 1923- DLB6
Hampton, Christopher 1946- DLB13
Handlin, Oscar 1915- DLB17
Hankin, St. John 1869-1909 ....DLB10
Hanley, Clifford 1922- DLB14
Hannah, Barry 1942- DLB6
Hannay, James 1827-1873 ....DLB21
Hansberry, Lorraine 1930-1965 ....DLB7
Hardwick, Elizabeth 1916- DLB6
Hardy, Thomas 1840-1928 ....DLB18, 19
Hare, David 1947- DLB13
Hargrove, Marion 1919- DLB11
Harness, Charles L. 1915- DLB8
Harris, George Washington 1814-1869 ......DLB3, 11
Harris, Joel Chandler 1848-1908 ....DLB11, 23
Harris, Mark 1922- DLB2; Y80
Harrison, Harry 1925- DLB8
Harrison, Jim 1937- Y82
Hart, Albert Bushnell 1854-1943 ....DLB17
Hart, Moss 1904-1961 ....DLB7
Hart, Oliver 1723-1795 ....DLB31
Harte, Bret 1836-1902 ....DLB12
Hartley, L. P. 1895-1972 ....DLB15
Harwood, Ronald 1934- DLB13

Cumulative Index

Hauser, Marianne 1910- Y83
Hawkes, John 1925- DLB2; Y80
Hawthorne, Nathaniel 1804-1864........................DLB1
Hay, John 1838-1905 ....DLB12
Hayden, Robert 1913-1980....................................DLB5
Hayes, John Michael 1919- DLB26
Hayne, Paul Hamilton 1830-1886.......................DLB3
Hazzard, Shirley 1931- Y82
Headley, Joel T. 1813-1897...................................DLB30
Hearst, William Randolph 1863-1951...............DLB25
Hearn, Lafcadio 1850-1904 ....DLB12
Heath, Catherine 1924- DLB14
Heath-Stubbs, John 1918-....................................DLB27
Hecht, Anthony 1923- DLB5
Hecht, Ben 1894-1964...............DLB7, 9, 25, 26, 28
Hecker, Isaac Thomas 1819-1888........................DLB1
Hedge, Frederic Henry 1805-1890 ....DLB1
Heidish, Marcy 1947- Y82
Heinlein, Robert A. 1907- DLB8
Heller, Joseph 1923- DLB2, 28; Y80
Hellman, Lillian 1906-1984..................................DLB7
Hemingway, Ernest 1899-1961.....DLB4, 9; Y81; DS1
Henchman, Daniel 1689-1761 ....DLB24
Henderson, Zenna 1917- DLB8
Henley, William Ernest 1849-1903...................DLB19
Henry, Buck 1930- DLB26
Henry, Marguerite 1902- DLB22
Henry, Robert Selph 1889-1970.........................DLB17
Henty, G. A. 1832-1902...DLB18
Hentz, Caroline Lee 1800-1856..........................DLB3
Herbert, Alan Patrick 1890-1971 ....DLB10
Herbert, Frank 1920- DLB8
Herbert, Henry William 1807-1858 ....DLB3
Herbst, Josephine 1892-1969...............................DLB9
Hergesheimer, Joseph 1880-1954......................DLB9
Herrick, Robert 1868-1938.........................DLB9, 12
Herrick, William 1915- Y83
Herrmann, John 1900-1959.................................DLB4
Hersey, John 1914- DLB6
Hewat, Alexander circa 1743-circa 1824 ....DLB30
Hewitt, John 1907- DLB27

Heyen, William 1940- DLB5
Heyward, Dorothy 1890-1961 and
 Heyward, DuBose 1885-1940....................DLB7
Heyward, DuBose 1885-1940 ....DLB9
Higgins, Aidan 1927- DLB14
Higgins, Colin 1941- DLB26
Higgins, George V. 1939- DLB2; Y81
Higginson, Thomas Wentworth 1822-1911.......DLB1
Hildreth, Richard 1807-1865.........................DLB1, 30
Hill, Susan 1942- DLB14
Himes, Chester 1909- DLB2
Hoagland, Edward 1932- DLB6
Hobson, Laura Z. 1900- DLB28
Hochman, Sandra 1936- DLB5
Hodgman, Helen 1945- DLB14
Hodgson, Ralph 1871-1962 ....DLB19
Hoffenstein, Samuel 1890-1947.........................DLB11
Hoffman, Charles Fenno 1806-1884................DLB3
Hoffman, Daniel 1923- DLB5
Hofstadter, Richard 1916-1970 ....DLB17
Hogan, Desmond 1950- DLB14
Holbrook, David 1923- DLB14
Hollander, John 1929- DLB5
Holley, Marietta 1836-1926.................................DLB11
Holloway, John 1920- DLB27
Holmes, John Clellon 1926- DLB16
Holmes, Oliver Wendell 1809-1894 ....DLB1
Home, William Douglas 1912- DLB13
Honig, Edwin 1919- DLB5
Hooker, Thomas 1586-1647 ....DLB24
Hooper, Johnson Jones 1815-1862.............DLB3, 11
Hopkins, Samuel 1721-1803 ....DLB31
Hopkinson, Francis 1737-1791 ....DLB31
Horovitz, Israel 1939- DLB7
Hough, Emerson 1857-1923 ....DLB9
Houghton, Stanley 1881-1913 ....DLB10
Housman, A. E. 1859-1936..................................DLB19
Housman, Laurence 1865-1959.........................DLB10
Howard, Maureen 1930- Y83
Howard, Richard 1929- DLB5
Howard, Roy W. 1883-1964 ....DLB29

Howard, Sidney 1891-1939 ....DLB7, 26
Howe, E. W. 1853-1937..............................DLB12, 25
Howe, Henry 1816-1893...............................DLB30
Howe, Julia Ward 1819-1910 ....DLB1
Howell, Clark, Sr. 1863-1936........................DLB25
Howell, Evan P. 1839-1905.............................DLB23
Howells, William Dean 1837-1920...................DLB12
Hoyem, Andrew 1935- DLB5
Hubbard, Kin 1868-1930 ....DLB11
Hubbard, William circa 1621-1704...................DLB24
Hughes, David 1930- DLB14
Hughes, Langston 1902-1967..........................DLB4, 7
Hughes, Richard 1900-1976 ....DLB15
Hughes, Thomas 1822-1896 ....DLB18
Hugo, Richard 1923-1982...............................DLB5
Hulme, T. E. 1883-1917..................................DLB19
Humphrey, William 1924- DLB6
Humphreys, Emyr 1919- DLB15
Huncke, Herbert 1915- DLB16
Hunter, Evan 1926- Y82
Hunter, Jim 1939- DLB14
Hunter, N. C. 1908-1971 ....DLB10
Huston, John 1906- DLB26
Hutchinson, Thomas 1711-1780 ....DLB30, 31

I

Ignatow, David 1914- DLB5
Imbs, Bravig 1904-1946 ....DLB4
Inge, William 1913-1973 ....DLB7
Ingraham, Joseph Holt 1809-1860...................DLB3
Irving, John 1942- DLB6; Y82
Irving, Washington 1783-1859.............DLB3, 11, 30
Irwin, Will 1873-1948....................................DLB25
Isherwood, Christopher 1904- DLB15

J

Jackson, Shirley 1919-1965 ....DLB6
Jacob, Piers Anthony Dillingham (see Anthony, Piers)

Jacobson, Dan 1929- DLB14
Jakes, John 1932- Y83
James, Henry 1843-1916................................DLB12
James, John circa 1633-1729 ....DLB24
Jameson, J. Franklin 1859-1937....................DLB17
Jay, John 1745-1829......................................DLB31
Jefferson, Thomas 1743-1826........................DLB31
Jellicoe, Ann 1927- DLB13
Jenkins, Robin 1912- DLB14
Jenkins, William Fitzgerald (see Leinster, Murray)
Jennings, Elizabeth 1926- DLB27
Jensen, Merrill 1905-1980..............................DLB17
Jerome, Jerome K. 1859-1927.......................DLB10
Jewett, Sarah Orne 1849-1909......................DLB12
Jewsbury, Geraldine 1812-1880......................DLB21
Joans, Ted 1928- DLB16
Johnson, B. S. 1933-1973...............................DLB14
Johnson, Diane 1934- Y80
Johnson, Edward 1598-1672.........................DLB24
Johnson, Gerald W. 1890-1980 ....DLB29
Johnson, Lionel 1867-1902 ....DLB19
Johnson, Nunnally 1897-1977 ....DLB26
Johnson, Pamela Hansford 1912- DLB15
Johnson, Samuel 1696-1772..........................DLB24
Johnson, Samuel 1822-1882............................DLB1
Johnston, Denis 1901- DLB10
Johnston, Jennifer 1930- DLB14
Johnston, Mary 1870-1936............................DLB9
Jolas, Eugene 1894-1952................................DLB4
Jones, Charles C., Jr. 1831-1893 ....DLB30
Jones, David 1895-1974.................................DLB20
Jones, Glyn 1905- DLB15
Jones, Gwyn 1907- DLB15
Jones, Henry Arthur 1851-1929....................DLB10
Jones, Hugh circa 1692-1760.........................DLB24
Jones, James 1921-1977 ....DLB2
Jones, LeRoi (see Baraka, Amiri)
Jones, Lewis 1897-1939.................................DLB15
Jones, Major Joseph (see Thompson, William Tappan)
Jones, Preston 1936-1979................................DLB7

Cumulative Index

Jong, Erica 1942- DLB2, 5, 28
Josephson, Matthew 1899-1978 ....DLB4
Josipovici, Gabriel 1940- DLB14
Josselyn, John ?-1675 ....DLB24
Joyce, James 1882-1941 ....DLB10, 19
Judd, Sylvester 1813-1853................................DLB1
June, Jennie (see Croly, Jane Cunningham)
Justice, Donald 1925- Y83

K

Kalechofsky, Roberta 1931- DLB28
Kandel, Lenore 1932- DLB16
Kanin, Garson 1912- DLB7
Kantor, Mackinlay 1904-1977.........................DLB9
Kaplan, Johanna 1942- DLB28
Katz, Steve 1935- Y83
Kaufman, Bob 1925- DLB16
Kaufman, George S. 1889-1961 ....DLB7
Kavanagh, Patrick 1904-1967...................DLB15, 20
Keane, John B. 1928- DLB13
Keeble, John 1944- Y83
Keeffe, Barrie 1945- DLB13
Keeley, James 1867-1934 ....DLB25
Kelley, Edith Summers 1884-1956 ....DLB9
Kellogg, Ansel Nash 1832-1886......................DLB23
Kelly, George 1887-1974.................................DLB7
Kelly, Robert 1935- DLB5
Kemelman, Harry 1908- DLB28
Kennedy, John Pendleton 1795-1870 ....DLB3
Kennedy, X. J. 1929- DLB5
Kent, Frank R. 1877-1958 ....DLB29
Kerouac, Jack 1922-1969.....................DLB2, 16; DS3
Kerouac, Jan 1952- DLB16
Kerr, Orpheus C. (see Newell, Robert Henry)
Kesey, Ken 1935- DLB2, 16
Kiely, Benedict 1919- DLB15
Kiley, Jed 1889-1962......................................DLB4
King, Clarence 1842-1901..............................DLB12
King, Grace 1852-1932..................................DLB12

King, Francis 1923- DLB15
King, Stephen 1947- Y80
Kingsley, Charles 1819-1875..........................DLB21
Kingsley, Henry 1830-1876............................DLB21
Kingsley, Sidney 1906- DLB7
Kingston, Maxine Hong 1940- Y80
Kinnell, Galway 1927- DLB5
Kinsella, Thomas 1928- DLB27
Kipling, Rudyard 1865-1936..........................DLB19
Kirkland, Caroline 1801-1864..........................DLB3
Kirkland, Joseph 1830-1893 ....DLB12
Kirkup, James 1918- DLB27
Kizer, Carolyn 1925- DLB5
Klappert, Peter 1942- DLB5
Klass, Philip (see Tenn, William)
Knickerbocker, Diedrich (see Irving, Washington)
Knight, Damon 1922- DLB8
Knight, John S. 1894-1981 ....DLB29
Knight, Sarah Kemble 1666-1727 ....DLB24
Knoblock, Edward 1874-1945........................DLB10
Knowles, John 1926- DLB6
Knox, Frank 1874-1944 ....DLB29
Knox, John Armoy 1850-1906 ....DLB23
Kober, Arthur 1900-1975 ....DLB11
Koch, Howard 1902- DLB26
Koch, Kenneth 1925- DLB5
Koenigsberg, Moses 1879-1945......................DLB25
Koestler, Arthur 1905-1983 ....Y83
Komroff, Manuel 1890-1974 ....DLB4
Kopit, Arthur 1937- DLB7
Kops, Bernard 1926?- DLB13
Kornbluth, C. M. 1923-1958...........................DLB8
Kosinski, Jerzy 1933- DLB2; Y82
Kraf, Elaine 1946- Y81
Krasna, Norman 1909- DLB26
Kreymborg, Alfred 1883-1966........................DLB4
Krim, Seymour 1922- DLB16
Krock, Arthur 1886-1974...............................DLB29
Kubrick, Stanley 1928- DLB26
Kumin, Maxine 1925- DLB5

Kupferberg, Tuli 1923- DLB16
Kuttner, Henry 1915-1958...............................DLB8
Kyger, Joanne 1934- DLB16

L

La Farge, Oliver 1901-1963............................DLB9
Lafferty, R. A. 1914- DLB8
Laird, Carobeth 1895- Y82
Lamantia, Philip 1927- DLB16
L'Amour, Louis 1908?- Y80
Landesman, Jay 1919- and
 Landesman, Fran 1927- DLB16
Lane, Charles 1800-1870.................................DLB1
Laney, Al 1896- DLB4
Lanham, Edwin 1904-1979 ....DLB4
Lardner, Ring 1885-1933 ....DLB11, 25
Lardner, Ring, Jr. 1915- DLB26
Larkin, Philip 1922- DLB27
Lathrop, Dorothy P. 1891-1980.....................DLB22
Laumer, Keith 1925- DLB8
Laurents, Arthur 1918- DLB26
Laurie, Annie (see Black, Winifred)
Lavin, Mary 1912- DLB15
Lawson, John ?-1711 ....DLB24
Lawson, Robert 1892-1957............................DLB22
Lawson, Victor F. 1850-1925 ....DLB25
Lawrence, David 1888-1973...........................DLB29
Lawrence, D. H. 1885-1930 ....DLB10, 19
Lea, Tom 1907- DLB6
Leacock, John 1729-1802...............................DLB31
Leary, Timothy 1920- DLB16
Lederer, Charles 1910-1976...........................DLB26
Ledwidge, Francis 1887-1917 ....DLB20
Lee, Don L. (see Madhubuti, Haki R.)
Lee, Harper 1926- DLB6
Lee, Laurie 1914- DLB27
Le Fanu, Joseph Sheridan 1814-1873.............DLB21
Le Gallienne, Richard 1866-1947 ....DLB4
Legare, Hugh Swinton 1797-1843...................DLB3

Legare, James M. 1823-1859..........................DLB3
Le Guin, Ursula K. 1929- DLB8
Lehmann, John 1907- DLB27
Lehmann, Rosamond 1901- DLB15
Leiber, Fritz 1910- DLB8
Leinster, Murray 1896-1975 ....DLB8
Leitch, Maurice 1933- DLB14
Leland, Charles G. 1824-1903 ....DLB11
Lenski, Lois 1893-1974..................................DLB22
Leonard, Hugh 1926- DLB13
Lerner, Max 1902- DLB29
Lessing, Bruno 1870-1940 ....DLB28
Lessing, Doris 1919- DLB15
Lever, Charles 1806-1872 ....DLB21
Levertov, Denise 1923- DLB5
Levin, Meyer 1905-1981 ....DLB9, 28; Y81
Levine, Philip 1928- DLB5
Levy, Benn Wolfe 1900-1973 ....Y81; DLB13
Lewis, Alfred H. 1857-1914...........................DLB25
Lewis, Alun 1915-1944..................................DLB20
Lewis, C. Day (see Day Lewis, C.)
Lewis, C. S. 1898-1963 ....DLB15
Lewis, Charles B. 1842-1924.........................DLB11
Lewis, Henry Clay 1825-1850.........................DLB3
Lewis, Richard circa 1700-1734.....................DLB24
Lewis, Sinclair 1885-1951 ....DLB9; DS1
Lewis, Wyndham 1882-1957 ....DLB15
Lewisohn, Ludwig 1882-1955 ....DLB4, 9, 28
Liebling, A. J. 1904-1963 ....DLB4
Linebarger, Paul Myron Anthony (see
 Smith, Cordwainer)
Link, Arthur S. 1920- DLB17
Linton, Eliza Lynn 1822-1898 ....DLB18
Lippmann, Walter 1889-1974........................DLB29
Lipton, Lawrence 1898-1975 ....DLB16
Littlewood, Joan 1914- DLB13
Lively, Penelope 1933- DLB14
Livings, Henry 1929- DLB13
Livingston, William 1723-1790 ....DLB31
Llewellyn, Richard 1906- DLB15

Cumulative Index

Lochridge, Betsy Hopkins (see Fancher, Betsy)
Locke, David Ross 1833-1888................DLB11, 23
Lockridge, Ross, Jr. 1914-1948........................Y80
Lodge, David 1935- DLB14
Loeb, Harold 1891-1974.................................DLB4
Logan, James 1674-1751..............................DLB24
Logan, John 1923- DLB5
Logue, Christopher 1926- DLB27
London, Jack 1876-1916............................DLB8, 12
Longfellow, Henry Wadsworth 1807-1882........DLB1
Longfellow, Samuel 1819-1892........................DLB1
Longstreet, Augustus Baldwin 1790-1870 ....DLB3, 11
Lonsdale, Frederick 1881-1954....................DLB10
Loos, Anita 1893-1981..................DLB11, 26; Y81
Lopate, Phillip 1943- Y80
Lossing, Benson J. 1813-1891......................DLB30
Lovingood, Sut (see Harris, George Washington)
Lowell, James Russell 1819-1891 ....DLB1, 11
Lowell, Robert 1917-1977.............................DLB5
Lowenfels, Walter 1897-1976.........................DLB4
Lowry, Malcolm 1909-1957..........................DLB15
Loy, Mina 1882-1966....................................DLB4
Ludlum, Robert 1927- Y82
Luke, Peter 1919- DLB13
Lurie, Alison 1926- DLB2
Lytle, Andrew 1902- DLB6
Lytton, Edward (see Bulwer-Lytton, Edward)

M

MacArthur, Charles 1895-1956.................DLB7, 25
MacCaig, Norman 1910- DLB27
MacDiarmid, Hugh 1892-1978.....................DLB20
MacDonald, George 1824-1905 ....DLB18
MacDonald, John D. 1916- DLB8
Macfadden, Bernarr 1868-1955.....................DLB25
MacInnes, Colin 1914-1976 ....DLB14
Macken, Walter 1915-1967 ....DLB13
MacLean, Katherine Anne 1925- DLB8

MacLeish, Archibald 1892-1982............DLB4, 7; Y82
Macleod, Norman 1906- DLB4
MacNamara, Brinsley 1890-1963..................DLB10
MacNeice, Louis 1907-1963.....................DLB10, 20
Madden, David 1933- DLB6
Madhubuti, Haki R. 1942- DLB5
Mailer, Norman 1923- DLB2, 16, 28; Y80, 83, DS3
Makemie, Francis circa 1658-1708 ....DLB24
Malamud, Bernard 1914- DLB2, 28; Y80
Mallock, W. H. 1849-1923...........................DLB18
Malone, Dumas 1892- DLB17
Malzberg, Barry N. 1939- DLB8
Mamet, David 1947- DLB7
Manfred, Frederick 1912- DLB6
Mangan, Sherry 1904-1961............................DLB4
Mankiewicz, Herman 1897-1953 ....DLB26
Mankowitz, Wolf 1924- DLB15
Mann, Horace 1796-1859..............................DLB1
Manning, Marie 1873?-1945 ....DLB29
Mano, D. Keith 1942- DLB6
March, William 1893-1954...........................DLB9
Marcus, Frank 1928- DLB13
Markfield, Wallace 1926- DLB2, 28
Marquand, John P. 1893-1960 ....DLB9
Marquis, Don 1878-1937 ....DLB11, 25
Marryat, Frederick 1792-1848......................DLB21
Marsh, George Perkins 1801-1882...................DLB1
Marsh, James 1794-1842..............................DLB1
Marshall, Edward 1932- DLB16
Martin, Abe (see Hubbard, Kin)
Martineau, Harriet 1802-1876......................DLB21
Martyn, Edward 1859-1923.........................DLB10
Masefield, John 1878-1967.....................DLB10, 19
Mather, Cotton 1663-1728........................DLB24, 30
Mather, Increase 1639-1723 ....DLB24
Mather, Richard 1596-1669 ....DLB24
Matheson, Richard 1926- DLB8
Mathews, Cornelius 1817-1889.....................DLB3
Mathias, Roland 1915- DLB27
Matthews, Jack 1925- DLB6

Matthews, William 1942-	DLB5
Matthiessen, Peter 1927-	DLB6
Maugham, W. Somerset 1874-1965	DLB10
Maury, James 1718-1769	DLB31
Mavor, Elizabeth 1927-	DLB14
Mavor, Osborne Henry (see Bridie, James)	
Maxwell, William 1908-	Y80
Mayer, O. B. 1818-1891	DLB3
Mayes, Wendell 1919-	DLB26
Mayhew, Henry 1812-1887	DLB18
Mayhew, Jonathan 1720-1766	DLB31
McAlmon, Robert 1896-1956	DLB4
McCaffrey, Anne 1926-	DLB8
McCarthy, Cormac 1933-	DLB6
McCarthy, Mary 1912-	DLB2; Y81
McCay, Winsor 1871-1934	DLB22
McClatchy, C. K. 1858-1936	DLB25
McCloskey, Robert 1914-	DLB22
McClure, Joanna 1930-	DLB16
McClure, Michael 1932-	DLB16
McCormick, Anne O'Hare 1880-1954	DLB29
McCormick, Robert R. 1880-1955	DLB29
McCoy, Horace 1897-1955	DLB9
McCullagh, Joseph B. 1842-1896	DLB23
McCullers, Carson 1917-1967	DLB2, 7
McDonald, Forrest 1927-	DLB17
McEwan, Ian 1948-	DLB14
McGahern, John 1934-	DLB14
McGeehan, W. O. 1879-1933	DLB25
McGill, Ralph 1898-1969	DLB29
McGinley, Phyllis 1905-1978	DLB11
McGuane, Thomas 1939-	DLB2; Y80
McIlvanney, William 1936-	DLB14
McIntyre, O. O. 1884-1938	DLB25
McKay, Claude 1889-1948	DLB4
McKean, William V. 1820-1903	DLB23
McLaverty, Michael 1907-	DLB15
McLean, John R. 1848-1916	DLB23
McLean, William L. 1852-1931	DLB25
McMurtry, Larry 1936-	DLB2; Y80
McNally, Terrence 1939-	DLB7
Mead, Taylor ?-	DLB16
Medoff, Mark 1940-	DLB7
Meek, Alexander Beaufort 1814-1865	DLB3
Meinke, Peter 1932-	DLB5
Meltzer, David 1937-	DLB16
Melville, Herman 1819-1891	DLB3
Mencken, H. L. 1880-1956	DLB11, 29
Mercer, David 1928-1980	DLB13
Mercer, John 1704-1768	DLB31
Meredith, George 1828-1909	DLB18
Meredith, William 1919-	DLB5
Merrill, James 1926-	DLB5
Merton, Thomas 1915-1968	Y81
Merwin, W. S. 1927-	DLB5
Mew, Charlotte 1869-1928	DLB19
Mewshaw, Michael 1943-	Y80
Meyer, Eugene 1875-1959	DLB29
Meynell, Alice 1847-1922	DLB19
Micheline, Jack 1929-	DLB16
Michener, James A. 1907?-	DLB6
Micklejohn, George circa 1717-1818	DLB31
Middleton, Stanley 1919-	DLB14
Millar, Kenneth 1915-1983	DLB2; Y83
Miller, Arthur 1915-	DLB7
Miller, Caroline 1903-	DLB9
Miller, Henry 1891-1980	DLB4, 9; Y80
Miller, Jason 1939-	DLB7
Miller, Perry 1905-1963	DLB17
Miller, Walter M., Jr. 1923-	DLB8
Miller, Webb 1892-1940	DLB29
Millhauser, Steven 1943-	DLB2
Milne, A. A. 1882-1956	DLB10
Mitchel, Jonathan 1624-1668	DLB24
Mitchell, Donald Grant 1822-1908	DLB1
Mitchell, James Leslie 1901-1935	DLB15
Mitchell, Julian 1935-	DLB14
Mitchell, Langdon 1862-1935	DLB7
Mitchell, Margaret 1900-1949	DLB9
Monkhouse, Allan 1858-1936	DLB10

Monro, Harold 1879-1932	DLB19
Monsarrat, Nicholas 1910-1979	DLB15
Montgomery, John 1919-	DLB16
Montgomery, Marion 1925-	DLB6
Moody, Joshua circa 1633-1697	DLB24
Moody, William Vaughn 1869-1910	DLB7
Moorcock, Michael 1939-	DLB14
Moore, Catherine L. 1911-	DLB8
Moore, George 1852-1933	DLB10, 18
Moore, T. Sturge 1870-1944	DLB19
Moore, Ward 1903-1978	DLB8
Morgan, Berry 1919-	DLB6
Morgan, Edmund S. 1916-	DLB17
Morgan, Edwin 1920-	DLB27
Morison, Samuel Eliot 1887-1976	DLB17
Morley, Christopher 1890-1957	DLB9
Morris, Richard B. 1904-	DLB17
Morris, William 1834-1896	DLB18
Morris, Willie 1934-	Y80
Morris, Wright 1910-	DLB2; Y81
Morrison, Toni 1931-	DLB6; Y81
Mortimer, John 1923-	DLB13
Morton, Nathaniel 1613-1685	DLB24
Morton, Thomas circa 1579-circa 1647	DLB24
Mosley, Nicholas 1923-	DLB14
Moss, Arthur 1889-1969	DLB4
Moss, Howard 1922-	DLB5
Motley, John Lothrop 1814-1877	DLB1, 30
Mowrer, Edgar Ansel 1892-1977	DLB29
Mowrer, Paul Scott 1887-1971	DLB29
Muir, Edwin 1887-1959	DLB20
Muir, Helen 1937-	DLB14
Munford, Robert circa 1737-1783	DLB31
Munsey, Frank A. 1854-1925	DLB25
Murdoch, Iris 1919-	DLB14
Murfree, Mary N. 1850-1922	DLB12
Murray, Gilbert 1866-1957	DLB10
Myers, L. H. 1881-1944	DLB15

N

Nabokov, Vladimir 1899-1977	DLB2; Y80; DS3
Nasby, Petroleum Vesuvius (see Locke, David Ross)	
Nash, Ogden 1902-1971	DLB11
Nathan, Robert 1894-	DLB9
Naughton, Bill 1910-	DLB13
Neagoe, Peter 1881-1960	DLB4
Neal, John 1793-1876	DLB1
Neal, Joseph C. 1807-1847	DLB11
Neihardt, John G. 1881-1973	DLB9
Nelson, William Rockhill 1841-1915	DLB23
Nemerov, Howard 1920-	DLB5, 6; Y83
Neugeboren, Jay 1938-	DLB28
Nevins, Allan 1890-1971	DLB17
Newbolt, Henry 1862-1938	DLB19
Newby, P. H. 1918-	DLB15
Newcomb, Charles King 1820-1894	DLB1
Newell, Robert Henry 1836-1901	DLB11
Newman, Frances 1883-1928	Y80
Newman, John Henry 1801-1890	DLB18
Nichols, Dudley 1895-1960	DLB26
Nichols, John 1940-	Y82
Nichols, Mary Sargeant (Neal) Gove 1810-1884	DLB1
Nichols, Peter 1927-	DLB13
Nichols, Roy F. 1896-1973	DLB17
Nicholson, Norman 1914-	DLB27
Niebuhr, Reinhold 1892-1971	DLB17
Nieman, Lucius W. 1857-1935	DLB25
Niggli, Josefina 1910-	Y80
Nims, John Frederick 1913-	DLB5
Nin, Anaïs 1903-1977	DLB2, 4
Nissenson, Hugh 1933-	DLB28
Niven, Larry 1938-	DLB8
Nolan, William F. 1928-	DLB8
Noland, C. F. M. 1810?-1858	DLB11
Noone, John 1936-	DLB14
Nordhoff, Charles 1887-1947	DLB9
Norris, Charles G. 1881-1945	DLB9
Norris, Frank 1870-1902	DLB12

Norris, Leslie 1921-	DLB27
Norse, Harold 1916-	DLB16
Norton, Alice Mary (see Norton, Andre)	
Norton, Andre 1912-	DLB8
Norton, Andrews 1786-1853	DLB1
Norton, Caroline 1808-1877	DLB21
Norton, Charles Eliot 1827-1908	DLB1
Norton, John 1606-1663	DLB24
Nourse, Alan E. 1928-	DLB8
Noyes, Alfred 1880-1958	DLB20
Noyes, Crosby S. 1825-1908	DLB23
Noyes, Nicholas 1647-1717	DLB24
Noyes, Theodore W. 1858-1946	DLB29
Nye, Bill 1850-1896	DLB11, 23
Nye, Robert 1939-	DLB14

O

Oakes, Urian circa 1631-1681	DLB24
Oates, Joyce Carol 1938-	DLB2, 5; Y81
O'Brien, Edna 1932-	DLB14
O'Brien, Kate 1897-1974	DLB15
O'Brien, Tim 1946-	Y80
O'Casey, Sean 1880-1964	DLB10
Ochs, Adolph S. 1858-1935	DLB25
O'Connor, Flannery 1925-1964	DLB2; Y80
Odell, Jonathan 1737-1818	DLB31
Odets, Clifford 1906-1963	DLB7, 26
O'Faolain, Julia 1932-	DLB14
O'Faolain, Sean 1900-	DLB15
O'Hara, Frank 1926-1966	DLB5, 16
O'Hara, John 1905-1970	DLB9; DS2
O. Henry (see Porter, William S.)	
Older, Fremont 1856-1935	DLB25
Oliphant, Laurence 1829-1888	DLB18
Oliphant, Margaret 1828-1897	DLB18
Oliver, Chad 1928-	DLB8
Oliver, Mary 1935-	DLB5
Olsen, Tillie 1913?-	DLB28; Y80
Olson, Charles 1910-1970	DLB5, 16
O'Neill, Eugene 1888-1953	DLB7

Oppen, George 1908-	DLB5
Oppenheim, James 1882-1932	DLB28
Oppenheimer, Joel 1930-	DLB5
Orlovitz, Gil 1918-1973	DLB2, 5
Orlovsky, Peter 1933-	DLB16
Ormond, John 1923-	DLB27
Ornitz, Samuel 1890-1957	DLB28
Orton, Joe 1933-1967	DLB13
Orwell, George 1903-1950	DLB15
Osborne, John 1929-	DLB13
Otis, James, Jr. 1725-1783	DLB31
Ottendorfer, Oswald 1826-1900	DLB23
Ouida 1839-1908	DLB18
Owen, Guy 1925-	DLB5
Owen, Wilfred 1893-1918	DLB20
Owsley, Frank L. 1890-1956	DLB17
Ozick, Cynthia 1928-	DLB28; Y82

P

Pack, Robert 1929-	DLB5
Padgett, Ron 1942-	DLB5
Page, Thomas Nelson 1853-1922	DLB12
Pain, Philip ?-circa 1666	DLB24
Paine, Thomas 1737-1809	DLB31
Paley, Grace 1922-	DLB28
Palfrey, John Gorham 1796-1881	DLB1, 30
Panama, Norman 1914- and Melvin Frank 1913-	DLB26
Pangborn, Edgar 1909-1976	DLB8
Panshin, Alexei 1940-	DLB8
Parke, John 1754-1789	DLB31
Parker, Dorothy 1893-1967	DLB11
Parker, Theodore 1810-1860	DLB1
Parkman, Francis, Jr. 1823-1893	DLB1, 30
Parrington, Vernon L. 1871-1929	DLB17
Parton, James 1822-1891	DLB30
Pastan, Linda 1932-	DLB5
Pastorius, Francis Daniel 1651-circa 1720	DLB24
Patchen, Kenneth 1911-1972	DLB16
Patrick, John 1906-	DLB7

Cumulative Index

Patterson, Eleanor Medill 1881-1948 .... DLB29
Patterson, Joseph Medill 1879-1946 .... DLB29
Paul, Elliot 1891-1958 .... DLB4
Paulding, James Kirke 1778-1860 .... DLB3
Payn, James 1830-1898 .... DLB18
Peabody, Elizabeth Palmer 1804-1894 .... DLB1
Pead, Deuel ?-1727 .... DLB24
Peake, Mervyn DLB15
Peck, George W. 1840-1916 .... DLB23
Penn, William 1644-1718 .... DLB24
Penner, Jonathan 1940- Y83
Pennington, Lee 1939- Y82
Percy, Walker 1916- DLB2; Y80
Perelman, S. J. 1904-1979 .... DLB11
Perkoff, Stuart Z. 1930-1974 .... DLB16
Peterkin, Julia 1880-1961 .... DLB9
Petersham, Maud 1889-1971 and
    Petersham, Miska 1888-1960 .... DLB22
Phillips, David Graham 1867-1911 .... DLB9, 12
Phillips, Jayne Anne 1952- Y80
Phillips, Stephen 1864-1915 .... DLB10
Phillips, Ulrich B. 1877-1934 .... DLB17
Phillpotts, Eden 1862-1960 .... DLB10
Phoenix, John (see Derby, George Horatio)
Pinckney, Josephine 1895-1957 .... DLB6
Pinero, Arthur Wing 1855-1934 .... DLB10
Pinsky, Robert 1940- Y82
Pinter, Harold 1930- DLB13
Piper, H. Beam 1904-1964 .... DLB8
Piper, Watty DLB22
Pisar, Samuel 1929- Y83
Pitkin, Timothy 1766-1847 .... DLB30
Pitter, Ruth 1897- DLB20
Plante, David 1940- Y83
Plath, Sylvia 1932-1963 .... DLB5, 6
Plomer, William 1903-1973 .... DLB20
Plumly, Stanley 1939- DLB5
Plunkett, James 1920- DLB14
Plymell, Charles 1935- DLB16
Poe, Edgar Allan 1809-1849 .... DLB3
Pohl, Frederik 1919- DLB8

Poliakoff, Stephen 1952- DLB13
Pollard, Edward A. 1832-1872 .... DLB30
Polonsky, Abraham 1910- DLB26
Poole, Ernest 1880-1950 .... DLB9
Poore, Benjamin Perley 1820-1887 .... DLB23
Porter, Eleanor H. 1868-1920 .... DLB9
Porter, Katherine Anne 1890-1980 .... DLB4, 9; Y80
Porter, William S. 1862-1910 .... DLB12
Porter, William T. 1809-1858 .... DLB3
Portis, Charles 1933- DLB6
Potok, Chaim 1929- DLB28
Potter, David M. 1910-1971 .... DLB17
Pound, Ezra 1885-1972 .... DLB4
Powell, Anthony 1905- DLB15
Pownall, David 1938- DLB14
Powys, John Cowper 1872-1963 .... DLB15
Prescott, William Hickling 1796-1859 .... DLB1, 30
Price, Reynolds 1933- DLB2
Price, Richard 1949- Y81
Priest, Christopher 1943- DLB14
Priestley, J. B. 1894- DLB10
Prime, Benjamin Young 1733-1791 .... DLB31
Prince, F. T. 1912- DLB20
Prince, Thomas 1687-1758 .... DLB24
Pritchett, V. S. 1900- DLB15
Propper, Dan 1937- DLB16
Proud, Robert 1728-1813 .... DLB30
Pulitzer, Joseph 1847-1911 .... DLB23
Pulitzer, Joseph, Jr. 1885-1955 .... DLB29
Purdy, James 1923- DLB2
Putnam, George Palmer 1814-1872 .... DLB3
Putnam, Samuel 1892-1950 .... DLB4
Puzo, Mario 1920- DLB6
Pyle, Ernie 1900-1945 .... DLB29
Pym, Barbara 1913-1980 .... DLB14
Pynchon, Thomas 1937- DLB2

Q

Quad, M. (see Lewis, Charles B.)
Quin, Ann 1936-1973 .... DLB14

Quincy, Samuel of Georgia birth date and death date unknown...DLB31
Quincy, Samuel of Massachusetts 1734-1789...DLB31

R

Rabe, David 1940-...DLB7
Raine, Kathleen 1908-...DLB20
Ralph, Julian 1853-1903...DLB23
Ramée, Marie Louise de la (see Ouida)
Ramsay, David 1749-1815...DLB30
Randall, Henry S. 1811-1876...DLB30
Randall, James G. 1881-1953...DLB17
Raphael, Frederic 1931-...DLB14
Rattigan, Terence 1911-1977...DLB13
Rawlings, Marjorie Kinnan 1896-1953...DLB9, 22
Ray, David 1932-...DLB5
Read, Herbert 1893-1968...DLB20
Read, Opie 1852-1939...DLB23
Read, Piers Paul 1941-...DLB14
Reade, Charles 1814-1884...DLB21
Rechy, John 1934-...Y82
Reed, Henry 1914-...DLB27
Reed, Ishmael 1938-...DLB2, 5
Reed, Sampson 1800-1880...DLB1
Reid, Alastair 1926-...DLB27
Reid, Helen Rogers 1882-1970...DLB29
Reid, James birth date and death date unknown...DLB31
Reid, Mayne 1818-1883...DLB21
Reid, Whitelaw 1837-1912...DLB23
Remington, Frederic 1861-1909...DLB12
Renault, Mary 1905-1983...Y83
Rexroth, Kenneth 1905-1982...DLB16; Y82
Rey, H. A. 1898-1977...DLB22
Reynolds, G. W. M. 1814-1879...DLB21
Reynolds, Mack 1917-...DLB8
Reznikoff, Charles 1894-1976...DLB28
Rice, Elmer 1892-1967...DLB4, 7
Rice, Grantland 1880-1954...DLB29
Rich, Adrienne 1929-...DLB5
Richards, I. A. 1893-1979...DLB27
Richardson, Jack 1935-...DLB7
Richter, Conrad 1890-1968...DLB9
Rickword, Edgell 1898-1982...DLB20
Riddell, John (see Ford, Corey)
Ridler, Anne 1912-...DLB27
Riis, Jacob 1849-1914...DLB23
Ripley, George 1802-1880...DLB1
Riskin, Robert 1897-1955...DLB26
Ritchie, Anna Mowatt 1819-1870...DLB3
Ritchie, Anne Thackeray 1837-1919...DLB18
Rivkin, Allen 1903-...DLB26
Robbins, Tom 1936-...Y80
Roberts, Elizabeth Madox 1881-1941...DLB9
Roberts, Kenneth 1885-1957...DLB9
Robinson, Lennox 1886-1958...DLB10
Robinson, Mabel Louise 1874-1962...DLB22
Rodgers, W. R. 1909-1969...DLB20
Roethke, Theodore 1908-1963...DLB5
Rogers, Will 1879-1935...DLB11
Roiphe, Anne 1935-...Y80
Rolvaag, O. E. 1876-1931...DLB9
Root, Waverley 1903-1982...DLB4
Rose, Reginald 1920-...DLB26
Rosen, Norma 1925-...DLB28
Rosenberg, Isaac 1890-1918...DLB20
Rosenfeld, Isaac 1918-1956...DLB28
Rosenthal, M. L. 1917-...DLB5
Ross, Leonard Q. (see Rosten, Leo)
Rossen, Robert 1908-1966...DLB26
Rossner, Judith 1935-...DLB6
Rosten, Leo 1908-...DLB11
Roth, Henry 1906?-...DLB28
Roth, Philip 1933-...DLB2, 28; Y82
Rothenberg, Jerome 1931-...DLB5
Rowlandson, Mary circa 1635-circa 1678...DLB24
Rubens, Bernice 1928-...DLB14
Rudkin, David 1956-...DLB13
Rumaker, Michael 1932-...DLB16
Runyon, Damon 1880-1946...DLB11

Russ, Joanna 1937- DLB8
Russell, Charles Edward 1860-1941 ....DLB25
Russell, George William (see AE)
Rutherford, Mark 1831-1913............................DLB18
Ryan, Michael 1946- Y82
Ryskind, Morrie 1895- DLB26

S

Saberhagen, Fred 1930- DLB8
Sackler, Howard 1929-1982 ....DLB7
Saffin, John circa 1626-1710 ....DLB24
Sage, Robert 1899-1962 ....DLB4
St. Johns, Adela Rogers 1894- DLB29
Salemson, Harold J. 1910- DLB4
Salinger, J. D. 1919- DLB2
Sanborn, Franklin Benjamin 1831-1917............DLB1
Sandburg, Carl 1878-1967 ....DLB17
Sanders, Ed 1939- DLB16
Sandoz, Mari 1896-1966...................................DLB9
Sandys, George 1578-1644 ....DLB24
Sargent, Pamela 1948- DLB8
Saroyan, William 1908-1981................DLB7, 9; Y81
Sarton, May 1912- Y81
Sassoon, Siegfried 1886-1967...........................DLB20
Saunders, James 1925- DLB13
Saunders, John Monk 1897-1940 ....DLB26
Savage, James 1784-1873 ....DLB30
Savage, Marmion W. 1803-1872 ....DLB21
Sawyer, Ruth 1880-1970 ....DLB22
Sayers, Dorothy L. 1893-1957 ....DLB10
Scannell, Vernon 1922- DLB27
Schaeffer, Susan Fromberg 1941- DLB28
Schlesinger, Arthur M., Jr. 1917- DLB17
Schmitz, James H. 1911- DLB8
Schreiner, Olive 1855-1920...............................DLB18
Schulberg, Budd 1914- DLB6, 26, 28; Y81
Schurz, Carl 1829-1906....................................DLB23
Schuyler, George S. 1895-1977 ....DLB29
Schuyler, James 1923- DLB5

Schwartz, Delmore 1913-1966 ....DLB28
Schwartz, Jonathan 1938- Y82
Scott, Evelyn 1893-1963 ....DLB9
Scott, Harvey W. 1838-1910 ....DLB23
Scott, Paul 1920-1978..DLB14
Scott, Tom 1918- DLB27
Scripps, E. W. 1854-1926.................................DLB25
Seabrook, William 1886-1945 ....DLB4
Seabury, Samuel 1729-1796.............................DLB31
Sedgwick, Catharine Maria 1789-1867..............DLB1
Seid, Ruth (see Sinclair, Jo)
Selby, Hubert, Jr. 1928- DLB2
Seredy, Kate 1899-1975 ....DLB22
Serling, Rod 1924-1975....................................DLB26
Settle, Mary Lee 1918- DLB6
Sewall, Joseph 1688-1769.................................DLB24
Sewall, Samuel 1652-1730 ....DLB24
Sexton, Anne 1928-1974 ....DLB5
Shaara, Michael 1929- Y83
Shaffer, Anthony 1926- DLB13
Shaffer, Peter 1926- DLB13
Shairp, Mordaunt 1887-1939...........................DLB10
Sharpe, Tom 1928- DLB14
Shaw, Bernard 1856-1950................................DLB10
Shaw, Henry Wheeler 1818-1885....................DLB11
Shaw, Irwin 1913- DLB6
Shaw, Robert 1927-1978............................DLB13, 14
Shea, John Gilmary 1824-1892........................DLB30
Sheckley, Robert 1928- DLB8
Sheed, Wilfred 1930- DLB6
Sheldon, Alice B. (see Tiptree, James, Jr.)
Sheldon, Edward 1886-1946............................DLB7
Shepard, Sam 1943- DLB7
Shepard, Thomas I 1604 or 1605-1649.........DLB24
Shepard, Thomas II 1635-1677 ....DLB24
Sherriff, R. C. 1896-1975................................DLB10
Sherwood, Robert 1896-1955 ....DLB7, 26
Shiels, George 1886-1949................................DLB10
Shillaber, Benjamin Penhallow 1814-
1890..DLB1, 11

Shirer, William L. 1904-	DLB4
Shorthouse, Joseph Henry 1834-1903	DLB18
Shulman, Max 1919-	DLB11
Shute, Henry A. 1856-1943	DLB9
Shuttle, Penelope 1947-	DLB14
Sigourney, Lydia Howard (Huntley) 1791-1865	DLB1
Silkin, Jon 1930-	DLB27
Silliphant, Stirling 1918-	DLB26
Sillitoe, Alan 1928-	DLB14
Silman, Roberta 1934-	DLB28
Silverberg, Robert 1935-	DLB8
Simak, Clifford D. 1904-	DLB8
Simms, William Gilmore 1806-1870	DLB3, 30
Simon, Neil 1927-	DLB7
Simons, Katherine Drayton Mayrant 1890-1969	Y83
Simpson, Louis 1923-	DLB5
Simpson, N. F. 1919-	DLB13
Sinclair, Andrew 1935-	DLB14
Sinclair, Jo 1913-	DLB28
Sinclair, Upton 1878-1968	DLB9
Singer, Isaac Bashevis 1904-	DLB6, 28
Singmaster, Elsie 1879-1958	DLB9
Sissman, L. E. 1928-1976	DLB5
Sisson, C. H. 1914-	DLB27
Sitwell, Edith 1887-1964	DLB20
Skelton, Robin 1925-	DLB27
Slavitt, David 1935-	DLB5, 6
Slick, Sam (see Haliburton, Thomas Chandler)	
Smith, Betty 1896-1972	Y82
Smith, Carol Sturm 1938-	Y81
Smith, Charles Henry 1826-1903	DLB11
Smith, Cordwainer 1913-1966	DLB8
Smith, Dave 1942-	DLB5
Smith, Dodie 1896-	DLB10
Smith, E. E. 1890-1965	DLB8
Smith, Elizabeth Oakes (Prince) 1806-1893	DLB1
Smith, George O. 1911-	DLB8
Smith, H. Allen 1906-1976	DLB11, 29
Smith, John 1580-1631	DLB24, 30
Smith, Josiah 1704-1781	DLB24
Smith, Lee 1944-	Y83
Smith, Mark 1935-	Y82
Smith, Michael 1698-circa 1771	DLB31
Smith, Red 1905-1982	DLB29
Smith, Seba 1792-1868	DLB1, 11
Smith, Stevie 1902-1971	DLB20
Smith, Sydney Goodsir 1915-1975	DLB27
Smith, William 1727-1803	DLB31
Smith, William 1728-1793	DLB30
Smith, William Jay 1918-	DLB5
Snodgrass, W. D. 1926-	DLB5
Snow, C. P. 1905-1980	DLB15
Snyder, Gary 1930-	DLB5, 16
Solano, Solita 1888-1975	DLB4
Solomon, Carl 1928-	DLB16
Sontag, Susan 1933-	DLB2
Sorrentino, Gilbert 1929-	DLB5; Y80
Southern, Terry 1924-	DLB2
Spark, Muriel 1918-	DLB15
Sparks, Jared 1789-1866	DLB1, 30
Spencer, Elizabeth 1921-	DLB6
Spender, Stephen 1909-	DLB20
Spicer, Jack 1925-1965	DLB5, 16
Spielberg, Peter 1929-	Y81
Spinrad, Norman 1940-	DLB8
Squibob (see Derby, George Horatio)	
Stafford, Jean 1915-1979	DLB2
Stafford, William 1914-	DLB5
Stallings, Laurence 1894-1968	DLB7, 9
Stampp, Kenneth M. 1912-	DLB17
Stanford, Ann 1916-	DLB5
Stanton, Frank L. 1857-1927	DLB25
Stapledon, Olaf 1886-1950	DLB15
Starkweather, David 1935-	DLB7
Steadman, Mark 1930-	DLB6
Stearns, Harold E. 1891-1943	DLB4
Steele, Max 1922-	Y80
Steere, Richard circa 1643-1721	DLB24

Stegner, Wallace 1909-	DLB9
Stein, Gertrude 1874-1946	DLB4
Stein, Leo 1872-1947	DLB4
Steinbeck, John 1902-1968	DLB7, 9; DS2
Stephens, Ann 1813-1886	DLB3
Stephens, James 1882?-1950	DLB19
Sterling, James 1701-1763	DLB24
Stern, Stewart 1922-	DLB26
Stevenson, Robert Louis 1850-1894	DLB18
Stewart, Donald Ogden 1894-1980	DLB4, 11, 26
Stewart, George R. 1895-1980	DLB8
Stiles, Ezra 1727-1795	DLB31
Still, James 1906-	DLB9
Stith, William 1707-1755	DLB31
Stoddard, Richard Henry 1825-1903	DLB3
Stoddard, Solomon 1643-1729	DLB24
Stokes, Thomas L. 1898-1958	DLB29
Stone, Melville 1848-1929	DLB25
Stone, Samuel 1602-1663	DLB24
Stoppard, Tom 1937-	DLB13
Storey, Anthony 1928-	DLB14
Storey, David 1933-	DLB13, 14
Story, Thomas circa 1670-1742	DLB31
Story, William Wetmore 1819-1895	DLB1
Stoughton, William 1631-1701	DLB24
Stowe, Harriet Beecher 1811-1896	DLB1, 12
Stowe, Leland 1899-	DLB29
Strand, Mark 1934-	DLB5
Streeter, Edward 1891-1976	DLB11
Stribling, T. S. 1881-1965	DLB9
Strother, David Hunter 1816-1888	DLB3
Stuart, Jesse 1907-	DLB9
Stubbs, Harry Clement (see Clement, Hal)	
Sturgeon, Theodore 1918-	DLB8
Sturges, Preston 1898-1959	DLB26
Styron, William 1925-	DLB2; Y80
Suckow, Ruth 1892-1960	DLB9
Suggs, Simon (see Hooper, Johnson Jones)	
Sukenick, Ronald 1932-	Y81
Sullivan, C. Gardner 1886-1965	DLB26
Sullivan, Frank 1892-1976	DLB11
Summers, Hollis 1916-	DLB6
Surtees, Robert Smith 1803-1864	DLB21
Sutro, Alfred 1863-1933	DLB10
Swados, Harvey 1920-1972	DLB2
Swenson, May 1919-	DLB5
Swope, Herbert Bayard 1882-1958	DLB25
Symons, Arthur 1865-1945	DLB19
Synge, John Millington 1871-1909	DLB10, 19

T

Tarkington, Booth 1869-1946	DLB9
Tate, Allen 1896-1979	DLB4
Tate, James 1943-	DLB5
Taylor, Bayard 1825-1878	DLB3
Taylor, Bert Leston 1866-1921	DLB25
Taylor, Charles H. 1846-1921	DLB25
Taylor, Edward circa 1642-1729	DLB24
Taylor, Henry 1942-	DLB5
Taylor, Peter 1917-	Y81
Tenn, William 1919-	DLB8
Tennant, Emma 1937-	DLB14
Terhune, Albert Payson 1872-1942	DLB9
Terry, Megan 1932-	DLB7
Terson, Peter 1932-	DLB13
Tesich, Steve 1943-	Y83
Thackeray, William Makepeace 1811-1863	DLB21
Theroux, Paul 1941-	DLB2
Thoma, Richard 1902-	DLB4
Thomas, Dylan 1914-1953	DLB13, 20
Thomas, Edward 1878-1917	DLB19
Thomas, Gwyn 1913-1981	DLB15
Thomas, John 1900-1932	DLB4
Thomas, R. S. 1915-	DLB27
Thompson, Dorothy 1893-1961	DLB29
Thompson, Francis 1859-1907	DLB19
Thompson, John R. 1823-1873	DLB3
Thompson, Ruth Plumly 1891-1976	DLB22
Thompson, William Tappan 1812-1882	DLB3, 11

Thomson, Mortimer 1831-1875..........................DLB11
Thoreau, Henry David 1817-1862......................DLB1
Thorpe, Thomas Bangs 1815-1878............DLB3, 11
Thurber, James 1894-1961....................DLB4, 11, 22
Ticknor, George 1791-1871................................DLB1
Timrod, Henry 1828-1867....................................DLB3
Tiptree, James, Jr. 1915-....................................DLB8
Titus, Edward William 1870-1952......................DLB4
Toklas, Alice B. 1877-1967..................................DLB4
Tolkien, J. R. R. 1892-1973................................DLB15
Tompson, Benjamin 1642-1714..........................DLB24
Tonks, Rosemary 1932-......................................DLB14
Toole, John Kennedy 1937-1969..........................Y81
Tracy, Honor 1913-..DLB15
Traven, B. 1882? or 1890?-1969........................DLB9
Travers, Ben 1886-1980....................................DLB10
Tremain, Rose 1943-..DLB14
Trescot, William Henry 1822-1898..................DLB30
Trevor, William 1928-..DLB14
Trilling, Lionel 1905-1975..................................DLB28
Trocchi, Alexander 1925-..................................DLB15
Trollope, Anthony 1815-1882............................DLB21
Trollope, Frances 1779-1863............................DLB21
Troop, Elizabeth 1931-......................................DLB14
Trumbo, Dalton 1905-1976................................DLB26
Trumbull, Benjamin 1735-1820........................DLB30
Trumbull, John 1750-1831................................DLB31
Tucker, George 1775-1861............................DLB3, 30
Tucker, Nathaniel Beverley 1784-1851..............DLB3
Tunis, John R. 1889-1975................................DLB22
Tuohy, Frank 1925-..DLB14
Turner, Frederick Jackson 1861-1932............DLB17
Twain, Mark (see Clemens, Samuel Langhorne)
Tyler, Anne 1941-......................................DLB6; Y82

U

Upchurch, Boyd B. (see Boyd, John)
Updike, John 1932-...............DLB2, 5; Y80, 82; DS3
Upton, Charles 1948-..DLB16

Ustinov, Peter 1921-..DLB13

V

Vail, Laurence 1891-1968..................................DLB4
Van Anda, Carr 1864-1945..............................DLB25
Vance, Jack 1916?-..DLB8
van Druten, John 1901-1957............................DLB10
Van Duyn, Mona 1921-......................................DLB5
van Itallie, Jean-Claude 1936-..........................DLB7
Vane, Sutton 1888-1963..................................DLB10
Vann, Robert L. 1879-1940..............................DLB29
Van Vechten, Carl 1880-1964......................DLB4, 9
van Vogt, A. E. 1912-..DLB8
Varley, John 1947-..Y81
Vega, Janine Pommy 1942-............................DLB16
Very, Jones 1813-1880......................................DLB1
Vidal, Gore 1925-..DLB6
Viereck, Peter 1916-..DLB5
Villard, Henry 1835-1900................................DLB23
Villard, Oswald Garrison 1872-1949..............DLB25
Vonnegut, Kurt 1922-............DLB2, 8; Y80; DS3

W

Wagoner, David 1926-......................................DLB5
Wain, John 1925-..DLB15, 27
Wakoski, Diane 1937-..DLB5
Walcott, Derek 1930-..Y81
Waldman, Anne 1945-......................................DLB16
Walker, Alice 1944-..DLB6
Wallant, Edward Lewis 1926-1962............DLB2, 28
Walsh, Ernest 1895-1926..................................DLB4
Wambaugh, Joseph 1937-........................DLB6; Y83
Ward, Artemus (see Browne, Charles Farrar)
Ward, Douglas Turner 1930-............................DLB7
Ward, Lynd 1905-..DLB22
Ward, Mrs. Humphry 1851-1920....................DLB18
Ward, Nathaniel circa 1578-1652....................DLB24
Ware, William 1797-1852..................................DLB1

Warner, Rex 1905-	DLB15
Warner, Susan B. 1819-1885	DLB3
Warren, Lella 1899-1982	Y83
Warren, Mercy Otis 1728-1814	DLB31
Warren, Robert Penn 1905-	DLB2; Y80
Washington, George 1732-1799	DLB31
Wasson, David Atwood 1823-1887	DLB1
Waterhouse, Keith 1929-	DLB13
Watkins, Vernon 1906-1967	DLB20
Watterson, Henry 1840-1921	DLB25
Watts, Alan 1915-1973	DLB16
Waugh, Auberon 1939-	DLB14
Waugh, Evelyn 1903-1966	DLB15
Webb, Walter Prescott 1888-1963	DLB17
Webster, Noah 1758-1843	DLB1
Weems, Mason Locke 1759-1825	DLB30
Weidman, Jerome 1913-	DLB28
Weinbaum, Stanley Grauman 1902-1935	DLB8
Weiss, John 1818-1879	DLB1
Weiss, Theodore 1916-	DLB5
Welch, Lew 1926-1971?	DLB16
Weldon, Fay 1931-	DLB14
Wells, Carolyn 1862-1942	DLB11
Wells-Barnett, Ida B. 1862-1931	DLB23
Welty, Eudora 1909-	DLB2
Wescott, Glenway 1901-	DLB4, 9
Wesker, Arnold 1932-	DLB13
West, Anthony 1914-	DLB15
West, Jessamyn 1902-1984	DLB6
West, Nathanael 1903-1940	DLB4, 9, 28
West, Paul 1930-	DLB14
West, Rebecca 1892-1983	Y83
Whalen, Philip 1923-	DLB16
Wharton, Edith 1862-1937	DLB4, 9, 12
Wharton, William 1920s?-	Y80
Wheatley, Phillis circa 1754-1784	DLB31
Wheeler, Charles Stearns 1816-1843	DLB1
Wheeler, Monroe 1900-	DLB4
Wheelwright, John circa 1592-1679	DLB24
Whetstone, Colonel Pete (see Noland, C. F. M.)	
Whipple, Edwin Percy 1819-1886	DLB1
Whitaker, Alexander 1585-1617	DLB24
Whitcher, Frances Miriam 1814-1852	DLB11
White, Andrew 1579-1656	DLB24
White, E. B. 1899-	DLB11, 22
White, Horace 1834-1916	DLB23
White, William Allen 1868-1944	DLB9, 25
White, William Anthony Parker (see Boucher, Anthony)	
White, William Hale (see Rutherford, Mark)	
Whitehead, James 1936-	Y81
Whiting, John 1917-1963	DLB13
Whiting, Samuel 1597-1679	DLB24
Whitlock, Brand 1869-1934	DLB12
Whitman, Sarah Helen (Power) 1803-1878	DLB1
Whitman, Walt 1819-1892	DLB3
Whittemore, Reed 1919-	DLB5
Whittier, John Greenleaf 1807-1892	DLB1
Wieners, John 1934-	DLB16
Wigglesworth, Michael 1631-1705	DLB24
Wilbur, Richard 1921-	DLB5
Wild, Peter 1940-	DLB5
Wilde, Oscar 1854-1900	DLB10, 19
Wilde, Richard Henry 1789-1847	DLB3
Wilder, Billy 1906-	DLB26
Wilder, Laura Ingalls 1867-1957	DLB22
Wilder, Thornton 1897-1975	DLB4, 7, 9
Wiley, Bell Irvin 1906-1980	DLB17
Wilhelm, Kate 1928-	DLB8
Willard, Nancy 1936-	DLB5
Willard, Samuel 1640-1707	DLB24
Williams, C. K. 1936-	DLB5
Williams, Emlyn 1905-	DLB10
Williams, Garth 1912-	DLB22
Williams, Heathcote 1941-	DLB13
Williams, Joan 1928-	DLB6
Williams, John A. 1925-	DLB2
Williams, John E. 1922-	DLB6
Williams, Jonathan 1929-	DLB5
Williams, Raymond 1921-	DLB14
Williams, Roger circa 1603-1683	DLB24

Williams, T. Harry 1909-1979 ....DLB17
Williams, Tennessee 1911-1983 ......DLB7; DS4; Y83
Williams, William Appleman 1921- DLB17
Williams, William Carlos 1883-1963 ....DLB4, 16
Williams, Wirt 1921- DLB6
Williamson, Jack 1908- DLB8
Willingham, Calder, Jr. 1922- DLB2
Willis, Nathaniel Parker 1806-1867 ....DLB3
Wilson, A. N. 1950- DLB14
Wilson, Angus 1913- DLB15
Wilson, Colin 1931- DLB14
Wilson, Harry Leon 1867-1939 ....DLB9
Wilson, John 1588-1667 ....DLB24
Wilson, Lanford 1937- DLB7
Wilson, Margaret 1882-1973 ....DLB9
Winchell, Walter 1897-1972 ....DLB29
Windham, Donald 1920- DLB6
Winthrop, John 1588-1649 ....DLB24, 30
Winthrop, John, Jr. 1606-1676 ....DLB24
Wise, John 1652-1725 ....DLB24
Wister, Owen 1860-1938 ....DLB9
Witherspoon, John 1723-1794 ....DLB31
Woiwode, Larry 1941- DLB6
Wolcott, Roger 1679-1767 ....DLB24
Wolfe, Gene 1931- DLB8
Wolfe, Thomas 1900-1938 ....DLB9; DS2
Wood, Benjamin 1820-1900 ....DLB23
Wood, Charles 1932- DLB13
Wood, Mrs. Henry 1814-1887 ....DLB18
Wood, William ?-? DLB24
Woodbridge, Benjamin 1622-1684 ....DLB24
Woodmason, Charles circa 1720- death date unknown DLB31
Woodson, Carter G. 1875-1950 ....DLB17

Woodward, C. Vann 1908- DLB17
Woollcott, Alexander 1887-1943 ....DLB29
Woolman, John 1720-1772 ....DLB31
Woolson, Constance Fenimore 1840-1894 ......DLB12
Worcester, Joseph Emerson 1784-1865 ....DLB1
Wouk, Herman 1915- Y82
Wright, Charles 1935- Y82
Wright, Harold Bell 1872-1944 ....DLB9
Wright, James 1927-1980 ....DLB5
Wright, Louis B. 1899- DLB17
Wright, Richard 1908-1960 ....DS2
Wylie, Elinor 1885-1928 ....DLB9
Wylie, Philip 1902-1971 ....DLB9

Y

Yates, Richard 1926- DLB2; Y81
Yeats, William Butler 1865-1939 ....DLB10, 19
Yezierska, Anzia 1885-1970 ....DLB28
Yonge, Charlotte Mary 1823-1901 ....DLB18
Young, Stark 1881-1963 ....DLB9
Young, Waldemar 1880-1938 ....DLB26

Z

Zangwill, Israel 1864-1926 ....DLB10
Zebrowski, George 1945- DLB8
Zelazny, Roger 1937- DLB8
Zenger, John Peter 1697-1746 ....DLB24
Zimmer, Paul 1934- DLB5
Zindel, Paul 1936- DLB7
Zubly, John Joachim 1724-1781 ....DLB31
Zukofsky, Louis 1904-1978 ....DLB5

DATE DUE